Where Rivers Meet

The Search for Peace with Justice

29th port: 02

To George,
with appreciation
and best wishes.
Wally

- For a copy of the complete Scottish Cultural Press catalogue please write to the publishers

Where Rivers

Meet

The Search for Peace
with Justice

From Primal Man to the Present Day

Wallace Allen Shaw
Foreword by Prof. Frank Whaling

SCOTTISH CULTURAL PRESS
EDINBURGH

First published 1997 by
Scottish Cultural Press
Unit 14, Leith Walk Business Centre,
130 Leith Walk, Edinburgh EH6 5DT
Tel: 0131 555 5950 ◆ Fax: 0131 555 5018
e-mail: scp@sol.co.uk
http://www.taynet.co.uk/users/scp

British Library Cataloguing in Publication Data
A catalogue entry for this book is available from the British Library

ISBN: 1 898218 83 8

Printed and bound by
Colour Books Limited, Dublin

Contents

About the Author

Wallace Allen Shaw was born in Crawfordsville, Indiana, where he graduated from Wabash College (BA in Philosophy). Post-graduate research brought him to New College, Edinburgh University, and he subsequently completed further degrees at Union Theological Seminary, New York City (MTh/BD in New Testament) and St Andrew's University (PhD in Practical Theology: the Content and Methodology of Religious Education).

He married Lesley Ballantine of Edinburgh in 1959 and served with the Methodist Church as Associate Minister in Bay Ridge, Brooklyn (where he was also Director of a Released Time School in Religious Education, and Chairman of the National Council of Christians and Jews for Brooklyn). Then he became a Minister in Westhampton Beach, Long Island.

Returning to Scotland in 1962 he became an Assistant Minister at St George's West Church, Edinburgh, and began writing the *Living Bible* series of textbooks for R.E. in Schools while awaiting his acceptance as a Minister by the Church of Scotland. In 1964 he became Minister of St Margaret's Parish Church, Glenrothes (where he also became Founder of Operation Friendship International, a multi-racial, multi-faith and multi-cultural youth venture affiliated to the United Nations as a Non-Governmental Organisation). From 1976 until his retirement in 1994, he was at Daniel Stewart's and Melville College, Edinburgh, where he became Chaplain and Head of the Religious Education Department (where his further writings included *The Gospel of Luke*, a teaching commentary, booklets such as *Between You and Me*, and manuscripts relating to his role as an N.G.O. Delegate to the United Nations). He was involved in the early development of Religious Education in Scotland. As a member of the Teaching Association, ATRESS, he served on the Secretary of State's Committee for the development of Religious Studies in Secondary Schools. He is a member of the Edinburgh Inter Faith Association.

"Wally" and Lesley have three children: Alison, married, living in Indianapolis, and Fiona and Andrew, living in Edinburgh. They have one grandson, Christopher.

Foreword

It is a pleasure to commend this book by Wallace Shaw, and that for two reasons: because it is so well done, and because it is so needed.

The attractiveness of this book lies in its width and imaginative insight. It ranges historically from Primal Religion with its beginnings in prehistory to the Bahá'í tradition which arose in the nineteenth century. It engages with early religious movements such as those of ancient Egypt, Qumran, and Greece and Rome; it looks at the monotheistic religions such as the Jews, Christians, and Muslims; it investigates Indian traditions such as the Hindu, Theravada Buddhist, and Sikh; and it explores Far Eastern traditions such as the Confucian, Taoist, Mahayana Buddhist, and Shinto.

In addition to its enviable width of coverage, it also creatively engages the insight of the reader. Included within its covers are imaginative attempts to enable one to get inside the worldview of other religions. Efforts are made to transport readers inside the thought-world of others and to allow them in some measure to see the universe as others see it. Structured dialogues and other insightful devices such as illustrations and charts help towards this end.

As well as being interesting, this book is also relevant and contemporary. Present-day issues are referred to, the language is modern and understandable, and the reader's experience is enlisted. The following pages will appeal not only to young people, teachers, and the educational world but also to others with a general interest in world religions.

Wallace Shaw is scrupulously fair in his discussion. He starts from where people are likely to be and takes them through empathy into the worldview of others, not least into the worldview of Christianity which can no longer be taken as read.

The human attributes of empathy, reason, concern, and thoughtfulness are brought convincingly to this work; it deserves to do very well.

Frank Whaling

Preface

There are *three* methods by which this book can be used:

1. As an Individual

One can use this book as a 'reader', identifying in one's own mind the role plays that are offered, as well as the responses to questions and statements as they arise.

2. For Class Use (see Appendix on p. 168)

At Daniel Stewart's and Melville College, Edinburgh, it was found that the writing of well organised notes in a notebook is an important discipline for effective learning. Notes should be written on important discoveries made from the content of each chapter, using its headings as captions. Notes also should be written on each introductory and concluding discussion. Questions and notes for comments should be written while listening to the dialogue presentations at the beginning of each section since each concludes with discussion. The Assignments need not be laboured; a few minutes writing brief essays will help each student to make a tentative reaction, and to further identify with each stance. The structure of each chapter is appropriate for Certificate Courses and Modules as well as for general Religious Education Classes.

3. Youth Clubs and Adult Discussion Groups (see Appendix)

This is a less formal and a less disciplined approach, without necessarily keeping a notebook. Members of the group(s) should be allocated parts from the cast listing in each of the four dialogues and from the **purely by accident** role play which can be found in italics at the beginning of each chapter.

An Existential Approach

Existentialists believe that our thoughts, our actions, even our feelings are determined not only by our current circumstances (both social and political) but also the circumstances from which we, as individuals, have arisen.

Existentialism therefore implies that it must be almost impossible to empathise with other individuals given that their own circumstances inevitably differ, sometimes radically, from our own.

"What is the use, then," you might ask, *"of having an 'existential approach' to a subject where the beliefs of the individuals concerned are so diverse that any mutual understanding is, by extension, unachievable?"*

Empathy is the key word, since this particular human talent allows us imaginatively to "enter" into the circumstances of others by "seeing" ourselves in their situation, in their shoes.

Think of method actors like Robert De Niro. They can make us believe in their portrayals because of their willingness to live, to the best of their ability, the lives of the people they portray. Method acting can involve changing what you think, wear, eat and do, where you live and even what you feel!

The more information we have about another person's circumstances, past and present, the more likely that, with some effort, we will be able to empathise, to come to an understanding of their existence.

This book offers that opportunity. For in this book those who have gone before us throughout history invite us to make their journey with them, to make their journey our journey so that through such empathy, through such tolerance and understanding, we can journey together in the search for peace with justice and meet as rivers meet.

Wallace Allen Shaw

To help seek objectivity and to help avoid prejudice, some commonly used terms are replaced by others: *e.g. Primitive Man* is replaced by *Primal Man*, and *AD* and *BC (Anno Domini* and *Before Christ)* are replaced by *CE* and *BCE (Common Era* and *Before the Common Era).*

Acknowledgements

In this edition I thank **Lesley Shaw** for initial corrections. I thank **Jean Williams** for further corrections, for the Multiple Choice Test, and for sharing with me the use of the original draft manuscript with classes at Daniel Stewart's and Melville College. Therefore, the students themselves are to be thanked for their co-operation, comments and critical evaluation which assisted with this revision. Further thanks are due to **Mariana Versteeg, Dr Ian Palin, Arzina Lalani, Ian Crosbie, Vivien Ballantine, Ralph Dunn, George C Cunningham, Dr James Russell, Dr Ernie Wilkins, Andrew Shaw** and **Ian Bruce**. I thank **Dr Ian Cameron** for the illustrations and for much further assistance. I thank **Dr Frank Whaling**, Professor of Religious Studies at the University of Edinburgh, for much encouragement through the Edinburgh Inter Faith Association and for writing the Foreword. I further wish to thank from Scottish Cultural Press: Jill Dick for having the vision of this book as a reader to provide imagination, and for her appropriate editing; and Carol Rodger for reformatting the manuscript.

The publishers acknowledge with thanks the permissions granted to use the following copyright material [pp. refer to this volume] (pp. refer to specific book):

BBC Worldwide Limited, [p.9]: *America*, Alistair Cooke.
By permission of Oxford University Press, [p.23]: *The Laws of Plato*, Jowett, B (trans.) 1920.
Mrs J Whiting-Moon, [pp.74–5]: 'The Laws of Manu', from *Religions of Man*, J S R Whiting.
HarperCollins Publishers Ltd: [pp.119–20] *The Way and its Power*, Arthur Waley; [pp.125–7] *The Analects of Confucius*, Arthur Waley.
The University of Chicago Press, [pp.12,13,14]: *Intellectual Adventure of Ancient Man*, Frankfort, Wilson, Jacobsen & Irwin.
Bahá'í Publishing Trust: [pp.132–3,138–42] *Gleanings from the Writings of Bahá'u'lláh*, Bahá'u'lláh, comp. and trans. Shoghi Effendi, rev. ed.; [p.136] *'Abdu'l-Bahá in London: Addresses and Notes of Conversations*, 'Abdu'l-Bahá, comp. Eric Hammond, 2nd ed.; [pp.129,142] *The Bahá'í Faith: An Introduction*, rev. ed., Gloria Faizi; [pp.143,144] *The World Order of Bahá'u'lláh: Selected Letters*, 1st pocket-sized ed., Shoghi Effendi; [p.142] *Bahá'í Prayers: A Selection*, rev. ed., Bahá'u'lláh, the Báb, 'Abdu'l-Bahá; [pp.135,139] *The Kitáb-i-Aqdas: The Most Holy Book*, rev. ed., Bahá'u'lláh; [pp.139, 140,141] *Tablets of Bahá'u'lláh revealed after the Kitáb-i-Aqdas*, Bahá'u'lláh, comp. Research Department of the Universal House of Justice, trans. Habib Taherzadeh with the assistance of a Committee at the Bahá'í World Centre, 1st US hardcover ed.; [p.139] *Kitáb-i-Íqán: The Book of Certitude*, Bahá'u'lláh, trans. Shoghi Effendi, 3rd ed.; [p.139] *Epistle to the Son of the Wolf*, Bahá'u'lláh, trans. Shoghi Effendi, 1st pocket size ed.; [p.140] *The Hidden Words*, Bahá'u'lláh, trans. Shoghi Effendi with the assistance of some English friends; [p.143] *Paris Talks: Addresses Given by 'Abdu'l-Bahá in 1911*, 'Abdu'l-Bahá, 12th rev. ed.; [p.140] *The Proclamation of Bahá'u'lláh to the Kings and Leaders of the World*, Bahá'u'lláh; [p.142] *Bahá'u'lláh and the New Era*, J E Esslemont, rev. 4th ed.

Symbols and their Meanings

Meaning

Primal Man — Animal as in a drawing by cave dwellers.

Ancient Egyptians — Pyramids as built for the pharaohs.

Ancient Babylonians — Two gods, meeting in the heavenly assembly.

Ancient Hebrews — Star of David, Mogen David, a relatively new symbol from the eighteenth century when it was felt required.

Ancient Greeks — Doric columns.

Ancient Romans — Laurel representing the authority of Caesar.

Qumram Community — Scrolls as found in the caves nearby.

Christians — Cross, the suffering and resurrection of Jesus Christ.

Muslims — Star which guides desert peoples and moon which lights the way through life.

Hindus — *Om* or *Aum*, the sacred sound symbolising what is beyond speaking about, Braham – the ultimate reality.

Buddhists — Wheel of the Law, indicating the Eight-Fold path to Nirvana.

	Sikhs	*Khanda*, the two-edged sword representing God's concern for truth and justice; the second and third swords representing God's temporal and spiritual power; and the circle, the unity of God.
	Shintoists	*Torii*, the gateway to a temple, representing bird perches as birds helped the gods in mythology.
	Dowists	Balance of *Yin* and *Yang* reflected in the Chinese view of the rhythmic cycle common to all life which, when in harmony, forms a whole.
	Confucians	Based on an imaginary Chinese painting of Confucius.
	Bahá'ís	Arabic representation of the "greatest name of God", *ya baha' al-abra* ("O Splendid of the most Splendid".)
	United Nations	Laurel of authority surrounding the world.
	Operation Friendship	Dove carrying an olive branch, symbol of peace, over the world.
	World Council of Churches	*Oikoumene*, a transliteration of the Greek letters of a word meaning, "the whole world together".
	Christian Aid	Figure representing every person in need.
	Fish: IXTHUS	Transliteration of the Greek letters forming together the word for fish and individually the initial letters for: *I* (Jesus), *X* (Christ), *TH* (of God), *U* (the Son), *S* (Saviour).
	Anchor	Safety in the saviour, as that which provides safety for a ship.
	IHS	Transliteration of the first three letters of the Greek word meaning Jesus.

The rich
will make temples for Siva.
What shall I,
a poor man,
do?

My legs are pillars,
the body a shrine,
the head a cupola
of gold.

Listen, O lord of the meeting rivers,
things standing shall fall,
but the moving ever shall stay.

Basavanna, leader of a medieval Hindu movement
(Translated by A K Ramanujan in *Speaking of Siva*, Penguin Classics, 1973)

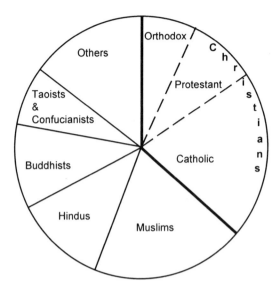

There are different ways of counting.
This is based on one type of census of
religious adherence and association.

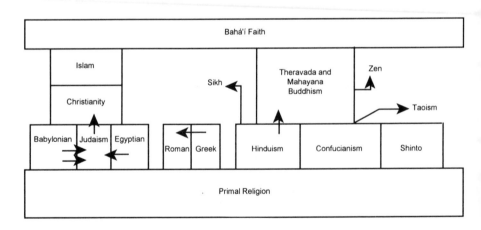

Historical flow-sheet to imply the influence of religions on each other.

Introduction

A teacher said to a class:

*It is **purely an accident** that I am older than you; you could just as easily have been my teacher. Therefore, I must treat you with respect, as if you were my teacher. And it follows that you must treat me with that same respect.*

What do you think of this? What if you were now a teacher and your teacher were your pupil? What kind of behaviour would you expect from him or her? What kind of attention, interest and respect would you want?

Jesus of Nazareth taught: *Do to others as you want them to do to you.* He meant that you should treat a person as if you were that person. Perhaps it is **purely an accident** that you are not that other person. *If* your Great Grandfather had not fallen in love with your Great Grandmother but with a different woman... *If* the child born to them had for some reason later moved to another country and had married someone of that culture and perhaps even of a different race and religion... *If* a child born to them had by chance met and married into yet another culture... *Then* you would be someone very different from the person you are.

No wonder it is silly as well as tragic that people throughout history have argued and fought, persecuted and killed those of other nations and cultures, races and religions.

A road sign says:

Drive carefully. The life you save may be your own.

The way we treat others has a way of coming back to us, like an Australian boomerang.

An American Indian doing a ceremonial dance; a Hindu washing, dressing and decorating the image of a god; a Taoist covered in a paper dragon, in a procession: they are so different from us. Their customs **purely by accident** seem so strange. Yet, what if you had been born of another nationality, another race, another religion, another cultural background? You could be that different person. Other people are no less strange to us than we are to them. If we can come to understand a person so different from us, we will know what we would be like if, **purely by accident**, we had been born that person. We also would know how we can have a constructive relationship with that person. It is easier to be friends with people you know and understand.

Isn't it strange that princes and kings,
And clowns that caper in sawdust rings,
And common people like you and me
Are builders of eternity.
Each is given a box of tools,
A shapeless mass and a book of rules;
And each must build ere life is flown
A stumbling block, or a stepping stone.
<Author unknown>

By looking at other ways of life and at the kind of person we might have been, we can learn how to tear down stumbling blocks that cause hatred, prejudice and war. And we can learn how to build stepping stones to love, justice and peace.

It is **purely by accident** that I am older than you; you could just as easily have been my teacher. What if you had been born not just a generation ago – as your teacher was – but a hundred years ago, or a thousand years ago or several thousand years ago? What would you be like? What kind of life would you be living? What would you believe? What would you think the world and the universe looked like? What would you think of heaven and earth? What would be your life style?

A journey in a spaceship to another planet would be quite an adventure. You – and certainly your children – may someday have that adventure. Some men and women already have travelled into outer space. We journey with them when we see films and pictures of their travels. With television *you* are there.

A journey back in time is no less an adventure. This is where you are going to begin this journey: thousands of years ago. And at each moment, as you make the journey mankind made down to the present time, you will encounter the kind of person you would have been if, **purely by accident**...

On our journey through time and from place to place there will be so much to see. What shall we look for?

In a class studying history, a pupil asked the teacher:

Why is history so often the history of war?

Why do so many of the dates we learn take us from one battlefield to another, from one war to another? Why is the story of mankind the story of war?

Sadly, so much of the story of mankind *is* the story of war. But there *is* much history that *is not* about people making war. Throughout history there have been those who were peacemakers and who *fought* for justice. They believed that merely being against war was not sufficient for being peacemakers. They believed that peace without justice is not peace.

So, as we make our journey we will find out how certain people at different places in our world came to discover how to make peace by doing justice and by loving mercy.

Our story begins with some of our distant ancestors, with what they thought and what they did. It continues with the story of more recent people and of people living today – their beliefs, their lives, their hopes and dreams. It is about how they were helped to be good neighbours through their purpose in life, their relationships with other people, and with the world around them.

On our journey, from the past to the present, we will learn to help ourselves as we learn to help others. For we could have had another life **purely by accident**.

————————————— **?** —————————————

"Purely by accident". To what extent do you believe this is true for your life?

Ancient Views of the Universe

CHARACTERS:
Narrator (Chairman), Cave Dweller, Ancient Egyptian, Ancient Babylonian, Ancient Hebrew

NARRATOR: *Purely by accident, four friends of yours lived several thousand years ago. Let us imagine what their conversation might be like if they were to appear together in our midst today. For our convenience, they will all speak English!*

I present to you a cave dweller, an Ancient Egyptian, an Ancient Babylonian and an Ancient Hebrew.

I would like to ask each of you to explain to us how you believe the world came into existence.

CAVE DWELLER: *Do you mean that it has not always been here? I find it difficult to think of this world not always being here or even of my cave not always being here. You mean there was a time when they weren't here?*

ANCIENT EGYPTIAN: *I think I can understand this cave dweller's attitude. As an Egyptian I come from the land of the Nile. I remember how my grandfather taught me that the Earth and the Sky created all things. I think he believed that as parents give birth to children, so the Earth and the Sky gave birth to everything else, including the Nile River.*

I believe, instead of this, that the great god Atum came out of a mass of water and made the Earth out of chaos by himself creating these first two gods, Earth and Sky.

ANCIENT BABYLONIAN: *As a Babylonian, I come from the land of two rivers: the Tigris and the Euphrates. I would agree that the earth was created, but I do not believe that Atum, a god, created the earth. I believe that Ti'amat, the Great Mother, was the creator. Ti'amat was not a god or goddess but a kind of demon.*

ANCIENT EGYPTIAN: *As an Egyptian, I do not understand how a demon could create anything. I can understand how a god that is all powerful could himself create two offspring, two children whom we Egyptians call Shu and Tefnut. Shu is the Air around us and Tefnut is the Moisture that we find in the Air, and in rain and rivers. These two, Shu and Tefnut, had children: Geb – the Earth, and Nut – the Sky-goddess.*

NARRATOR: *Do you believe that Atum, your god, was himself created?*

ANCIENT EGYPTIAN: *Yes, Atum was made out of the waters that existed so long ago. In these waters – the primeval waters at the beginning of time itself – there dwelt eight strange creatures. There were four frogs and four snakes, male and female, and they brought forth Atum, the creator Sun-god. These frogs and snakes were, among other things, the Ocean and chaotic Matter, Boundlessness, Darkness and the Wind.*

3

Atum, the Sun-god, made everything else out of water – all plants and animals.

NARRATOR: *What do you think of this, Ancient Babylonian?*

ANCIENT BABYLONIAN: *It is strange indeed. I believe that the chaos and waters out of which the creator-god was made was an enemy and not a friend. Ti'amat, the demon, was the Great Mother of many beings. This demon made the gods; and one of them, Marduk, led the others in a battle against Ti'amat and killed this demon. No longer did the force of evil control creation. Out of what was left of Ti'amat, with the evil removed, the Earth and the Universe – what you call the stars and the planets – were constructed.*

NARRATOR: *Then you agree that gods were themselves created out of the primeval waters?*

ANCIENT EGYPTIAN: *Yes, I come from the land of the Nile. Our river runs through the centre of the land. On both sides there are mountains. All is in balance: as one looks up the Nile, to the left is the valley and then mountains and to the right is the valley and then mountains. All is symmetrical. And underneath the Nile and the land on both sides is the primeval water that holds up the earth and the sky. The sky itself is the underbelly of a giant cow with its feet resting on the four corners of the earth. Nut, the Sky-goddess, changed herself into this cow in order to hold the sky above the earth for ever and ever. The sky was lifted up by Shu, the Air-god. Re, the Sun-god, is to this day still sitting on the cow and from up there he rules the universe with the help of Nut. Each evening, Nut, the Sky-goddess, gives birth to the new stars and each morning she gives birth to the new sun, her "golden calf".*

ANCIENT BABYLONIAN: *I, too, believe that underneath the earth is water. However, since I come from "the land of two rivers" – the Tigris and the Euphrates, I do not believe that the earth is symmetrical. For in any direction I look I see uneven ground: mountains here, valleys there. I do not believe that the earth has four corners. The earth, I would agree, is rather flat, but I believe that this flat earth is inside a gigantic bubble. The bottom of this bubble holds the water of the rivers and seas from falling down. The top of the bubble is the dome we see above us. Holes in the dome let water come down on us in the form of rain when the gods wish to pour it on us. The sun, the moon and the stars dance across the dome. The gods have fun playing catch with the sun and the moon, as by day and night they have their ball games.*

NARRATOR: *I must now ask how our Ancient Hebrew pictures the universe.*

ANCIENT HEBREW: *I believe that the universe was created by one God who was never himself created because He always has and always will exist. Time, itself, He created. My ancestors – the ancestors of the Hebrew people – came from the land of the Babylonians – the land of the two rivers. So we share with the Babylonians the belief that the sky is like a dome. Above the dome are the lights of heaven. But we believe that underneath the earth are the dark and gloomy shadows of Hades.*

Many of our more recent ancestors lived in Egypt and, as slaves, helped to build the Pyramids. There we learned about Re, the Egyptian sun-god. But we do not believe in the many gods of our Babylonian and Egyptian neighbours. We believe that God is one and that, although He dwells with us, He so often has revealed himself to us from the mountain tops – like Mt. Sinai where he gave us the Ten Commandments, and like Mt. Zion where we built a temple and our holy city of Jerusalem.

We, too, have a river: Jordan. We think of it as the boundary line which some of our ancestors crossed when they came into our country from Egypt.

We want to have peace with our Babylonian and Egyptian neighbours. There have been too much injustice and too much bloodshed between us.

NARRATOR: *I am certain that, whatever we believe about the creation of the earth, we all want to live in a just world and in a peaceful world.*

Our cave dweller has not said much. Therefore, we will let our cave dweller have the last word.

CAVE DWELLER: *I believe that gods dwell in all things. How the world was created – if it was created – I do not know. This does not matter to me. Three things do matter: my family, how I can get food for my family, and how I can keep my enemies from taking from me what little I have. Perhaps I can learn how to stop taking from my enemies what little they have. Perhaps I can learn how to make my enemies my friends. Maybe our descendants, those who come after us, can create a new world – where everyone has his needs met and therefore has no desire to fight.*

"Peace, man."

NARRATOR: *Thank you; I think we all share your hope. I want to thank each of you for joining us today.*

?

1. Why do you think many cave dwellers believed that the earth was never created but has always existed?
2. Belief in primeval waters is the belief that waters existed before the earth was created and that these waters support the earth from underneath the place where the people live. This assumes that the earth is flat. Why do you think the Ancient Egyptians believed that God – Atum, or Re as he came to be called – was made out of primeval waters?
3. Why do you think that the Ancient Babylonians believed that a creator-god was himself made by a demon who had to be defeated in a battle to let good rule over evil?
4. Why do you think that the Ancient Hebrews believed in one God rather than in many gods, and that He, Himself, was never created?
5. How can it be that the kind of country ancient man lived in influenced his view of creation? Why did it make a difference to him whether, for example, his land was symmetrical or not and whether it had one river or two? What other things do you think influenced ancient man's view of life?
6. *"Man has always been a war-mongerer, always will be and nothing can change his nature."* What do you think about this statement?
7. Reread the last comments by the Cave Dweller. Do you share these hopes? What are some of the things you think need to be done to fulfil them? What is the most important thing that needs to be done?

Primal Man
The First Peacemaker

Assume that **purely by accident** you have been born several thousand years ago and are part of a primal tribe. Say these sounds and see if anything happens:

Da a dada
Da a dada
Da a dada
    Da kata kae
Di a didi
Di a didi
Di a didi
    Di kata kae

If it was not raining before you said this chant, is it raining now? If it was raining, is it now raining more heavily? If nothing has happened, do you think that if you continued for several hours or through the night it might start raining?

These sounds were chanted by a certain primal tribe whenever rain was needed to provide water for drinking and for the growing of crops.

If, **purely by accident**, you had been the one who first spoke these words, then these may have been your thoughts:

All around me is fighting. When will the rain come again? The people have no water to drink unless they go to the one pool of water that is left. People are fighting for the land that the pool is on. He who has a big club or a strong spear takes the water for his family and tribe and keeps everyone else away. We

have the water now. But soon another tribe will come with bigger clubs and stronger spears and take the water hole from us.

When we have water we do not share it with those who have none. When others have water, they do not share it with us. When will the rains come?

I will pray to the rain-god for water:
"Da" ... "Dada" ... "Da a dada".

The rain does not come. There is no water from the sky. I must try again.

"Di" ... "Didi" ... "Kata kae".

The rain-god does not send rain. He must want a longer prayer.

"Da a dada, da a dada,

6

Da a dada, da a dada;
Da kata kae.
Di a didi, di a didi,
Di a didi, di a didi,
Di kata kae".
Still no water from the sky. I will teach the
chant to others in the tribe. If we speak
loudly enough and long enough, maybe it
will please the rain-god and he will answer
with water from the sky.

The First Peacemaker

And so throughout the day and into the night your tribe continues to chant the sounds you have taught it. In the morning hours it begins to rain. The tribe shouts louder and louder. It rains more heavily. It pours. The pool of water overflows. Other pools are filled. There is no more fighting. There is peace in the land.

The cave dweller feared the unknown and believed that spirits were to be found in all things. He believed that all objects were like himself and acted on purpose, for good or ill. He believed that the stone that he stumbled over, and that hurt his foot as he ran through the forest, intended to hurt him. He had offended it in some way. So he made a sacrifice and asked the stone for forgiveness. He knew that when he, himself, struck someone he intended to do him harm. So when nature struck him – with lightning or bad weather or even a branch – it did so with purpose, perhaps in anger.

Primal Man reasoned by analogy, from the known to the unknown. *I move; the wind moves. Therefore it must be like me. I speak; the wind speaks. Therefore it must be like me. I think and plan before I act; therefore the wind must think and plan before it acts. I must do all I can to keep in the favour of the wind.*

Primal Man's religion was his response to the unknown. His first laws were a series of *dos* and *don'ts* to appease the gods and to avoid offending them.

Primal Man did not know an inanimate world. All things were alive. Even stones had life. The thunderstorm could water parched ground and save the crops. It also could rain death upon the harvest and upon the people in bad storms. Primal Man knew nothing about *low fronts* and scientific explanations given by the weatherman on television. Belief that god or gods or spirits dwell in all things is called *"pantheism"*.

Primal Man had many myths. These myths were imaginary stories about the gods. (Myths are poetic ways of thinking of, or describing, the unknown power or powers behind all things.)

Today we see the sun rise in the morning and fall in the evening and we explain this in terms of the earth moving around. Today we see colours and we describe them as wavelengths. We have a dream while sleeping and we understand it as a vision of our subconscious mind. Primal Man did not have science to give him such explanations. The sun rose because the sun-god chose to bring the light of a new day. The different colours were caused by the different moods of the gods – bright cheerful gods, dark sombre (and perhaps to be feared) gods. He believed that dreams were given by a god during sleeping hours to terrify him or to inspire him or to forewarn him of some coming event. Dreams were just as real to Primal Man as what happened to him when he was awake. He had no reason to think otherwise. In his myths he would mention dragons and two-headed monsters alongside monkeys and rabbits. His dream world and his awake world were one and the same world.

If he wanted to harm his enemy he would make a bowl and draw a picture of his enemy on it and then smash the bowl. This he believed would bring real harm to his enemy.

When his friend returned from a hunting party bringing food for his family and for the tribe, he would dance and shout so that the celebration could be seen by the gods. Part of the meat would be broken off and burnt as a thanksgiving offering to feed the gods. The smoke would carry the burnt meat up to the sky-god, the moon-god, the sun-god, the rain-god – and to all the food-gods. Being made happy, they would assure the next hunting party of success.

Primal Man expressed his hopes and longings in the pictures he drew on the walls of caves, and in the objects he made: totem poles, charms and altars on places he considered sacred.

Primal religion can be found in our world today. The Kikuyu tribe of East Africa worships the god, Ngai. The people believe that lightning is a weapon Ngai sends down as a spear to warn them. Thunder is a cracking of the joints in Ngai's legs as he walks.

A Bantu tribe of Namibia worships Ndjambi whose holy name, *Karunga,* was heard for the first time by missionaries only after they had lived with the tribe for twenty-five years.

A Bantu tribe of Transvaal worships Ra-Luvhimba, *Father Eagle.* When something bad happens the women chant, *Lu, Lu, Lu...* When something good happens, like being saved from an accident, these words are shouted:

Ra-Luvhimba has saved me...
Ra-Luvhimba has saved me...
Ra-Luvhimba has saved me...

Drought brings sacrifices and the shouting of these prayers, hands clapping:

Ra-Luvhimba, give us rain... give us health... Ra-Luvhimba, give us rain... give us health...

The people have a mythological story of their god speaking through a great flame on top of Matopo Hill (in Namibia), a story that parallels the Hebrew story of Yahweh and the burning bush on Mt. Sinai.

The Maori tribe of Polynesia have a religion that is kept as a guarded secret. Its people must promise, on fear of death, not to talk about their god and never to speak his name. They make no offerings or sacrifices to him. They never speak his name, as the ancient Hebrews did not speak the name *Yahweh* for they thought it was too holy.

The Delaware Indians worship Kaong whose name means, *the great "I am", the one who creates,* just as *Yahweh* is a form of the Hebrew verb *to be* and means *the great existence from which comes all that exists.*

Tanka is worshipped by the Dakota Indians. They believe that Tanka is greater than man in the same way that man is greater than the buffalo. (Sadly, the white man killed off the buffalo that roamed the American plains.)

To think of God in the imagery of man, as a god who speaks and a god who walks, is called *anthropomorphism* (pronounced an-thro-po-mor-fism). The Pawnee Indians of Nebraska believe that Tirawa, the name they use for God, is a Great Power but in no way a Great Person. At night this Power moves through the darkness to protect. It is unusual to find a primal religion that is not *anthropomorphic.*

We must take care that we show respect for forms of primal religion in our world today. Many American Indians were forced to become Christians on fear of death by early missionaries. Many of the Indians who held to the primal beliefs of their ancestors suffered persecution and humiliation.

1. Say the chant, *Da a dada*, again. Can you bring on the rain? How do you think this chant came to be spoken?

2. What do you believe the first peacemaker was like? In what ways can we be peacemakers (a) with our spoken words? (b) with our written words? (c) with our drawings or carvings? (d) with song and dance? and (e) with our actions, the things we do?

3. Consider these words about the persecution of the Native American by certain Christian invaders:

    "One unforgettable story tells of a native king who would not renounce his religion and was about to be burned at the stake. As he felt the first fires lap his body, he was for the last time offered the rite of baptism. He refused, saying he feared that, if he accepted, he might 'go to heaven and meet there only Christians'." (from *America*, Alistair Cooke)

    Do you have any feelings about the way some primal tribes, Native Americans and people of other religions, have been strongly persuaded to become Christians? What do you think Jesus of Nazareth would have thought of this?

Ancient Egyptians
All Men are Created Equal

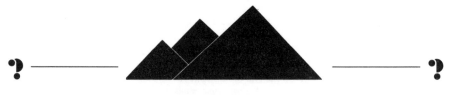

1. Do you believe that there is life after death?
2. If so, what do you believe that that life is like?
3. Do you believe that all people who live in your country should have equal rights? Why or why not?

Assume that **purely by accident** you are living several thousand years ago in Ancient Egypt. As an Ancient Egyptian you probably believe in many gods and believe that there was a time when they did not exist. You believe that Atum, the creator god, came out of primeval water, somehow creating himself. He created his own children, the god Shu (Air) and the goddess Tefnut (Moisture). Their children by his creative power, are Geb (the Earth) and Nut (the Sky). He made Geb so that he would have land on which to stand and on which a temple could be built at Heliopolis so that people would worship him.

Later, Atum came to be known as Re (the Sun god).

As an Ancient Egyptian you look around you. You see the Nile running through a fertile valley and on either side is desert and then the mountains, which (with the Mediterranean Sea to the North) box in the world as you know it. The Nile flows North to this sea. Almost all the people – 99 percent – live on the land that is fertile. And only three percent of the land at this time was fertile.

The geography of the land determines your beliefs. The earth seems to be between the mountains, forming the base of a huge rectangular box. The earth is the floor or bottom of the box. The top, the sky above, is simply the belly of a gigantic cow whose feet rest on the four corners of the earth. Around the walls on the inside of the box a river flows on a kind of balcony, carrying planets being sailed by Re (the Sun god) and Isis (the Moon god) like children sailing toy boats around a pond.

This is not surprising or strange to you. You think from the known to the unknown. You know how important the Nile is to you and to Egypt and so you assume that the gods must have **their** own water.

You think to yourself:

Man moves by boat, therefore the sun must move by boat too. Other gods must form the crew for this boat. The gods must think and act like people. People like to receive gifts, and so gods, too, must like gifts.

So you and others give gifts to Pharaoh, your

leader, who throws them into the Nile when you want it to rise, to overflow and irrigate the land.

You believe that each day and night are cycles of life and death. As the sun rises in the East and sets in the West, you believe that all goods brought in by traders from the East are from the Sun god and you give thanks in prayer:

O Re, all good wood – cedar, cypress and juniper – fresh myrrh and ebony and clean ivory... baboons, apes, greyhounds and panther skins, all come from thee. Praise to thee, O Re.

Evening and morning are death and life. You pray to the Sun god to bring the life of each new day:

O Re, when thou settest on the western horizon, the land is in darkness in the manner of death, but when thou risest on the eastern horizon, the land is again in light and all life is renewed. Let all beasts prance upon their feet and everything that flies or flutters join with man in saying, "Praise to thee! O Re".

And you believe that when death comes, the world hereafter is like the one here. As the Sun god finds the earth at the birth of each new day to be the same, so life after death (the birth of life beyond death) is like a new day and you believe that you will awake after death to the same kind of world, the heavenly Egypt. Therefore, you hope to be buried with all the things you have needed in this life for you will need them for the next life. You will need a boat with a sail for travelling southwards, which is upstream on the heavenly Nile. And you will need a boat without a sail for travelling northwards, which is downstream on the Nile.

The picture language of Ancient Egypt is called, *hieroglyphics*. Three examples are:

(mountain)

(Egypt, the land between the mountains)

(foreign land)

Ancient Egyptians believed that they, alone, were real people. They considered people who lived outside Egypt to be like animals. And yet, when a foreigner came into Egypt for trading, he was considered to be a person because he was on Egyptian soil. Only people in Egypt were considered to be human and yet *all* people in Egypt were considered to be human, whatever their race, religion or previous nationality.

Therefore, an important contribution of Ancient Egypt was its lack of racial, religious and national (at least when in Egypt) prejudice. When, almost 4000 years ago, some Hebrew people settled in Egypt, they were welcomed in peace. You may know the story about how Moses, one of the Hebrews, led his people out of Egyptian captivity in what is called *the Exodus*. The name of Moses comes from Egyptian for *leader* (as in the name of Pharaoh Rameses or Re-moses, Re the Sun god's leader, and Tutmos or Tut-moses, the god Tut's leader).

All people in Egypt were considered equal. An Egyptian code stated that all people were created by Atum to have equal opportunity:

I relate to you the four good deeds which my own heart did for me... in order to silence evil. I did four good deeds...

I made the four winds that every man might breathe thereof like his fellow in his time. That is the first of the deeds...

I made the great flood waters that the poor man might have rights in them like the rich man. That is the second of the deeds.

11

I made every man like his fellow. I did not command that they might do evil, but it was their hearts that violated what I had said.

I made that their hearts should cease from forgetting the west, in order that divine offerings might be made to the gods of the provinces.

The gifts of wind, water, human bodies and opportunities for worship equally were given to all people in Egypt.

Therefore, all people were under the same law to do good in return for good being done to them. *Give to others the kindness they give to you.* The Ancient Egyptian people may have looked down upon foreigners outside their land, but they otherwise believed that the gods demanded that they show kindness to *all* within their land, regardless of race, religion and nationality.

Is it not sad that by about 600 BCE (when the following poem was written) the Egyptians believed they had betrayed their ancient beliefs?

To whom can I speak today?
*   One's fellows are evil;*
*   The friends of today do not love.*
To whom can I speak today?
*   The gentle man has perished,*
*   But the violent man has access to*
*   everybody.*
To whom can I speak today?
No one remembers the lessons of
*   the past;*
No one at this time does good in
*   return for good being done to him.*
(from *Intellectual Adventure of Ancient Man*, Frankfort, et al.)

1. What were the four great deeds which Ancient Egyptians believed that the god Atum had done which made them all equal?
2. What were other *lessons of the past* which Ancient Egypt gave to peace and justice?
3. If you were now an Ancient Egyptian, what advice would you give to the world today?
4. Give some examples of duties that you have if you are to protect the rights of others.
5. What do you believe is the significance to the Ancient Hebrews of the fact that they lived in Egypt for part of their early history? (Consider from the Bible: Genesis 41:39–43, Exodus 1:8–14, and Exodus 3:1–10.)

Ancient Babylonians
The First United Nations?

1. Do you believe that nations should make treaties promising that they will not attack each other?
2. What are some examples of such treaties in our world today?
3. How are these treaties enforced?
4. What are some of the rules or regulations that protect you and others at school or college, at work or at home?
5. What happens when these rules are broken?

Assume that **purely by accident** you are living several thousand years ago in Ancient Babylonia (sometimes called *Mesopotamia)*. You live in a land that appears circular, for in any direction you look the horizon seems to be an equal distance away. The earth appears to be flat, although you know that the ground is uneven with mountains here and valleys there. You look up and the heavens appear to enclose around you, beyond a gigantic bubble. There must be, you think, doors in the dome. For during the day it seems that a god throws a ball (the sun) across the sky and at night another god must throw another ball (the moon) across the sky. You think that the gods must be opening doors in the dome to use the sky for playing games of catch. Water is kept by the gods in a vast pond above the sky and they pull out plugs when they want the rain to fall. If you dig a deep hole, water may come up out of the ground and so you believe that the flat earth rests on water which itself must be kept from falling down

by more land below it.

You live in a land that, unlike Egypt, does not have mountains protecting it on either side from its enemies. Valleys between the hills make your country wide-open to attack. This makes you feel insecure and threatened. Also, you live in a land of two rivers, the Tigris and the Euphrates. They are not, like the Nile, usually predictable and friendly. You do not know when one of them will suddenly rise and flood your crops, or fall and leave them ruined in a thirsty land.

Someone in your country has written:

The rampant flood which no man can oppose,
Which shakes the heavens and causes earth to tremble,
In an appalling blanket folds mother and child,
Beats down the canebrake's full luxuriant greenery,
And drowns the harvest in its time of

13

ripeness...
(translated from Cuneiform in *Intellectual Adventure of Ancient Man*, Frankfort, et al.)

Your crops may be drowned by torrential rains, or smothered by dust in the dry season.

Further, you believe that because such disorder of nature surrounds you, your survival depends upon a disciplined order willed by decision of the gods.

The land between the curve of the Tigris and Euphrates rivers brings a *Fertile Crescent* of civilisation. Old villages have expanded into city-states ruled by a general assembly of all adult free-men. You live in a *Primitive Democracy,* limited by excluding slaves and children – and probably women – from the right to vote. Otherwise, it is unusually representative for the world of that day. A council of elders makes day-to-day decisions, but in times of crisis all adult free-men assemble and vote. In an emergency, a king might be appointed to make necessarily swift decisions; but when the crisis is over, so also is the king's term of office.

You, and others in Ancient Babylonia around you, believe that the gods make their decisions in the same way. There is a heavenly *assembly of the gods* which decides all things. This heavenly council has Anu (the god of heaven) as its leader and Enlil (god of the storm) at his side. Every person has an individual god representing him. You believe that the god who represents you on this council looks after your interests, though he can be over-ruled by a vote against your favour and for the benefit of others.

Because nature seems to be so chaotic, you believe that all things were created out of chaos by Ti'amat, an evil demon goddess who was killed in battle by Marduk. With the evil removed, everything on earth and in the universe was constructed by the god Anu out of what was left of Ti'amat. Anu (Father of the gods) is not only the god of the sky, he is the sky itself. Enlil (Lord Storm) is god of

the storm and also is the storm itself. Enlil is master of all things under the sky. Enki (Lord Earth) is the source of the life-giving waters of the two rivers and of all the wells which spring from the vast sea of water below the earth. The gods have control over all things and dwell in all things. All things are alive and have the personality and will of the god or goddess within them. Even salt, which preserves as well as adds flavour, is alive.

You can call on any god to help you. If you believe you are suffering some kind of witchcraft from someone who wishes you harm, you might call on Lord Salt to rescue and preserve you:

O Salt, created in a clean place,
For food of gods did Enlil destine thee.
Without thee no meal is set out in Ekur,
Without thee god, king, lord, and prince do
*   not smell incense.*
I am ...... (give your name), the son of ......
*   (give your father's name),*
Held captive by enchantment,
Held in fever by bewitchment.
O Salt, break my enchantment! Loose my
*   spell!*
Take from me the bewitchment! – And as my
*   Creator*
I shall extol thee.
(from Maqlu, Tablet VI, in *Intellectual Adventure of Ancient Man*, Frankfort, et al.)

Being an Ancient Babylonian, before you play a reed or stringed instrument you might pray to Reed or to String to make your music awe-inspiring. (As today, before you do any writing you might pray to Lord Biro to let the words flow correctly.)

You believe that the ear, and not the brain, is the god of wisdom and learning. To make yourself more clever you perhaps pray to Ea (from which we get our word, *ear*). You believe that Babylonia is the centre of the earth and, therefore, that the universe also has such a power-centre. All the gods are bound together in Marduk.

You look out and see a Ziggurat, an artificial mountain built of sun-dried bricks to form a temple tower to your city god. You believe that there is a heavenly city with a large staff of divine and human servants. One god is a door keeper to the holy of holies within the temple. He admits those who are to meet the city god who, himself, is protected by two armed body-guards.

Another god is the chief butler who supervises the preparation of all food and drink. A further god is the coachman who cares for the city god's chariot. There are heavenly musicians and drummers who entertain the city god and soothe him when he is upset. There is a divine chief of police, a divine gamekeeper and even a divine inspector of fisheries. Menial work is done by human beings. You believe that everyone, when he dies, has a heavenly task to do. Man was created to be a servant of the gods. If he is obedient, he can expect to receive favours and rewards. Because you believe this, you sometimes write letters to the heavenly god who is your representative. Because he is busy, he may not always hear your prayers but at least he will respond to your written correspondence!

So one day you write a letter that forms the deepest prayer you have ever offered. In wedge-shaped Cuneiform characters you write to your divine representative:

Our land is so open to invasion. Wars have been numerous. When our people have been strong, our army has gone out and conquered others, bringing back the bounty of slaves and the wealth of plundered goods. When our people have been weak, we have been invaded and many of our people have been carried off as slaves while those left behind have been stripped of their possessions. Now that we are strong, can we use this strength to impose peace and justice upon the peoples around us and upon ourselves?

It is done. An international peace treaty is drawn up and enforced.

This is how you believe your prayer was answered. By the power of Marduk, Anu directed an assembly of the gods to consider the request made by you through your representative god. The assembly votes to instruct your king through a dream to send soldiers to all the surrounding countries bearing the instruction that these countries are to send representatives to Babylon on a certain date to draw up a treaty. The instructions state that any country that does not adhere to this will be destroyed by the Babylonian army.

The various surrounding countries send representatives, and the treaty is drawn up and voted on by the international assembly of representatives. There is peace for many years creating a cradle of ancient civilisation.

One of the important contributions of Ancient Babylonia was its primal democracy. It forced the drawing up of such a treaty. **Purely by accident** you could have been the peacemaker who provoked the treaty. And the Babylonian assembly where it took place could be called the prototype or ancient foundation of what we call today the *United Nations.*

A part of this contribution by Ancient Babylonia was the Hammurabi Code. Discovered in the winter of 1901–02 in excavations at Susa, it originally contained about 4000 lines of Cuneiform writing on 51 columns of laws given by Hammurabi, the king of Babylon (*c.* 1955–1913 BCE), almost 4000 years ago. The Hammurabi Code contains laws which were gathered from sources including West Semitic (very early Hebrew or Jewish) tribes. The following is a translation of part of the introduction:

*When lofty Anu, king of the Anunnaki, and
   Enlil, lord of heaven and earth,
who determine the destinies of the country,
   appointed Marduk, the first born*

son of Enki, to execute the Enlil functions
  over the totality of the people, made him
  great among the Igigi, called Babylon by
  exalted name, made it
surpassingly great in the world, and firmly
  established for him in its
midst an enduring kingship whose
  foundations are as firmly grounded as
those of heaven and earth – then did Anu and
  Enlil call me to afford well-being to the
  people,
me, Hammurabi, the obedient, god-fearing
  prince, to cause righteousness to appear in
  the land,
to destroy the evil and the wicked, that the

strong harm not the weak
and that I rise like the sun over the black-
  headed people, lighting up the land.

(From *Hammurabi's Code*, exhibited in the
Louvre Museum, Paris; a translation of the
Cuneiform writing)

Hammurabi thought that his purpose in life
was to bring righteousness (justice) to his
people, and *that the strong harm not the
weak* requires strict self-discipline among
those who are strong. Does this also mean
more than simply leaving the weak alone?
Did he not imply that *Peace without Justice
is not Peace*?

1. Why did the Ancient Babylonians believe that their creator god was himself created out of chaos?
2. What was the value of its *primal democracy?*
3. Is the entire world open to attack today?
4. What is the United Nations doing to try to prevent this?
5. What countries today are particularly vulnerable (a) to drought and (b) to flood?
6. *That the strong harm not the weak:* how can this protection be provided by (a) a school, (b) a home, (c) a work place, (d) a community, and (e) a government? In what ways does this require justice?
7. *Peace without justice is not peace.* Why do you agree or disagree?

Ancient Hebrews
Land of Hope and Glory
Swords into Ploughshares

? ——————————— ——————————— ?

What names of people, places and events come to your mind when you think of the Ancient Hebrews and their Scriptures (what Christians call *The Old Testament* and Jews call *The Tenakh*)? Draw up as long a list as possible.

Assume that **purely by accident** you are an Ancient Hebrew and are living in the year 539 BCE. You were born in Babylon during the time of the Jewish Exile, and have grown up there.

You know how your view of the universe is much like that of your Babylonian friends who have influenced your thought. You believe that the earth is flat. You look up and see what seems to be a dome. At night you think that the light of heaven shines through holes in this dome as specks of twinkling light. Below the earth, you believe, is Sheol or Hades – the underworld, the place of the dead, with its gloomy, dark shadows.

You are familiar with Hammurabi's Code. You also know about the Babylonian Creation Myth and the Babylonian story of a great flood. These stories have had their influence on you and are finding their way, in a Hebrew form, into your Sacred Scriptures, many of which have been written during the Exile.

You've seen a Hebrew scroll entitled, *Genesis* (beginnings) which was brought to your Synagogue (your school and place of worship). It tells about how Abraham, *the Father of Israel*, led nomadic tribes from the Ancient Babylonian city of Ur, near where the Euphrates River empties into the Persian Gulf, to Palestine. It tells how food shortage forced the tribes to travel on down into Egypt. The city of Ur was second only to Babylon as the largest city in Mesopotamia. Ur had a gigantic Ziggurat and you reflect on how your ancestors must have been familiar with the Babylonian religion, Hammurabi's Code and its teaching: *let not the strong harm the weak.* You know how, when your ancestors arrived in Egypt, they were well treated in accordance with the Ancient Egyptian principle of equality. Your ancestors were different from the Egyptians in race, religion and culture and yet the Egyptians welcomed them into their land. You recall how, according to your new Scriptures, Joseph, a descendent of Abraham, became a leader in Egypt (Genesis 41:41). In Egypt, your ancestors encountered and benefited from the principles of equal rights.

17

After your ancestors had been in Egypt for some 600 years, there was a pharaoh, Rameses II, who believed that the Hebrews had become too strong and that they might fight against Egypt. (They had supported the Hyksos invaders against Egypt so there was cause for this Egyptian fear.) So the pharaoh made the Hebrews slaves to help build new pyramids and cities (see Exodus 1:8–10). You know from your Sacred Writings the legends of how one of your ancestors, Moses (the name is Egyptian for *leader*), in a burning bush on top of Mount Horeb, encountered the presence of God who revealed his name to be Yahweh, Hebrew for *I am who I am* (or *I am the Great I am* or *I am the Great Being;* see Exodus 3:14).

You know the story of the Exodus, the journey from Egyptian captivity to a Promised Land. You believe that Yahweh revealed to Moses on Mount Sinai *Ten Commandments* which were written on two stone tablets and carried in an ark to the Promised Land. You know stories about how some of your ancestors passed eastwards around the Dead Sea, crossed over the Jordan river and entered the Promised Land, victoriously destroying the city of Jericho and by Yahweh's instructions slew the men, women and children who lived there (see Joshua 6:21).

The slaughter continued because the people who lived in Palestine had war chariots and it took a number of years for the conquest to be complete.

Kings were chosen for their military success: Saul for slaying thousands and David for slaying in the tens of thousands (see I Samuel 18:7). You know how the next king, Solomon, built Jerusalem and a temple to Yahweh, but did so by treating the tribes as his slaves. The northern tribes broke away and formed their own kingdom. You know how, in spite of the efforts of prophets like Elijah and Amos to reform the people, the Northern Kingdom was destroyed by the Assyrian army (722 BCE) and the northern tribes were dispersed. When the Assyrian army turned southwards, the Southern Kingdom was saved by the gold and silver of Jerusalem being given to the Assyrians as tribute money.

You know how the Southern Kingdom was strong only when its neighbours were weak. When the Babylonian Empire took over from the Assyrians, its king Nebuchadnezzar was not so willing to allow Judah to remain free. He marched his army against Jerusalem (596 BCE), taking a number of its leading people into Exile in Babylon. Then he returned again and after a terrible siege he destroyed the city and Solomon's temple to Yahweh and carried more Hebrews off into Exile in Babylon.

You reflect on how, once again, Hebrew people were in the land of the Tigris and the Euphrates rivers:

By the waters of Babylon,
* there we sat down and wept,*
* when we remembered Zion...*
How shall we sing the Lord's song
* in a foreign land?...*

(Psalm 137)

You know how one answer to that question was found at the end of that song which you have sung so many times:

O daughter of Babylon...
* Happy shall be he who takes your*
* little ones*
*   and dashes them against*
*   the rock!*

Your mind goes from prophet to prophet, seeking an answer. From the prophet Amos:

Hear this word that the Lord has spoken
against you, O people of Israel... which I
brought up out of the land of Egypt:
"You only have I known

of all the families of the earth;
therefore I will punish you
for all your iniquities ".

(Amos 3:1–2)

And you think to yourself:

To be chosen by God does not mean to be
chosen for special privileges but for extra
responsibilities and for higher expectations.
The nation has fallen short. Good people
have been badly treated <Amos 2:6>, some
people have lorded it over others <2:14>,
the rich have used bribery to gain power
while ignoring the needs of the poor <5:12>,
people have made a display of their worship
and the giving of offerings while betraying
God with ill-treatment of their neighbour
<5:21>, and dishonesty in business and in
the market place has been common <8:4–6>.
Because the high expectations were not met,
the judgement has been severe. The message
of Amos was relevant to the Southern
Kingdom of Judah. If only she had listened!

And you reflect on words from the prophet
Micah:

It shall come to pass in the latter days
    that the mountain of the house of the Lord
shall be established as the highest of the
mountains...
    and many nations shall come, and say:
"Come, let us go up to the mountain of the
Lord,
    to the house of the God of Jacob;
That he may teach us his ways
    and we may walk in his paths. "
For out of Zion shall go forth the law,
    and the word of the Lord from Jerusalem.
He shall judge between many peoples,
    and shall decide for strong nations afar
off;
and they shall beat their swords into
ploughshares,
    and their spears into pruning hooks;

nation shall not lift up sword against nation,
    neither shall they learn war any more...

(Micah 4:1–3)

And you think to yourself:

The day of peace with justice shall come. The
weak shall be like the lame who walk – they
shall have equal power.

(Micah 4:7)

And you reflect on words from the prophet
Jeremiah:

The Lord said to me, "Do not say, I am only
a youth, for to all to whom I send you you
shall go, and whatever I command you you
shall speak... "

(Jeremiah 1:7)

And you think to yourself:

The message of Jeremiah must be taken
seriously. Even though I am young, as was he
when he began speaking as a prophet, I can
be strong like a fortified city <Jer. 1:18>. I
do not need to be like so many political and
religious leaders who do not seek after that
which is lasting <2:8>. I do not need to be
like "clever" people who glory in their
wisdom, or like the mighty who glory in their
power, or like the rich who glory in their
wealth <9:23>. I do not have to follow the
crowd.

You think of a message from the prophet
Ezekiel:

I was among the exiles by the river Chebar,
the heavens were opened and I saw visions of
God.

(Ezekiel 1:1)

And you think to yourself:

The people of the world are like a valley of

19

dry bones that are separate and lifeless without hope. There does not seem to be a common purpose. The bones can be joined together with flesh added and the spirit of God can bring a new life to them <Ez. 37>. The day will come when the exile will be over. We shall return to Zion and rebuild Jerusalem. The people of the world can turn to one centre and come to it like rivers flowing to a common pool. The brotherhood of all men some day will be a reality. And I can help make it so.

And these thoughts lead you on to the message of the prophet Isaiah (Second Isaiah, of the Exile):

Comfort, comfort my people,
*   says your God.*
Speak tenderly to Jerusalem,
*   and cry to her*
that her warfare is ended,
*   that her iniquity is*
*   pardoned,*
that she has received from the Lord's hand
*   double for all her sins.*
A voice cries:

"In the wilderness prepare the way of the Lord,
*   make straight in the desert a highway for our God.*
Every valley shall be lifted up,
*   and every mountain and hill be made low;*
the uneven ground shall become level,
*   and the rough places a plain.*
And the glory of the Lord shall be revealed,
*   and all flesh shall see it together,*
*   for the mouth of the Lord has spoken."*

(Isaiah 40:1–5)

End of the Exile

In the year 539 BCE the Persian army defeated the Babylonians in battle and became the overseers of the Hebrew people. Cyrus, king of Persia, made a decree that all the Hebrews in Babylonia were free to return to their homeland. After fifty years the Hebrew people in Exile were reunited with those in their homeland. They began rebuilding Jerusalem and the temple.

1. What do you believe was the influence on the Ancient Hebrews by (a) the Egyptians, (b) the Babylonians and (c) the Persians?
2. Consider the contributions of the Exile to the Ancient Hebrews towards principles for (a) peace and (b) justice.
3. What hope do you believe a Jew living in your country today might have for Israel? What do you think he might mean by *Shalom*, the Hebrew word for *peace?*

Early Views of Education

⫙ ◯ 🌀 ✝ ☪

CHARACTERS:
Narrator (Chairman), Ancient Greek *(c.* 500 BCE; an Athenian), Ancient Roman *(c.* 300 BCE), Member of the Qumran Community *(c.* 50 CE), Early Christian *(c.* 100 CE), Early Muslim *(c.* 700 CE)

NARRATOR: *Purely by accident, five friends of yours lived several hundred years ago, though at different times. Let us imagine how they would describe education during their eras, if they were to appear together in our midst today. For our convenience, they will all speak English!*

I present to you an Ancient Greek (an Athenian) who lived about 2500 years ago, an Ancient Roman who lived about 2300 years ago, a member of the Jewish Qumran Community who lived about 1950 years ago, an Early Christian who lived about 1900 years ago, and a Muslim who lived about 1300 years ago. I would like all of them to explain their views of education.

I now ask our Ancient Athenian to give his view of education.

ANCIENT ATHENIAN: *"Kaire,"* (greetings). *As an Ancient Greek, I believe that the most important thing for mankind is education. If you do the beginning of anything correctly, then the end will be right – just as if you go down the right road, with perseverance you will eventually get to the right place. The purpose of education is to help you choose the right road and then to give you the skills to journey on it. I believe that such education is the birthright of every child.*

Yet, my country was originally founded on slavery. It is for the slave to do the work. Anyone else is a fool if he works with his hands, for he would forfeit his right to be a citizen. No tradesman or farmer should work. He should simply oversee his slaves and make certain that they complete their tasks efficiently. Education, then, is not for learning how to work or how to make money through labour. Education is for making use of your leisure time, which should be all of your time. School should help you to learn how to get others (parents, teachers and dining hall ladies) to do your work for you.

So, should you study mathematics? Yes, of course; but not to learn how to add up accounts. It should be learned as a pure science for the good of your own soul. Anything that is learned for practical purposes is not education. The practical work is done by slaves; so it is unbecoming for a free citizen to be involved in that.

NARRATOR: *You're very lucky, then, not to have been a slave! I, myself, must say that I don't believe in slavery; but do continue. Do you mean that it is wrong to use school to prepare for a job? How is one going to learn how to heal the sick or design a building or teach unless he is given certain skills through education?*

21

ANCIENT ATHENIAN: *These, to be sure, belong to the art of learning. They require a higher degree of knowledge. They also are of great benefit to the community. Further, to become a businessman or a merchant is worthy of training at school, but only if one is to be involved in big business and large trading agreements, perhaps importing from many parts of the world and selling throughout the country. Education, however, must be that which develops the quality of honesty in all your dealings. The good businessman is not the one who makes a lot of money but the one who honestly presents his goods without any misrepresentation. To be trained in agriculture means to be trained to manage a very large farm or raise many hundreds of sheep. One best learns about a job by being on the job, learning through working, being an apprentice – perhaps with your father. Preparation for a job ought not to be done in a classroom.*

NARRATOR: *If, then, education is not for storing up a lot of information, if it is not for teaching a man a trade or to help him make money, what is it for?*

ANCIENT ATHENIAN: *The aim of Athenian education is to help Athenians to love beauty, to love Athens and to serve Athens in times of peace and war. It is virtuous men who make the best citizens. Therefore, education is for culture and virtue – not to make money but to become a good person and a good citizen, to show consideration for others and respect for moral values – to desire excellence for men. This is why we spend so much time studying music, playing the lyre, memorising the words of the poets and learning drama and how to act: to desire excellence for men.*

NARRATOR: *And for women? What about girls and women?*

ANCIENT ATHENIAN: *A woman can remain totally uneducated. Why should there be schools for girls to go to? Indeed, a girl should remain in seclusion, the less seen or heard the better. If a girl knows how to keep a house orderly and to take wool and make clothes, that is enough. She should have sense enough to let the maid-servants do the spinning.*

NARRATOR: *What if a girl wants to follow the same pursuits as a man?*

ANCIENT ATHENIAN: *What! I cannot even think of such an idea! It is irrational! Now, I hear that Sparta is giving education to girls; but we in Athens are above doing that. Education is for boys. And the best education, if you can afford it, is being in a class of one. This means having a private tutor to mould your character. Most important of all, education must last until the end of life. It's when the boy has left school, no longer requiring a tutor, that his real learning begins. A boy may leave school but he must never leave "learning". This is why the development of character and right attitude is so important at school. Only if you do the beginning of something correctly will the end be right. Only a good man can be a good learner.*

NARRATOR: *What do the rest of you say to this?... I call on our Ancient Roman.*

ANCIENT ROMAN: *I agree that education is important. I agree that it should help develop character – honesty and the hatred of all that is evil and unjust. Further, I agree that a boy should grow up healthy and strong in mind and body, and learn to serve the country in times of peace and war. But I do not believe education is for one's own cultural development but to fulfil one's duty to the gods, the state and the family. Reverence for the gods is essential.*

I believe that the family carries on the fine tradition of Rome. A boy should be taught by his father and his school how to speak in public in the forum. He should learn self-control, respect for the law and the institutions of his country, and show respect for his parents. He should grow up to be what his parents want him to be. A girl should be taught by her mother how to be modest, virtuous, industrious and skilled in the duties of the household. All adults should show respect and even reverence for every boy and girl.

I agree with the Greek philosopher, Plato, who wrote:

"It is more important to give respect to our children than to give gold. Parents should set the best example and never do or say anything shameful. For the best instruction stands not in precept, but in the consistent practice of what we teach."

(from *The Laws of Plato*, Jowett, B (trans.))

With this respect, education can be an initiation into a traditional way of life. Without tradition there is no motivation for living the good life.

I agree that education should not be for making money – that is, money should not be the aim; for that leads to a craving of material things rather than for being a good citizen. For the boy, this means having a job that helps his country, Rome. For the girl, this means being a good wife and mother. There is no need for formal education in a school.

A boy must be honoured by wearing a purple band on his toga, exactly like the senators. For he carries the law and acts as a priest with religious duties in the home. He must wear a bulla, a round, flat, hollow leather disk around his neck, like a locket. This charm is to ward off the influence of the evil eye.

We Romans do not have schools. A child's main influence until the age of seven is his mother. Then, the boy is attached to the care of his father who must be his constant companion and his main teacher. He assists his father as an apprentice to his trade, business or on the farm. When his father goes to the assembly in the forum, so must the son go to listen to the public debates. From his father he learns the laws and history of Rome, and physical exercises – to throw the javelin, to fight in armour, to ride a horse, to box. Perhaps from his grandfather he will learn to read, to write clearly and even to swim. It is important that the boy marry into a good family; it is unimportant whether that family has wealth.

In short, it is the responsibility of parents, and not teachers in a school, to make their life work the nurture and education of their children, to initiate them into the way of Roman life.

When a boy is about fifteen or sixteen years old, he exchanges his toga with its purple stripe and begins wearing the plain white toga of a Man, and he removes the bulla from his neck. He is taken to the forum and, after a sacrifice to the gods, he has his name entered on the tabularium, the list of names of full citizens. Only then does someone outside the family, a mentor, help him to launch into the service of Rome. A mentor assists him usually for about a year.

<This was the pattern of Roman education down to about 240 BCE. When the empire began developing, with the fathers taken off to war, a school system was established as a father-substitute.>

NARRATOR: *So, the fact that there was no school in Ancient Rome in 300 BCE doesn't mean that there was no learning! Let us ask a member of the Qumran Community in Ancient Israel to tell us about his view of education.*

MEMBER OF THE QUMRAN COMMUNITY: *When I was a Jewish child, I went to school at my local synagogue during the week and worshipped there on the seventh day of each week, the Sabbath day of rest. I learned how to read and write Hebrew. I learned many stories from the Scriptures – such as the creation stories in Genesis, the freedom of my people in Exodus, the laws in Leviticus and Deuteronomy, hymns from the Psalms and a collection of prayers. Then when I was about ten, my parents decided to associate me with a community that has about four thousand members throughout Palestine. All are Jewish men and live in communities away from cities and villages. My community, Qumran, is in the desert near the Dead Sea and houses about two hundred men. We want to keep the covenant with God, promise to obey his laws and be faithful to the best of the Hebrew religion. As Moses led the Israelites into the wilderness to receive the law, so we live in the desert to keep the law, to reaffirm our faith in God. In this way we hope to help remove the darkness of evil in the world and bring the light of righteousness and truth. The Torah, the Laws of God as revealed to Moses and explained by the prophets, I believe, have become badly interpreted. But there are now new prophets and teachers in the land and one of these, at Qumran, has become my teacher and the teacher of other men who have joined our community. We call him, "the Teacher of Righteousness" who will help usher in the new age of the Kingdom of God with peace and justice. We believe that as our priest before God, our teacher speaks the message of God.*

We have to prepare ourselves to receive his message. We have to seek communion with the eternal presence of God so that as children of light we can receive the light of wisdom and love. This means that we live a highly disciplined life, away from all earthly desires.

Ours is an age of great expectation. Our community is near where the Jordan River empties into the Dead Sea. There, just a few years ago, John the Baptist was preaching and baptising, crying out in the wilderness that the Kingdom of God is at hand. We heard rumours that about twenty years ago a Jewish teacher by the name of Joshua (or Jesus) of Nazareth was baptised by John and then taught disciples and followers about the Kingdom of God.

We, too, have baptism and we are disciples of our own teacher. Indeed, we have a deep pool at Qumran in which our members wash, as a ritual for seeking a new life.

At the age of ten I began a thorough study of the laws and covenant of God. When I was twenty, I was publicly brought before those who were members of the community; and I was tested on my knowledge and moral character. Then for a year I was on probation and all my possessions were handed over to a trustee, reserved for common ownership of the community. I was given a further testing at the end of the year, voted on, and admitted to the table of fellowship and full membership of the Qumran Community.

I own nothing. In my total poverty as a student, I work at a stone table studying the law and copying scrolls, and I work in the community garden raising crops. I join in the services of worship and prayer. My life has been one of study and obedience to the Qumran Teacher of Righteousness who is God's representative for my guidance and life. Finally, I would want to make it quite clear that I do not believe in slavery. It is a violation of God's law. He gave freedom to the Jewish people. He would want them to extend it to others.

NARRATOR: *We have heard from our Ancient Athenian, our Ancient Roman, and this Member of the Jewish Qumran Community. I call, now, on an Early*

Christian to give us his view of education,
that of a Christian around 100 CE.

EARLY CHRISTIAN: *In his First Letter to
the Corinthians, Paul wrote that "God will
destroy the wisdom of the wise". Paul
believed that God has chosen the foolish
things of the world to ultimately reveal truth.
In its early days, Christianity has attracted so
many simple, humble, uneducated people and
I believe that it must always be open to them.
Jesus once put a child in the midst of his
disciples and said, "Unless you become like
one of these, you can in no way enter the
Kingdom of Heaven". Therefore any view of
life which excludes the simple-minded people
of this world is a violation of my religion.
One can be very limited in one's ability to
think and still be a Christian.*

*And yet, I know through the Gospels that,
as a Jewish rabbi (teacher), Jesus taught that
one must love God with all the mind as well
as the heart, soul and strength. I believe,
therefore, that faith is open to the simple-
minded but demands all of that mind. Many
Early Christians cannot read or write, but
they can think and Christianity should
challenge all of that thinking.*

*As Paul also wrote in his First letter to the
Corinthians, "When I was a child, I spoke
like a child, I thought like a child, I reasoned
like a child; when I became a man, I gave up
childish ways".*

*When Paul visited Ancient Athens, he saw
people worshipping many idols and then one
inscribed, "to the unknown god". He said
that Jesus had come to reveal this unknown
god. Paul talked to Epicurean and Stoic
philosophers about their Greek and Roman
gods. The greatest wisdom of man, and the
aim of education, should be to know God and
God's way for man. It is not the way of
intellectual arrogance, but it is the way of
wisdom and truth. Yet all the wisdom in the
world does not, in itself, make one a good
man.*

*Jesus was brought up in a carpenter's
home in Nazareth. He learned a trade from
his father. He received the Jewish education
of his day. As one from the Jewish Qumran
Community has just told us, Jewish education
for all boys began at an early age. Jesus
went to school at his local synagogue in
Nazareth during the week and worshipped
there on the Sabbath day. He learned how to
read and write Hebrew, he learned stories
from the Scriptures and numerous prayers.*

*In homes where a Jewish family became
Christian, the synagogue continued to be the
school for the children until Christians were
barred from the synagogue. Gentile families
who became Christians continued normal
education for their children according to the
tradition of their culture, until Roman
persecution made Christianity illegal.*

*We have not set up schools for our
children because of the fear of persecution
and because we expect the Second Coming of
Christ at any moment. There is no point in
preparing for life in the world when we
expect the world shortly to become the
Kingdom of God.*

*Where education is important is for those
joining the Church. For this purpose, the
accounts of the teachings of Jesus which we
have in the Gospels were written.*

NARRATOR: *Now I call on our Early
Muslim to speak.*

EARLY MUSLIM: *I believe in the teachings
of the Jewish prophets, in the teaching of the
prophet Jesus of Nazareth, and in the
revelation of the prophet Muhammad as contained in the Qur'an. I believe that education
should lead to knowledge of the will of God
and the surrender of one's life to him.*

*I believe that the aim of education is to
help one to learn about the Truth that is from
God. God has shown his Truth through the
teachings of prophets: from Adam, through
Noah, Moses, Jesus and others in this golden*

chain of prophets. Muhammad (peace be upon him) brought revealed words of Truth and guidance. The Qur'an, the book revealed to the prophet Muhammad (peace be upon him), is the last of these words of guidance. The most important aim of education is to discover the Word of God, informing a person of his Creator, of the purpose of creation and how to live a fulfilling and rewarding life at peace with himself, with all others, and with his Creator.

Islam is an Arabic word. It is derived from two roots, one SaLiMa, meaning peace and the other SaLLiMa, meaning submission. Islam is a way of life, a commitment to surrender one's will to the Will of God and

as such to be at peace with the Creator and all that he has created. As God is One, so all of his creation is one and indivisible. The religious and secular are one and two sides of the same coin. Therefore the oneness of God means the oneness of life. Distinctions of race, colour, caste, wealth, and power disappear. Education, for a Muslim, therefore, ought to be for peace and justice.

NARRATOR: *For giving their views on education, I wish to thank the Ancient Athenian, the Ancient Roman, the Member of the Qumran Community, the Early Christian and the Early Muslim.*

❓

1. Which one of the five positions do you most agree with? Why? What, in your view, are its weaknesses, if any?
2. Which one of the five positions do you least agree with? Why? What, in your view, are its strong points, if any?

Ⅲ ○ ♥ ✝ ☉

Ancient Greeks
All Things in Moderation

With which of the following statements do you *Agree* and with which do you *Disagree?* Give reasons for your answers.

1. *Water is the substance of all things.* (Thales, *c.* 585 BCE.)
2. *Everything is composed of monads* (atoms), *tiny particles which cannot be seen.* (Anaximander, *c.* 546 BCE.)
3. *Air is the substance of all things.* (Anaximenes, *c.* 540 BCE.)
4. *All is change and in constant flux. You cannot step into the same river twice because new waters are ever flowing.* (Heraclitus, *c.* 500 BCE)
5. *As notes are to music, so numbers are the clue to all things... The square on the hypotenuse is equal to the sum of the square of the other two sides.* (Pythagoras, *c.* 510 BCE.)
6. *All is one; change is illusion.* (Parmenides, *c.* 450 BCE.)
7. *Know yourself; the unexamined life is not worth living.*
8. *It is better to suffer evil than to do it.*
9. *Say what you mean; mean what you say. Choose your words carefully.*
10. *No one would do evil if he really knew its consequences.*
11. *Knowledge is essential to goodness.* (7–11 attributed to Socrates, 469–399 BCE.)
12. *You learn best in discussion with others, putting together your best beliefs with theirs.*
13. *You can never really know anything until you understand its relationship with other things.*
14. *Be guided by universals, seeking to know the general form behind the specific ideas.*
15. *You cannot know a thing (or person) itself, but only a false image of it.* (12–15 attributed to Plato, *c.* 427–347 BCE.)
16. *The good is that at which everything should aim. Like an archer, aim above a mark if you wish to hit it.*
17. *The middle way is the best way; avoid extremes.*
18. *Courage is the golden mean between cowardice and rashness.*
19. *The chief end of man is happiness, not pleasure. Happiness is well-being for others as well as for yourself.*
20. *Man is a charioteer being pulled by two horses:* Reason *and* Emotion. *Keep them side by side, running together. Beware lest one dominates the other.*
21. *Virtue is developed by habit. You learn by doing the right thing repeatedly.*
22. *Justice is virtue applied to your treatment of your neighbour.*

23. *Practical wisdom is knowing how to obtain the end.*
24. *Art is making rather than doing.*
25. *One learns best by himself and can best increase his own knowledge.*
26. *To study music has the power of producing a certain effect on the moral character of the soul.* (16–26 attributed to Aristotle, *c.* 384–322 BCE.)

Assume that **purely by accident** you are an Ancient Greek living in about the year 200 BCE. Your land of Greece is a land of mountains. It has a jagged coastline on three sides with numerous islands. The Mediterranean Sea lies to the South, the Ionian Sea to the West and the Aegean Sea to the East.

You were born in Athens. You think to yourself:

For many of us, it is as important to have power on the seas as to have it on land. We have several hundred cities which are independent states. And there are numerous peasant villages, all independent of each other. Some are supported by farming and the raising of animals, others are supported by commerce.

My ancestors were primarily farmers and shepherds. This means that villages were first collections of farmers and were self-sufficient. They did not have kings to whom the land belonged; it belonged to the people.

Every adult man has voting rights. We are a limited democracy like the Ancient Babylonians, but without their unity. Everyone in a community tends to be of one blood relationship.

At the top of the social scale are those people who have fought in battles, either on land or sea. They have been awarded most of the land. So the wealth belongs mostly to those of military background. Certainly only members of the tribe can own land.

In the middle are free farmers, then landless agricultural labourers, merchants and craftsmen. Then there are the resident foreigners who do not enjoy equal rights,

even the right to vote.

At the very bottom end of the social scale are the slaves, gained through the spoils of warfare.

All these city states and villages have different constitutions, with magistrates, a senate and an assembly. The magistrate is the priest of the community who decides religious matters, becomes the general of the army in times of war, and (with the advice of his senate) decides matters of justice that have been carried to the assembly of the people.

The cities offer centres of commerce, administration, and religious observance and have been fortified for military defence. Our Athenian navies have made foreign conquests, bringing much wealth and allowing farmers to specialise. But in difficult years, farmers have had to borrow money at high interest rates, using their land to guarantee payment. If they cannot make one of the payments, they lose their land and are almost reduced to the status of slaves.

Athens, the great port city, is the largest city-state with about 40,000 male adults. Other city-states, including Sparta, have less than 5000 citizens (male adults).

Some of our people are really land hungry. They want more trade outlets and are setting up colonies through lands around the Mediterranean Sea.

Now, instead of bartering, we are using money. The agora, the market-place, originally a place for religious and political assembly, is a centre for business. Some craftsmen and merchants, by using slaves, are getting very rich. Many believe that "money makes the man", that money is the

*measure of all things. I'm not so sure.
Certainly if I were a slave I wouldn't believe
that.*

*In the early days of my country, religion
flourished. It contained stories of tribal gods.
Before we had a written language, the myths
were told by word of mouth from one
generation to another. There were magical
practices and superstitions based on spring
and harvest festivals. These survived after
our development of ideas of philosophy and
science. Drama, poetry, art, music and
dancing expressed beliefs in magic and the
gods. A written language made possible the
writing down of great heroic epic poetry such
as the Iliad and the Odyssey (in the eighth
century BCE). But these were essentially
centred on human, rather than divine, tales.
They prepared the way for the decline of the
priest and the rise of the poet as the
inspiration of Greek culture. The religious
took second place to the secular. The
independence of the city-states encouraged
the independence of thought and a sense of
freedom from dependence upon religion. It
was thought that man's achievement was free
to develop through hard work. He could
move from an animal-like roaming to a
system of order and justice – under Zeus, but
through human effort.*

*I believe in Zeus and other gods. Yet it is
not religion but philosophy that is the main
influence on my life.*

Religion

A myth is a story used to explain the world,
nature, and questions about the meaning of
life and death. In Ancient Greece, myths
were about both gods and goddesses. A
shepherd, competing for grazing land and
concerned over the protection of his sheep by
night, might create a story about a strong,
masculine sky-god and how he helps keep
the sheep from danger and being taken by an

enemy. This god is to him like having a
defending army.

However, a farmer living within the
protection of a peaceful, agricultural community might imagine a story about the
fruitfulness of the earth-mother goddess to
explain the source of nourishment for his
crops.

In Greece, as elsewhere, the first forms of
worship were adoration of natural objects
such as trees, rocks and animals. Then
reverence was given to man-made objects
such as weapons, fire, certain tools, and roof-
pillars – important for his survival. Religion
was influenced by beliefs from many lands
including Egypt, Babylonia and Palestine.

As the circumstances varied – new leaders,
invasions, migrations, the growth of towns,
changing social patterns – the various
mythological stories produced a hierarchy of
gods and goddesses peculiar to these
circumstances and different from one
community to another.

The characteristics of a god or goddess
could change. In trade with the Eastern
world, the people of Crete (1000 years before
Classical Greece, 700 years before Homer)
came to believe in a bull-like god who had
three stages of his life: that of a youth, a
priest-king and a dying animal. He was the
son of Rhea, the great Mother goddess.
Various stories were told of him being born
at Knossos and at Mount Dicte.

Then when the mainland became powerful,
it acquired this bull-god but equated him with
Zeus, its sky-god. There are stories of Zeus
being born in Arcadia and also in Messenia.
When the Olympic Games became so
important, stories were told about how Zeus
was born in Olympia. This was an attempt to
explain how the Games were founded.

Rhea (known also by other names) bore
other children, indeed one each year as a
symbol of her respect for her worshippers by
bringing a new harvest. It was believed that
her own fruitfulness was a reminder to the

fields to bear a good harvest and to the flocks and herds to multiply. Each year she had a new consort (sexual companion) who was slain during the seed time, with his body and blood scattered and sprinkled over the fields to fertilise them. Then she chose another partner to father another child.

Each community had its mythological stories showing how the partner was slain. In Mysia he was drowned, in Thrace he was torn to pieces by women, in villages around Mount Ida he was bled to death, in Elis he was flung from a moving chariot, in Crete he was slain by a double-headed axe.

When the god-companion became favoured by the people, stories were told about how he was not slain but a sacrifice was substituted for his death. And the god became a king-like figure, surpassing in authority the goddess.

The Greek's basic need, of course, was food. As he developed villages and cities, his need became protection through power. Stories about a fertility-goddess explained how he got food. Stories about a protection-god explained his source of power. Stories about the god Zeus evolved from his being merely a consort of the earth-goddess who died (or was killed) annually to the immortal, never-ageing, supreme god and divine ruler. Stories of arguments and quarrels between goddesses and gods were myths to explain the struggle between old forms of worship (fertility cults, harvest festivals, etc.) and the new forms of worship (praise for the protector-god, prayers for success in battle, etc.).

Earlier, a man left his family to marry into – and join – the family of his bride. Later, this practice changed and instead it became the custom for the bride to leave home to live with her husband in the house of his father. Her brother would inherit the family possessions; where before, her father's home would be inherited by herself and her husband.

An early myth tells the story of the god Menelaus who went to Sparta to live with his wife, Helen, the (supposed) daughter of the king. Eventually he became the successor to his father-in-law's throne. A later myth tells the story of Odysseus who persuaded his bride, Penelope (daughter of a Spartan chieftain), to go with him to his home on the island of Ithaca.

Eventually, twelve gods and goddesses emerged to have chief authority and dwelled with Zeus, their lord – and for some, their father – in palaces around his stronghold on Mount Olympus. They were:

- ZEUS (ruler and father; giver of laws and good and bad fortunes, defender of liberty and justice, protector of property, and giver of the harvest.)
- POSEIDON (brother of Zeus; lord of the seas)
- HERA (goddess guardian of marriage and childbirth)
- DEMETER (sister of Poseidon; corn-goddess on whom survival depends)
- APOLLO (son of Zeus; played the lyre; god of light, youth, prophecy and music)
- ARTEMIS (twin sister of Apollo; giver of fertility)
- APHRODITE (mother of Eros, the god of love; goddess of love)
- ARES (son of Zeus and Hera; god of war)
- HEPHAESTUS (god of fire and magic)
- HERMES (son of Zeus; god of luck, wealth, roads, dreams, and patron of merchants and thieves)
- ATHENE (daughter of Zeus; patron goddess of Athens)
- HESTIA (later replaced by Dionysus, protector of theatres and drama)
- ASKLEPIOS (god of medicine)

Most Greeks believed that gods and goddesses, though unseen, were present everywhere. They looked like people (anthropomorphic) though they were far more attractive in appearance and had far nobler minds. They were excellent craftsmen and any person with talent was thought to have received a special gift from them. Therefore one was under obligation to use one's talent to the best of one's ability, but without pride. Pride would offend the gods and violate the basic maxim, *"All things in moderation, nothing in excess"*. Vanity was considered to be an extreme of self-appreciation.

The gods also stood above the moral restrictions of people. Because the gods were free to engage in sexual exploits, it did not mean that people had that right. The gods and goddesses were not bound by inflexible rules, dogmas or doctrines. The stories of how they were created did not determine human creation. There was no conflict between religion and science. Indeed, all scientific discoveries were considered to reflect divine power. The people would practice medicine and also worship Asklepios, the god of healing, believing that there was no conflict in doing both.

In towns and cities the Greeks worshipped their gods in beautiful temples built to honour them. In the sixth century BCE human sacrifice was replaced by animal sacrifice and gifts of fruit and flowers. Religious ceremonies included solemn processions through the streets, the singing of hymns (writings of poets, set to music), the saying of prayers, and orderly rituals which closed with the worshippers eating the sacrificed animals.

There were sceptics (doubters) and atheists (non-believers) among the intellectuals and eventually science and secular (non-religious) philosophy became strong in Greek thinking with mythology being unimportant.

Philosophy

The development of cities (with their market places used for political debates) and travel (with its commercial and cultural contacts throughout the Mediterranean world) brought much enlightenment.

In the seventh and sixth centuries BCE, reason and experience of life gave birth to philosophy and science. Principles were sought for understanding man and the order of nature. Thales, Anaximander, Anaximenes, Heraclitus, Pythagoras and Parmenides have been mentioned; and there were other contributors at this time.

The most original creation in Athenian culture was drama, developed from primal religious rituals and tribal initiations connected with the god, Dionysus. From this beginning came Greek tragedies and comedies. Greek architecture and sculpture reached their height with the Temple of Zeus at Olympia (*c.* 460 BCE) and the Parthenon at Athens (*c.* 440 BCE). Herodotus became the *"Father of History"* when he wrote a critically constructed account of the Persian Wars (*c.* 440 BCE).

"Philosophy" is from two Greek words for *"love"* and *"wisdom"*. Socrates, the *"Father of Philosophy"*, questioned principles of justice and behaviour, and current political and moral answers. As a citizen of Athens, he initially was permitted to speak critically of its conduct, education and political affairs; but he finally was imprisoned and put to death. He wanted discussion to be the means of educating practical men, seeking the best in themselves and their relationships.

Plato, a student of Socrates, wrote *dialogues* in which he portrayed his great teacher in conversation with certain individuals seeking wisdom and others (the Sophists) whom he believed were blocking the road towards truth with their closed minds. He founded a school (the Academy) with which he tried to create an ideal pattern for educating leaders for society.

Aristotle, the most famous pupil of Plato and himself the teacher of Alexander the Great, founded a new kind of school, the

Lyceum (*c.* 335 BCE) which made Athens a centre of learning which included mathematics, astronomy, physics, botany, zoology, geography, debate and all areas of philosophy. It became a school drawing in students from all over Greece.

Alexander the Great's conquest of the East (including Palestine in 333 BCE) formalised and expanded the Greek Empire. Then, in little more than a hundred years, Greece came under the domination of Rome (*c.* 200 BCE– 300 CE).

————————————— **?** —————————————

1. Thucydides became the *Father of Scientific History* when he wrote a careful account of the Peloponnesian War and proposed that *Knowledge of the past helps us to understand and interpret the future.* (a) Is this true? (b) Should history also be the study of peace as well as war? (c) If so, how?
2. What is the difference between a myth, a legend, and a folk-tale?
3. *Religion, to the Ancient Greeks, was a form of escape, like watching television.* To what extent do you believe this statement is true? To what extent do you believe the practice of religion today is a form of escapism? Is religion merely a form of escape?
4. Some Ancient Greeks used mystery religions to try to guarantee a better life in the afterworld, life after death. In what ways is religion used to try to guarantee this today? Should this be its main purpose?
5. **Philosophy** is often divided into five parts:
   Metaphysics, concerning questions about existence;
   Epistemology, concerning questions about knowing;
   Ethics, concerning questions about morality;
   Logic, concerning questions about reasoning; and
   Aesthetics, concerning questions about beauty.
   State a question about each part *and* give two possible answers to each question.

III

Ancient Romans
Pax Romana

? ———————— ———————— **?**

1. Do you believe that you should follow in your father/mother's footsteps? That is, to what extent do you believe that you should have the same life style and vocation as one of your parents?
2. To what extent should you believe in the institutions (i.e. church, school, club, political party) supported by your parents?
3. Should education be for the purpose of inducting you into the traditions of the nation? If not, why not and what do you think is its purpose?
4. What traditions of your nation (aspects of its life) would you like to help preserve for the next generation?
5. To what extent do you hope that your children will have the same type of life that you have?
6. Which of the following statements do you agree with. Do you think you are an Epicurean or a Stoic? A mixture of both? Neither? Why?

Epicurean

1. Happiness is the chief goal in life.
2. Happiness is through pleasure which leads to peace of mind.
3. Eat, drink and be merry for tomorrow you may die.
4. Enjoy what you have to the full.
5. Mental joy is the greatest kind of joy.
6. Do not worry about the past or anticipate the future; live in the present moment.
7. Religion is unnecessary.

Stoic

1. Let reason, which is good, rule passion/emotion, which is bad.
2. There is one god: Jupiter, the god of discipline.
3. The world is good; do not try to escape from it.
4. Treat others as rational beings; this is Roman law.
5. The undisciplined life is not worth living.
6. Keep a stiff upper lip; do not let any emotions show.
7. Accept the religion of the nation.

Assume that **purely by accident** you are living about two thousand years ago in Rome under the emperor Augustus (reigned 27 BCE–14 CE).

Some of your earliest ancestors entered Italy from North Africa, by way of Spain and a western land route, and settled on the coast near Genoa.

Others arrived between 3000 and 2000 BCE as invaders from the north bringing metal and the new age of military development through bronze weapons. They built defensive camps raised on stakes, the prototype of the Roman camp.

A third wave entered from the north in the eleventh century BCE armed with iron, though they were illiterate and their culture was not as advanced as that of the Egyptians and Babylonians at that time. Classical Greek culture was coming to birth, when the Romans who were later to conquer Greece were still uncivilised in the sense that they were a rural society with no cities. It was during this Iron Age that the foundation was laid to Roman religion: belief in the survival of the dead (either transported to another world or hovering as spirits in this one), belief in gods not as individual beings (as in Greek polytheism where many gods had begun as humans) but as forces, spirits, dwelling in things.

A fourth layer of civilising effect came with invaders in the ninth century BCE. They were the Etruscans from Asia Minor to the East, and by water routes they brought skills of painting, sculpture and metal work, a desire for good living and commerce. They also brought the art of writing which they may have learned from the Greeks.

A fifth and final wave of ancestral immigrants came to Southern Italy from Greece in the eighth century BCE eventually building more Doric temples in Italy and Sicily than were ever built in Greece itself. (Links with Greek culture had preceded them by five hundred years.) Not until then was the city of Rome founded.

The Greek influence continued and Roman spirit gods were eventually upgraded to become equivalents of Greek deities with which they were assimilated. But Roman religion had varied from age to age. Jupiter was eventually assimilated with the Greek god Zeus, but to his earliest worshippers he was neither like a god nor like a human. He was just a stone, the spirit in the stone.

Every Roman house had a shrine. As a Roman at the age of sixteen you take off the *bulla* charm from around your neck and put on a new *toga*. This was the coming of age ceremony called *Officium Togae Virilis.*

To bind yourself to a contract or business deal you go into the temple of Jupiter, pick up a stone and make an oath:

If I knowingly deceive you and break this contract, may Jupiter, without harm to the City or the citadel, cast me forth as I cast this stone.

Then you throw the stone as far as you can.

To ratify a treaty, a priest kills a pig with a flint-stone from the temple of Jupiter and says:

If the Roman People shall be the first to transgress this treaty by common consent and of malice aforethought, then Jupiter do you on that day strike the Roman People even as on this day I smite this pig, and smite it harder because you are stronger and more mighty.

The tradition of using a stone came from the Neolithic Age, when stones were used as axe-heads, and was carried over into the Iron Age. Thus, metal-users held to the earlier tradition in honouring Jupiter, the god of light and sky and the great protector of city and state.

In the same way you consider Mars as the god of war whom you have assimilated with the Greek god Ares, and yet you hold to his primitive attributes of a spirit in growing crops. The month of March (to which he gave his name) is a time when you celebrate his festival, for it launches the season of good weather, not only the time for crops to grow but also the best time to wage war.

Quirinus, the third in the triad of *high* gods of Rome, was also a god summoned in war. He was a god with no mythology or human identity in his primitive form when he was more an *it*, a lifeless thing, than a *living person*. A priest would anoint the gods and in this way acknowledge them as having a life-giving force, which Romans called *numen*. The word means *nod* and suggests that a god need not do anything but give a nod if it wishes to meet your need.

At the end of each year (23rd February by the Roman calendar) you and your neighbours meet at the stone which marks the separation of your properties. You sacrifice a pig or lamb and the *numen* (spirit) protects your boundary from feuds between you, and from aggressors attacking you, for another year.

You believe in gods and goddesses galore, deities for all seasons, circumstances, and for all things. And you are often not certain whether they are male or female and so often you begin your prayer, *Be you a god or a goddess...*, implying that you do not know which, but also revealing the primal roots of your religion where divinity was more an *it*, a thing, than a *person*.

Your worship is a development of liturgy that grew out of primal religion. You are interested in gaining personal and material rewards for yourself and your family. Your worship does not demand any moral obligations. You please the gods only so that they will please you. Your desire is not, *Thy will be done*, but *my will be done*.

At first Roman religion was for the clan (the family) and was totally domestic. From this developed the state cult with its public days of obligation, public festivals. The fighting season ended in October, requiring purification after all the bloodshed. On the 15th a chariot race was held, with a horse (representing the corn-spirit) from the winning team being sacrificed to Mars. Its tail was cut off and carried by a runner to the Regis. There it was hung up with its blood dripping sacrificially onto the altar and then used by the Vestal Virgins for purification. The shields were stored away, symbolising that the season for battle was over.

Each December you celebrate Saturnalia, the winter festival time for partying, not realising that originally it was a religious festival connected with farming. As the focus of life has changed from the rural settlement to the urban state, so the simple primitive ritual of the family hearth, directed by the father, has been superseded by the elaborate liturgy of a State religion, highly organised by special priests and priestesses. The common denominator of magic meant that the self-centred aim continued. What was *good for the family* merely became what was *good for the state*. *My will be done* became *our will be done*. Gods and goddesses please note: you exist to serve *us*.

The purpose of building temples was no different from the purpose of building altars of mounds of earth perhaps covered by a crude roof. Through the Etruscan and Greek influences, representations of deities were placed within the temples. The *numina* (nods) no longer were spirits; they had become personified. *Numina* were no longer *its*; they now had to be *hes* and *shes*, gods and goddesses in the images of men and women and for the purpose of meeting human needs. Animism (belief that animals have immortal souls) and pantheism (that spirits are in all things) developed into anthropomorphism (belief that spirits could be represented by human images). The first Roman temple may have been built in the first year of the Republic, 509 BCE.

By the Christian era, the Hellenisation of Roman religion was complete:

(Roman – Greek)

gods
Jupiter – Zeus
Neptune – Poseidon
Mars – Ares
Apollo – Apollo
Vulcan – Hephaestus
Mercury – Hermes

goddesses
Juno – Hera
Minerva – Athena
Diana – Artemis
Venus – Aphrodite
Vesta – Hestia
Ceres – Demeter

With the Roman acquisition of Greek mythology (stories of divine escapades), the anthropomorphism was extensive.

Then came an event that brought about a dramatic change in Roman religion. The disasters of the Second Punic War (Hannibal, 218–201 BCE) suggested that the gods were not on Rome's side. The rituals of the State had not maintained the favours of the gods. Someone else's will was being done.

So the Romans did five things to appease the gods:

1. They changed the Gladiatorial games in the Forum from *man against beast* to the more civilising (?) formula of *man against man*. However this did not appear to be enough to woo the gods.
2. Therefore they reverted to human sacrificing. The Romans tried burying alive Greek and Gallic men and women in the Forum. But the gods were seemingly unimpressed.
3. So the Romans tried to draw the gods' attention to extra-ordinary events (*i.e.* a statue *unnaturally* falling on its face, a volcano *strangely* erupting), suggesting that Rome was special. The gods were unpersuaded and their sympathies were still not gained.
4. So the Romans placed Greek gods side by side with Roman ones to suggest the authority of two impressive civilisations. The gods were still unimpressed.
5. Then the Romans added the pride of the Orient to their authority. When Hannibal was defeated but still at large in southern Italy – and to surpass the power of his elephants – they sought possession of the statue of Cybele, the Great Mother from Pessinus (near modern Ankara) in Galatia. But would King Attalus I of Pergamum release her? Yes, he was persuaded to stay on the right side of Rome. It was only a year after the Great Mother arrived by boat and was placed in the temple of Victory that Hannibal left Italy for good.

The Great Mother was the first eastern deity to enter Rome; she was followed by others from the East, including Asia and Egypt. (This look to the East continued in the arrival of Judaism and Christianity. The Christian Church in Rome was to be founded by two immigrant Jews: Peter and Paul.)

Meanwhile, Greek philosophy came to Italy. Epicurus (born 341 BCE) offered a secular (without belief in a god) philosophy of escape, peace and quiet. Aristotle had taught that happiness was the chief goal in life. Epicureanism developed this idea. At its best, it interpreted this happiness as well-being and peace of mind: not worrying about the past nor anticipating the future, but appreciating the present moment in contemplation with freedom from dependence upon material things. At its worst, it interpreted this happiness as pleasure, self-indulgence, sensual excess and dependence on material things. Rome tended to degrade Epicureanism and popularise the saying, *Eat, drink and be merry, for tomorrow you may die* – live to the full not with self-examination but with self-indulgence. Horace and Lucretius became Roman proponents of Epicureanism.

Then there was Zeno, the father of Stoicism. He was the son of a Phoenician merchant in Cyprus and came to Athens in 314 BCE. Unlike Epicurus, Zeno had a strong belief in God, the God of vigorous reason and the search for truth. He taught that divine reason controlled the laws of the universe and that it was also the source of human reason which ought to control human life. To conform to this reason (to obey its laws) alone led to the good life. Epicureans denied divine Providence; Stoics believed that it ruled the world and ought to rule the human heart. Stoicism, with its vigorous discipline, was to become the religion of the Roman army. It was Pantheistic without belief in a transcendent God. Seneca became its Roman proponent. And Jews who settled in Rome found a waiting audience. Though few Romans became Jews, many placed Yahweh, the God of the Jews, alongside Egyptian and Greek gods.

Augustus renewed and revitalised Rome, creating for it the image of an eternal city and established effects of a *Pax Romana*, Roman Peace, praised by poets. Virgil and Horace, though they claimed to be Epicureans, gave literary additions to the religious revival. Horace called for the restoration of the temples. Augustus sanctioned emperor worship in the East, where people had been used to thinking of rulers as gods, to induce absolute loyalty to the state and its traditions. (Emperor worship was later extended to the West.)

As a Roman living under the reign of Augustus, you have a religion which is eclectic (drawn from many sources) yet lacking dogmatism. You are under no compulsion to believe any particular statement of faith or to worship in any particular way. You have been encouraged to worship and keep the festivals more for political reasons than for religious ones. You are bathed in philosophy, scepticism, mysticism, emotionalism and paganism. You hope that *Pax Romana* will last forever.

?

---

1. Consider your views on the following statements:
   a. *To our children we should bequeath self-respect and not god.* (From the *Laws*, Plato 427–347 BCE: Athens.)
   b. *The aim of education is to produce self-control, combined with dutiful affection to parents, and kindliness to kindred.* (Cicero, 106–43 BCE.)
   c. *It is by obeying the gods, O Roman, that you rule the world.* (Horace, 65–08 BCE.)
   d. *Cuius regio, eius religio*: Whose is the realm, his is the religion.
   e. *We must take care that the child, who is not yet old enough to love his studies, does not come to hate them.* (Quintillion, c. 40–118 CE.)
   f. *Friendship is one of the world's supreme values, and a school supplies friendships which are never open to the boy with a private tutor. In a school the boy learns not only what he is taught, but what others are taught as well.* (Quintillion, paraphrased by William Barclay in *Educational Ideals in the Ancient World*, p. 176.)

2. Roman education was *not the kind of education which consists in amassing facts, or acquiring certificates, or obtaining degrees. It was initiation into a way of life.* (William Barclay, *op. cit.* p. 157.)

   Do you think that the examination system should be continued, changed or abolished? Why?

3. *Roman religion and education were both founded on tradition. Both were initiations into a traditional way of life.*

   Do you think that this was a good thing? What traditions do you think should be maintained by you for the benefit of the next generation?

   ()

Qumran Community and the Dead Sea Scrolls
Ancient Voices Cry from the Wilderness

? ──────────   ────────── **?**

With which of the following statements do you *Agree* and with which do you *Disagree?* If you disagree, briefly explain why.

1. The world has ceased to live by the laws of God as interpreted by prophets of old and these urgently need to be re-examined.
2. A righteous teacher who seeks to usher in a new age of peace with justice should be listened to and obeyed.
3. It would be a good thing if I could get away into a remote place and live in a community committed to studying the laws of righteousness and living by faith in God.
4. Thorough preparation, firm self-discipline and communion with the eternal presence of God are required of one who desires to receive the light of wisdom and love.
5. One's knowledge of righteousness and one's morality of character should be periodically examined.
6. The day will come when evil will be at an end and righteousness and justice will prevail. Meanwhile, one ought to try to belong to the community of righteous people however few that remnant may be.
7. All things are divinely ordained and planned, even the struggle between good and evil in society and in the individual souls of men and women.
8. The need for peace with justice is so urgent in the world today that your community should organise a rota whereby study of the way to achieve this should continue day and night (24 hours a day, seven days a week), with you participating every third night.
9. Before being fully admitted to a community, one should have a probationary period in three stages, each lasting a year.
10. A priestly leader should be assigned to every group of ten students.
11. All meals should be eaten in common, with teachers and pupils entering the dining hall in groups ordered according to knowledge and good character.
12. There will be a last judgement when the body will be raised and flesh will become immortal with the soul.
13. Humility, patience, simplicity, obedience, fidelity and purity are virtues to be prized.

39

14. Everyone should bring whatever he owns and all the money he has into the community when joining it so that all, including one's strength and knowledge, can be shared in common ownership.
15. Vows of allegiance should annually be made to the rules of the community by all who wish to remain in it.
16. I should continue learning and studying throughout my life.

The extent to which you agree with the above sixteen statements suggests the extent to which you believe your community should be like the Qumran Community. We have already considered the view of education in the Qumran Community (see p. 24). This community was more than an educational institution, however, and membership in it was seen to be membership for life. Many scholars believe that it was from this community that the Dead Sea Scrolls apparently came.

The most important archaeological discovery of the twentieth century. This is how the Dead Sea Scrolls have been described. Father de Vaux (a Roman Catholic priest, biblical scholar and archaeologist) assisted with the translation of the Scrolls in Jerusalem and led the excavations of Qumran.

How were the Dead Sea Scrolls discovered and identified?

One day in February or March 1947, a fifteen year old boy of the Taamirah tribe of Bedouins by the name of Mohammed adh-Dhib (meaning *the wolf*) and one or two companions were walking along a cliff-face in the hills of Judea, five miles from where the Jordan river empties into the Dead Sea and less than two miles from the shore of the Dead Sea. The area is called *Jeshimon*, meaning *land of appalling desolation* – rugged desert land. Why was he there? According to one story, he was a shepherd boy looking for a lost sheep or goat. According to another, he was a traveller seeking refuge from a storm. According to yet another story, he was on his way to Bethlehem with goods (perhaps smuggled across the Jordan). For some reason he crawled into a cave. Inside he found some pottery jars. From several that were broken there protruded leather scrolls wrapped in linen, badly decomposed.

To simplify an involved story, it can be stated that Mohammed and his friends took some of the scrolls to a Muslim sheikh in Bethlehem, their market town destination. The sheikh sent them to a merchant who was a member of the Syrian Orthodox Christian Church at Bethlehem who then informed another merchant in Jerusalem.

Eventually a Dutch biblical scholar suggested that the largest scroll was a copy of the book of Isaiah. It was about a year after their discovery that William Albright, an eminent American professor who had been sent photographs of parts of the scrolls, proclaimed them *the greatest manuscript discovery of modern times*. Millar Burrows, an American scholar in Jerusalem, claimed, *The Isaiah scroll is the oldest known manuscript of any book of the Bible.* Yet scepticism prevailed; the authenticity was questioned.

Then fragments of manuscripts found in excavations of the cave in February 1949 were taken to London. Dr Harold Plenderleith, a chemist in charge of the research laboratory at the British Museum, spent three months trying to separate leaves of leather by softening them with controlled humidity under glass and then hardening them with refrigeration. He put about a hundred pieces together like a jigsaw.

Articles began appearing in the world's press – in English, Danish, Dutch, French, German, Hebrew, Italian, Norwegian, Spanish and Swedish. Many more languages followed. There was keen interest throughout the world.

In 1951, a *carbon-14* test on a piece of linen cloth verified the date of the wrapping of one of the scrolls to be around 33 CE, plus or minus 200 years (*i.e.* between 167 BCE and 233 CE). Coins and other artefacts found in the first and other caves suggested that the Dead Sea Scrolls were hidden in the caves around 70 CE and were written during the century or so before that.

In all, forty caves in the area contained scrolls and these included almost all the books of the Old Testament (the Jewish Tenakh), several biblical commentaries and other writings including a Manual of Discipline and a hymnbook for a monastic-type community. In all, remains of about 100 scrolls were found. But where had the scrolls come from and why had they been placed in the caves? Many scholars believed that the answers were to be found nearby in the desert beneath the cliffs.

How was the Qumran Community excavated and identified as the place where the Dead Sea Scrolls were written?

When Father de Vaux and others excavated the first cave in 1949, they inspected a sand-covered ruin that lay in the desert, about a mile away, called *Qumran*. It appeared to be the remains of a small Roman fortress, but its proximity was tantalising. Did anything lie beneath the sand?

Two years later he returned with a team of seventeen men and began digging. Among their discoveries they uncovered a main building 118 feet by 94 feet, a large room with a wall nine feet high, a plastered bench and a complete jar identical to those used for storing the manuscripts in the cave. Most important, there were Roman coins from about the time of the birth of Jesus but none after the time of the first Jewish revolt against Rome (66–70 CE) or later.

Other archaeological evidence suggested that a community had been built and used for about a hundred years before it was destroyed by an earthquake known to have severely shaken the area in the Spring of 31 BCE. Then, after the gap of about a generation, the remaining foundations were built upon and the area re-used during and following the time of Jesus, abruptly ending during the Jewish revolt of 66–70 CE. Archaeological evidence suggested 70 CE as the last possible date for the copying of the manuscripts of the Dead Sea Scrolls.

Later excavations of Qumran identified an upper storey above the main hall as being a scriptorium, a room for copying manuscripts. It had three tables. The largest was about 16 feet long and 20 inches high. The tables were too far from the kitchen to have belonged to a dining hall. Further, there were a bronze and also a clay ink stand. The conclusion of many scholars: this was the very place where the Dead Sea Scrolls were written. In them, we have the actual literature written and read by the Qumran Community, the very copies they made and used.

It is an historical fact that in 68 CE when the 10th Legion was sent from Rome to Palestine to suppress the Jewish revolt, Jerusalem was destroyed and a blitz subdued Judea. Vespasian left a garrison at Jericho in 69 CE (mentioned by Josephus, the historian). The conclusion of Father de Vaux is supported by many scholars: the members of the Qumran Community, seeking to preserve their library, sealed their scrolls in jars and hid them in the nearby caves. The Roman garrison attacked and destroyed Qumran. Members of the community fled or were slaughtered. The scrolls were not retrieved and were forgotten for almost 1900 years. The caves protected what has been called *the best kept secret of the ages.*

Shortly after visiting some of the caves, observing the excavations at Qumran, seeing the Dead Sea Scrolls in the Hebrew museum in Jerusalem and meeting with Father de Vaux, the present writer made the following paraphrases based on the scholarship of Professor Millar Burrows and Professor Theodore Gaster.

The Manual of discipline of the Qumran Community
(paraphrased selections):

If you wish to join the community you must pledge yourself to respect God and man; to live according to our rules; to do what is good and upright in the sight of God, in accordance with what he has commanded through Moses and through God's servants, the prophets; to keep far from all evil and to cling to all good works; to act truthfully and righteously and justly without stubbornness, lust or other manner of evil; to help bind the community together in mutual love.

You must declare your willingness to serve truth by bringing all of your mind, all of your strength, and all of your wealth into the community so that your mind may be purified by truth, your strength controlled by righteousness and justice, and your wealth used for the common good. You must carry out your orders to the letter. You must be punctual with your work.

When you enter the community, your relationships with others will be critically examined. You will then be given a particular rank by the standard of your understanding and performance so that order can be

maintained and the work of all in the community be effective. You will be promoted for integrity and demoted for waywardness.

If you have a grievance against someone, you must reveal it truthfully, humbly and humanely. You are not to speak to him angrily or arrogantly or in a bad mood. You are not to bear hatred in your heart. If you have a charge against someone, deal with it there and then. Do not nurse a grudge. Furthermore, you must not speak about it publicly unless you can prove it by witnesses.

This is how you are to relate to others in the community. Obey your superior in all matters of work. All are to eat together, worship together and take counsel together.

Every third night you are not to go to bed but are to stay awake reading, studying the law and worshipping together.

If you disrupt a class, you will be suspended for ten days.

If you go to sleep in the classroom, you will be suspended for thirty days.

If you miss a class without good reason, you will be suspended for ten days.

If you walk about naked in public, you will be suspended from the community for six months.

If you indulge in raucous, inane laughter, you will be suspended for six months.

If you slander your neighbour, you will be regarded as outside the community and suspended for one year. If you slander the entire community, you will be expelled and never permitted to return.

Do what Scripture instructs when it says, "Prepare a way in the wilderness, make straight in the desert a highway for our God."

The Damascus Document associated with the Dead Sea Scrolls
(paraphrased selections):

Now listen, all you who know the right thing

to do: do it. Do not harm those who are known to you. God loves the truth and He wants you to know the truth. Do not be stubborn or difficult. Think before you act. Will it bring hurt to others? Then do not do it. Will it help others? Then do it. Do not follow those who are foolish. They are not strong but weak. And when you have done wrong, tell those who would help you to put things right again.

Do not bear a grudge. This makes you and others unhappy.

Share what you have with those who have greater need.

This day God will help you in ways that you might not believe if you were told. But if you are puffed up and think too highly of yourself, God will bring you low. Woe to him who takes what does not belong to him; one who steals does not find true joy. Joy is given to those who are kind.

There are rules in our community. What you are to do, do. And what you are told not to do, do not do.

Do not be stubborn. Love learning, for learning is from God.

True friendship is forever. You make true friends by sharing, helping, by hard work, by carefully listening and by kind speaking.

Now, from the beginning of this day until the coming of night be true to those who teach righteousness and be thankful to God who opens your heart to love and your mind to wisdom.

Today is the day for you to bring joy and peace and love to others as God will bring them to you.

Hymn of the Initiates
(paraphrased selections):

God, you are all that is Right and Highest
        in my life.
In my life, you are the cause of all Goodness,
        the source of knowledge,

the top of all my great moments.

Therefore, first thing in the morning
        and last thing in the evening,
I will say good things about you.
When I eat and drink I will give you thanks.

Whenever I am distressed I will turn away
        from thoughts of my plight
to join with others in praise of you.

I will cause no revenge
        because you only are the judge.
Nor will I be envious
        when those who do wickedness
steal rewards.
Nor will I conceal my anger or forget
unrighteous men
        until you bring justice.

I will not crave the lowest standard;
Nor shall anyone hear coarse words from my
mouth.
Instead, I will speak of all that is good,
        the bountifulness of God.

Blessed are you, O my God;
Apart from you no man's way is perfect,
        and without your will nothing good
happens.

The Books of the Initiates
(paraphrased selections):

It is you, O God, who lifts up my heart
        and brings me good cheer.
Amid the sorrow of mourning,
        amid havoc, comes your word of
peace.
When I am afraid,
        there comes your word of courage.
When I suffer,
        there comes your conquering word.

I give thanks to you, O Lord.

You have raised up a remnant,
men of truth and sons of light,
men of abundant compassion.
No wealth can equal your truth.

Further information about Qumran and the Dead Sea Scrolls

Probably the sect included male celibates living at Qumran and had associating families in nearby settlements. (Evidence: the Manual of Discipline, the Damascus Document and skeletons including women and children in the Qumran cemetery.)

Membership in the Community was considered to be a sign of divine election, being part of a faithful remnant of God's chosen people, Israel.

Believing they were helpless and weak, members claimed dependence upon God for wisdom and righteous living. The study of God's laws (in Scripture) and prayer were considered as essential preparations for the kingdom of God.

There were two anointed-ones (messiahs) expected in the future: one, a king, and the other, a high priest.

When the Old Testament of the Revised Standard Version (Common Bible) was being finalised in 1948, it was thought that the book of Isaiah would have to be translated all over again in light of the Dead Sea Scroll which was so much older than any known manuscript. Yet possibly only thirteen sentences had words needing to be changed. (These can be found as footnotes in the RSV "Common Bible".) Scribes copying biblical manuscripts always tried to be as accurate as possible. We should not be surprised that there were perhaps thirteen errors in modern translations of Isaiah revealed by the scroll. We should be surprised that there were not more caused by scribes making mistakes.

Many copyists wrote *by ear* rather than *by eye*; that is, often the scrolls were dictated – one person reading and several copying. Before 1948, Isaiah 21:8 was translated *then a lion cried* or *then he cried like a lion*. But in Hebrew, *lion* and *he who saw* sound alike. The Dead Sea Scroll translates, *then he who saw cried*. *Lion* came into Biblical manuscripts seemingly through a later scribe listening to dictation and writing the wrong word.

Jesus was baptised by John in the Jordan River during the time the Qumran Community was active just a few miles away. The Gospel of John states that Peter, Andrew, James and John were present with Jesus. Some scholars believe that John the Baptist and/or some of the disciples, or even Jesus himself had some association with the Qumran Community. It seems likely that at least they knew about it. It was into this wilderness that the gospels, in their stories of his temptation, state that Jesus went.

What happened to those who survived the Roman destruction of Qumran by fleeing from the community? Did some of them eventually become Christians?

There is much affinity between the language of the Dead Sea Scrolls and the New Testament. For example, the Qumran Community considered themselves to be *the elect of God*. (Compare this with Titus 1:1 and First Peter 1:1.) They considered themselves to be *Children of Light*. (Compare this with Luke 16:8; John 1:7–9, 8:12 and 12:36; Ephesians 5:8; and Thessalonians 5:5.) They belonged to a *temple of God*. (Compare this with First Corinthians 3:16–17 and Ephesians 2:20–22.) They had to choose between the *two ways* of good and evil. (Compare this with Matthew 7:13f. and Luke 13:23f.)

However, in the Dead Sea Scrolls there is no reference to suffering, death or resurrection related to the teacher of righteousness. *Teacher of righteousness* referred to a continuing office, not to a particular individual. Further, at Qumran there was a common meal but no Communion or Eucharist.

Nevertheless, the Dead Sea Scrolls enrich our understanding of Judaism in the period in which Christianity arose. They help us to understand the Jewish *Tenakh* (the Christian Old Testament). They also give us information for better understanding of the climate out of which Christianity grew. They help us to better understand New Testament language and literature.

In their own right, the Dead Sea Scrolls and the excavations at Qumran describe a quest for peace and justice, in ancient voices crying out in the wilderness of Judea.

?

What do you believe is the significance of Qumran and the Dead Sea Scrolls in the search for peace with justice?

Christians
Do Unto Others...

1. Consider several specific ways in which Christians are involved in seeking to help meet human need in areas such as hunger, thirst, illness, poverty, the nuclear threat, unemployment, industrial relations and inter-personal relationships.
2. What do you believe is the most important characteristic of the Christian Church? (*i.e.* Its services of worship? Pastoral care? Providing funeral services? Wedding services? A particular area of meeting human need?)

Assume **purely by accident** that you were born almost 1900 years ago into an early Christian family in Jerusalem. Your view of the universe is that of a flat earth with a dome up above it through which, you believe, at night the light of heaven shines through holes as specks of twinkling light. Below the earth, you believe, is Sheol or Hades – the underworld, the place of the dead with its gloomy, dark shadows.

You are familiar with the Scriptures of the Jewish religion. You have seen copies of scrolls that contain the journeys of Paul and some of his letters to the early Christian communities established by his missionary travels which carried Christianity through Asia Minor to Rome. You have seen copies of scrolls which contain stories of the life and teaching of Jesus. Your father's parents were Jews who became Christians through the preaching of Peter, other disciples, and James (the brother of Jesus). Your grandparents also met Paul when he returned from one of his missionary journeys. Your father was

baptised at the time his parents became Christians. You have been brought up in a Christian home. The year is 97 CE. These are your thoughts:

I believe that Jesus was the greatest prophet and teacher of God's truth who ever lived. He brought a message demanding that we love all people, even our enemies; that we avoid greed and the craving for material things; that we must use what we have in helping all in need. Jesus demanded that we live by belief in God, as Elijah had demanded before him; in the justice of God, as Amos had before him; in the mercy of God, as Hosea had before him; in the hope in God, as Isaiah had before him; in the vision of peace, as Ezekiel had before him; and that we share in the suffering of God, as Jeremiah had done before him. As these prophets had been sent by God to proclaim the message of God's way for us, so also, I believe, was Jesus sent. So first of all, I believe that Jesus was a great prophet and teacher of righteousness sent by God.

Further, I believe that Jesus fulfilled the longing of Israel for the Messiah – the new king and suffering servant – whose coming would be prepared for by the return of Elijah. I believe that the voice of John the Baptist crying in the wilderness, "Prepare the way of the Lord", was the voice of Elijah. Some have believed that John the Baptist was the Messiah, but I believe that John himself taught that the one who came after him would be greater than him. I believe that John the Baptist was Elijah who was expected to return before the Messiah came.

I believe that Jesus was about 30 years old when he was baptised by John. Jesus was tempted, as all people are tempted, to base his life on the search for possessions, power and popularity. All three of these temptations he totally resisted, living instead in poverty, servitude and rejection. He sought to serve God only. He was rejected not only by the people of Nazareth where he had lived but also by the authorities here in Jerusalem who put him to death after a brief three years teaching and ministering to the physical and spiritual needs of crowds of people in Galilee and Judea.

Jesus became one with the outcasts and poverty-stricken, hungry people of this world; and he died for them as for all people that they and all might live in the kingdom of God here and now. I believe that Jesus rose from the dead and that because he lives we too can live in righteousness now and throughout eternity as part of the kingdom of God, by the power of the Holy Spirit. I believe that God was in Christ reconciling the world to himself and reconciling the peoples of this world to one another.

I believe, therefore, that anything that I do that sides with this reconciliation is good and that anything that I do which violates this reconciliation is evil.

A few years before I was born, there was a Jewish uprising to overthrow the Roman rule

here in Palestine. Some Christians joined with certain Jews in trying to gain freedom from the terrible yoke. A Roman army was sent to subdue the people here. Jerusalem and many villages in Judea were destroyed. My parents' home was among so many that were torn down. There is still the persecution of Jews and Christians for we share in common the unwillingness to reject the worship of God and our obedience to him alone. Five years before the Roman army was sent to subdue us, there was the fire in Rome for which the Emperor Nero blamed Christians even though Christians did not cause it. So now there is a double reason why Christians are persecuted. Many of my family's friends, and some of my own, have been put to death.

These are hard times for one to be a Jew or a Christian. Jews and Christians alike are one under a common persecutor. Jesus, whom my Jewish friends acknowledge as a prophet, taught that we should love our enemies and do good to those who hate us. This is hard for us to do. I believe that soon Jesus will return and fully establish the kingdom of God. Until that day, I hope that Jews and Christians will live in peace together by the teachings of all the prophets. However, there have been tensions between us. Already there has even been bickering between Christians. It would be sad if there became divisions in the Church. As Paul taught, "In Christ there is neither Jew nor Gentile, neither slave nor free, neither male nor female". (From the Bible, Galatians 3:28.)

It would be sad if ever Christians should persecute others because of their religion or race or nationality. As a Christian I must believe that all are my brothers and sisters, one brotherhood of mankind under the fatherhood of God.

Until the kingdom of God breaks in upon me and upon this world, I believe that I live in the presence of the risen Christ and there-

fore that I ought to live or die for his goal of a just and peaceful, reconciled world.

Background

In 312 CE Christianity became the official religion of the Roman Empire following the Emperor Constantine's *conversion* (he was never baptised, though he professed Christian faith). Rome itself was sacked by Alaric in 410. Following years of glory, the Roman empire crumbled.

The Eastern part of the empire, centred on Constantinople, did not fall. The Bishop of Constantinople claimed to be the new head of Christendom. Then, following the development of doctrinal differences, the Greek-speaking Eastern Orthodox Church was finally severed from the Latin-speaking Western Roman Church in 1054.

Between 1095 and 1270 there was a series of Crusades, launched with the high ideals of proclaiming the Christian message to the world but which was tarnished by the sad realities of the battlefield and the craving of booty. The Crusaders slaughtered many Jews, Muslims and others.

Then there were many Christians who showed spiritual and mental strength: like St Francis of Assisi (1181–1226) and St Thomas Aquinas (1224–1274). There was further disruption in the sixteenth century. In 1517, the German Monk Martin Luther posted his *ninety-five theses* and the Reformation was further developed by John Calvin in Switzerland and John Knox in Scotland.

Meanwhile, self-reform (the Counter Reformation) was being developed within Roman Catholicism by Ignatius Loyola (1491–1556) who founded the Jesuits, and by many others before and after him. The Roman Catholic Church wasted no time in embarking on a period of internal correction. Scripture was recognised as a source of truth alongside tradition.

Today there are noticeable divisions within the Church. Yet despite the fragmentation of institutionalised Christianity into innumerable churches, despite the errors and inquisitions through 2000 years, and despite the differences presented to the world, still there is a yearning for the gospel of reconciliation as expressed by one of the most-sung hymns:

... We are not divided, All one body we,
One in hope and doctrine, One in charity...

Do not all Christians acknowledge one God? Do not all declare loyalty to one Lord? Do not all find a central symbol of their faith in the Cross? Do not all Christians believe that these should be the factors of motivation in their lives? All are thereby placed under the obligation to acknowledge the brotherhood of all mankind and are challenged to practice – in charity – what they preach.

Perhaps, as far as Christianity is concerned, the whole is greater than the sum of its parts.

Consider this prayer for the Catholic (universal) Church:

O Gracious Father, we pray for your holy Catholic Church. Fill it with all truth, in all peace. Where it is corrupt, purify it; where it is in error, direct it; where in anything it is amiss, reform it. Where it is right, establish it; where it is in want, provide for it; where it is divided, reunite it; for the sake of your son Jesus Christ, our Lord. AMEN.

Consider also this prayer attributed to St Francis of Assisi:

Lord, make us instruments of your peace;
where there is hatred let us sow love;
where there is injury, pardon;
where there is doubt, faith;
where there is despair, hope;

*where there is darkness, light; and
where there is sadness, joy.*

*O Divine Master, grant that we may not so
much seek
to be consoled as to console;
to be understood as to understand;
to be loved as to love;
for it is in giving that we receive;
it is in pardoning that we are pardoned;
and it is in dying that we are born to eternal
life.*

What is Christianity?

Where do we begin an answer? Obviously it
is a religion; or is it? Dietrich Bonhoeffer
(the Christian pastor and theologian who was
put to death by personal order of Adolf
Hitler) wrote about what he called
religionless Christianity.

Obviously, at least it is a statement of
belief; or is it? Let us ask, What do Christians
believe? Do they not all believe in the
Apostles' Creed which is recited in many
Churches throughout the world? One English
form is:

*I believe in God, the Father Almighty,
creator of heaven and earth.*

*I believe in Jesus Christ, his only Son our
Lord. He was conceived by the Holy Spirit
and born of the Virgin Mary. He suffered
under Pontius Pilate, was crucified, died,
and was buried. He descended to the dead.
On the third day he rose again. He ascended
into heaven, and is seated at the right hand
of the Father. He will come again to judge
the living and the dead.*

*I believe in the Holy Spirit, the holy
Catholic Church, the communion of saints,
the forgiveness of sins, the resurrection of the
body, and the life everlasting.*

For hundreds of millions of Christians the
110 words of the Apostles' Creed state the
central convictions of their faith. This creed
is repeated countless thousands of times
every day in every part of the world by
Christians of many churches. It is used in
services of worship by Roman Catholics and
by most Protestants as one of the principal
traditional affirmations of the Christian Faith.
This form of the creed dates back to the
seventh century, developing from a more
basic form of the third century. Although it
was not written by the apostles, it developed
out of earlier, simpler confessions of faith
belonging to the time of the Early Church.

Yet there are many non-orthodox
Christians today who acknowledge creeds as
traditional statements of faith but who do not
accept them as essential to being a Christian.
The Unitarian Church (which many would
claim to be within the Christian category)
rejects belief in creeds and their Trinitarian
(Father, Son and Holy Spirit – three persons)
implications. Unitarians also deny belief in
the divinity of Christ. Another view of
religion which claims to be Christian but
denies belief in God is *Christian Atheism.*
This view is expressed by the American
professor of religion, Thomas Altiser, in his
book, *Is God Dead?*

However, since its birth at Pentecost
almost 2000 years ago, the Christian Church
has usually centred on one forceful
conviction: the divinity of Christ. The belief
that God sent his Son to earth in the person
of Jesus who lived as humans live and
suffered as humans suffer, separates
Christianity from all other religions.

Yet during the 2000 years since Jesus lived
and died, churches have developed such a
diversity of belief and practice that it is
sometimes difficult to recognise that they
have all acknowledged the same Lord:

- The glittering spectacle of an Easter Mass
  in St Peter's, Rome;
- The stillness within the bare walls of a

Quaker meeting house;
- The squatting circle of Congo tribesmen around the white-haired medical missionary;
- The chanting monks cut off from the world on the forbidden peak of Mount Athos;
- The walk through Selma, Alabama, with black and white hands held together, and the singing of *We shall overcome*;
- The cross carried in ecumenical solemnity from church to church on Good Friday;
- The figure, alone, kneeling in the chancel of a French cathedral;
- The families sitting in their cars at a drive-in service;
- The thousands pressing forward in Wembley Stadium at the appeal of an evangelist;
- The wraithlike figures kneeling in perpetual adoration before the altar in a Quebec convent;
- The sea of faces swaying, the sound of speaking in tongues to the beat of clapping hands;
- The host of variations of baptisms, confirmations, Eucharists, weddings, funerals, Sunday morning and evening and week-day services.

And so much more – *Christians at worship.*

- The rebuilding of the abbey at Iona from which a ministry of healing, social service, pastoral care, industrial reconciliation and social concern reaches out to a nation;
- The mixed group of Protestants and Catholics called together to work for a society whose priorities are mutual respect, the participation of all, and the sharing and stewardship of resources at the Corrymeela Community in Northern Ireland;
- The Tear Fund providing food, water and medical care for a suffering village;
- The projects of Christian Aid, organised through the World Council of Churches, giving immediate and long-term help to disaster victims;
- The non-denominational school providing years of education for an orphan boy living on another continent, linked to him only by the concern of a Catholic priest;
- The church youth club in a peaceful Scottish New Town establishing *Operation Friendship*, a structure for international, multi-racial, multi-faith, and multi-cultural exchanges for young people, not least in Northern Ireland but also for an increasing number of other countries;
- The isolated priest or vicar or minister, or Home Missionary, or layman or laywoman, reaching out a hand to the alcoholic or addicted, bereaved or distressed, rejected or lonely individual and seeing the situation through, co-ordinating other help required;
- The hastily convened meeting to seek some form of constructive action in the wake of yet another factory or pit closure;
- The church hall converted for use as a work shop for some who otherwise would be unemployed;
- The group in a protest sit-in voting *no* with its demonstration against something it feels unjust or destructive.

And so much more – *Christians trying to help meet human need.*

?

---

1. Put the Beatitudes of Jesus (from the Bible, Matthew 5:3–10) into your own words.

(Here each one is quoted from the *Common Bible* followed by explanatory notes and a translation based on a commentary by William Barclay:)

The Beatitudes

a. *Blessed are the poor in spirit, for theirs is the Kingdom of Heaven.*
This is about realising that you cannot go it alone. It is the opposite of being *proud in spirit*. So:
O the joy of the one who knows that he is not the greatest, that he needs others to help him, and who therefore doesn't show off. He is the kind of person who lives the simple life, putting his trust in God to bind him into fellowship with others. He'll never be alone.

b. *Blessed are those who mourn, for they shall be comforted.*
This is about having a heart so sympathetically broken for the world's suffering that you really care. So:
O the joy of the one who is so sorry for those whose hearts are broken that he does whatever he can do to get their smiles back. He too will have a happy smile.

c. *Blessed are the meek, for they shall inherit the earth.*
This is about being angry at the right time and never at the wrong time, for you know your own weaknesses. So:
O the joy of the one who doesn't blame others for what is his own fault, who knows that two wrongs don't make a right; for by not losing the place, his emotions are under control. He is a leader among men, and the whole world is at his feet.

d. *Blessed are those who hunger and thirst for righteousness, for they shall be satisfied.*
This is about being more concerned for doing right than for being wealthy. So:
O the joy of the one who hungers and thirsts so much for what is right that when he hears of someone who is really hungry or thirsty, or otherwise in need, he gives until it hurts or even until he feels good. He doesn't want to gain at the cost of others; for he who gives most, receives most.

e. *Blessed are the merciful, for they shall obtain mercy.*
This is about identifying with another person in such a way that you can even think the way he does; such empathy helps him to know that you really care for him. We all want to believe that we are understood. So:
O the joy of the one who puts himself in the place of others so that he sees as if with their eyes and feels as if with their feelings; for that is what others will do for him. He will receive their sympathy when he is sad and their comfort when he is hurt.

f. *Blessed are the pure in heart, for they shall see God.*
This is about having the right aim in life and not letting anything cloud your vision of it. So:
O the joy of the one who does his best in truth and love because he has aimed for the best. That is where he finds God.

g. *Blessed are the peacemakers, for they shall be called the sons of God.*
This is about making right relationships with other people so that you can honestly say, *shalom*: peace be with you, I wish you well and therefore you can count on me. So:
O the joy of the one who can be counted on to make friends of enemies, who not only stops fights but starts friendships; for he not only is God's son, he is doing

God's work.

h. *Blessed are those who are persecuted for righteousness sake, for theirs is the Kingdom of Heaven.*

This is about suffering for what you know to be right. So:

O the joy of the one who suffers when he is doing what he knows is right, for those whom he is helping will be his friends forever.

2. Do you *Agree* or *Disagree* with a–g? How would you answer h?
   a. The Christian Church should stay out of politics. It should not make any *official* political pronouncements, or otherwise *meddle* in politics.
   b. Clergy should keep their political views to themselves.
   c. Christian laity (non-clergy) have the right to be politically involved.
   d. All Christians have the obligation to be involved in political issues but should try to base their views on the life and teachings of Jesus and his concern for justice and mercy as foundations for the peaceful Kingdom of God on earth.
   e. Religion is the cause of all the major problems (and many minor ones) in our world. Therefore, the first step to solving these problems is to destroy religion. Christianity is a religion; therefore, Christianity should be destroyed.
   f. It is not religion but the abuse of religion that is one of the main causes of problems in our world. Religion is like a hammer. Used wisely, it can help one build; used foolishly, it can help destroy.
   g. In his ministry, Jesus ran afoul of both the extremely conservative and the extremely radical religious and political forces in Palestine.
   h. How would you express your beliefs concerning *either* the relationship between Christianity and politics *or* your evaluation of religion.

3. Consider the following facts about the four Gospels at the beginning of the New Testament and then answer the questions.
   a. Matthew, Mark and Luke are not three totally different accounts of the life of Christ. They have much in common, including the same general outline of Jesus' life which differs from that of John. They are commonly referred to as the *synoptic gospels* (*synoptic* means *to see together*) because they can largely be put into parallel columns.
   b. 95 percent of Mark is found in Matthew and 65 percent of Mark is found in Luke.
   c. Only 30 verses of Mark do not appear either in Matthew or Luke.
   d. Verses in Matthew which do not appear in Mark are not to be found in Luke either. Verses in Luke which do not appear in Mark are not to be found in Matthew.
   e. Matthew and Luke each have over 1000 verses. Mark has under 700.
   f. Where Matthew and Luke do not follow Mark's order, they disagree between themselves.
   g. The Gospel of John differs from the synoptics in order and content.

What conclusions do you draw? What is the significance of the *synoptic problem* for understanding Christianity?

Muslims
Submission to the Most High

? ——————————— ——————————— **?**

1. What do you believe is meant by the word *God*?
2. Muslims and many others believe in a Last Judgement where one will either be rewarded for good deeds done or punished for evil deeds done. What further details would you give to what is meant by *Last Judgement*? How would you explain the meaning of *delights of heaven* and *terrors of hell*?
3. Is there such a thing as a *Holy War*? Comment.
4. What are some ways in which a person can help someone of another religion and from another country feel at home in Britain?
5. If we are given the freedom to express our own views about religion, how can we show that we accept the responsibility of respecting the views of others? What limits, if any, do you believe should be given to this respect?

Assume that, **purely by accident**, you were born in Mecca, Arabia (today called Saudi Arabia), in about the year 68 AH (*c.* 700 CE). You live in a community that is surrounded by mountains and desert, isolated by an ocean of sand. You live in an age of ignorance and superstition, when many people worship numerous spirits and powers (including fire) and numerous gods and goddesses (including al-Uzzah, the planet Venus, regarded as a goddess), making idols of stone and wood. The various tribes fight constantly, female infant children are often buried alive, and almost everyone is illiterate. Each tribe lives by its own laws and there is an emphasis upon grabbing what one can during one's life, with no belief in life after death. You live at a time when there are around Mecca a number of Jews and Christians, some of whose ancestors had fled from Roman persecution in the first century. Many of the Christians are bickering among themselves and some are living immoral lives. There is the longing for a new prophet, a descendant of Abraham. This is also a time when Mecca is a major centre of commerce with much trade by camel caravan especially with Egypt, Israel and Syria. These are your thoughts:

"Bismillshi 'rrahmani 'rrahim."
       <a transliteration of Arabic for "in the Name of the One God, All-Merciful, All-Loving">.

When I was born, the first words ever spoken to me were spoken by my mother into my ear as a new born child. She said, "I bear witness that there is no god but God and Muhammad is the Prophet of God." *Every day of my life I confirm my belief in this.*

My people have been descendants of Ishmael, a son of Abraham. The leading and strongest tribe is the Quraish, in charge of the Ka'ba, the cube which I believe was built by Adam and was rebuilt after the flood and which holds the sacred Black Stone given to Ishmael by the angel Gabriel.

On the 12th day of the month of Rabi-ul-Awwal a little over a hundred years ago <in the year 570 CE> *a child was born here in Mecca to Aminahy, the wife of Abdullah* <Arabic for "servant of God">, *the son of Abedul Muttalib of the Quraish tribe. The child was named Muhammad* <the Praised One> *and Ahmad* <the Most Laudable>. *Later he came to be known as al-Amin* <meaning trustworthy/faithful one> *on account of his character, especially his honesty. But before the child was born his father, Abdullah, died. And his mother died when he was only six. Al-Amin was cared for first by his grandfather, but when his grandfather died two years later, this orphan child was cared for by his uncle, Abu Talib, a merchant.*

The boy noticed that sometimes his uncle was cheated in business, even by Christians. His uncle would exchange goods and find out later that what he had received was sand instead of grain. The boy longed for a way of life which would inspire honesty. One day, when he was twelve, he was accompanying his uncle on a trading mission towards Syria when they met a Christian monk named Bahira. The monk, having seen a cloud following the trading party, thought that it was a sign; and, pointing to the boy, he said, "This is the greatest Prophet." The boy to whom he was referring we call the Prophet Muhammad, may God bless him and give him peace!

One day a quarrel broke out concerning repair work on the Ka'ba <Arabic for "cube">. *The argument was over who should lift the sacred Black Stone into its place. It was agreed that the first man to come to the Ka'ba the next day would be the one who would decide the dispute. Muhammad* <Arabic for "Highly Praised is God"> *was the first to arrive the next morning. He decided the dispute by spreading out a robe, placing the Black Stone on it, and having the tribal leaders each take hold of the robe and carry the Black Stone to its place. He solved the problem and from that moment he was called al-Amin* <the "trustworthy/faithful one">.

A widow by the name of Khadija heard of Muhammad's honesty and ability. Her wealthy husband had left a large merchant's business. She offered al-Amin a large sum of money to take a camel caravan to Syria. He accepted and was very successful. On his return, Khadija suggested that they get married. They did, when he was 25 and she was 40.

Muhammad often went into the desert to meditate about the Creator and to reflect on the meaning of life and his purpose in it. One day when he was in the Cave of Hira'a on Jabal-al-Nor <Arabic for "Mount of Light">, *a hill outside Mecca, his favourite place for meditation, he had a vision. He saw an angel in the form of a man with feet astride the horizon and with a piece of brocade on which there was writing. This voice from heaven said, "Read". He replied, "I cannot read". Three times the angel told him to read or recite, and he finally did. Then he heard a voice saying, "O Muhammad! Thou art the Apostle of God and I am Gabriel."*

Muhammad was trembling when he arrived home. When she heard what had happened, Khadija, his wife, told him that God was speaking to him through words brought by the archangel Gabriel. She took Muhammad to Waraka, a Christian teacher, who claimed that Muhammad was the prophet foretold in ancient books.

Muhammad, may God be pleased with him!, kept his views secret for three years then received a message from God to preach as his prophet. At first only his wife (Khadijah), a former slave (Zayd, whom he freed and adopted as a son), a cousin (Ali) and two friends (Abu Bakr and Uthman) believed him to be a prophet. They were the first Muslims.

At first in Mecca and later in Medina, he received many revelations from God which he taught to his friends who taught them to others. He went to Safa, the hill in the centre of Mecca, and spoke to multitudes of people.

Though the numbers of Muslims began to grow, persecution in Mecca became harsh. For ten years he preached about the one and only God, the Compassionate and Merciful, to those who lived in Mecca and to those who came there as pilgrims to the Ka'ba or on business. The Meccans were angry because they wanted to worship many gods and goddesses, bowing down to idols of stone and wood and many made their living from making these idols. Those of the higher classes were angry because, according to Muhammad (peace be upon him), God demanded higher moral standards; and all people should be treated as equal. The Prophet's early adherents were mainly slaves and poor workers who received verbal ridicule and even physical punishment. Many fled to other parts of Arabia, some fled across the Red Sea into Ethiopia. Six visitors to Mecca from Yathrib <300 miles to the north-east> became Muslims and later the Prophet fled there <in the year 622 CE>. There he met with much success. <The name Yathrib was changed to Madinat al-Nabi (meaning "the city of the Prophet") shortened to "Medina".> The year of this flight (Hijra) from Mecca marked the turning point and is the first year of my calendar, 1 AH <Anno Hijra, meaning "the year of the flight">.

At the beginning of each year, on the first day of the month of Muharram, I along with

all Muslims listen to stories of how the Prophet and his friends made their flight. Medina is the second most sacred city to any Muslim. It was from there that Islam flourished and spread rapidly. It was there that Muhammad established a modest building for use as the first mosque where special services were held each Friday. Muhammad was a preacher, teacher, judge, statesman and general. He was both a religious and a political leader who pronounced the commands of God.

Although Muslims were repeatedly attacked by groups of armed men from Mecca who sought to destroy the stronghold of the new religion, opposition subsided and in 8 AH Muhammad (may God bless him and give him peace!) was able to return to Mecca in triumph and the Ka'ba was dedicated to God, Exalted is He! Ever since, Mecca has been a place of pilgrimage and is the holiest place in Islam.

When Muhammad (peace and blessing be with him) died, Abu Bakr became the first Caliph, then Umar, then Uthman and then Ali, cousin and son-in-law of the Prophet. Internal controversy over leadership followed and eventually resulted in two principal sects: the Shias and the Sunnis. I believe that soon the faith will be supreme in the world.

I believe that throughout the ages God has sent many messengers or prophets. Among them were Abraham, Moses and Elijah, Amos, Micah, Isaiah, Jeremiah, Jesus and Muhammad (peace and blessings be upon him!). I believe that Muhammad (peace be upon him!) was "the seal of the prophets", the last and therefore the greatest messenger whom God sent to teach people what they should believe and how they should live. I believe in one God, Allah, the Magnificent. I believe that words given by God to Muhammad were written down in the Qur'an <Arabic for "read out loud"> which I believe is the most sacred book. I read from it every day and read completely through it every month, though I also study what Christians call "the Bible". The Qur'an is about the same length as the New Testament. Any Muslim who has memorised all of the Qur'an is called a Hafiz <meaning "memoriser">. I have learned much of it by heart and hope some day to be a Hafiz. Meanwhile I am trying to live by the Qur'an and its 114 Suras <"chapters">. It is sacred to me. I wash my hands before I touch it. And I would never place it on the floor nor put anything on top of it. Because Muhammad (peace be with him!) could not write, he appointed special scribes to record the special revelations of the Qur'an which were given to him by God.

I try to follow the teachings of the Qur'an. I pray five times a day. When the time comes that I have a job, I will give 1/40th of my income to charity and this beyond my normal obligations of giving. Meanwhile, I try to help those who are less well off than myself. I fast during the daylight hours of the month of Ramadan to help instil self-discipline. It is easy for me to keep the law of pilgrimage because I live in Mecca, though I help welcome Muslims who want to come here at least once in their lifetime to visit the Ka'ba. I live in a city that only Muslims are allowed to enter. I adhere to the teachings of the Qur'an not to drink alcohol, or eat pork or ham, or gamble in any way, or lie, steal or cheat.

Yet it is not just avoiding what the Qur'an teaches as the wrong things but doing what it teaches as the right things of life that I seek to maintain.

Sadly there has been much bloodshed between Christians and Muslims even over the few years since the new faith was born. I believe that the early fighting led by the Prophet himself was defensive because of the prejudice and persecutions of my people by Christians.

At Medina, Muhammad (peace be upon him!) declared that Jews and Christians "shall practise their religions as freely as the Muslims". **I believe that this may be the first charter of freedom of conscience in human history.** Should ever Muslims try to force others to become Muslims, I believe that this would be a violation of the teachings of God.

Many Christians condemn Muslims for having more than one wife, but this custom in our land makes certain that all women are cared for. It is true that when Khadija died, the Prophet came to have several wives at the same time, particularly when he was between 55 and 60 years old. When his friend Zaid divorced Zainab, the Prophet married Zainab. This was good. He believed that the protection of the rights of women was a duty given by Allah (exalted is He!); and divorced and widowed women were to be respected, not degraded as they had been. The Prophet taught that sexual relations should only take place within marriage.

Muhammad (peace be with him!) believed that fighting was justified only if it was jihad <"holy war"> for the faith, which would lead to paradise for those who fought in it. He taught that Medina must be set up as an independent state so that it could be free from Mecca's dominance and be based on God's laws. The Prophet was once wounded in battle. He did not endorse aggressive war, but only justified war fought as a last resort after all attempts at peace had failed and when one's own people were being unjustly treated.

The Prophet returned to Mecca and dedicated the Ka'ba to God. He died two years later at the age of 62 <in 632 CE>. I believe that he was the final messenger of God and brought, in the Qur'an, his final message.

I hope to live by this message all my days, God willing.

What is Islam?

Islam, whose over a billion adherents

compose one-fifth of the world's population, is built partly on the foundation of Christianity which itself was formed on the foundation of Judaism. In Britain, Islam is related to the Judeo-Christian heritage although its birthplace was Arabia rather than Palestine. Today there are three basic kinds of Muslim: Traditionalists (seeking revival), Modernists (seeking reformation), and Secularists (seeking revolution). Due to transliterations of Arabic sounds into English letters, words like Muhammad, Qur'an and Hijrah are spelled in a variety of ways (*e.g.* Mohammed, Koran, and Hegira). Muslim means *one who submits*. Allah (al=the, lah=God) means *the God*. Muhammad means *highly praised*.

The Qur'an

Qur'an (or Koran) is the use of English letters for the sounds of the Arabic word meaning *recitation*. (This is called, *transliteration*.) Muhammad had his scribes write down the revelations on flat stones, shoulder blades and ribs of dead animals, and even on palm leaves. The final collection was probably edited by the third Caliph (successor), Uthman. The Qur'an is slightly shorter than the New Testament. It contains 114 Suras (chapters), the longest having 186 ayats (verses). Orthodox Muslims believe that the original Qur'an contains the words of God and is written on a tablet at the side of God's throne in Heaven. It is the Word of God in the form of a book. In Arabic, the Qur'an is in rhyming prose which is lost in English translations. (Arabic is written from right to left, like Hebrew.) The Qur'an is used in mosques but is never put on display.

Muslims believe that Judaism and Christianity have been fulfilled by Islam. The Qur'an states of God:

He (Allah) *has revealed to you* (Muhammad)

the Book with the truth, confirming the scriptures which preceded it; for He has already revealed the Torah (law) *and the Gospel* (Good News) *for the guidance of men, and the distinction between right and wrong.*

(Sura 3:3–4)

The Qur'an regards Jesus of Nazareth highly but denies that he was uniquely the Son of God. It states that God has no material form and that incarnation is impossible, as also is a Trinitarian (God in three Persons) view of God as Father, Son and Holy Spirit:

Speak nothing but truth about Allah. The Messiah, Jesus, son of Mary, was no more than Allah's apostle... So believe in Allah and His apostles and do not say, "Three"... Allah is but one God. Allah; forbid that He should have a son.

(Sura 4:171)

There are two references to the birth of Jesus in the Qur'an:

When the angel said: "Mary! God has chosen thee and purified thee and chosen thee above the women of the world ... be obedient to thy Lord and humble thyself... God gives thee good news with a word from Himself whose name is the Messiah, Jesus, son of Mary, worthy of regard in this world and the hereafter, and one of those who are near to God..." She said, "My Lord, how shall there be a son born to me as no man has touched me and I am not unchaste?" He said, "So shall it be, God creates what He pleases; when He has decreed a matter, He only says to it, 'Be', and it is."

(Sura 3:40–47)

And she conceived him and then withdrew herself with him to a remote place. And the throes of childbirth compelled her to take herself to the trunk of a palm tree. She said:

57

"Oh, would that I had died before this..."

(Sura 19:22–24)

Muslims, then, believe that Jesus had a miraculous birth. But they do not believe that Jesus suffered and was crucified, for he was too great a prophet. They believe that either the story of the crucifixion mistakes Jesus for someone else, or he came down from the cross and was revived. Muslims do not believe in the resurrection or ascension of Jesus:

And (the Jews) saying: "We have killed the Messiah, Jesus, son of Mary, the apostle of God"; and they did not kill him nor did they crucify him, but he was made to resemble (one crucified) ... and they certainly did not kill him...

(Sura 4:157)

Besides the Qur'an there is the "Hadith" (saying) which gives further details on "Sunna" (the rules of life). Different types of Muslims, such as the Sunni and Shi'a Muslims, give different interpretation to the Hadith. Unlike the Qur'an, the Hadith is open to criticism by Muslims.

The Five Pillars of Islam

There are five foundations on which Islam is built.

1. The Creed

The First Pillar of Islam is "Shahada" or "Kalimah" (declaration of truth). All Muslims believe "la ilaha illa'llah; Muhammad rasulu'llah". This transliteration from Arabic means, "There is no God but Allah; Muhammad is the Messenger (Prophet) of Allah." These words, in Arabic, appear on each mosque. Every person is meant to be God's servant.

2. Prayer

The Second Pillar of Islam is "Salat" (regular worship/prayer). There are two main kinds of prayer. One type is performed, with actions (called "rak'ahs") as well as words, five times a day: at sunset (which is also the beginning of the Jewish day), bedtime, dawn, noon and afternoon. Every mosque has minarets (tall towers) where the "Muezzin" gives the call to prayer which may be amplified by loudspeakers. Muslims have elaborate rituals of washing hands, face and feet before prayer and of facing Mecca. Heads are always covered during prayer. Men wear a "topi" (small cap) and women wear a "burka" (a shawl which covers the head and shoulders). Inside a mosque there is a "mihrab" (niche) or "qibla" (direction) wall which lies in the direction of Mecca. Islam has no organised priesthood. Each community elects an "imam" (leader) to lead prayer. Sandals and shoes are always left outside a mosque. Found at the beginning of the Qur'an, the Muslim prayer most equivalent to the Lord's Prayer of the Christian is

THE EXORDIUM

IN THE NAME OF ALLAH
THE COMPASSIONATE
THE MERCIFUL

Praise be to Allah, Lord of the Creation,
The Compassionate, the Merciful,
King of Judgement-day!
You alone we worship, and to You alone
we pray for help.
Guide us to the straight path,
The path of those whom You have favoured,
Not of those who have incurred Your wrath,
Nor of those who have gone astray.

(Translated into English, N J Dawood)

A second type of prayer is called "du'a" (supplication/petition). It is less formal and may be said anywhere, at anytime. Women usually pray at home rather than in a mosque.

3. Charity

The Third Pillar is "Zakat" (purification). Each Muslim is required to give financial support to his religion. Then, after calculating certain deductions (i.e. rent, mortgage, debts, clothes, travel) he is required to give a further 1/40th (2½%) of his income or wealth to the poor and less fortunate, perhaps through charities set up by Islam. Imam Al-Ghazali, whom many Muslims believe to be a great Muslim teacher, wrote about the three degrees of Charity and their importance:

The lowest degree is where you place your brother on the same footing as your slave or your servant, attending to his need from your surplus...
At the second degree you place your brother on the same footing as yourself...
At the third degree, the highest of all, you prefer your brother to yourself and set his need before your own. Self-sacrifice is one of the fruits of this degree...
Two brothers are likened to a pair of hands, one of which washes the other.

Charity, then, to the Muslim, is not limited to a specific amount beyond which he can claim to have perfectly fulfilled the law. The charity of love has no boundaries.

Charity purifies because giving to those less fortunate than yourself will make you more generous and friendly and will help build the world as a community without the barriers of greed, competition, rivalries and class distinctions.

The Muslim promises to give charity believing that if he avoids it he will get his deserved punishment on the Day of Judgement.

4. Fasting

The Fourth Pillar of Islam is "Saum" or "Sujam" (fasting). From sunrise to sunset, throughout the month of Ramadan (the ninth month in the Islamic year, which has thirteen lunar months), the Muslim does not eat or drink. Though pregnant women, the old and the sick are exempt from this rule, others only eat or drink after dusk. In hot countries this rule emphasises all the more the need for self-discipline.

Ramadan marks the time when Muhammad received the first revelation of the Qur'an from God. How did Muslims know when dawn had come or when dusk arrived? The test of light was that a dark thread can be distinguished from a light one. Today, determined by its location, each Muslim community has printed times of sunrise and sunset for each day of Ramadan. The penalty for breaking the fast without good reason is to be obliged to provide a meal for 60 people or to fast for 60 further days. Fasting helps one to know what it is like to be poor and to have no food, and it encourages one to share what one has with those who are in need.

5. Pilgrimage

The Fifth Pillar of Islam is "Hajj" or "Hadj" (Pilgrimage). Every Muslim is required to go to Mecca at least once in his lifetime, as a sign of his quest for a purified commitment to God. Only Muslims are allowed into the sacred city of Mecca.

Preparations for Hajj begin many months in advance and friends and relatives bring good wishes. Special clothing must be put on before arrival in Mecca: two pieces of white seamless towelling for men and long white cotton dresses (with a covering for the head) for women. In this way all who enter Mecca seek to look alike in equality and for unity. The pilgrims begin calling out to God, "Labbaika", meaning "I am here at your service". They hear the voice of the muezzin calling them to prayer. They must show a particular Islamic permit for entering the city. Important experiences include walking seven times around the Ka'ba (a cube 15 metres long, 10 metres wide and 14 metres high, also called the "Bait-ul-lah", the "House of God"), hoping to get close enough to kiss the sacred Black Stone (an oval stone 18 centimetres in diameter which is secured in the south-east corner). Tradition holds that the stone was given to Ishmael, Abraham's son, by the angel Gabriel, and was originally white but turned black due to the sins of those who saw it. Pilgrims then go on to Mount Arafat, 21 kilometres away, to pray from noon to sunset. Other acts recall stories found in Genesis 22 (from the Jewish Torah, part of the Christian Bible) recalled in the Qur'an, Sura 37:100–111. Some men dye their beards red to show that they are Hajjis, men who have made the pilgrimage. On their return home, they may decorate the outside of their houses with pictures of things they have seen.

Expansion of Islam

Islam spread farther and more quickly than any other religion and has always given special toleration to Christians and Jews, except by extremists (found in many religions). Within 20 years it dominated the richest principalities of the Near East: Syria fell in 635 CE, Iraq in 637, Palestine in 640, Egypt in 642, and the entire Persian empire in 650. Then it spread eastward to India, westward to the Atlantic, across the Straits of Gibraltar, into Spain, Portugal and France. Masses of conquered subjects embraced the new dynamic faith and way of life. Then, in one of history's decisive battles, the Arabs were halted by the Franks at Tours in 732. Yet within a hundred years Islam was well established from France to China and from Spain to India.

Culturally, the ninth–eleventh centuries were golden ages in Islam. Exposed to the Graeco-Roman, Byzantine and Persian heritages (to which it added its own brilliant culture), art, philosophy and poetry flourished in its Empire and mathematics and medicine advanced. The Arabs preserved the culture of civilisations. During the time Christians were involved in their militant crusades, Islam established the first university, founded by Fatimid Shi'a at the al-Azhar mosque in Cairo. When Europe was engulfed in the Dark Ages, it was the Arabs who preserved Greek medicine, astronomy and philosophy. They gave to the world, through this preservation and distribution, paper making from China and the form of numbers from India. Although the Arab Empire was overrun by the Turks in 1258, the Turks eventually became Muslim, carrying the empire into the twentieth century.

When the Arab army under Omar conquered Jerusalem in 637, Omar ordered that a mosque be built on the site of the ruins of the Jewish temple, and around the altar used from even before the time of Solomon. This Mosque of Omar, the "Dome of the Rock", is perhaps the oldest Muslim building outside Arabia and is built on a site sacred to Jews and Christians. (Tradition claims that one night during his tenth year as a prophet, Muhammad went to Jerusalem and ascended into Heaven from the site of this rock.)

In an age of marked male chauvinism, Muhammad taught that girls as well as boys were gifts of God. He condemned the (then) common practice of killing baby daughters. In an age of extensive polygamy, when a hundred wives was not unheard of, he taught, "Of women who seem good in your eyes, marry but two, or three or four; and if you fear you shall not act equitably, then one only."

Just as the Christians are divided into two main divisions (the Catholics and the Protestants) the Muslims too are divided into two main branches: the Shi'a and the Sunni. All Shi'a accept that the Prophet designated Ali as the successor whereas the Sunnis accept him as the fourth caliph.

Today, the Shi'as (Shi'ites) tend to give close allegiance to their Imams (as they prefer to call their Caliphs), whom they believe are infallible and are the successors to Muhammad in their interpretations of the Qur'an. The Sunni tend to give more authority to their community. There are numerous other groups, such as the Sufis ("wearers of undyed wool") who are mystics concentrating on prayer, self-denial and spiritual exercises such as whirling dances. All Muslims consider the Qur'an to be sacred literature. Shi'as live mainly in Iran, Iraq, Lebanon and India. Most Muslims today are Sunnis who compose about 80 percent of all Muslims.

Britain has over a million of the world's billion Muslims. Hundreds of thousands of Muslims in Britain are immigrants from Urdu-speaking Pakistan which until 1970 was a Commonwealth country. Muslims have also come from other countries and, of course, many have been born in Britain. In Britain, besides those who have come from poor villages, are those who are teachers, doctors and lawyers. Muslims may eat meat if it has been slaughtered in a special way, but never any pig-product (bacon, ham or pork). Many Muslims maintain their customs of dress and life, emphasising hard work. All Muslim boys are circumcised, either shortly after birth or around the age of twelve or even later.

Islam is not just a way of belief, it is, further, a way of life with a strong communal spirit. It is a faith for all people, of every race, language, nationality and background. A true Muslim uses Islam as a "religion of peace and justice".

To the Muslims, therefore, religion and life, faith and politics, are inseparable:

Daylight

In the Name of Allah, the
Compassionate, the Merciful
By the light of day, and by the fall of night,
your lord has not forsaken you, nor does he
despise you.
The life to come holds a richer
prize for you than this present life. You shall
be gratified with what your Lord will give
you.
Did He not find you an orphan and
give you shelter?
Did He not find you in error and
guide you?
Therefore do not wrong the
orphan, nor chide away the beggar. But
proclaim the goodness of your Lord.
(Sura 93)

---------------------- **?** ----------------------

1. Why, do you believe, have many black Christians become Muslims?
2. What do you believe are the pressures brought to modern Muslims from secularisation on the one hand and modernisation on the other?
3. Why should Muslims never be called "Muhammadans"?
4. Would you be prepared to go without lunch today? Or without eating during daylight for a month? Why do Muslims fast during Ramadan?
5. Compare the prayer in Sura 1 from the Qur'an (see above under PRAYER) with the Lord's prayer in Matthew 6:9–13 or Luke 11:2–4 from the Christian Bible.
6. Compare and contrast several characteristics of the Koran and the Bible.
7. Compare and contrast the life of Muhammad with that of Jesus.

8. Orthodox Muslims believe that the Qur'an is the Word of God in the form of a book and that the original Qur'an is to be found on a tablet at the side of the throne of God in Heaven. How do you think this relates to the Christian idea of Jesus as the Word of God in a person, or to the Bible as the Word of God? *"The phrase 'Word of God' is used in many ways and is therefore ambiguous."* Comment.

9. How does Islam build upon the foundations of Judaism and Christianity?

10. Christianity teaches that man is a sinner in need of a saviour. Islam teaches that man is born innocent and is free to follow God or not, to do good or to do evil. How do you evaluate these two views of life?

11. The "Shar'ia" (the "clear path" of Islamic Law) gives instructions on living. For example, one recent Shar'ia rule is on dress and states that one should not "ape the trends set by money-making non-believers in Paris and London". Do you think this is good advice?

12. Some liberal Muslims today believe that the Black Stone was originally a meteorite which the Arabs believed had been sent by God, and that some of the stories about the life of Muhammad should be interpreted as legend. What is your view, and how would you explain the visions of Muhammad and the creation of the Qur'an? Can you respect those whose views are different from your own?

13. "For a Muslim to be turned away from a mosque because of the colour of his skin would be unthinkable, yet many Christian Churches practice apartheid, turning coloureds or blacks away from church doors." Comment.

14. *"As sons and daughters of Adam and Eve (through descendency of the first of our species as they themselves were evolved through lower forms of life), we are all brothers and sisters... We are all fellow passengers aboard Spaceship Earth. Need our inner worlds be so far apart?"* (Muhtar Holland). Comment.

15. If you were the headmaster of a school that had Muslim students or the manager of a factory employing Muslims, would you allow them to stop studying or working at times for prayer? In the dining hall or canteen, would you provide food suitable to their laws? What else would you do or not do? Justify your answer. Write a short memo either for teachers in your school or for the foremen at your work.

16. Which of the following express your views?
    a. *"There is no such thing as a 'holy' war."*
    b. *"All war is holy if a person is supporting his own nation with physical force, and it is always right for him to do so."*
    c. *"War can be justified only to the extent that it denies exploitation and extends true freedom, meaning freedom with justice."*
    d. *"Terrorism, like all aggression, should be resisted – and forcefully if necessary."*
    e. *"Anyone, regardless of his religion, who supports fanatics and militant subversion betrays the teachings of the Hebrew prophets, of Jesus of Nazareth, and Muhammad. Herein can be identified bad Jews, bad Christians, bad Muslims and simply the evil person, the one who betrays the will of God. Equally, anyone who supports governments who maintain injustice violates these teaching. Herein there may be a dilemma in certain circumstances."* Comment. How would you solve this dilemma?

The Eastern Search for Unity

CHARACTERS:
Narrator, Hindu Guru (sitting in yoga form, legs crossed in front of him, wearing a Sacred Thread over his left shoulder and under his right arm, a ring on his finger), Buddhist Monk (white robe, barefoot, begging bowl; sitting in lotus position), Zen Buddhist Monk (white robe, barefoot, begging bowl; lotus position), Sikh Guru (wearing a turban, sitting cross legged, hands folded in front).

NARRATOR: *We have been searching for the way to peace with justice. So far we have met a number of people of ancient or early views of life. You may recall our cave dweller, our Ancient Egyptian, our Ancient Babylonian and our Ancient Hebrew. You may also recall our Ancient Greek, our Ancient Roman, the Member of the Qumran Community, the Early Christian and the Early Muslim.*

So far we basically have been looking at civilisations that directly influenced Western thought and culture. Today we make a transition. We turn to the East. It is true that because of trade and migration, and even the journeying of armies, that Western civilisation and Eastern civilisation have had much cross fertilisation of ideas. Nevertheless, we turn now to the first of two dialogues with people from the Eastern world.

__Purely by accident__, four members of our community lived in a different part of the world many years ago. Let us imagine what their conversation might be like if they were to visit us today.

It is my pleasure to present an Ancient Hindu guru (or teacher) from India, an early Buddhist monk from China, a Zen Buddhist monk from Japan and a Sikh guru from the Punjab province of India. I would like each of you to tell us about your view of life. Let us begin with our Ancient Hindu.

HINDU GURU: "OM... Let us meditate upon the adorable light of the radiant sun. May it stimulate our mind. OM..." *And I do mean to say, "our mind", and not, "our minds". For our mind is, in reality, one. I am part of you and you are part of me, in reality. The divisions we see around us are but illusions.*

We were told to assume __purely by accident__ that I, as a member of your community, had been born at a different time and in a different place. But in this earlier cycle of my life I __was__ born at a different time and in a different place. Indeed, I have been born on numerous occasions. Although I have been sitting among you in this room, many years ago I was a Hindu guru in India, and I am merely now returning to a previous life. It is not, "__purely by accident__".

I believe that when the world was created, the gods sacrificed a primitive giant, Purusha, out of which they made the world. From the head of Purusha came the Brahmins, the priestly caste. From his arms

63

came the Kshatriya, the warrior caste. From his thighs came the Vaisya, the tradesman caste. And from his feet came the Sudra, the farmer and manual worker caste. Then there were others below this, the Outcastes.

I have been born many times into this world, each time into a higher or lower caste, or even into a non-human form such as a tree or a snake, determined by how I lived in my previous existence. And after I die, I will be reborn into my next existence depending upon how I live in this life. A Brahmin who is greedy in this life may become a pig in his next reincarnation. For with the privileges of his high station in life come extra responsibilities and his misdeeds are considered more serious than those of lower estates. The higher the climb, the greater the fall. In my previous lives, I have been a pig, a worm, an ant, a blade of grass. But then, perhaps, so have you. You and I are part of the cycles of creation. Invariably we do not know what our previous cycles were or what our future cycles will be.

Such are the higher and lower forms of life. The caste system merely classifies them. There are these four main castes and thousands of sub-castes. Everyone has his station in life and he must live according to its rules.

There are millions of gods, but also there is only one God. The Vedas declare, "Reality is one."

Reality is not to be found in this world of change. It is found only in Brahman. My view of the universe is this. Brahman, being the Absolute, is one. It is indivisible and unchangeable, beyond action and inaction, beyond good and evil. But within Brahman, as within a seed, is the power of life. When it, Brahman, shows this power in the creation of a universe, it takes the form of Maya, the material world that we see and feel. This world has come from Brahman like heat rising from a fire. This universe is not God, neither is heat the fire from which it comes.

Yet heat comes from fire and cannot exist without it. You and I come from Brahman and we cannot exist without it.

So this world, Maya, is a projection of God, though it is not God. It is a projection of Reality, but it is not Real.

This world itself is part of a cycle. It will exist for a little more than four thousand million years and then will be destroyed by fire or water and return once again to Brahman. Time and time again this creation process will be repeated.

Brahman comes in three forms. As the god Brahma, it created our universe. As the god Vishnu, it sustains the universe. And in the form of the god Shiva, it will eventually destroy the universe to make way for a new one in the continuous cycle, birth and rebirth, of universes. For when this universe is destroyed, it will not materially disappear but will merely change form, and in the next cycle it will become the substance for yet another universe.

But all is one, all is Brahman. For you and me to discover this and to know it, is for you and me to realise that this world around us is not reality. Here, we do not really exist. For true existence is Brahman. All is one. You and I are one. For us to really know that would be for us to break from the cycles of rebirth and to make a final return to Brahman with all the bliss that would mean... OM... Peace... Peace... Peace... OM...

NARRATOR: <Looking over at the Buddhist and inviting him to speak, but saying nothing.>

BUDDHIST MONK: "OM... Let us meditate upon the adorable light of the radiant sun; may it stimulate our mind. OM..." ... "All that we are is the result of what we have thought: it is founded on our thoughts, it is made up of our thoughts." ... "A tamed mind brings happiness." ...

"Whatever a man thinks about continually, to that his mind becomes inclined by the force of habit." ... "Undertake to observe the rule: to abstain from taking life; to abstain from taking what is not given; to abstain from sensuous misconduct; to abstain from false speech; to abstain from intoxicants as tending to cloud the mind." ... "OM... Let us meditate upon the adorable light of the radiant sun; may it stimulate our minds." ... *OM... Peace... Peace... Peace... OM...*

NARRATOR: <Looking over at the Zen Buddhist, acknowledging that he is next to speak. And continuing to look at him.>

ZEN BUDDHIST MONK: <Having been meditating, lotus position, with your back straight and arms folded across your waist, you look down your nose without moving... After a pause, you lift your right hand to the level of your head, with elbow squared... You wait for absolute silence and then:> "OM..." <Then waving your hand:> *Do you feel that?* <Waving your hand again:> *Do you feel that?* <Waving your hand yet again:> *Do you feel that? When you can honestly say that you feel that, then you will know that you have arrived at unity, and the state of blissful nirvana is yours! ... OM... Peace. Peace. Peace... OM...*

NARRATOR: *We now await hearing what our Sikh guru (or teacher) has to say.*

SIKH GURU: "Ik oanker; wahe Guru ji ki fateh!" <Repeat three times.>

NARRATOR: *And that means, "God is one being; victory to God! God is one being; victory to God! God is one being; victory to God!"*

I wish to thank our Hindu guru, our Buddhist monk, our Zen Buddhist monk and our Sikh guru for their contributions. It would be appropriate for you to make small donations into the begging bowls of the two monks. Thank you.

？

What are your reactions to the above comments?

Hindus
Reverence for Life

With which of the following statements do you *Agree* or *Disagree?* What is your answer to h?

a. One should not kill any living animal.
b. One should not eat meat.
c. The cow is a holy animal; it should be treated with respect.
d. To be a hermit is better than being a householder, which itself is better than being a student. To be a holy man is better than either of these. To be one with God is best of all. (The four stages of Jnana Veda Yoga – Path of Knowledge; from the *Laws of Manu, c.* 200 BCE.)
e. *All that you do, all that you eat, all that you give away should be done as an offering to the Supreme Personality of the Godhead. ... Be free from reactions to good and evil deeds* (to what others do), *and you will be liberated.* (Bhakti Yoga – the Path of Love, from the *Bhagavad-Gita.)*
f. *Each day you must honour your parents and ancestors. Give shelter to guests, alms to the poor and feed animals especially cows. Divide your food into three parts: for guests, for animals and for your family. Do everything without thought for your own gain, popularity or personal pleasure. To avoid it being for selfish reasons, your work should be done as a sacrifice to the gods.* (Karma Yoga – Path of Works.)
g. Right action depends upon clear thinking. You should clear your head (1) by not harming others and by not lying or stealing, (2) by right relationships, (3) by sitting properly for meditation, (4) by good breathing, (5) by being alone, withdrawing your mind from worldly concerns, (6) by concentrating on that which is sacred/divine, (7) by meditation in a way that frees you from time and place, and (8) by becoming totally absorbed into your true self. (Raja Yoga – Path of meditation.)
h. If you were to choose between the four Yogis (d–g: Path of Knowledge, Path of Love, Path of Works and Path of Meditation), which would you select; and how would you then allocate second, third and fourth places?

Around 1800 BCE, almost 4000 years ago, and about the same time as Abraham was leading the nomadic Hebrews from Mesopotamia into Palestine, nomadic horse-men crossed the Himalayan mountains from the north-west into India. They called themselves *Aryans* (Nobles). They came on horses and in chariots, destroying the cities of the Indus (Indian) people, and then settled by the Indus River. The Aryans found a religion already developed, but the mixture of the two cultures seems to have inspired the creation of religious songs, prayers and stories. Aryan priests composed ṣongs about many gods of the sky as they made sacrifices to them. Then their teachers taught about the one holy Power behind the universe (Brahman) and the ideas of rebirth.

The religion developed and expanded throughout the country, contributing the greatest amount of sacred literature of any culture throughout history.

Assume that, **purely by accident**, you were born in India in about the year 500 BCE. These are your thoughts:

"OM... Let us meditate upon the adorable light of Savitri, god of the sun. May it stimulate our mind. OM..."

When I was born, the three letters which make up the sacred syllable AUM <often written as OM> *were written on my tongue with a pen dipped in honey. The letters represent the three main gods of my ancestors, Brahma, Vishnu, and Shiva. The next samskara* <ceremony> *came ten days after I was born: I received my name. All samskaras take place in front of sacrificial fires with everyone chanting.*

Because I was born into the Sudras <unskilled worker, lowest> *caste, I did not receive a Sacred Thread. But children of the three other castes receive this as a sign that they are prepared spiritually for their education.*

Each father gives a prayer as his child stands in front of a fire:

"Oh my child this Sacred Thread is most purified and will lead you to the knowledge of the Absolute. The natural source of the Sacred Thread is the Lord himself and it is bestowed again and again for eternity. It gives long life and favours thoughts of God. This thread I put round you. By the grace of God, may it gave you power and brilliance. OM, let us meditate on the glorious light of the Creator; may he enlighten your mind."

The colours are white for Brahmins (priestly caste), red for Kshatriyas (warrior/ ruler caste), and yellow for Vaisyas (farmer/ merchant caste). The colour identifying my caste, the sudras (unskilled worker caste), is black. Then there are the untouchables, the outcasts, who do menial work. They do not have a Sacred Thread either. But to the upper three castes, the Sacred Thread is given sometime between the ages of seven and thirteen. It is made of three strings, each with nine strands in the appropriate colour, and is symbolic of the debt owed to Brahman. It is worn over the left shoulder and under the right arm.

The child's teacher then says:

"Oh, my pupil, I accept you as one of my children. From now on your happiness and sorrow will be my happiness, and my sorrow."

A boy's head is shaved to remove any bad karma and to mark the start of his journey in the first of four stages of life, the life of a student.

I look out on the world and I see mountains and valleys and rivers – at first they look permanent, everlasting. But I know that the mountains are wearing down and the valleys are filling in, and the rivers are ever changing. Each day comes with its moon being replaced by the sun in endless cycles. I watch a caterpillar changing into a butterfly. All seems to be born and then reborn into a different form of life. Grass is eaten by a cow and becomes food which itself is transformed into milk. The cow dies and becomes fertiliser for new plants, which are themselves the life substances for more cows.

Such is reincarnation and the cycles of rebirth from plant life into animals, from animals to humans, from one human to another, perhaps ascending towards Brahman, perhaps descending away from it, until finally moving to the top of the recycling system and becoming one with Brahman, like water in a river changing and returning to the source from which it came.

What is the way towards union with Brahman? Pure thought, strict self-control, total detachment, absolute truth, with non-violence, acceptance and compassion towards all living creatures.

This does not mean a dreary life. Colourful, lively festivals, elaborate temple ceremonies, marriage feasts, the sound of drums and cymbals, the sight of swaying elephants and processions – these all show that life is to be enjoyed.

As we make our way up and down the cycles, we pass through the various castes. The four castes are further divided into over 3000 subcastes. The goldsmith and the grocer are in the same general merchant caste but in different subcastes.

We are put into castes according to the quality of our previous life. The quality of my present life will determine at what level I enter my next form.

My ancestors thought that they were being watched over by the eye of the sun god, who would reward the doer of good and punish the doer of evil. I know, however, that many bad people receive undeserved rewards in this life and many good people receive undeserved suffering. This goes against my sense of justice, unless, as I believe, the appropriate reward or punishment is given out in the next cycle of life.

In 4000 million years this world will be destroyed and become fire and water again and flow back to Brahman, which will then create another cycle of existence.

The world is maya, material. I can see, feel and touch it. But it is not the real world for only Brahman is real. This world is like heat rising from a fire. It is not the fire; but it comes from fire and depends upon fire. Without fire it would not exist. Without Brahman I would not exist. How can I seek

oneness with Brahman?

All is one; life is illusion. I see a table as different from a chair, a person of one nation as different from another.

My need is to get beyond this way of seeing things – getting rid of my "self", my own way of seeing things. Instead, I must come to see Brahman in my self and my self in Brahman, to fulfil myself in it. I need to understand self-realisation truly to be God-realisation by losing my self and my separate identity (which is an illusion) and letting it flow back into the oneness of Brahman, like a bowl of water being poured back into a river and then flowing into the ocean. Why would I want to be a finite person when I can take on infinity and know total bliss?

We have a room in our house with the image of a god in it. I don't really worship the god. It is a symbolic, representation – a manifestation of Brahman. Therefore I wake the god up in the morning, give it food, bathe it, put clothes, jewellery and flowers on it, and then tuck it into bed at night.

This might not be the manner of worship of a more educated Hindu, yet I am not mocked. Nor do I mock others. No Hindu looks down upon his less educated brothers who worship in a more crude manner. We see in this variation, rather, a stage in the development of man, or even as evidence of the cycles of reincarnation towards enlightenment. For me to mock someone practising a more primal form of worship would be a sign that I was further, than I thought I was, from recognising the unity of all things. In any case, the worship of an image is not really idolatry, perhaps, but the art of embracing the whole universe in a little object.

It saddens me when people ridicule the way others worship. My outlook and practices may appear different from yours, but are they? How many of you had a doll when you were young? Do you remember – or do you pretend to have forgotten – how you couldn't get to sleep at night if you

didn't have your teddy bear? Did anyone
mock you, laugh at you? How would you
have felt if someone had? Was not your love
for your doll a training-ground for loving
people? So it is with those who make images
of gods, because they are unable in this life,
in this incarnation, to understand God in his
true form. They need symbols. I need
symbols. And we need symbols relevant to
our own situation.

People of different religions are like
pilgrims climbing a mountain in the mist,
unable to see the others climbing the same
hill on parallel paths. Only when they reach
the summit and the mist is left behind, can
they see that there are many ways to the top.

I hope the day will come when everyone
tolerates the views of others and no one
thinks that he has all the answers. Maybe
then we will have no war and maybe then
everyone will be treated as equal and the
world will be just. Meanwhile, I will seek
peace in my own way. OM... Peace...
Peace... Peace.

What is Hinduism?

Today in cities and villages, on street corners
and in country lanes throughout India, gurus
(religious teachers) discuss their views of
God and man. They are listened to by
countless *shishyas* (disciples) and by-
standers. Today there are about 500 million
Hindus in the world (1/10th of the world's
population), of which about 500 thousand are
in Britain. This means that only about one in
every thousand Hindus lives in Britain.

Hinduism is perhaps the oldest living
religion in the world. It is the foundation of
several other Eastern religions. As Judaism
was the foundation for Christianity and
Islam, so Hinduism was the foundation for
Buddhism, Jainism and Sikhism. Today it is
influencing Western thought.

Hinduism is the simplest, yet also the most
complex religion. Hindus believe in one
eternal Spirit called Brahman, yet they also
believe in many gods. Indeed, there are over
300 million Hindu deities, all with names.
There are almost as many Hindu deities as
there are Hindus. Hinduism is a kind of
polytheism (belief in many gods) within
monotheism (belief in one God).

The fact that there are many languages in
India encourages there to be many forms of
religion. Hinduism is not one religion but
many; it is an encyclopaedia of religions.
Each village has its own interpretation of
faith and each family has its own shrine. Yet
there is a mutual tolerance.

Hindu Gods

There are gods in the form of animals and
humans, demons, ghosts, and even heavenly
dancing girls. Even the gods seem to form
themselves into castes. There are gods for all
seasons and circumstances. There is Agni, the
god of fire; Ushas, goddess of dawn;
Savitri/Surya, the sun god; Vayu, the wind
god; Yama, god of death; Varuna, god of the
sky; Sarasvati, goddess of learning; Ganapati,
the elephant-headed god of wisdom and
success. There is Indra with a thousand eyes,
Brahma with four heads and Ganesha with
perhaps sixteen arms, symbolic of the
overwhelming power of Brahman.

Brahman is the Godhead, the unity of the
Spiritual Force, the holy Power, the great
Spirit, and the supreme Soul of the Universe.
Brahman is referred to as IT, not as a person.
Brahman is everywhere, yet it is other. What
is Brahman? It is:

...infinite in the east ... south, ... west, ...
north, above and below, and everywhere
infinite ... unlimited, unborn ... not to be
conceived.

(from the *Upanishads*)

Brahman is represented by three principal gods, Brahma (creator god), Vishnu (sustainer god) and Shiva (destroyer god).

Brahma (not to be confused with Brahman) is represented by four heads which he needed when he was searching for his daughter, according to a Hindu story. Brahma lives on Mount Meru where his wife, Sarasvati (the goddess of the creative arts), rides a peacock. Out of matter that already existed, Brahma created the universe. When the universe ceases to be, there will still be matter for another universe. Nothing which exists is completely destroyed; nothing which is destroyed completely stops existing. There is simply a change in form, a conservation of energy. Physical things (maya – the world of appearances) and spirituality are completely different. A person can be physically alive in this world and yet have his spirit with Brahman. Brahma misbehaved and is not honoured today.

Vishnu was originally the god of the sky. His wife is Lakshmi who rides through the heavens on a man-bird named Garunda. Peculiar to Vishnu is that he can be incarnated in various forms, such as a fish or a tortoise, as Rama, whose wife Sita is the incarnation of Lakshmi, and as Krishna. Indeed, Vishnu has been incarnated in nine avatars (forms). Lord Krishna was the eighth avatar, Buddha the ninth avatar; and some Hindus believe that Vishnu has already had a tenth avatar, in the form of Jesus Christ.

Shiva was originally the god of the earth. He has horns and three faces or eyes to see the past, present and future. He has four hands. One holds creation, another is destructive, another gives people salvation and the other one gives them protection. One hand points to the toe and place where the soul can find refuge, and thereby reveals no need to fear. Wrapped around him is a serpent symbolising the endless cycle of life. Shiva lives on Mount Kailasa. Sometimes he rides a bull with his arm around his wife, Parvati. He can dance magnificently on the back of a dwarf. Shiva is Lord of the dance through whose dancing the universe is fortified with energy.

The two main types of Hindus today are the Vaishnavas (who worship Vishnu the preserver) and the Shaivas (who worship Shiva the destroyer of all things, preparing the way for rebirth). Those who worship Vishnu put a white U on their foreheads with a red vertical line through the middle of it giving the appearance of three vertical lines. Those who worship Shiva put three horizontal yellow lines across their foreheads. This allows the two main types of Hindus to be identified easily.

Hindu Sacred Writings

There are two types of Hindu sacred writing. First there is *shruti* (Sanskrit for *revelation*). This is the kind of writing traditionally believed by Hindus to be of divine origin. It includes the *Vedas* and the *Upanishads*. Second there is *Smriti* (Sanskrit for *tradition*). This is the kind of writing acknowledged to be of human origin and is of secondary importance. It includes the *Mahabharata* (with the *Bhagavad-Gita*), the *Yama* and the *Laws of Manu*.

Revelation

Veda means *knowledge* (of God). The *Vedas* are four books which were written in Sanskrit between 1500 and 800 BCE and contain sacred hymns and prayers. The *Rig Veda* (*Knowledge of Praises*) was chanted by priests:

A hymn to Agni, God of Fire

I praise Agni, the chosen priest, god, minister of sacrifice,
The sacrificial priest, most generous giver of

wealth.
Worthy is Agni to be praised by living and by
ancient seers:
He shall bring the gods here to us.
Through Agni man obtains wealth, yea,
plenty, growing day by day,
Most rich in heroes, glorious.
Agni, the perfect sacrifice which you
encompass about
Truly goes to the gods...

A hymn to Ushas, Goddess of the dawn

In all ages has the goddess Dawn shone, and
shows her light today, endowed with riches.
So will she shine on coming days; immortal
and undecaying, she moves on in her own
strength.
In the sky's borders has she shone in
splendour: the goddess has cast off the veil of
darkness.
Dawn approaches in her magnificent chariot,
awakening the world with purple horses...

Daily Prayer

We meditate on the loving light of the sun-
god, Savitri;
May it stimulate our thoughts.

It is called Indra, Mitra, Varuna and Agni
And also Garutman the lovely-winged in
heaven.
The real is one, though known by different
names:
It is called now Agni, now Yama, now
Matarishvan.

(from the *Rig Veda*)

Upanishad means *sitting down together*. The
Upanishads are sacred books consisting of a
collection of discussions between gurus and
their disciples, written between 800 and 300
BCE:

The secret of immortality is to be found in
purification of the heart, in meditation, in

realisation of the identity of the Self within
and Brahman without. For immortality is
union with God.
Thou Brahman art man, Thou art woman.
Thou art the dark blue bee and the green
parrot with red eyes. Thou hast the lightning
as Thy child. Thou art the seasons and the
seas. Having no beginning, Thou dost abide
with all pervadingness, from where all things
are born.
OM...
May Brahman protect us,
May he guide us,
May he give us strength and right
understanding.
May love and harmony be with us all.
OM. ... Peace – Peace – Peace.
Of that goal which all the Vedas declare,
which is implicit in all penance, and in
pursuit of which men lead lives of continence
and service, of that will I briefly speak.
It is – OM.
This syllable is Brahman. This syllable is
indeed supreme. He who knows it obtains his
desire.
It is the strongest support. It is the highest
symbol. He who knows it is reverenced as a
knower of Brahman.
The Self, whose symbol is OM, is the
omniscient Lord. He is not born. He does not
die. ...
Know that the Self is the rider, and the
body the chariot; that the intellect is the
charioteer, and the mind the reins.
The senses, say the wise, are the horses;
the roads they travel are the mazes of desire.
The wise call the Self the enjoyer when he is
united with the body, the senses, and the
mind.
When a man lacks discrimination and his
mind is uncontrolled, his senses are
unmanageable, like the restive horses of a
charioteer. But when a man has
discrimination and his mind is controlled, his
senses, like the well-broken horses of a
charioteer, lightly obey the rein.

71

He who lacks discrimination, whose mind
is unsteady and whose heart is impure, never
reaches the goal, but is born again and
again. But he who has discrimination, whose
mind is steady and whose heart is pure,
reaches the goal, and having reached it is
born no more.

The man who has a sound understanding
for charioteer, a controlled mind for reins –
he it is that reaches the end of the journey,
the supreme abode of Vishnu, the all-
pervading. ...

Like the sharp edge of a razor, the sages
say, is the path. Narrow it is, and difficult to
tread! ...

That in which the sun rises and in which it
sets, that which is the source of all the
powers of nature and of the senses, that
which nothing can transcend – that is the
immortal Self.

What is within us is also without. What is
without is also within. He who sees difference
between what is within and what is without
goes evermore from death to death. ...

The immortal Self is the sun shining in the
sky, he is the breeze blowing in space, he is
the fire burning on the altar, he is the guest
dwelling in the house; he is in all men, he is
in the gods, he is in the ether (air), he is
wherever there is truth; he is the fish that is
born in water, he is the plant that grows in
the soil, he is the river that gushes from the
mountain – he, the changeless reality, the
illimitable! ...

Man does not live by breath alone, but by
him in whom is the power of breath. ...

That which is awake in us even while we
sleep, shaping in dream the objects of our
desire – that indeed is pure, that is Brahman,
and that verily is called the Immortal. All the
worlds have their being in that, and no one
can transcend it. That is the Self.

As fire, though one, takes the shape of
every object which it consumes, so the Self,
though one, takes the shape of every object in
which it dwells.

As air, though one, takes the shape of
every object which it enters, so the Self,
though one, takes the shape of every object in
which it dwells.

As the sun, revealer of all objects to the
seer, is not harmed by the sinful eye, nor by
the impurities of the objects it gazes on, so
the one Self, dwelling in all, is not touched by
the evils of the world. For he transcends
all...

Him the sun does not illumine, nor the
moon, nor the stars, nor the lightning – nor,
verily, fires kindled upon the earth. He is the
one light that gives light to all. He shining,
everything shines. ...

The whole universe came forth from
Brahman and moves in Brahman. Mighty and
awful is he, like to a thunderbolt crashing
loud through the heavens. For those who
attain him, death has no terror...

OM ... Peace – Peace – Peace.

OM ... Hail to the supreme Self!

The syllable OM, which is the imperishable
Brahman, is the universe. Whatsoever has
existed, whatsoever exists, whatsoever shall
exist hereafter, is OM. And whatsoever
transcends past, present, and future, that also
is OM.

All this that we see without is Brahman.
This Self that is within is Brahman.

This Self, which is one with OM (AUM),
has three aspects, and beyond these three,
different from them and indefinable – the
Fourth.

The first aspect of the Self is the universal
person, the collective symbol of created
beings, in his physical nature. ...

The second aspect of the Self is the
universal person in his mental nature. ...

The third aspect of the Self is the universal
person in dreamless sleep. ...

The Fourth, say the wise, is ... pure unitary
consciousness, wherein awareness of the
world and of multiplicity is completely
obliterated. It is ineffable peace. It is the
supreme good. It is One with a second. It is

the Self. Know it alone!
This Self, beyond all words, is the syllable
OM. This syllable, though indivisible,
consists of three letters: A-U-M. They
represent the three aspects of the self,
physical, mental, dreamless sleep. ...
The Fourth, the Self, is OM, the indivisible
syllable. ...
Before creation, all that existed was the
Self, the Self alone. Nothing else was. Then
the Self thought: "Let me send forth the
world."
He sent forth these worlds: the highest
world, above the sky and upheld by it; the
sky; the mortal world, the earth; and the
world beneath the earth.
He thought: "Behold the worlds. Let me
now send forth their guardians." Then he
sent forth their guardians. ...
OM ... Peace – Peace – Peace.
(from the *Upanishads*)

Tradition

One Hindu writing, the *Mahabharata*, is
three times the length of the entire Christian
Bible. It is the world's longest poem and
contains about three million words. The
Bhagavad-Gita (*Song of God*) is part of this
long work, and was written between 400 BCE
and 100 CE. It is a call to serve God through
love as revealed by Krishna, the eighth
manifestation of Vishnu. What Krishna asks
for is love:

I am Brahman. Within this body there is life
immortal that shall not perish. I am the truth
and the joy forever... He who takes refuge in
me shall pass beyond Maya... He who
regards with an eye that is equal friends and
comrades, the foe and the kinsmen, the vile,
the wicked, the men who judge him... he is
the greatest...
Just fix your mind upon Me, the Supreme
personality of the Godhead, and engage all

your intelligence in Me. Thus you will live in
Me (Krishna, as God) always...

Reincarnation

As a man casts off his worn-out clothes
And takes on other new ones in their place,
So does the embodied soul cast off his worn-
out bodies
And enters others new...

Four Castes

When they divided primeval man,
Into how many parts did they divide him?
What was his mouth? What his arms?
What are his thighs called? What his feet?

The Brahmin was his mouth,
The arms were made the Prince (Kshatriya),
His thighs the common people (Vaishya),
And from his feet the serf (Shudra) was
born...

Duty

Better one's own duty to perform, though
void of merit,
Than to do another's well;
Better to die within the sphere of one's own
duty;
Perilous is the duty of other men...

Yoga

Let the Yogin ever integrate himself
Standing in a place apart,
Alone, his thoughts and self restrained,
Devoid of earthly hope, nothing possessing.

Let him for himself set up
A steady seat in a clean place,

73

Neither too high nor yet too low,
With cloth or hides or grass bestrewn.

There let him sit and make his mind a single
point;
Let him restrain the motions of his thought
and senses,
And engage in spiritual exercises (yoga)
To purify the self.

Remaining still, let him keep body, head and
neck
In a straight line, unmoving;
Let him fix his gaze on the tip of his own
nose,
Not looking round about him.

There let him sit, his self all stilled,
His fear all gone, firm in his vow of chastity,
His mind controlled, his thoughts on Me
(Krishna, as God)
Integrated, yet intent on Me. ...

(from the *Bhagavad-Gita*)

The *Yama* (*Abstentions*) and the *Laws of
Manu* (*Man*, like Adam; written 200–100
BCE) are further writings acknowledged to be
humanly created.

*(1) Do not destroy or injure anything. (2) Do
not lie. (3) Do not steal. (4) Do not be
envious. (5) Do not overeat or overdrink or
over-indulge in sex. (6) Keep yourself clean
inside and out. (7) Be contented. (8) Practice
self-discipline, tolerance, patience and
mental calmness. (9) Educate yourself. (10)
Try to surrender your mind to the Higher
power.*

(from the *Yama*)

Rules for the Student, the first of four stages

*Let him not injure others in thought or deed;
let him not utter speeches which make others*

*afraid of him, since that will prevent him
from gaining heaven. ... Let him abstain from
money, meat, perfumes ... substances
flavouring food, women ... and from doing
injury to living creatures ... and from the use
of shoes and an umbrella, from desire, anger,
covetousness, dancing, singing ... from
grumbling, idle disputes ... and lying, from
looking at or touching women.*

Rules for the Hermit, the third of four stages

*When a householder sees his skin wrinkled
and his hair white ... then he may resort to
the forest... Abandoning all food raised by
cultivation, and all his belongings, he may
depart into the forest, having committed his
wife to his sons, or accompanied by her... Let
him wear a skin or tattered garment; let him
bathe in the evening and in the morning, and
let him always wear his hair in braids; the
hair of his body, his beard, and his nails
being unclipped ... and give alms according
to his ability. ... Let him live without a fire,
without a house, wholly silent, subsisting on
roots and fruits. ...*

Rules for the Holy Men, Sadhus, the fourth of four stages

*Take no thought of the future, and look with
indifference upon the present. Departing
from his house fully provided with the means
of purification let him wander about
absolutely silent and caring nothing for
enjoyments that may be offered to him. Let
him always wander alone, without any
companion, in order to attain final
freedom... He shall neither possess a fire,
nor a dwelling, he may go to a village for his
food, but be indifferent to everything ...
concentrating his mind on Brahman. A*

*potsherd in place of an alms bowl ... and
coarse worn-out garments, life in solitude
and indifference towards everything, are the
marks of one who has attained liberation. ...
Let him bless when he is cursed ... sitting* (in
yoga position), *entirely abstaining from
enjoyment.*

(from the *Laws of Manu, c.* 200 BCE)

Hinduism and the Western World

If to the Western world Hinduism appears as
a primitive form of superstitious practices, it
could be argued that the Western world has
misunderstood entirely what the Hindu view
of life is all about. The Western world, today
engulfed in materialism and militarism, has
much to learn from – and benefit from –
Hinduism. In an age of anxiety,
contemplative meditation can bring peace of
mind. (The British Fellowship of Healing
makes use of a form of this.)

How has Hinduism survived? It has
absorbed new ideas and has accepted new
religions. It added Buddha to its pantheon of
gods when he died in the sixth century BCE.
When Muslims entered India in the eleventh
century CE, the Hindus accepted them almost
as a sect of their own religion, and added
Muhammad to their long list of recognised
Holy Men. (Muslim Pakistan was carved out
of India in 1947.)

It is understandable, therefore, why after
perhaps 1900 years of encounter with
Christianity, only two percent of India is
Christian. Hinduism has simply absorbed
much of Christianity. Today, gurus teach the
Sermon on the Mount (Matthew 5–7) along
with *reverence for life.* Some Hindus even
consider Christ as the 10th *avatar* (form) of
Vishnu. Some of them have suggested that
Jesus spent from age fourteen to thirty, some
of the *silent years* (about which the Gospels
make no mention), in India. Some other

Hindus believe that the 10th avatar will not
come for another 425,000 years.

Ramakrishna, a Brahmin priest in Calcutta
in the nineteenth century, taught that
Krishna, Buddha, Jesus and Allah were all
names for the same force or reality. He mixed
Hinduism, Buddhism, Christianity and Islam.
One of his disciples, Swami Vivekananda,
taught:

*If... there is ever to be a universal religion it
must be one which will hold no location in
place or time; which will be infinite, like the
god it will preach; whose sun shines upon the
followers of Krishna or Christ, saints or
sinners, alike; which will not be in the
Brahmin or Buddhist, Christian or Islamic,
but the sum total of all these, and still have
infinite space for development, which in its
catholicity will embrace in its infinite arms
and find a place for every human being...*

He taught that Hinduism contained the
essence of that religion.

Mahatma Gandhi taught:

*I maintain that India's great faiths are all-
sufficing for her. Apart from Christianity and
Judaism, Hinduism and its off-shoots, Islam
and Zoroastrianism, are living faiths. No one
faith is perfect. All faiths are equally dear to
their respective adherents. What is wanted,
therefore, is living friendly contact among
the followers of the great religions of the
world, and not a clash among them in the
fruitless attempt on the part of each
community to show the superiority of its faith
over the rest. ...*
*In order to attain a perfect fellowship,
every act of its members must be a religious
act and an act of sacrifice. I came to the
conclusion long ago, after prayerful search
and study and discussion with as many
people as I could meet, that all religions are
true and, also, that all had some error in*

them; and the whilst I hold by my own, I should hold others as dear as Hinduism; from which it logically follows that we should hold all as dear as our nearest kith and kin and that we should make no distinction between them. So, we can only pray, if we are Hindus, not that a Christian should become a Hindu; or if we are Muslims, not that a Hindu or a Christian should become a Muslim; nor should we even secretly pray that anyone should be converted; but our inward prayer should be that a Hindu should be a better Hindu, a Muslim a better Muslim and a Christian a better Christian. That is the fundamental truth of fellowship.

Gandhi was assassinated in 1947 while trying to reconcile Hindus and Muslims. Martin Luther King, Jr., was assassinated in 1968 during the Civil Rights struggle in America where he advocated Gandhi's principles of non-violence and tolerance.

The Vedanta Hindus teach:

God has made different religions to suit different aspirants, ties and countries... One can ascend to the top of the house by means of a ladder or a bamboo or a staircase or a rope, so diverse are the ways and means to approach God, and every religion ... shows one of these ways. ... The devotee who has seen God in one aspect only, knows Him in that aspect alone.

Perhaps Hinduism is not the most primal religion today. Some believe that it holds within its grasp the most modern perspective and is the best suited to resolve the problems of conflict and intolerance in our world.

———————————— ❢ ————————————

1. *A particular Christian living in India called himself a "Hindu Christian". When asked to demonstrate how he prayed, he stood on his head in a yoga position and meditated for ten minutes.* Do you think that "Hindu Christian" is a contradiction in terms? Do you think that Hinduism has anything to gain from Christianity? If so, what? Has Christianity anything to gain from Hinduism? If so, what?
2. Should there be a warrior caste in society and, if so, should it be held in high regard? What does it mean for a warrior to be a peacemaker?
3. Is religious exclusiveness a form of bigotry? Can it cause suffering?
4. Is the caste system an attempt to justify the very divisions in life which Hinduism seeks to destroy? If so, how would you resolve this paradox?
5. Hinduism claims that this world is an illusion and yet many Hindus are involved in political reform, education, civil rights, and public health – some of Britain's finest doctors are Hindus. How would you explain this paradox?
6. Are all ways to God equally valid? If not, should they nevertheless be given equal respect? How can one hold to his own views of life and yet show respect to people whose views are different from his own?
7. *If Jesus said, "I am the way...; no one comes to the Father but by me" (John 14:6), the meaning of these words is much more in line with the beliefs of Hindus who show reverence for life than with the actions of the Crusaders who claimed to believe that Jesus was the way. Some Hindus are more Christian than many Christians. For one to say, "Christ is the only way", is not sufficient for identifying him as a Christian.* Comment.

8. *Fair is fair. A Christian who supports missions to India and would want Hindus to listen carefully to what Christian missionaries teach, should himself seek out Hindus and set aside time to listen carefully to what Hindu gurus are saying in Britain today. Indeed, he is under obligation* "in the name of Christ" *to do just that. Otherwise, he is not treating others the way he would want them to treat him or someone representing him.* Comment.
9. What are some arguments in favour of vegetarianism?
10. To seek truth means to practice harmlessness. Comment.
11. If you believed in karma and rebirth, how would this affect what you did today?
12. What do you believe is the difference between yoga and prayer?
13. *Britain has a class system on which it bases salaries. Financially, it seems, at the top are company presidents and directors. Then lawyers and doctors. Then salesmen, labourers and politicians. Then teachers and clergy. At the bottom are students and the unemployed. The **only** difference from a caste system is that perhaps one can move from one class to another in this life.* Comment.
14. *"No one faith is perfect. All faiths are equally dear to their respective followers. What is wanted, therefore, is living friendly contact among the followers of the great religions of the world, and not a clash among them in the fruitless attempt on the part of each community to show the superiority of its faith over the rest."* (Mahatma Gandhi). Comment.

ॐ

Theravada Buddhism
The Small Raft
(The Southern Way)

? ——————————   —————————— ?

1. Which of the following do you believe is the best definition of religion?
   a. That which requires a belief in God, in gods or in the supernatural.
   b. That which offers worship and such cultic practices as offerings or sacrifices, having priests or other types of clergy.
   c. That which offers *ultimate concerns* in life.
   d. That which holds *peace and justice* as its aim.
   e. That which ought to be option adding and horizon extending in education.
   f. That which begins when people are trying to understand the things that are happening to them.
2. Specifically, what do you believe is the purpose of life?
3. By what principle do you think you live?
4. Do you believe that there is life beyond death? If so, what do you think the after-life is like?
5. Why do you think there is suffering?
6. Do you find that often your thoughts are frivolous and uncontrolled, not least when trying to study or concentrate? To what extent are peaceful surroundings essential? Does listening to music help? If so, what kind of music? Does going for a walk help you to think things through? If so, why? What else is helpful to keep you from being confused and muddled?

Over 500 million people, more than 1/10th of the world's population, are Buddhists. Theirs is a gentle way of life which requires, however, strict self-discipline. They have inspired, some believe, the noblest perceptions of thought ever developed by mankind. Buddhism contributed the great Tang Dynasty culture to China during the seventh to tenth centuries CE. It brought civilisation to Japan. It is not so much a religion as a way of life.

Many people define religion in terms of that which requires belief in God. By this definition, Buddhism is not a religion. Some Buddhists do not believe in God, or in gods, or in the supernatural. This is true in spite of the fact that Buddhism is based on the foundation of Hinduism and grew out of Hindu culture of India. Since most people would include Buddhism in a list of religions, perhaps a better, more useful definition of religion is *that which concerns one ultimately*. Many Buddhists believe that one's ultimate concern is to focus on the way to Nirvana, release from the wheel of rebirth. There are other useful definitions of *religion* too. It comes either from the Latin word *religare* (meaning *being bound*) or from *relegere* (meaning *gather together*).

Buddhism, like all religions, has variations. The three main divisions are so different that they themselves virtually form three different religions.

The first of these divisions is **Theravada Buddhism**, the *Way of the Elders* (*thera* = elders; *vada* = way), found in Southern Asia especially in Sri Lanka, Burma, Thailand and Laos. Such Buddhists emphasise that one can arrive at Nirvana only by one's own achievement, making one's own way. In this *do it yourself religion*, one crosses the sea of self-desire, following the teachings of the Buddha, on one's own. One only needs a small raft, big enough for one person.

The second of these divisions is **Mahayana Buddhism**, the *Way that is big* (*maha* = big; *yana* = way), found in Northern Asia in Tibet, Korea, Cambodia, Vietnam, Taiwan, China and Japan. It emphasises that Buddha came to earth to help man towards Nirvana and many of its adherents believe that Buddha can be worshipped. Mahayana Buddhists believe that it is better to help others gain Nirvana than to gain it for themselves. Therefore, they believe that the raft must be big enough to take other people, as well as themselves, on the journey. They refer to Theravada Buddhism as Hinayana, *Small raft* (hina = small; yana = way or raft), the size for one person only. *Small raft*, unfortunately, can appear derogatory.

A form of Buddhism which developed from Mahayana is **Zen** (meaning *meditation*). Zen is an extremely important form of Buddhism; and since it is so different from Mahayana, it will be considered separately in

a further chapter.

People often speak of Buddhism as if it were one religion. This would be like calling Judaism, Christianity and Islam one religion. The three forms of Buddhism that we are considering relate and yet perhaps have even greater differences from each other than do these other three religions.

The present chapter, then, is basically concerned with Theravada Buddhism, though it forms a necessary introduction both to Mahayana Buddhism and to Zen (as Judaism forms a necessary introduction to Christianity and Islam).

Assume that **purely by accident** you were born about the time of Jesus of Nazareth but in the country of Sri Lanka (previously called Ceylon). These are your thoughts:

I live on an island off the south tip of India. This island and India were once Hindu, but about 600 years ago a considerable change was taking place. Small communities were being swept into larger ones, old ways of living were being challenged by new ones. It was an age of insecurity with considerable suffering. People were asking fundamental questions: What is the purpose of life? What is the best way to live? Is there anything beyond life? Why is there suffering?

Some said, "Enjoy life and turn your back on suffering; pretend it is not there!" *Others said*, "Cut yourself off from the world; live the ascetic life; be on your own, for at least you can trust yourself!"

Into such an age of change, a Hindu prince was born by the name of Siddhartha Gautama. His father, of the warrior caste, was so wealthy that the family lived not in one palace but in three – one for the cold season, one for the hot season and one for the season of rains.

The boy was very good at sports; and at the age of 16, in an archery contest, he won the first prize of a wife for himself: beautiful Yashodara. They lived in luxury, had a son and were very happy. However, Gautama was not content. One day he left his sheltered life and arranged to be driven out of the palace in a chariot. He encountered suffering for the first time. He saw an old man, "broken-toothed, grey haired, crooked and bent of body, leaning on a staff, and trembling in every limb". The prince had never seen an old man before. He wondered if all people moved towards this form of decay and suffering. Then he saw a sick man (perhaps a leper) and wondered why there was illness. Then he saw a dead man being carried to a burning place. This man's death, and the grief of his family, troubled him.

"Why is there old age, sickness and death?" he pondered.

Then he saw a Hindu monk who was a hermit and had cut himself off from the world; the monk looked calm and serene. The prince decided to become such a monk and renounce the world.

So when he was 29, Gautama left his wife and baby son to find the solution to the riddle of life's suffering. He cut off his hair, put on a yellow robe, took a begging bowl and joined two Brahmin (Hindu) monks. For two years he tried meditation in the Hindu tradition. He meditated "upon the adorable light of the radiant sun... OM..." He joined five ascetic Hindu holy men (hermits). For five years he listened to their teaching. He tried mortification of the flesh, self-flogging, extensive fasting almost to the point of starvation. For six years he sought the solution to the riddle of Man's suffering and the way to escape from the imprisonment in this world caused by the cycles of reincarnation. He wanted to arrive at the state of existence in which there is no suffering nor sorrow.

Then one day, when he was 35, he sat in meditation under a Bo tree (the sacred Bodhi tree) at Bodh-Gaya, near a tributary of the Ganges River. He decided he would not move from the tree until he had found the answer

to the riddle of suffering and had attained enlightenment.

Through the hours of that night he first recollected his former births, then he gained a view of the entire world, then he realised the effect of greed upon life, then (like a fire with no more fuel) he became tranquil. He had reached perfection. When dawn broke, the sky was bright; there was heavy wind, thunder and rain from a cloudless sky.

He had visions. Mara, the evil one, tempted him with the world's wealth and gaiety, if he would depart from his quest. Mara attacked him with rain, rocks and weapons; but Gautama was unmoved. The fingers of his right hand, pointing downwards and calling on the earth beneath him, symbolised his steadfastness.

Mara and his evil armies were defeated.

After 49 days of meditation and rapture, Siddhartha Gautama attained enlightenment and came to be known as the Buddha, the "Enlightened one".

At first, Gautama the Buddha wanted to keep the discovery to himself and be satisfied with his own salvation; but he put this selfishness aside and, instead, went to Benares and found the five Hindu holy men, the ascetics with whom he had travelled. He preached to them about the path to enlightenment. One day he returned to his father's palace, but he stood silent at the door with an alm's bowl in his hands. For 45 years the Buddha taught throughout northern India. His simple teachings had more popular appeal than the elaborately involved teaching of many of the Hindu gurus.

Then when he was 80, Gautama the Buddha ate some poisonous mushrooms. These were his dying words to his disciples: "Work out your salvation with diligence." He went directly to the final Nirvana, the place of his dreams, permanent reality, the end of suffering, the peace that passes all understanding. His body was burned with great reverence, and his bones and teeth were enshrined as relics in dagobas (temples).

I believe that there were many Buddhas before Gautama and that there will be many more to come. I do not worship him as many people worship God or gods. I give ultimate value to the principle of enlightenment, the way to Nirvana, which he represented. This is why statues of Buddha are not meant to be life-like, resembling Gautama. They look detached and impersonal.

When I was a four year old boy I took part in a lavish initiation ceremony to recall Gautama the Buddha's renunciation of the world. First I dressed up in princely clothes symbolising the luxurious youth of Gautama. Then I removed these and put on rags to represent his decision to forego riches and worldly pleasure. Then my head was shaved and I was given a monk's yellow robes. After I put these on, I took a begging bowl for alms and said the Three Refuges: "I seek the refuge of Buddha; I seek the refuge of the Dharma (the law); I seek the refuge of the Sangha (the order of monks)." *By saying these words, I became a Buddhist. Shortly afterwards, I spent several weeks in a monastery.*

I have gone to dome-shaped dagobas which house the carefully preserved relics of Gautama's body. I have often walked with many other Buddhists around a dagoba keeping it on my right (a practice called "circumambulation") *and have made offerings of food, flowers, incense or even of coconut oil lamps. I have not worshipped the Buddha, rather I have paid him homage to show respect for the Buddhist Way. Because the number of relics of the Buddha's bones and teeth are limited, many dagobas contain other reminders of the Way, such as images and sacred writings. I have spent much time helping with the building of dagobas and their upkeep. I believe I also gain merit through making offerings of food and flowers, through pilgrimages, meditation,*

helping to feed the monks and by taking part in public ceremonies. I can gain merit even by sweeping the pavement to save tiny creatures from being stepped on. Most of all, I meditate upon the teachings of the Buddha. My goal in life is to attain Nirvana through enlightenment, and release through this from the cycles of rebirth. I know that at all times I must show the utmost of self-discipline and must follow faithfully the Middle Way of Buddha's teachings. I believe that I can attain Nirvana only on my own. After all, Gautama the Buddha had no help along the way.

Teaching (Dharma)

As Christianity was built on the foundation of Judaism and therefore accepts many of its teachings, likewise Buddhism was built on the foundation of Hinduism and accepts many of its teachings. Thus Buddhism accepts reincarnation, that all living things go through cycles of birth, death and rebirth. A man, by good deeds, might even be born as a god and live a long life in heaven; but even gods must die and be reborn as men. Further, a saint is considered to be above the gods by the quality of his life. Buddhism accepts the doctrine of karma, that good works and good living in this life affect the level of further rebirths. Buddhism accepts the belief that this world is full of suffering and sorrow from which one should seek release. It accepts the way of renunciation, stating that the removal of greed and selfishness is the way of release.

But while Hinduism and Buddhism share the same objects, they disagree on methods. Many Hindu holy men believed in inflicting pain on themselves and withdrawing from society. Gautama the Buddha taught that, although self-indulgence and greed led to suffering, neither self-injury nor attempts at escape from the world were useful. He prescribed the *Middle Way* between self-indulgence and gratification on the one hand and self-injury and asceticism on the other. The Middle Way is the way of calm detachment.

Gautama the Buddha renounced the caste system, instead believing that all people are equal in the possibility of gaining spiritual release. The Buddha did not teach a belief in God, that the human spirit is part of an entity which does not change. Instead, he taught that the self is in constant change. The way of losing all greed and earthly craving is the way to knowing the self and is the way towards Nirvana, ultimate permanent reality.

This way requires extensive effort. By doing good deeds and self-denying acts of generosity, one can become rid of selfish desires. How long will it take to attain this release? It may take not only many years; it may take many lives in the cycles of reincarnation. Yet when enlightenment breaks through, it breaks through suddenly.

Scriptures

The scriptures of Theravada Buddhists were originally written in Pali. Surviving fragments date from about 250 BCE. They are called *Tripitaka*, meaning *Three Baskets*. The first basket is the DISCIPLINE Basket which contains rules for monks and nuns. The second basket is the TEACHING Basket which contains the message of Buddha and his disciples, and legends about the Buddha (such as his previous lives). The third basket offers COMMENTARY on the Buddha's teaching. The *Pali Canon* consists of 45 enormous volumes.

Gautama the Buddha is believed to have spoken his two great teachings – the Four Noble Truths and the Noble Eight-fold Path – in his first sermon at Benares, as stated in the basic literature of early Buddhism called, *"Discourse on the Turning of the Wheel of the Law"*.

The Four Noble Truths

1. *SUFFERING is universal, the situation of all.*
2. *The CAUSE of suffering is craving, selfish desire.*
3. *The CURE of suffering is the elimination of this craving.*
4. *The WAY to eliminate this craving is the "Middle Way" through the Noble Eight-fold Path.*

The Noble Eight-fold Path

1. *RIGHT KNOWLEDGE or belief/ viewpoint.* (Accept the Four Noble Truths and their implications.)
2. *RIGHT INTENTION or resolve/values.* (Stop thinking of I, me, mine; and seek purity of heart, willing one thing and being determined to succeed in love.)
3. *RIGHT SPEECH or words.* (Think before you speak, being helpful and not hurtful; no deceit or lies, boasting or gossip.)
4. *RIGHT CONDUCT or action/behaviour.* (Live to benefit mankind; act unselfishly and charitably, obeying the Five Precepts, overcoming evil with good.)
5. *RIGHT MEANS OF LIVELIHOOD.* (Choose your vocation wisely; the more your work or job helps others, the more it helps you towards Nirvana.)
6. *RIGHT EFFORT.* (Using meditation, develop willpower for the highest moral standards.)
7. *RIGHT MINDFULNESS.* (Using meditation, become wholesome to help you see yourself, others, things and truths in the best light.)
8. *RIGHT CONCENTRATION.* (Using meditation, go beyond your knowledge, thought and behaviour, your worries and desires – cooling off/extinguishing *("Nirvana")* the flame of your earthly self and greed.)

All Buddhists believe that the third and fourth of these teachings (RIGHT SPEECH, what we say, and RIGHT ACTION, what we do) are extended in a code for living called the Five Precepts (these and the Three Refuges are chanted daily):

The Five Precepts

1. *Abstain from taking life*
2. *Abstain from stealing*
3. *Abstain from sexual misconduct*
4. *Abstain from lying*
5. *Abstain from intoxicants which cloud the mind.*

Monks have five more: (6) Eat moderately and before noon. (7) Do no dancing, singing or acting, nor observe these. (8) Do not use perfume or jewellery. (9) Do not sleep on a comfortable bed. (10) Do not receive gifts of gold or silver.

A further five are sometimes added: (11) Do not gossip. (12) Do not be envious. (13) Do not be malicious. (14) Do not swear. (15) Seek the truth. Rules of Monastic Restraint from a Book of Discipline include: *If a monk, whether he dwells in a village or in solitude, should take anything not given, he should no longer live in the community. ... From anger, malice, and dislike to accuse falsely a pure and faultless monk of an offence which deserves expulsion, intent on driving him out of the religious life, deserves suspension. ... To persist, in spite of repeated admonitions, in trying to cause divisions in a community which lives in harmony, deserves suspension... To refuse to be admonished by others about the non-observance of the rules deserves suspension.*

Some other teachings attributed to Gautama the Buddha

It is the mind which gives to things their quality, their foundation, and their being: whoever speaks or acts with impure mind, sorrow follows him as the wheel follows the steps of the draught ox. It is the mind which gives to things their quality, their foundation, and their being: whoever speaks or acts with purified mind, happiness accompanies him as a faithful shadow.

There are two extremes, O Monks, which must be avoided. One is the life of pleasure, which is base and ignoble contrary to the spirit, unworthy, vain. The other is a life of extreme asceticism which is dreary, unworthy, vain. The Perfect, O Monks, kept aloof from these two extremes and discovered the Middle Path which leads to rest, to knowledge, to enlightenment, to Nirvana.

Here, O Monks, is the truth about pain. Birth, old age, sickness, death, separation from what we have, are pain. The origin of pain is the thirst for pleasure, the thirst for existence, the thirst for change. And here is the truth about the suppression of pain – the extinction of that thirst through the annihilation of desire.

Heedfulness – the path unto the Deathless. Heedlessness: the path that leads to Death. The heedful ones never die. The heedless are as dead already.

O disciples, everything created must perish. A man must separate from everything he has loved. Do not say, "We no longer have a master": when I am gone my teaching shall be your master. (These are claimed to be among the Buddha's last words.)

Gautama Siddhartha died at the age of 80 in about the year 483 BCE. During the next 300 years Buddhism spread throughout India and onto the island of Ceylon. The great Indian emperor, Asoka, made many conquests and reigned from 269 to 237 BCE. When he endorsed Buddhism, he denounced war and formed the peaceful principles of Buddhism into a state religion. He also assisted Buddhism to spread to other countries. He sent a Buddhist monk by the name of Mahinda (possibly his son) to Ceylon. Mahinda taught the message of Buddhism to King Tissa of that country.

The teachings of Theravada Buddhism spread into the Middle East during the Greek Empire (around the third–second centuries BCE), largely due to trade. (Ancient Aramaic scripts of some Buddhist scriptures were found in Afghanistan a few years ago.) Some scholars believe that Buddhism had an influence on the teachings of Jesus, of Nazareth, a town near the trade routes.

Although its teachings, traditions, art and culture spread throughout Asia, Buddhism largely died out in India, its birthplace. There, it was mostly absorbed into Hinduism from which it had come, and the remaining parts were eliminated by the Muslim conquest. India gave birth to Buddhism, but there have been relatively few Buddhists in India since the twelfth century CE.

However, Buddhism in its Theravada form has continued to dominate Ceylon, Burma and Thailand. And in its Mahayana, Zen and other forms the impact has been overwhelming on Indonesia, Tibet, Korea, Vietnam, Cambodia, China and Japan.

Today, Buddhism is influencing the world, not least Europe and North America. During the Vietnam War, a Buddhist monk showed his protest by sitting in the yoga position, pouring gasoline over himself and burning himself to death. Fighting and war in any form is repugnant to Buddhism. Many would claim that it is the most peaceful and least militant religion in the world. Its word for love (*metta*) means *a calm, unemotional detachment from the world* rather than a strong passionate attachment to another person. And it has shown how passion can be destructive. It offers something positive to a world in which *love* has been so abused.

?

1. The sixth century BCE has been called *an age of enlightenment*. It was a time when Greek philosophy was beginning to develop. It was the century of the Jewish exile in Babylon which has been called *the Golden Age of Israel's history* – the age of Second Isaiah, Jeremiah and Ezekiel, the *Father of Judaism*. It was the time of Siddhartha Gautama and the beginning of Buddhism. How would you explain the importance of that century?

2. In the sixth century BCE, India was caught up in an age of rapid changes: the transition from rural into urban life meant that many old life-styles appeared irrelevant and new questions and problems arose. The Hindu Brahmins (priests) were mainly concerned with offering sacrifices and other cultic practices.
   a. What are the basic changes in your country today?
   b. To what extent do you believe the Christian Church is too concerned with cultic practices, maintaining large buildings and a pattern of religion irrelevant to the needs of the new society?
   c. What specifically do you think the clergy and laity (non-clergy) should be doing about this?
   d. What are some things that you believe you can do about this?

3. Some who knew him in his youth predicted that Prince Gautama would become either a great religious teacher or a great king who would conquer and rule over all of India. Religious or political/military leader: which would you rather be and why?

4. Prince Gautama's parents wanted him to be a political/military leader. What were your parents' hopes for you and to what extent did you wish to fulfil them?

5. During your childhood, in what ways were you protected from unpleasantness and from observing suffering? Why? Are there forms of unpleasantness and suffering in the world that you feel obliged to try to remove? How? Why?

6. TWO LIVES. Compare the temptation stories of Gautama (with Mara under the Bo tree) and Jesus (with Satan in the Wilderness – see Matthew 4:1–11 and Luke 4:1–13). Are these stories legends? Why do you think they came to be written? In what other ways would you compare the lives of Gautama *the Buddha* and Jesus *the Christ.*

7. TWO TEACHINGS. What are some comparisons between the teachings of Gautama and Jesus?

8. To what extent do you endorse the moral teachings of Buddhists? Do you believe in:

   a. *having tolerance for the views of others?*
   b. *being non-violent, refusing to hurt or harm (as well as kill) those who disagree with you or who might be your enemies?*
   c. *showing respect for each individual no matter how different his life style?*
   d. *showing love for animals and insects?*
   e. *showing respect for the realm of nature and man's environment, spoiling none of its beauty?*
   f. *believing in the fundamental spiritual equality of all human beings, regardless of nationality, race or culture?*
   g. *believing that appreciation of art, literature and music motivates reflection on the things that make for peace?*
   h. *showing dissatisfaction with materialism?*
   i. *having peace and serenity of mind?*
   j. *searching for freedom from the constant changes in this life?*
   k. *living by a high moral code of self-discipline?*
   l. *believing in the wrongness of stealing?*
   m. *believing in the wrongness of sexual misconduct?*
   n. *believing in the wrongness of using drink or drugs which cloud the mind?*
   o. *eating with moderation?*
   p. *not being malicious?*
   q. *not swearing?*
   r. *seeking the truth?*
   s. *not gossiping or being vicious in speech?*
   t. *seeking a vocation/job which helps others?*
   u. *acting unselfishly?*
   v. *making use of meditation?*
   w. *accepting the superiority of personal moral conduct over external religious rites and ceremonies?*
   x. *believing that worry is a fruitless waste of time and not the way to tranquillity?*
   y. *being a monk as a possible way to self-fulfilment?*
   z. *the Four Noble Truths and the noble Eight-fold Path?*

9. Buddhism developed in India and then almost entirely departed from it. Britain has been called a *Christian* country and yet membership in Christian Churches is declining and represents a minority view of the people living here. Do you believe that some day Christianity will largely disappear from Britain? Why, or why not? If so, what do you believe will take its place?

10. The two extremes: materialism (over-indulgence, greed and sensuality) and

asceticism (self-denial and withdrawal from society): to what extent do you believe you are an extremist and in which direction? What would you need to do to arrive at the *Middle Way*.

11. Buddhism demands personal character of a high moral standard but is not based upon aggressive social ethics. Are tolerance and personal example always the best ways to react to injustice? Explain your answer.

12. Asoka, king of India, renounced fighting when he became a Buddhist. He replaced his soldiers with missionaries. How would you evaluate this? Can missionaries be militant, destroying the freedom of belief with manipulative salesmanship? How do you think Buddhist monks avoid this today?

13. Do you believe that meditation has any value, or is it a waste of time?

14. Compare and contrast Nirvana and Heaven.

✸

Mahayana Buddhism
The Large Raft
(The Northern Way)

? ———————— ⊕ ———————— ?

Do each of the following exercises for at least a minute.
1. a. Breathe quietly, mentally counting 1–10 *AFTER* each breath.
    b. Breathe quietly, mentally counting 1–10 *BEFORE* each breath.
    c. Do you feel any difference between a and b? If so, try to explain it.
2. Breathe quietly, thinking about the good things and happy times in your life and wishing yourself well.
3. a. Breathe quietly, thinking about someone you like and wishing him/her well.
    b. Breathe quietly, thinking about someone you do not get on well with, and wishing him/her well.
    c. Breathe quietly, thinking about all the people in the world and wishing them well.

The second form of Buddhism is Mahayana (*maha* = *large/great*; *yana* = *raft/vehicle/circle*) Buddhism found especially in Tibet, Mongolia, Korea, Cambodia, Vietnam, Taiwan, China and Japan. Basically it endorses most of the teachings of Theravada (*the Way of the Elders*) Buddhism and its interpretation of the life and teaching of Gautama the Buddha. But Mahayana Buddhism emphasises that it is better for one to help others attain Nirvana than to attain it for oneself. This led to the development of elaborate rituals, more complex places of worship and complicated forms of art. (There is an evolution in the portrayal of the Buddha in sculpture, represented at first by a symbol such as a wheel or a tree and later in human

form.) Alexander the Great, the Greek warrior, invaded Punjab in 326 BCE and brought the influence of Greek art and architecture to Buddhism.

About 200 years after Gautama's death, some of his disciples began teaching a more popular form of Buddhism that was more easily adapted to the needs of ordinary people, not least because they did not need to become monks to gain enlightenment. Believing that one's own Nirvana must be secondary to that of others, they emphasised that the raft on which one travels across the pilgrimage in life must allow room for other people. Because this doctrine came to be known as Mahayana (*the large raft*), its adherents sometimes called the other form,

Hinayana (*the small raft*) in perhaps a belittling as well as descriptive way to refer to Theravada Buddhism. The new teachings were brought to China shortly after the time of Jesus.

Consider that **purely by accident** you were born in China about a thousand years ago. These are your thoughts:

I am a "Bodhisattva" <"sattva" = essence; "bodhi" = enlightenment>, a future-Buddha. I believe that someday I will become a Buddha and enter Nirvana, but not before all mankind has entered. I do not want Nirvana just for myself. I want to have numerous rebirths in the future so that I can help others in their pilgrimage towards Nirvana. Between rebirths, I believe that Bodhisattvas reside for long periods of time in the heavens. I believe in Amitabha <Amida> Buddha, the "Buddha of Infinite Light" to whom I pray and whom I believe is not and never has been an actual historical person. Amitabha lives in a kind of heaven which is called "Great Western Paradise", or the "Pure Land" to which all good Buddhists can hope to go. I do not worship idols or images of Amitabha Buddha because I believe that the images are merely focal points for concentration, not for the Buddha himself.

One does not have to be a monk to gain paradise, the jewelled paradise of harmonious music and radiant light, which has colourful trees everywhere. I believe that Amitabha Buddha sits in paradise on a lotus seat, on a gold mountain surrounded by his saints.

Yes, I give reverence to Gautama the Buddha, and I believe in his teachings. I believe that it is significant that when Gautama gained enlightenment he did not go immediately into Nirvana. He remained to teach others the way, not just through wisdom for themselves but equally through compassion for others.

I believe that Gautama the Buddha was the fourth avatar <rebirth, appearance on earth> of Amitabha Buddha.

Sacred Writings

Mahayana Buddhists accept the Tripitaka (the three baskets of **DISCIPLINE**, **TEACHING** and **COMMENTARY**) as sacred. The four Noble Truths, the Noble Eightfold Path and the Five Precepts are among their basic beliefs which they share with Theravada Buddhists. However, they consider to be sacred other writings which they call Sutras (*Threads*). Sutras are so numerous that no one has ever read them all.

(Re-read the quotations from the *Tripitaka* and other writings given on pp. 82–84, for these are basic also to Mahayana Buddhism.)

Sutras (teachings of the Buddha)

In the Japanese edition, Sutras consist of over 100 volumes which have been extended to over 325 volumes by Tibetan Buddhists.

On Meditation (Yoga)

After he has passed his day in keeping his mind collected, the self-possessed man should shake off his sleepiness and spend also the night in the practice of Yoga. When threatened with sleepiness you should constantly mobilize in your mind the factors of exertion and fortitude, of stamina and courage. You should repeat long passages from the Scriptures which you know by heart, expound them to others and reflect on them yourself. In order to keep awake all the time, wet your face with water, look round in all directions and fix your eyes on the stars. With your senses turned inwards, unmoved and well-controlled, with your mind undistracted, you should walk about or sit down at night. Fear, zest, and grief keep sleepiness away; therefore cultivate these three when you feel drowsy...

You are further asked to apply mindfulness to your sitting, walking, standing, looking, speaking, and so on, and to remain fully conscious in all your activities. The man who has imposed strict mindfulness on all he does, and remains as watchful as a gatekeeper at a city-gate, is safe from injury by the passions, just as a well-guarded town is safe from its foes. No defilement can arise in him whose mindfulness is directed on all that concerns his body. On all occasions he guards his thought, as a nurse guards a child. Without the armour of mindfulness a man is an easy target for the defilements, just as on a battlefield someone who has lost his armour is easily shot by his enemies. A mind which is not protected by mindfulness is as helpless as a sightless man walking over uneven ground without a guide. ... Therefore you should super-intend your walking by thinking "I am walking", your standing by thinking "I am standing", and so on; that is how you are asked to apply mindfulness to all such activities.

Then, my friend, you should find yourself a living-place which, to be suitable for Yoga, must be without noise and without people. First the body must be placed in seclusion; then detachment of the mind is easy to attain. But those who do not like to live in solitude, because their hearts are not at peace and because they are full of greed, they will hurt themselves there, like someone who walks on very thorny ground because he cannot find the proper road. ...

Sitting cross-legged in some solitary spot, hold your body straight, and for a time keep your attention in front of you, either on the tip of the nose or the space on your forehead between the eyebrows. Then force your wandering mind to become wholly occupied with one object. If that mental fever, the preoccupation with sensuous desires, should dare to attack you, do not give your consent, but shake it off, as if it were dust on your clothes. Although, out of wise consideration, you may habitually eschew sense-desires, you can definitely rid yourself of them only through an antidote which acts on them like sunshine on darkness. There remains a latent tendency towards them, like a fire hidden under the ashes; this, like fire by water, must be put out by systematic meditation. As plants sprout forth from a seed, so sense-desires continue to come forth from that latent tendency; they will cease only when that seed is destroyed. When you consider what sufferings these sense-pleasures entail, by way of their acquisition, and so on, you will be prepared to cut them off at the root, for they are false friends. Sense-pleasures are impermanent, deceptive, trivial, ruinous, and largely in the power of others; avoid them as if they were poisonous vipers! The search for them involves suffering and they are enjoyed in constant disquiet; their loss leads to much grief, and their gain can never result in lasting satisfaction. A man is lost if he expects contentment from great possessions, the fulfilment of all his wishes from entry into heaven, or happiness from the sense-pleasures. These sense-pleasures are not worth paying any attention to, for they are unstable, unreal, hollow, and uncertain, and the happiness they can give is merely imaginary.

But if ill-will or the desire to hurt others should stir your mind, purify it again with its opposite, which will act on it like a wishing jewel on muddied water. Friendliness and compassion are, you should know, their antidotes; for they are forever as opposed to hatred as light is to darkness. A man who, although he has learned to abstain from overt immoral acts, still persists in nursing ill-will, harms himself by throwing dirt over himself, like an elephant after his bath. For a

holy man forms a tender estimate of the true
condition of mortal beings, and how should
he want to inflict further suffering on them
when they are already suffering enough from
disease, death, old age, and so on? With his
malevolent mind a man may cause damage to
others, or he may not; in any case his own
malevolent mind will be forthwith burned up.
Therefore you should strive to think of all
that lives with friendliness and compassion,
and not with ill-will and a desire to hurt. For
whatever a man thinks about continually, to
that his mind becomes inclined by the force
of habit...

(from *Manda the Fair*,
words attributed to the Buddha)

Lo! like a fragrant lotus at the dawn
Of day, full blown, with virgin wealth of
scent,
Behold the Buddha's glory shining forth,
As in the vaulted heaven beams the sun!
    Greed is the real dirt, not dust;
Greed is the term for real dirt.
The wise have shaken off this dirt,
And in the dirt-free man religion lives.
    How excellent a moral life pursued till
death!
    How excellent a well-established faith!
    And wisdom is for men a treasure which
brings merit,
    And which the thieves find very hard to
steal.
    The man of wisdom who did good,
    The man of morals who gave gifts,
    In this world and the next one too,
    They will advance to happiness.

On the Practice of Introversion

No distractions can touch the man who's
alone both in his body and mind.
Therefore renounce you the world, give up
all discursive thinking!

Thirsting for gain, and loving the world, the
people fail to renounce it.
But the wise can discard this love, reflecting
as follows:
Through stillness joined to insight true,
His passions are annihilated.
Stillness must first of all be found.
That springs from disregarding worldly
satisfactions.

To share in the life of the foolish will lead to
the states of woe;
you share not, and they will hate you; what
good comes from contact with fools?

Good friends at one time, of a sudden they
dislike you,
You try to please them, quite in vain – the
worldly are not easily contented!

Self-applause, belittling others, or encouragement to sin,
Some such evil is sure to happen where one
fool another meets.

Two evils meet when fools consort together.
Alone I'll live, in peace and with
unblemished mind.

The fools are no one's friends, so have the
Buddhas taught us;
They cannot love unless their interest in
themselves impels them.

Trees do not show disdain, and they demand
no toilsome wooing;
Fain would I now consort with them as my
companions.

Fain would I dwell in a deserted sanctuary,
beneath a tree, or in a cave,
In noble disregard for all, and never looking
back on what I left.
Fain would I dwell in spacious regions
owned by no one,
And there, a homeless wanderer, follow my

own mind.

*A clay bowl as my only wealth, a robe that
does not tempt the robbers,
Dwelling exempt from fear, and careless of
my body.*

*Those who travel through Becoming should
regard each incarnation
As no more than a passing station on their
journey through Samsara.*

*So will I ever tend delightful and untroubled
solitude,
Bestowing bliss, and stilling all distractions.*

*And from all other cares released, the mind
set on collecting my own spirit,
To unify and discipline my spirit I will strive.*

(from *Practices of a Bodhisattva*
by Shantideva, a Mahayana writer
of the seventh century CE)

On Karma

*1. A single rule you set aside, or lying words
you speak,
    The world beyond you ridicule – no evil
you won't do!
2. Better for you to swallow a ball of iron
red-hot and flaming with fire,
    Than on the alms of the people to live,
while immoral, indulgent, intemperate.
3. If it's suffering you fear, if it's suffering
you dislike,
    Just do no evil deeds at all – for all to see
or secretly.
4. Even a flight in the air cannot free you
from suffering,
    After the deed which is evil has once been
committed.
5. Not in the sky nor in the ocean's middle,
    Nor if you were to hide in cracks in
mountains,
    Can there be found on this wide earth a*

*corner
    Where karma does not catch up with the
culprit.
6. But if you see the evil others do, and if you
feel you disapprove,
    Be careful not to do likewise, for people's
deeds remain with them.
7. Those who cheat in business deals, those
who act against the Dharma,
    Those who swindle, those who trick – not
only harm their fellow-man,
    They hurl themselves into a gorge, for
people's deeds remain with them.
8. Whatever deeds a man may do, be they
delightful, be they bad,
    They make a heritage for him; deeds do
not vanish without trace.
9. A man will steal while profit seems to lie
that way.
    Then others steal from him, and so the
thief by thieving is undone.
10. The fool, while sinning, thinks and hopes,
"This never will catch up with me".
    Wait till you're in the other world, and
there the fate of sinners learn!
11. The fool, while sinning, thinks and hopes,
"This never will catch up with me".
    But later on there's bitterness, when
punishment must be endured.
12. The fool does evil deeds while unaware of
what they lead to.
    By his own deeds the stupid man is burnt,
as though burnt up by fire.
13. The fools, unwise, behave as though they
were their own worst enemies,
    Committing many evil deeds which issue
then in bitter fruits.
14. Not is an action called "well done,"
which brings suffering in its train,
    Of which we reap the fruit quite glad, in
happiness, with joyous heart.
15. In hot pursuit of their own joys they
laugh when they do evil deeds.
    They'll weep with pain and misery, when
they receive their punishment. ...*

(from the Sanskrit *Dharmapada*)

The Death of Gautama the Buddha

In measured steps the Best of Men walked to his final resting place – no more return in store for him, no further suffering. In full sight of his disciples he lay down on his right side, resting his head on his hand, and put one leg over the other. At that moment the birds uttered no sound, and, as if in trance, they sat with their bodies all relaxed. The winds ceased to move the leaves of the trees, and the trees shed wilted flowers, which came down like tears. ...

In his compassion the All-knowing, when he lay on his last resting place, said to Ananda, who was deeply disturbed and in tears: "The time has come for me to enter Nirvana. Go, and tell the Mallas about it."...

The Mallas, their faces covered with tears, came along to see the Sage. They paid homage to Him, and then, anguish in their minds, stood around Him. And the Sage spoke to them as follows: "In the hour of joy it is not proper to grieve. Your despair is quite inappropriate, and you should retain your composure! The goal, so hard to win, which for many aeons I have wished for, now at last it is no longer far away. When that is won – no earth, or water, fire, wind of ether <*air*> is present; unchanging bliss, beyond all objects of the senses, a peace which none can take away, the highest thing there is; and when you hear of that, and know that no becoming mars it, and nothing ever there can pass away – how is there room for grief then in your minds? At Gaya, at the time when I won enlightenment, I got rid also of this body, the dwelling place of the acts accumulated in the past. Now that at last this body, which harbours so much ill, is on its way out; now that at last the frightful dangers of becoming are about to be extinct; now that at last I emerge from the vast and endless suffering – is that the time for you to grieve?...

"It is indeed a fact that salvation cannot come from the mere sight of Me. It demands strenuous efforts in the practice of yoga. But if someone has thoroughly understood this my Dharma, then he is released from the net of suffering, even though he never cast his eyes on Me. A man must take medicine to be cured; the mere sight of the physician is not enough. Likewise the mere sight of Me enables no one to conquer suffering; he will have to meditate for himself about the gnosis <*wisdom*> I have communicated. If self-controlled, a man may live away from Me as far as can be; but if he only sees my Dharma then indeed he sees Me also. But if he should neglect to strive in concentrated calm for higher things, then, though he live quite near Me, he is far away from Me. Therefore be energetic, persevere, and try to control your minds! Do good deeds, and try to win mindfulness! For life is continually shaken by many kinds of suffering, as the flame of a lamp by the wind."...

Thereupon the Buddha turned to his Disciples, and said to them, "Everything comes to an end, though it may last for an aeon. The hour of parting is bound to come in the end. Now I have done what I could do, both for myself and for others. To stay here would from now on be without any purpose. I have disciplined, in heaven and on earth, all those whom I could discipline, and I have set them in the stream. Hereafter this my Dharma, O monks, shall abide for generations and generations among living beings. Therefore, recognize the true nature of the living world, and do not be anxious; for separation cannot possibly be avoided. Recognize that all that lives is subject to this law; and strive from to-day onwards that it shall be thus no more! When the light of gnosis has dispelled the darkness of ignorance, when all existence is seen as without substance, peace ensues when life draws to an end, which seems to cure a long sickness at last. Everything, whether stationary or movable, is bound to perish in the end. Be ye therefore mindful and vigilant! The time for my entry into Nirvana has now arrived! These are my last words!"

And when the Sage entered Nirvana, the earth quivered like a ship struck by a squall, and firebrands fell from the sky. The heavens were lit up by a preternatural fire, which burned without fuel, without smoke, without being fanned by the wind. Fearsome thunderbolts crashed down on the earth, and violent winds raged in the sky. The moon's light waned, and, in spite of a cloudless sky, an uncanny darkness spread everywhere. The rivers, as if overcome with grief, were filled with boiling water. Beautiful flowers grew out of season on the Sal trees above the Buddha's couch, and the trees bent down over him and showered his golden body with their flowers. ...

(from *The Acts of the Buddha*, written in the first century CE: from a Tibetan translation, *Buddhist Scriptures*)

History

By trade routes through the Himalaya Mountains, Buddhism spread into China shortly after the time of Christ. By sea routes from Korea, it reached Japan. In the seventh century CE the Japanese Prince, Shotoku Taishi, established Buddhism as a national religion. In the eighth century CE a mixture of (a) Mahayana Buddhism, (b) a form of Hinduism which had pronounced practices of magical and mystical forms and (c) traditional Tibetan practices of the worship of demons yielded Tibetan Lamaism. Today, the Dalai and Panchen Lamas are considered by their followers to be living incarnations of some of the Buddhist holy beings of the past.

1. What are the differences between Theravada Buddhism and Mahayana Buddhism? Which one do you prefer? Why?
2. With which of the Buddhist teachings on karma do you agree?
3. What is yoga and how would you evaluate it?

Zen Buddhism
The Way of Meditation

?̣ ——————————— ——————————— ?̣

1. A man has fallen over a cliff, hanging on to a branch with his teeth. Assume you are that man. Someone asks you, *What is "Zen" <"meditation">*? What is your initial answer?
2. On a separate small piece of paper, write down what you consider to be the most important word. Now, throw it away into a waste basket. Have you really thrown it away? If you think so, then also put an answer you did not give into the waste basket.
3. Take a flower in your hand (a drawn picture will do), hold it up and gaze at it in absolute silence. Now smile. Reflect on these words by Tennyson:
   "Flower in the crannied wall, I pluck you out of the crannies.
   I hold you here, root and all in my hand, little flower.
   If I could but understand, what you are, root and all, and all in all,
   Then I should know what God and man is."
   Now crush the flower. Now ask yourself, *Do I know what God and man is?*

Assume that **purely by accident** you were born in Japan about 500 years ago. You are a Zen Buddhist. These are your thoughts:

I think that there is no point to believing in God. Indeed I find such a belief to be a barrier to enlightenment. So too, I believe, is the use of any words as if they were sacred. Not any scripture, not any form of ritual or worship, not incense, not chanting, not the wearing of gorgeous robes: none of these are the means to enlightenment. Such props of religion may be ways of attracting attention, they may add beauty and help create an atmosphere for tranquillity; but they offer nothing for real peace.

Indeed the mind must be freed from all such focus if I am to attain enlightenment.

Words considered to be sacred may help take us to the bottom of the mountain, but they have no further value and that on which they are written might as well be burnt to bring warmth to the body. For the mountain cannot be climbed with such relics. As an adult throws away the toys of childhood, so must the true mountaineer get rid of relics. He climbs best who has the lightest load. So much of what is considered by many to be religion is really a burden. I must be free from all of this.

Should I then search for truth? No, not the truth found by intelligence and reason. No.

The expert believes that he understands more and more about less and less – that what seemed to be a simple quest at first, is really complex. The expert believes that the more he learns, the more he has yet to discover.

This does not mean that I must avoid the quest for knowledge, but that I must seek to go beyond knowledge to enlightenment. And that does not require less discipline, but more. The way to enlightenment is not the easy way, the way of sloth. Indeed each moment of my day is spent either meditating or working in the fields. I must want the influence of Zen as much as a man held under water wants fresh air.

But this is not finding life to be a burden. As the story goes:

"Two monks, returning home, came to a ford where a pretty girl was waiting, not wanting to get her clothes wet. One monk picked her up in his arms, crossed the stream and having put her down, walked on. The other monk was horrified and continued to be angry as they walked mile upon mile. The first monk said, 'That girl? I put her down at the ford. Are you still carrying her?'"

I believe that it is where thinking ends that Zen begins. Thinking and believing can put me in a cage trying to reach out to other people's thoughts. Zen, however, is a breaking through locked doors, throwing them open and letting the light flood in. Anything that will thrust me into this is of value.

My goal is Satori <the Zen term for enlightenment.> It is a leap from thinking to knowing. Since it lies beyond thinking, I cannot describe it; but I believe it will liberate me from all forms of bondage and let me escape from the wheel of birth and death, birth and death in endless circles. Satori may come to me slowly, or quite suddenly, or not at all. But I hope it comes for it will make me a new person.

To help me along this path I will now meditate on a koan:

"A long time ago, a man kept a goose in a bottle. It grew larger and larger until it could not get out of the bottle any more. The man did not want to break the bottle, nor did he wish to hurt the goose. How would I get it out?"

Zen

Japan's best known contribution to Buddhism is the Zen school. Zen is a sect of Mahayana, the Northern school of Buddhism. *Zen* (from the Chinese word, *Ch'an*, which is from the Sanskrit word, *Dhyana*) means *meditation*. In our search for peace with justice, we have arrived at undoubtedly the most difficult religion to understand.

Zen offers no belief in God or gods or the supernatural. It offers no dogma or set of beliefs. It is a way of thinking, acting, and being. It is totally rational, yet beyond reason. It describes the indescribable, like revealing a sunrise to a blind person. It is sudden awareness, enlightenment, knowing that one's mind is part of All-mind. It is the leap from thinking to knowing; and it is knowing without thinking. Zen is **seeing** the sound of a storm, **hearing** the beauty of a tree – for it is beyond one's senses. It is the *Middle Way*, yet above the two of which it is between. It is not the *Middle Way* of moderation. Who would want to be half way between good and evil? The Middle Way of Zen Buddhism is a synthesis on a higher plain, showing that the opposites were always one. All things are one.

Zen is, then, like seeing with a third eye and discovering that this eye is the other two.

"What is Zen?" asks a mathematician.

A Zen master might give this answer: *"Zen is the third point of a triangle, related to the other two points not by the connecting lines but by the triangle itself. The third point of a triangle is **all** that is within the triangle, and **all** that is outside the triangle as well. The* *third point of the triangle, therefore, is not the third point. To call it the third point is to miss the point. When you know that the third point of a triangle is not a point at all, but the sum of all points together and yet not the total number – when you know that – then you will have arrived at Nirvana."* With these words a Zen Master might try to answer the question, but it is not the answer, for the answer is not in words.

The words of Zen often do not make sense; but words themselves are weak and detached symbols. A word is never what it represents; it is always a false label. Could you be summed up in one word, even by your name? Could you be totally explained in many words, even thousands of words? Labels are false stereotypes. True wisdom, therefore, comes without words. It comes through experience, yet it is not the experience.

Zen Buddhists acknowledge that Gautama the Buddha was the first Patriarch. They believe that an Indian Buddhist by the name of Bodhidharma was the 28th successive patriarch and that he came to China in the sixth century CE. They consider Bodhidharma as the formal founder of the Zen school of Buddhism (though in an elementary form, Zen had entered China in the first century CE). Bodhidharma introduced the element of *Satori*, the immediate experience of truth, into Buddhism. He is often depicted in Zen art with a beard and looking somewhat fierce. Tradition claims that he was last seen as an old man carrying a sandal on his head. (Not because he was mad, but because he was trying to say something.)

Zen teaching spread from India to Ceylon, Burma, Siam, Cambodia, China, Korea, Japan and Tibet. Today its presence is increasing in Europe and North America.

There are two main sects of Zen. There are the **Rinzai** who make extensive use of the koan, an unsolvable riddle. Then there are the **Soto**, who teach that *the practice of meditation is enlightenment.* The Soto do not use koans for they believe that the Buddha nature is here and now in the practice of meditation.

"What is the sound of one hand clapping?" This is a koan. What is your answer?

Zen, like Mahayana Buddhism, teaches that Theravada Buddhism is wrong to suggest that one can attain Enlightenment by his own efforts. Zen Masters provide important assistance towards Nirvana. They often use tough measures, even force such as a blow on the face, to try to bring on the jolt of sudden Enlightenment, or more likely to describe the real solution to a koan as being like a blow in the face.

Zen Masters often use humorous stories. Zen itself is like a good joke, you either see it or you do not. For the joke itself is spoiled when words are used to explain it.

Question: *"What is the difference between a hen?"*

Answer: *"One leg is both of the other."*

If the question is not meaningful, neither is the answer an answer. Yet it is the answer, but not in words.

To try to *explain* Zen is impossible. The above is merely an attempt by someone who has studied it for many years and who feels no nearer to understanding it. A Zen Master might reply, *"Why try to understand it? Why not try to experience it?"* This now is what we shall try to do, letting Zen *speak* for itself.

Zen Buddhist Teachings

(Re-read the Scriptures of Buddhism given on pp. 82–83 and 88–92. They belong to Buddhism and belong to the wealth of literature, tradition and experience on which Zen is founded.)

Those who perform meditation for even one session
Destroy innumerable accumulated sins;

how should there be wrong paths for them?
The Paradise of Amida Buddha is not far.

(a Zen verse, from *The Song of Meditation*)

Empty-handed I go, and behold, the spade is
in my hand;
I walk on foot, yet on the back of an ox am I
riding,
When I pass over the bridge
Lo, the water floweth not; it is the bridge
doth flow.

If you have a staff I will give you one; if not, I
will take it away.

(attributed to Basho, a ninth-century
Korean monk; all that he said when
asked to give a sermon)

"When a man comes to you with nothing,
what would you advise?"
"Nothing."

(answer attributed to Joshu,
a famous Zen Master)

One in All,
All in One –
If only this is realised
No more worry about your not being perfect.

Better than one thousand verses
Where no profit wings the word,
Is one solitary stanza
Bringing peace of mind when heard.

What do you mean by "looking into your own
mind"?
To turn one's vision into the source of the
mind, and completely abstain.

When we think we know something, there is
something we do not know.

(Prof. D T Suzuki, a Zen teacher)

I look at the sea.
I enter the rival sea.
How hard to walk on!

I give myself to the sea.
Where now is the sea, am I?

(in the form of a Japanese Zen *"tanka"*,
from *Zen Buddhism*, Christmas Humphreys)

He who knows does not speak; he who speaks
does not know.

(*Tao Te Ching*,
a saying often used by Zen Buddhists)

Zen Koans

What is the reason of Bodhidharma's coming
from the West?

We all know what two hands clapping are
like.
What is the sound of one hand clapping?

If all things are reducible to the One, to what
is the One to be reduced?

How many elephants are there on a blade of
grass?

Does a hill go up or down?

What is "mu" (nothing/not)?

When a monkey goes around a tree, does the
tree go around the monkey?

(in the form of a Zen koan,
by William James,
American philosopher and psychologist)

There are over 1700 Zen koans. The Zen Master may repeat a koan over and over to his pupil until he "sees" it. Or before it is seen, he may choose a new one. When the "answer" comes, it is described to be like a blow in the face. Zen Buddhists also set their own koans for they believe that life itself is a koan.

Zen Monastery

In a Zen Buddhist monastery, something like the following schedule will be kept:

4.30 a.m.: get up.
5.00–7.00: meditation
7.00: breakfast, of a simple rice-gruel
8.00: group meditation
9.00: teaching from a Zen Master and quizzes using koans
10.00–12.00: free time
12.00: lunch
1.00 p.m.: private meditation
2.00–4.00: work outdoors, gardening, etc.
4.00–5.30: meditation and quizzes using koans
5.30: evening meal
7.00: meditation
8.00: lecture
9.00: go to bed.

The timing is done by the use of incense sticks in front of a statue of the Buddha. When a stick burns down, a bell is rung: perhaps signalling the monks to walk quickly around the hall. When the next incense stick burns down, a bell may signal the monks to meditation. This walking and meditating may be done in rotation for several hours. If a monk falls asleep while meditating, the Master will certainly wake him up, perhaps hitting him with a piece of wood.

"What are those?" asked a Zen Master.
"Those are birds flying," replied the monk.
"Where are they now?"
"They are gone," replied the monk.
The Master grabbed the monk's nose and twisted it. *"Are they really gone?"* he asked.

?

1. Imagine you are watching running water (perhaps while filling a bath or sitting by a river). SEE the water flowing. Is it restful? Can you let your mind flow instead of the water? What do you think this means?
2. Now you are swimming in the ocean. Describe this not in terms of the waves flowing over you but of you flowing over the waves.
3. Gaze at a painting or listen to music. Let yourself *be* the artist or the composer. Try to HEAR the painting or SEE the music.
4. *"If any man be unhappy, let him know that it is by reason of himself alone."* (Epictetus, a Greek slave) To what extent do you believe that it is not an event but your response to an event which may make you unhappy?
5. *"If you can meet with Triumph and Disaster and treat those two impostors just the same..."* (Rudyard Kipling) How can you attain such a disposition?
6. *"One ought to get so far as to become entirely independent of the accident of one's external surroundings."* (Count Keyserling) To what extent do you believe you should try to become detached from the world around you?
7. *"Even without thought-processes one can be useful to other beings. For one can be like the sun or moon whose rays light up all things, like the wishing jewel which can create anything, like the great earth which has the power to produce all things."* (from *Buddhist Scriptures*, Penguin, p. 216) Should one seek to be to others like the radiance of the sun? How can one attain such constructive charisma?
8. *"What you think is what you are."* To what extent do you believe this Zen statement is true?

9. *"Though a man should conquer a thousand times a thousand men in battle, he who conquers himself is the greatest warrior."* (Comment.)

10. *"Love is the law."* Do you agree? What are the dangers when this is interpreted literally, rather than metaphorically? Can you give some illustrations of metaphor in the Bible? What are some of the problems that are caused by metaphoric sayings in religious literature (not least the Bible) being interpreted literally?

11. *"Any man's death diminishes me because I am involved in mankind. And therefore never send to know for whom the bell tolls. It tolls for thee."* (John Donne) Do you agree? Why or why not?

12. Some Buddhists have interpreted Zen as a religion for warriors, emphasising rigorous self-discipline and contempt for death, and have engaged in battle without questioning its justification. Other Buddhists have interpreted Zen as a religion which accepts no war as just or holy. How would you explain these two opposed views from the same religion?

13. Many Buddhists (Theravada and Mahayana) believe that Nirvana belongs to some future "there and then" at the end of their cycles of life as many Christians believe that Heaven belongs to some future time at the end of life. Other Buddhists (Zen) believe that Samsara (Nirvana) belongs to the present moment "here and now", as other Christians believe that Heaven is here and now, the Kingdom of God in the midst. (*E.g. "Blessed are the poor in spirit for theirs is the kingdom of heaven."* From *Matthew* 5.) Which of the two emphases do you believe is more important? (Or are they both equal, or both unimportant?)

14. *"Lord, give me the serenity to accept what cannot be changed, the courage to change what ought to be changed and the wisdom to know the one from the other."* (A prayer by Reinhold Niebuhr, a Christian theologian.) Some critics of Zen Buddhism believe that Zen has a major fault: that Zen Buddhists accept life as it is rather than seek to change it. Is this criticism justified? To what extent can Zen help one to come to terms with circumstance, changing what ought to be changed, yet finding serenity when it is appropriate?

15. *"There are only three things in the world: one is to read poetry, another is to write poetry, and the best of all is to live poetry!"* (Rupert Brooke) What does this mean? Do you agree?

16. *"What I do to my disciples is to liberate them from their own bondage with such devices as the case may need."* (Wei Lang, Sixth Chinese Zen Patriarch) What is your bondage? Has it really been caused by yourself? What device do you think might bring release? Will it require great courage and tremendous effort?

17. *"A Theravada Buddhist climbs a wall, sees Nirvana and jumps over into it. A Mahayana Buddhist climbs a wall, sees Nirvana and climbs back down to help others over. A Zen Buddhist..."* How would you finish the statement? Which of these is closer to describing your attitude to life?

18. You have just sat an examination. You feel you may have failed. If you worry about it and are afraid of failing, you will not get on with more study for other exams. This means that you have failed already. If, on the other hand, the result is that you realise that you should have worked harder in preparation for it and you start to knuckle down, then you have passed the *"real"* exam. It is the experience that matters. If you have learned in the process, you are further ahead than some who have passed or have a higher mark. Learn to live successfully with failures. There are more to come. Failure is a necessary part of any journey to success. (Comment.)

19. *"Three cars have two, four and six cylinder engines, respectively. The first uses all*

of its power. The second uses half of its power. The third also uses half of its power. Which one is the most powerful?" Why is the answer, *"Not the second or the third"*? As a parable, what does the story mean when applied to yourself? Why is it irrelevant that power is not determined merely by the number of cylinders?

20. Question: *"Is the horizon up or down?"* Answer: *"It is both in motion."* Question: *"Why is a part greater than the whole?"* Answer: *"Because the whole is complete and finite, while a part is unfinished, changing, and therefore infinite."* (Comment.) Why are the questions meaningful and why are the answers true? Is all language merely metaphor?

21. How can you use Zen constructively in preparation for homework assignments? How can you make the doing of homework a Zen experience?

22. A monk asked, *"Ever since ancient times many people have left their homes and loved ones to enter the gates of Buddhism and study Zen meditation. They expend a great amount of time and energy on disciplined, contemplative training. What is it they gain?"* A Zen Master answered, *"Nothing."* Try to explain why he said this.

✸

Sikh

Baptism of the Sword

? ———————————   ——————————— ?

Do you *Agree* or *Disagree* with the following statements?

a. *"There is One God; He is the Supreme Truth."* (the *Mool Mantra*, from the *Japji*)
b. God dwells in all people; and He created all people to be equal as part of the one brotherhood of mankind.
c. Because it is a gift from God, one's own body should be treated with care. Therefore, alcohol and tobacco should not be used; and hair, a source of strength, should not be cut.
d. All people should be treated equally – regardless of race, religion and nationality, whether rich or poor, whether men or women. One ought to show kindness to all people.
e. One should live a life of service to others.
f. Animals were created to serve man. Therefore, meat can be eaten; but animals should be treated with kindness.
g. Each person has had numerous cycles of birth, death and rebirth.
h. Only God can release one from this re-incarnation.
i. One should work hard "with hands, head and heart".
j. One should acquire wealth in order to share it. One should give not expecting to receive in return. Avoid selfishness.
k. One should give at least ten percent of one's income to charity.
l. One should never deceive another person.
m. The simple life is a better life.
n. One should not be superstitious, or practice black magic or believe in astrology.
o. Gambling is wrong.
p. Provide help for the family. Do not be an ascetic or use a begging bowl.
q. The views of others should be tolerated.
r. One should be prepared to die for one's faith if necessary.
s. It is morally wrong to allow rape and murder of defenceless people. One should be prepared to die to defend the weak from ruthless treatment.
t. One should be prepared to fight for justice.
u. Fasting brings no merit.
v. *"One reaps what one sows."* (the Law of Karma)
w. One does not go to heaven or hell when one dies. Heaven and hell are conditions of

life in this world.
x. War is justified if it defends freedom and opposes injustice. *"When all other means have failed, it is righteous to draw the sword."* (Guru Gobind Singh)
y. Leisure time is necessary time. One should make time for physical recreation, hobbies, seeing films, watching television and reading good books. But avoid entertainment that corrupts or is anti-social.
z. A place in the court of God can only be obtained if one does service to others in the world.

Assume that **purely by accident** you were born about a hundred years ago of Sikh parents in Northern India in the Punjab (near the border of Pakistan and Afghanistan beyond the Thar Desert). These are your thoughts:

I live in "Punjab" which means "five streams", and refers to streams which flow from the Himalayan Mountains into the Indus River. It makes me sad to think that many years ago, here in India, Hindus and Muslims fought each other. Guru Nanak was a Hindu who was attracted by Islam, but he wanted to bring the two together into one brotherhood by founding a new religion.

Guru Nanak married and had several children. He worked in business and farming and then, at the age of 30, he became a wandering teacher. One day while bathing in a stream he had a vision of God giving him a cup of sweet nectar. God said to him, "Go and repeat my name, and make others do so. This cup is a pledge of my regard."

Nanak taught that, by worshipping the one God, Hindus could be freed from the endless cycles of re-birth. He travelled far, even to Mecca, the centre of Islam. Having settled at Kartarpur, he composed many songs. He insisted that his community have a kitchen where food was freely served to all who came, whether Sikhs or not.

Shortly before he died at the age of 65, he appointed Guru Angad as his successor. Angad compiled the Granth, the Sikh holy book.

It was the Muslim leader Akbar who gave us the land on which the Golden Temple and our holy city, Amritsar, was built.

I was "baptised by the sword" and became a member of the Khalsa <the Sikh community>. *In this ceremony I was instructed to love God, to study the scriptures and to serve mankind. I was told to always wear the five Ks, the **KESH*** <uncut hair>, *the **KANGA*** <a comb to keep the hair in place under a turban for men or a scarf for women>, *the **KARA*** <a steel bracelet, symbol of unity, on the right wrist>, *the **KACHS*** <shorts worn by men and women, originally to give free movement in battle> *and the **KIRPAN*** <a short sword symbolic of protecting the weak and defending one's faith>. *After praying, I read aloud from the Granth. Then the baptism amrit* <nectar> *of water and sugar was stirred in a large iron bowl by a Khanda* <a double-edged sword>. *The senior Sikh read the Japji* <a poem by Guru Nanak>, *including the words which since then I have used every day in my devotions:*

"There is One God
He is the Supreme Truth."

Other Sikhs present knelt in the warrior's position, squatting with the left knee on the floor and the right knee raised ready to help me rise into combat if an enemy should appear. All present read in turn from the scriptures and a prayer was given. Then I squatted in the warrior's position and was given the baptismal nectar to drink. Nectar was also sprinkled five times on my eyes, hair and hands. Then the words, "Wahe Guru ji ka Khalsa" <"the Khalsa is the chosen of God"> *were spoken. I responded with "Wahe Guru ji ki fateh"* <"Victory to God">. *Singing and praying concluded the service. This was followed by all present eating mixed food of flour, water, sugar and melted butter.*

I believe that if I keep my baptismal vows I can reach Nirvana and freedom from re-incarnation. Therefore, I must meditate every day, live a good life in service to others and always be tolerant of the beliefs and ways of life of others. Depending on my quality of life I will move nearer or further from Nirvana.

Nanak taught that his followers should pray each day. I rise before dawn every day, have a bath (to symbolise the washing of my soul) and then I meditate on the name of God who is within me and within all people. I repeat the Japji poem written by Nanak and the Jap written by Gobind Singh. Whenever possible I then go to the gurdwara to worship with others. At dusk I join with the family sitting in front of the Granth. We cover our heads and take off our shoes and bow out of respect for this Guru. We meditate on two hymns. We each use the mala <a loop of thread with 108 knots> *to help us repeat "Wahe Guru"* <"Wonderful Lord"> *in our worship of God. I believe that this helps us to be humble and to serve others.*

I am glad that at the gurdwara all are welcomed and that all are invited to eat together afterwards – rich and poor, young and old, teachers and students, Sikhs and non-Sikhs. There must be no barriers. I believe in "baptism of the sword". I believe that it is right for Sikhs to fight for justice and to defend our faith with the sword. I must defend the weak from ruthless treatment. I must always remember those who were beaten, shot, cut up or burnt alive and who could not make any resistance. I must remember the martyrs of my faith.

This, then, is my prayer:

"May Sikhism find a loving place in our hearts and serve to draw our souls towards

Thee. Save us, O Father, from lust, wrath, greed, undue attachment and pride. ... Grant... the gift of faith, the gift of confidence in Thee. ... Grant that we may, according to Thy will, do what is right. Give us light, give us understanding. ... Forgive us our sins. ... Help us in keeping ourselves pure. ... Through Nanak may Thy Name forever be on the increase. ... Hail Khalsa of the Wonderful Lord who is always victorious."

There are about ten million Sikhs in the world today. There are about 300,000 Sikhs in Britain, 320,000 Hindus and a million Muslims (out of a British population of about 68 million). Although there are different sects, the Sikh religion developed from Indian culture and a mixture of Hinduism and Islam.

From Hinduism came a belief in re-incarnation and the transmigration of the soul at death from one body to another. From Islam came a firm belief in one God and the one brotherhood of man under God without any caste distinctions.

The Ten Sikh Gurus

1. **Guru Nanak** (1469–1534) was the founder of Sikhism and lived in the Punjab when it was part of the Muslim Mogul Empire. He tried to combine Hindus and Muslims into one brother-hood by abolishing the caste system and by simplifying the cultic practices of ritual, ceremony and pilgrimage. He was an extremely gentle person.

2. **Guru Angad** (1504–1552) created a way of writing the Punjabi language. He also organised education for young children and started building gurdwaras as places of worship and learning.

3. **Guru Amar Das** (1479–1574) discour-aged suttee, the practice of widows

cremating themselves on the funeral pyre of their husbands. He reinforced the practice of communal eating to help make certain that the caste system was abolished. He made the langar (communal kitchen) an essential part of each gurdwara.

4. **Guru Ram Das** (1534–1581) selected the site for the Sikh holy city, later called Amritsar, on land given by Akbar, a Muslim Emperor. He also made an artificial island for the site of the temple.

5. **Guru Arjan** (1563–1606) organised the building of the Golden Temple at Amritsar and completed the Granth, the Sikh sacred writings which include the teachings of Nanak and other teachers before and after him, including Muhammad. He was imprisoned by a Muslim emperor and tortured to death. Continuing Muslim persecution pro-voked the Sikhs into military revolt against their Islamic rulers.

6. **Guru Har Gobind** (1595–1644; the son of Arjun Dev) founded the Sikh army to defend the faith and introduced *"baptism of the sword"*.

7. **Guru Har Rai** (1630–1661; grandson of Arjun Dev) avoided politics but tried, unsuccessfully, to make peace with the Muslim Emperors.

8. **Guru Har Krishan** (1656–1664; the son of Har Rai) became leader of the Sikhs at the age of five and died of smallpox when he was nine.

9. **Guru Tegh Bahadur** (1621–1675; another son of Har Rai) was executed for refusing to become a Muslim.

10. **Guru Gobind Singh** (1666–1708; son of Teg Bahadur) made the Sikhs the strongest power in North-western India. He instituted the baptismal ceremonies called "*Pahul*" and wrote the second collection of sacred scriptures. He declared that there would be no more human gurus but that the Granth would be the immortal guru, to be called *"Guru Granth Sahib"* ("Holy Book which is Lord").

Sikh Scriptures

The Adi Granth ("first book") was compiled over a period of 200 years by several Gurus. This first sacred collection contains hymns written by Nanak and others, together with a number of Hindu and Muslim writings. It is considered the final Guru and is called *"Guru Granth Sahib"*. It begins with the Mool Mantra ("chant") and the Japji, the most important Sikh hymn, on the value of God:

There is one God
He is the Supreme Truth. ... (Mool Mantra)

As he was in the beginning: the Truth,
So throughout the ages,
He has ever been: the Truth,
So even now he is Truth immanent,
So forever and ever he shall be
Truth eternal...

Let compassion be thy mosque, let faith be
thy prayer-mat, let honest living be thy
Koran, let modesty be the rules of observ-
ance, let piety be the fasts thou keepest.

In such wise strive to become a Muslim:
right conduct thy Kaaba; truth thy prophet,
good deeds thy prayer,
submission to the Lord's will thy rosary;
Nanak, if thou do this, the Lord will be thy
protector...

Kabir, where there is divine knowledge there
is righteousness;
where there is falsehood, there is sin.
Where there is covetousness, there is death;
where there is forgiveness, there the Lord
is...

The extent to which you agreed with the 26 statements at the beginning of this chapter suggests the extent to which you agree with the Sikh religion.

Sikhs believe that all religions began with good purposes and are but different roads leading to the same goal. To what extent do you agree?

Sikhs believe that worship helps them to be humble and to serve others. How do you evaluate worship for yourself? Where do you find your motivations?

The Way to Life

CHARACTERS:
Narrator (Chairman), Japanese Shintoist (Kami no Michi), Chinese Taoist (pronounced Dowist), Chinese Confucian, Member of the Bahá'í Faith

NARRATOR: *We have come a long way in our search for peace with justice. So far we have met a number of people of ancient or early views of life. You may recall our Cave Dweller, our Ancient Egyptian, our Ancient Babylonian and our Ancient Hebrew, our Ancient Greek, our Ancient Roman, the member of the Qumran Community, the Early Christian and the Early Muslim. They presented views that have directly influenced Western thought and culture.*

More recently we met an Ancient Hindu guru from India, an Early Buddhist monk from China, a Zen Buddhist monk from Japan and a Sikh guru from the Punjab province of India. Their views also have influenced Western thought.

***Purely by accident**, four members of a group were born in other cultures outside our country towards the end of the last century. They have come to join us today.*

It is my pleasure to present a Japanese Shinto Priest, a Chinese Taoist <pronounced Daoist>, a Chinese Confucian and a Bahá'í. I would like each of you to tell us about your view of life. Let us begin with our Japanese Shinto Priest.

SHINTO PRIEST: *The Japanese name for my view of life is "Kami no Michi". It means, "the Way of the Gods". "Kami no Michi" is*
the official religion of Japan. In Chinese, "Kami" is written as "Shin" and "Michi" is written as "Tao" <pronounced Dao>. "Shin-Tao" (or "Shinto") is the Chinese word for "Kami no Michi", the Way of the Gods. Shinto was the name given by the Buddhists who wanted to distinguish "the Way of the Gods" (Shin-Tao) from the Way of Buddha (Buddha-Tao).*

"To" or "Tao" <pronounced as Dao> means the "Way". "Shin" means the "Gods". Shinto therefore means, "the Way of the Gods". Shinto is the official religion of Japan. Buddhism and Zen and other views of life are also found in Japan. But Shinto is its main cultural heritage as Christianity is the main cultural heritage of Britain.

"Kami" is Japanese for "spirit" or "god". I believe in thousands of gods because I believe that spirits or gods dwell in all things. It is Kami that makes things unusual and even inspiring. There is Kami in the music you enjoy listening to; it attracts you and inspires you. It is Kami that makes this building special and this desk so interesting. When you look at the sun, or see the rain coming down, or hear the thunder and feel awe-struck, it is Kami. When you look at a mountain or a stream or even this chair, it is Kami that makes it special. "Kami" means "spirit" or "upper" or "above" or "above

106

the ordinary" or "unusual". Anything can be unusual; everything is unusual. Gods, people, animals and all things in nature – trees, grass, stones, flowers – all are related because all have a Kami-nature, the same divine spirit in them, whether alive or dead. Our ancestors had Kami in them. I believe that I should honour them in order to pay respect to Kami.

I say to you, "Respect Kami by doing what you think you should do. Let your conscience be your guide." We were all born with a sense of right or wrong. We do not need to learn about morals or values; we know these already. This is why, although I am a priest, I do no preaching or teaching. I have nothing to teach you. The way of the gods is the way you know you should go. So go; let nothing hold you back. Don't feel uneasy or think that there is anything wrong with you. Go through the gateway of life knowing that Kami will go with you.

NARRATOR: *Thank you. Now I call on our Chinese Taoist <pronounced Daoist>. What do you believe is the way to life?*

TAOIST: *Although Taoism <pronounced Dowism> is found in Japan, it originated in my country of China. We have just heard how "Kami no Michi", the way of the gods, is popularly known by the name Shinto, a Chinese name: Shin-to or Shin-Tao <pronounced Shin-Dao>. Tao means way. As a Taoist <pronounced Daoist>, I believe, however, not in the way of the gods. Nor do I believe that the spirit naturally dwells in me and that therefore I can let my conscience be my guide. I believe that Tao – the Way – is the ultimate mystery behind everything in the world and indeed the universe. We cannot naturally grasp it. We need much learning and mystical insight, some connection between ourselves and that which is beyond us.*

Consider the way the universe works: the turning of the earth, the movement of the

planets, the order of the universe. There is not only a **pattern** or method by which the universe works, there is also a **power** or force that causes it to work. When there is an earthquake or a tornado, something seems to be wrong or destructive in the working of the planet, something that is not according to its intended pattern nor to its constructive power. And yet it is what happens; it is part of the changing order. When things go well, Yang is in control; when things go badly, Yin is in control. Yet the universe needs the balance of both: Yin and Yang.

I believe that my life is like that – a mixture of Yang and Yin. I have my good days and my bad days. But I must be in flow with nature. Tao is the way I should order my life so that it is in accord with the pattern – the plan – of the universe. I believe that I should work **with** nature, not against it. I believe that I should go with the flow of nature, like going down a stream rather than fighting against it.

Tao, the Way, can keep my life in perfect balance; but I cannot be told the Way. I must find Tao for myself. When I do, my life is at peace – like floating leisurely down a stream on a raft.

Therefore, the symbol of Taoism is not the open gateway of Shintoism but the two parts of a circle called Yin and Yang. Yin and Yang are the twin forces that govern nature and all of life. Yin is the dark part and Yang is the light part. "Yin" means the "dark side" of a mountain – the shadow. Yang means the "sunny side" of a mountain – the sunlight. Yin is like the darkness of winter and Yang is like the brightness of summer. Yin is like the colours of blue or black; Yang is like the colours of white or red. Yin is the power that gives softness, moisture and change. Yang is the power that gives firmness, dryness and solidity. Yin is like all that is feminine and Yang is like all that is masculine. Yin is often represented by a tiger and Yang by a dragon.

Life needs both Yin and Yang, but both in balance, both involved with each other. This is why, in the symbol of my religion, the two are bound together.

I must not let conscience be my guide because my conscience may not be in tune with nature. I must not let specific moral teachings be my guide because what is appropriate for one person may not be appropriate for another. What I can do is prepare myself for finding Tao by living with peaceful simplicity, by keeping myself physically fit like a strong tree and by not thinking too highly of myself or ignoring the needs of others. As Lao Tzu, the father of Taoism, said, "Let nature take its course."

NARRATOR: *Thank you. Now, what does our Confucian believe is the way to life?*

CONFUCIAN: *I believe that Tao is the great law of life. Confucius said, "We must not be separated from the Tao for one moment."*

I believe, however, that Confucius gave the teachings which help me to find the way. "Peaceful simplicity", yes. "Humility", yes. "Heeding the needs of others", yes. But I would be more specific than that. Confucius used an important word – "li". "Li" means "the ideal standard of conduct". If one is devoted to "li" he will help to order human relationships that alone can let peace and harmony reign throughout the world. There are five relationships that you and I must get right. First, between the RULER and his SUBJECTS. Second, between FATHER and SON. Third, between HUSBAND and WIFE. Fourth, between OLDER BROTHER and YOUNGER BROTHER. And fifth, between OLDER FRIEND and YOUNGER FRIEND. These are the "five great relationships". I believe that I must take them seriously. I believe that I must work them out carefully.

SUBJECTS must be loyal but this requires that RULERS must be benevolent. SONS must be respectful, but this requires that FATHERS must be loving. WIVES must be obedient, but this means that HUSBANDS must be supportive. The YOUNGER BROTHER must be co-operative, but this means that the OLDER BROTHER must be gentle. The YOUNGER FRIEND must be helpful, but this means that the OLDER FRIEND must be considerate.

The family matters. It is the hub of society. Indeed, society is just only when the ruler treats his subjects as if they were his children.

Confucius said, "If the ruler is virtuous, the people also will be virtuous."

Shintoists let nature take its course. Taoists turn to nature to understand the order they seek for themselves. I believe that I can know the order of nature only by looking inside myself. Let my chief concern be the forming of right relationships with other people. The divine spirits, what some call "the gods", do not matter. It is our ancestors who have given us our real heritage.

NARRATOR: *What is the way to life? Our Shintoist has said, "The way to life is to let nature take its course." Our Taoist has said, "The way to life is to let nature **set** our course." Our Confucian has said, "The way to life is to look within ourselves in order to find the way of nature." I wonder how our Bahá'í is going to answer the question, "What is the way to life?"*

BAHÁ'Í: *I have been most interested to hear that you have been searching for peace with justice. I believe that there can be no peace without justice, nor can there be justice without peace. The story of man's search for these two necessities of life has been a long one. Primal man, Ancient Egyptians, Babylonians, Hebrews, Greeks, Romans, the Qumran Community and Early Christians and Muslims – a Western search – has* brought a great legacy to each one of us.

The Hindus, Buddhists, Zen Buddhists, and Sikhs – an Eastern Search – has added to this legacy. Further to the Eastern search, you are beginning today a consideration of Shintoism, Taoism and Confucianism and adding to this the Bahá'í Faith, which seeks to bridge East and West.

The Bahá'í Faith was founded in Ancient Persia (what today we call Iran) which lies to the North of the Persian Gulf and somewhat East of Ancient Babylonia, and lies between the Western and Eastern world. The aim of the Bahá'í Faith is to build a bridge between East and West, between all people wherever they may live on this planet earth – regardless of nationality, race, culture, yes, and even of religion, that all the barriers might be removed so that we might have one world built on a firm foundation of justice and peace.

You have discovered how Judaism was the foundation for Christianity and Christianity for Islam. So too was Islam a foundation out of which developed the Bahá'í Faith. Judaism, Christianity, Islam and the Bahá'í Faith – each in turn added to the prophetic message.

A prophet is a spokesman for God, a teacher of righteousness, someone who has been called by God to speak a message explaining the way to peace with justice and justice with peace: for example, Elijah, Amos, Hosea, Micah, Isaiah, Jeremiah and Ezekiel. A Prophet, with a capital P, is a Manifestation or Messenger of God possessed of the divine Spirit. Such were, I believe, Moses, Krishna, the Buddha, Jesus and Muhammad.

I believe that Moses, Jesus and Muhammad were great prophets. I believe that through Moses God gave the fundamentals of His law. I believe that through Jesus (called "the Christ" by Christians) God gave a further explanation of his Word of truth that was required for

man's understanding of how he should live. I believe that through the prophet Muhammad other revelations from God were given. I believe that the founder of the Bahá'í Faith was the Prophet the Báb, who was followed by Bahá'u'lláh, another great teacher of righteousness and Manifestation of God.

Today, you have listened to a Shintoist, a Taoist and a Confucian. They, too, have something to teach us about the Way to life. I believe that what they have called Tao – the Way – is their search for the Way God would have man live in peace and justice. I am seeking to understand the Way of God for his people. Although I do not believe in many gods as Shintoists do, nor in ancestor worship as the Taoists do, nor in Heaven rather than God as Confucianists do. (Confucius was a humanist and the idea of God as such did not appeal to him.) Nevertheless, my beliefs have much in common with theirs. Man must take seriously the flow of nature and give greater respect for the natural world. We must appreciate the way of nature and seek its harmony. We must look within ourselves and others and find in mankind the Tao – the Way to life. I believe that this is in the nature of man, of every man, because the Spirit of God – the Spirit of love, unity, justice, peace, reconciliation – dwells within us, between us and beyond us. This Spirit of God, I believe, created the world of nature and the nature that is in the world – the mountains and rivers, the trees and flowers, the plants and animals.

The originator of the Bahá'í Faith was the Báb. Báb means "door" – door to the truth. Báb means "gateway" – gateway to life. Báb means "Way", the Tao. In 1850, the Báb was put to death in Persia (Iran), martyred for his faith. Bahá'ís are being persecuted today as you listen to me speaking. So often prophets and their followers have been rejected.

Somehow the people of this world must respect the basic human right of freedom of belief. Yet so much more is urgently required.

Somehow we must find the Tao – the Way –
to let our beliefs work for reconciliation
rather than for division and confrontation.

As Bahá'u'lláh taught:

"O people of Justice! Be as brilliant as the
light and as splendid as the fire that blazed
in the Burning Bush. The brightness of the
fire of your love will no doubt fuse and unify
the contending peoples and kindreds of the
earth. ..."

As 'Abdu'l-Bahá, appointed successor to
Bahá'u'lláh, said:

"The gift of God to this enlightened age is
the knowledge of the oneness of mankind and
of the fundamental oneness of religion."

What is the way to life? If mankind can
decide to work together, the way will become
revealed. Indeed it already has been
revealed.

There is an old saying, "Where there's a
will, there's a way." There is a way. What
man needs is the will to live it.

NARRATOR: I wish to thank our Shintoist,
our Taoist, our Confucian and our Bahá'í.

1. Where do you agree/disagree with the above views?
2. How do you evaluate the following statements?
   a. Shintoism: "The Way to life is to let nature takes its course."
   b. Taoism: "The Way to life is to let nature set our course."
   c. Confucian: "The Way to life is to look within ourselves in order to find the Way of nature."
   d. The Bahá'í Faith: "The Way to life is the way to peace with justice, the way of the prophets, the way of unity."

Shintoists
Let Nature Take its Course

Do you *Agree* or *Disagree* with the following statements? Can you briefly give reasons for your answers?

1. Nature is the binding force by which all things are held together.
2. The peaceful unity of mankind can be attained by people being in tune with nature.
3. One should live by the example of nature and then let nature take its course.
4. No one needs a creed or statement of faith to live by.
5. No one has the right to do whatever he wants to, whenever he wants to, regardless of the effect it has on others.
6. Let your conscience be your guide.
7. One should love the spirit in nature.
8. The best place for a shrine or place of worship is in a garden full of flowers, in a forest filled with trees, or alongside a stream.
9. My land is protected by the spirits of my ancestors.
10. Only a clean mirror gives a good reflection. The mirror of my conscience must be kept free of the dusts of envy, meanness, inconsideration, hatred, revenge, anger, pride and selfishness.

Assume that **purely by accident** you were born of Shinto parents in Japan at the beginning of the twentieth century, shortly before the First World War. These are your thoughts:

I believe that in the beginning the world was divided into a pure heaven above and impure water below. Izanagi, the Kami-spirit of man, and Izanami, the Kami-spirit of woman, stirred the water with a spear and made an island of land on which to get married and live together. They made Kami-spirits of trees, plants and winds. The Izanami, the

Kami-spirit of woman, died and began to decompose. When she realised that Izanagi saw her in this decaying state, she divorced him. Izanagi, with total disapproval, washed himself in the ocean. Suddenly the moon goddess came out of his right eye, the sun goddess out of his left eye and the storm god out of his nose.

But the storm god, Susanoo, destroyed the rice fields of the sun goddess, Amaterasu. In revenge, Amaterasu, the sun goddess, hid in a cave of heaven and made the world dark. Some Kami-spirits hung a mirror on a sakaki tree and this enticed Amaterasu to come out,

making the world bright again. In this way,
the changes from day to night, and night
back to day, were made.

Amaterasu, the sun goddess, sent her
grandson, Ninagi-no-Mikoto to rule the
island. Ninagi-no-Mikoto made his grandson
the first divine emperor of the islands. <A
variation of this Shinto myth is that
Amaterasu sent her son to rule the island. He
married the daughter of Mount Fuji, and it
was their grandson who became the first
emperor.> The island is my country of Japan,
and I regard the emperor as a god.

I do not believe that there is any force of
evil within man. Consider the trees and
flowers and all of nature. They have the
Kami-spirit and do not contain evil. Consider
birds and animals. They have the Kami-spirit
and know naturally what to do. So, too, with
man. His instinct tells him whether something
is the right thing to do or not.

However, although man within himself is
good, nevertheless he can do wrong by
violating his conscience.

Since there is no force of evil, there is no
original sin, only original good. This does
not mean that everything anyone does is
good. Because man has been born with the
Kami-spirit within him, he knows the
difference between good and evil, right and
wrong; therefore he should follow his
conscience. Yet he can have his conscience
fogged over by evil spirits, the "magatsuhi",
and do the evil he wishes to avoid. Like a
good tree which does not grow straight if its
way is blocked, or like a mirror which gives a
poor reflection if it is not free of dust, so a
man will not do that which he knows is right
if he is confused.

I do not have to fight against evil by
following a set of disciplinary rules. Rules
would make me of less value than a bird or
animal, a tree or flower. This does not mean
that I have the right to do whatever I want to,
whenever I want to, to whomever I want to,
and that nobody has the right to stop me.

Indeed, my conscience sets a very high
standard of behaviour. My conscience comes
from the Kami-spirit. Therefore, I must
follow "Kami no Michi" <Japanese for the
"Spirit way">, the "Way of the Gods"
<Shinto or Shen-Tao in Chinese>.

Because the Kami-spirit dwells in all
things, all things are related and bound
together into one through Kami. All the
world of nature – land, water, plants, birds,
animals, people and goods – is part of the
Kami in the natural world. The world is
constantly changing – crops grow, plants
and animals change, grow and reproduce,
people move through childhood, adulthood
and old age. The forces that bring these
changes in the world are Kami. Wind, rain,
thunder, storms – these phenomena are
Kami. The sun, moon, mountains, rivers,
oceans, land: these objects are Kami. Dogs,
cats, foxes, birds, fish: these creatures are
Kami. The spirits of our ancestors, of ourselves and the people around us, are Kami.

We can sense the Kami within these things
when we regard them with awe, like noticing
the splendour of harvest time, the colours of
a rainbow, the beauty of a sunset, the
wagging tail of a dog, the heritage and
memories of our ancestors.

I believe that my land of Japan is protected
by the Kami of the ancestors of the people
who live there. I believe that Kami protects
me and helps me throughout my life: in my
student days to help me do my homework and
pass exams, in my adulthood to protect my
home and family, and in my old age to help
me to withstand disease. Animals and insects,
birds and fish, are also protected by Kami. I
must show respect for nature and its living
creatures because of the Kami-spirit that
dwells within.

Kami does not depend upon my beliefs. So
I have no need for creeds. Therefore I have
no superiority over people whose outlook on
life is different from my own. Anyone can
believe anything and still be a Shintoist. One

does not even need to know what one believes, or whether one believes in anything. All one needs to do is follow the Way of the gods, the Way of Kami. One does this by rituals, and even these do not have to be of any particular type so long as they are carried out with care, showing respect for Kami.

Shintoism is tolerant of every view of life and adaptable to every type of life. I must not point out wrongs or find fault in what others believe or do, for to do so makes them feel guilty and me to feel superior. Instead, I must try to bring honour to my ancestors. The natural way to do this is to be honest, generous, fair and tolerant. Shinto – the Way of the gods – is the Way of doing things to show respect.

If one lives by rules and regulations, one seeks to respect the law. If one lives to bring honour to one's ancestors, one seeks to respect Kami, the Spirit-god. If one lives by rules, then changes in society may make these irrelevant or out of date. If one lives to bring honour, one is free to change with the changing needs of society.

I wish to go the Way of nature, but I want to see that Way clearly. I do not want anything to cloud my view like dust clouds over the reflection of a mirror. Envy, meanness, inconsideration, hatred, revenge, anger, pride and selfishness are the dusts that cloud the Way. If I wipe off the dust, I can see the Way clearly.

Because of the dust, however, I often do the wrong that my conscience tells me to avoid, or I avoid the right that my conscience tells me I should do. Therefore, every day I perform rites of purification and then say this prayer:

"Awe-inspiring Izanagi, Kami-spirit of man, when you performed the rite of purification facing the sun, in the land covered with green trees at the mouth of a great river, the great Kami of Purification, Haraedo-no-Kami, appeared. Give us purification for all our sins, misdeeds and pollutions. Cause the Heavenly Kami, the Earthly Kami and all others to give us purification. Please listen to me and speak."

Every day I pray to my guardian Kami. I have a Kamidana ("god-shelf") with three boxes containing items from the Kami-world (for example, a stone, a hair from my dog, some paper). I purify myself, rinsing my mouth out with water and then pouring water over the tips of my fingers.

Then I offer the Kami-spirit some rice and a bowl of tea. I tell the Kami-spirit what I have been doing at school, what marks I have received for my homework and exams. I thank the Kami-spirit for any especially good things that have happened to me. I praise the Kami and ask it to remember my family, friends and community. Sometimes I write down my prayers on a slate, telling the Kami something special I would like to have happen to me.

I have made the required pilgrimage to the shrine of Amaterasu, the Sun-Goddess, at Ise. Also I have climbed Mount Fuji with other Shintoists. I was first taken to a shrine when I was a month old. I go to one on special occasions.

I believe that "the True Way is one and the same, in every country and throughout heaven and earth".

Japanese Shinto Writings

It was Buddhism that brought the art of Chinese writing to Japan. From the sixth century CE, when Buddhism entered Japan, Buddhism offered a superior, more refined literature, priesthood, culture and religious structure than there had been before. Yet permission was sought from Amaterasu, the Shinto Sun-goddess herself, for building Buddhist temples and images in Japan. The Sun-goddess was considered to be identical to the light (enlightenment) of Buddha. Shintoism was reinterpreted in the light of

Buddhism and the Shinto temples became Buddhist. This was for political reasons, for dictators had taken over Japan, supported by Buddhist leaders.

Shinto (Shen-Tao) is Chinese for "The Way of the gods". Shinto, although a Japanese religion, is usually called by its Chinese name. Its oldest writings date no earlier than the eighth century CE. They are (1) "Nihongi" (the *Chronicles of Japan*) with their long list of names of gods and goddesses, creation myths and an account of Buddhism coming to Japan from China and (2) "Kojiki" (the *Record of Ancient Things*).

The Sun Goddess fixes her Temple

The Great Goddess, Amaterasu, said: "The province of Ise, of the divine wind, is the land whither repair the waves from the eternal world, the successive waves. It is a secluded and pleasant land. In this land I wish to dwell." In compliance, therefore, with the instruction of the Great Goddess, a shrine was erected to her in the province of Ise.

(from *Chronicles of Japan*)

In the eighteenth century CE, after years of domination by Buddhism, and especially by Zen, there was a Shinto revival in Japan. Two of the Shinto writers in this revival were Motoori and Hirata who wished to return to traditional Shintoism, rejecting its Buddhist influences:

The Goddess Amaterasu (the Kami of the sun) offers the one true way

The True Way is one and the same, in every country and throughout heaven and earth. This Way, however, has been correctly transmitted only in our Imperial Land. ... The "special dispensation of our Imperial Land" means that ours is the native land of the Heaven-Shining Goddess who casts her light over all countries in the four seas. Thus our country is the source and fountainhead of all other countries, and in all matters it excels all the others.

(from *Motoori, Precious Comb-box 6*)

In all countries, as if by common consent, there are traditions of a divine being who dwells in heaven and who created all things. These traditions have sometimes become distorted, but when we examine them they afford proof of the authenticity of the ancient traditions of the Imperial Land. There are many gods, but this god stands at the centre of them and is holiest of all.

(from *Hirata, Summary of the Ancient Way 1*)

In 1868, Shintoism became the official religion of Japan, replacing Buddhism as the most prominent religion. The emperor was considered to be a descendant of the Sun-Goddess and the one to be worshipped.

?

1. In 1946, following the Second World War, the victorious Allies, through General Douglas MacArthur, insisted that the Japanese Emperor Hiro Hito no longer be considered to be divine.
   a. What do you believe is meant by *the divine right of kings*?
   b. What, if any, do you believe are the dangers of a political leader of a country

claiming to be the moral leader with unquestionable righteousness?

2. Re-read the teachings quoted above under the heading **THE GODDESS AMATERASU OFFERS THE ONE TRUE WAY.**
    a. Wherein do you agree/disagree with these teachings?
    b. What good, if any, comes from people believing that their country is the best? Is there any danger in nationalistic pride?

3. Consider the statement: "I don't see anything wrong in it?" Can you be wrong when you think you are right? If so, give some examples.

4. Is it always right to follow your conscience? If not, give some examples of immoral acts based on one living by his conscience.

5. Can you think of some occasions when you should seek the advice of others? How do you decide whether you should heed their advice?

6. Can anything that you think is **wrong** for others to do ever be **right** for you to do?

7. Would you like to live in a home, school, town, country or world where there are no rules? Why/why not?

8. *"I have the right to do whatever I want to, whenever I want to, to whomever I want to, and nobody has the right to stop me."* Comment.

9. Shintoists believe that the eight dusts clouding the mirror of one's conscience are **ENVY, MEANNESS, INCONSIDERATION, HATRED, REVENGE, ANGER, PRIDE** and **SELFISHNESS**
    a. Which one of these do you believe is worst? Why?
    b. What, if anything, do you believe should be **taken from** this list?
    What, if anything, do you believe should be **added to** this list?

10. *"It is one thing to know the difference between right and wrong; it is quite another thing to do the right."* (*"The good I want to do is what I avoid; the evil I want to avoid is what I do. Who can save me from this body of death?"* Paul: in the Christian Bible, *Romans* 7:19–25)
    a. How do we know the difference between right and wrong?
    b. How are we able to do the right and avoid doing wrong? (What is the source of motivation and how can we put it to use?)

11. *"Let nature take its course."* How would you evaluate this statement?

Taoists
The Way of Acceptance
(The Lowest Road)

Do you *Agree* or *Disagree* with the following statements? Can you justify your response?

1. One's ancestors should be honoured.
2. In creation, there evolved many different heavens to which spiritually-minded people journey after death to live together in eternal happiness.
3. There are both good and evil spirits in the natural world – in people, animals, plants, rocks, water, etc.
4. People are not distinctively superior to other creatures or objects in the natural world. (The NSPCA is just as important as the NSPCC.)
5. Mankind should not try to conquer nature for his own benefit, but rather he should seek harmony with nature for his spiritual satisfaction.
6. One should appreciate beauty and order in nature and seek to live accordingly.
7. Man, earth (including animal and plant life) and Heaven are one indivisible unity ruled by Tao (pronounced Dao), the Way and law of nature.
8. Only when one conforms to this Way of nature, does one enjoy peace and help extend it to others.
9. When one disturbs this harmony with nature, Heaven and nature are disturbed and catastrophes occur.
10. Man is not above nature. Indeed, only by subordinating oneself to nature's Way, can one's life be constructive and meaningful.
11. All is in constant change. Nothing remains the same for even a moment.
12. Yang (the positive force, represented by heaven and the sun) and Yin (the negative force, represented by the earth and rain) must be kept in balance. The one may prevail at one moment, and the other at another moment; but they should both be accepted.
13. Everything contains Yang and Yin. In nature they are in harmony. Together, in harmony, they are always good.
14. The source of the harmony of Yang and Yin, and the principle of their order, is Tao – the Way, the road, the law of life for everything, and the channel of peace.
15. Governments should not interfere with the ways of nature and the natural Way of mankind. *Laissez faire;* leave it alone.
16. The nature of man is peaceful. Man is not, by nature, a warmonger. But when he is

not in line with nature, he is not in line with peace.
17. Joyful rituals and ceremonies please the good spirits.
18. Rituals of exorcism (the casting out of demons), the practice of magic and the wearing of lucky charms can check the power of evil spirits.

Assume that **purely by accident** you were born in China of Taoist parents and of peasant background about 100 years ago. Recall the words on p. 107 about Yin and Yang. These are your thoughts:

Like all primitive people, thousands of years ago my ancestors believed that powerful forces dwelled on land and water. They observed these in both the splendour and the terror of nature. The harvest depended upon the sun and rain and the regularity of the changing seasons. The seasons themselves depended upon the order of the universe.

My ancestors developed various rituals for giving thanks when the harvest was plentiful and the elements of nature were favourable, and to gain the attention of "shen" <"Good spirits"> *for continuing to bring good fortune. My ancestors had other rituals for guarding themselves against "kuei"* <"bad spirits"> *that brought misfortune. They believed that danger lay everywhere in the form of demons in certain animals, birds, fish and dragons. Whenever considering marriage, birth or death – choosing a partner, building a home or digging a grave – my ancestors believed that the help of experts in the laws of "feng-shui"* <literally "wind-water"> *should be sought.*

For countless centuries, shen and kuei were appeased by sacrifice. At first they were real, more recently they have become symbolic – paper images of houses and possessions are burnt. When food is offered today, it is eaten by the donors themselves. Every year when I was young, a priest came to my house and made a doorway out of paper and set up an altar and images of gods. This protected my health for another

year and I believe it made me better when I was sick.

When shen, good spirits, are sought, the ceremonies are joyous and fun – in a carnival atmosphere. When the ceremony has the purpose of exorcising kuei <casting out bad spirits>, *the atmosphere is solemn. Always, however, the ceremony must be performed with strict observance of tradition. People, animals, plants, rocks and water are all part of the natural world. There are many different heavens where my ancestors went when they died.*

Yang and Yin hold all nature in balance. The principle is Tao, the Way of nature. Through Tao all things have been given their shape, their place and their role to play.

*I believe that my aim in life is to seek harmony with all things. If I achieve this, I will be in accord with Tao and thereby find peace and enlightenment. To achieve this, I must not interfere with nature's Way by meddling in the affairs of nature. Such meddling and interfering is the cause of **all** ills of society, **all** that is wrong in the world. I must let nature take its course. "What is contrary to the Tao soon perishes."*

When I die, I want to be a good spirit, not a demon. I must follow Tao. I owe it to my ancestors. How else do I really honour them? How else can I bring them happiness, except by following Tao?

I wish everyone lived by Tao – simply and naturally, without selfishness. I wish there was no interference with the Way of nature. Hopefully, the day will come when all people are in good fellowship and show brotherly love, the natural Way to relate to all other people. This means the end of ambition, competition and aggression for the

117

individual and the end of interference by governments in nature's Way. The day of peace is the day when all people will be in partnership with nature.

Taoism

Over a billion people live in China today. (There are about 40 million Taoists, about 1:25.) The cultural heritage of China was defined by the influence of three people who lived in the sixth century BCE: **Siddhartha Gautama** the founder of Buddhism; **Lao Tzu** (sometimes transliterated as Lao-tse), the founder of Taoism; and **Confucius**, the founder of the religion that bears his name. The sixth century BCE also produced the beginnings of Greek philosophy in persons like Anaximander, the father of Atomic Physics, and Pythagoras, the mathematician. It was also the century that encircled the Jewish exile during the time of prophets like Jeremiah, Second Isaiah and Ezekiel (called the "Father of Israel").

Christianity refers to God, the plan of God (providence) and the teachings of God and his prophets, using three different terms to mean three different things. Taoism uses one word to mean three different, although related, things: (1) Tao is the mystery behind the universe, what many other religions call God; (2) Tao is the way the universe works, the system of Yin-Yang (explained on pp. 108–109), which relates to what some call the providence of God; and (3) Tao is the Way the individual can link his life to the Way the universe works, using the Power ("Te", pronounced De) available to him for peace, avoiding any struggle against the flow of the universe, which relates to what some call the teachings of God and His prophets.

The name, Lao Tzu, literally means "Old Master" (from the claim that he was conceived at the age of 60 by a shooting star and lived to be 160). Most of what is stated about Lao Tzu is legendary. Tradition claims that he was born around 600 BCE on a farm in the province of Honan in Central China. He may have been a great scholar and teacher who became a curator of the Imperial archives at the court of Chou and resigned because of disagreements with the Chinese leaders of that day. Tradition claims that after a period of meditation in his old age, he journeyed westward riding in a cart pulled by two black oxen. A gatekeeper asked him to write down his view of life. Within a few days Lao Tzu had written the *Tao Te Ching*. He left his writings behind and journeyed on over a mountain pass, never to be seen again. There is also the tradition that he ascended into a heaven.

Lao Tzu taught that one should seek harmony with the "Way of nature" (Tao), rather than with the way of civilisation, in order to be at one with the supreme governing force behind the universe. When Mahayana Buddhism came to China from India in the first century CE, Taoism developed into a formal religion. By the second century CE, idolatry, superstition, and the use of lucky charms caused worship to be reduced to magic and mysticism, though the influence of Buddhism continued.

Modern science and the teachings of Communism have weakened Taoism. Nevertheless, its concept of Tao, simplicity of living, the oneness of nature and the inner joy through a simple life continue to be in evidence. Recently, China has allowed freedom of worship.

For almost 4000 years, Chinese people have had ancestral shrines. Many Chinese people today do not make use of shrines to honour their parents. Yet the idea continues that "family" means more than simply those who are living under one roof.

It is said that *"half the soul of China is Taoist"*. Its writings, such as the *Tao Te Ching,* are revered and read. Lao Tzu is still honoured.

The way that may yet triumph in China is the lowest way, running down stream with the river, becoming one with the balance of nature.

Taoist Literature

The *Tao Te Ching* (pronounced Dao De Jing), with additional Taoist literature, is one of the two moulding influences on traditional Chinese thought. The other is the teachings of Confucius and his disciples. In the twentieth century, the teachings of Chairman Mao ("The Little Red Book") set out to replace these with the influence of Chinese Communism.

The *Tao Te Ching* is attributed to Lao Tzu who is traditionally considered to be the founder of Taoism. Tao means *"Way"* and Te means *"Power"*. *"Tao Te Ching"* means the *"Way and its Power"* (the book of the Right Way). It contains only about 5000 words, less than twenty times the number of words on this page. It is commonly referred to as *The Book of the Way;* it begins:

The Way that can be spoken is not the Eternal Way;
The Name that can be named is not the Eternal Name.
It was from the nameless that Heaven and Earth sprang...
This same mould we can but call the Mystery,
Or rather the Darker than any Mystery,
The Doorway from where issued all Secret things.

(Way 1)

Actionless Activity

The Sage relies on actionless activity,
Carries on wordless teaching,
But the myriad creatures are worked upon by him; he does not disown them.

He rears them, but does not lay claim to them,
Controls them, but does not lean upon them,
Achieves his aim, but does not call attention to what he does.

(Way 2)

Against imposed knowledge and laws – for simplicity

Banish wisdom, discard knowledge,
And the people will be benefited a hundredfold.
Banish human kindness, discard morality,
And the people will be dutiful and compassionate.
Banish skill, discard profit,
And thieves and robbers will disappear...
Give them Simplicity to look at, the uncarved Block to hold,
Give them selflessness and fewness of desires.

(Way 19)

Against War

Soldiers are weapons of evil.
They are not the weapons of a gentleman...
Even in victory there is no beauty.
Who calls victory beautiful is one who delights in slaughter. ...

Repay evil with Good. ...
Love is victorious in attack, and invulnerable in defence.
Heaven arms with love those it would not see destroyed. ...

He who contains within himself the richness of Tao's virtue is like a babe.
No poisonous insects can sting him, nor can any fierce beasts seize him,
Nor can birds of prey strike him.
He who attains Tao is everlasting.

119

*Though his body may decay, he never
perishes.*

*He who by Tao proposes to help a ruler of
men
Will oppose all conquest by force of arms;
For such things are wont to rebound.
Where armies are, thorns and brambles
grow.
    The raising of a great host is followed by a
year of dearth. ...
    This is against Tao, and what is against
Tao will soon perish.*

(Way 30)

Tao created all – do not abuse nature

*Tao gave them birth;
The "power" of Tao reared them,
Shaped them according to their kinds,
Perfected them, giving to each its strength...
So you must, Rear them, but not lay claim to
them.
Control them, but never lean upon them,
Be chief among them, but not manage them.*

This is called the mysterious power.

(Way 51)

The Three Treasures

*I have three Treasures. Guard them and keep
them safe.
The first is **LOVE** <mercy/pity>; the second
is **MODERATION** <simplicity>; the third is
NOT TRYING TO BE FIRST <humility>.
With **moderation**, one will have **power**.
Through **humility** one can continually
develop **talent**.* <If one tries to be first, one
will fall behind; if one claims to be first, one
will stop growing.>

(Way 67)

After this "Classic of the Way" *(Tao Te Ching)*, other writings developed the teachings of Tao, especially with explanations of Yin-Yang.

In 1978 the Chinese people's Congress guaranteed religious freedom and set up a department of religion, with representatives of various religions, to advise the Communist government.

?

1. Christians believe that man was created to have dominion over animals and objects. Taoists believe that although people have an important part to play in the world of nature, they are not distinctively superior. What view do you hold towards these statements, and why?
2. Christians believe, *"In the beginning was the Word."* (John 1:1). Taoists believe, *"Through Tao all things have been given life and form."* What, if anything, do you think is the difference between *"Word"* and *"Tao"*? (Chinese translations of the New Testament use the word *"Tao"* for *"Word"*, describing Jesus as the Tao of God, and God himself as Tao, and the teachings of Jesus as Shen-Tao.) What is your view of these uses of the word *"Tao"*? Do Christianity and Taoism have anything in common? How would you relate the teachings of Jesus with the teachings of Lao Tzu?
3. How would you explain the influence of the great thinkers of the sixth century BCE upon history?
4. *"Lord, give us the serenity to accept what cannot be changed, the courage to change what ought to be changed, and the wisdom to know the one from the other."*

(Reinhold Niebuhr, Christian theologian). Does the first part of this prayer reflect sentiments shared by Taoists? Does the second part? How would you decide in a situation whether you needed *"serenity to accept"* or *"courage to change"*?

5. *"Do not try to teach others the way they should use their reason; but show them the way you use yours."* (Descartes, seventeenth-century French philosopher). People in a room make their way to the door by different movements because they are situated in different places and perhaps facing different directions. The way out for one might be by going to the left, while the way out for another might be by going to the right. Taoists believe that no one can tell another how to find the Way; the other person must find it for himself. To what extent do you think this is true?

6. *"He who by Tao proposes to help a ruler of men will oppose all conquest by force of arms, for such things rebound. ... This is against Tao. What is against Tao will soon perish"* (from Way 30). Do you agree? Why/why not?

7. Explain the theory of Yin-Yang: soft-hard, wet-dry, changing-solid, feminine-masculine, passive-active, silence-noise, black-white, the rhythm of winter-summer – each in balance, each in relationship with the other, forming a mixture. Do you take a Taoist interpretation of this Way of nature, Yin and Yang?

8. A boy got a bicycle as a present. (Is that good?) He had an accident on it and broke his leg. (Is that bad?) This caused his aunt to give him a computer. (Is that good?) The computer was stolen. (Is that bad?) The thief was caught. (Is that good?)... Are good and evil relative and dependent upon each other? Tell your own Yin-Yang story.

9. *"No one can float on water if he fights it. Indeed, become like water. Note how it changes shape when it is put in containers of different shape. Water seeks its own level, the lowest level, the common level of nature. Seek that level. Follow the example of water. Take the lowest path, the simplest road, the easiest principle. Those who fuss, never achieve. The Way never acts, yet all action is done through it."* What do you think of this moral metaphor and its advice?

10. What is the difference between conquering nature and befriending it? Give illustrations of each. Which do you prefer?

11. *"I lift up my eyes to the hills. ..."* (Psalm 121). Western religion tends to look and consider *"hills"* and *"heaven above"* as metaphors for its search for what is best in life. Churches are built on hills or in prominent positions to be noticed, with spires that point upward. Taoists look down and find in ravines and valleys their metaphors for the Way. Their temples are built to blend in with nature. Which metaphor do you find most helpful – up or down? Many modern Christian theologians are writing about God as the "Ground of all Being", the "Foundation of life". Do you believe that these metaphors are useful?

12. There are two main types of Taoists: those who follow the teachings and those who emphasise cultic practices. Many Taoists have a philosophical rather than a religious approach to the Way. Other Taoists make use of temples, ritual, priests and even magic. Many Christians emphasise teachings over worship, and others consider ritual important. Which view do you find more useful?

13. Do you wear a lucky charm? Why/why not?

14. It is said that "Pure Land" Buddhism caused Taoism to add rituals and worship to its religion, while an early form of Taoism led to the development of Zen which does not make use of worship. What do you believe are some of the ways religions and cultures are influencing each other today?

Confucians
Honour for our Ancestors
(Right Relationships)

? —————————————   ————————————— ?

Decide whether you *Agree* or *Disagree* with each of the following statements. Give reasons.

1. Finding happiness for oneself and others here and now, in the present life, is what matters. Life in the hereafter (if there is such) is unimportant.
2. The way to happiness is through right relationships with other people.
3. Religious art is inspired by reverence for nature rather than by reverence for God or gods.
4. To be a student is far more important than to be a priest. Learning matters; worship does not matter. The teacher is second in importance only to the student.
5. There is no such thing as original sin. Man was born with original goodness which he must seek to apply.
6. *"If a man in the morning embraces the Tao* (Way), *then he may die the same evening without regret."* (Confucius.)
7. *"As to the Tao, we must not be separated from it for a single moment."* (Confucius.)
8. Peace depends upon all people being devoted to *"li"*, the ideal standard of conduct determining right relationships between husband and wife, parent and child, older brother and younger brother, older friend and younger friend, and ruler and subject.
9. One should revere the customs of the past.
10. Ancestors should be honoured. *"To serve those now dead as if they were living, is the highest achievement of true filial* (brotherly) *piety."* (Confucius.)
11. *"What you do not want done to yourself, do not do to others."* (Confucius.)
12. Sound character is the root of a good civilisation.
13. *"If the ruler is virtuous, the people will be virtuous."* (Confucius.)
14. *"Absorption in the study of the supernatural* (God, gods, spirits) *is most harmful."* (Confucius.)
15. *"To devote oneself earnestly to one's duty to humanity, and while respecting the spirits to keep them at a distance, may be called wisdom."* (Confucius.)
16. *"The duty of children to their parents is the fountain whence all other virtues spring."* (from the Confucian *Classic of Filial Piety*.)
17. It is wrong to rest in the middle of the day.
18. Although it should not end there, charity should begin at home.

19. *"Education in music and dance is education for living harmoniously with other people."* (Confucius.)
20. To revive ancient customs is the way of restoring peace, happiness and prosperity.
21. A good ruler is one who loves and protects the common people.

Assume that **purely by accident** you were born of Confucian parents in China about a hundred years ago. These are your thoughts:

I believe that Master K'ung <K'ung Fu-tse, or Confucius> was born in North-central China in a town called Tsou and that his father, Shu He, may have been of royal descent. The death of his father shortly after his own birth, meant that Master K'ung was brought up in poverty by his mother. He may have become an orphan when he was just a young lad. He married when he was about 20 and had a son and a daughter; but I believe that, although he was well educated and worked as an overseer of public fields and as an inspector of grain markets, he always knew poverty and identified with the common people of China. He had special interests in archery and music.

I do not know much more about his life, but I know that he was disillusioned over the endless warmongery of district rulers who fragmented the country. He appealed to what he believed was China's more peaceful past and began studying ancient records, laws and history and collecting folk music. Strife provoked him to seek a way for peace. He collected together many stories, poems and sayings of many Chinese people. These he passed on to his many students.

Master K'ung lived at a very troubled time in the history of China. Government officials were inefficient and dishonest. He believed that Heaven itself had called him to bring about a change in society, to transform human relationships from misery to happiness. Everything that made for happiness, prosperity, mental health and emotional well-being was from the Tao <the Way> of

T'ien <Heaven>; and everything that made for unhappiness within and between people was the result of opposition to this Tao.

Master K'ung believed that he could train young men to themselves become moral teachers. He was an extremely strict teacher himself and demanded hard work from his students. He knew that justice and peace required clear thinking and considerate action. He found that young minds were more open to development than old ones. The older people scorned and even mistreated him, ignoring his teaching.

When he was about 60 years old, Master K'ung went on a journey searching for a job in government in which he might have strong influence on his country. But no job that matched his ability was offered to him. Disappointed, he returned to his home and his life of teaching. Then he died after a number of illnesses.

Master K'ung taught, "If a man in the morning embraces the Tao, then he may die the same evening without regret." *But what is the Tao, the Way? It is not the return to nature; it is the living of right relationships. Only if relationships of people are right, can the society in which they live be good.*

These are the Five Virtues through which Master K'ung believed a person could come into harmony with the Tao of Heaven and tap the endless resources of its happiness and power:

1. *"Jen" – love and compassion for other people.*
2. *"Yi" – justice tempered by this love and compassion.*
3. *"Li" – right observation of ritual which shows respect for others, especially our*

ancestors.

4. *"Chih" – wisdom, the knowledge of the Tao of Heaven.*

5. *"Ch'i" – sincerity, being devoid of hypocrisy through total surrender to the Tao of Heaven.*

I believe that I must use the Five Virtues with great care to attain "li", the ideal standard of conduct. I must show this conduct in the Five Relationships of which I am a part. These Five Relationships are those between:

husband *and* **wife;**
parent *and* **child;**
older brother *and* **younger brother;**
older friend *and* **younger friend;** *and*
ruler *and* **subject.**

Master K'ung taught that relationships are right only when people are acting on the principle, "What you do not want done to yourself, do not do to others." *A wife should be obedient, but her husband must be righteous towards her; a father should show love, but his son must also show respect; a younger brother should show humility, but the elder brother must show gentleness; a younger friend should give honour, but the older friend must be humane; a subject should be loyal, but a ruler must be benevolent and not take advantage. Indeed, Master K'ung taught that* "a good emperor is like a caring father." "If the ruler is virtuous," *he taught,* "the people will also be virtuous."

Thus Master K'ung's view of the great society is that it is like a great family in which all mankind will seem like one man in harmony – and in which all will treat others humanely, the old being held in high regard and the helpless being cared for.

I believe that if everyone is devoted to "li", the ideal standard of conduct, then all human relationships will be rightly ordered and an ideal society will result with harmony, peace and justice throughout the land.

No wonder even emperors have said these words in the honour of Grand Master K'ung:

"Great art thou, O thou of perfect wisdom. Full is thy virtue, thy doctrine complete. Mortals have never known thy equal. All kings honour thee. Thine ordinances and laws have come down to us in glory. Filled with awe we clash our symbols and strike our bells."

I wish to follow the teachings of one who discouraged war and who urged all men to live as brothers in a great community which reflects the Tao of Heaven. My country has had almost 2500 years of benefit from the teachings of Master K'ung. May China never seek prosperity in a way which violates this peace.

Background

The religious heritage of the billion people living today in China is Taoist and Confucianist (dating from the sixth century BCE) and Mahayana Buddhist (imported from India in the first century CE). Before the arrival of Communism, these three religions were considered to be three parallel roads to the same destination. Their teachings were considered to be in harmony with each other, emphasising the importance of family unity and the essential goodness of human nature. In the third century BCE, a Taoist writer by the name of Chuang Tzu included stories and teachings of Confucius for Taoism (in much the same way as many Jewish writers today refer to and endorse the teachings of Jesus of Nazareth).

Confucius is the Latinised name given by Jesuit missionaries to K'ung Fu-tzu, meaning "Grand Master K'ung". Confucius's full name was K'ung Chung-ni. He was born about 551 BCE in the Chinese province of Shantung, and died about 479 BCE. He used the word *T'ien* (Heaven) to designate that which was divine. *T'ien* does not mean God in the Western sense of a being, but a complex form of Love-Powers which enter the hearts of those who live by the Tao. Confucius wrote:

"The power of spiritual force in the universe – how active it is everywhere! Invisible to the eyes, impalpable to the senses, it is nevertheless inherent in all things and nothing can escape its operation."

Of the three pillars of Chinese religion, Confucianism is more a formal ethical system than it is a religion with priests as found in Taoism and Mahayana Buddhism. Yet as the years passed, some temples were built in the honour of Confucius and he became an object of veneration, though seldom considered as divine. By the second century BCE, sacrifices were being offered to him at his tomb and the Emperor Wu made Confucianism the fundamental discipline for training government officials. By the seventh century CE, shrines were being built to Confucius.

Progressively, Confucius was called *"Duke"*, *"Prince"*, *"Venerable Sage"*, *"Sacred teacher of Antiquity"* and, by some, even *"god"*. There are, however, no statues or images of Confucius. The focus of Confucian temples is usually a tablet inscribed with his name.

Early in the twentieth century many Chinese began believing that Confucianism, with its regard for the past, had kept the nation from developing the science and technology necessary for progress and prosperity in the modern world. Many Chinese began believing that China must change or perish. Confucianism began being ridiculed or simply ignored. Ironically, the Chinese warlords who promoted Confucianism because it upheld traditional loyalties themselves violated the peacefulness which Confucius himself sought for China.

Writings

It is claimed that Confucius wrote five books called "classics". These are the *Books of History, Poetry, Rites and Changes* and the *Annals of Spring and Autumn*. But he himself claimed to be a "transmitter" and not a "creator". He probably wrote little himself, his teachings being recorded later by his disciples to preserve his view of ethics. In the first century CE these writings were engraved on stones and copied by rubbing with ink. This means that no errors have entered the manuscripts for almost 2000 years.

Confucius tells of his Progress

At fifteen I set my heart upon learning. At thirty I had planted my feet firm upon the ground. At forty I no longer suffered from perplexities. At fifty I knew what were the biddings of Heaven. At sixty I heard them with docile ear. At seventy I could follow the dictates of my own heart, for what I desired no longer overstepped the boundaries of right.

Confucius speaks of order and morality

Govern the people by regulations, keep order among them by chastisements, and they will flee from you, and lose all self-respect. Govern them by moral force, keep order among them by ritual, and they will keep their self-respect and come to you of their own accord.

He who rules by moral force is like the pole-star, which remains in its place while all the lesser stars do homage to it.

If out of the three hundred Songs I had to take one phrase to cover all my teaching, I would say, "Let there be no evil in your thoughts".

125

The search for goodness

The Master said: "Without Goodness a man cannot for long endure adversity, cannot for long enjoy prosperity."

Wealth and rank are what every man desires; but if they can only be retained to the detriment of the Way he professes, he must relinquish them.

Poverty and obscurity are what every man detests; but if they can only be avoided to the detriment of the Way he professes, he must accept them. The gentleman who ever parts company with Goodness does not fulfil that name.

(4:2, 5)

Duties of Rulers

Duke Ai asked: "What can I do in order to get the support of the common people?"

The Master said, "Approach them with dignity, and they will respect you. Show piety towards your parents and kindness towards your children, and they will be loyal to you. Promote those who are worthy, train those who are incompetent; that is the best form of encouragement."

(2:19–20)

The Negative Golden Rule

The Master said: "Never do to others what you would not like them to do to you."

(from the *Analects of Confucius*. 15:23)

The Foundation of Virtue

The duty of children to their parents is the foundation whence all other virtues spring.

(from the *Classic of Filial Piety*)

The Mean or Middle Way

The Master said: "Perfect is the Mean in action, and for a long time now very few people have had the capacity for it. I know why the Way is not pursued. It is because the learned run to excess and the ignorant fall short."

The Five Great Evils

The Master said, "Repay injury with justice and kindness. He who offends against Heaven has none to whom he can pray. Man is the representative of Heaven, and supreme above all things. There are five great evils. The man with a rebellious heart who becomes dangerous; the man who joins vicious deeds to a fierce temper; the man who is knowingly false; the man who treasures in his memory foul deeds and repeats them; the man who follows evil and spreads it."

From the writings of the Taoist Chuang Tzu, *c.* 369–286 BCE, come further teachings attributed to Confucius, of which the following are a selection:

Do you know what it is that destroys virtue, and where wisdom comes from? Virtue is destroyed by fame, and wisdom comes out of wrangling. Fame is something to beat people down with, and wisdom is a device for wrangling. Both are evil weapons – not the sort of thing to bring you success...

Confucius said, "Make your will one! Don't listen with your ears, listen with your mind. No, don't listen with your mind, but listen with your spirit. Listening stops with the ears, the mind stops with recognition, but spirit is empty and waits on all things. The Way gathers in emptiness alone. Emptiness is the fasting of the mind. ..."

Confucius said, "In the world, there are two great decrees: one is fate and the other is duty. That a son should love his parents is fate – you cannot erase this from his heart. That a subject should serve his ruler is duty – there is no place he can go and be without his ruler, no place he can escape to between heaven and earth. ... If you act in accordance with the state of affairs and forget about yourself, then what leisure will you have to love life and hate death? Act in this way and you will be all right. ... "

Confucius said, *"Life, death, preservation, loss, failure, success, poverty, riches, worthiness, unworthiness, slander, fame, hunger, thirst, cold, heat – these are the alternations of the world, the workings of fate. Day and night they change place before us and wisdom cannot spy out their source. Therefore, they should not be enough to destroy your harmony; they should not be allowed to enter the storehouse of spirit. If you can harmonise and delight in them, master them and never be at a loss for joy, if you can do this day and night without break and make it be spring with everything, mingling with all and creating the moment within your own mind – this is what I call being whole in power." ...*

———————— ❓ ————————

1. Which of the above teachings attributed to Confucius do you consider most important? Wherein do you *agree* or *disagree* with the statements?
2. "All Chinese are Confucianists when they are successful, and Taoists when they are failures." (Dr Lin Yutang, Chinese scholar) Does everyone have one philosophy or religion in life in times of peace and prosperity and another in times of war and poverty?
3. A country must look to the past if it is to preserve the best of its heritage. **And** a country cannot look to the past and also open the way to the future. With which of these statements do you agree more, and why?
4. Which is more descriptive of your country today: clinging to the past or looking to the future? Are these in conflict?
5. "Confucius had only contempt for law courts; and his great disciple, Mencius, developed the idea of benevolent government. Without protection of civil rights, the idea that our rulers should or would love us like parents is naive to the extreme." (Dr Lin Yutang) Do you agree?
6. Confucianism is based on the belief that right relationships develop a just society. Communism is based on the belief that a just society cultivates right relationships. Which do you believe must come first, **good people** or a **good state**? Why?
7. Moral teachers outlast politicians. Do you agree?
8. A student is more important than a teacher and a teacher is more important than a soldier. Do you agree?

Bahá'ís
Unity in Diversity
(Peoples of the World Unite!)

? ——————————————— ?

Do you *Agree* or *Disagree* with each of the following statements? Give reasons.

1. *"Let not a man glory in this, that he loves his country; let him rather glory in this, that he loves mankind."* (Bahá'u'lláh, to Prof. E G Browne of Cambridge University.)
2. *"Beware of prejudice; light is good in whatsoever lamp it is burning. A rose is beautiful in whatsoever garden it may bloom. A star has the same radiance whether it shines from the East or from the West."* ('Abdu'l-Bahá.)
3. There should be no idle rich who are lazy nor idle poor who beg.
4. Except for medical purposes, one should avoid drugs and intoxicating liquor.
5. A good marriage contributes to the health of the individual and of society.
6. Parents have no right to arrange marriages for their children, but their consent should be sought. Their consent must not be withheld because of prejudice (discrimination against class, colour, religion or nationality) on their part.
7. It is not enough to love each other. A good marriage requires being well-suited for each other; marriage should not be rushed into but built on solid foundation.
8. A good person is not merely good in himself or herself. He must live and work in harmony with all other people.
9. Work that does not seek unity is wasted. A person working towards social or religious reform on his own or with an isolated group may inadvertently be working against others of like mind with wasteful duplication or wasted effort. Resources should be pooled, instead of individuals spending their precious hours, days and years of their lives working on their own without co-operating with others. Peace can only come through the unity of all in constructive work.
10. It is not sufficient to work for one's own benefit or even for that of one's own family, school, factory, firm or religion. One must seek a larger aim.
11. Take great care not to be unkind to those who disagree with your view of religion. If you believe you have discovered a truth, beware lest in sharing it you belittle those who refuse to accept it.
12. The plan of God for this age is the unity of the entire human race.
13. The unity of mankind must come before the problems facing the world can be completely solved.
14. Prejudice keeps people apart, the oneness of religion binds them together.

15. Education is not complete without the teaching of spiritual standards and giving great attention to the training of character.
16. Men and women are equal in the sight of God and must have equal rights. Neither sex should be allowed to be, or even feel, superior to the other.
17. An auxiliary language should be developed so that all mankind will have a common means of communication, supplementing the existing languages that preserve cultural heritages.
18. There should be unity in diversity and diversity in unity. Individuals, groups and nations should have a common bond and a mutual aim while also having the right to be different.
19. True religion and true science are always in agreement. They should be accepted as allies. They are the two wings of humanity. Unless both are strong, mankind cannot soar to the heights of progress. True religion can never oppose scientific facts.
20. Science and technology provide the tools. Religion shows how they should be used.
21. *"Science without religion leads to materialism and destruction; religion without science breeds fanaticism and superstition."* (From *The Bahá'í Faith,* by Gloria Faizi, p. 81.)
22. Work done in the spirit of service to others is not only a religious obligation; it is a form of worship.
23. Through graduated taxation of those whose income exceeds their needs, the state must provide for those who are unable through misfortune to provide for themselves and their families.
24. **Profit-sharing**: Besides fair wages a labourer should benefit directly from the profits he helps create. (Compare, from the Christian Bible, *II Timothy* 2:6)
25. **Prophet-sharing**: Religions should show mutual respect for the prophetic voices that have been heard throughout the history of mankind.
26. Tyranny is a cause of poverty and starvation. Voluntary sharing is a solution; war and bloodshed are not.
27. Society has evolved through tribe, city-state and nation towards the age of a world commonwealth of independent nations. Love for one's own country is no longer the highest form of loyalty.
28. Every individual must abandon at the outset the idea that *he* is right and everyone else is wrong.
29. A world tribunal, democratically elected by all nations, should peacefully and justly settle all international disputes.
30. A uniform system of currency, weights and measures should be developed to assist international relationships.
31. War is a curse which diverts energy and wealth away from the advancement of living standards, education, the arts and the elimination of disease.
32. The development of nuclear weapons is forcing nations to urgently seek ways to abolish war. These ways will lead to "The Lesser Peace" and that in turn will lead to "the Most Great Peace", the Golden Age of Peace with Justice as foretold by the Messengers of God who already have announced His Plan for mankind.
33. Modern means of travel and communication have removed the physical barriers between nations; and international industry has created economic inter-dependence between nations. Nevertheless, man is still clinging to the outmoded stereotypes of history. Mankind must be freed from tunnel-vision and near-sightedness.
34. In the past, many priests, monks and other professional clergy did gallant work which must not be belittled or forgotten. However, the days for a professional

priesthood are over. Now each individual must do his own unbiased searching and accept full responsibility for his own beliefs and actions. Yet, having formed his own opinions, he should not disregard the opinions of others or cling to a closed-minded dogmatism.

35. **Fire by friction**: *"The shining spark of truth cometh forth only after the clash of differing opinions."* ('Abdu'l-Bahá.)

36. One ought not to belittle or mock the beliefs of others.

37. One should beware of siding with one political party over another lest he betray the unity which rises above political differences. Also, one should seek the unity which rises above all racial, religious, cultural and national insularity.

38. One should support *The Universal Declaration of Human Rights* of the United Nations.

39. Worship should be practised in such a way as to reflect the unity of all mankind. One's worship should be seen as a symbol of one's unity with all people.

40. *"The Glory of Humanity is the heritage of each one. ... All are equal before God. He is no respecter of persons."* ('Abdu'l-Bahá.)

41. One should *"...revere all the founders of the world's religions and regard the scriptures of all the world's religions as sacred."*

42. Spiritual teachings of all religions are in harmony and reflect eternal truth. Social teachings of all religions, moral laws and traditions of practice and observance are appropriate to cultural development and must be allowed to differ because they are not eternal truths.

43. Differences within and between religions often occur at best because of changing human need and at worst because of distortions made by human failings.

44. It is at times of human decay throughout history that prophets have been sent for human renewal.

45. *"Truth is one in all the religions and by means of it the unity of the world can be realised."* ('Abdu'l-Bahá.)

46. *"If only men would search out truth, they would find themselves united."* ('Abdu'l-Bahá.)

47. As light reflected from a mirror continues to shine after the mirror is destroyed, so the soul survives death. The soul is spiritual and not material reality.

48. There is no force of evil. Evil is but the absence of good or it is the lesser degree of good, as darkness or twilight is the absence of light.

49. As food feeds the body, so prayer feeds the human spirit. Yet life, in true service to mankind, is itself a prayer of praise and service to God.

50. *"Marriage is the foundation of a good family; good families, in turn, are the foundations of a stable civilisation."*

51. There is but one race – the human race.

52. One should support the United Nations Association, help establish branches of the World Congress of Faiths and willingly participate in inter-faith activities.

53. One should not support a group which is only interested in its own well-being or is provincial in outlook.

54. Every individual has the right to self-expression.

55. The true patriot is one who not only loves his country but one who loves the world.

In the INTRODUCTION to the search for peace with justice through this study of world religions, the first words you read were these:

A teacher said to a class:

"It is purely an accident that I am older than you; you could just as easily have been my teacher. Therefore, I must treat you with respect, as if you were my teacher. And it follows that you must treat me with that same respect."

You were asked what you thought of this. You were reminded that Jesus of Nazareth taught, *"Do to others as you want them to do to you,"* and that He meant that you should treat a person as if you were that person. Then you read:

"Perhaps it is purely an accident that you are not that other person. If your Great Grandfather had fallen in love not with your Great Grandmother but with a different woman... If the child born to them had for some reason later moved to another country and had married someone of that culture and perhaps even of a different race and religion... If a child born to them had by chance met and married to yet another culture... Then you would be someone very different from the person you are.

"No wonder it is silly as well as tragic that people throughout history have argued and fought, persecuted and killed those of other nations and cultures, races and religions...

"An American Indian doing a ceremonial dance – a Hindu washing, dressing and decorating the image of a god – a Taoist covered in a paper dragon, in a procession: they are so different from us. Their customs seem so strange. Yet, what if, purely by accident, you had been born of another nationality, another race, another religion, another cultural background? You could be that different person. Other people are no less strange to us than we are to them. If we can come to understand a person so different from us, we will know what we would be like if, purely by accident, we had been born that

person. We also would know how we can have a constructive relationship with that person..."

Since you first read those words you have added to your general knowledge of World Religions and to man's search for peace with justice by making this introductory study of Western and Eastern Religion.

At the beginning of each group of religions you have met people who **purely by accident** were born in different cultures at different times in history, who suddenly appeared in your midst, role-playing parts which, except by the accidents of birth, could have been them. Whoever was that Primal Man, that first peace maker and justice builder?

Then within each unit you have been requested to assume that **purely by accident** you were someone of the particular faith being considered.

Now you are asked to make this assumption for the last time here:

Assume that, **purely by accident**, you are a member of the Bahá'í Faith and one of almost 7000 people from all over the world who gathered at the Royal Albert Hall in London to mark the 100th Anniversary of Bahá'u'lláh's declaration of his mission. It is April, 1963. You enter the hall and are seated. As informal conversations continue with people waiting for the meeting to begin, you consider the scene. These are your thoughts:

What a gathering of people! All the colours of humanity!

All these various accents I'm hearing. So many different countries represented. It's almost like being at the United Nations. And yet we are not here representing different races, cultures, religions or even nations. We all believe that there is one race – the human race – and that differences of culture and religion are not really differences. We all believe that there is one God and one

brotherhood of mankind. Different
nationalities? No, we all consider ourselves
to be citizens of the world! We don't
represent different peoples and places. We
were united as one even before we met here
and even before we became Bahá'ís. We're
all of one stock. We're all "sons of Adam"
and there's nothing we can do about it except
to face up to that fact and live accordingly.

Differences? Plenty to be seen; but they
are not real differences. That young Black in
African dress is struggling to speak French
to that chap who looks as if he just got off an
Air France flight. I wonder, how good is the
Frenchman's Swahili? We need that international auxiliary language now. I know that
those who are going to speak to us at this
celebration wish we had it now. Some day...!

That woman over there in the blue and
gold sari. With the number I've seen like her,
the Air India flight must have been full. They
undoubtedly needed several planes. These
two next to me: a Cockney Londoner and a
Brooklynese New Yorker? No wonder
Churchill said that Britons and Americans
have everything in common except language.
He knew first hand – his Grandmother was
from Indiana and had a Hoosier twang. His
and successive British governments have
welcomed Bahá'ís fleeing from persecution in
Iran. I wonder how many here have
themselves suffered persecution or suspicion
elsewhere than in Iran.

We're different because we don't honour
bigotry and fanaticism and the separating
differences. Neither did the Prophets. None
of them – not the Prophets Moses, Jesus,
Muhammad, the Báb or Bahá'u'lláh
(Manifestations of God), nor the lesser
prophets: such as Amos, Jeremiah and John
the Baptist. They all suffered persecution too.
Not that I can claim to be like them. There's
plenty in my own life to sort out. "Judge not,
that you be not judged," taught Jesus. It's all
right for a Messenger of God to judge, but
then he proclaims the judgement of God: to

awaken, to challenge, to renew – for peace
with justice – for the true unity of all
mankind – "Unity in diversity", the central
teaching of our faith, the urgent need for
humanity.

This crowd seems to be from everywhere.
And here we are together. "What a good
thing for brethren to dwell together in unity."
<Psalm 133:1>. I wonder, how many of over
150 nations with Bahá'ís are represented
here, and how many of the over 400
languages into which our teachings have
been translated are represented here today?
How much unnecessary effort can be saved
when everyone in the world has a second
language in common? One translation will
serve the world, freeing so much energy for
other work towards unity. What energy
saving! What correction to so much
unnecessary misunderstanding! A major
barrier removed. Everyone in the world able
to talk to everyone else, having a common
language to help remove suspicion and to
encourage the awareness of a common
humanity. Yet also we need to have separate
languages to protect cultural diversity and
freedom.

So most of us have come here by plane.
That wouldn't have been possible a few years
ago. And those of us from this island have
benefited from this being the age of the train
– and the speedy journey by bus and car.
How much modern developments in travel
and communication have helped make this
the age for peace. And now the Russian
sputniks, American space rockets and the
promise of satellites beaming television
programmes world-wide. So much is
happening in this age. The world has become
one neighbourhood, old prejudices and
barriers are breaking down. "East and West
– never the twain shall meet." No Bahá'í
wrote those words. Instead Bahá'u'lláh
taught:

"There can be no doubt whatever that the
people of the world, of whatever race or

religion, derive their inspiration from one heavenly Source, and are the subjects of one God." (from *Gleanings from the writings of Bahá'u'lláh*, p. 216)

Man has conquered space. Now he must conquer the nearest space of all: the human heart.

Science and its technology are helping. True science and religion are in harmony, like the wings of a bird. Separately, the one leads to materialism and selfishness and the other leads to prejudice and superstition. But together...! Man can fly like a seagull. Someday, perhaps, someone will write a parable about man learning to fly like a seagull.

Now, I must reflect on the event of 100 years ago that we are celebrating today. What were those words? Bahá'u'lláh wrote to the Shah his own account of that experience in prison 100 years ago – in 1863:

"During the days I lay in the prison of Tehran, though the galling weight of the chains and the stench-filled air allowed me but little sleep, still in those infrequent moments of slumber I felt as if something flowed from the crown of my head over my breast, even as a mighty torrent that precipitates itself upon the earth from the summit of a lofty mountain. Every limb of my body would, as a result, be set afire. At such moments my tongue recited what no man could bear to hear.

"O King! I was but a man like others, asleep upon my couch, when lo, the breezes of the All-Glorious were wafted over me, and taught me the knowledge of all that hath been. This thing is not from me, but from One who is Almighty and All-Knowing. And he bade me lift up my voice between earth and heaven, and for this there befell me what hath caused the tears of every man of understanding to flow... His all-compelling summons hath reached me, and caused me to speak his praise amidst all people."

Bahá'u'lláh was in prison among other followers of the Báb and also among

murderers and robbers – 150 in all. Chains were heavy on his shoulders, binding him so that he could neither stand up nor sit down. Much of what little food he received was poisoned. Every day one of the Báb's followers was taken and shot; but on the way, each in turn came to receive a blessing from Bahá'u'lláh. He had tried to keep their spirits up, getting them to chant prayers:

"God is sufficient unto me; He verily is the All-Sufficing!"

Back would come the refrain:

"In Him let the trusting trust."

Even the Shah in his palace nearby could hear the loud noise of their singing and chanting.

For four months Bahá'u'lláh was in prison. His body bent under the weight of chains as Jesus' body had been bent by the weight of carrying his cross. And Jesus had heard the heavenly voice at his baptism with a summons: "This is my beloved Son, in whom I am well pleased", *and had received the gift of the Spirit like a dove descending upon him. So Bahá'u'lláh received his calling. Many such experiences were common to all the Prophets. And so Bahá'u'lláh received his all-compelling summons that night 100 years ago: he was the one foretold by the Báb.*

Yet the story of the Bahá'í Faith began before 1863 and that day in a prison cell. It began before time itself, it began in the plan of God for his Creation. It is this that makes our gathering from so many countries and races so important today.

Persia!

The historical story began in or near Persia. <Known to us today as Iran.> *In Biblical times, it was from Ur in Mesopotamia that Abraham began his journey, about 1800 BCE. Many of the leading Jews spent most of the sixth century BCE in Babylonian Exile. It was the age of the prophets Jeremiah, Second Isaiah and Ezekiel. It was the Golden Era in Israel's history. When Babylonia was* conquered by the Persians, the Jews were freed to return to Israel and rebuild their temple. Cyrus, king of the Persians, gave them considerable help.

It was from Persia that at least one of the three Wise Men came, according to a legend surrounding the birth of Jesus in the Gospel of Matthew. The legend states that he was a follower of the Prophet Zoroaster and that he journeyed to Bethlehem in Judea and to the place of the humble birth of a descendant of Abraham: the Holy Messenger of God, the Prophet Joshua (the Hebrew name of Jesus) considered by many to be the Christ. The words he spoke eventually pervaded the whole Mediterranean world of the Roman Empire – with the special help of Paul, Peter, Luke, and others – then throughout Europe and Britain and on to the New World of the Americas and beyond.

I believe that it is significant that Islam was built on the foundation of Christianity as Christianity was built on the foundation of Judaism.

The site of Solomon's Temple, the centre for Jewish worship, in turn also became sacred to Christians – as it was to Jesus himself – and then was used as the site for a Mosque, the Dome of the Rock, built on the place where Muslims believe Muhammad, who was in the line of the Prophets, made, one night, a journey into heaven itself.

The Báb!

Most directly of all, Persia became in God's plan the birthplace of Sayyid 'Ali-Mohammed, born on 20th October, 1819, in the city of Shiraz in Fars, the seat of Persian beginnings. The early 1800s were years of decline in Persia. Religious and political leaders mismanaged the people and burdened them with unjust leadership. Sayyid 'Ali-Mohammed, filled with great wisdom and virtue, claimed to be the "Bearer of a new Revelation from God" from his own religious experience lasting through the night

of 23rd May, 1844 – a date that has become an annual Holy Day of observance in the Bahá'í calendar.

As with the lives of all Prophets, there were many divine signs to support 'Ali-Mohammed's credentials as a Messenger of God. Unlike John the Baptist, he was an independent Manifestation of God, a Prophet who brought special laws and revelations. Yet, like John the Baptist before him, he was a voice crying in the wilderness, announcing one who would come after him. It was at a gate, the Gate of Shiraz, that Mulla Husayn, who – like Simeon of whom Luke wrote – believed he would not die until he saw the Promised One. Mulla Husayn became the Báb's first follower, later writing of that moment: "Excitement, joy, awe, and wonder stirred the depths of my soul."

Sayyid 'Ali-Mohammed came to be known as the Báb <Arabic for "Gate"> – the Herald sent to prepare the way, the way that would bring the dawn of a new age of Peace proclaimed by all the Prophets of old. The Báb told his disciples to be lamps of righteousness:

"Ponder the words of Jesus addressed to His disciples, 'Let your light shine before the eyes of men'."

So they did let their light shine with the power of the Holy Spirit that had engulfed Abraham, Moses, Jesus and Muhammad, and their followers and those of John the Baptist, with whom the Báb, to some extent, can be likened.

The Báb was then 25 years old. Six years later he had been imprisoned in the Chihriq fortress near the Russian and Turkish borders. Some of his prison guards came under his persuasion as some of Paul's had when he was a prisoner in Rome. But the Báb had threatened the pompous positions of too many unjust religious and political leaders. Like Jesus, he had foretold his own martyrdom, and at a mock trial bearing similarities to that of Jesus, he was sentenced. After three years of imprisonment, the Báb was led out into the public square at Tabriz and in the noontide heat of a summer's day, his life ended before a firing squad – with a jeering crowd like one in Jerusalem over 1800 years earlier. He was 30 years old.

So too ended the life of one of his followers, Tahirih <Arabic for "the Pure One">, referred to as the Persian Joan of Arc, becoming the first woman suffrage martyr with these words: "You can kill me as soon as you like, but you cannot stop the emancipation of women!"

Bahá'u'lláh!

Bahá'u'lláh's father, a Minister of State, gave him a noble birth and named him Husayn-'Alí. When his father died, he accepted the family duties as the eldest son, but declined the position at court offered to him.

The burden of the martyred Báb fell upon him. Bahá'u'lláh had become his follower at the age of 27, six years before the Báb died. It was the Báb who had selected the name, 'Bahá'u'lláh' <Arabic for "The Glory of God">. He never met the Báb, though he had much correspondence with him. He had tried to rescue Tahirih on several occasions, like someone unwilling to stand back and let others be bullied and tormented unrighteously.

When the Báb died, Bahá'u'lláh tried to reason with the authorities that the new religion must be tolerated. For this, he was thrown into the "Black Pit" at Tehran prison, and his home was seized and pillaged. When freed, he was forced to journey Westwards, like Abraham before him. An edict of the Shah had expelled him into exile. On the fierce mid-winter journey, his wife, his son 'Abdu'l-Bahá – aged eight – and daughter Bahiyyih – age six – joined him. He journeyed through a wilderness, as Moses, Elijah, Jesus and Muhammad had before him.

During his years in Baghdad he did much

writing: the sacred books of **Hidden Words**, **The Book of Certitude**, **The Seven Valleys**, and **The Four Valleys** and so many other papers.

Then the Sultan of Turkey summoned Bahá'u'lláh to Constantinople <now Istanbul>, the centre of the declining Ottoman Empire. In a garden by the Tigris River – at the same time as General Grant was preparing for a decisive battle at Vicksburg which would lead to the end of the American Civil War and the end of slavery – Bahá'u'lláh proclaimed that he was the one foretold by the Báb and promised by prophets of old. That day marks the most important festival in the Bahá'í year. 'Abdu'l-Bahá was then 19 and shared with other members of the family his father's suffering.

They travelled past the ruins of Nineveh, the great Assyrian capital to which the Prophet Jonah had reluctantly gone and of which Christians sing:

"Lo, all our pomp of yesterday
Is one with Nineveh and Tyre!"
    <Recessional, by Kipling>
Then they went by steamer along the coast of the Black Sea to Constantinople, the site of Constantine's New Christian Rome and later the site of a major battle during the Crusades. But Bahá'u'lláh had been born too late to have any effect upon the Christian militaristic fanaticism of that era, though not too late to challenge the corruption, injustice and mismanagement of the Ottoman court. He wrote to the Sultan Abdul-Aziz:

"We behold in thee the foolish ruling over the wise, and darkness vaunting itself against the light... Hath thine outward splendour made thee vain-glorious? ... It shall soon perish." <from Kitáb-i-Aqdas, 89, p. 53>

Bahá'u'lláh tried to get the Sultan and Napoleon III to avoid abusing their power. Instead they consorted together and oppressed millions of people, making councils of war rather than peace.

The response of the Sultan was to make

*Bahá'u'lláh's exile more secure: life
imprisonment for Bahá'u'lláh and his family
in the castle originally built by the Christian
Crusader Knights of St John around AD
1100, which they called St Jean d'Arc – on
the site of Acre, the "Strong City" mentioned
in the book of Psalms – and was made the
Christian capital of Palestine until the
Crusaders were forced out. It was to become
the penal colony of the Ottoman Empire.*

*This meant an eleven day sea voyage,
stopping at Smyrna, one of the cities for
which the Biblical book of Revelation was
written <Rev. 1:11>, across the
Mediterranean Sea to Alexandria and Port
Said in Egypt, to Jaffa, from where Jonah set
sail on his run-away voyage in the Biblical
parable, where Crusaders often landed on
the way to Jerusalem, and which was to be
Bahá'u'lláh's own first landing in Palestine.
Then on to Acre where Bahá'u'lláh would
spend the next 24 years in teaching and
further writing, including the Book of Laws
(his most important) and where he would
have further influence on his son, 'Abdu'l-
Bahá – then 24.* <'Abdu'l-Bahá would take
his father's teachings personally to London,
Edinburgh, Paris, New York, Montreal,
Chicago and San Francisco – throughout
Europe and North America, where he would
be welcomed by Bahá'ís and so many
others.>

*When they arrived in Acre the family were
taken to cells <in a building that has been
preserved>. They suffered typhoid, dysentery
and malaria, with inadequate food and
without medical help. 'Abdu'l-Bahá, 40 years
later in London, said:*

"…I was happy all that time in that prison.
When one is released from the prison of self,
that is indeed release! For that is the greatest
prison." <from *'Abdu'l-Bahá in London*, p.
120>

*Perhaps he was reflecting upon the
teachings of Paul who wrote:*

"For freedom, Christ has set us free; stand

fast therefore, and do not submit again to a
yoke of slavery." <Galatians 5:1>

*The Sultan had charged Bahá'u'lláh with
"crimes against humanity". A man who saw
the charges posted against Bahá'u'lláh in
Acre joined with others in plotting his death,
but when he arrived at the cell he found
himself changing heart – like Joseph of
Aramathea who was a member of the
Sanhedrin that condemned Jesus to death but
who somehow was changed and gave his own
tomb for the body of Christ – and like Saul
who breathed threats against the Christians
but who, on his way to persecute them, had a
transforming experience on the Damascus
Road and became Paul the Apostle.*

*The mountain behind Haifa is Carmel
<Cerem-El is Hebrew for "the Vineyard of
God">. Here, over 2000 years earlier, Elijah
had forced a contest with the false prophets
of Ba'al, to call Israel back to the worship of
Yahweh. Solomon sang of the beauty of
Carmel; Jesus undoubtedly travelled there, a
mere day's journey from Nazareth. There,
when allowed to leave his prison cell,
Bahá'u'lláh showed his son where he wanted
the Shrine of the Báb to be built to house the
Báb's remains. On Carmel, Bahá'u'lláh
wrote his "tablet of Carmel" that would
make this mountain of the Lord the centre of
the new world faith. There, Bahá'u'lláh
stayed in a tent for three months shortly
before he died in 1892, entrusting in his Will
the burden of leadership of the new world
religion to his son, 'Abdu'l-Bahá.*

'Abdu'l-Bahá!

*The Báb was like John the Baptist
proclaiming the coming of the Messiah.
Bahá'u'lláh was like Jesus the Christ
ushering in the Kingdom of God. 'Abdu'l-
Bahá was like Paul taking the message to the
Empires of the world.*

*Already the followers numbered in the
hundreds. Shortly they would be numbered in
the thousands and tens of thousands and then*

millions until the world would be united.

So here in the Royal Albert Hall 7000 have gathered. Nearby in the City Temple just over half a century ago, 'Abdu'l-Bahá – then almost 70 years old – gave his first public speech to a packed congregation. In it he said:

"The gift of God to this enlightened age is the knowledge of the oneness of mankind and of the fundamental oneness of religion. War shall cease between nations, and by the will of God the Most Great Peace shall come; the world will be seen as a new world, and all men will live as brothers."

Then in 1912, having spent 40 years in exile and prison, 'Abdu'l-Bahá travelled on to America – speaking in churches, synagogues, temples, mosques, universities and charitable institutions. On a May afternoon he laid the cornerstone of the Mother Temple of the Bahá'í Faith in Wilmette, Illinois, just outside Chicago, near the Northwestern University campus. <It was as a drama student at Northwestern that the present writer watched this magnificent house of Worship being built which led to his forty years of study of world religion.>

On his journey back to Palestine, 'Abdu'l-Bahá stopped again in London, travelled on to Oxford and then spent several days in Edinburgh.

Thousands greeted 'Abdu'l-Bahá wherever he went. Theodore Roosevelt, later to become President of the United States and who was to help set up the League of Nations following the First World War, greeted him. Alexander Graham Bell <born in Edinburgh> *who invented the telephone was just as interested in the messages to be sent around the world as in the method of sending them. He had 'Abdu'l-Bahá a number of times to his home. Andrew Carnegie, the Scottish philanthropist who built so many libraries throughout the United States and elsewhere, wrote to 'Abdu'l-Bahá that he was just as interested in the contents of the books they*

housed as he was in the buildings that housed them. 'Abdu'l-Bahá wrote back to Bell:

"Today the most important object of the Kingdom of God is the promulgation of the cause of universal peace and the principle of the oneness of the world of humanity."

During the next eight years, 'Abdu'l-Bahá laboured for that "Most great Peace". During the First World War he organised a section of Palestine for the growing of wheat to help feed a hungry world. He gave freely to the poor who faced starvation.

Then he died on a late-November morning in 1921. Over 10,000 gathered on top of Mount Carmel for his funeral: the consuls of several nations; leaders of Jewish, Christian and Muslim communities; Arabs, Greeks, Turks, Armenians, Jews, Egyptians, Americans, and Europeans. Troops of Baden-Powell's Boy Scouts marched in the procession. The prayers were in many languages and forms.

Shoghi Effendi!

In his Will, 'Abdu'l-Bahá named Shoghi Effendi, great-grandson of Bahá'u'lláh, as "Guardian" of the Faith. (Three generations of one family were to take up the banner.) Shoghi Effendi was studying at Oxford University. Though at first "shattered" by the news from the master's Will, he accepted the daunting role. During his 36 years as "Guardian" he was to organise the structure of the Faith into providing the groundwork for a World government, which has had considerable influence on the formation and work of the United Nations.

Shoghi Effendi summarised the teachings of Bahá'u'lláh with these words:

"The Bahá'í Faith recognises the unity of God and of His Prophets, upholds the principle of an unfettered search after truth, condemns all forms of superstition and prejudice, teaches that the fundamental purpose of religion is to promote concord and harmony, that it must go hand-in-hand with science, and that it constitutes the sole and ultimate basis of a peaceful, ordered and progressive society. It inculcates the principle of equal opportunity, rights and privileges for both sexes, advocates compulsory education, abolishes extremes of poverty and wealth, exalts work performed in the spirit of service to the rank of worship, recommends the adoption of an auxiliary international language, and provides the necessary agencies for the establishment and safeguarding of a permanent and universal peace." <see *A Crown of Beauty*, Braun and Chance, pp. 5–6.>

In November 1957, while on a visit to London, Shoghi Effendi died and was buried here. Now it is six years later, 7000 Bahá'ís have gathered here from all over the world. (The Bahá'í Universal House of Justice, proposed by Bahá'u'lláh to be the supreme administrative institution of the Faith, has just been selected by representatives of 56 nations.) Undoubtedly all of the 7000 attending this assembly will make a pilgrimage to his grave, before we leave London to seek to continue the work of the Prophets for justice and for that "Most Great Peace".

Bahá'í Scriptures: selections from the writings of Bahá'u'lláh

Bahá'í scriptures include the teachings of the Báb, Bahá'u'lláh and 'Abdu'l-Bahá, as Christian scriptures include the teachings of Moses and Jesus Christ, as well as John the Baptist, Peter, Paul and others.

(Letters and headings have been added to aid reference for discussion. *GWB* – *Gleanings from the Writings of Bahá'u'lláh*.)

A: The Oneness of Humanity
There can be no doubt whatever that the people of the world, of whatever race or religion, derive their inspiration from one heavenly Source, and are the subjects of one God.

(from *GWB*, p. 216)

B: Accept all true prophets
Beware, O believers in the Unity of God, lest ye be tempted to make any distinction between any of the Manifestations of His Cause, or to discriminate against the signs that have accompanied and proclaimed their Revelation. ... Be ye assured, moreover, that the works and acts of each and every one of these Manifestations of God... are all ordained by God, and are a reflection of His Will and Purpose.

(from *GWB*, p. 59 – cf. *Matthew* 7:14–20)

C: All true prophets teach the same faith
If thou wilt observe with discriminating eyes, thou wilt behold them all <the Manifestations of God> *abiding in the same tabernacle, soaring in the same heaven, seated upon the same throne, uttering the same speech, and proclaiming the same Faith. ... Wherefore, should one of these Manifestations of Holiness proclaim saying: "I am the return of all the Prophets," He, verily, speaketh the truth.*

(from *GWB*, p. 52)

D: Why true prophets appear to differ
The measure of the revelation of the Prophets of God in this world, however, must differ. Each and every one of them hath been the Bearer of a distinct Message, and hath been commissioned to reveal Himself through specific acts. It is for this reason that they appear to vary in their greatness.

(from *GWB*, pp. 78–9)

E: False gods are created by man's imaginings
There can be no doubt whatever that the

peoples of the world, of whatever race or religion, derive their inspiration from one heavenly Source, and are the subjects of one God. The difference between the ordinances under which they abide should be attributed to the varying requirements ... of the age in which they were revealed ... Arise and, armed with the power of faith, shatter to pieces the gods of your vain imaginings, the sowers of dissension amongst you.

(from *GWB*, p. 217)

F: Why true prophets were persecuted

Leaders of religion, in every age, have hindered their people from attaining the shores of eternal salvation, inasmuch as they held the reins of authority in their mighty grasp. Some for the lust of leadership, others through want of knowledge and understanding, have been the cause of the deprivation of the people. By their sanction and authority, every Prophet of God hath drunk from the chalice of sacrifice ... What unspeakable cruelties they that have occupied the seats of authority and learning have inflicted upon the true Monarchs of the world, those Gems of divine virtue.

(from *Kitáb-i-Íqán*, pp. 10–11 – cf. *Matthew* 5:12)

G: The aim of true faith is unity and love

The fundamental purpose animating the Faith of God and His Religion is to safeguard the interests and promote the unity of the human race, and to foster the spirit of love and fellowship amongst men. Suffer it not to become a source of dissension and discord, of hate and enmity.

(from *GWB*, p. 215 – cf. *I Corinthians* 13)

H. How the world can be healed

That which the Lord hath ordained as the sovereign remedy and mightiest instrument for the healing of all the world is the union of all his peoples in one universal Cause, one

common Faith. This can in no wise be achieved except through the power of a skilled, an all-powerful and inspired Physician.

(from *GWB*, p. 255)

I: Useful work is a form of worship

It is incumbent upon each one of you to engage in some occupation – such as a craft, a trade or the like. We have exalted your engagement in such work to the rank of worship of the one true God ... Waste not your hours in idleness and sloth, but occupy yourselves with what will profit you and others.

(from *Kitáb-i-Aqdas*, p. 30 – cf. *Matthew* 20:6)

J: The value of knowledge

Knowledge is as wings to man's life, and a ladder for his ascent. Its acquisition is incumbent upon everyone ... In truth, knowledge is a veritable treasure for man, and a source of glory, of bounty, of joy, of exaltation, of cheer and gladness unto him ...

(from *Epistle to the Son of the Wolf*, pp. 26–7)

K: When is the time to lift up the spirits of others? How?

This is the Day whereon the Ocean of God's mercy hath been manifested unto men, the Day in which the Daystar of His loving-kindness hath shed its radiance upon them, the Day in which the clouds of His bountiful favour have overshadowed the whole of mankind. Now is the time to cheer and refresh the downcast through the invigorating breeze of love and fellowship, and the living waters of friendliness and charity ... Forget your own selves, and turn your eyes towards your neighbour.

(from *GWB*, pp. 7–9)

L: A Beatitude

Blessed is he who preferreth his brother before himself.

(from *Tablets of Bahá'u'lláh*, p. 71)

139

M: How to use religion – and how not to use religion

O ye that dwell on earth! The religion of God is for love and unity; make it not the cause of enmity and dissension.

(from *Tablets of Bahá'u'lláh*, p. 220)

N: How to treat those who disagree with you

Consort with all men, O people of Baha, in a spirit of friendliness and fellowship. If ye be aware of a certain truth, if ye possess a jewel, of which others are deprived, share it with them in a language of utmost kindliness and goodwill. If it be accepted, if it fulfils its purpose, your object is attained. If anyone should refuse it, leave him unto himself, and beseech God to guide him. Beware lest ye deal unkindly with him.

(from *GWB*, p. 289)

O: Dangers that come from knowing what is true and from doing what is right

Blessed are the learned that pride not themselves on their attainments; and well is it with the righteous that mock not the sinful, but rather conceal their misdeeds, so that their own short-comings may remain unveiled to men's eyes.

(from *GWB*, p. 315)

P: Courtesy

We, verily, have chosen courtesy, and made it the true mark of such as are nigh unto Him. Courtesy is, in truth, a raiment which fitteth all men, whether young or old. Well is it with him that adorneth his temple therewith.

(from *Proclamation of Bahá'u'lláh*, p. 20)

Q: How should one live?

Be generous in prosperity, and thankful in adversity. Be worthy of the trust of thy neighbour, and look upon him with a bright and friendly face. Be a treasure to the poor, an admonisher to the rich, an answerer of the cry of the needy, a preserver of the sanctity of thy pledge. Be fair in thy judgement, and guarded in thy speech. Be unjust to no man, and show all meekness to all men. Be as a lamp unto them that walk in darkness, a joy to the sorrowful, a sea for the thirsty, a haven for the distressed, an upholder and defender of the victim of oppression. Let integrity and uprightness distinguish all thine acts. Be a home for the stranger, a balm to the suffering, a tower of strength for the fugitive. Be eyes to the blind, and a guiding light unto the feet of the erring. Be an ornament to the countenance of truth, a crown to the brow of fidelity, a pillar of the temple of righteousness, a breath of life to the body of mankind, an ensign of the hosts of justice, a luminary above the horizon of virtue, a dew to the soil of the human heart, an ark on the ocean of knowledge, a sun in the heaven of bounty, a gem on the diadem of wisdom, a shining light in the firmament of thy generation, a fruit upon the tree of humility.

(from *GWB*, p. 285 – cf. *Matthew* 5:3–16)

R: What is faith?

The essence of faith is fewness of words and abundance of deeds…

(from *Tablets of Bahá'u'lláh*, p. 156 – cf. *James* 1:14–16)

S: Justice is essential, not least for one who desires God

O Son of Spirit! The best beloved of all things in My sight is Justice; turn not away therefrom if thou desirest Me, and neglect it not that I may confide in thee. By its aid thou shalt see with thine own eyes and not through the eyes of others, and shalt know of thine own knowledge and not through the knowledge of thy neighbour… Verily justice is My gift to thee and the sign of My loving-kindness. Set it then before thine eyes.

(from *Hidden Words*, p. 2 – cf. *Micah* 6:8)

T: Religious education

The source of crafts, sciences and arts is the power of reflection. Make ye every effort that out of this ideal mine there may gleam forth such pearls of wisdom and utterance as will promote the well-being and harmony of all the kindreds of the earth.

(from *Tablets of Bahá'u'lláh*, p. 72 – cf. *Matthew* 28:20)

U: A universal language

The day is approaching when all the peoples of the world will have adopted one universal language and one common script. When this is achieved, to whatsoever city a man may journey, it shall be as if he were entering his own home.

(from *Tablets of Bahá'u'lláh*, p. 166)

V: The true patriot

It is not his to boast who loveth his country, but it is his who loveth the world.

(from *GWB*, p. 95)

W: World citizenship

The earth is but one country, and mankind its citizens.

(from *GWB*, p. 250)

X: The right aim in life – unity

O contending peoples and kindreds of the earth! Set your faces towards unity, and let the radiance of its light shine upon you. Gather ye together, and for the sake of God resolve to root out whatever is the source of contention amongst you.

(from *GWB*, p. 217 – cf. *I Corinthians* 1:10)

Y: Love must be universal

All men have been created to carry forward in ever-advancing civilisation... To act like the beasts of the field is unworthy of man. Those virtues that befit his dignity are forbearance, mercy, compassion and loving-kindness towards all the peoples and kindreds of the earth.

(from *GWB*, p. 215 – cf. *Colossians* 3:11)

Z: The true man

That one indeed is a man who, today, dedicateth himself to the service of the entire human race.

(from *GWB*, p. 250 – cf. *Matthew* 25:31f.)

AA: A message to the world's leaders

O ye the elected representatives of the people in every land! Take ye counsel together, and let your concern be only for that which profiteth mankind, and bettereth the condition thereof, if ye be of them that scan heedfully... Be vigilant, that ye may not do injustice to anyone, be it to the extent of a grain of mustard seed... Compose your differences, and reduce your armaments, that the burden of your expenditures may be lightened... Rest not only your power, your armies, and treasures. Put your whole trust and confidence in God, who hath created you, and seek ye His help in all your affairs... Know ye that the poor are the trust of God in your midst. Watch that ye betray not His trust, that ye deal not unjustly with them... My object is none other than the betterment of the world and the tranquillity of its peoples. The well-being of mankind, its peace and security, are unattainable unless and until its unity is firmly established... God grant that the light of unity may envelop the whole earth and that the seal, "the Kingdom is God's", may be stamped upon the brow of all its peoples.

(from *GWB*, pp. 11, 250–2, 254, 286 – cf. *Luke* 1:1–4ff. and *Acts* 1:1ff.)

BB: Stewardship of time and talent

O Friends! Be not careless of the virtues with which ye have been endowed, neither be neglectful of your high destiny. Suffer not your labours to be wasted through the vain imaginations which certain hearts have devised. Ye are the stars of the heaven of understanding, the breeze that stirreth at the break of day, the soft-flowing waters upon which must depend the very life of all men ... Be ye guided by wisdom in all your doings, and cleave ye tenaciously unto it ... With the utmost friendliness and in a spirit of perfect fellowship take ye counsel together, and dedicate the precious days of your lives to the betterment of the world and the promotion of the Cause of Him Who is the Ancient and Sovereign Lord of all.

(from *GWB*, pp. 84 and 196–97, – cf. *Luke* 10:30f.)

CC: A Prayer

O my God! O my God! Unite the hearts of Thy servants, and reveal to them Thy great purpose. May they follow Thy commandments and abide in Thy law. Help them, O God, in their endeavour, and grant them strength to serve Thee. O God! leave them not to themselves, but guide their steps by the light of knowledge, and cheer their hearts by Thy love. Verily, Thou art their Helper and their Lord.

(from *Bahá'í Prayers*, 59, p. 61 – cf. *Matthew* 5:7f. and *Colossians* 4)

?

1. *"My religion consists of a humble admiration of the illimitable superior spirit who reveals himself in the slight details we are able to perceive with our frail and feeble minds. That deeply emotional conviction of the presence of a superior reasoning power, which is revealed in the incomprehensible universe, forms my idea of God."* (*The Universe and Dr Einstein*, by L Barrett, p. 106.) Do you agree? What forms your idea of God? Whether or not you believe in God, do you believe that those who do should seek unity for all? Do you believe that those who do not believe in God should seek unity for all? What kind of unity?

2. *"Bahá'u'lláh teaches that the Messengers of God are not to be set up as rivals in the world, each competing with the others for the homage of the human race. They are like teachers in the same school."* (From *The Bahá'í Faith*, by Gloria Faizi, p. 32.) Do you agree? Why, or why not?

3. *"The world in the past has been ruled by force, and man has dominated over woman by reason of his more forceful and aggressive qualities both of body and mind. But the balance is already shifting; force is losing its dominance, and mental alertness, intuition, and the spiritual qualities of love and service, in which woman is strong, are gaining ascendancy. Hence the new age will be an age less masculine and more permeated with the feminine ideals, or, to speak more exactly, will be an age in which the masculine and feminine elements of civilisation will be more evenly balanced."* ('Abdu'l-Bahá, *Bahá'u'lláh and the New Era*, p. 141.) To what extent do you believe this is true? What is your evidence?

4. To what extent do you believe that the story of the founding of the Bahá'í Faith parallels that of Judaism and Christianity? Compare the role of the Báb with Elijah and John the Baptist; Bahá'u'lláh with Isaiah and Jeremiah, and the Jewish idea of "Messiah", and Jesus; and 'Abdu'l-Bahá with Maimonides, Hertzl (the founder of Zionism), Peter (who was with Jesus from the beginning of his ministry and who many would claim to be his appointed successor), Paul and Christian missionaries. How would you compare the mission of Bahá'ís and Christians today?

5. *"Both the founders of religions and the pioneers of science have suffered scorn and denial from their contemporaries. Conflict has arisen among their followers as a result of human error usually caused by ignorance and prejudice."* What

illustrations from history can you give to support this? What about today?

6. *"Genuine independent investigation demands of men much more than a blind acceptance of a faith taught by someone else. Bahá'u'lláh explains that each person must detach himself from inherited belief and prejudice. He must abandon at the outset the idea that he is right and everyone else is wrong."* What is meant by (a) "blind acceptance" and (b) "inherited belief and prejudice"? Does this mean (a) that all faiths are blind and (b) that you should reject with impunity all the beliefs of your parents and/or society?

7. Bahá'ís believe that universal education is important so that all can read and write and have access to information which should not be confined to certain teachers or religious authorities. They believe in an independent search for truth where one discovers for himself and makes his own quest for truth. This does not mean that he should not listen to others or consider their views. It does mean that the relationship between a student and a teacher should not be one of slave to master. In school, how can one show respect without submitting to the view that teachers have all knowledge and students are totally stupid? Can Student Councils help abolish domination in education? Can teachers block the road to true inquiry? How? Can students? How? What should/can/must be done about this?

8. *"When you meet those whose opinions differ from your own, do not turn away your face from them. All are seeking truth, and there are many roads leading thereto... Do not allow differences of opinion, or diversity of thought, to separate you from your fellow-men, or to be the cause of dispute... Rather, search diligently for the truth and make all men your friends."* ('Abdu'l-Bahá, *Paris Talks*, 15.9, p. 46.) Assuming that many of your opinions differ from your parents, colleagues and friends, how can you search for truth and yet make others your friends (a) at the office (b) at home, parents/family, and (c) elsewhere, other relationships – including the old woman on the bus?

9. Do you believe that statement 45 (p. 131) is really true? What are you prepared to do with those who do? What changes would this make to your life?

10. Do you believe that statement 46 (p. 131) is really true? What are the practical implications of this statement on your life?

11. Steps towards world unity that are considered important by Bahá'ís include (a) the elimination of extremes of wealth and poverty within and between nations, (b) an international language, (c) a democratically elected world government, (d) preserving human rights and arbitrating inter-national problems, and (e) a common system of currency, weights and measures. In what order of importance would you place those which you consider important? What would you add to this list?

12. Shortly before the Second World War, Shoghi Effendi, the "Guardian" of the Bahá'í Faith, wrote about a world society:

"In such a world society, science and religion, the two most potent forces in human life, will be reconciled, will co-operate, and will harmoniously develop. The press... will be liberated from the influence of contending governments and peoples. The economic resources of the world will be organised, its resources of raw materials will be tapped and fully utilised, its markets will be co-ordinated and developed, and the distribution of its products will be equitably regulated.

"National rivalries, hatreds, and intrigues will cease, and racial animosity and prejudices will be replaced by racial amity, understanding and co-operation. The causes of religious strife will be permanently removed, economic barriers and restrictions will be completely abolished, and the inordinate distinction between

classes will be obliterated. Destitution on the one hand, and gross accumulation of ownership on the other, will disappear. The enormous energy dissipated and wasted on war, whether economic or political, will be consecrated to such ends as will extend the range of human inventions and technical development, to the increase of the productivity of mankind, to the extermination of disease, to the extension of scientific research, to the raising of the standard of physical health, to the sharpening and refinement of the human brain, to the exploitation of the unused and unsuspected resources of the planet, to the prolongation of human life, and to the furtherance of any other agency that can stimulate the intellectual, the moral, and the spiritual life of the entire human race." (from *World Order of Bahá'u'lláh,* p. 203)

Do you share these expectations? Do you believe they are just? What do you believe needs to be done (or needs to stop being done) if the world is to turn its "swords into ploughshares"? What can you do (a) now? (b) through your job or vocation? and (c) in your leisure time?

13. In 1931, Shoghi Effendi wrote:

    "The call of Bahá'u'lláh is primarily directed against all forms of provincialism, all insularity and prejudices. If long-cherished ideals and time-honoured institutions, if certain social assumptions and religious formulae have ceased to promote the welfare of the generality of mankind, if they no longer minister to the needs of a continually evolving humanity, let them be swept away and relegated to the limbo of obsolescent and forgotten doctrines. Why should these, in a world subject to the immutable law of change and decay, be exempt from the deterioration that must needs overtake every human institution?" (from *World Order of Bahá'u'lláh,* p. 42)

    What do you think should be "swept away"? How can this be done and yet show respect for those who disagree?

14. Over one of the nine archways at the Bahá'í Temple in Wilmette, Illinois, that over-looks Lake Michigan near Chicago, are inscribed these words of Bahá'u'lláh:

    "So powerful is unity's light that it can illumine the whole earth.
    Consort with the followers of all religions with friendliness.
    The source of all learning is the knowledge of God...
    All the Prophets of God proclaim the same Faith."

    Do you agree? Why?/Why not?

15. *"Let those who read them <the teachings of Bahá'u'lláh> consider well with themselves whether such doctrines merit death and bonds, and whether the world is more likely to gain or lose by their diffusion."* (Prof. E G Browne of Cambridge University, after visiting Bahá'u'lláh.) What is your verdict?

16. Would your verdict on the last quotation be the same if it meant the confiscation of your property, stoning, flogging, exile, imprisonment, separation from family, or even an early death for yourself?

17. What do you believe is the message of hope and love for **all the peoples and nations of both East and West**?

18. *"All the world's problems, strife and wars are caused by religion."* Discuss. Identify problems not caused by religion. Identify solutions offered by religion.

19. For **peace with justice**, what common ground ought there to be
    a. within each religion;
    b. between religions; and
    c. between religion and secular society?

Multiple Choice Questions
The Western Approach

Either use an answer grid or number 1–80.

1. Concerning the creation of the world, cave dwellers tended to assume that
   a) the world was always here. b) it came down from the sky. c) it was made by their ancestors. d) it was formed by a giant. e) it was made by a demon.
2. The Ancient Egyptians believed that in the beginning there existed
   a) earth. b) sky. c) water. d) air. e) a and b.
3. Ancient Egyptians called the creator god
   a) *Atum.* b) *Re.* c) *Tefnut.* d) *Ti'amat.* e) c and d.
4. The power of creation according to the Ancient Babylonians was the great Mother demon goddess called
   a) *Atum.* b) *Re.* c) *Tefnut.* d) *Ti'amat.* e) c and d.
5. A Myth can be
   a) a legend about God or gods/Goddesses. b) a poetic way to explain anything unknown. c) a true story. d) an allegory with one point. e) *either* a *or* b.
6. Primal Man's religious beliefs were shaped by
   a) fear of the unknown. b) stories of imaginary creatures. c) the gods. d) war. e) prophets.
7. Primal Man believed that spirits were to be found in
   a) water. b) air. c) natural objects. d) people. e) all of these.
8. *"Da a dada"* was a primal chant to the
   a) sun god. b) wind god. c) rain god. d) creator god. e) war god.
9. The belief that gods dwell in all things is called
   a) anthropomorphism. b) humanism. c) pantheism. d) monotheism. e) polytheism.
10. To think of God or gods in the imagery of man is called
    a) anthropomorphism. b) humanism. c) pantheism. d) monotheism. e) polytheism.
11. Belief in many gods is called
    a) anthropomorphism. b) humanism. c) pantheism. d) monotheism. e) polytheism.
12. The Ancient Babylonians believed that the sun and moon crossed the sky
    a) by the energy of gods within them. b) because gods used them for playing games of catch. c) so that gods could use them for watching man. d) by their own power. e) chasing each other.
13. The Babylonian who drew up an ancient code for living was
    a) Anu. b) Enlil. c) Hammurabi. d) Marduk. e) Rameses.
14. The purpose of this Babylonian code was to bring
    a) justice. b) discipline. c) power. d) religion. e) happiness.

15. *"Moses"* (as in *Rameses* or *Ra-Moses*) is from the Egyptian word for
    a) god. b) goddess. c) demon. d) leader. e) prophet.
16. The ancient civilisation that believed that the earth was flat and had a dome above it with holes that let in the heavenly lights, and underneath was the underworld, was
    a) Primal Man. b) Ancient Egyptians. c) Ancient Babylonians. d) Ancient Hebrews. e) Ancient Greeks.
17. The ancient civilisation that believed that the earth was flat and that the gods sailed the sun and moon as boats across the sky, which was the bottom of a gigantic cow, was
    a) Primal Man. b) Ancient Egyptians. c) Ancient Babylonians. d) Ancient Hebrews. e) Ancient Greeks.
18. The ancient civilisation that taught that *"all men are created equal"* was
    a) Primal Man. b) the Ancient Egyptians. c) the Ancient Babylonians. d) the Ancient Greeks. e) the Ancient Romans.
19. The ancient civilisation that taught that *"the strong should not hurt the weak"* was
    a) Primal Man. b) the Ancient Egyptians. c) the Ancient Babylonians. d) the Ancient Greeks. e) the Ancient Romans.
20. An artificial mountain built of sun-dried bricks to form a temple to a city god is called
    a) a pyre. b) a pyramid. c) a ziggurat. d) an idol. e) a statue.
21. The Jewish scriptures were originally written in
    a) Greek. b) Latin. c) Arabic. d) Hebrew. e) Hieroglyphics.
22. The Hebrew tribes originally came from
    a) Mesopotamia. b) Canaan. c) Egypt. d) Greece. e) Rome.
23. The *"Father of Israel"* who led the tribes from there around 1900 BCE was
    a) Elijah. b) Abraham. c) Moses. d) Joshua. e) Joseph.
24. *"Yahweh"*, the Hebrew name for God, literally means
    a) Leader. b) Divine. c) King. d) the Grand Master. e) the Great *"I am"*.
25. The Jewish king who built the temple in Jerusalem was
    a) Saul. b) David. c) Solomon. d) Elijah e) Jeremiah.
26. In the sixth century BCE, Jerusalem was destroyed and many of the Jews were taken captive into
    a) Babylonia. b) Egypt. c) Canaan. d) Rome. e) Assyria.
27. This period of captivity lasting over 50 years is called the
    a) Diaspora. b) Exodus. c) Exile. d) Pilgrimage. e) Journey.
28. The prophet (or prophets) who taught that the day will come when people *"shall beat their swords into ploughshares, and their spears into pruning hooks; nation shall not lift up sword against nation, neither shall they study war any more"* was (or were)
    a) Amos. b) Micah and Isaiah. c) Jeremiah. d) Hosea. e) Ezekiel.
29. The prophet who suffered punishment and imprisonment in Egypt in the sixth century BCE was
    a) Amos. b) Micah. c) Jeremiah. d) Second Isaiah. e) Ezekiel.
30. The prophet who had a vision of a valley of dry bones and believed people had lost unity and the Spirit of God was
    a) Amos. b) Micah. c) Jeremiah. d) Elijah. e) Ezekiel.
31. In 539 BCE the Jews were free to return to Palestine because their captors were defeated by the
    a) Assyrians. b) Persians. c) Greeks. d) Romans. e) Philistines.
32. Who issued a decree to enable the Jews to return to their homeland and paid for their rebuilding of the temple?
    a) Cyrus. b) Nebuchadnezzar. c) Hezekiah. d) Caesar. e) Ezekiel.

33. The Hebrew word for peace is
    a) *Kaire.* b) *Yahweh.* c) *Elijah.* d) *Shalom.* e) *Yom.*
34. The ancient civilisation that set up a kind of first United Nations was
    a) Egypt. b) Babylonia. c) Israel. d) Greece. e) Qumran.
35. To an ancient Athenian Greek, which of the following was **not** an aim of education?
    a) honesty. b) practical skills. c) culture. d) philosophy. e) duty.
36. Which of the ancient peoples considered the most important duty to be *"duty to the state"*?
    a) Babylonians. b) Egyptians. c) Greeks d) Romans. e) the Qumran Community.
37. *"Philosophy"* is from two Greek words meaning
    a) the love of wisdom. b) the system of justice. c) the Manual of Discipline. d) human exploits. e) the good life.
38. *"Ethics"* is the examination of
    a) discipline. b) love. c) wisdom. d) culture. e) morality.
39. He has been called, *"the Father of Atomic Physics"*. Around 550 BCE, this Greek taught: *"Everything is composed of monads* (atoms), *tiny particles which cannot be seen."* His name was
    a) Thales. b) Anaxamander. c) Anaximenes. d) Heraclitus. e) Parmenides.
40. He has been called, *"the Father of Philosophy"*. He taught, *"Know thyself; the unexamined life is not worth living"*. He wanted discussion to be the means of educating practical men, seeking the best in themselves and their relationships. His name was
    a) Heraclitus. b) Parmenides. c) Socrates. d) Plato. e) Aristotle.
41. He was the tutor of Alexander the Great. He taught, *"avoid extremes; the middle way is the best."* He founded a new kind of school, the Lyceum, which made Athens a centre of learning which included Mathematics, astronomy, physics, botany, zoology, geography, debate and all areas of philosophy. He was
    a) Heraclitus. b) Parmenides. c) Socrates. d) Plato. e) Aristotle.
42. The chief god of the Greeks, believed to be the defender of liberty and justice, was
    a) Apollo. b) Poseidon. c) Mars. d) Jupiter. e) Zeus.
43. The phrase, *"**my** will be done,"* (for the benefit of **my** family and **my** country) could best sum up
    a) Greek philosophy. b) Roman religion. c) Qumran religion. d) Christianity. e) Islam.
44. A treasure-house of scrolls, probably written by the Qumran Community, was found in 1947 in caves near the
    a) Red Sea. b) Dead Sea. c) Sea of Galilee. d) Mediterranean Sea. e) Persian Gulf.
45. Scholars believe that the scrolls were hidden to save the community from Titus when he marched the Tenth Roman Legion into Palestine. He destroyed the temple in Jerusalem, and much of Judea, in about
    a) 600 BCE. b) 70 BCE. c) 1 CE. d) 70 CE. e) 600 CE.
46. These scrolls included copies of
    a) most of the books of the Jewish *Tenakh,* the Old Testament. b) a Manuel of Discipline. c) a song book. d) b and c. e) a, b and c.
47. The Qumran Community were
    a) Greeks. b) Romans. c) Jews. d) Christians. e) Muslims.
48. In the Qumran Community, if someone disrupted a class he would be
    a) told to be quiet. b) put on detention. c) suspended for ten days. d) expelled from the community. e) put to death.
49. In the Qumran Community, on a rota basis, everyone stayed up for study and prayer.
    a) every night. b) every third night. c) once a week. d) once a month. e) once a year.

50. Which of the following was **not** an aim of the Qumran Community?
a) common ownership of property. b) knowledge of God. c) world peace. d) skills to earn a living. e) righteous living.
51. The word *"celibate"* can mean
a) priest. b) unmarried. c) teacher. d) prophet. e) king.
52. The leader of the Qumran Community was called
a) *"prophet"*. b) *"scribe"*. c) *"abbot"*. d) *"Teacher of Righteousness"*. e) *"Master"*.
53. The statement *Justice is virtue applied to your treatment of your neighbour* is attributed to
a) Thales. b) Anaximander. c) Parmenides. d) Heraclitus. e) Aristotle.
54. Stoics believe that
a) religion is unnecessary. b) religion is important and there is one god: the god of discipline. c) reason, which is good, should rule passion, which is bad. d) happiness is the chief goal in life. e) a and b.
55. Roman culture developed
a) before the Greeks. b) after the Greeks. c) at approximately the same time as the Greeks. d) not at all, but remained in a primitive state. e) totally independent of the Greeks.
56. To an ancient Roman, which of the following was **not** an aim of education?
a) induction into traditions. b) development of character. c) respect for the law and institutions. d) equality between the sexes. e) respect for the state religion.
57. To bind themselves in a business deal, ancient Romans often
a) slaughtered a lamb and shared it. b) drew up a witnessed legal document.
c) made an oath and threw a stone. d) both a and b. e) both a and c.
58. The Roman pagan winter festival which was later replaced by Christmas on the 25th of December was called
a) *"Hogmanay"*. b) *"Sabbath"*. c) *"Pax Romana"*. d) *"Saturnalia"*. e) *"Passover"*.
59. Belief that animals have immortal souls is called
a) pantheism. b) anthropomorphism. c) animism. d) monotheism. e) polytheism.
60. *"Pax Romana"* means Roman
a) bread. b) gods. c) praise. d) loyalty. e) peace.
61. Classical Roman religion and architecture was most influenced by the classical
a) Persians. b) Greeks. c) Egyptians. d) Jews. e) none of these.
62. The chief Roman god was
a) Jupiter. b) Neptune. c) Mars. d) Apollo. e) Mercury.
63. Elijah, Amos, Hosea, Isaiah, Second Isaiah and Ezekiel were among the Hebrew
a) kings. b) seers. c) priests. d) military leaders. e) prophets.
64. Jesus was baptised by
a) Elijah. b) Isaiah. c) John. d) himself. e) no one.
65. Jews and Muslims acknowledge that Jesus was a
a) king. b) god. c) Messiah. d) prophet. e) priest.
66. The Roman Emperor Nero blamed Christians for starting the fire in Rome about
a) 1 CE. b) 65 CE. c) 312 CE. d) 514 CE. e) 900 CE.
67. Christianity became the official religion of Rome under Constantine about
a) 1 CE. b) 65 CE. c) 312 CE. d) 514 CE. e) 900 CE.
68. A formal Christian statement of belief is called a
a) gospel. b) testament. c) creed. d) charity. e) parable.
69. Between 1095 and 1270 CE, many Jews, Muslims and others were tragically slaughtered by people who claimed to be Christians and were called
a) Covenanters. b) Reformers. c) Crusaders. d) Zealots. e) Idolaters.

70. The German monk who launched the Reformation was
    a) John Calvin. b) John Knox. c) Martin Luther. d) Thomas Aquinas. e) Ignatius
    Loyola.
71. The one who helped develop Roman Catholic self-reform (the Counter Reformation) and
    who founded the Jesuits was
    a) John Calvin. b) John Knox. c) Martin Luther. d) Thomas Aquinas. e) Ignatius
    Loyola.
72. Christians number about a billion people of whom the ratio of Protestants to Roman
    Catholics is about
    a) one to five. b) one to two. c) one to one. d) two to one. e) five to one.
73. The Corrymeela Community where Catholics and Protestants live and work together is in
    a) America. b) Northern Ireland. c) Scotland. d) Germany. e) Russia.
74. Christian Aid, which seeks to help meet human need throughout the world, is organised
    through
    a) the Iona Community. b) the Corrymeela Community. c) the Church of Scotland.
    d) the Church of England. e) the World Council of Churches.
75. The Iona Community, which rebuilt the abbey on Iona (from which it has spread), is
    deeply involved in
    a) the healing ministry. b) pastoral care. c) social service. d) industrial reconciliation.
    e) all of these.
76. Operation Friendship, which promotes international understanding and which celebrated
    its 30th Anniversary in 1995 with over 25,000 youth exchanges between twelve countries,
    was founded by a youth club in
    a) Liverpool, England. b) Dublin, Ireland. c) Belfast, Northern Ireland. d) Glenrothes,
    Scotland. e) Honfleurs, France.
77. About 95 percent of Mark is found in
    a) Matthew. b) Luke. c) John. d) both Matthew and Luke. e) both Luke and John.
78. The Gospel which is distinctive from the other three in both order of events and content is
    a) *Matthew.* b) *Mark.* c) *Luke.* d) *John.* e) none of these because there are no basic
    differences in order and content between any of the Gospels.
79. The Ecumenical movement is
    a) a Protestant Missionary Society. b) a Quaker Movement. c) a Roman Catholic
    Missionary Society. d) offering an opportunity for all people in all Churches to work
    together. e) a group of priests and ministers.
80. The Golden Rule is, *"Do unto others as*
    a) *they do unto you."* b) *you do not do unto them."* c) *you would do unto them."* d) *you
    would want them to do unto you."* e) *they do not do unto you."*

Religious Pursuit
Muslims and the Eastern Approach

Many of the questions here are covered in the text. Those that are not have an asterisk (*) after them. The answers and the additional information required can be found at the end, pages 161–67.

Muslims
Submission to the Most High
1. What does the Arabic word *Islam* mean?
2. What does the Arabic word *Muslim* mean?
3. What does the Arabic name *Muhammad* Mean?
4. What does the Arabic word *hafiz* mean?
5. When was Muhammad born, and when did he die?
6. What is a *subha*?*
7. Do Muslims consider God as "Father"?
8. What does *mosque* mean; and what are its identifying characteristics?*
9. On what day should all male Muslims go to a mosque; and why do they not believe that this is a day of rest?*
10. How fast does a camel travel?*
11. What can be the size of a large camel caravan?*
12. How far from home do camels sometimes travel in caravans?*
13. What goods did camels carry to or from Mecca in the time of Muhammad?*
14. What were the chief dangers faced by travelling merchants? *
15. What does AH mean and what date would a Muslim give 2000 CE?
16. How long is the Qur'an?
17. Except for the ninth one, with what words does each of the 114 Suras begin?*
18. How many pilgrims come to Mecca each year?*
19. What does *Caliph* mean?*
20. Why should one not call a Muslim a *Muhammadan*; and what does using this term say about the one who uses it?*
21. What is *id-al-Fitr* (or *Eid-ul-Fitr*)?*
22. What is *Id-al-'Adha*?*
23. What is *Meeled ul-Nabi*?*
24. What is *Hijrah Day*?
25. Why do Muslims not believe in baptism?*
26. In what are Muslims buried?*
27. What is a *mosaic*?*

28. What is a pilgrimage?
29. What does *Shahada* (or *Kalimah*) mean; and what is the First Pillar?
30. What does *Salat* mean; and what is the Second Pillar?
31. What does *Zakat* mean; and what is the Third Pillar?
32. What does *Saum* (or *Sujam*) mean; and what is the Fourth Pillar?
33. What does *Hajj* (or *Hadj*) mean; and what is the Fifth Pillar?
34. What are some of the 99 "Beautiful Names" for God found in the Koran?*
35. What does *Qur'an* (or *Koran*) mean?

Hindus
Reverence for Life

1. To what did the Indus River give its name?
2. What do Hindus call the Spiritual Source?
3. What is the Hindu name for the creator god?
4. What do Hindus call the highest caste?
5. What is a Hindu teacher called?
6. What is the teacher's disciple called?
7. What is the name given to the illusion of the material world?
8. What is the name Hindus give to one who practices yoga?
9. What is the name Hindus give to works/deeds which determine the next life cycle?
10. What do Hindus believe is the cause of suffering in this life?
11. Do Hindus believe that the soul dies?
12. What does reincarnation mean?
13. What is "the law of karma"?
14. According to Hinduism, does God decide your fate?
15. What does a *tilaka* (red spot) of washable powder in the centre of a Hindu woman's forehead mean?*
16. Who dominates and controls a Hindu family, giving an allowance to the marriage partner?*
17. By whom and when are these words spoken: *"With utmost love to each other may we walk together... May we make our minds united."*?*
18. Why do Hindus tend not to weep at a funeral?
19. How is a Hindu body disposed of during a funeral?*
20. What is the name of the best community for one to die in; and what is the most sacred river in which to have one's ashes scattered?*
21. What happens to a person who (a) kills a priest or (b) steals from a priest?*
22. Do Hindus hope for the kingdom of God on earth?
23. What is the classical language of India?
24. What is the word for caste in this language?*
25. What is the word for a Hindu temple?*
26. What is the Hindu symbol for life?*
27. How does a Hindu man pray?*
28. Do Hindus worship images?
29. What god does *Krishna* represent?
30. What do the three main forms/faces of Brahman (God) represent?
31. Is the *Taj Mahal* a Hindu temple?*
32. What is the name of the Mother goddess in Hinduism?
33. What are the characteristics of Sanskrit?*

34. What is the *Rig Veda*?
35. What does *Upanishads* mean?
36. What is the path of severe exercise or discipline called in Hinduism?*
37. Is there another "Way to *Brahman*"?*
38. What does the place name *Calcutta* mean?*
39. What does *Krishna* mean?*
40. According to Hinduism, what is the underlying unity of all things?
41. What is the Hindu belief called that considers that all things have a common unity, that all is God and God is all?*
42. What is the Hindu belief called that states that God is in all things, but that He/it also remains beyond man?*
43. When did Britain rule India?*
44. What are verses of Hindu scriptures called?*
45. To what type of religion does Hinduism refer?
46. Who is a Hindu?
47. Who was the founder of Hinduism?
48. How old is Hinduism?
49. What binds diverse Hindu people together?
50. What is *yoga*?
51. What is the creed of Hinduism?*
52. What name is given to that part of Brahman that is in all living things (*i.e.* your soul)?
53. Why should one respect all living things?
54. Why does Brahma, the creator god, have four heads each facing a different direction?*
55. What name is given to the form of Brahman that is a god who preserves life and is the god of goodness and love?
56. What name is given to the form of Brahman who destroys things so that new things can be created, and who is pictured as the lord of the dance?
57. What are the parts of a Hindu temple?*
58. Do worshippers remove shoes before entering a Hindu temple?*
59. How does one know whether a Hindu worships Viushnu or Shiva?
60. What ritual might a Hindu carry out upon waking?*
61. What is the best known Hindu prayer?*
62. To keep track of the 108 times this prayer is said, what is the string of 108 prayer beads called?*
63. What is the name given to the service of worshipping a god?*
64. What is the *Navarati*?*
65. What is the *Divali* Festival?*
66. What is the Festival of *Shivarti*?*
67. What is the Festival of *Holi*?*
68. What is the Festival of *Rama-navami*?*
69. What is the Festival of *Janamashtami*?*
70. What does *Samsara* mean?*
71. What does *Mukti* mean?*

Theravada Buddhism
The Small Raft
(The Southern Way)

1. What is the third largest religion in the world; and how many adherents does it have?

2. What are the three main types of Buddhism?
3. Buddhism is the state religion of what countries?
4. Theravada Buddhism is the dominant religion of what country?
5. About what percentage of people in Sri Lanka are Buddhists?*
6. Buddhism initially developed out of what religion?
7. Was Buddhism ever the dominant state religion of India?
8. What does *Buddha* mean?
9. What was the name of the Prince who became the Buddha in the sixth century BCE?
10. What are the traditional dates for his birth and death?
11. Where was he born?
12. What legends surround his birth?
13. What legendary evidence do many Hindus give that Gautama the Buddha was the ninth incarnation of Vishnu?*
14. What was the name of Siddhartha's wife?
15. What four signs (the Four Passing Sights) did Gautama see when he was 29 years old?*
16. Where did Siddhartha become the Buddha?
17. Where did he give his first teachings?
18. What happened to Gautama the Buddha's son and wife?*
19. How old was Gautama the Buddha when he died?
20. What four beliefs does Buddhism share with Hinduism?
21. Where, when and in what language were the canon (early official scriptures) of Buddhism written?
22. Why are Buddhists vegetarians?
23. What animals are the most privileged in Buddhism?*
24. Do Buddhists believe in the immortality of the soul/spirit?*
25. What are acts, good or bad, called which raise or lower one in the chain of rebirths?
26. What is the doctrine taught by the Buddha called?
27. Does Buddhism take account of a person's social stature?
28. As a religious teacher, what did Buddha teach about God?*
29. What is the symbol of Nirvana?*
30. What is release from the Wheel of rebirth called?
31. What is the symbol of Gautama the Buddha's calling on the earth to witness the steadfastness of his aim?*
32. What are the duties of a Buddhist monk?*
33. What property does a Buddhist monk own?*
34. Are any Buddhist monks married?*
35. Are Buddhist monks strict pacifists?
36. What must one do to become a Buddhist monk?*
37. To what are secondary schools often attached in Buddhist countries?*
38. How is the monk's robe worn?*
39. Who often practise medicine in Buddhist countries?*
40. How do Buddhist monks spend their time?*
41. How are statues of Buddha positioned? *
42. Why are some statues of Buddha so large?*
43. What is the meaning of a statue of the Buddha in the lotus position with his left hand resting on his lap and his right hand touching the ground?*
44. What is the meaning of a statue of Buddha with the knuckles of the fingers together, thumbs above and touching?*
45. What is the meaning of a statue of the Buddha with the right hand pointed up, the elbow at

right angles and the thumb and first finger forming a circle (or when the hands are folded, one across the other, on the lap)?*

46. What is the meaning of a statue of the Buddha with the tips of the fingers of the right hand touching the chin?*
47. Why do many statues show Buddha lying on his side?*
48. Why do Buddhists sometimes hang garlands on the mirrors of their motor vehicles?*
49. What is a Buddhist place of worship called?*
50. The Christian community is called the Church; what is the Buddhist community called?*
51. Do Buddhists have prayers, services of worship or sacraments?*
52. Are there Buddhist ceremonies at birth, beginning of adolescence, marriage or death?*
53. Why do Buddhists not offer sacrifices or prayers to Buddha?*
54. When Buddhists go to temples, do they worship as a congregation?*
55. What is the *Wessk* (or *Vesak*) Festival?*
56. What is the Water Festival?*
57. How does one become a Buddhist?*
58. What do you call someone who practices yoga?
59. Does Buddhism offer different types of meditation for different types of people?*
60. Do Buddhists believe that man has a soul which forms a spiritual link with God?*
61. To where did Buddhism spread from India?
62. When do Buddhist monks carry umbrellas?*
63. Must one take off his shoes before entering a Buddhist temple?*
64. Where and for how long did Gautama the Buddha teach?
65. What are the basic Buddhist scriptures called; and where were they written?
66. *Buddha* is the name of what person?*
67. Do Theravada Buddhists believe that women can attain Nirvana?*
68. Do Theravada Buddhists believe that someone can help you reach Nirvana?
69. Is Theravada Buddhism a "do-it-yourself religion" whose founder is seen as a teacher and not as a saviour to whom one prays?
70. What name is given to the ideal Theravada Buddhists?*
71. Can the laity (non-monks) gain enlightenment?
72. Why, according to Buddhism, do people have accidents or misfortune?*
73. What do Buddhists believe is the cause of war?*
74. What do Buddhists believe is the way to peace?*
75. Do Buddhists believe in burial?*
76. Has a Buddhist ever been Secretary General of the United Nations?*
77. With what words does a Theravada Buddhist begin each day?*
78. How does a Buddhist give a blessing?*
79. What are the symbolic meanings of the basic architectural shapes of a Theravada temple?*

Mahayana Buddhism
The Large Raft
(The Northern Way)

1. What additional practices of Mahayana Buddhism distinguish it from Theravada?*
2. What are translations of the Buddha's teachings and new writings in Sanskrit called?
3. What is the Festival of Lanterns?*
4. What is the spiritual leader of Mahayana Buddhism in Tibet called?
5. What is the favourite prayer of Tibetan Buddhists?*
6. In what three forms can statues of Buddhas be found?*

7. About what percentage of the population of Thailand are Buddhists?*
8. In Thailand, because many teenagers spend part of their time as monks, what are often attached to monasteries?*
9. How long is the collection of Chinese Buddhist Scriptures?*
10. In China, what two other religions rival the popularity of Mahayana Buddhism?*
11. In Japan, what national cult exists side by side with Mahayana Buddhism?
12. An *Arhat* is a Theravada Buddhist striving for his own perfection before presuming to lead another towards Nirvana. What is the name given to a Mahayana Buddhist seeking first to help others towards Nirvana, believing that he cannot enter Nirvana until everyone else has?
13. In Tibet, where do one third of the population live?*
14. In Japan, what form of Buddhism is most popular?*

Zen Buddhism
The Way of Meditation

1. Today, about what percentage of Japanese are Buddhists?*
2. How many sects of Buddhism are there in Japan today?
3. What are the two main types of Zen?
4. Who is acknowledged as the founder of Zen?
5. What does *Zen* mean?
6. What is the Zen word for "Enlightenment"?
7. What two other religions were drawn on in the development of Zen?
8. Does a Zen Buddhist who believes that he has arrived at Satori have any reason to consider himself superior to, or even different from, someone who is not Enlightened?*
9. What does a Zen Buddhist believe is moving when he sees a flag blowing in the wind: the flag, or the wind?*
10. Do Zen Buddhists believe one can understand Zen?*
11. Which do Zen Buddhists believe is more important: moral action or spiritual knowledge?*
12. What is a good answer to, "What is Zen?"*
13. What is *Samsara*?
14. What are the signs of *Satori*, Zen awakening?*
15. Are Zen monks like Christian monks or priests; what are they like?*
16. What is a Zen Master called?*
17. Is Zen an escape from life?*
18. Can drink or drugs bring Satori?*
19. What are the characteristics of a Zen Buddhist?*
20. What is easier than knowing about Zen?*
21. Does Zen depend upon IQ and mental ability?*
22. What is the name given to the type of meditation used by Zen Buddhists?*
23. What is the Zen word for the "sitting" in meditation?*
24. Is Zen a religion?*
25. Is Zen atheistic, teaching there is no God or gods?
26. In Zen art, what does "Taming the Ox" signify?*
27. What is the bull a symbol of in Zen art?*
28. What does a herdsman represent in Zen art?*
29. What is one called who claims to be in the direct line of the Buddha's experience and therefore is able to teach it?*
30. Can an arrogant Zen Buddhist be in Satori?*

Sikhs
Baptism of the Sword

1. What does *Sikh* mean?*
2. Who was the founder of the Sikh religion?
3. Where was he born and when did he live; what were his dates of birth and death?*
4. What main belief do Sikhs share with Hindus?
5. What main belief do Sikhs share with Muslims?
6. When does a Sikh boy begin wearing a turban?*
7. What is the Sikh symbol of the Brotherhood?*
8. When were the Sikhs defeated by the British and the Punjab incorporated into British India?*
9. Following the fighting of Sikhs with Muslims and Hindus, when did the Indian government recognise the Punjab as an independent Sikh province?*
10. What additional names are given (a) to all baptised boys and (b) to all baptised girls?*
11. Are infant Sikh children taken to the gurdwara for dedication to the service of God?*
12. How is a Sikh child's name chosen?*
13. Are Sikhs forced to marry partners chosen by their parents?*
14. What is a Sikh place of worship called?
15. What does each Sikh place of worship contain?*
16. What is found outside a Sikh place of worship?*
17. In the Sikh religion, do worshippers stand or sit?*
18. What do Sikhs do after worship?
19. Why do Sikhs after worship invite all, including non-Sikhs, to share their food?*
20. Where do Sikhs believe God is?*
21. Why do Sikhs meditate?*
22. Do Sikhs have priests?*
23. What is the main place of Sikh pilgrimage?*
24. Is this temple on a hill?*
25. What is *Baisakhi*?*
26. What is *Diwali*?*
27. Why does someone wave a *chauri* (a silver sceptre with animal hairs) over the Granth when it is read?*
28. Why do Sikhs teach that they should not cut their hair?
29. In Britain today, about how many Sikhs are there and what is their ratio to Muslims and to West Indians?*
30. To whom does the term *Guru* refer for Sikhs?
31. How many gurdwaras are there in Britain today?*
32. Does a gurdwara contain an altar or statues?*
33. Do Sikhs believe in miracles?*
34. What percentage of the population of India is Sikh?*
35. Do Sikhs eat meat?
36. What are the 5 ks of Sikhism?

Shinto
Let Nature Take its Course

1. What is the Japanese word (transliterated by English letters) for "spirit", "god", "upper" or "above the ordinary"?
2. What is the Japanese word for "the Way of the Gods"?

3. What is the Chinese word for "the Way of the Gods"?
4. When did the Shinto religion begin?*
5. Who was its founder?*
6. How many gods/spirits are to be found in Shintoism?*
7. Does Shintoism have women priests?*
8. Do Shintoists confess "sins"?*
9. What is the *Misogi* (or *Kessai*) rite of purification?*
10. What is the *Harai* (or *Oharai*) rite of purification?*
11. What is a *nusa* (or *Haraigushi*)?*
12. What looks like a hut with an upstairs room with a mirror representing a god, can only be entered by priests, and has a place outside for ceremonial dances?*
13. At a shrine, how do Shinto priests arouse the Kami-spirits?*
14. Do Shintoists carry charms to keep evil spirits away?*
15. Do Shintoists have festivals?*
16. Why do Shintoists hang holly branches and sardine heads outside their homes, and shout, "Come in, good fortune", while throwing beans out of a window?*
17. When was the first Japanese emperor?*
18. With what are the cultic practices of Shintoism preoccupied?*
19. What does a Shinto woman do with some of the first rice cooked each day?*
20. What is *saki*?*
21. Do many Japanese Christians follow the national faith of Shintoism today?*

Taoists
The Way of Acceptance
(The Lowest Road)

1. What is the Chinese word (in English letters) for "Way"?
2. What is the Chinese word for "Power"?
3. What is Chinese for "the Way and its Power"?
4. Who, according to tradition, wrote this "Book of the Way"?
5. When things go well, what do Taoists believe is in control?*
6. When things go badly, what do Taoists believe is in control?*
7. Do Taoists believe that the Way can be taught?*
8. What is the symbol of Taoism?
9. What does *Yin* mean?
10. What does *Yang* mean?
11. Do Taoists believe that your conscience should be your guide?
12. How long is the *Tao Te Ching*?
13. Where can one find information about Yin-Yang?*
14. Do all Taoists practice religious rituals?*
15. What are the two main types of Taoism?*
16. How does Taoist worship reflect Yin-Yang?*
17. What gods are found in most Taoist temples?*
18. Do some Taoists worship other gods, goddesses and even Buddhas and the Jade Emperor?*
19. What is a Taoist temple called?
20. What do many Taoists sacrifice?
21. What do they then do with the sacrifices?
22. What is often burnt within a Taoist temple in honour of ancestors?*

23. What is the "Passing through the Door" ceremony?
24. What is the Dragon Boat Festival?*
25. What is the Festival of the Eighth Moon?*
26. How might a Chinese Taoist family honour a saintly female ancestor?*
27. How might a Taoist priest exorcise an evil spirit and thereby cleanse a temple?*
28. What might a Taoist family use if a Taoist temple was not available?*
29. What is the Taoist symbol of immortality?*
30. Why do many Chinese Taoists walk along under long paper dragons in their festivals?*
31. When was Buddhism introduced into China?
32. How did Buddhism influence Taoism?
33. How did Taoism influence Buddhism?

Confucians
Honour for our Ancestors
(Right Relationships)

1. What are the four main views of life which have influenced Chinese thought?
2. What Eastern religions teach that the basic nature of man is good and not evil?*
3. Which of these "religions" is less a religion than it is a formal ethical system defining personal relationships in an ideal moral order, solidly based on family unity?
4. In what century did Confucius live?
5. What are the Five Virtues taught by Confucius?
6. What are the Five Relationships which Confucius taught must be kept right?
7. Since the time of Confucius 2500 years ago, what has maintained the fabric of Chinese society in spite of times of chaos and disorder?*
8. What relationship did Confucian emperors seek with their subjects?
9. Is Confucius considered to have been a humanist, believing in the nature of man rather than the power of God or gods?
10. What does the name *Confucius* mean?
11. Was Confucius the originator of many teachings?
12. What is *the Classic of Filial* (brotherly) *Piety*?*
13. Do priests have charge of Confucian temples?*
14. What inscription is on the tomb of Confucius?*
15. What words are claimed to be the last of Confucius?*
16. Do Confucian temples contain images of Confucius?
17. What do Chinese mean by "family"?*
18. What did Confucius teach as the source of all goodness?
19. When did China become Communist?*
20. Who is known as the "patron saint of scholars"?*

Bahá'ís
Unity in Diversity
(Peoples of the World Unite!)

1. What is the youngest of the world's religions?*
2. When did it begin?*
3. Where and when did it celebrate the 100th Anniversary of Bahá'u'lláh's all-compelling summons that he was the one foretold by the Báb?
4. Who are the co-founders of the Bahá'í Faith?

5. What does *Bahá'í* mean?*
6. In how many countries are Bahá'ís found today?*
7. Is the Bahá'í Faith a sect of Islam?
8. Who was Sayyid 'Ali-Muhammad?
9. Who was the Báb?
10. What does *Báb* mean?
11. What were the followers of the Báb called?*
12. How were many of the followers of the Báb treated by some in authority in Iran?
13. What effect did the persecution of the Báb and his followers have?*
14. Did any who claimed to be the Báb's followers persecute others?*
15. How did the Báb die?
16. Why was he put to death?*
17. Where was the Báb buried; who chose the site; who built the original shrine; and who extended the structure in the 1930s and the outer superstructure in the 1950s?*
18. Who was Mirza Husayn 'Ali?
19. Where and when was Bahá'u'lláh born?
20. Was Bahá'u'lláh born in poverty or wealth?
21. What does *Bahá'u'lláh* mean?
22. How did he get this name?
23. Where and when did Bahá'u'lláh come to believe that he himself was the Holy One (prophet)?
24. What were among his main interests of study?*
25. Who were called "the Father and Mother of the poor"?*
26. How old was Bahá'u'lláh when he became a follower of the Báb?
27. When did he meet the Báb?
28. Who was the first person to believe in the mission of Bahá'u'lláh?*
29. What does *'Abdu'l-Bahá* mean?*
30. Who was known as "The Master"?*
31. How did 'Abdu'l-Bahá become Head of the Bahá'í Faith?
32. How old was 'Abdu'l-Bahá when his father died?*
33. How many children did he have?*
34. Who said, "My house is the home of laughter and mirth"?*
35. Where was 'Abdu'l-Bahá during the years of 1901–08?*
36. Where, besides Britain, did 'Abdu'l-Bahá personally spread the Bahá'í Faith?
37. What happened to 'Abdu'l-Bahá during the First World War?*
38. Who took Haifa in order to free someone being threatened with crucifixion on Mount Carmel by the Turks?*
39. In recognition of his work for peace, on whom did the British Government confer a knighthood after the First World War?*
40. When, where and how did 'Abdu'l-Bahá die?*
41. What are the twin pillars of the World Order of the Bahá'í Faith as specified in the last Will of 'Abdu'l-Bahá?*
42. Whom did 'Abdu'l-Bahá appoint as "Guardian" of the Bahá'í Faith in his Will and Testament?
43. What principle work, besides leading the movement, was done by the Guardian?*
44. Who were the "Hands of the Cause of God"?*
45. Who succeeded Shoghi Effendi as the Guardian?*
46. What do Bahá'ís believe is the most likely cause of war?*
47. What is the cure for this cause of war?*

159

48. What can lead to the consciousness of the oneness of mankind?*
49. What are the two wings which, if not in conflict, are both necessary to help mankind soar to the heights?
50. How many races do Bahá'ís believe there are?
51. Do Bahá'ís fast?*
52. Do Bahá'ís have ministers or clergy?
53. Are Bahá'ís pacifists?*
54. Can Bahá'ís be married in Scotland without a civil service?*
55. What distinctive clothing do Bahá'ís wear?
56. Do Bahá'ís believe that we are on a collision course with disaster and that there is nothing we can do about it?
57. What are the Bahá'í scriptures called?
58. Into how many languages have its scriptures been translated?*
59. What scriptures are read during a Bahá'í service?*
60. Is there a sermon?*
61. Is there an organ?*
62. Who may worship with Bahá'ís?*
63. How many months are there in the Bahá'í calendar?*
64. When is the Bahá'í New Year?*
65. What precedes the Bahá'í New Year?*
66. What are the democratically elected local assemblies called?*
67. At what age may a boy or girl become a member of the Bahá'í community?*
68. At what age may a Bahá'í vote in a Bahá'í election?*
69. Who may contribute to the Bahá'í Fund?*
70. Where are the shrines of the Báb and Bahá'u'lláh?
71. How many Bahá'ís have been tortured to death?*
72. How many centres of Bahá'í worship are there in the world today?*
73. Is there a Bahá'í Temple in Britain?*
74. What are the distinctive features of a Bahá'í Temple?*
75. What are found around or near a Bahá'í Temple?*
76. Where is the World Centre of the Bahá'í Faith?*
77. Where is the Bahá'í Universal House of Justice?
78. How often is there an election of the members of the Universal House of Justice?*
79. As a Non-Governmental Organisation, is the Bahá'í International Community linked with the United Nations?*

Multiple Choice Test Answers

1: A. 2: E. 3: A. 4: D. 5: E. 6: A. 7: E. 8: C. 9: C. 10: A. 11: E. 12: B. 13: C. 14: A. 15: D.
16: D. 17: B. 18: B. 19: C. 20: C. 21: D. 22: A. 23: B. 24: E. 25: C. 26: A. 27: C. 28: B. 29: C.
30: E. 31: B. 32: A. 33: D. 34: B. 35: B. 36: D. 37: A. 38: E. 39: B. 40: C. 41: E. 42: E. 43: B.
44: B. 45: D. 46: E. 47: C. 48: C. 49: B. 50: D. 51: B. 52: D. 53: E. 54: E. 55: B. 56: D. 57: C.
58: D. 59: C. 60: E. 61: B. 62: A. 63: E. 64: C. 65: D. 66: B. 67: C. 68: C. 69: C. 70: C. 71: E.
72: B. 73: B. 74: E. 75: E. 76: D. 77: A. 78: D. 79: D. 80: D.

Religious Pursuit Answers

Muslims
Submission to the Most High

1: submission (to the will of God). 2: One who has submitted. 3: Highly Praised (is God).
4: Memorizer. 5: 570 CE–632 CE (2 AH). 6: 99 beads to help Muslims remember and reflect on the 99
"Beautiful Names" for God. 7: No. 8: Place of prostration; a dome symbolising the universe and the
dome of faith, four towers (minarets) at the corners of the outer square symbolising the other four Pillars
of Faith, one wall – with a niche (*mihrab*) and pulpit (*minbar*) to its right – faces Mecca. There are no
seats or pews but there may be carpets or rugs on the floor. There are no sculptures or pictures but there
may be writings and patterns on the walls and ceilings. A screen in front of the place for women
separates them off from men. A mosque is used as a school in evenings and as a community centre.
9: Friday, midday prayer; Muslims believe that Allah never needed a rest. 10: About 2 ½ miles per hour.
11: Up to 2500 camels and 200 merchants and guides. 12: 1500 miles. 13: Spices, perfumes, dried fruit,
silk, cereals, edible oils, etc. 14: Severe heat of the day, bitter cold of the night, wild animals, and
bandits. 15: Anno Hijra (Arabic for "breaking old trees" or "migration"); 1420 AH. 16: Almost the
length of the New Testament. 17: *In the name of God, the Compassionate, the Merciful*; because the
Koran is about the teachings and identity of God. 18: Over a million. 19: *Successor*. 20: Because a
Muslim does not follow and obey Muhammad but God, who alone is to be worshipped; one who calls a
Muslim a "*Muhammadan*" shows his own ignorance of the main belief of Islam. 21: *Festival of the
breaking of the Fast*, the end of Ramadan; a joyful occasion with special foods, the giving of presents
and wearing new clothes. 22: *Festival of Sacrifice*, an animal is sacrificed to recall the substitute for
Abraham's child. 23: *Birthday of the Prophet*, to recall Muhammad's life and teachings. 24: *New Year*,
the day Muhammad left Mecca for Medina. 25: Because Muslims believe that all children are born free
of sin. 26: In the clothes in which they made their pilgrimage. 27: Small pieces of glass, pottery or
wood, etc., arranged in a pattern. 28: Visit to a holy place. 29: *Declaration of Truth*, the CREED.
30: *Regular Worship/Prayer*, PRAYER. 31: *Purification*, CHARITY. 32: *Fasting*, FASTING.
33: *Pilgrimage*, PILGRIMAGE. 34: The One, Creator, Knower, Hearer, Forgiver, Very Patient, Guide,
Protector, Provider, Answerer of Prayer, Merciful, Judge, etc. 35: *Read out loud/recite*.

Hindus
Reverence for Life

1: To Hinduism/Hindu and to India/Indian. 2: Brahman. 3: Brahma. 4: Brahmin. 5: A guru.
6: Shishya. 7: Maya. 8: Yogin. 9: Karma. 10: Bad karma in the last life. 11: No, it migrates from one
body to another. (Samsara means "to flow together, transmigration".) 12: The transmigration of the *jiva*
(soul) to another body. 13: Your position in this life has been determined by the quality of your last life
(how good or bad you were then). It is irrelevant whether you receive now more or less than what you
deserve for this present life since your real reward/punishment comes in the next one. 14: No, you
determine your own fate; there is no such thing as good or bad luck. Each person sets his own destiny in
his next life by the quality of his *karma* (works) in his present life. 15: That she is married. 16: The
Hindu wife. 17: By the husband at his wedding, as part of his marriage vow. 18: Because it is
considered a release from this life of illusion to a new and better life. 19: Burnt (cremated) on a pyre
(pile) of wood with the ashes put in a cloth. 20: Benares; in the Ganges River with the hope of going

161

directly to Brahman. **21**: In his next life he/she will be reborn: as a dog, donkey or bull; or a thousand times as a spider or snake. **22**: No, they believe instead that life in this world is the testing and developing place for the soul. **23**: Sanskrit. **24**: *Varna*, meaning "colour". **25**: *Mandir*. **26**: The cow, the symbol of all creation. **27**: Sitting bare to the waist with legs crossed in front of him, facing the East, the direction of the rising sun. Usually alone, whether in the worship room of his house or even when in a temple. Often beginning with the Mother of the Vedas: *"OM…"*. He may use prayer beads or meditate on a single sentence. He may offer flowers or food to the god. **28**: No, they understand these images to be only symbols of the spirit. **29**: Vishnu. **30**: The three aspects of his nature: creator, sustainer, destroyer. **31**: No, it is Muslim. **32**: Kali. **33**: Related to Greek and Latin and written left to right (unlike Hebrew and Arabic). The letters are squarish with a line along the top. **34**: Among the oldest of Hindu scriptures, a collection of over 1000 hymns sung by priests while offering sacrifices to the gods of the Aryan tribes who invaded India about 1500 BCE. **35**: *Sit down near*, a collection of discussions between Hindu gurus and disciples. **36**: The *Way of Yoga*, a yoking control of mind and body. **37**: Yes, the *Way of Devotion* as explained in the *Bhagavad-Gita*, the *Gita* (song) of the Lord, through the incarnation of Krishna. **38**: *Kali-ghat*, the "steps of *Kali*", the Mother goddess. **39**: Black, identifying a manifestation of god with dark-skinned Indian people. **40**: Brahman. **41**: Monism. **42**: Modified Pantheism. **43**: From 1857–1947, when India gained its independence and Muslims in the North were allowed to form their own state of Pakistan. **44**: Mantras. **45**: Many types, some simple and some complex, some polytheistic (belief in many gods) and some monotheistic (belief in one God). Hinduism does not refer to a single group of beliefs and practices. **46**: Anyone who is born into (or has chosen to go into) the traditional Indian pattern of society, with its variety of beliefs and practices and has not chosen a different pattern (*i.e.* by becoming a Christian or a Muslim). **47**: There was no single prophet or founder, but a variety of sages and holy men who laid its foundation in writing from about 1500 BCE but with traditions going back to Primal Man. **48**: Older than its sacred writings which date to the Aryan invasion of 1500 BCE; as old as India or Primal Man. In this sense, no religion could be older. **49**: Their land and its common source of cultural practices and also the writing of the *Ramayana* and *Mahabharata*, a common literature. **50**: Meditation, the Way from bondage to Samsara. **51**: It has none. **52**: *Atman*. **53**: Because they all contain Atman. **54**: To show that he has knowledge of all things in the universe. **55**: *Vishnu*. **56**: *Shiva*. **57**: A central shrine containing the image of a god on the west end, and with a tall tower above, perhaps symbolic of a sacred mountain. In front is an assembly hall. The entrance is on the east side towards the rising sun. Below steps is the statue of a bird or animal on which the god rides. A pool for ritual bathing may be nearby. **58**: Yes, and they must bathe and put on clean clothes before they move from the hall into the shrine room. **59**: He worships *Vishnu* if he has three vertical lines on his forehead and he worships *Shiva* if he has three horizontal lines there. **60**: He puts the right foot on the ground first, saying a prayer acknowledging the creation; cleans his teeth and tongue; has a bath and then eats breakfast and says prayers. **61**: *Gayatri Mantra*: *"OM…; let us meditate upon the light of Savitri, the radiant sun; may it stimulate our mind."* **62**: A *mala*. **63**: *Puja*. **64**: A nine day festival to *Durga/Kali*, the divine symbol of motherhood, in September or October. Fireworks and sparklers. Effigies of the demon *Ravana* are burnt. **65**: Festival of Light: a four day festival in October or November (the New Moon), marking the end of the old year, beginning the New Year. Celebration of the victory of light over darkness. Bright lights and decorations, wearing new clothes. Presents are given and greeting cards are sent. **66**: Dancing through the night to *Shiva*. **67**: Spring Festival: a five day festival in late February or early March to celebrate the Spring harvest and the season of love. Stories of *Rama*, the god of love, and *Krishna* are dramatised. Coloured water is thrown over everyone for fun, recalling the story of Krishna teasing the milkmaids. **68**: Celebration of *Rama's* birthday in March or April with an image of Rama carried around. **69**: Krishna's Birthday Festival. **70**: "To flow together/ transmigration", cycle of rebirth. **71**: Release from Samsara.

Theravada Buddhism
The Small Raft (The Southern Way)

1: Buddhism, about 500 million. **2**: Theravada (the "Elder's Way/Raft/Vehicle"), Mahayana (the "Large Raft") and Zen. **3**: Burma, Thailand, Tibet and Laos. **4**: Ceylon. **5**: About 60%. **6**: Hinduism. **7**: Yes, during the reign of emperor Asoka, in the third century BCE. **8**: Literally, "Awakened One" or "Enlightened One", from *budh* meaning "to awake". **9**: Siddhartha Gautama. **10**: *c.* 563 and *c.* 483 BCE.

11: Near Kapilavastu, 100 miles north of Benares, in Nepal. **12**: Signs in the sky, miraculous healings and earthquakes. **13**: That as an infant he spoke in a lion's voice, "I am the chief in the world; this is my last birth." **14**: Yashodara. **15**: an old man, a sick man, a dead man (representing suffering) and then a monk (representing the peace that a Hindu monk could receive). **16**: Under a Bo tree (symbolising the tree of knowledge) at Bodh-Gaya, near a tributary of the Ganges River. **17**: In Benares. **18**: Legend states that his son became a monk and his wife at least desired to follow his teachings. **19**: 80 years old. **20**: Rebirth; *karma*; the world as a place of sorrow; and renunciation of earthly passion as the way to wisdom and enlightenment. **21**: In Sri Lanka (Ceylon), in the first century BCE. (based on third century BCE oral tradition) in the Pali language. **22**: Because they respect all life and do not kill animals. **23**: Monkeys, from Hindu mythology: monkeys formed a bridge to help Rama rescue his wife from a demon who had carried her off to an island. **24**: No, man has no soul to spiritually link with God, gods or any supernatural power. **25**: Karma. **26**: Dharma, simply stated and illustrated by stories and parables. **27**: No, Buddhism rejects any form of caste system. **28**: Nothing; he taught that true happiness comes through man controlling his own mind which is not a gift from God or gods nor does it come through any form of worship. **29**: A reclining Buddha. **30**: Nirvana, from *va* meaning "blow", as to blow out the fire (of greed), the cessation of pain. **31**: The right hand pointing downward. **32**: Above all he must set an example of the Buddhist way of life, pointing towards Nirvana. Mahayana monks also might officiate at funerals, perform ceremonies in the temples of monasteries and provide the religious education for youth. **33**: None – except a yellow (orange in Mandalay) robe, a begging (alms) bowl for food, a needle, a string of 108 beads used when meditating on the qualities of Buddha, a razor to keep his head shaved, a filter for straining insects from water (so that even in his drinking he causes no suffering). **34**: Some are (in Korea and Japan), but most are celibate. **35**: Usually, because this is implied by the rule against harming any living thing. **36**: Shave the head and eyebrows, give up all belongings, take vows of chastity (except in Korea and Japan), eat only what is put in one's alms bowl, beg only in silence, diligent meditation and study, live in a monastery, wear a yellow robe and go barefoot or wear sandals. **37**: Monasteries. **38**: The yellow cloth is wrapped around the body leaving the right arm and shoulder uncovered. **39**: Monks, offering herbal remedies. **40**: Staying in a monastery (normally during the rainy season), meditating, studying the Dhamma, travelling, teaching, serving as a schoolmaster or doctor and reciting sayings to aid health, the harvest, etc. **41**: Standing, sitting or reclining; and the positions of the hands depict aspects of Buddha's teachings. **42**: Many Buddhists believe that the larger the statue the more effective a visit to it will be. **43**: Strength comes from the earth. **44**: Buddha giving a blessing. **45**: Teaching positions. **46**: Thinking position; tradition claims that Buddha used this form when he sat under the Bo tree. **47**: The position in which it is believed that Gautama the Buddha died. **48**: To remind them of the Buddha's teachings. **49**: The Sangha (meaning "assembly"). **50**: The Sangha. **51**: No, though they may meditate (including in front of statues of Buddha). **52**: No, these are unimportant to a Buddhist. However, a Theravada priest might be invited to recite a "Buddha-word" in the house to bless a new-born child, at a marriage or at a funeral. **53**: They do not believe that Buddha is God nor that there are any immortal gods. **54**: Theravada Buddhists do not worship at all (they do not believe in God/gods); their meditation is as individuals. They bow before the Buddha, kneel, and prostrate themselves – their palms on their foreheads, saying the "Three Jewels". **55**: Lasting 3 days in May, it commemorates the birth and enlightenment of Buddha with decorations in homes and streets, and presents are given to monks and those in need. The beginning of the Buddhist year. **56**: During New Year, water is splashed on people as floats pass by, as in the Hindu Festival of Holi; but here the water refers to cooling Brahma's head when it was cut off by a king – note the legacy of Hinduism. **57**: One says, "Adoration to Buddha, the Blessed One, the Worthy One, the Fully Enlightened One." One faces a statue of Buddha, incense is offered and one says words of confession (including for sins in past lives), acknowledging that they were due to greed, anger and ignorance, and resolving not to commit them again; and then one says the Three Refuges and accepts the Five Precepts. **58**: A yogin. **59**: Yes, see *Buddhist Scriptures* (Penguin paperback, pp. 116–21), to find the form most suited to you. **60**: No. **61**: To Ceylon, Burma, and Thailand (Theravada) and to Tibet, Mongolia, Korea, China and Japan (Mahayana). **62**: When their heads have just been shaved, for protection from the sun. **63**: Yes. **64**: Northern India, for 45 years. **65**: The *Pali Canon, in Ceylon.* **66**: Of no person; it is not a name but is Sanskrit for "fully enlightened"; a description and not a name. **67**: No, they have bad karma; they therefore desire to have sons who can become monks. **68**: No, it is reached only by your own right living (following the Five Precepts, etc.); it is "do-it-yourself": your acts of merit can hasten the moment of Nirvana's arrival. **69**: Yes, salvation is seen as coming through one's own actions and not through a God or gods. **70**: "Monks"; in some countries (like Thailand and Burma) almost all male Buddhists spend at least several weeks as monks as part of their education. **71**: Yes, but less likely; women are not considered to be second class or inferior. **72**: Because of bad karma (deeds) in previous lives. **73**: Human greed which leads to violence. **74**: Get rid of greed. **75**: No, cremation. **76**: Yes, U Thant. **77**: The Three Refuges: "I seek the refuge of Buddha; I seek the refuge of the Dharma (the law); I seek the refuge of the Sangha (the order of monks)." **78**: By putting his fists together with the thumbs pointing towards each other. **79**: From the bottom up: rectangle=earth, then the oval=air, then the circle=fire, then the horizontal line=water, and on top the vertical line=wisdom.

Mahayana Buddhism
The Large Raft (The Northern Way)

1: Superstition, magic, fortune-telling, the reverence towards images in temples, and numerous miracles. **2**: Sutras, considered by Mahayana Buddhists to be sacred. **3**: A Mahayana festival for the dead, with offerings made to the dead and lighted candles placed in paper boats to guide their spirits. **4**: The Dalai Lama, considered to be the reincarnation of Kwanyin, the Being of Compassion in the Lotus Scriptures. **5**: "Hail to the Jewel of the Lotus." **6**: Standing, sitting or reclining on their hands. **7**: About 90%. **8**: Secondary schools. **9**: About 100 volumes, totalling perhaps 200 times the length of the Christian Bible; but unlike the Bible, it is written entirely in highly stylised form, much of which is in verse. **10**: Taoism and Confucianism. **11**: Shintoism. **12**: Bodhisattva. **13**: In Buddhist monasteries. **14**: A form of Mahayana: "Pure Land" Buddhists who worship Amida Buddha, Lord of the Western Paradise.

Zen Buddhism
The Way of Meditation

1: About 50%, of whom most are Zen Buddhists. **2**: More than 12. **3**: Rinzai and Soto. **4**: Bodhidharma (sixth century CE in China), though Zen originated with Gautama the Buddha. **5**: From *Ch'an* (Chinese) which is from *Dhyana* (Sanskrit): *Zen* means "meditation". **6**: *Satori*. **7**: Confucianism and Taoism. **8**: No. **9**: Neither; his mind. **10**: No, one can only experience it. **11**: Neither; they are reciprocal, each spilling over into the other. **12**: "That's it." **13**: Cycles of rebirth. **14**: Increasing serenity, a sense of flow, and the feeling that things are right (with achievement and security becoming unimportant). **15**: No, they take no vows (are not "set apart"), do not officiate at worship (there is none), they usually marry, are free to leave a monastery whenever they wish, and are not considered mediators between man and God (in whom they do not believe). **16**: The *Roshi*. **17**: No, an escape into it, a new way of experiencing it. **18**: No, they cloud the mind, blocking *Satori*. This is the reason Buddhists do not use alcohol or drugs. **19**: Humility, humour, poverty, highly motivated but without selfish ambitions (for wealth, honours, praise), tolerant non-dogmatic, joyful, open-minded, often smiling and laughing. **20**: **Feeling** it. **21**: No, it has to do with character. **22**: *Zazen*. **23**: *Za*. **24**: Yes, if religion is defined as something that can give meaning to life. No, if religion is defined as belief in God or gods or as something with a ritual or dogma. **25**: No, it simply avoids theological arguments and presses for an ultimate All-ness, of which everyone is part. **26**: Since the twelfth century it has represented "Satori". **27**: The mind. **28**: A yogin, one who meditates. **29**: A Zen Master. **30**: No, because *Satori* means **self-less** enlightenment.

Sikhs
Baptism of the Sword

1: From Sanskrit *S'ishya*, meaning "disciple". **2**: *Guru* ("spiritual teacher") Nanak. **3**: Near Lahore (now called *Nankana Sahib*) in Punjab; 1469–1534. **4**: Re-incarnation. **5**: God is one. **6**: As soon as he can tie one. **7**: The turban. **8**: In 1850. **9**: In 1966. **10**: a) Singh, Guru Gobind's family name (meaning "Lion"); and (b) *Kaur* ("princess"). **11**: Yes. **12**: It must begin with the first letter of the first verse on the page appearing when the Granth is opened at random. **13**: No, though the parents often advise. **14**: The *gurdwara* (the "house of the guru", referring to God as *Guru* and to the *Guru Granth*, the Sikh Scriptures). **15**: The Granth (also found in an upstairs room in a Sikh home and read every day), a drum and harmonium and a stringed instrument (*sitar*), and a community kitchen (*langar*). **16**: A flag with the Sikh symbol and the words *ik oanker* ("God is one Being") are painted on the front. **17**: Sit. **18**: They have a common meal together. Non-Sikhs are welcome. **19**: To show that all are equal before God. **20**: Within every person. **21**: To search for God within themselves. **22**: No, any man or woman can lead worship. **23**: The Golden Temple at Amritsar, the centre of the Sikh faith. **24**: No, on low land. One must walk steps down to it, symbolising humility. **25**: The Sikh New Year Festival on 13 April, to celebrate the beginning of the summer season and the birthday of Sikhism (when in 1699 Gobind Singh established the *Khalsa*). In 1919 British troops killed or wounded over 2000 Sikhs who refused to disperse. **26**: The Hindu Festival of Light used by Sikhs as a Festival of Freedom to celebrate the release of Guru Har Gobind, by the Muslims. **27**: As a sign of respect for its authority and to keep the flies away from the reader. **28**: Because strength lies in their hair (acknowledging the story of Samson in Judges 6), because Buddha, Jesus and Muhammad had long hair and because it is useful living tissue (it absorbs solar energy and contains much vitamin D). **29**: 250,000; 2:1 and 3:1. **30**: It is limited to the spiritual guides and revealers of truth of Guru Nanak and his 9 successors. Only in Sikh Scriptures is it used of God himself and more generally of religious teachers. **31**: Over 80. **32**: No. Besides worship, it is used as a social centre and has a communal kitchen attached. **33**: No. **34**: 2%. **35**: Yes, although since grain is much more available in the Punjab, there is little tradition of eating meat except at weddings and feasts. Meat is never cooked in the free kitchen. **36**: *Kesh* (uncut hair and beard), *Kangha* (comb), *Kara* (steel wrist band), *Kaccha* (short trousers), *Kirpan* (sword).

Shintoists
Let Nature Take its Course

1: *Kami*. **2**: *Kami no Michi*. **3**: *Shinto* (*Shen-Tao*). **4**: *c.* 650 BCE, although some of its practices date back to 1000 BCE and its writings did not appear until *c.* 800 CE. **5**: No founder. **6**: About 8 million *Kami*. **7**: Yes; there are over 15,000 men and about 500 women Shinto priests. **8**: No, they have rites of purification which they believe make confession unnecessary. **9**: A Shinto ceremony performed by oneself – *i.e.* self-denial of large meals or meat, bathing in cold water, meditation in an awkward, uncomfortable position, unlike most forms of yoga. **10**: A Shinto ceremony performed for one by a priest – *i.e.* waving a *nusa* (*haraigushi*) back and forth over a house or car to make it safe. **11**: A purifying wand with paper and flax streamers. **12**: A Shinto shrine, called a *jinja*, literally meaning a "Kami-house". **13**: By clapping their hands. **14**: Usually. **15**: Yes, using drama and worship. **16**: To usher in the spring, the *Setsubun* Festival. **17**: *c.* 660 BCE. **18**: Purity and cleanliness, symbolised by a mirror. **19**: She places it on the god-shelf. **20**: Wine made from rice. **21**: Yes; also many Japanese Buddhists follow the national faith of Shinto.

Taoists
The Way of Acceptance (The Lowest Road)

1: *Tao*. **2**: *Te*. **3**: *Tao Te Ching*. **4**: *Lao Tzu*, sometimes spelled *Lao-tze*. **5**: *Yang*. **6**: *Yin*. **7**: No, each person must find it for himself. **8**: Two parts of a circle: Yin the dark part – blue or black – and Yang, the light part – white or red. **9**: Literally, the "dark side" (of a mountain), the shadow, darkness of winter, the power that brings softness, moisture, change – feminine. **10**: Literally, the "sunny side" (of a mountain), brightness of summer, the power that brings firmness, dryness and solidity – all that is masculine. **11**: No; and unlike Shintoists, Taoists believe that one should let nature take its course. **12**: Only about 5000 words. **13**: From the *Book of Chuang Tzu*, written around the third century BCE, perhaps about the same time as *Tao Te Ching*. **14**: No, not the *Tao Chia* type. **15**: *Tao Chia*, using the Power (*Te*) which comes to one who adapts himself to Yin-Yang; and *Tao Chiao*, using religious practices, priestly rituals and magic to encounter *Tao Chun*, the Lord of the Earth, who directs Yin-Yang. **16**: Coming from opposite directions, two assistants of the Taoist Master will alternate their singing as they approach the sacred ground, illustrating how Yin and Yang alternatively dominate nature. **17**: The supreme god, *San-tsing* (the trinity/three pure ones). The three forms are *Yuh-Hwang Shang-ti*, creator and source of truth; *Wan-chang*, the god of education and learning; and *Lao Tzu*, the founder of Taoism who was deified – made a god – after his death. **18**: Yes. **19**: A *kuan*. Its walls are designed to keep out evil spirits. The gateway is usually guarded by two large stone lions. **20**: Rice, fruits, cakes, vegetables and even cows. **21**: They eat the offerings; the gods only absorb the essence. **22**: Incense is burnt, and perhaps also candles, money and even chickens. **23**: An annual celebration up to the age of 16 by which a person goes through an archway (of heavy paper) about 2 metres high and a metre across, set up by

Taoist priests. Noise is made with songs and trumpet sounds calling on gods to protect the one passing through. Rice is offered as sacrifice. All the family, holding candles, follow through the archway as a priest chases away evil spirits with his sword. **24**: A small boat is made of paper, with figures lining the sides to form a guard of honour. The festival boat is burnt allowing the gods to be transported back to their heavens. **25**: A Taoist festival. **26**: By gathering in a temple, on the anniversary of the ancestor's birthday, placing offerings of incense, flowers, fruit and tea on a table and having a robed Taoist priest call on their patron goddess to invoke blessings on their ancestor. **27**: In ceremonial dress, holding a sword in his right hand and a small metal bowl of water in his left hand, he takes water into his mouth and spits it out to purify the atmosphere. **28**: Use a Buddhist temple or meet elsewhere. **29**: The peach. **30**: To drive away evil spirits. **31**: In the first century CE by Chinese traders and merchants carrying silk to western markets through India. "Pure Land" Buddhists and Zen (*Ch'an*) Buddhists are the two main types in China. **32**: Pure Land Buddhists brought temple worship and cultic practices to Taoism. **33**: An early form of Taoism (without cultic practices) helped with the development of Zen Buddhism.

Confucians
Honour for our Ancestors (Right Relationships)

1: Buddhism, Taoism, Confucianism and Communism. **2**: Buddhism, Taoism and Confucianism have no concept of original sin. **3**: Confucianism. **4**: Sixth century BCE. **5**: *Jen*, love and compassion; *Yi*, justice; *Li*, right observation of ritual showing respect for ancestors; *Chih*, knowledge of the Tao of Heaven; and *Ch'i*, Sincerity. **6**: Father/son; elder brother/younger brother; husband/wife; elder friends/younger friends; rulers/subjects. **7**: Solidarity of the family. **8**: That of father to children. **9**: Yes. **10**: Grand Master K'ung (*K'ung Fu-tzu*). **11**: No, he claimed to be a transmitter, not a creator. **12**: The basic scripture of Confucian ethics. **13**: No, they are under the control of scholars called "mandarins". **14**: "Confucius, the Primal Sage". **15**: "The great mountain must fall. The strong timber is broken. The wise man fades as does the plant." **16**: No, only tablets inscribed with his name. **17**: All ancestors living and dead, as well as all in the household. **18**: Heaven (*Shang Ti* or *T'ien*). **19**: 1949. **20**: Confucius. Daily sacrifices were made to him in Chinese schools.

Bahá'ís
Unity in Diversity (Peoples of the World Unite!)

1: The Bahá'í Faith. **2**: Two hours and eleven minutes after sunset on 22nd May, 1844, when the Báb made his Declaration; the Bahá'í calendar dates from *Naw-Ruz*, 1844. **3**: In London in 1963. **4**: The Báb and Bahá'u'lláh. **5**: "Followers of the prophet Bahá'u'lláh". **6**: About 350 countries, territories and major island groups. **7**: No, it is as distinct from Islam as Islam is from Christianity and as Christianity is from Judaism. One should not use the term "Bahá'í-ist" for the same reason as one should not use the term "Muhammadan": to do so implies the worship of a person. **8**: A descendent of the Prophet Muhammad whom Bahá'ís call, the *Báb* ("Gate"). **9**: He claimed to be the gate to a new age of peace and universal brotherhood; and he was the one who announced the coming of a greater messenger who would further prepare the way for uniting the world in universal brotherhood. **10**: It is Arabic for "Gate". **11**: *Bábis*, "followers of the Gate". **12**: By persecution: cruel torture and slaughter. **13**: It dramatically increased the number of followers. **14**: Yes, two (perhaps misguided by despair) attempted to assassinate the Shah, in the same way as demented Christians blamed Jews for the death of Jesus. This led to massacres of the Bábis (followers of the Báb). **15**: After imprisonment, by a firing squad: at noon on 9 July, 1850, in Tabriz. **16**: Because he taught that Islamic laws and ceremonies concerning prayer, fasting, inheritance, marriage, divorce, etc. needed to be revised: Muslims believe that Muhammad was the "Seal of the Prophets" and therefore anyone who claims that there can be subsequent divine revelation is considered to be a blasphemer and a heretic. **17**: On Mount Carmel – Bahá'u'lláh; 'Abdu'l-Bahá; and Shoghi Effendi. **18**: The son of a leading minister at the court of the Shah; he came to be known as Bahá'u'lláh. **19**: In Tehran, Persia (Iran) on 12th November, 1817. **20**: Extreme wealth of a noble family. **21**: It is Arabic for "the Glory of God". **22**: It was a name mentioned by the Báb. **23**: In the "Black Pit" dungeon of Tehran, in 1852; he publicly declared his mission there in 1863. **24**: Islam, Iranian literature and calligraphy. **25**: Bahá'u'lláh and his wife, by how they shared their wealth. **26**: 27 years old. **27**: He never did except through correspondence. **28**: 'Abdu'l-Bahá, his eldest son (age 9), after Bahá'u'lláh had been in prison. **29**: "The servant of *Baha*" ("the Splendour of God"). **30**: *'Abdu'l-Bahá*, by his father.

31: By his father's Will and Testament. **32**: Age 48. **33**: Nine, of whom five died young. **34**: 'Abdu'l-Bahá. **35**: In prison in 'Akka, near Haifa. **36**: By way of Egypt, throughout Europe and North America. **37**: He was a prisoner of the Turks, but he spent his time setting up agricultural projects near Tiberias to provide wheat for the people of Palestine. **38**: General Allenby, who then cabled London, *"Have today taken Palestine. Notify the world that 'Abdu'l-Bahá is safe."* **39**: 'Abdu'l-Bahá: he accepted the honour but never used the title. **40**: On 28 November, 1921, in Haifa, Israel, following years of imprisonment, and then liberation by General Allenby. **41**: One, a Guardian of the Faith with authority for interpreting scripture; and two, an elected Universal House of Justice to make decisions on all other matters. **42**: Shoghi Effendi Rabbani, his eldest grandson, then 24 and a student at Balliol College, Oxford. **43**: Considerable writing, of which about a million words have been published, including a history of the First Bahá'í Century. Further, he translated Bahá'í literature from Persian and Arabic into English. **44**: Bahá'ís without administrative duties, appointed by the Guardian to help guide the faith. **45**: No one; he had no children and the Universal House of Justice could find no way to make an appointment. **46**: Prejudice (of religion, race, class and nation) which creates division and hatred. **47**: Consciousness of the oneness of mankind which alone can lead to that unity essential for destroying prejudice. **48**: Universal education so that everyone can make an independent search for truth and open-mindedness; so that no one believes that he alone is right and everyone else is wrong. **49**: Religion and science, together devoid of superstition and materialism. **50**: One, the human race. **51**: Yes, those in good health and aged 15–70 fast from sunrise to sunset each day from 2nd–20th March. **52**: No; every Bahá'í is a Bahá'í teacher by what he says and does each day of his life. **53**: No, but they seek to find peaceful solutions and to be peacemakers. **54**: Yes; in 1978, Parliament approved the appointment of Bahá'í Marriage Officers. **55**: None. **56**: No; mankind is on the threshold of the age of peace. He can do many things to hasten it and to counteract the delaying action of injustice, ignorance, war and disunity. **57**: There are many collections, including *The Book of Certitude, The Hidden Words* and *The Seven Valleys* written by Bahá'u'lláh. **58**: In over 670. **59**: Selections from the scriptures of any religion may be used. **60**: No; nor is any administrative activity permitted in the House of Worship itself. **61**: No, nor any musical instrument; but music of all religions can be sung. **62**: Anyone, regardless of his religious beliefs, cultural background, nationality or race. **63**: 19 months of 19 days each with 4 (or 5) extra days to bring the 361 days into line with the lunar calendar (and Leap Year). **64**: The Winter Equinox, 21st March, called *Baha*, Arabic for the "Splendour" (of God). **65**: The 19 days of fasting, during the 19th month of *Sultan*, Arabic for "Sovereignty". The months are named after qualities of God. **66**: Spiritual Assemblies. **67**: Age 15, though he/she may be registered as a Bahá'í by his/her parents as a child or infant. **68**: Age 21. **69**: Only Bahá'ís; they do not solicit funds from non-Bahá'ís. **70**: Near Acre, around the coast from Haifa and by Mount Carmel. Nearby is the World Administrative Headquarters of the Bahá'í Faith and the Universal House of Justice, its supreme governing body. Bahá'ís also make pilgrimages to many places scared to the memory of the Founders of Judaism, Christianity and Islam. **71**: Thousands. **72**: Over 100,000, but there are only a few Temples. **73**: Not yet. There are 6 completed so far – in America, Uganda, Germany, Australia, Panama City and Samoa. (The King of Samoa is a Bahá'í.) One for India is under construction and others are being planned. **74**: A mixture of Roman and Muslim architecture (arches and a dome); it has 9 sides – symbolic of wholeness and unity and all-inclusiveness, as 9 includes all other digits. **75**: Beautiful gardens and extra buildings, with more being constructed. The Wilmette Temple outside Chicago already has a Home for the Aged and nearby is the Bahá'í Headquarters for the USA. Projects include a hospital, hospice, and a home for orphans. The House of Worship is the centre out of which develop social, educational and humanitarian needs; but it is only used for worship. **76**: Haifa, near Acre. **77**: On Mount Carmel. **78**: Every 5 years. **79**: Yes, it has permanent representatives at the UN headquarters in New York, and in Geneva, and with the UN Environment Programme (UNEP) in Nairobi. It has full consultative status with the UN Economic and Social Council (ECOSOC) and the UN International Children's Emergency Fund (UNICEF). It is represented on the UN Offices of Public Information (OPI). Bahá'ís co-operate with the UN to achieve World Peace, universal human rights and full economic and social development of all peoples and nations. Bahá'ís believe that many of their fundamental beliefs are reflected in the UN's *Universal Declaration of Human Rights* and the *Declaration of the Rights of the Child.*

167

Appendix
To use the book within a group situation

It has been assumed throughout that the reader is interested in the book from a personal, singular point of view. However, by noting the following guidelines, the book can quite easily be adapted for group use – either school, university, community or, on a more personal level, between two or three individuals. For most chapters, a pen and notebook should be available.

The questions both before and after the chapters may be answered either orally or on paper. Many may be converted into group discussions or debates.

For specific use in a group in a school or college course, see "For Class Use" in the Preface. Some teachers will want to see and mark the notebook for continuous assessment of preparation and note-taking skills.

Ancient Views of the Universe

Props: Improvised costumes and anything that helps to identify the characters.
Setting: The cast should be sitting at the front of the group in a semi-circle on both sides of the narrator. Stand when you speak, and speak clearly so that all can hear.
Instructions: All listening carefully, taking notes under the headings of "Cave Dweller", "Ancient Egyptian", etc. Write down questions as well as information and comments in preparation for the discussion at the end.

Primal Man: The First Peacemaker

"Da a dada": this chant can either be performed in unison or some other repetitive form.

Ancient Egyptians: All Men are Created Equal

Things to do:
Draw a picture of the Ancient Egyptian view of the universe and briefly explain it to others in your own words. To what extent do you believe that a person's view of the universe can affect his view of life and its value?

Ancient Babylonians: The First United Nations?

Things to do:
Assume that you desire peace and justice. Also, imagine that you are an Ancient Babylonian and that you believe you have a god or goddess who is a personal representative for you in a heavenly council. Write a letter to him or her.

Project:
Begin a project on the United Nations. Begin collecting articles, pamphlets and literature about the UN. Make up a poster.

Ancient Hebrews: Land of Hope and Glory

The introductory question can be used within groups as well as individuals.

Things to do:
1. Draw a picture of the Ancient Hebrew view of the universe and briefly explain it in your own words.
2. Under the title "A Year to Remember", write as if you were an Ancient Hebrew to explain why 539 BCE was such a year.

Early Views of Education

Props: Improvised costumes and anything that helps to identify the characters (i.e. the Ancient Roman might wear a toga with a purple band, and around his neck a leather, hollow disk).
Setting and Instructions: the same as before.
A discussion should follow the role play.

Things to do:
Write an essay entitled "One view of Education", in which you examine one of the views of education mentioned in terms of its value for today.

Ancient Greeks: All Things in Moderation

Group discussion following the initial questions:
a. Where do you agree with others in your group? Where do you disagree? Why?
b. Which quotation strikes you as most significant? Why?

Things to do:
Write a short essay entitled "All things in moderation", referring to the Ancient Greeks and also to your life today.

Ancient Romans: Pax Romana

Things to do:
Write an essay "Pax Romana", explaining the relationship between the Roman view of religion and peace, and the extent to which you believe that it offered real peace.

Qumran Community: Ancient Voices Cry from the Wilderness

Additional question to introductory questions:
With which of the above is your verdict different from the majority in the group? Can you justify your minority view?

Things to do:
1. Compile together for a school a brief *Manual of Discipline* which you would like to think might be dug up in 2000 years time. Seal it in a container and bury it.
2. Write a short essay with the title "A day in my life at Qumran".

Christians: Do Unto Others

Additional tasks at the beginning of the chapter:

1. Bring to the group a newspaper or magazine clipping that shows at least one of the involvements as outlined in Q4b by a group of Christians.
2. Create two columns on a sheet of paper: use as a heading for the left one, *Things I know about Christianity;* and use as a heading for the right one, *questions I have about Christianity.* Using three horizontal lines, divide the double page into four sections and identify them as *Church, Bible, Life of Jesus* and *Teachings of Jesus.* Take about ten minutes to fill in the eight categories with as many statements as you can. For example, the four categories on the left might respectively begin: Mother Teresa worked among the poor in Calcutta... There are four Gospels... Jesus was baptised in the Jordan River... Blessed are the poor in spirit for theirs is the kingdom of heaven.
3. a. *Where do we come from? What are we? Where are we going? How do we get there?* Write brief notes to your own personal answers to these four questions.
   b. Why do you believe others give different answers to these questions? How do you think they might differ?
4. a. Write brief notes to the answers (to the four questions) which you initially believe are given by Christianity.
   b. Why do you believe various Christians might give differing answers?
   c. Why do people who agree on where they want to go, often disagree on how to get there?

Additional questions and tasks for the end of the chapter:

1. Further to the introduction of the chapter, how do your views compare with those of others in your group?
2. Make a poster with the clippings that have been brought (see additional task above and Q4b.)
3. Write a short essay entitled 'A day in my life in the early church'.

Muslims: Submission to the Most High

Things to do:
Write an essay entitled "A Day in my life as a Muslim".

The Eastern Search for Unity

At the end of this role play, the Buddhist and Zen-Buddhist monks can go around the group collecting food (they are forbidden to handle money) in their bowls. What are your reactions to this role-play?

Hindus: Reverence for Life

Additional questions to ask after this chapter:
Should school assemblies be expressions of tolerance reflecting the variety of views held by pupils and teachers? If so, give specific recommendations for changes and give specific suggestions for content. Put these in writing and give them to those who are in charge of the assemblies.

Things to do:
1. Write notes on the important qualities of Hinduism.

2. Write an essay entitled "A day in my life as an early Hindu".

Theravada Buddhism: The Small Raft

Things to do:
1. Write an essay entitled "A day in my life as a Theravada Buddhist".
2. The Buddhist Code of discipline for living in a monastery is called a *Vinaya*. Draw up a Vinaya for either your school/college/workplace, or your home.
3. Compare some of the teachings of Buddha with some of the teachings of Jesus.
4. Put the Noble Eight-Fold Path into your own words, making it apply to your life.

Mahayana Buddhism: The Large Raft

Things to do:
Write a short essay with the title "A day in my life as a Mahayana Buddhist".

Zen Buddhism: The Way of Meditation

The introductory question to this chapter should be undertaken, within a group situation, by individuals reading out the Zen stories and koans. Others in the group can then undertake tasks 1a–c. Alternatively, pre-record the stories (as suggested) so that the whole group can participate at the same time.

Things to do:
Do one of the following:
1. Write an essay entitled, "A Day in my Life as a Zen Buddhist".
2. Put the Noble Eight-fold Path (see p. 82) into your own words, making it relevant to your own life. Which part do you think you need to develop most urgently? How do you think you can do this?
3. *"He who has Zen is based upon a rock which the rival seas of the opposites cannot trouble. What is more he has Zen."* What does *"based upon a rock"* mean here? Read Matthew 7:24–27, the Parable of the Two Builders, at the end of the "Sermon on the Mount". What does *"built on a rock"* mean here? Compare and contrast the two statements in a short essay entitled, "Two Rocks".
4. "Zen and the Search for Peace with Justice". Write a short essay with this title.
5. Write a Satori-type story describing an experience you have had of seeing a mountain, walking through a garden, field, or stream, or observing birds or animals, or having a special moment while reading a book, making a new friend, visiting a relative, or returning home after a time away.
6. Write your own koan. Now, try to answer it.
7. Read *Zen and the Art of Motorcycle Maintenance* by Robert Persig, or *Through the Looking-Glass* by Lewis Carroll. Write a paragraph describing **your** experience of reading this Zen-type literature.

Sikh: Baptism of the Sword

Things to do:
Write a short essay entitled, "The Sikh Quest for Peace with Justice".

The Way to Life

Things to do:
Write an essay entitled, "My Present View of the Way to Life".

Shintoists: Let Nature Take its Course

Things to do:
Write a short essay entitled *either*
1. "Nature's Way of peace with Justice", or
2. "Dusts on my Mirror" (see discussion question 9).

Taoists: The Way of Acceptance

Have members of the group standing or sitting in different positions and directions, and blindfolded. Now have a *volunteer* try to direct at the same time all of them to the door.

Things to do:
Write an essay entitled, "The Taoist Way to Peace with Justice".

Confucians: Honour for our Ancestors

Things to do:
Write an essay entitled either, "Confucius's Way to Peace with Justice", or "The Five Virtues and the Five Relationships of Confucius".

Bahá'ís: Unity in Diversity

Circle the numbers in the introductory questions of those you would most like to discuss and write out *two* of those that you believe are most important.)

Discussion:
Consider the introductory questions. Listen to the views of others as carefully as you express your own.

Things to do:
1. Write down your comments on one of the introductory questions.
2. Write down your comments on one of the quotations from the teachings of Bahá'u'lláh.
3. Assume that 'Abdu'l-Bahá, in his travels throughout Europe and America, visited your classroom and that you were living at that time. Write an essay entitled, "A Faith to Live By?"

Select Bibliography of Quotations and Special References

'Abdu'l-Bahá, *'Abdu'l-Bahá in London: Addresses and Notes of Conversations,* comp. Eric Hammond, 2nd ed. (London: Bahá'í Publishing Trust, 1987)

'Abdu'l-Bahá, *Paris Talks: Addresses Given by 'Abdu'l-Bahá in 1911,* 12th rev. ed. (London: Bahá'í Publishing Trust, 1995)

Bahá'u'lláh, *Epistle to the Son of the Wolf,* trans. Shoghi Effendi, 1st pocket size ed. (Wilmette, Ill: Bahá'í Publishing Trust, 1988)

Bahá'u'lláh, *Gleanings from the Writings of Bahá'u'lláh,* comp. and trans. Shoghi Effendi, rev. ed. (London: Bahá'í Publishing Trust, 1978)

Bahá'u'lláh, *The Hidden Words,* trans. Shoghi Effendi with the assistance of some English friends (London: Nightingale Books, 1992)

Bahá'u'lláh, *The Kitáb-i-Aqdas: The Most Holy Book,* rev. ed. (London: Bahá'í Publishing Trust, 1993)

Bahá'u'lláh, *Kitáb-i-Íqán: The Book of Certitude,* trans. Shoghi Effendi, 3rd ed. (London: Bahá'í Publishing Trust, 1982)

Bahá'u'lláh, *The Proclamation of Bahá'u'lláh to the Kings and Leaders of the World* (Haifa: Bahá'í World Centre, 1973)

Bahá'u'lláh, the Báb, 'Abdu'l-Bahá, *Bahá'í Prayers: A Selection,* rev. ed. (London: Bahá'í Publishing Trust, 1975)

Bahá'u'lláh, *Tablets of Bahá'u'lláh revealed after the Kitáb-i-Aqdas,* comp. Research Department of the Universal House of Justice, trans. Habib Taherzadeh with the assistance of a Committee at the Bahá'í World Centre, 1st US hardcover ed. (Wilmette, Ill: Bahá'í Publishing Trust, 1993)

Barclay, William, *Educational Ideals in the Ancient World* (Collins, 1959)

Conze, Edward (trans.), *Buddhist Scriptures* (Penguin Classics, 1959)

Cooke, Alistair, *America* (BBC Worldwide Limited, 1973)

Dawood, N J (trans.), *The Koran* (Penguin Classics, 1956, 4th revised edition 1974)

Effendi, Shoghi, *The World Order of Bahá'u'lláh: Selected Letters,* 1st pocket-sized ed. (Wilmette, Ill: Bahá'í Publishing Trust, 1991)

Esslemont, J E, *Bahá'u'lláh and the New Era,* rev. 4th ed. (London: Bahá'í Publishing Trust, 1974)

Faizi, Gloria, *The Bahá'í Faith: An Introduction,* rev. ed. (New Delhi: Bahá'í Publishing Trust, 1986)

Frankfort, Wilson, Jacobsen and Irwin, *Intellectual Adventure of Ancient Man* (The University of Chicago Press)

Humphreys, Christmas, *Zen Buddhism* (William Heinemann Ltd.)

Jowett, B (trans.), *The Laws of Plato* (Oxford University Press, 1920)

Mascaro, Juan (trans.), *Upanishads* (Penguin Classics, 1965)

Ramanujan, A K, *Speaking of Siva* (Penguin Classics, 1973)

Revised Standard Version of the Bible (Thomas Nelson & Son, 1952)

UNESCO, *The Sacred Writings of the Sikhs* (Allen & Unwin)

Waley, Arthur, *The Analects of Confucius* (Allen & Unwin)
Waley, Arthur, *The Way and its Power* (Allen & Unwin)
Whiting, J S R, *Religions of Man* (Stanley Thornes Publishers Ltd, 1983)

D0545225

21 FEB 2014		

You can return this item to any library but please
note that not all libraries are open every day.
Items must be returned on or before the due date.
Failure to do so will result in overdue charges.
Items may be renewed unless requested by
another customer, in person or by telephone, on
two occasions only. Your membership card number
will be required.
Please look after this item – you may be charged
for any damage.

Headquarters:
Information, Culture & Community Learning,
Town Hall, Bournemouth BH2 6DY

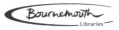

THE
HANSIE CRONJÉ
STORY

AN AUTHORISED BIOGRAPHY
Written by Garth King

●

MONARCH
BOOKS
Oxford, UK

ACKNOWLEDGEMENTS

The publisher would like to thank the following people for their availability to be interviewed and for their valuable contribution to the book:

Family
Ewie Cronjé (Father)
San-Marie Cronjé (Mother)
Bertha Cronjé (Hansie's widow, who married
  Jacques du Plessis on 12 June 2004)
Frans Cronjé (Brother)
René Cronjé (Frans' wife)
Hester Parsons (Sister)
Gordon Parsons (Hester's husband)
Frans Cronjé Snr (Cousin)
Wiester Strydom (Uncle)
Hansie Strydom (Grandfather)

Mentors
Johan Volsteedt (Grey College Head Master
  and cricket coach)
Ray McCauley (Pastor)
Peter Pollock (Cricket selector and spiritual
  guide)
Tich Smith (Business mentor and spiritual
  guide)
Les Sackstein (Lawyer)

Friends
Waksie Prinsloo (School and university)
Stephan van Schalkwyk (School and
  university)
Jaco Swanepoel (School and university)
Johan Laubscher (School and university)
Louise and Wouter Klopper (Bloemfontein)
Gordon and Marge McNeill (Fancourt)
Garth le Roux (Fancourt)
Norman Minnaar (Cricket sponsor and
  Fancourt)
Raymond van Staden ('Body guard',
  intelligence during King Commission)
Wendy Sherrin (SA Film Industry)

Dave Hooper (Pastor in George)
Franklin Stern (Fancourt)
Jean Safers (Fancourt caddy)

Teachers
Emma Wessels (Grey College)
Tommie Cronjé (Grey College)

Cricket
Kepler Wessels (SA Cricket)
Jonty and Kate Rhodes (SA Cricket)
Allan Donald (SA and Free State Cricket)
Boeta Dippenaar (SA and Free State Cricket)
Corrie van Zyl (SA and Free State Cricket)
Craig Matthews (SA Cricket)
Roger Brown (Free State Cricket)
Gary Kirsten (SA Cricket)
Daryll Cullinan (SA Cricket)
Andrew Hudson (SA Cricket)
Eddie Barlow (Free State Cricket Coach)
Bob Woolmer (SA Cricket Coach)
Craig Smith (SA Cricket Physiotherapist)
Ali Bacher (CEO, United Cricket Board
  of SA)
Alan Jones (Former Australian rugby coach
  and media personality)
Tim Noakes (SA Sports Science Institute)
Justin du Randt (SA Sports Science
  Institute)
Andy Capostagno (Cricket commentator)
Neil Manthorp (Journalist)

Other
Anne Warmenhoven (Clinical psychologist)
Howard Buttery (Bell Equipment, Hansie's
  employer)

CONTENTS

FOREWORD

By Frans Cronjé
Hansie's older brother

There are many facets to *The Hansie Cronjé Story*, but the theme that stands out most clearly is that of choices and their consequences. The daily choices that Hansie made determined his destiny. In the preface of his book, *The Great Divorce*, C.S. Lewis wrote:

You cannot take all luggage with you on all journeys; on one journey even your right hand and your right eye may be among the things you have to leave behind. We are not living in a world where all roads are Radii of a circle and where all, if followed long enough, will therefore draw gradually nearer and finally meet at the centre: rather in a world where every road, after a few miles, forks into two, and each of those into two again, and at each fork you must make a decision. Even on the biological level life is not like a river but like a tree. It does not move towards unity but away from it and the creatures grow further apart as they increase in perfection. Good, as it ripens, becomes continually more different not only from evil but from other good.

I do not think that all who choose wrong roads perish; but their rescue consists in being put back on the right road. A sum can be put right: but only by going back till you find the error and working it afresh from that point. Never by simply going on. Evil can be undone, but it cannot 'develop' into good. Time does not heal it. The spell must be unwound, bit by bit, 'with backward mutters of disserving power' – or else not. It is still 'either-or'. If we insist on keeping Hell (or even earth) we shall not see Heaven: if we accept Heaven we shall not be able to retain even the smallest and most intimate souvenirs of Hell. I believe, to be sure, that any man who reaches Heaven will find that what he abandoned (even in plucking out his right eye) has not been lost: that the kernel of what he was really seeking even in his most depraved wishes will be there, beyond expectation, waiting for him in 'the High Countries'.

The first question that I was asked by the media when we publicly announced this project was: "Why write the book?" My answer is three-fold:

Firstly, I believe that Hansie's life was such a rich mixture of success, failure and drama that there is a wealth of experiences to learn from, by studying his life. In September 2001 Hansie spoke at a dinner in Stellenbosch and made the comment:

"Someone once said that life can only be understood backwards, but it has to be lived forwards. Therefore, it is wise to learn from the mistakes and achievements of the many men and women that have gone before us. I certainly don't stand here saying that I know everything or anything at all, but hopefully by the end of my short speech tonight you will be able to take something from my life and learn from the many mistakes that I have made and from some of the good things that I have done."

I often told Hansie, after the King Commission, that I thought it was necessary to write a book about his experiences, so that people could learn from his life. His answer was always that you cannot tell a story until it is finished and ready to be told. The story is now finished, and it is ready to be told.

The second reason for writing this book is that I believe that it is important to tell the Hansie Cronjé story in an accurate and well-balanced way. Since April 2000, many journalists have written articles and some have even written books about Hansie, but most of those were one-sided and often inaccurate. We, as Hansie's close family, have never made ourselves available for any in-depth interviews, partly because we have learnt to distrust many people in the international media (there are of course some exceptions to that list).

Thirdly, we would like to give some kind of closure to the many people from all over the world who have supported and prayed for our family throughout the King Commission and beyond Hansie's death. We thoroughly appreciate this support and I would like to mention that most of the support that we have received, apart from the many South Africans, came from India, Pakistan and Sri Lanka. With God's help and their support we have been able to bear Hansie's loss and the media onslaught.

This book is the culmination of two years of planning and research and 12 months of writing and editing. It was a journey that included many moments of joy, mixed with some deeply emotional experiences. Over 30 people were interviewed by the author and their views form the basis of the book. (The names of the interviewees appear in a list in the Glossary in the front of the book.)

Among those interviewed were all of Hansie's close family, many friends, former team-mates and a few people who were critical of Hansie. Garth King also did his own extensive research. Another aspect that added tremendous value to the book were the findings of Anne Warmenhoven, a clinical psychologist who made the research she'd done for her PhD thesis on emotional intelligence, called "A psycho biographical study of Wessel Johannes 'Hansie' Cronjé", available to the author.

In telling Hansie's story we had to make a few decisions. The hardest decision was what to include and what to leave out. In the end we decided that this book would not be a book filled with cricket statistics and detailed descriptions of matches. The two "Hansie and the Boys" books by Rodney Hartman cover those aspects very well. Neither did we attempt an in-depth investigation into corruption and match-fixing in cricket. We merely gave enough of an outline of the King Commission, for the reader to have an understanding of Hansie's involvement with the bookies. Instead we chose to focus on the human side of Hansie and tried to uncover as much of his personality as possible.

It is important to note that the independent voice of the author is evident throughout the book, often in the first person. In some instances there were disagreements among Hansie's family and friends about the conclusions that Garth drew, and in other instances there were disagreements about the interpretation of certain events and experiences. Sometimes both sides of the story were voiced, but mostly the author decided on the most likely version. The entire editorial team went to great depths to check the authenticity of the various stories, but sometimes the only research to go by was the interviewee's recollection of an event. Therefore it is possible that some individuals may have slightly different versions of the same story. We chose to include those stories in any case, as we felt that they add to the richness and depth of the book.

From the start we decided that it would be best if the book were not written by a family member, but rather by an independent writer without any strong preconceived views about Hansie. Garth had never met Hansie, neither did he closely follow his career, nor is he a sports journalist. His views are fresh, articulated from a platform of extensive access to the memory banks of Hansie's family and close friends.

Be that as it may, the entire Cronjé clan and Bertha (Hansie's widow) are in agreement that the book, as a whole, is a well-balanced and accurate story of Hansie's life, and it is our sincere hope that you will enjoy the book and that it will make a lasting impression on your own life.

May you make the many decisions in your own life with wisdom

Frans Cronjé
Cape Town, June 2005

CHAPTER ONE

BOY IN A STORM

I n Bloemfontein in the Free State Province of South Africa, the dome of blue sky seems wider, higher, longer and brighter.

The natural landscape in winter is shades of grey greens, red browns and straw yellows. There are hard, bushy plains and a few rising, encircling russet and tan hills around a spring – Spitzkop, Brandkop, Naval Hill, Ferreira's Kop: rocky, flat-topped sentinels heaving up from the flat earth and surrounding the big town. The population consists of those of Dutch and French descent known as Afrikaners; a smattering of recently-arrived Taiwanese; the Sotho, whose great King, Moshoeshoe, held back white and black enemies from his Thaba Bosigo mountain fortress; some Tswana; some Griqua, of old mixed European, Far East and African lineage, and others of more recent British, European and African descent. The dominant groups, numerically, politically and socially, are the Afrikaners and the Sotho.

Even with legislated segregation a thing of the past, these different tribe-like groupings mostly do not co-mingle. They still live in their separate spaces, some out of choice, many because of economic imperatives and also because they simply continue to stay where they have always stayed – next to their neighbours and friends. The wheels of change grind slowly in Bloemfontein. Generally, black and white are largely separated by sets of long and straight railway tracks slicing through the town, which neatly and efficiently divide.

In its Karoo Sequence landscape, Bloemfontein is at the centre of South Africa. It's an Afrikaner heartland, a Ruritania of sorts, one of the last truly Afrikaner cities, located in what was once the old Boer Republic of the Orange Free State.

The cosmopolitan and globalised cities of Durban and Johannesburg are far away; the haughty old courtesan, Cape Town, is nearly 1 000km to the south-west. Tourists don't often stop here; they're just passing through en route to other destinations.

On the mostly flat expanses and seemingly endless straight roads of the central Free State Province, they say you can see for ever. Time, a straight line, gradually dips over the endless circle of clear horizons.

In winter great sheets of white frost are spread over generous suburban, khaki kikuyu lawns, on almost countless sports fields of many kinds, and on the tresses and tufts of the open veld. The frosted fields of Bloemfontein make for brutal games of rugby. Falling on the ground is like falling on concrete. In June, July and August the air is sharp, raw and clean. At night, the cold bites like an angry puffadder.

On summer afternoons, lofty clouds of white, grey, purple, violet, black and blue billow up – frequently in many different textures, layers and weird forms for miles into and across the sky, transforming an austere panorama into shocking scenes of the Creator's wild opulence.

Massive, mobile cumulus stacks, pregnant with great waters, gather into cumulonimbus mountains of fantastic vastness and solemnity. Sometimes, dust storms raising hell on scores of kilometres of ploughed farmland convect into the atmosphere, sucked into the monstrous cathedrals of droplets. Blood-brown dust mingles with the electric storm clouds.

This story begins on such an afternoon. On a day that God made. When boys had rejoiced, and were glad in it.

A tall and athletic boy, with big, hazel laughing eyes, a neatly shorn head of stiff black-brown curls above bushy eyebrows, stood in the wide and long back-yard of his family's suburban home at 246 Paul Kruger Avenue, in the genteel Bloemfontein suburb of Universitas.

Cricket stumps were placed near a corrugated asbestos wall running along the side of the property. The wall had several holes in it, which stand to this day, where hard cork balls had breached after repeated and explosive deliveries. Over the years, most of the large and small windowpanes on one side of the home had been broken by the unruly garden games of the sport-mad children.

Hansie Cronjé, 10, was at the crease.

Bowling was young Allan Donald, a lanky and powerful boy with a long, quick and brutal arm and furious expression. Fielding were Hansie's older brother, Frans, and younger sister, Hester, as well as the three Bojé brothers, Nicky, Louis and Fourie.

At the end of the garden were three willow trees. Hansie had claimed the one at deep midwicket as his own when, as a six-year-old boy, he saw the garden for the first time. The other two trees stood at deep square leg and long-on.

In the late afternoons of summer, such backyard cricket matches were a regular feature of life.

Allan, at the end of his 15-yard run-up, turned around. He gave Hansie a stare and then charged in towards the boy. Hansie repeatedly tapped his old bat on the lawn, concentration on his face. The hard cork ball slammed into the greasy kikuyu turf and bounced speedily and wickedly for the middle stump. The young batsman, with fluid and electric grace, moved forward, hit the ball with the meat of the bat, and sent it screaming past Allan. The ball slammed into a wire fence at the opposite end. "Four runs!" shouted Hansie, revealing even white teeth, which shone out of a darkly tanned and open, pleasant face. "And that is his fifty – the crowd goes mad…" Hansie commentated himself and showboated a little as the other players smiled at his antics.

A drop of rain splashed on Hansie's brow. He looked up into the sky. The boys and Hester heard a low boom and then ducked in alarm as lightning struck close by. The horizons jumped with more jagged cracks of white light in the now blue-black sky tinged with a muddy red.

The clouds directly above, heavy with the blood-dust, began to void. Quickly, amid the crazed cacophony of repeating thunder, absurdly large droplets sheeted down in aggressive cascades.

It had been a hot day. The air was still warm, and the children stood for a while in the garden, getting wet, tilting their heads to the sky and opening their parched mouths to the globs of water. Relentlessly, the rain drummed down, soaking the lawn. Puddles gathered in the many flower and shrub beds. Hester and the boys ran inside. That game was over for now.

The children, after a quick towel-dry, galloped to the lounge to watch a sports video, a much-favoured form of entertainment. Their rugby heroes, in the days of the sports boycott of South Africa, were the Welsh champions who had captured hearts and minds globally with their rugged flair and sporting spirituality. The images of the victorious mud-splattered gladiators were inspirational, irresistible and hugely exciting, and the boys idolised players like Williams, Bennett and Edwards.

After a short, noisy discussion, *The Crowning Years* – highlights of the glory days of the Welsh rugby team of the 1970s – lost out to *The Greatest Match*. For the boys, this was the match of all matches: the game between the British Barbarians and the All Blacks played on 27 January 1973. They had watched it repeatedly for the wonderfully exciting, running rugby displayed as the Barbarians romped to victory by 23 points to 11.

As the sights and sounds of *The Greatest Match* swelled within them, they watched and listened with joy to the rousing song of a jubilant Wales crowd: "Guide Me, O Thou Great Jehovah". The Welsh folk hymn echoed in the rugby stands, urging on the victorious – revitalising the discouraged.

Outside the storm ended. The dark clouds moved on across the plains, watering the thirsty veld. The bass booms and mighty lashes receded until there was silence. In the stillness, the glossy veneer of water in the sunlight transformed the world. Fresh scent and sight of a newness of life was everywhere. The moistened fragrance of clay-rich soil, thorn trees, roses, veld bushes and grasses, even distant Merino sheep flocks, maize fields and old sandstone buildings, caressed the senses. Faintly acrid steam, not unpleasant, rose in soft hanging clouds from the long and wide tarred road outside the house.

The commentary of Cliff Morgan and the singing and roars of the Welsh crowd in the stands of Cardiff Arms Park spilled out of the lounge into the garden and into the street. The boys sat bolt upright as Phil Bennett caught the ball deep inside his own half. With 15 All Black players in front of him and very little support, he started running – and then that flawless side-step – two, three, four All Blacks unsuccessfully trying to tackle him. Eventually the Barbarian support caught up and with uncanny flair and wonderful hands, the ball was passed around to half the team before Gareth Edwards scored arguably the best try in world rugby history.

Excitement boiled up inside young Hansie. With a loud "*Ja!*" and "*Kom ouens!*", he jumped out of his chair and dashed from the lounge. The other boys and Hester looked at each other, mystified for a few moments before they heard the back door swing open and saw Hansie kick an old leather rugby ball onto the lawn. Hansie sprinted after the ball, water and mud splashing as he ran.

In a flash the teams were onto the lawn too. Hester, even though she often played rugby with the boys and could hold her own very well, had her limits and retreated into her girlishness. She watched them play from the lounge and told her mom: "They are completely mad", to which her mother replied, "No, they're just boys."

The boys had often talked about and dreamed of playing rugby in the mud, like their heroes in Wales. Now the wet and muddied lawn of 246 Paul Kruger Avenue was magically transformed into a Cardiff Arms Park Stadium.

They formed two teams: The "British Barbarians" and the "All Blacks". This Barbarian side included fullback J P R Williams, flyhalf Phil Bennett, scrumhalf and captain Gareth Edwards, all of the glorious Welsh. The boys appropriated their heroes' identities and began to play with joy.

They formed up and played a rousing game, enjoying the now spongy kikuyu lawn, with its red-orange clay soil seeping through the grass's mat. Now and again they'd crash into a garden bed, splashing mud. In the background, the video was still playing at nearly full volume, and the roar of the crowd, distinct, reverberated in their heads and hearts. The glory of the game was simply real. Heroic exploits consumed half an hour. Backwards and forwards the magic played on, as they tackled hard, ran wildly, falling exultantly into puddles.

At the game's end they were covered in mud, with grass burns borne proudly on knees. They looked at each other and laughed madly. Frans ran off and got hold of the garden hosepipe, spraying them all and himself thoroughly until the mud washed off the rugby heroes.

Hansie, gripped now by a new impulse, looked around with a naughty smile and began to peel off his clothes, shouting, "Ten push-ups for the last one in!"

They all followed suit and dashed for the swimming pool. Six naked boys vaulted and bombed into the water, almost in unison, splashing, shrieking and laughing wildly.

Tannie Chrissie Bojé (the Bojé brothers' mom), followed by Hester, suddenly walked through the back door, onto the patio near the pool. Mrs Bojé smiled at a blushing Hester as all six boys dived under the water, vainly trying to conceal their nudity. Giggling bubbles floated up from their mouths and nostrils.

Later, after modesty had been restored, the Bojés and Allan said their respectful good-byes to Tannie San-Marie Cronjé – there was homework to be done if they didn't want to face the cane the next day.

Hansie went back to the pool, swimming quietly and thoughtfully. In the lounge, Frans removed the video tape that had now played out. The second tape caught his eye. He inserted *The Crowning Years* and hit the play button. The last section of the tape began to screen. It was a summary of the Welsh team's best tries that decade; in the background their supporters sang "Guide Me, O Thou Great Jehovah".

Hansie dived under the water. The floor mosaic of a fish rippled. The sun-starred pool swirled as the liquid blue moved around the boy's lanky, light brown body. Hansie looked, wide-eyed, at the mosaic and then broke the surface. Clambering out, he sat next to the pool and gazed up at the washed sky, feeling the warm sunlight on his face.

From the lounge, the hymn floated through the house and into the garden.

Guide me, O Thou Great Jehovah,
Pilgrim through this barren land;
I am weak, but Thou art mighty;
Hold me with Thy powerful hand:
Bread of Heaven, Bread of Heaven,
Feed me now and evermore.
Feed me now and evermore.

Open now the crystal fountain,
Whence the healing stream doth flow;
Let the fiery, cloudy pillar
Lead me all my journey through:
Strong deliverer, strong deliverer,
Be Thou still my strength and shield.
Be Thou still my strength and shield.

When I tread the verge of Jordan,
Bid my anxious fears subside:

Death of death, and hell's destruction,
Land me safe on Canaan's side:
Songs of praises, Songs of praises
I will ever give to Thee.
I will ever give to Thee.

— Wilfred Williams, 1714-91

CHAPTER TWO

TRAILBLAZERS

The Promised Land

The countless springbok are my flock
Spread o'er the unbounded plain

— Thomas Pringle

En wij weten dat dengenen, die God liefhebben,

alle dingen medewerken ten goede, namelijk dengenen,

die naar zijn voornemen geroepen zijn.

— The Bible, Romans 8:28

Hansie Cronjé, born in 1969, was the robust genetic product of hardy farmers of Dutch and French ancestry – obstinate, pious, freedom-loving people, many of whom trekked away from the British-occupied territories in the south and east of the country.

The Cronjé treks took place some time before the Great Trek when thousands of Boers travelled far, far away from the Cape Colony, many of them keen to escape from the arrogant English and their taxes, jurisdiction and language policy.

Poverty, drought, land-hunger, large families with sons needing their own farms, forced Anglicisation, equality before the law with blacks – all these also played a part in these journeys into the promise offered by an untamed interior vastness.

The earlier trekboers were a semi-nomadic pastoralist group. They were a Calvinist people of the Book and drew a strong analogy between their quest for freedom and that of the ancient Jewish race that had fled from the slavery of Egypt's Pharoah. Once, after trekking northwards for seemingly endless days, pushing back frontiers, they believed they had reached the Nile and named the river they found as such. Rocky edifices at times were thought to be ruins of Egyptian pyramids.

With guns, the Bible, the sjambok and resolute purpose they colonised great chunks of the African sub-continent's interior. Quasi-European, a wild people apart. A new race of Africans. Afrikaners.

The first Cronjé forebears in South Africa, brothers Pierre and Etienne (or Estienne) Cronier, had been christened in Rouen, Normandy, France in 1671. The French Huguenot brothers arrived in Table Bay on 3 September 1698, on the ship *Driebergen* – ten years after the first wave of persecuted Protestant French Huguenots landed in Cape Town.

The Croniers were taken by the Dutch authorities to the Berg River in the Drakenstein Valley, where both were given farms. Pierre's farm was named Versailles and Etienne was given two farms – Champagne and Olyvenhout. Etienne never married, so the family legend is that all South African Cronjés stem from Pierre. Both brothers were members of the Church Council of the local French-speaking Huguenot congregation in Drakenstein, a congregation that exists today in the form of the Paarl Nederduits Gereformeerde Kerk (Dutch Reformed Church). The brothers worked hard and soon became prosperous.

Governor Jan van Riebeeck of the Verenigde Oostindische Compagnie (Dutch East India Company) had landed in Table Bay some 40 years before the arrival of the Croniers, to establish a refreshment station for ships en route to and back from the Far East. This event had signalled the start of Europe's colonisation of southern Africa.

Pierre and his wife Susanne (née Taillefer, widow of Jean Garde) were married in 1709 and had three children – two daughters and a son, also named Pierre, who later married Susanna Roi, daughter of Jean Roi and Maria le Febvre.

The Cronjé clan moved on to Swellendam, in an easterly direction. From Swellendam these trekboers moved again by ox wagon to Graaff-Reinet, into the arid and majestic Great Karoo, a vast and desert-like interior. From there the now-named Cronjés moved on to Colesberg. Francois Johannes (Cornelius) Cronjé had hunted in the Rouxville district in 1819 and had "found the land immediately east of the Caledon River unoccupied". When drought struck in the 1820s and 1830s it was there that he directed his wagons. The Cronjés were moving incrementally towards the centre of the land mass of southern Africa, covering many long hundreds of often unchartered kilometres. Their relentless nomadic pastoralist push was achieved before the Great Trek of the Boers from the British-controlled Cape Colony, which began in the first half of 1800. Their pioneering spirit was strong and they were arguably the first reconnaissance scouts of the Great Trek's rugged pioneers. *Voorlopers*. The ones in front. The trailblazers.

When at last the Cronjés chose to settle in the Promised Land of the Orange Free State with its grassy, sun-baked, open-savanna plains and herds of wild antelope, they were speaking Dutch, not French. The Huguenots had been thoroughly absorbed into the Afrikaners, as these Africans of Dutch descent now called themselves.

At the time of the Great Trek of the 1830s, many groups of Dutch-French descent moved up from the Cape Colony into the central plains where the Boers would eventually create the Orange Free State Republic in 1854, despite strong resistance from a resident English-speaking community in Bloem-fontein, the capital.

In this new land, the migrating herds of springbok in the central plains of South Africa reportedly numbered in the millions. Such was the force and sheer multitude of these mind-blowing migrations of *trekbokke*, that herds of sheep and cattle in their path would sometimes be compelled to join in the march or be trampled to death. In time, the Afrikaners found that the deep and rich, black and red clay soil of the Free State plains also produced good crops of maize and wheat, and that the summer rains were reasonably consistent. Cattle were kept mainly for small dairy herds. Successful Merino sheep farming would come later.

At the centre of the growing rural settlements were the local congregations of the Dutch Reformed Church. Farmers funded the construction of these Calvinistic cathedrals of the plains, churches with towering spires that could be seen for many miles. Here the faithful gathered every quarter, coming from far and wide, often travelling many days, to attend *nagmaal*, or holy communion, These were times not only of religious observance but also, for many farming families, the only times in the year when friendships and family ties could be renewed, when courting could take place, when trading and gossip could be enjoyed in the extended Afrikaner family.

Interviewed at his home in Bloemfontein, Hansie's father, Ewie Cronjé, spoke with precise detail about his family: "My father – also named Frans Johannes Cornelius Cronjé – was born in 1904 in the area between Rouxville and Smith-field. My mother was a Swanepoel from Dewetsdorp. In those days, our farm was mainly a Merino sheep farm. There was also lots of hunting: blesbok and springbok mostly."

This sacred connection to the land, to hunting for food, to wide and desolate spaces, to tribal introspection, to the church, is still in the blood of the many Afrikaner families of Bloemfontein.

This is a people moulded by a deep and ancient form of Calvinism, which gained new life and rugged vigour on the open vistas of Africa, away from the atheistic and agnostic "isms" of Europe. A hearty work ethic, self-reliance, fear of God, absolute reverence for the Bible, and an inward-looking, fierce love of the elevated *volk* and *vaderland*, so entwined with the stories of the conquest of Canaan, were emphasised. The consideration of such characteristics is essential if one wants to understand Hansie Cronjé.

Hansie, whose name is recorded in Grey College annals as "W J Cronjé", got his names from a long line of Wessel Johanneses. This is one of the old traditions still observed by many Afrikaner families: first sons are named after their father's father and second sons after their mother's father.

Hansie's mother, Susanna Maria "San-Marie" Strydom, was born in 1944. Her father and grandfather were both named Wessel Johannes Strydom. (Hansie's maternal grandfather was still alive in 2005 at the ripe age of 93, living in Bloemfontein.)

The first sign of the sporting gene in the Cronjé and Strydom lineage was when Wessel Johannes "Hansie" Strydom senior started playing bowls in Winburg and later in Theunissen in the Free State. On farms in these two districts, he ran Merino sheep, a dairy and some crops. His Winburg farm at the confluence of Leeuspruit, the Vet and Groot Vet Rivers was named Junction Spruit and was still in the hands of the Strydom family in 2005.

Hansie senior was educated at Kingswood College in Grahamstown, "so that he could learn English", in order to make his way in the increasingly sophisticated bilingual arena of the Union of South Africa under the British Crown, and it was there that he played cricket for the first time and saw the likes of sporting greats such as the rugby footballers Bennie and Stanley Osler, the Moffets and the Slaters, in action. In the period 1920-32, the Springbok flyhalf (and later captain) Bennie was to South Africa what Jonny Wilkinson was to the English in 2004. The magical blending of Afrikaner and South African English sporting excellence was at the starting blocks.

Later, against the monolithic adherence of Afrikaners to the fascist National Party, Oupa Hansie would stand for the less conservative United Party in a general election in the Winburg constituency, setting the scene for a fairly liberal, inclusive political approach. Hansie's paternal grandfather, Oupa Frans, also supported the United Party.

Frans Johannes Cornelius Cronjé (FJC) had matriculated from Hoërskool Voortekker in Bethlehem in the Free State and then studied at Grey University College in Bloemfontein (now Free State University) before moving on to the Grootfontein Agricultural College and finally the Sydney Technical College in Australia, where he studied sheep and wool farming. At the time, there were at least eight South Africans studying at the Sydney College in the 1920s. One wonders about the origins of the town named Cronjé near Adelaide in Australia.

At all these colleges FJC played hooker in their rugby teams. On his return to South Africa he worked for the Farmers' Co-operative Wool and Produce Union Limited, and then started farming in the 1930s in the Bethulie district on a farm called Ebenhaezer – where Hendrik Petrus Jacobus and Nicolaas Everhardus ("Ewie") Cronjé were born in 1933 and 1939 respectively.

Ebenhaezer, which means *"Tot hier toe het die Here ons gehelp"* (God helped us to this place) was about 25km west of the then fine agricultural town of Bethulie.

From the verandah of the farmhouse one could see eastwards to a flat country-side, with the small rocky hillocks near Bethulie faintly visible. To the west, little koppies and ridges sheltered grazing springbok and to the south was the 2 250km Orange or Gariep River. Today the farm lies under many metres of the waters of the Gariep Dam, South Africa's largest fresh water source, with a capacity of six billion cubic metres.

Oupa Frans was reputedly much like his grandson Hansie. "At the age of 25 he looked just like Hansie, same build, same face, also tall. He was a popular man in the south and south-eastern Free State. He never spoke badly of anybody – a wonderful, brain-clever man, like Hansie," said Ewie. "His family, community, province and country were high on his list of priorities. He loved his sheep – he knew his sheep like few sheep farmers did. He was an excellent speaker and never used notes, and was a deacon and elder in the Dutch Reformed Church."

From Bethulie the family moved to a farm near Bloemfontein in 1951 and FJC died in 1968, a year before Hansie was born. At that time FJC was a civic leader and had served for five years as president of the Central Agricultural Society, today known as the Bloemfontein Show.

Ewie Cronjé's mother, Elizabeth Maria Susanna (nee Swanepoel) and FJC both played tennis for Bethulie. FJC also performed the role of rugby referee in Bethulie at times. Bethulie in those days was a big town with a great love of sport. In 1950, for example, Bethulie led Free State University 6-3 at half-time, a situation which today would be laughable.

Experience in leadership roles, liberal tendencies, and a familial love of sport had by now been refined in the blood and bone of the Cronjés.

BLOEMFONTEIN was founded in 1846 by Major Henry Douglas Warden, the British Empire's Resident of the Orange River Sovereignty, who bought the land from a farmer for £37 pounds 10s. Numerous theories exist about the origin of the city's name: it it is said to refer to the flowers that grew at the source of a spring, to a local chieftain named Jan Bloem, and to a much-loved ox named Bloem, who was notorious for jumping over kraal fences.

After the withdrawal of the British from the Orange River Sovereignty in 1854, Bloemfontein became the capital of the Boer's Orange Free State Republic, which was incorporated into the Union of South Africa as the Orange Free State province, later to become the Free State Province, after South Africa's first democratic elections in 1994.

Anthony Trollope, the British author, who visited Bloemfontein in the 1870s, wrote:

The town is so quiet and seems to be so happy and contented, re-moved so far away from strife and want and disorder, that the beholder as he looks down upon it is tempted to think that the peace of such an abode is better than the excitement of Paris, London or New York.

There is an atmosphere of general prosperity about Bloemfontein which is apt to make the dweller in busy cities think that though it may not quite suit himself, it would be good for everybody else and thus there comes upon him a question of conscience as he asks himself whether it should not be good for him also.

The 192-hectare nature reserve, Naval Hill, slap-bang in the middle of the Free State's provincial capital, is an excellent vantage point from which to consider Bloemfontein. Why, one may ask, call a lone flat-topped 'koppie' in the centre of the interior Naval Hill? The reason is that during the Anglo-Boer War, Lord Roberts sent in a naval brigade to man the look-out position, which offers a panorama of the surrounding flat land, and views of spitzkop, Brandkop and Ferreira's Kop to the south.

One of several famous Cronjés was the Boer fighter, General Pieter Arnoldus Cronjé, who was a successful commander in the early stages of the Anglo-Boer War of 1899-1902, defeating the British at Magersfontein and laying siege to Mafikeng.

However, Lord Roberts's thrust on the central front precipitated the sur-render of Cronjé's 4 000-strong force in 1900 at the Battle of Paardeberg in the Orange Free State, near Bloemfontein. He was disgraced by this surren-der in the eyes of some Afrikaners and labelled a *hensopper* (hands upper).

After the war he became a member of a travelling show that toured the United States re-enacting scenes from the Anglo-Boer War. He returned to South Africa and died a lonely and unhappy man, according to some history text books.

To the south of Naval Hill, one catches a glimpse of the National Memorial to the 26 370 Boer women and children who died during the Anglo-Boer War. There, a sandstone obelisk marks the site of the ashes of the great English social worker and reformer, Emily Hobhouse, whose compassion for the Boer women and children in British concentration camps is honoured and remembered. Despite Emily's good services, there remains a residue of anti-English feeling among some elderly Afrikaners.

About 40 Cronjé families – apparently all descended from Pierre Cronjé – live in Bloemfontein today.

Locals refer to Bloemfontein as a "10-minute city" – meaning that one can cross town from any point and only take 10 minutes to get to one's destination. Ample, well-maintained, long and wide roads criss-cross the city.

From the crest of Naval Hill one can easily see how small the city really is, and get a fine sense of why Trollope admired it. It is lovely in its way, mild and prosperous-looking, with generous homes and beautiful gardens and distant semi-formal and informal settlements.

From the hill one can also see the old Ramblers Cricket Club, where Hansie's father as captain of the Free State team in 1967, played against Bill Lawry's Australians and held them to a draw. In that game, Ewie bowled 25 overs, with 12 maidens, and took three wickets for 44 runs. His batting score was 70 not out.

One can also catch sight of the Free State Rugby Stadium and Springbok Park, also known as Goodyear Park, where Hansie walked onto the field in 1990 in his bright orange uniform, captain of the Free State team at the age of 21.

CHAPTER THREE

A SOLID GROUNDING

Dad was always Hansie's hero.

— Frans Cronjé, Hansie's brother.

"Oom Ewie", as he is respectfully known throughout Bloemfontein, or "Ewie" as the cricketing fraternity knows him, is a former rugby, cricket and tennis champion and long-serving provincial and national sports administrator. He remembers the most minute detail about sport and sporting events. His brown eyes seem to glaze over at times, as if consumed by his thoughts when discussing his favourite subject. But he mostly has the frank and direct look of a man who is used to commanding other men in a simple and friendly manner. He ponders questions thoughtfully, slowly and methodically delving into himself and carefully pulling out measured answers. A cautious, intelligent, noble Afrikaner. A pious stoic.

Sport is in the very fibre of the Cronjés. And like Hansie, Ewie was and is bound to Grey College, to Bloemfontein, to the Free State, and to South Africa, in that order. Generally, his preferred method of interaction with the world today is through the telescopic lens of the sporting life, zooming in on all its great triumphs, nigh-unbearable losses, and bitter disappointments.

The retired, still-shattered don of Free State sport spends many of his daily hours in a brown leather armchair in a small and comfortable TV lounge, which, like many other parts of the generously-proportioned Cronjé home, holds almost innumerable trophies and other memorabilia of glorious years gone by. Hansie years. Years that have now ended with contrasting emotions of great pride and joy, and tragic loss, heartache and, yes, some unresolved anger towards Hansie's old persecutors. Forgiving one's enemies, even for such stalwarts of the Christian faith, is often a process, not an event.

Ewie and his wife, San-Marie, know that Hansie made some serious mistakes in his life and they are certainly not blind to that. It is not that they think that Hansie's critics are beyond the pale. They can understand why some didn't like Hansie at all, and felt let down by him.

A large photographic portrait of Hansie – one of many in the house – glows bright and proud in the entrance hall, a guardian angel watching cheerfully and man-fully over all those who enter. Youthful and pulsing with joy; this depiction of a young Hansie in his prime provokes painful and ambiguous feelings for all who pass by.

Ewie is by any standard obsessed with sport – and not just cricket and rugby. Also golf, tennis and bowls, and that's just for starters. In 2004 he retired from a long and massive contribution to Free State sport and its administration as Director of Sport for the University of the Free State.

At that time Ewie was still recovering from prostate-cancer surgery, and was watching sport on TV night and day, every day, for long and curiously intense hours when he was not playing bowls enthusiastically with San-Marie, his patient and dignified partner.

His enthusiasm for bowls is characteristically relentless and competitive. That driving impulse to win – to be the best, to play the game hard and well and often, to practise repeatedly, to think carefully and cleverly about strategy and technique – is still there, as strong as ever.

For Ewie, sport is therapy for the heartache. But cricket is sometimes hard to watch and the tears come easily, as they have always come easy for the Cronjé family, who seem to have curious mixtures of iron-hard resolve and soft emotions in their make-up. It is a not unpleasant character twist, a trait that seems to balance out the family members nicely, making the seeming sport automatons touchingly human and accessible. Hearts of flesh, not of stone. As a family they have always been known for their gentle hospitality, friendliness and courtly good manners.

In the 1940s, soon after he started walking, Nicolaas Everhardus "Ewie" Cronjé started playing a cricket of sorts on the family's Bethulie farm Ebenhaezer with his Sotho playmates, the sons of his father's farm workers.

Bethulie, then a bustling little centre for prosperous white sheep farmers, started out as a London Missionary Society station in 1829. A prisoner-of-war camp was situated in the Bethulie district during the Anglo-Boer War, and many women and children died there at the hands of their British captors. Francois and Koot, two of Ewie's great-uncles, died during that war in other British concentration camps. Many have not forgotten the British atrocities and it certainly had not been forgotten then in the 1940s and 1950s, even by the liberal Cronjé clan.

Because of all the time he spent with the Sotho boys, little Ewie quickly became proficient in Sesotho, a skill that would stand him in good stead as a sports administrator and communicator in the Free State context.

"My older brother, Hendrik Petrus Jacobus Cronjé, and I used to play with these boys and we played a crude form of cricket. We didn't have a bat. We had a garage wall as the wickets. We drew a half circle on the ground in front of the wall and we would roll a tennis ball towards the 'batsman', who stood in the half circle. The 'batsman' would kick the ball away," Oom Ewie said, relating his first exposure to the game that would play such an important part in his life.

Later, the tennis ball was replaced by a cork ball and the hard and scruffy little black and white feet were exchanged for a toy cricket bat from OK Bazaars, the local supermarket. "It was tough. The boys bowled fast and we faced that hard ball without gloves, without pads or a box. But we all loved the games."

Ewie's Sotho playmates called him "Baby" and his brother Hendrik, "Thabo". In a curious way this was a tribute, and an indication of mutual affection as many Afrikaner boys in those days were called "*kleinbaas*" (little boss) by their black friends.

After school in the mornings, Ewie and Hendrik would quickly get any bothersome homework out of the way (or not), and then set up their next game of cricket. The nearby farmhouse's windows had wooden shutters, but young Hendrik and Ewie were often simply too lazy to close them, and smashed more than a few panes in their enthusiasm. "My dad never used to complain, but my mother used to chase us and give us a good hiding when it happened," Ewie said matter of factly. "After a window broke, my father always used to say, 'Hell! It must have been good shot, Ewie'." Many years later, Ewie would say much the same thing to his own window-breaking sons, Frans and Hansie.

As these games developed they took on a purer form of the *rooineks'* game. After Ewie's father bought the OK Bazaars bat, the boys found an axe and chopped out the shapes of "stumps" on a bluegum tree near the farmhouse. The seven boys, who included Hendrik, Ewie, Tantjies, Ramayani, Lebusa, Boytjie and Tutu, played relentlessly, winter and summer, continuing their games when the family moved to another farm close to Bloemfontein called Kromspruit. Even there, the windows were not safe, and the occasional hidings from Ma for shattered glass continued, as did the wry, supportive responses from Pa.

At that time, only English boys played organised cricket in Bloemfontein, where Afrikaners outnumbered the English about three to one, a ratio which is changing these days even more in the Afrikaners' favour. Few Afrikaners played cricket in South Africa at all, at any level, then. The game was clearly seen as one for *souties* (a derogatory term for English South Africans that derives from their being seen to have one foot in England and the other foot in South Africa, with their private parts dangling in the salty sea.)

But down on those prosperous Free State farms a revolution in South African cricket was brewing, one of enduring and dramatic proportions. The simple joy of the game, played with a passion and ferocious will to win by "Baby" and "Thabo", was later to be refined to the nth degree at sports crazy Grey College in Bloemfontein.

Enthusiasm for the game was not only fed by the mutual joys of farm cricket. "In the summer of 1946/7 we went down to the coast after the shearing. We arrived in Cape Town and my dad took us to the Newlands Cricket Stadium where we saw our first big games – Western Province versus Eastern Province, and Western Province versus Natal. Currie Cup matches."

Ewie remembers that Dudley Norse, the Springbok captain, scored over 100 for Natal against Western Province and that Anton Murray, who also played for South Africa, scored more than 100 for Eastern Province against Western Province. "There was a fantastic atmosphere. We sat under the oaks."

Of course, Ewie enjoyed every second, watching the game intently, barely noticing Table Mountain, majestic in the background. At that time, sturdy little Ewie, a veteran of innumerable farm cricket matches, was only seven years old.

Oom Ewie is convinced that the Cronjés' fascination with cricket stemmed mainly from the family's friendship with the affable and worldly-wise hotelier, David Marks, owner of the Royal Hotel in Bethulie. Marks was a keen cricketer, who as a youngster had played for South Western Districts against the 1927 MCC team that came to South Africa.

Few towns in South Africa have not had a Royal Hotel at some stage in their histories. Before the unholy rush to the cities in later decades, towns like Bethulie were busy, profitable centres of good social activity.

Marks was one of the few English speakers in Bethulie – Jews were very often the only English speakers in small Free State towns – and the friendship between the successful Boer farmer and the Jewish hotelier was a fortuitous conjunction of cultures, one that would pay dividends for South African cricketing excellence decades later. Frans Johannes Cornelius Cronjé's easy-going acceptance of and close friendship with an English-speaking Jew in a deeply conservative Afrikaans town was unusual. Once again, the Cronjés' enlightened and fresh, open approach to life helped them to forge ahead of the pack.

⬤

Young Ewie arrived at Grey College, Bloemfontein, in 1951 and soon started playing tennis. Formal cricket followed, after "one chap who played under-12 cricket was ill and the coach asked who could play because they needed an 11th man. I put up my hand, thinking bravely that my foot cricket and bluegum-tree matches with the boys on the farm would stand me in good stead.

"'Where did you play?'" they asked.

"In Bethulie, on the farm," came Ewie's response.

That was good enough for the coach. The beaming, confident little *plaasjapie* was just too cheerful and confident to resist. In the same year, Ewie was picked for the under-12 A side to play against St Andrew's in Bloemfontein.

At Grey in the 1950s there was an overseas professional employed at the college named Dennis Smithson, who began to refine the form of the enthusiastic farm boy, who was at that time one of the few Afrikaans-speaking boys in the parallel-medium school showing any interest in the English sport.

Before he turned 15, this natural-born player would be picked for the Grey College 1st XI. He eventually played for the Free State Schools side in the national showcase of provincial schools' talent, the Nuffield Tournament.

Innate Cronjé leadership, sportsmanship and intelligence also found expression through the exploits of Ewie's older brother Hendrik, who played for Grey College's first teams in rugby, tennis, cricket and athletics. Many years later, both Hendrik and Ewie had two sons, and all four of them attended Grey College. Hansie had an older brother at Grey, just like his dad did.

Ewie's father, Frans Johannes Cornelius Cronjé, was compelled to do what Ewie himself would one day do for his own sons. He travelled. A lot. Transporting children to and from Bloemfontein, to Port Elizabeth, to Durban, to East London, Pretoria, Cape Town, in an endless, almost every-weekend pilgrimage, criss-crossing the country by rail, car and bus in pursuit of trophies and the joy of the games. For this, Bloemfontein was perfectly placed in the centre, the heart of South Africa.

Ewie's mother, Bessie (Elizabeth Maria Susanna Cronjé), was also supportive. "She used to coach tennis. She taught me how to deal with nerves," said Ewie. "Because she got so nervous during my matches she calmed me," he offered, perhaps implying that as Mom was doing the worrying he could get on with the match. This strange dynamic also seemed to work for Hansie and his dad in later years.

Development of big-match temperament was a thick vein in the Cronjé body corporate and Ewie soon became renowned for his cool and calm attitude during major sporting events. The trick was ridiculously simple. Ewie adopted the same attitude to Hansie that his dad and mom had to him. In Ewie's own words, "No pressure, just good luck. No advice. Just play well and enjoy the game. I tried to do the same with our kids."

Young Ewie was also Grey College's cheerleader, or *rasieleier*, lustily urging the school along in their battle songs on the sporting fields and in their regular morale-boosting, robust singing in the school assembly hall before the big rugby and swimming galas. Cricket matches were somehow too dignified to sing at, or about.

Like his son Hansie, Ewie had a reputation of being a prankster, a showman-leader and jokester. His antics as a Grey College cheerleader are legendary and, until recently, he occasionally performed this role at the Grey College assembly at the request of the pupils, rocking and rolling around like a mad Elvis, shaking his leg in robust buffoonery; poking fun at the opposition, making crude comments about the appalling "vomit"-coloured school uniforms of the enemy, about their namby-pamby ways, their useless tactics, their ugly girlfriends and so on. "All good clean fun," said Ewie.

When Ewie matriculated in 1957, a year in which he played Nuffield Cricket, he was the only Afrikaans-speaking boy in the Free State team. Thirty years later, when Hansie captained the Nuffield cricket side in 1987, there were only two English-speaking boys.

Near the end of his schooling Ewie wanted to study agriculture, but Mr J M B "Johan" Faure, the principal, counselled, "*Boet*, if I see your science marks, it's not a good idea. You must do a BA."

Ewie was disappointed. "All my people farmed. I was the first one not to farm. Maybe I just played too much sport. Sometimes I'm really sorry about that."

But not even the ancient tug of farming could stop the sports colossus. The Cronjé cricketing dynasty was now on track. Such genetic and visionary pulses continued when Ewie started studying for his BA at the University of the Orange Free State (UOFS) from 1958, later graduating with a BEd in 1966. Ewie represented the university at first team level in rugby, tennis and cricket.

Ewie's sporting career never missed a beat as the years rolled by: he played tennis for the Free State for 12 years, and was for three years chosen for the National Students Team. Ewie also played for the Free State cricket team for 11 years – three years of them as captain. Amazingly, Ewie also played for the UOFS first teams in table tennis and squash. Somehow, he managed to complete his BEd and soon afterwards was approached by the headmaster of Grey, Mr A K Volsteedt, to teach and to coach sports at his old alma mater.

Although Ewie taught the English boys at the school Afrikaans, it was principally his cricket and tennis coaching duties that consumed his time and interest. No doubt he was chosen for that role, rather than for his academic qualifications. Today, Grey pupils still dominate the junior provincial tennis teams.

His cricket-coaching successes at Grey were also phenomenal. In the 1960s his pupils usually made up nine or ten of the Nuffield XI – Morné du Plessis, a future Springbok rugby captain, was captain of the 1966 Free State Schools team. In the 1965 team was Johan Volsteedt, who would later have a massive influence on Ewie's two sons.

It was during this time that the young teacher got involved in provincial sports administration. He served on the Free State Tennis Committee, the Free State Cricket Committee and was chairman of the Bloemfontein Junior Tennis Organisation. He was also a Free State Nuffield selector and team manager.

This explosion of administrative activity did not put a brake on his sport playing – in 1964 he won seven of his nine matches at an inter-provincial tennis tournament in Pretoria, for example. As Free State cricket captain, his 70 not-out against Australia in 1967 stood as a Free State record until Hansie improved on that in 1994 by scoring 251 runs against the Aussies.

In 1969, shortly after Ewie's father passed away at 64 after a heart attack, Ewie noticed an advert in *Die Volksblad* for a Sports Organiser at UOFS. "I loved teaching, but I wasn't good at it. I knew that I would much rather organise a tennis tournament than mark papers."

He applied and got the job. UOFS was the last Afrikaans university to start a sports office and now the sports dynamo was at the helm of Free State sports development.

Five years previously, Ewie had noticed the glamorous Bloemfontein Teachers College Carnival Queen, a blonde beauty named Susanna Maria Strydom.

Like Ewie, San-Marie was a farm child, another Free Stater through and through. She started her education at a farm school, delivered there by an old horse called Japie, who plodded to and from the school with the cartload of kids and nobody at the reins.

These happy carefree days were rudely interrupted when her parents decided she needed to go to an English school to learn to speak that language, and she was dispatched to the private Epworth Methodist School for Girls in Pietermaritzburg, Natal, where she formed an excellent friendship with the Afrikaans-speaking headmistress, Suzie Kachelhoffer.

"In those days in the Orange Free State, English children were forbidden to attend state Afrikaans schools and Afrikaners were forbidden to attend state English schools," explained San-Marie. "Epworth was a hard road. But I was happy. Mrs Kachelhoffer was a lay preacher in the Methodist Church. She had a big influence on my life. I'm forever grateful for that Christian school." The strong foundation laid then in that little girl would never leave her, and today San-Marie practises a Christianity that is deeply felt.

From Epworth, San-Marie moved to the Bloemfontein Teachers' College. There she met Ewie, who had called in one evening with the intention of introducing her to his best friend, Wessie Marais. After a good look at the blonde bombshell Ewie decided to keep her for himself. San-Marie's studies were consequently interrupted by her marriage to one of Bloemfontein's most eligible bachelors, who by all accounts seemed to be in a hurry to get to the honeymoon.

San-Marie eventually – after completing her diploma in pre-school teaching through the University of South Africa – taught at Grey College's Primary School and at one time one of her tennis pupils was none other than little Kepler Wessels.

First-born Frans Johannes Cornelius was born on 15 May 1967 and named after his paternal grandfather. Wessel Johannes "Hansie" was born on 25 September 1969 and named after his maternal grandfather. San-Marie wanted him to be known as Wessel because he had a cousin whose nick-name was Hansie, but her father (Hansie's namesake) protested, saying, *"Dan kan jy hom net sowel Gat doop en Petunia noem!"* [Then you might as well christen him Backside and nickname him Petunia!]

Hester Sophia was born on 11 November 1970 and named after her maternal grandmother.

●

Ewie, in the midst of a full bloom of Bloemfontein sporting culture in the 1970s and 1980s, was a busy man, night and day. "I kept the household going," said San-Marie, "and tried to stand in for Ewie whose time was consumed with his own sport, teaching and administrating. The children hardly saw him. I was also working. It wasn't always easy, but the children attended schools where the teachers really cared for them."

Ewie, now entrenched in the UOFS Sports Office, served there for 35 years. He presided over an incredible surge in the construction and development of a whole range of sports facilities and endeavours in Bloemfontein, as the city became increasingly sports-mad with the advent of television in South Africa in 1974.

"At UOFS, we had a five-year plan to catch up to Maties (Stellenbosch University) and Tukkies (Pretoria University). In 1978 we were arguably the second-best sporting university, after Tukkies," said Ewie.

Increasing interest in sport in Bloemfontein – centred around the sprawling, almost endless grounds of the University of the Orange Free State and the organisational and sporting talents of that institution – meant more bums on seats, more sponsorships. A whole range of achievements were notched on Ewie's belt – too many to mention here.

All this was the platform on which Hansie Cronjé was raised. And under Hansie and Ewie, the early '90s were the golden years of Free State cricket.

Did the Cronjés insist that their sons play cricket, or play sport? "We encouraged them," said Ewie, "but we did not insist on their playing any sport. If Hansie had come to me and said he wanted to be an opera singer, I wouldn't have been upset. I would've said, 'Be an opera singer and enjoy it, my boy.'"

Oom Ewie's Perfect South African Cricket Pitch

In his slow, bass voice, carefully enunciating his measured Bloemfontein English, guttural, with expectorated "G" sounds and rough, rolling "R"s, Oom Ewie describes the fine craft of good pitch construction and maintenance.

His brown eyes sparkle with pleasure under the bushy grey eyebrows and the old-fashioned spectacles as he speaks of the best pitch attainable. Apart from his skills as player and administrator, he also has a passion for caring for and building new sporting fields. He loves to talk of these things; these sacred things of earth and plant and sporting stewardship. This farmer's son speaks of the hallowed turf wicket with ponderous agricultural detail born of rich experience and many years of practised trial and error, as a Bethulie farmer would speak of his maize fields, lovingly tended and gratefully harvested.

"The first thing is, you dig the ground out, you dig out a whole strip: 20.12 metres long and 2.64 metres wide. Then you fill up with broken glass and ash for moles. On the sides put asbestos board to keep kikuyu from shooting through and the moles from getting in.

"Drainage must be good. You don't want the pitch to get water-logged, so there must be a slightly domed curve to it. This must be rolled flat. Above the glass comes compost and sand and black or red clay soil. Then the pitch must be planted with runners or squares of the grass mat you're going to use.

"When you plant grass it must be fine grass: skaapplaas, bayview, Harrismith, Cape royal, damkweek... You've got to get to a farm dam that's empty and have a look there – the fine grass will be on the floor of the dam.

"The grass should be planted in two inches of black clay – that is what I like. Skaapplaas and damkweek can be found in the Bloemfontein district. It comes from the Tierpoort Dam. The Goodyear Springbok Park stadium pitch is skaapplaas grass. Damkweek is one of the best but for me skaapplaas is the ideal.

"Before you plant the grass you must put a good fertiliser underneath. In the joins of the planted squares, or among the runners, you must put more clay. It must be black clay. The clay must be very fine.

"The best clay in the world is from San-Marie's brother's farm at Junction Spruit in Winburg. It binds well and it is very hard. You must make the clay damp, but not too wet. If it's too wet it packs onto the roller. You must roll it damp, not wet. Compact it and let it bake in the sun. It gets very hard and makes the pitch faster and more bouncy and true than any other I have known – and it lasts."

According to Ewie, the pitches in India and at Port Elizabeth's St George's Park break up after a few days. Pitches become untrue and result in luck playing too large a part in the game.

"Hansie," he says, "was uncannily capable of 'interpreting' cracks when he batted, carefully noting the precise lie and rudiments of the cracks and intuitively and instantaneously responding to the ball's exact placement within them."

Part of the secret was that Hansie knew cricket pitches intimately. "When I was preparing the pitches at the University of the Free State, Hansie and Frans had to often drive the rollers, and lay or remove the tarpaulins, depending on the weather. Ground staff worked 9 to 5 but because I was responsible for pitch maintenance, I'd take the boys to the pitches after hours and on weekends – especially in the early mornings – to keep things in good order. I'd point things out to Hansie and Frans about the pitches. Hansie knew pitches intimately, from start to finish and was a past master of Bloemfontein wickets. It was one reason for his success. Pitches. That's where the actual game takes place."

At Goodyear Springbok Park, later that afternoon, I walked onto the field and strolled to the pitch with Frans Cronjé, Hansie's brother. There it was: Tierpoort Dam skaapplaas on black clay from Junction Spruit farm. Neatly rolled and gently domed.

I gazed up at the stands, at the blocks of white, orange, blue and green chairs, the sloped grass incline, at the presidential suites, where a proud but often nervous Ewie used to watch his sons play, at the corner of the field where Hansie's blonde British girlfriend Debbie Coleman used to cause a sensation by sun-tanning on the grass in her small bikini during matches.

There was the mid-wicket Cow Corner by the eucalypts, where Hansie used to repetitively slog-sweep the ball out of the large ground. There were the change rooms, where raucous displays of bonhomie after astounding, unlikely wins would erupt in Hansie's day.

Visible from the pitch is the nearby Bloemfontein Zoo. The occasional sounds of vervet monkeys, chacma baboons and peacocks, and the roar of lions, could be heard.

I knelt down and stroked the beautiful skaapplaas mat, its slightly-curled leaf blades and runners tightly interwoven, softly bristling on the bed of hard and smooth, baked clay. My fingers glided sensuously over the tight, green-greasy maiden-fur mat. A perfect and true pitch, for bounce and speed, such as only the Free State could provide.

A classic groundsman's legacy.

CHAPTER FOUR

STABILIS

After all, you have to ask yourself why they put a scoreboard next to the field.

If winning wasn't important, why would you need to keep score?

— Mr Johan Volsteedt on the subject of competition

Grey College Bloemfontein is an intimidating place. For 150 years it has been a potent and successful mix of pompous English colonial tradition and super-Afrikaner Zeitgeist. The school credo, Stabilis, means "steadfastness".

The school's imposing Edwardian sandstone main building was designed by Sir Herbert Baker's office, and its sprawling 60ha campus, set in the heart of Bloemfontein, encompasses six cricket fields, eight rugby fields, a new gymnasium headed by a biokineticist, a rugby stadium, 20 cricket nets, four soccer fields, an Astroturf hockey stadium comparable to the best in the world, an Olympic-size swimming pool, 20 tennis courts, four squash courts, four grass hockey fields, a grass athletics track, fly-fishing dam and table-tennis venue.

Old Greys have included more than 100 South Africa representatives and many SA Schools representatives. Names like Ryk Neethling, Morné du Plessis, Ollie le Roux, Pieter and Helgaard Muller, Naka Drotske, Kepler Wessels, Hansie Cronjé, Nicky Bojé, Boeta Dippenaar, Jaco Reinach, LJ Van Zyl and Johan Cronjé. Grey College is regularly rated among the top three in rugby and hockey in the country and by 2005 had produced six cricketers and 28 rugby players who had represented South Africa in international sport.

When Old Greys meet, they use the Grey College handshake: the two small fingers of the right hand tucked into the palm. The sign of the brotherhood. The handshake that can do wonders for your business, or your career and standing in some corridors of power and influence.

Hansie's brother, Frans, and I took a tour of the immaculate and parklike school campus and everywhere we went we were greeted by a respectful "*Môre, Meneer*" ("Good morning, Sir") and a direct, open and friendly look from the boys we passed on their way to the weekly morning assembly. Tradition, mutual respect, Christianity and discipline characterise the school.

Throughout the year, the sports teams of Grey College compete over weekends against most of the country's best schools. Because of Grey's reputation as a sporting school, the other schools put in a huge amount of preparation during the weeks that lead up to their matches with Grey, and they often make this the highlight of their sporting year. This means that almost every weekend the Grey boys have to face psyched-up opponents, and there is no room for making mistakes.

Certain schools make for even bigger battles and sometimes it is like war. Schools like Queen's College, Afrikaans Hoër from Pretoria, Paul Roos Gymnasium and Maritzburg College. But the longest-standing battle, and the fiercest of all, is the one staged between Grey College and its old, and now formidable enemy, the Grey High School of Port Elizabeth, which is also named after Sir George Grey, the British governor of the old Cape Colony. Over 500 boys travel by train to compete in a wide variety of sports, alternating every year between Bloemfontein and Port Elizabeth. We visited the day before this annual Derby in 2004.

About 20 minutes before assembly, the 1 000-odd high-school boys filed into the hall, packing in like sardines. The youngest ranged right up against the podium, pushed forward from behind by the tight crush. Another bank of boys sat down on chairs on an upper tier at the back of the hall. Every single boy was impeccably neat and tidy, with short cropped hair, a clean white shirt and grey trousers, tie knot pushed right up against the closed collar button, shirt tucked in, striped blazer buttoned up.

As Frans and I stood outside the hall, what appeared to be spontaneous singing began. This was no thin, compulsory stuff. The cries were vocalised with shocking vehemence. Song after song, chant after chant was voiced in great waves of enthusiastic energy.

> ... For when the men of College come you know
> College Happyland, Happyland
> I'm going to stay at College till I die
> College Happyland, Happyland
> I'm going to live at College till I die

Another song they sang is still Ewie's favourite:

> Let every good fellow now lift up his voice
> Vive le Grey College
> And sing to the health of the school of his choice
> Vive le Grey College...

Frans, a former full-time Christian missionary who now owns a film production company in Cape Town and who played professional provincial rugby and cricket in South Africa for the better part of a decade, had been invited to speak at the assembly. Later we filed in through a door at the back of the stage with the teachers and took our seats on the podium. As we did so, the boys stood to attention, a thousand intent eyes gazing respectfully and attentively at the adults on the stage. The sea of faces showed no signs of cynicism, or hints of rebellion. During the late '70s and most of the '80s Hansie would have been one of those twinkling in the firmament of arguably one of the world's most incredible and classic sporting schools. That day, the boys stood quietly among the scores of honour boards that cover most of the wall space, many of them containing the name of the legend "W J Cronjé", who made his debut for the Grey College 1st XI cricket side at the age of 14, captained the Orange Free State Nuffield Week cricket side, captained the Grey First XV rugby side, and captained the Orange Free State Craven Week rugby side. (Hansie was a hard-working eighth man, known for his good ball skills and ability to read the game.)

The headmaster, Johan Volsteedt, stood at the rostrum and quickly spoke of the need for servant-hood to those less fortunate, added a stern warning against arrogance and then proceeded to quote from Proverbs 13:

> *He who ignores discipline comes to poverty and shame,*
> *But whoever heeds correction is honoured ...*
> *He who walks with the wise grows wise,*
> *But a companion of fools suffers harm.*
> *Misfortune pursues the sinner,*
> *But prosperity is the reward of the righteous...*
> *A poor man's field may produce abundant food,*
> *But injustice sweeps it away...*

A hymn was sung, proudly at a shockingly loud volume, in wonderful contra-diction to the State's systematic attempts at the removal or emasculation of Christianity at schools. The boys' voices, in perfect and practised unison, blended manly and boyish tones in lusty praise of the eternal Trinity: Father, Son and Holy Spirit.

It was impossible not to be impressed by the rough glory of it.

After Volsteedt had spoken, Frans was introduced as the guest speaker. He also quoted from Proverbs, this time from Proverbs 3, verses 5 and 6:

> *Trust in the Lord with all your heart and lean not on your own understanding;*
> *in all your ways acknowledge Him and He will make your paths straight.*

Frans then delivered a quick and hearty sermonette about how to make the right decisions in life, and used examples from the life and lessons of Penny Heyns, the

South African Olympic gold medallist swimmer. The four basic points were that one must have a purpose in life; that one must have core values, that is, those found in the Bible; that God's guidance must be sought through prayer; and that a good mentor must be identified and activated.

Frans then went on to say that "if your ability is to win all your matches then you must win all your matches" and "the way that you play sport is the way you play the game of life". The end of his speech was met with loud and sustained applause. As honoured guests, Frans and I were then given silver cups engraved with the school crest by the school captain and his deputy, followed by a brutally hearty handshake and yet more applause.

The assembly ended formally with the singing of the prayerful national anthem, "Nkosi Sikelel' iAfrika" ("God Bless Africa"), and the school song:

> Aan Bloemfontein se Westekant,
> Die oudste in Oranjeland,
> Staan ons Grey Kollege heg en sterk,
> Beroemd vir spel en goeie werk.
> Standvastig soos ons voorgeslag –
> In ons verlede lê ons krag –
> Streef ons karaktervas en trou
> Na eenheid wat 'n nasie bou.
>
> Ons driekleur-vaandel wapper fier,
> Ons bou 'n eenheidstoekoms hier,
> Ons mikpunt bly wat hoogste is,
> Ons wagwoord immer STABILIS!

After the two songs I sat transfixed under the solid stinkwood beams. The teachers remained seated as the boys, without prompting, turned around and faced the centre of the hall. They put their arms around each other's shoulders, and then in perfect unison, bent down. A knotted and knitted sea of muscular, blazered backs stooped, presenting a striped carpet. For long seconds there was absolute stillness. Then suddenly, raucously, they roared out the school's war cry: *Guske malaya waa, Guske malaya gee, Who are, who are, who are we? We are, we are GCB, We lead at work, we lead at play! We are Grey, Grey, Grey, Grey College!*, stamping their feet, backs rippling and undulating, rejoicing in their hard-earned excellence and readiness for the rugby battle that their heroes – the sacred First XV – would tackle that Saturday. This display of school pride continued for some time after the assembly. (In 2004 they ended up losing to Grey High, but until that weekend the Grey College First XV had not lost a single match in almost four full seasons. And this triumphant spree included winning a Schools World Cup of sorts where some of the world's best rugby schools competed. Being used to winning almost all your matches is how Hansie learnt to play his sport.)

Earlier that morning I had met the principal, Mr Johan "Vollies" Volsteedt, in his office, with Frans Cronjé at my side. Volsteedt, who studied law for a while, and was once the Free State cricket coach, is an intense and wiry man with mischievous pale blue eyes, thinning brown hair and a somewhat brutal and uncompromising intellect. As a boy at Grey, Volsteedt's cricket coach was for a while Hansie's father, Ewie. His father, A K Volsteedt, had been principal before him. That's how it is at Grey – sons and fathers, fathers and sons – the torch passes on. Families and friends intertwine down the generations.

He regarded me warily, with what appeared to be restrained pugnacity, probably wondering what kind of animal I was, apparently only partly convinced by the endorsement of Frans, Hansie's imposing bear of a brother.

It wasn't a particularly good time to interview the eccentric Free State legend, arguably one of the most powerful and influential men in Bloemfontein, the undisputed *baas* of an inner sanctum. He was making notes for his weekly address to the boys, answering the telephone, looking at his computer screen, his secretary wandering in and out. Not the best of interviews, but I got the picture of young Hansie's world.

Questioned about corporal punishment and its comparatively recent outlawing in the "new" South Africa, Volsteedt replied, "In Hansie's day corporal punishment was routine here. A very good routine. For sure. Sure, Hansie got whacked, for example when he occasionally bunked classes. Sometimes before a big rugby match Hansie and his mates would go and have coffee at the tuckshop instead of attending maths classes. We would just go and fetch them and whack them and put them back in the class. This was really a game that they played with me," he remembered fondly.

In a curious tone of mixed pride and possibly hidden exasperation, he told of an exercise that the boys of the school were required to do. It seemed an attempt to recapture some of the stern old discipline that had been partially thwarted over the years as the humanistic, deterministic and relativistic values of some parents (and the State) were challenging the old school ethos. Increasingly, I learnt from a Grey teacher later, boys were being protected by parents from the consequences of their actions – even Grey is not immune to this creeping modern malady. Grey boys had been formally asked searching questions about what rules they would like to live by at the school. The boys' answers had come in and had been synthesised into the following: "Grey gentlemen do not need rules. We are co-responsible for maintaining the following values and conduct: 1. Pride/standards. 2. Integrity. 3. Unity/teamwork. 4. Spirit/loyalty." This credo was binding and the boys uphold it in the sternest way possible themselves, not leaving it up to the teachers to discipline those who step out of line.

"We demand absolute loyalty to the school," Volsteedt said simply and harshly. This was no joke. It was said with the full force of intellect and discipline.

When challenged on the school's legendary obsession with sport, the head-master demurred. "Last year in the Free State we had the second-best matric [final-year] academic results in the province. The state gave us R150 000 as a reward for the result. The best results in the Free State came from Grey's Afrikaans sister school, Oranje. We're not going to compete with them," he said, humorously admitting defeat to the sisterhood. Who can compete with our girls? He also pointed proudly to Grey's award-winning music ensemble. No further evidence of focus on the arts was offered, other than the comment, "We have drama too."

Tellingly, he added: "What is important is that we play our sport to the best of our potential. If we fail to do that, we are shamed. After all, you have to ask yourself why they put a scoreboard next to the field. If winning wasn't impor-tant, why would you need to keep score?" The implication, one can argue, is that if Grey loses they have failed to extend themselves to their full potential. Competitiveness gone berserk, one could say. Such awful competitiveness was in Hansie's marrow.

"If we lose, we lose," Volsteedt continued. "We do it graciously, just like we do if we win. At our school you will never see someone throwing his hands in the air, embracing or kissing someone, or falling on somebody when we win. We just don't do it. This etiquette is not taught by us, but taught by the generations, by the matrics themselves. Our matrics have a very strong role to play in the school. They are the people who determine the atmosphere in any given year. There is no way the matrics in 2004 would ever say they cannot achieve the peaks and successes of the 2003 matrics. That's what makes us strong on a con-tinual basis. Every year tries to improve on the previous year. It's been like that for a long, long time.

"Our school songs are like hymns to us, so we put them in the hymn book," he said, with a hint of self-mockery.

So sport is a religion in the school? "No, I never said that. An old teacher here once said that at this school rugby is a religion and all the other sports are just sects. This is really not true anymore. We have spent more money on hockey at this school than any other sport. We have Astroturf that is second to none. Our soccer facilities are probably the best of any school in SA."

When one considers how expensive it is to send one's children to a private school, it is incredible to think that Grey is a government school, and that the school fees are lower than those of most popular schools in the country today. The creation and maintenance of Grey's world-class facilities are possible due to the Old Grey network, which ensures that traditions are maintained and flexed. "They give generously," explained Volsteedt.

The Grey heritage is strongly linked to Sir George Grey's honourable attempts to bridge the Boer-Brit divide, finding expression in parallel-medium education (English and Afrikaans are the languages of instruction but separate classes mean the boys receive their education in their preferred language) and the curious British Empire inflections at what today is a school complement that is 70 percent Afrikaans. This robust marriage has stood the test of time, producing luminaries such as Bram Fischer, the communist anti-apartheid activist who died in 2004.

Volsteedt said, "It is fortunate that our name is 'Grey', which fits in nicely with our attitude to colour. We are all Grey here. Not black or white." The first black kids were admitted to the school in 1993 and about one in 10 boys in the Afrikaans classes is "not white" and nearly half of those in the English classes are "not white". "We don't look at colour," said Volsteedt, "we look at loyalty to the school."

To get your son accepted at Grey is a fairly difficult exercise though, because the number of boys that attend the school is restricted to around 1 000. When sons are born, they're booked in and preference is given to the sons of Old Greys. Many sports-oriented families across the country send their sons to Grey, making it a deep repository of genetically and psychologically endowed athletic excellence.

Volsteedt will always have an unshakeable belief in the primacy of Grey College and its lofty traditions, a wild passion for Grey and the Old Grey network. He is the epitome of all that was and is good (and bad, depending on your point of view) in the South African pedagogics of yesteryear and he provides a key to understanding Hansie Cronjé. The gutsy maleness, the aloof leader, the mischievous streak that bubbles up at the most unlikely moments, the relentless self-discipline, the focused intensity of playing to win, the pious yet robust wisdom, all distinguish Volsteedt, and the Grey ethos. This template was stamped deep into Hansie's personality. Volsteedt effectively functioned as Hansie's massively influential third parent for the better part of his high school years and way beyond that, to the very end.

He was a potent and enduring mentor. A cricket coach, a coach for life. It seems that Volsteedt decided whatever Hansie had done, he was still a Grey boy and thus, in Volsteedt's eyes, worthy of forgiveness and compassion when repentance was evident. But it went further than that. Hansie, once the school captain (the same rank as head boy in other schools), has retained his place of honour at

Grey and is remembered with a ferocious and forgiving love, the 'iron love' of good boys and good men. A wild love that cannot be broken. His achievements stand, blemishes washed away by the blood. His memory will always be held dear. Always. His portraits and sporting memorabilia still have their place of honour in the hallowed halls of the school and in the sports stadium building.

Hansie was always a golden boy in Volsteedt's eyes. "His father, Ewie, taught me at Grey so I knew the family. Frans was born on the school grounds where I also live and I noticed Hansie's talent as a sportsman in primary school."

Wessel Johannes "Hansie" attended Grey from the first grade to the last. Towards the end of his school career, he was chosen as captain of the South African Schools cricket side. One of his team-mates was Jonty Rhodes, who later became his closest friend and team-mate in the national cricket side. For good measure, he also dabbled in the editorial of the school newspaper, *Stabilis*. In his final year, aged 18, he was the school captain of 1 100 boys. "He was decent, loyal and had integrity," said Volsteedt. "He knew how to handle adults and his own peer group. He was a fantastic link between the boys and the teaching staff. He had an open mind and an easy way of handling problems and discussing matters.

"In some years, the school captains have a tremendous impact on the school. Hansie was one of those." He was someone the boys would listen to. When he walked onto the podium there would immediately be silence. The sheer force of his presence demanded it.

●

While visiting Grey College, I also met with long-standing teacher Tommie Cronjé (a very distant relation of Hansie's) and two other teachers, Miss Emma Wessels and Jaco Swanepoel. Tommie and Miss Wessels had been teachers when Hansie was at Grey, and Jaco had been Hansie's mate at school before he became a teacher. They had all known Hansie well.

It was a cold winter's day and frost was still on the school's lawns. We sat, cramped up in the small office, with the boys' rugby anthems still drifting up the staircase from the hall. While Frans's benign but vigilant presence may have modified their comments to an extent, they seemed to open up, and express themselves well, if a little cautiously, in English, their second language, despite my occasional encouragement to them to speak in Afrikaans.

"Hansie stood out as a leader who was well balanced and who had a fine sense of humour," said Tommie Cronjé, a boyish gentleman in his 50s, with a fine mop of grey hair and the athletic build of a 30 year old. "Whenever he gave his opinion the others would pay very close attention. In a discussion, when there was a problem to be solved, everybody, even the teachers, looked towards him for the answer. It was a natural thing. He didn't force this on anybody; it was simple and natural leadership. Strangely, he seemed to have all the answers. He was not feared, he was respected. Part of his charm was that he was so approachable, especially for the younger pupils of the school. He was an ideal leader to go to, because he always had a sympathetic ear."

Cronjé and Miss Wessels pooh-poohed allegations that have surfaced in a few books and articles over the years that Hansie was a sly and calculating bully. "He may have had a few enemies but I'm sure this enmity, if it existed, was the result of jealousy or envy." Their response was echoed by Jaco.

Miss Wessels added that despite Hansie's gargantuan sporting commitments – in his earlier Grey years he played tennis too – he was "balanced" and still managed to get 70% averages in his subjects at school. "He never had to prepare for anything he did, he just seemed to be perpetually ready for anything that was thrown at him. He was always ready to catch the ball."

It is noteworthy that the school captain is primarily chosen by the schoolboys themselves and "once they have chosen, they carry him along and live with their choice, whatever the consequences," said Jaco. "They stand or fall together." When Hansie fell, his brothers fell with him. When Hansie staggered to his feet, he was cheered onwards and upwards.

The teachers all concurred that Hansie was well behaved and respectful in class. He would at times disagree with teachers, "but he always did so in a way that did not seem arrogant".

The exceptional nature of Grey begs the question: to what extent did the school's ethos influence Free State cricket and the subsequent heady transformation of South African cricket in the late '80s and early '90s? The short answer to that is simply that Grey produced Kepler Wessels and Hansie Cronjé and had arguably nearly everything to do with South Africa's cricketing successes, with these two men at the helm.

After the interview, Frans and I continued our stroll around the Grey campus, noting the generously proportioned old wood-and-corrugated iron tuckshop, where Hansie and his mates had had their cheeky coffee breaks. We wandered to the small wall of remembrance nearby – a recent and modest construction, where the ashes of just a few recently deceased Old Greys had been deposited behind grey slate squares. Overhead, the hadedas cried in their plaintive, mocking way as they flew over the frosty cricket and rugby fields. Grey College soccer teams and rugby teams were getting ready for the long journeys to Saturday morning's fixtures in Port Elizabeth. They stood about around their buses, talking happily, laughing and playing. The sun shone warmly on the centre of Bloemfontein.

Grey, for now, is still seated on its throne. Still remembering its own. Still channelling the wild exuberance of boys into the joyful old pursuits of their fore-fathers. Still flying banners that are noble, ethical, valiant and true. Striving towards the disciplined mastery of self, in homage to the past. Fearing God. The torch is being passed on still. Stabilis!

CHAPTER FIVE

A BOY'S BOY

Hansie's Paradox

Boyhood is a most complex and incomprehensible thing.
Even when one has been through it, one does not understand
what it was. A man can never quite understand a boy,
even when he has been the boy.

— G K Chesterton

Was jy ooit al eensaam?

Was jy ooit al dronk?

Was jy ooit al sewe jaar in Bloemfontein se tronk?

Ja ek was al eensaam

Ja ek was al dronk

Ja ek was al sewe jaar in Bloemfontein se tronk

— a local folk song of unknown origin that Hansie used

to sing as a child and a young man

Hansie was always a boy at heart. In a way, it was a unique case of arrested development – a man forever mischievous; strangely immature and moody at times, but yet very mature as a young leader at other times. It was this often appealing naughtiness that made Hansie who he was. It was also what contributed to his trouble in later life.

That, at any rate is this author's perception, garnered after listening carefully to what many close friends and family members say about him.

With the aura of the invincibility of youth, he took on some serious bastards and lost the game. *What was he thinking?* Part of the answer to that question may be that he was thinking like a naughty teenager, a teenager with a fresh and pioneering, amoral approach to the challenges of life.

Hansie's paradox, perhaps, was that he was a very mature child, but a curiously immature adult. His natural personality was simple, humble, mostly openly friendly, and the relentless burden of complex responsibilities often made it impossible to flex that properly. He was also rabidly competitive and wore the mask of a stern, iron leader, especially on the field. And somehow it fitted well.

Hansie was a leader of males from the time he was at primary school and probably before. This leadership was natural, inherited, and it was also learnt and reinforced at the feet of his dad, his older brother Frans, Johan Volsteedt, Kepler Wessels, Eddie Barlow, Ray McCauley and Peter Pollock. All strong men and stern. And all of them with strong streaks of surprising, mischievous charm. Boys' boys. Men's men.

His powerful leadership abilities resulted in perpetual commanding roles throughout his life. Almost from the beginning, he assumed captaincies, and they were regularly allocated to him as a matter of course. The burden at times weighed heavily, especially towards the end of his career, when relentless cricket, marred by long spells of up to four months away from home, by political inter-ference, long periods of boredom, by the loneliness of a strong captain who was thought to be invincible and self-sufficient, cooped up for months, *stoksiel alleen* in a psychological sense, in the soulless hotel-chain bedrooms of India, England, Australia and other countries, unable to escape, to be normal, to walk about without being jostled. At times it seemed to suck all the joy from the very game he loved.

For a man who had taken on every responsibility handed to him from his earliest days, a man for whom almost every moment was spent in an adoring public's eye, whose professional life demanded such iron control, the lucrative world of the bookies must have seemed strangely exciting and intoxicating. Perhaps Hansie saw this as a place where a boy's mad and irresponsible adven-tures could be had, as an opportunity to rebel against the constant pressure from himself and everyone else to fulfil the role of a paragon of virtue. On the other hand, pushing the boundaries was just something that Hansie did – like running the Two Oceans Marathon (56km) at the age of 19 and bungee-jumping from the highest possible place in Africa, the Storms River Bridge (216 metres).

Hansie's uncle, Oom Wiester of Junction Spruit, relates a telling incident involving his nephew. He makes much of it to this day. At the height of Hansie's career as the national team's captain in the late 1990s he was on a blesbok hunt on the farm, when inner turmoil found expression on the flat expanse of that shrub-by Free State *soetveld* farm.

The Cronjés' connections to the land have always been strong. As boys Frans and Hansie would ride Shetland ponies on their uncles' and grandfather's farms and, with their Strydom cousins on Junction Spruit, would shoot pigeons with catapults and make biltong from the meat or braai the little carcasses. They would fish for carp, yellowfish, barbel and mudfish in the Vet Rivers, and would often join in the annual springbok and blesbok hunt as marksmen in their own right. The boys were given small cattle herds as gifts from Oupa Hansie Strydom and in that way also shared in the *soetveld's* largesse.

Every year Oom Wiester culled about a dozen blesbok on his 2 000ha farm and since his primary-school days, Hansie and his brother Frans had participated in many such hunts.

The hunters were placed at various vantage points, on little hills mostly, where they would take what little shelter was afforded by the odd small tree, large bush, or rock. Oom Wiester would get the blesbok herd moving in the direction of the concealed hunters in his old Corona bakkie.

Earlier in the day, the cussing, rough, but likable Boer had tried out his newly acquired .375 rifle while sitting in the bakkie's cabin. He had rested the barrel on the pick-up's windowsill and taken aim at a handsome blesbok ram. As he fired, the seismic force of the retort of the gun had unexpectedly shattered the windscreen, frightening the daylights out of the gruff old farmer. He was shaken a little by that somewhat portentious episode, but another surprise was in store for Oom Wiester that day.

"I noticed that the blesbok herd had moved past Hansie's position, without his reacting. I went looking for him and found him sitting quietly under a *wag-'n-bietjie* tree, ignoring the hunt. His .303 rifle lay next to him and he was gazing into the distance. "*En nou?*" (And now?) asked his uncle.

Hansie replied, "*Oom*, did you know that I have had one big problem in my life? I have never been a child. I've never had the privilege of being a child? Do you know how nice it is just to sit here and be still?"

Oom Wiester interprets Hansie's surprising revelation as follows: "Hansie had to be an adult when he was a child. He never had the time to sit and think like a child. On that day, Hansie had shared something very important. It came from his heart."

Later, after Hansie and his fellows had skinned the buck, they cut out the livers with their long hunting knives as they dissected the small dark brown, black and white antelope.

Nearby, the gutted and skinned animals lay in a heap at the back of the bakkie. Rivers of crimson blood flowed in furrows off the bakkie's tailgate, dripping steadily and pooling on the orange clay soil. Blesbok eyes gazed sightlessly at the bright blue and swarms of malachite flies hovered over the glossy carcasses.

The men made a fragrant smoky fire with some nearby thorn-tree twigs and branches on a russet-brown sandstone koppie, and surveyed the Free State *platteland* scene. They threw the juicy, deep red organs onto the coals. The smell of the burning food was as always, exquisite, spiritual, recalling an ancient hunters' tradition. When the livers were nicely charred, the men prised them off the coals with sticks, placed them on a flat, altar-shaped rock, and seasoned them with coarse rock salt.

The providence of God's veld, as always, was enjoyed and appreciated. Uncharacteristically quiet, Hansie had silently munched the aromatic and pungent meat. For once, there was no cocky banter from him. The only sound came from the little crackles and low hissing of the fire, and distant birdsong. The bleak silence was at once deeply comforting and unbearably sad.

Overhead, high up, a fish-eagle surfed the surging updrafts. Childhood and innocence had seemed to wisp away, like the little column of smoke in the soft breeze, disappearing into the heavens. Gone forever.

When Frans Cronjé was born, Ewie was a housemaster at Leith House, one of the Grey College hostels. Among his babysitters in those early days were hostel boarders, later to become Springbok rugby greats, Morné du Plessis and Dawie Snyman. Sports heroes influenced the Cronjé children from the start.

Hansie was born with two teeth in his mouth, a mop of thick black hair and the characteristically pronounced eyebrows. Ewie, by then, had been appointed Sports Organiser at the UOFS and San-Marie was a nursery school teacher. The Kontiki Pre-Primary School, where San-Marie was the principal, eventually became so popular there was a long waiting list.

Both Frans and Hansie skipped crawling, instead sliding their buttocks along the floor, using their heels to propel themselves forward. Conventional wisdom has it that crawling is an essential milestone in the development of a child, that missing out on this "vital" stage is a presage of problems to come. Yet both were great athletes in the making. Hansie only walked at 16 months and up to then he couldn't even stand up against a chair. Even when he did start to walk, he fell down frequently and would simply stay seated and wait quietly and patiently for someone to come and pick him up. He struggled with athletics as a little child, which just made him work harder to be good at sports. Before they went to nursery school, Hansie and Frans were playing "rugby", cricket and "golf" whenever they could.

Ewie and San-Marie, with their three children eventually moved to 246 Paul Kruger Avenue, Universitas, when Hansie was seven. The children, catching sight of the garden for the first time, immediately noted the three evenly-spaced willow trees and had run helter-skelter for them, each claiming one as his own.

The spacious new house was perfectly placed. Down the road were both the Grey College and the University of the Orange Free State campuses, as well as the Universitas Dutch Reformed Church. The children could walk or cycle to school;

Ewie could walk to work and come home most days for lunch, but would often only return in the late evenings after cricket practice. Saturdays especially were a blur of sporting activity.

Hansie's quick and vibrant ways soon caught the attention of his teachers at Grey Primary, and the University of the Orange Free State's Education Department came to see Ewie and San-Marie and said that Hansie's IQ tests showed clearly that he was a "gifted" child. They were asked if they would be interested in allowing Hansie to attend special classes at the faculty for such children. Hansie's parents refused because "we wanted our children to all grow up evenly balanced. We never had the idea that we should push them to make sure they reached the top".

Typically, for middle-class white Bloemfontein at that time, several servants tended the garden, washed dishes, cleaned the house, made beds and cooked meals for the endless, hungry streams of visitors, mostly young people. (Farm worker families living on the farms of the Cronjé clan would have taken it as a personal insult if employment at that home had not been forthcoming.)

Jessie was the Cronjé's sleep-in domestic worker and she always knew that she had to cook more than what was necessary for the family alone. A typical weekday's lunch would include a roast lamb with all the trimmings, breakfast would be the traditional sausage dish, *pap en wors*, and supper would be another cooked meal with meat. *Biltong* would often be eaten between meals. There was a seemingly endless supply of meat from the farms.

The home soon came to be known as "the five-star hotel", partly because the Cronjés were five in number, but also because their hospitality was so generous. Guests constantly filed in and out – boys and girls from the nearby schools, as well as many of the overseas cricketing pros and coaches who were assured of hearty meals, fun and laughter and a home from home. In a sense, 246 Paul Kruger Avenue became the heart and soul of Free State cricket.

This great tradition of hospitality was still evident in the summer of 2004 when I spent many long days, lodged in Hansie's old bedroom, interviewing San-Marie, Ewie, Hansie's sister, Hester, and Frans and other family members and friends. For them it was often a painful and difficult process. Sitting on the stoep near a massive red bottlebrush tree in full and shocking-red bloom, tears welled up every now and again in Hester's blue eyes. In her high-pitched, girlish and melodious voice, she spoke of a keenly felt and ferocious love for her brother, forgiving him lavishly, lashing out at critics, even at those within the close family, who at times had expressed disappointment and anger, however cautiously.

She gazed at the fine, large garden, alive with pigeons, doves, weavers, mousebirds, wagtails and Eurasian bee-eaters in the Pride-of-India, thorn, ash and camphor trees. Nearby were roses – Iceberg, First Prize, Little Red Hedge, Queen

Elizabeth and Hansie's favourite, Germiston Gold. Hester remembers well the cricket games on the lawn and how Hansie and Frans would inject water into tennis balls and shave off half of the balls' fur to make them swing through the air and move like a cricket ball. Hester's femininity had not precluded her from playing backyard rugby and cricket with the boys regularly until she was about 20.

She slowly dredged up her fond recollections of her brother. The little things, little shining narratives of memory.

She remembered how Hansie, in grade one, had bought a chocolate cake at a school cake sale for his mother and how he had, while waiting for his mom to fetch him, decided to "decorate" the cake with discarded sucker sticks, little stones, sand, twigs and leaves. The cake was lovingly presented to San-Marie. "He was so proud of his beautiful cake," Hester said.

She remembered how Hansie, 8, and his partner in crime Louis Bojé, Nicky's brother, perched in Hansie's willow tree and *kleilatted* the inviting rump of their neighbour's domestic worker through a window as she worked in the kitchen. And how the outraged neighbour had phoned San-Marie and complained stridently about this outrageous mischief. For a while, San-Marie had refused to believe it, until she saw the giggling boys sitting in the tree with their willow-whip weapons, tipped with little balls of red clay.

Hester recalled how Frans and Hansie were belted by Ewie if they made a noise when Ewie was trying to get in his regular Sunday afternoon nap. "Dad would say, 'Go to your room!' and fetch his belt." The boys would meekly go to the main bedroom, bend over and receive several lashings on their behinds.

"When the boys got hit I used to cry for them, but they would always treat any hidings they got as a big joke and laugh about them afterwards." Hansie, she said, received more hidings than Frans did. He had an endless capacity for pranks and jokes and he often practised these on his sister. "And I always felt he used to somehow manage to avoid being punished. He used to get away with it as a matter of course, but was always willing to accept responsibility when it got out of hand."

Hester mentions Sundays with special affection. "When Hansie was young, Sunday, at least, was the one day of the week when there were no formal sporting commitments. Just family time. Church time. We'd come back from church on Sunday morning and Dad would buy the Sunday newspaper and a packet of cheese curls and we'd each get a chocolate." It was a day of rest. A day for going to church, the Sunday *braai*, being alone as a family, catching up on family news. A day of snoozing and lying around the pool. A day of social garden cricket and rugby games. As the years rolled by, formal sports matches infringed hungrily on the Sabbath and this was unquestioningly accepted by the Cronjés. The sanctuary of the one day of family time without sport, without work, was breached and family life after that was never quite the same.

Hansie in his teens was charming, very attractive. Tall, dark and handsome, witty and full of life – a great hit with the girls. He knew how to handle them; he knew how to handle people. "Hansie dated my friends, one after another, and he broke many hearts," recalled Hester wryly. "I used to cry because when he broke up with them, those girls would stop coming to our house and I had no one to play with.

"I sometimes used to say, 'This *bloomen* cricket! Everything in our family is about cricket.' But I came to see that if it hadn't been for the cricket, we would never have seen so much of the country. All our holidays revolved around sport. And we travelled up and down the country, attending the games that Hansie and Frans played in.

"But it wasn't as though they had no time for me. Hansie was always willing to help where he was needed. I was terrible at maths and often I couldn't complete my homework. I used to wake Hansie before sunrise to ask his assistance with some of the formulas and he would then try to explain it all to me." If it got to the point where Hansie was frustrated with Hester's lack of mathematical ability, he would just complete the homework for her himself.

"Hansie and Frans were good boys," Hester continued. "With all the cricket they played they never got up to things like smoking and drinking, like some of their peers did. Cricket kept Hansie out of trouble. But in the end, cricket was the trouble."

In July 2004, San-Marie was still shell-shocked by the explosions of misfortune around her son. She remembered very little about his babyhood, as if tragedy had expunged parts of her memory. In a curious way, San-Marie seemed overly composed, as if she were blocking off the helter-skelter pain of the previous four years.

"Hansie was such an easy child," she said. "He always meekly did as he was told. He was the victim, I suppose, of middle-child syndrome, not getting the attention that the oldest received, or the youngest got.

"For example, I never had to say 'go and do your homework', or 'time for bed'. He would come and say good night and tuck himself in. Doing his own thing. So easy. In retrospect, I think he did lack attention from Ewie and myself at times."

Even when Hansie was in kindergarten his sense of duty was marked. "If I dropped him off late for school, he would simply drop his satchel and run like mad for the classroom, so afraid he was of being late.

"He took part in all school activities. In primary school he would immediately get his homework done before a packed afternoon of sport, Monday to Friday. At night, even as a young boy, he'd finish his homework without prompting and see to it that his bag was packed. He was like that his whole life, always preparing for what lay ahead."

"From the start," said San Marie, "he simply decided he wanted to be a good cricketer and he went flat out for it.

"As a little boy he had a very mature way of thinking, of organising his life and organising himself. Planning for the future. He set himself goals."

While Ewie and San-Marie never really put pressure on their kids to succeed and perform well, it can be said that they didn't have to. Grey College was there for that, and self-discipline and exacting high standards in sport in particular were internalised by the pliant but spirited boys. "We supported our kids. Ewie never coached them, but he spoke endlessly about sport. They discussed things about the game of cricket. They always had a high regard for Ewie's knowledge of sport. Hansie idolised his father."

Despite Ewie's pretence of a relaxed attitude towards the achievements of his sons, he was highly strung. Sometimes he was too nervous to watch Hansie play, leaving the TV room at critical moments, unable to watch. At cricket matches he would sometimes wander off and disappear when Hansie was batting in difficult circumstances. "He never watched without neuroses. He couldn't simply relax and enjoy the game," said San-Marie.

There was a stage when Hansie, aged 13 or 14, was battling to get runs and had had a run of poor form. Ewie had told Hansie then, "I'll give you ten cents for every run you score in future." In his next big match Hansie scored a century, noting the runs in his diary and carefully multiplying them by 10, a practice that would continue down the years.

Hansie, it seems, was definitely attracted to money and status from an early age. Frans commented, "It was incredible how money also seemed to 'find' him. When we would go away on a cricket tour as primary or secondary school teams, we would be placed with families who hosted us for the evening or for the weekend. I would almost always find myself with a family that was not so wealthy, but Hansie would always be with the wealthiest family at the school. It became a standing joke."

●

Hansie's cricketing prowess was clearly evident from the start. By grade one both Hansie and Frans were playing cricket regularly, a game they had started to play from the time they could walk. On one occasion when Hansie was about 10 years old, he took a wicket while bowling off-spin and immediately turned around to the teacher-umpire with a broad smile and said, "Hell, Sir, I am good, hey?" When he was 10 he played for the Grey Under-13 side and by the time he was 14 he was playing for Grey's Under-19 First team.

"Taking part in sport was natural because of my involvement in sports playing and administration," said Ewie. "Hansie always enjoyed running. He quickly realised the importance of being fit to play the game of cricket. He didn't have the physical strength that some other boys had, so rugby wasn't a good choice for him, but he made a success out of it in any case.

"Hansie lived in the shadow of Frans, but he came into his own after Frans left school. As a young boy Hansie always thought that he had to do what Frans did. If Frans played in the forwards then he wanted to be a forward. If Frans was a bowler then he thought he must bowl too.

"In grade one, the teacher asked them their names and Hansie said 'my name is Wessel Johannes Cornelius Cronjé', adding the 'Cornelius' that is Frans's third name. At high school Hansie picked the same subjects Frans had chosen."

The relationship between the brothers was always good. The only time they ever had words was when they argued about who was going to bat first in their garden games, or whether someone was out or not. Hansie looked up to Frans, who was a strong, easy-going and likable role model – a strong protector who took pride in his little brother's successes.

But the time came when Hansie was taller than his older brother and he could no longer fit into Frans's discarded school uniforms. It marked the moment that Hansie stepped out of the shadow of his older brother. "While Frans was a good mentor and a good standard for him, there came a point when Hansie needed to go his own way," said San-Marie. Later on Hansie often commented that he thought that Frans may even have had more talent than himself, but that he (Hansie) was just fortunate to have had the opportunities at the right time and to use them well.

Frans, Hansie and Hester learnt to speak English rapidly because throughout their childhood overseas pros frequently made 246 Paul Kruger Avenue their home-from-home. The children not only learnt English, they learnt the rudiments of cricket at the feet of international masters of the game, such as Colin Bland (a Rhodesian who had played for South Africa and was one of the greatest fielders of all time), and Arnold Sidebottom and Neil Hartley (two former Yorkshire cricket players and coaches), who were playing for Free State and coaching at schools.

These men knew that they could drop in on the Cronjés any time, when the dubious pleasures of the hotel became a little too sad and lonely and the home-cooked meals called loud and clear. "In those days," said Frans, "professionals were not paid well and the hearty meals at the Cronjés' were understandably popular."

Frans recalled that Neil Hartley's sponsored car was an ugly brown, second-hand Datsun, the battery of which was strapped onto the engine block with insulation tape. "He once left the keys in the ignition, and left it running, with a R10 note on the windscreen, begging someone to steal it," said Frans. "No-one took up the offer to steal the car, but someone did steal the R10 note!"

"The pros not only taught us to speak English, they taught us that English people were no different from Afrikaners. They gave us healthy perspectives on socio-political issues. In the past, we had always seen cricket as an English sport and rugby as an Afrikaans one. That changed, of course and soon I found that I had as many English as Afrikaans friends. I enjoyed the English sense of humour and their challenging awareness," said Frans.

For all they learnt from visiting pros, the sports coaches at Grey loomed large in the boys' lives, exercising powerful influences over their charges, much more so than ordinary teachers. The biggest influence came from Johan Volsteedt. In his speech as school captain on his final day at school, Hansie made special mention of Mr Volsteedt's influence on his life and thanked him for it.

During my first visit round of interviews in Bloemfontein, Frans and I met Waksie Prinsloo and Stephan van Schalkwyk at Waksie's comfortable Bloemfontein suburban home, full of active kids and the ever-present brown leather couches of bourgeois Bloemfontein. These two mates of Hansie's had been with him throughout the Grey school years in the same year group. Waksie, a short, tough guy with a friendly, strong and high-pitched clear tenor voice, spoke with deep fondness and humour of the man and the boy.

Waksie, who has the not unusual distinction of never having been on a losing team during his 12 years of rugby at Grey, was in the same year as Hansie. He remembered one of their rugby coaches, Mr "Lappies" Labuschagne, who some-times, at the end of a rugby practice, would tell them what they needed to do at their next practice. Lappies would sometimes not even show up for that practice, knowing full well that the boys would carry out his instructions to the letter despite his absence.

"That is the kind of trust that is expected at Grey. Lappies would let you write a test and walk out of the classroom, and I can assure you that not one of the students ever cheated. That typifies Grey," said Waksie.

Stephan added, "Lappies used to hit us with a blackboard duster if we got below 80% for his tests. He would take it as a personal insult if we didn't perform adequately."

Like many of Hansie's friends, the boys all stayed in the same neighbourhood, played rugby and cricket together, went to church together, played together con-stantly. A tight weave of social fabric. Church had an added attraction: girls. At Sunday School the boys could sit and interact with females at close quarters. Most of the girls would have come from Oranje Hoërskool, Grey's Afrikaans sister school, and they were teasingly referred to by the Grey boys as "Oranje busse" (Orange buses).

"Hansie was an excellent tennis player," said Stephan, "but at the age of 16 he had to choose between cricket and tennis, and tennis was the inevitable victim."

Stephan and Hansie had played doubles together. "My grandparents lived in Aliwal North, which had some excellent clay courts. So we would go and stay there and play tennis. Hansie loved to slide on the clay when he played, showing off to any watching girls. I remember once when he did a show-off slide, he accidentally did the splits and ended up in a heap on the court. The girls laughed and he was very embarrassed."

Waksie recalled the Grey Primary championship finals when he partnered Hansie against Stephan and Jamie Hills. "Hansie was the number-one tennis player at the school. The match was a hard one and Hansie made his opponents increasingly irritated during the match. Hansie chirped and sledged them out of the game. On one occasion, Stephan caught a ball from Hansie before it bounced, well over the back line and Hansie insisted on taking the point because it hadn't bounced before the catch. For days afterwards, Hansie mercilessly teased them about losing the match."

Waksie made the point that "in our culture winning was really important. It was everything. Hansie was always incredibly competitive about just about everything in life, to the point of being an absolute bastard. Even when he was just playing putt-putt, or touch rugby."

Like Waksie, Hansie never lost a rugby match in which he played for Grey, from grade one to matric. The only game they didn't win was when they played in Craven Week for Free State. Hansie was the captain and the entire Free State schools team was made up of the Grey First XV. After drawing the game 11-11 they had all sat there crying. "Crying like babies, in Paarl," said Waksie.

While competition against opponents was one thing, camaraderie and brotherhood amongst mates was another, even when it came to girls. Girls – they loved Hansie to bits and he worked his way through a substantial band of female admirers at high school.

In their matric year, Hansie, Jaco Jacobs and Waksie were each dating beautiful "Oranje busse". It was three weeks to the all-important Matric Ball. Waksie recounts: "I decided to break up with my girl and Hansie asked me, 'Did you split up?' I said yes and Hansie said, 'I should do that as well'. Jaco said, 'Me too, let's do it together.'"

Hansie's girlfriend, Vanessa van Viegen, approached Hansie the next day and said, "Listen Hansie, I heard a rumour you want to split up with me?" Hansie denied it, but the next day he went to Jaco and said, "When are we going to split up with our girls?" Jaco said, "I already did", and Hansie replied, "I'll have to as well now."

"He phoned her right after that and broke up with her," said Waksie.

They all agreed that when the golden boy split up, there was always another girl lined up, waiting anxiously to take her place.

Before Hansie and Frans reached their teens, a regular visitor started hanging out with the boys. His name was Allan Donald.

I interviewed Allan in Bloemfontein, at his rambling old home in Bayswater, which was being renovated. His English wife, Tina, a beautiful blonde from Birmingham, served us coffee, while Allan's little son, Oliver, scampered around, climbed trees and threw balls unexpectedly at his dad.

"I remember arriving at Grey in grade six and I had already heard about these famous Cronjé kids. I befriended them and I was soon playing cricket 'test matches' in the Cronjé's back yard. In winter it was all-out rugby in the garden.

"Sometimes Oom Ewie used to be the referee, the umpire and the groundsman. All of us, including Oom Ewie, took these backyard matches seriously and they were played with passion and great competitiveness," said Allan.

"Our cricket teams at primary school were unstoppable. Sometimes, we bowled out teams for five or three runs." Generally Allan would take most of the opposing side's wickets and Shaun Lamude would take the rest. "We used to be very disappointed if the other side got more than 20 runs. We always hoped that we would bat first as a team so that we could at least get a decent knock in. If we batted second the match was quickly over."

Frans notes that Allan bowled almost as fast at primary school as he would as an adult. "Allan was one of the finest athletes I ever played sport with, even as a young boy."

Allan, when he was busy with his national service in the South African Defence Force at the Tempe infantry base, spent many long hours at the Cronjé home during his numerous "sports passes". "On Fridays, I used to ask the boys what they were doing at the weekend. There were numerous sleep-overs. I can remember there were kids everywhere, and nearly always there were six or more kids playing cricket in the garden.

"What a calm and fantastic captain Hansie was, even in a backyard game. He was almost too humble. Some critics say he should've been tougher – but he was tough inside. He was too humble as a person. People used to say: 'How can he remain so calm and focused and still be in charge of what he was doing?'"

Corrie van Zyl (who played for Free State and South Africa, coached the Free State side, was assistant coach of the South African side and in 2005 was the coach of the Goodyear Eagles) is himself an Old Grey and offered an insight into the influence Grey had on Hansie and the boys, and the success of South African cricket under his captaincy.

"I started playing cricket because of Grey. I never grew up watching cricket on TV because there wasn't any cricket on TV. My dad, Corrie senior, played rugby for Free State and he wasn't into cricket at all. It was an Englishman's game. Eventually, I was introduced to the game by Joubert Strydom, who was also Hansie and Frans's friend. When Frans and Hansie made their debuts for Free State, Joubert was the Free State captain.

"We started to play cricket in backyards while in primary school, then cricket started up at Grey because of Vollies [Johan Volsteedt, the headmaster]. Vollies transformed Grey by making cricket a significant sport, not only played by English guys.

"In those early days, only a few Afrikaans boys and lots of English boys played the game. But slowly this process gave rise to Afrikaans cricketers like Kepler Wessels, myself, Allan Donald and Hansie. Soon, Afrikaner boys were clamouring to play." Added to this was the inspirational Ewie Cronjé, critically located in the bosom of respectable Afrikanerdom.

"It wasn't TV, or even radio that got us into cricket. In retrospect, it was those backyard games played all over Afrikaans Bloemfontein, similar to the games played at 246 Paul Kruger Avenue, so full of boyhood pleasure and competitive spirit."

Soon, little Hansie Cronjé was sitting under the flowering jacaranda trees, manning the scoreboard at the Ramblers' Cricket Club, earning R5 for a three-day game and being given a lunch-time hamburger and Coke. Completely in love with cricket.

But, as Hester had said, while cricket kept Hansie out of trouble, in the end cricket was the trouble.

CHAPTER SIX

AN ORANGE SUNRISE

Shimla Shimla

Punjabee

Peshawar Peshawar

Irawagee

We are we are GUC

— traditional war cry of the rugby teams of Free State University

(formerly known as Grey University College)

I think you won this trophy one year too early.

Next year you're going to talk money, not cricket.

— cricket coach JohanVolsteedt, prophesying on the night Free State won

the inter-provincial Benson & Hedges day-night series in 1989.

Orange, white and blue. Blue for the big sky. White for light, for purity. Orange for Dutch William of Orange, for the red-rich soil, for the glowing sun. And on the old South African Republic flag, there is a centrepiece made up of three flags: the Union Jack, the old flag of the Boer republic of the Orange Free State, and the *Vierkleur* of the old Transvaal Republic.

An African-European symbol of a whites-only African state, born of the conventional Afrikaner national socialism and English colonial wisdom of the times.

The flag of apartheid. But also a flag that is simply a part of history, a symbol of the old Republic of South Africa, with all its hideous warts and carbuncles, in the 1960s, 1970s and 1980s. The flag of Hansie's childhood, his teens and his young adulthood. Containing the proud flags of his forefathers. You can't wish away that history.

Apartheid, of course, was appalling; as appalling as any form of brutally imposed social and political engineering.

In the Bloemfontein of Hansie's youth, there was only one hotel in the city that would accept guests who were not white, and that was where all the overseas players stayed, whatever their ethnicity. Players of colour were not allowed to reside in any white area, bar the "international" Cecil Hotel, now derelict and forlorn in the ghettoising Central Business District. And officially they were also subject to a host of other apartheid laws, which, for example, forbade inter-racial sex, insisted that toilets were racially segregated and imposed a curfew on the movements of blacks, who were not officially allowed to be in white areas at night. As Hansie grew into a young man, some of these laws were repealed, especially in the 1980s, but not all.

But tottering apartheid didn't stop the little surge of black pros into the Free State side: Alvin Kallicharran from Guyana, Vanburn Holder, Sylvester Clarke and Franklyn Stephenson from Barbados, and Omar Henry from Stellenbosch near Cape Town. These were immensely talented international cricketers who all helped to electrify Free State cricket. The world started to take notice of a young side of Afrikaners who were radically committed, superbly athletic and who never seemed to give up, whatever the odds. At the helm was a young captain who behaved like a mature 30-year-old world-beater, and whose smile lit up Springbok Park.

A bright new day was dawning. A big, orange sun peeped above the flat horizon of the Free State *platteland*.

⬤

Jonty Rhodes first met Hansie in 1982 at the Perm Week for primary schools. Hansie played for Free State and Jonty for Natal. Later, they both played for the South African Schools side in 1986 and in 1987 Hansie was the captain and Jonty the vice captain.

Their relationship grew steadily, helped along by the fact that Digby and Tish (Jonty's parents) and Ewie and San-Marie quickly became great friends, too. All were teachers and, like Hansie, Jonty had been raised in a strict and Christian milieu that was also sports-besotted and authoritarian.

Jackie McGlew, then the South African convenor of selectors, had identified Hansie as a possible national squad captain when Hansie was just 18.

Even in those early days, his wicket was always vital to the opposing side. Jonty recalls vividly how elated the Natal side was when Hansie's wicket fell in their game against the Free State Schools team in 1987. It really was like winning the match, although the match was drawn because of rain.

"Even at that young age he was a prolific scorer. Always hungry for runs," Jonty said.

But besides that, it was his leadership that really shone brightly. Jonty remembers when the SA Schools side played against Free State in December 1987. "The fearsome fast bowler Allan Donald was the opening bowler for the Free State side, and Allan had already played in rebel tests against Kim

Hughes's Australian side. The boys in the schools side were absolutely petri-
fied to face him."

Hansie and Jonty opened the batting. "I had hardly scored a run when Allan
pinned me on the elbow and I had to retire." (In the next year another Allan
Donald ball hit Jonty on the head, hurting him severely and aggravating his
epilepsy condition.) While Jonty did come back and score 20, Hansie had played
"Sling" and the other bowlers deftly, achieving a century.

"At just 18, Hansie had an incredible, calming influence during that match.
Without his input most of the guys would've been gibbering idiots," said Jonty.

●

Around the time of Hansie's selection for the Free State side at the age of 18
in 1988, Ewie and San-Marie had no idea of the greatness brewing in their
young son.

"We never thought Hansie would be a cricketer for the national side
because a national side didn't exist in those isolation days. We never gave it a
thought, we were just simply too pleased when Hansie played for Free State,"
San-Marie said.

"Both our sons wanted to go and play English county cricket immediately
after school and we said 'no'. I said, 'No, you have to study first. What you do
with your degree after that I couldn't care.'

"We realised that Hansie and Frans needed something to fall back on. Hansie
was always very aware of falling behind, of being left behind by his peers. Even
though he was earning far more than they were in cricket, he had repeatedly
said, 'I'm being left behind, because by the time I go into a profession they are
going to be established.'

"One day, without discussing it with us, he woke up and got all dressed up and
was clutching a little briefcase. I said, 'Gee, you're looking smart, where are you
going to?'

"Hansie replied, 'I'm looking for work.' He went to Les Sackstein, the family
lawyer, and shadowed him for a while – he wanted to see if he would enjoy a legal
career. At the time, Hansie had just started playing cricket for the Free State."

In the early 1980s, Free State cricket was a decidedly quaint, relaxed English
pastime; an opportunity to be with the boys and to simply have a right old booze-
up after the game. As wonderful and enjoyable as that old-fashioned idyll was, it
tended not to win matches and was not going to take Free State cricket out of
the B-Section.

In those early years Corrie van Zyl was a strong influence on Hansie, and
vice versa. "When I started playing for Free State in the early '80s the province

was still in the B-Section," Corrie recalled. "Cricket in the Free State, then, was played simply because guys loved the game, especially its social aspect. It was a fun pastime, not a profession, or a mission in life. I got the impression when I started playing that some guys just enjoyed getting away from their wives. In those days the team practised for an hour or two on Mondays and Wednesdays only. There was little preparation for matches and physical fitness wasn't an issue really.

"That was not the way we were brought up at Grey. When I played for Grey it took a lot of hard work in order to get into and continue to play for the first team. We were taught to prepare properly, we were taught about life. We were taught that one didn't just do something, you always did it to the best of your ability."

The Old Greys in the team, Hansie, Frans Cronjé, Corrie, Louis Wilkinson and the captain, Joubert Strydom, wanted things to change from the hail-fellow-well-met, amateur social games, to some hard-core competitiveness and a missionary zeal, dedicated to victory at almost any cost.

The transition to the new athleticism began in July of 1988. Hansie and Corrie were by far the fittest guys in the team, but not super-fit. The team soon started a pre-season fitness programme that was basically just running round the field at Grey.

This early move towards top-class fitness was a team decision, spurred on by Joubert, Corrie, Frans and Hansie.

"Initially I did quite well in the team," said Corrie, "but in the second year I got dropped. And that changed my whole attitude. I wanted to play for Free State. The humiliation of being dropped was terrible for me. That's when I started training. That's when in the winter I went to bowl on my own. That's when I started running. I ran in the afternoons on my own. It was then that things started happening for me. I took responsibility for my own fitness outside the team training. I knew if I wanted to retain my place in the team I needed to be as fit as I could be."

Physical fitness at Grey was emphasised in all the sports. "We always trained that way. We were always totally prepared. There was an emphasis on total preparation, though, rather than just simple fitness."

This attitude was something that Hansie subscribed to in thought and deed. To win, you had to do more than the best of your opponents did.

As the older, less-fit, less-focused Free State cricketers started leaving, or being dropped from the team, and the new players, mostly Old Greys, were flowing in, things really started to sparkle. The fresh young men, brains washed clean, bodies hardened in the Grey ethos, started to turn Free State cricket around, planning its exit from the doldrums of the B-Section.

"We used to run at Grey College's athletic oval grass track, and from the start Hansie stood out. Every afternoon we used to compete in a 4km run, then go to the Kloppers' Gym and work out there. We all understood how important it was for us. Soon, the rest of the team joined in. It became the norm, and we all decided that this was the way forward," said Corrie.

Some of the toughest sessions took place in Bloemfontein's second highest building, the Sanlam Park Building. The players would run from the gym and then sprint up and down the 30 storeys of stairs a few times before running back.

There was also a new attitude to the technical aspects of the game. In winter the team bowled and batted regularly in a converted badminton hall, and at the cold and hard outside nets, where the ball felt like a hard piece of ice; the red leather-covered sphere handled in the frosty climate until hands were red and raw.

"We knew that to be the best at your game you had to be physically fit. But also, achieving radical fitness taught us something about ourselves and taught us something about our team-mates, about their grit, their endurance, their fighting spirit," said Corrie. This regime began and was initially maintained without a coach. The team members were doing it for themselves. All they needed to sharpen the edge even further was a good coach and some overseas pros.

Corrie acknowledged, though, that the Free State team in the 1980s went to extremes when it came to fitness. "It was hell sometimes and we felt that if we could get through those sessions, we could get through anything!"

In the cruel Free State mid-winter the team would get up at dawn and run wearing balaclavas to Happy Valley, get to the hill and then sprint up the winding tracks. A run such as that one would take place nearly every single day of the year.

The Free State team became infused with a kind of holy zeal that was unparalleled in South African provincial cricket at the time. "We didn't want to be a Free State team that everybody would beat in two days. We felt that this was one thing – getting super-fit – that would improve our chances."

Corrie took careful note of Hansie. "From the beginning, Hansie said he wanted to play for South Africa. He wanted it badly. He was incredibly infectious in his will to win; you could see it in the way he prepared, in his relentless enthusiasm. I simply knew that Hansie would become a national player."

The regular runs became insanely competitive. "We got really silly, I suppose," said Corrie. "We began by breaking away from the pack in the last 100m to win the race, but after a while we began pulling away after the first lap on the daily 4km run on the athletics field at Grey. Hansie was usually the winner. He soon became the fittest member of the team and it stayed that way. He worked harder than anyone."

In this atmosphere, Hansie naturally started assuming a leadership role in a way that was seamless. "He constantly raised the bar in terms of fitness levels" – something he would do during his captaincy of the national team, too.

The harsh regime was accepted. Everyone wanted it. There was no debate about it, no irritation about the relentless and demanding new ethos. Hansie's way, the Grey way.

Free State cricket was stuck in the B-Section until 1985. In 1980, no one in Bloemfontein could be found to head the Free State Cricket Union, such was the public disinterest. Ewie volunteered and started the building process. In 1984, the South African Cricket Union CEO Dr Ali Bacher said that an "Afrikaans team" (all the provincial teams, barring the Free State and to some extent Northern Transvaal, were dominated by English-speaking South Africans) needed to be allowed to play in the A-Section. There was huge resistance from most of the bigger provinces. Their argument was that Free State cricket was far too weak to hold its own against the stronger sides and that their inclusion in the A-section would be to the detriment of South African cricket. To facilitate this affirmative action, it was decided to allow Free State to field three overseas players during the 1987/88 season: initially, Sylvester Clarke, Allan Lamb and Alvin Kallicharran. Along with these three fine cricketers, Mike Procter, who had just retired from playing cricket, was appointed Free State's first-ever full-time coach. Procter and these pros had a big and lasting impact on Bloemfontein, culturally and cricket-wise, opening the eyes of many of the blind to the goodness of other races and cultures, not to mention the finer points of hard-core international cricket.

Free State managed to make it to the final of the Castle Currie Cup in that 1987/88 season, where they lost to the Transvaal "Mean Machine" of Clive Rice. Allan Lamb had a brilliant season for Free State, breaking all kinds of records and he was well backed-up by a brutal pace attack from bowlers like Sylvester Clarke, Allan Donald, Corrie van Zyl, Bradley Player and Johan van Heerden. When Lamb had to fly back to England for two weeks, a replacement batsman had to be found, and this was Hansie's break.

His debut was an extremely tough match and the entire game was over before tea on day two. Rice, as captain of the Transvaal side, always managed to convince the Wanderers groundsman to prepare a "snake pit" of a green pitch to bat on. His philosophy was simply to intimidate the opponents and he backed his own bats-men to score more runs than the other teams would. (Such tactics are no longer allowed and provincial sides now lose valuable points and receive a heavy fine if they leave too much grass on the pitch.)

Hansie didn't get any runs in the first innings but then top-scored in the Free State second innings of 54, with 16 runs. Frans also played in that match and recalled how, batting with Hansie, he sometimes feared for his younger brother's safety as West Indian bowler, Rod Estwick, pounded Hansie with short-pitched deliveries that hit him on the chest and forearm. Hansie fought through it well, though, and his 16 runs would have been worth a lot more on a normal batting wicket.

By now the Free State Cricket headquarters had moved away from Ramblers. Under Ewie's guidance, a lovely cricket oval had been built on the university campus, which had grass embankments all around. Free State supporters packed out these embankments to support their "new" team. These matches soon became such a popular social event that the clouds of hanging smoke from the braais sometimes affected visibility.

At the start of the 1988/89 season, Johan Volsteedt was appointed to replace Procter as Free State coach. And so the influence of Volsteedt on Hansie and the Free State continued.

Free State games moved to Springbok Park, the stadium that Ewie had helped to build in 1989. Cricket was now firmly on the social map of Bloemfontein – excitement buzzed as Hansie and the boys started succeeding against the big provinces. Backyard games spread like a virus among Afrikaans schoolboys. When the Free State team played, crowds flocked to Springbok Park. The show was on the road – and Hansie was Bloemfontein's No. 1 pop star by far.

Volsteedt (who coached the side from 1988/89 to 1990/91) had a simple philosophy about cricket: "Cricket is ultimately a preparation for the rest of your life. The way you play cricket is the way that you live your life. So when you play cricket, you have to do it well."

Joubert Strydom was captain and Hansie started cementing his place in the Free State top order. During this time, his brother, Frans started playing rugby for the Free State as hooker, and was not permanently in the Free State cricket side.

The first big trophy that Free State won was the Benson & Hedges Night Series. The final was played at Newlands, where the young team beat mighty Western Province in 1989 against all odds. No one gave Free State, batting first, even a remote chance of winning. Hansie played a big role in the victory, scoring 70 runs, and the team's total after 45 overs was 213. Western Province, with sterling players like Peter Kirsten and Adrian Kuiper, went in to bat and were bowled out for 170. It was a remarkable victory.

Free State, like all the other teams in South Africa, was allowed to field two overseas players. The Yorkshireman, Ashley Metcalfe, was one and the other player was a fiery fast bowler from Leicestershire called Gordon Parsons.

In the semi-final, Free State had played the Impalas (a combined B-section team) at Virginia in the Free State and Hansie had knocked up 105 – if he hadn't done so, Free State would never have made it to the final.

As Hansie got his first limited-overs century, his best mate Waksie Prinsloo, somewhat inebriated, ran onto the field and put a beer to Hansie's mouth in celebration. The security guards came running to capture the hooligan. Waksie outran them back to the stands and jumped a barrier, but one of his feet got hooked in the fence, and he went tumbling over the side, not to be seen again for some time.

In the dressing room after the final there was raucous pandemonium as the Free State team savoured the victory over Western Province. But coach "Vollies" was quiet. Much too quiet. When Hansie asked him why he wasn't excited, the coach replied, prophetically, "I think you won this trophy one year too early. Next year you're all going to talk money, not cricket."

Volsteedt now says, "I don't think I was wrong when I said that." Lucre has a way of unsettling everything, of distorting and toxifying. Intriguingly, he added, enigmatically, "Cricket is now a small piece of dust in my life."

When Hansie was selected as Free State captain in October 1990, he didn't score a run for two or three matches. "Hansie told me I must drop him from the team, that he didn't deserve to be in it," remembered Volsteedt. "And I said, 'There's no chance of that.' I told him that he was going to be a very good captain, and a very good player. I work like that at Grey College also. I take a long time to work out who should be in the team, but when I make up my mind, they are made to play. From when he was a schoolboy, I knew that Hansie had the hallmark of greatness." This despite some flaws Hansie needed to work on: "He was so tall he played forward easily, and sometimes played forward to the wrong ball. But the game came to him easily; the ramifications of the game came to him easily."

Volsteedt is careful to point out that cricket is a complex game that requires brainpower. "Comparing cricket to any other game is like comparing chess to snakes and ladders. It's true. In cricket your mind has to work forward for days. And you have to plan ahead on the field, not in the dressing room."

There came a time when Free State cricket felt it necessary to replace Volsteedt with a new coach and Hansie felt very strongly that Eddie Barlow was that person. Eddie had played for South Africa in the '60s and '70s in one of South Africa's greatest teams that included players like Ali Bacher, Trevor Goddard, Graeme and Peter Pollock, and Mike Procter. Eddie was a fiery and controversial character who always bubbled over with self-confidence and energy.

Hansie and Oupa Hansie Strydom.

Oupa Frans and Ouma Bessie Cronjé.

8 April 1995. Hansie's uncles, aunts and cousins, as well as Oupa Hansie and Ouma Hester
Strydom celebrated the marriage of Hansie and Bertha

The Cronjés spent most December holidays on the Natal South Coast. Pictured right are Hester, San-Marie, Frans, Ewie and Hansie.

Hansie, about 18 months old.

Hansie, San-Marie and Frans on the Durban Beachfront.

Hester, Frans and Hansie with Ewie (seated) in the pool at 246 Paul Kruger Avenue.

The three Cronjé siblings prepare to race

Wide-angle view of the 'test-match ground' garden at 246 Paul Kruger Avenue.

Bird's eye view of Bloemfontein taken from Naval Hill.
1. C.R. Swart Building; 2. Free State Rugby Stadium;
3. Goodyear Park Cricket Stadium; 4. Sanlam Plaza;
5. Grey College; 6. Brandkop;
7. Klipkerk Dutch Reformed Church; 8. Ramblers Club.

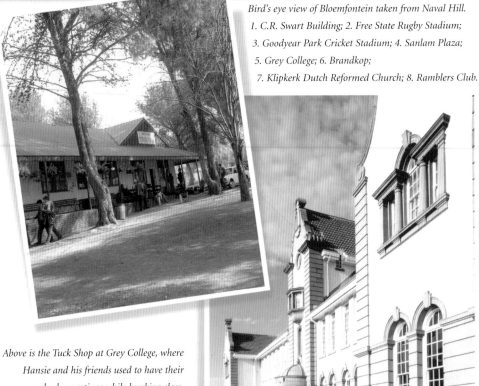

Above is the Tuck Shop at Grey College, where
Hansie and his friends used to have their
cheeky meetings while bunking class.
Right is the Main Building of the school.

At home with Alvin Kallicharran. Behind Kalli is his wife Nazli.

The Cronjé family in a photograph taken by Die Volksblad *in 1984. Hansie was 15 years old at the time.*

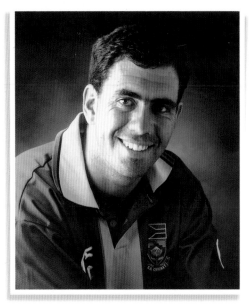

Grey College Primary, 1982

*Hansie, Hester and Frans on Hansie's first day at
school in January 1976.*

South African Cricket Captain 1999.

School Captain, Grey College, 1987.

The Free State under-13 cricket side in 1981. Hansie is seated second from right in the back row. He is seated between Jaco Swanepoel and Neil Hartley. Three players went on to play Free State Provincial cricket with Hansie. They are Phillip Radley (front row, extreme left), Kosie Venter (front, third from left) and Louis Bojé (front, fourth from left).

Hansie captained the Free State under-19 side in 1987. (Hansie is pictured seated between the two coaches). Seated second from right is Louis Bojé, and on the floor on the extreme right is Waksie Prinsloo. The coach at the back is Mr Lappies Labuschagne. On Hansie's right is Mr Dries van de Waal. Three players in the back row went on to play for the rugby Springboks: Ruben Kruger and Pieter Muller (third and fourth from right), and Charl Marais (on the extreme right).

Captain of the Grey College First Rugby Team in 1987.
Pictured on Hansie's left is Louis Bojé, Charl Marais (4th from right) and Ruben Kruger (far right).

Hansie and Marilize Borchard (centre, back) at the Grey Matric Farewell in 1987. Also pictured are Stephan
van Schalkwyk (left, back), Adri Hechter (right, back) and Waksie Prinsloo (centre, front).

The 1988/89 Free State team. Back, from left to right: Johan Volsteedt, Ashley Metcalf, Johan van Heerden, Allan Donald, Joubert Strydom, Frans Cronjé, Corrie van Zyl, Dave Ferrant. Front: Gordon Parsons, Robbie East, Hansie, Rudolph Steyn and Louis Wilkinson.

Springbok Park (Goodyear Park, as it is known today).

November 1991. The first Indian tour by a South African side. Mother Teresa on the left, the Taj Mahal below in the middle.

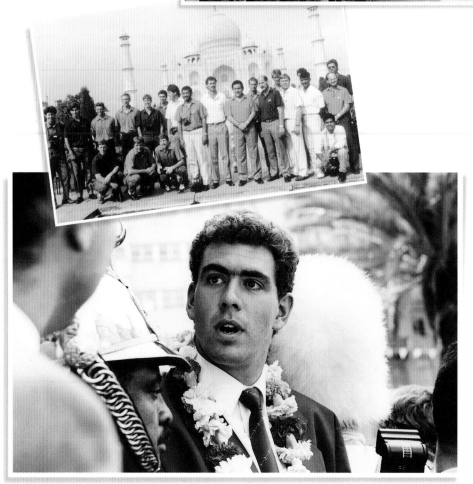

In opening Springbok Park on 20 September 1989, Ewie released a pigeon while Gordon, Hansie and Frans looked on, dressed in orange.

Hansie and Debbie in 1990

Bertha, Hansie, Gordon and Alexandrea at Ludgrove in England, 1995.
Hansie got into trouble for trying to take a photo with Princess Di in the background.

Hansie's medium-paced bowling was especially effective in One Day cricket and he often managed to break important partnerships.

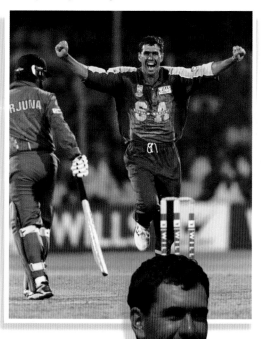

Below: Celebrating a Nantie Hayward wicket with Mark Boucher.

Managing a rueful smile after being given out LBW by Pakistani umpire Javed Akhtar at Headingley, Leeds. It was during the final Test Match against England. Hansie was one of nine Akhtar LBW victims. Only two of those were English.

Hansie carrying Fanie de Villiers off the field after the win against Australia in Sydney, 1994. The other player is Errol Stewart.

Hansie perfected and was famous for his slog sweep.

Celebrating Jonty Rhodes's century at Lord's in London, against England

Hansie, Vollies and Kepler at Lord's, in 1994. This picture hangs proudly in Volsteedt's office, sporting the simple caption "A promise kept".

Spiritual mentor and former body-builder, Pastor Ray McCauley.

Eddie Barlow coached Free State for one season and managed to transform the team into one of the most successful teams in the country.

Hansie and Bertha's wedding day on 8 April 1995.
The flower girl is Alexandrea.

Jonty Rhodes was most probably Hansie's closest
friend throughout his career and beyond.

In 2005 Eddie and his wife, Cally, lived in Cardiff in Wales. Eddie's response to my questions via e-mail helped me to understand the impact that this giant of South African cricket had on Free State. "I was on a visit to Free State in the early '80s, publicising my little coaching manual and went out onto a field where I was surrounded by a group of very dirty and noisy young schoolboys. At the front stood a young, tousled-headed lad with clear brown eyes shining in a dusty and sweaty face. Dying to ask a question, his hand was held high to the sky. *'En wie's jy?'* (Who are you?) I asked.

"'*Hansie Cronjé, Meneer. Is Meneer regtig 'n Springbok krieketspeler?*' (Is Sir really a Springbok cricketer?)

"'*Ja*,' I replied.

"'*Jussus*,' he said.

"'Why are you so dirty?' I asked.

"'It's from the fielding, Sir. Always fielding. Maybe that one run can win the game for us.' I had just met the person who was to be one of the best captains South Africa has ever seen and I had to stifle the smile of joy welling up from my stomach.

"'May we now go to the nets?' he asked.

"Hansie, from our first meeting, was to me, the perfect example of a fine person, cricketer and captain. When I came to Free State to coach in 1991, he was well on the way to becoming one of the best. As captain and coach we had a tremendous rapport and he was open to any innovations that I might suggest to make the team perform better. He certainly led by example, as the stats will prove, and his one ambition in life was to play for South Africa.

"Free State at that time was a backwater of cricket but when I left they had three in the SA side, not due solely to me, but to Hansie's determination to improve his team and make them winners. He was an unselfish captain who cared about his team, but cared as much as I did about winning. Off the field he was a man who enjoyed life and could be a great giggler, dissolving into fits of laughter when told a funny story. He, was above all, the man who gave his all for South Africa and who was so proud to wear the green and gold. When I went to Johannesburg in 1998, to assist Bob Woolmer during the West Indies tour, I had no kit and Hansie lent me some of his with the admonition, 'Hey, Coach, make sure you give this back to me.' He had earned the right to wear it and he did so with pride."

"Barlow took this young side with potential and made it the best in the country," said Corrie van Zyl. "He took us from a so-so side to a very good side, because he made us believe in ourselves. He showed us that only through hard work could you get there. But Eddie also put in the hours himself. He worked hard with the guys."

Hansie took the Barlowisms and made them his own. "Eddie was into basics and firm principles. He believed that there was only a certain way you could play cricket: 'practise the way you play'. He brought to South Africa a professional attitude of practising twice a day. At 8am promptly, the guys would get on the bowling machine. Early in the morning Eddie would make sure that the groundsmen had prepared the pitches correctly so that we got the best out of the practice," recalled Corrie.

On Mondays, Eddie would up the speed and frequency of the bowling-machine's balls, causing havoc with the batsmen, and say, "You're batting like a dog's arse." By Thursday he would change the settings, setting the machine slower, making the batsmen believe they were improving markedly in a short space of time. By Friday, Eddie's praises were ringing in their ears. "He used to make us feel we were totally prepared. Ready to win the Saturday game."

Eddie was a controversial coach. His simple, tough approach to the game often ticked off many egoistic high-class professionals who resented being treated like schoolboys. But his attitude worked well in the Bloemfontein context, and the young team was quite at home with such harsh but familiar and conservative authoritarianism. "We were willing to learn. Eddie wanted things done his way and we were quite happy to go along with it. If he said 'jump' we would all just accept it and jump even higher than he asked. We all wanted to go the extra mile and Eddie was exactly the right person for the job," said Corrie.

Eddie transformed Free State cricket with his back-to-basics approach: getting the small things right, believing in your own abilities. He carefully added a psychological component to Free State's preparation – building up the players mentally, getting them to believe totally in themselves as winners, sticking with them when they underperformed. Such a regime was perfect for Hansie and he blossomed under Barlow, who had a powerful effect on him.

By then, provincial sides were only allowed one overseas player per side. Barlow had no hesitation in signing Franklyn Stephenson, the tall fast bowler from Barbados. Western Province and Boland spin bowler, Omar Henry, also signed on for Free State in the same year.

In the racist atmosphere of the Free State of that time this was a significant milestone. In the past, the overseas players such as Clarke, Kallicharran and Stephenson were not seen as local players of colour, but had a curious "honorary white" status by virtue of their importance as international cricketers. But now for the first time, a South African of colour was to play as a local in the team, and the nonsense of apartheid was becoming increasingly obvious to some old-style Afrikaners. Cricket was helping to break down barriers.

And team bonhomie was cutting through the cords of separatism, which had yet to release its grip on South African society.

Frans recalled an incident that infuriated the Cronjé family. "In the 1988/89 season, it took a lot of explaining to get Kallicharran admitted to Bloemfontein's Universitas Hospital. We had played squash at the university and suddenly Kalli doubled-up with pain. He had pinched a nerve in his back and couldn't move. The university ambulance picked him up and took him to hospital. It was only after we kicked up some serious fuss that he was finally admitted to the hospital and treated. Kalli was very gracious about the whole incident, but I know that it left a scar behind his always smiling exterior."

At 246 Paul Kruger Avenue, the pros were welcome guests whatever their race. How ludicrous that their sitting down to a *boerekos*-laden dining-room table, swimming in the pool and using the toilets should have shocked conservative whites. But it was a different time then and Frans's girlfriend (and now his wife), René, commented on how unique an experience it was for her in the early days of their courtship to sit at the same table and be friends with black people.

The Cronjés ignored racial differences on the team as a matter of course. A cricketer, after all, was just a cricketer.

Sitting in the players' section, with its grand view of a pristine Springbok Park (now called Goodyear Park) in Bloemfontein, on a warm and invigorating spring day is a pleasant enough experience. The immaculate fast-green outfield, the good and bouncy fast wicket, the enthusiastic young men of the rainbow nation in white playing an excellent four-day game. But the only apparent enthusiasm in the large 15 000-seater stadium is the occasional "Howzat!?" from the bowler as he probes for an LBW decision.

Take the match between the Free State Eagles and the Highveld Lions in 2004. There were some great cricketers playing: Nicky Bojé, Boeta Dippenaar, Roger Telemachus, Andrew Hall, to name but a few. And Allan Donald, as assistant coach of the Eagles, was seen striding around the field encouraging the players. Yet only a handful of supporters witnessed the game from one small section of Hansie's old hallowed ground. In the press box nearby, the radio commentators and sporting journalists were doing their job. But was anyone listening? Would a significant number of readers read what they wrote? Would anyone care?

One of the stalwarts of provincial cricket today is the assistant coach of the Johannesburg-based Highveld Lions, the Englishman Gordon Parsons, who is also married to Hester Cronjé. He is not pessimistic about provincial and national cricket, but that should, perhaps, be balanced by the fact that he is employed by the South African cricket authorities.

A fast bowler who also batted usefully in his heyday, Gordon, now 45, hails from Slough, and has been a professional cricketer since 1976. He played county cricket for Leicestershire and Warwickshire before moving to South Africa as a professional, playing for Boland and Griqualand West, and then moving to Virginia and Bloemfontein in 1988 and playing for the Free State.

Quiet and softly spoken, Gordon clearly recalled meeting Hansie in the summer of 1987. Hansie and Deon Jordaan (a school friend of Hansie who also played for Free State) were practising in the nets at the Ramblers Club and Gordon strolled over, offering to bowl to Hansie for a while. "After that we had a cool drink together and I was impressed by the 17-year-old's questions. He asked me about his weaknesses. He asked me how I would bowl to get him out."

After coaching the Free State Under-24s for a while, Gordon Parsons was called up in 1988 to play for Free State, along with young Hansie and Frans Cronjé. "In the 1988/89 season Hansie started to relax in the top-class cricket arena and scored above 50 with regularity," Gordon said.

Gordon moved on to the Harvinia Club, then a strong club and one of the best in the Free State, helped along nicely at the time by the gold price, which meant superb cricketing and club facilities in the mining town of Virginia, about 145km from Bloemfontein. Although he was based in Virginia, many inter-club matches were in Bloemfontein and like the other overseas professionals, he stayed at the Cecil Hotel.

"Hansie soon invited me to stay with his family at 246 Paul Kruger Avenue when I needed accommodation in Bloemfontein. The Cronjé household was always open to cricketers and the family took a special interest in the overseas professionals."

Gordon said that during an away game in Port Elizabeth in the 1988/89 season, he and Hansie and their girlfriends made up a foursome at the local putt-putt course. "I let Hansie win, and from that point our relationship grew and I started to become a regular visitor at the Cronjé home," he said with a smile. At the time Hansie was involved in a long-standing relationship with an Oranje Hoërskool girl, called Marelize Borchard.

"The Cronjé family," said Gordon, "was unbelievably close. I couldn't believe how well they got on with each other. There was never any animosity about anything. They seemed to live to please each other. They were so empathetic, towards each other and towards those around them."

In one sense, said Gordon, they were a normal, middle-class Bloemfontein family. "They were heavily into religious principles. Unbelievably hospitable. Their house was daily filled with visitors, who stayed for lunches and suppers. They didn't seem to have any racist attitudes at all, welcoming players of all colours with equanimity and joy. They weren't rich; they struggled to pay the bills. Their grocery bill must've been huge."

Gordon was 30 when he began to notice young Hester Cronjé, 19, and think of her as more than a friend. The romance didn't get off to a good start as he was already dating someone else and for a while he vacillated between the two women, eventually fixing on the young and naïve Hester. "The age difference, the cultural differences and the toing and froing to England were a huge concern to Mr and Mrs Cronjé, but they didn't interfere and allowed Hester to make her own choices."

This "hands-off" approach to their children was typical of Ewie and San-Marie, who generally allowed their offspring to make their own choices in life with little or no open criticism and certainly no obvious censure – just a stoic belief in their children's basic goodness, that *alles sal regkom*, and that mistakes will eventually be learnt from.

At the age of 21, Hansie became the captain of worldly-wise cricketers like Gordon. "From the start, Hansie was a great captain," said Gordon. "He was relentless and disciplined, but he never got too fanatical. He got me to start running. Hansie was very competitive, very motivated and very naughty, in the schoolboy sense.

"I always respected him, despite the fact that he was ten years younger. As a captain at practice, on the field and in planning and coaching sessions he behaved like a mature 30-year-old. In training and preparation, he always led from the front, obsessed with the basics, with getting the small things right. He required it. He demanded it. And it was meekly and happily given by all the players, young and old, experienced and inexperienced."

Even today, Gordon grapples with his understanding of Hansie's complexities. "Sometimes I can't put my finger on his character. He had a spiritual quality that was impossible to define. His mature leadership abilities reminded me strongly of the great captains of world cricket, like Mike Brearley and Ray Illingworth. Even when Hansie wasn't batting well, his captaincy alone was worth his place in the team."

His leadership was innate and it was characterised by an obsessive attention to detail. "This, I think was one of the things he learnt from Eddie Barlow. He made average players feel like world-beaters."

Gordon also remembered Hansie's competitive streak. Playing in a crunch Free State Club Championship match against the University of the Orange Free State at the end of the club season, Gordon was in line for a big financial bonus if he won the game, and he was excited because Harvinia had put up a good total in their innings. Hester was at the ground watching nervously. "She remarked earlier that she hoped we (Hansie and Frans) would do well, but that we would lose," said Frans.

Frans and Hansie were furious about a bad umpiring decision while Harvinia were batting, and it was made worse when the same umpire gave three university batsmen out LBW, causing the students to be three wickets down for not too many runs. That meant that Hansie and Frans were batting together to save the match. According to Gordon, Hansie nicked a beautiful outswinger from Gordon and was caught behind.

Hansie didn't walk and was given "not out". Gordon sulked, and as he walked past Frans, he said tearfully, "Your *boet* nicked that." To add insult to injury, Hansie went on to score 100, hitting boundaries over Gordon's head.

Gordon was in Hansie's Free State team for three seasons (1988/89, 1989/90 and 1990/91) before his career as a player received a serious blow from a shoulder injury sustained three weeks after his marriage to Hester in 1991. After that, he coached the Free State B-side, which included the likes of Boeta Dippenaaar, Nicky Bojé and Frans Cronjé, before he was appointed head coach of the North West Dragons in Potchefstroom in 1995.

What crops up often in discussion about the days when he played with Hansie is the happy togetherness of the team then, the tight social fabric that knitted them together, a "family" team that was always happy to socialise together after matches and practices and on weekends. They went regularly to Ritchies's restaurant and pub in their free time.

There was a feeling of belonging to a great wave of change, knowing in their hearts that they were part of a magical march to success. The players were happy to mentor and be mentored, hungry to learn and teach in an atmosphere of high excitement and rugged commitment, to each other and the cause of Free State cricket. This was in contrast to the ethos today, where provincial players lead significantly separate lives outside their formal duties. It is as if the happiness has been torn out, as if a sense of joy and noble purpose has been eviscerated.

Perhaps in those early days, the family ties that pulsed out from the homes of the Bojés, the Cronjés, the Strydoms and others contributed. Family values were at the core of this young side's mental and physical health and strength.

But now the good old days are gone. And what is in their place? Empty stadiums. The bonhomie so reminiscent of Free State and South African cricket in Hansie's day is gone.

●

Hansie's appetite for practical jokes was large. Volsteedt, at first glance a stern character with a great sense of dignity, remembers many such pranks when he was Free State coach. "Hansie enjoyed making a fool of me, even when he was a schoolboy, but he had the knack of doing it in such a way that everyone appreciated it – even the victim."

Once, when Free State was playing in the Nissan Shield at Springbok Park, the team were sitting together in the stands when Volsteedt stood up to see and greet someone nearby. Suddenly, young Hansie lunged forward and pulled the coach's trousers down to his ankles. The team hooted with laughter at "Vollies'" embarrassment.

"We once went to Natal on tour and stayed at Umhlanga Rocks. The team was scheduled to leave the next morning at 8am," recalled Volsteedt. "Hansie told the receptionist to give everyone in the team a wake-up call at 4am. He had his own room, and slept on blissfully until a more godly hour."

Hansie's pranks included buckets of ice in team-mates' beds, apple-pied beds, and buckets of water propped up against hotel doors, which splashed forwards when the door was opened by the occupant. Similar escapades were later practised with the same glee by the deceptively taciturn Kepler Wessels.

On more than one occasion Hansie announced that the bus's keys had been lost and would send the team on a fruitless search for the "missing keys" – until Hansie would eventually "find" them. Once, driving along a road in Sea Point, Cape Town, he sent the vehicle into a wild 180-degree spin, much to the annoyance of his brother and the terror of the other sleepy occupants of the vehicle. A favourite trick would be, while the team were dozing peacefully on the road, to quietly tune the vehicle's radio just off a radio station's frequency and then suddenly turn the volume up to the max, waking his team-mates suddenly to the mad hell of distorted sound.

But if anyone tried to turn the tables, Hansie would get unreasonably grumpy; he seemed to insist on having the last laugh in the succession of silly jokes. Perhaps this is another illustration of his competitiveness, relentless in everything he did.

Volsteedt recalled an incident that occurred after a Free State match at Newlands, Cape Town. The Free State team had had a hell-raising night in a post-match party. "I drove the team in a minibus early the next morning – we had a 6am plane to catch. As we were driving along, Hansie suddenly said, 'I want you to turn left here and go to that building over there'.

"When I asked why, he urgently repeated his request: 'Please just go to that building.'"

Volsteedt insisted on knowing why the detour was necessary and Hansie replied, "I just want to pick up my name. I threw it away there last night."

Johan Laubscher, a school friend of Hansie's, recalled, "Hansie always made his friends feel special and it seemed like he had a lot of time for each individual. He also had a great sense of humour. Once, he introduced me behind my back as a golf pro, knowing full well that I do not play golf at all. I was perplexed by all the golf questions from complete strangers, until I later discovered Hansie's prank. He reminded me of this for a long time, very proud of his own joke."

Hansie's Grey College mates, Stephan van Schalkwyk and Waksie Prinsloo, were at Free State University with him and played a large part in his life. They fondly recalled many humorous Hansie incidents relating to cars.

After he finished school, Hansie's first car was an old Volkswagen Beetle. Waksie Prinsloo said, "Hansie took me for a drive and later asked me if I wanted to try the car out. While I was battling to find the reverse gear, he said, 'Stop here, I will show you how to find the reverse gear.' We stopped and changed seats. Hansie then told me to 'sit like a girl'. I did so and then Hansie grappled with the reverse gear, and in the process he touched my leg several times. With a broad grin, Hansie had said, 'That's why I bought this car!'"

Waksie remembered another incident that is a good example of Hansie's daredevil mischievousness. Waksie was using his dad's new Ford Sierra as his own dilapidated Volkswagen Golf had broken down.

He had parked the car on the varsity campus and, returning to it later, found to his dismay that all the hubcaps had been removed. He knew his father would "crack" and was eager to avoid this. But the hubcaps cost about R200 each and Waksie didn't have that kind of money.

Hansie's solution was simple: "We'll steal them back... Let's wait until there's a smart function at the Sand du Plessis Theatre and find a nice Sierra with some hubcaps." The next day they cased the joint. "There was no real security," said Waksie, "but one guy was walking around, so we had to be careful."

They spotted a spanking new Sierra with just the right hubcaps. The boys decided to make a game of it. They took turns: one would remove two hubcaps, while the other kept watch and timed him to see who could do it in the fastest time.

While Hansie kept watch, Waksie made short work of two hubcaps in five seconds. Hansie was suitably impressed and challenged. Now it was his turn while Waksie kept watch. Hansie glided deftly to the first wheel. But something was wrong. The hubcap wouldn't come off. Sweating now, Hansie had screamed under his breath, "The thing doesn't want to come off!" Perversely, Hansie's hubcaps were tied onto the wheel with plastic straps. Waksie, sweating too, frantically scoured the lot for the patrolling guard. They were on the point of giving up and getting the hell out of there, when Hansie somehow managed to wrench the hubcaps free.

They made their escape with the four hubcaps, triumphant. Later that evening, Hansie and Waksie had walked together to the Cronjé home. Waksie had a habit of touching his face periodically. He had not noticed that his hands were coated with black rubber and that his face was full of dark smudges. As they walked into the house, Ewie Cronjé asked, "Waksie, why is your face so black?" Waksie mumbled some pathetic story far from the truth, while Hansie "laughed his head off".

"Hansie," said Waksie, "was immensely proud of this whole escapade and told everybody the story of the stolen hubcaps."

But the next week, Waksie got his comeuppance. He had his old Golf back and it had failed to start because of a flat battery. Hansie helped him push-start the vehicle at night and in the process Waksie went through a stop street without putting the car's lights on. A traffic officer stopped him and issued two fines: one for going through a stop street and another for travelling at night without headlights.

The fines' total exactly matched the value of the hubcaps.

While at university, Hansie had little time to study, nevertheless, with his usual intelligence and self-discipline, he managed a respectable BCom in four years, a remarkable achievement considering how cricket consumed his time and focus.

Waksie and future Springbok rugby player Ruben Kruger stayed in a student digs dubbed Bonkers. Here Hansie was a periodic but fairly regular visitor, drinking a beer or two and playing cricket on the lawns with his old mates. Cricket was not only a profession; it was also damned good fun. His appetite for the game was insatiable.

The Free State University has about 23 000 students and the campus is laid out on a massive 425 morgen which includes an impressive array of sports facilities. Today the students come from all over Africa, including Kenya, Eritrea, Uganda, Zambia, Lesotho, Namibia and Zimbabwe. In Hansie's day, all the students were white.

An old bicycle shed attached to the Abraham Fischer Hostel (affectionately known as Vishuis) has been converted by the students themselves into the Ewie Cronjé Room. Initially, this caused some consternation among the high-ups because "permission" had not been granted. But eventually the university bosses relented. "I've given them cricketing stuff of my dad's and Hansie's," said Ewie, obviously pleased by this grassroots recognition for the Cronjé contribution to cricket.

He proudly pointed out, "In the 1980s I wanted to make Free State University cricket big. When Hansie started playing cricket at varsity in 1988 all members of the UOFS first team were Old Greys."

Today, the still sports-mad university has six cricket fields, eight rugby fields, two soccer fields, 18 tennis courts, five hockey fields, six netball courts, several basketball courts, 20 squash courts, several badminton courts and an Olympic-size swimming pool. Most of the fields are floodlit at night, because the students mostly practise after dark.

And then of course there is the Varsity Cricket Oval, where Hansie started his provincial career in 1988, the same year he started his BCom. He played there for three years before the 15 000-seater Springbok Park was built. The Oval, with its grass embankments can fit in 5 000 people.

Hansie played eighth man in the UOFS under-20s rugby team and was a regular and fanatical supporter of the Shimlas, the university's 1st XV.

In a 1990 video of a Shimla match against archrivals Potchefstroom University, Hansie's manic exuberance for victory is wonderfully evident. His mate, Louis Bojé, had just converted a winning penalty kick from behind the halfway line in the dying moments of the game. Frans and Waksie also played in the game. Hansie, with toothy smiles, the very picture of delight, rushed onto the field from the spectators' stands and helped to carry the hero off. Exultation at winning was a hallmark of Hansie's character and he always supported his friends and Frans when they played any sport, frequently carrying them from the field on his shoulders when victorious.

Jonty Rhodes ruefully admitted that it took him five years to complete his degree, and that his first salary for Natal was R3 000. "I walked out of varsity with nothing in the bank, even after several years of first-class professional cricket. "But while he was still a student, I remember Hansie talking about buying a house, taking out a bond, getting a tenant in it. By the time he left varsity after four years he had an asset portfolio."

In a Cronjé family video clip circa 1991, filmed at 246 Paul Kruger Avenue, a beautiful 25-year-old Yorkshire woman, Debbie Coleman, gazes into the camera with a curious mixture of boldness and timidity. She seems a little overwhelmed by the raucous, often unintelligible bonhomie around her. She seats herself coyly, looks conscious of herself as a curiosity, her shapely legs coiled up underneath her.

Hansie's English girl from England.

It was precisely her other-worldliness, her exotic appeal that probably drew Hansie. His relationship with her epitomised his coming of age, his statement of independence as a man, a man who was just beginning to take on the world, to savour the world, to make his own mistakes.

Debbie was the daughter of Brian Coleman, a Yorkshire umpire-coach who had moved to the Free State a few years earlier. She had come to visit her dad and taken a shine to the strange and exotic world of Bloemfontein, and the handsome, polite and robust young Afrikaners had, no doubt, piqued her interest. She soon had a job as an aerobics instructor at the Kloppers' Gym, where the Free State cricket team was regularly at work.

With her large brown eyes, lovely white teeth and her carefully styled blonde hair, she was hard to resist; an interesting example of forbidden fruit in a town renowned for its Calvinistic piety.

Her supple antics at Kloppers Gym made for an intoxicating vision, and she soon had a young Hansie under her spell. His sometimes tempestuous relationship with her lasted for nearly two years, from around the time of his ascendancy to Free State captain at the age of 21.

Gorgeous Debbie provided a feast for the eyes at cricket matches. At Springbok Park she would soak up the sunshine on the sloped banks of Cow's Corner, shedding her bikini top and lying there outrageously in her G-string. The exposure meant, of course, the regular lingering of the TV cameras on Hansie's girlfriend's shapely form.

Hansie's relationship with her shocked some members of his family. For the first time in his life, he was being openly rebellious. Hansie, according to some family members, sometimes snuck her into his room overnight at 246 Paul Kruger Avenue, apparently without the knowledge of his parents. It was provocative behaviour in the Christian Bloemfontein context, especially in those years.

His relationship with Debbie coincided with his new rock-star status, and his persona was battling to find its ground. For the first time in his life, he was exposed to public criticism: either he was accused of being "Captain Grumpy" or, when he tried a more carefree and friendly approach, of being too relaxed and *windgat*.

Said René, "Debbie was a fun-loving, warm and friendly girl who loved Hansie deeply, perhaps too much. She was someone with a different value system. She gave Hansie a new way of seeing things, new answers to his questions about life."

At first, Hansie distanced himself from anyone – even his family – who tried to interfere with or criticise his relationship with Debbie. He drifted away from the Church's teachings on sex before marriage.

"Hansie," said René, "highly valued his relationships, and loyalty to people close to him was one of his highest priorities. I saw Hansie go through a very painful and difficult separation from Debbie, a process that took more than a year.

"Later, when Hansie got a contract to play in Norden, he saw it as an opportunity to get Debbie back to England – in her home country where she could have the support of her own family and friends – to spend a last few happy weeks together before breaking the relationship off with clear finality."

●

There is a curious connection between India, Pakistan and the Free State, in the names of the university's first and second rugby teams.

A name for the teams was sought around 1920. The first rugby side lost a game and the students decided that a new war cry was needed to help the team win. Kêppie Landau opened a world atlas and running his finger along the foothills of the Himalayas, came upon the names Peshawar, Irawa (now the Ravi River) and Shimla. From these a new chant was devised. Shimla was adopted as the name for the first team and Irawa for the second.

CHAPTER SEVEN

CAPTAIN KEPLER

There are four things in life that never return: a spoken word,
a shot arrow, time elapsed and a lost opportunity.

— Alan Jones, to the South African side on the night before their first match

against Australia after isolation.

On the release of Nelson Mandela by President F W De Klerk in 1990, the future of South African cricket was suddenly bright. The world wanted the feisty, long-untested South Africans back on the global playing fields.

After more than two decades of sporting isolation, after fractious and unhappy rebel tours, world cricket started to unlock the stadium turnstiles and change-room doors.

A sudden and momentous opportunity arrived as India and Pakistan called off their 1991 Test Series because of heightened political tension between the two old enemies. Ali Bacher, Geoff Dakin and Krish Mackerdhuj of the United Cricket Board of South Africa, went to an International Cricket Council (ICC) meeting in London and arrived back in South Africa on a bright Sunday, 1 November 1991 with great news. During the meetings in London, the Indian cricket authorities had invited the South African side to India to play three One-Day International matches.

With six hours' notice, a South African team was rapidly selected and organised to tour India and on Thursday, 7 November 1991, they were in their striped green and gold blazers and ties, ready to fly from Johannesburg airport to Calcutta. Clive Rice was captain and the team mainly consisted of experienced provincial players: Jimmy Cook, Andrew Hudson, Mandy Yachad, Kepler Wessels, Peter Kirsten, Adrian Kuiper, Brian McMillan, Dave Richardson, Tim Shaw, Clive Eksteen, Richard Snell, Allan Donald and Craig Matthews. It would be a swansong of sorts for some of the older players who had been deprived of normal world competition for all their cricketing lives, due to the apartheid-isolation years.

None of them had any experience of playing for their country, although Kepler Wessels had earned his batting stripes in Australia. The Old Grey warrior had faced the challenge of sports isolation by uprooting and moving to Australia, where he settled in and played 24 Tests for that country.

His cricketing ability had already made him Hansie's hero at Grey College. Videos of Kepler's astounding Australian cricketing adventures had been shown again and again to the young star cricketers at the school. His batsmanship was closely watched and carefully analysed, over and over. After his Grey College years, Hansie had watched Kepler's progress with deep interest and Grey pride. Before they even met, Hansie was already a disciple of the stern master of his craft.

After being falsely accused of helping to organise a rebel tour to South Africa, Kepler was effectively hounded out of his adopted country. He then moved to Port Elizabeth in South Africa, and led Eastern Province cricket to new heights.

The recently formed United Cricket Board of South Africa (UCB) also selected four "development" players for the Indian tour, who were to come along for the ride of a lifetime: Hansie Cronjé, Faiek Davids, Derek Crookes and Hussein Manack. Hansie was ecstatic, even though he knew he was an appendage of sorts and that he wouldn't get to play on the tour. The young Afrikaner had only been overseas once before – a month-long holiday in England with Ewie and Frans back in 1988, when the three of them had stayed with former Free State pro, Alvin Kallicharran, and his family in Birmingham.

India was as exotic a destination as one could imagine for the South Africans. Its strangeness was made even more poignant by the fact that, until 1976 no person of Asian descent was allowed to stay in the Free State for more than 24 hours. Part of the racist rationale at the time of the introduction of this law was that Indians and other Asians would overwhelm white business hegemony in the province.

The specially chartered Boeing, packed with the UCB executive, the team and many South African cricket supporters (including Ewie and San-Marie), finally landed in Calcutta. The temperature was 35° Celsius, with a humidity factor of 95%. Jago Dalmaia, president of the Indian Cricket Board, met them on the plane and a large and exuberant welcoming party greeted the South Africans on the runway. Every member of the touring party received a garland and dash of paint on the forehead to welcome them.

Many thousands of people swarmed the Dumdum airport building in the overwhelming reception. Hansie was amazed and somewhat unnerved by the spectacle.

The airport crush was spectacular enough, but the South African entourage were at a loss for words as they ventured into Calcutta by bus, surrounded by a convoy of cars and 300 mopeds. What was normally a 30-minute drive to the hotel turned out to be a ponderous three-hour epic.

As the team bus trundled along slowly, stopping regularly, a cheer went up inside the bus at the sight of UCB executive member, Douglas Maku, driving one of the Cricket Association of Bengal scooters that buzzed by.

At least 2 000 000 people lined the streets between the airport and the hotel in anticipation of the "new" international team on the circuit. Everywhere, smiling faces waved UCB flags, mopeds constantly buzzed the bus, the riders grinning and waving. Heads popped out of windows of battered cars, shouting greetings. India's magnificent largesse, its deep fervour for the game, was in rampant display, as if a thousand peacocks had spread out their fantails, strutting about in high excitement. It was a glorious return to the fold for players who'd been considered the sporting world's outcasts.

India. Always overwhelming, magnificent and opulent. Brimming with joy and beauty, and lurking with danger. A land of mighty and unseen forces and gods.

Hansie stared wide-eyed at this complex and beautiful new world, drinking in the endless spectacle. He was entranced.

At the Oberoi Hotel, "barriers of khaki-clad policemen stood shoulder to shoulder at the entrance, and enabled the overwhelmed cricketers to scramble from the bus to the foyer. A milling crowd remained outside throughout the South Africans' stay. Each arrival, each departure would be a rousing adventure," wrote Edward Griffiths in his book, *Kepler: The Biography*.

The following day, after a nets practice, the entire touring party piled into the buses again to visit Mother Teresa of Calcutta. The contrast between their five-star hotel and the Sisters of Mercy complex could not have been greater. The poverty, disease and desperation of the truly poor was laid bare. The reality of suffering and squalor, and the compassion of Christ through His servants, provided a sobering contrast to all the frenzied glamour.

⬤

A book of Mother Teresa's quotes is proudly displayed on a coffee table in the living room at 246 Paul Kruger Avenue. San-Marie's favourite, which she often quoted to Hansie, is: "God sent me to the world in order to love those that no-one else wants to love, so that they would know there is a God."

Christian concern for the poor was something that San-Marie was fond of teaching her children, and Frans commented, "Hansie's desire to help others less fortunate than himself was a trait which Mom noticed very early in his life. He often demonstrated a real concern for those who were less privileged." Such concern was to be especially noticed in his unselfish role in development cricket in later years, a fact that Ali Bacher remarked on time and again.

The visit to Mother Teresa had an enormous impact on Hansie and his mother. San-Marie's account of it follows:

I had read and heard of the work of Mother Teresa and thought I had a picture in my mind of what she was like…but I soon realised how wrong my mental picture was. The reason for our visit to her home was to hand her R10 000 as a gift from South Africa and the cricket team. After travelling through the slums of Calcutta, our bus came to an abrupt standstill and we looked at the surrounding area in amazement. I couldn't believe that this was where a world figure would live and work. Could this be home to any human being of fame?

We entered a very narrow alleyway…in desperate need of paint and brush. Disease, leprosy, Aids hung in the air…I almost wanted to stop breathing right there amongst the disease-infected walls. There, right in front of us, overhanging a very ordinary wall, was a signboard simply reading 'Mother Teresa'. That was all. We stood like sheep in silence, waiting in a cramped foyer. The cricketers were up front. I stood up on my toes, desperately wanting to catch the first glimpse of what was to come.

Young nuns in white and blue kept telling us to keep the visit short. All of them carried worried expressions on their faces. They appeared very nervous, almost agitated with our call… I later learned that Mother Teresa had been very ill. She had received a pacemaker to counteract a heart condition.

I didn't see her arrive, instead I saw our cricketers disappearing one by one. Then I realised they were going down on their knees to be blessed and be given a prayer card. Hansie was still just as tall as she was, even though he was kneeling. Tears started flowing … it was a very emotional moment.

My turn came… Whatever I expected, dreamt of finding, was way out and unreal to this moment in time. There before me stood the little five-foot-tall lady, dressed in her distinctive white sari with blue edging, her drooping shoulders and her face furrowed by the deep wrinkles that time had etched. Her blue-grey eyes looked tired and faint. I looked into a face that spoke to your deepest soul within. With her over-sized hands she gave me a yellow card that read:

"THE FRUIT OF SILENCE IS PRAYER
PRAYER IS FAITH
FAITH IS LOVE
LOVE IS SERVICE
SERVICE IS PEACE

Mother Teresa"

To this day I carry it in my wallet wherever I go. Special words from a special lady.

How humble I felt after this uplifting moment. The tiny figure showed little of Christ's mighty power within her. I asked myself, could this be the person who showed no fear – who influenced lords, princes and kings? This was her home, no fuss and frills, only a massive Cross on the staircase with her Jesus on it … her inspiration, her life, her all.

The ladies were invited to visit her children's hospital next door. Rows and rows of people queued for their daily rations of rice… a mere bowl for each family. What mattered most was that it was given with love. Upon entering the hospital, no cameras were allowed. An atmosphere of death hung around. Sickly, very sickly, deformed children lay on shining floors and beds. The tender care they received was evident. The sight cannot really be put in words… My only consolation was at least they would die having been loved… They could at least smile upon death for Mother Teresa had given them hope. Most of these were children left out on the streets to die. They would also know that a Loving Father was waiting to welcome them into eternal life.

She told us, "For me every individual matters. I believe in person-to-person contact. I see Jesus in every one of them and since there is only one Jesus, the person that I am talking to at that moment is the only person in the world at that moment." She knew the need in all humans to be loved and be treated as special even if it was but for a short time. Her secret in life was the centrality of Christ. She and all who worked for her were channels, or instruments of Christ and His love… All was done for the Glory of God.

Little did I know in nine years' time my own life would come to a standstill … and Mother Teresa's imprint would help me carry my own little cross.

On a Sunday morning, 10 November 1991, South Africa played their first match against India.

Eden Gardens is a massive and intimidating stadium, taking in about 100 000 people. Tens of thousands of fans milled around outside the stadium trying vainly to enter, to watch their captain Mohammed Azharuddin and his team do battle with the South Africans.

The team, including the development players, walked onto the field to greet the crowd, bowing and putting their hands together in a prayer-like greeting. "The crowd just cheered and cheered. I'll never forget it," said Hansie in the Rodney Hartman book *Hansie and the Boys*.

Throughout the match, the noise was deafening. Fireworks were ignited when the Indian side performed well and at times the stands were on fire. Clouds of acrid sulphur wafted around the space. Thousands of policemen patrolled the stands, and misbehaving individuals were given a sharp crack with a long, stout stick. The spectacle was worthy of any hot-blooded Bollywood epic – and one of the world's greatest cricketing moments.

Back at 246 Paul Kruger Avenue, Debbie Coleman, Allan Donald's wife Tina, Frans and his wife, René, were in front of the TV at 5 am – as was most of South Africa – to watch the start of the game. It was a defining moment in the nation's history: the match signalled new political, social and sporting beginnings.

The South Africans were overpowered by the Indian side. A small, 17-year-old batsman, Sachin Tendulkar, was especially noticeable.

●

From Calcutta the touring party went to Agra and, after the obligatory visit to the serene Taj Mahal, the team and officials enjoyed a banquet at the palace of Prince Scindia. The second match in Gwalior was also lost, but in the third match in New Delhi, the South African team started finding their feet and managed a win.

While Hansie and his development mates never played, it was a multi-faceted experience for them all, etched in the brain and spirit.

It was around this time that Kepler Wessels first noticed Hansie. "I'd heard about him, of course, but I saw him then for myself. We arrived one night, midnight, in Agra, I think, and we got off the plane. All our baggage was on a truck at the hotel and for some reason the [staff] were not available to off-load. We stood around waiting, and everybody was tired and irritable. So Hansie simply jumped onto the baggage mountain and started taking down the suitcases and 'coffins'. This prompted others to do the work too. Then I could see that he had natural leadership, was a servant-leader, doing what it takes to get things done, however small.

"I've always known that you can't manufacture or teach leadership. I think you're born with it. There's no question Hansie was a natural-born leader of men and this small incident was merely the first confirmation of what I continued to see clearly in his life," Kepler confirmed.

The short and exotic trip affected Hansie deeply and the taste of international cricket had made him even more determined to fulfil his destiny. But he knew that to achieve glory, he would have to continue to do what he always had – work harder and train longer than anyone else.

From his schooldays, Hansie was perceived as a boy who knew what he wanted in his sporting, personal and academic life, setting goals to achieve his aims and working conscientiously and relentlessly to that end. In his short life up to then, he had captained many school and provincial teams. "In all these captaincy roles he had proved that he was without match when it came to dedication and conscientiousness. Hansie was someone who had always 'led from the front'. He had always been the fittest and most hardworking member of every team he had ever been part of," said Frans. Few would disagree.

●

Back home in the Free State, Hansie became even more ferociously committed. The young Free State captain kept on driving himself and his team-mates to be fitter and better than they had ever been. His own cricketing performances, especially in One-Day matches, were impressive. With Eddie Barlow as coach and Hansie as captain, the Free State team was fast becoming the new force to be reckoned with in South Africa.

Hansie's capacity for hard work was complemented by extreme self-discipline. While other players were taking well-earned rest periods, Hansie would be out training. Delayed gratification characterised his lifestyle. "If he got invited to a party that was during training time, he would either make a plan to do the same amount of hours earlier in the day, or he would try to reschedule the event so that he could go," said Gordon, Hansie's brother-in-law.

●

In 1992 came the announcement of the squad to go to the World Cup in Australia. Hansie had expected the same team that toured India to be picked, but the South African selectors surprised nearly everyone – and angered not a few – by going with young talent like Hansie, Jonty, Mark Rushmere and Andrew Hudson. Convenor Peter van der Merwe, Tony Pithey, SK Reddy, Rushdi Magiet, Lee Irvine and Peter Pollock were brave men who had the guts to do what would turn out to be in SA cricket's best interests. Kepler Wessels was to replace Clive Rice as captain. Mike Procter was appointed as coach and Alan Jordaan as manager. A new and adventurous era had begun.

"I was really glad to see Hansie and Jonty in the team," recalled Kepler. "They were young, energetic and both had a very strong work ethic. They were exactly the type of players that I wanted to have in the side. I had a vision to turn the South African side into the fittest side in the world and with players like them we could do it.

"With Hansie, I knew that he would go beyond the call of duty, working harder than what was required." Echoing what has been said previously, Kepler explained, "At Grey College it was a big thing to be the best that you could be, and never to back down, to look the opposition in the eye and take them on. We believed in establishing our authority, very much like the Australian mentality of today.

"At Grey, too, we also planned, and we strategised and eventually it started happening. At school we used to have team meetings – pretty much like we have at top level – and really plan matches like a military campaign."

But the inclusion of young lions did mean that the side was inexperienced, and that posed a bit of a problem. "For this reason I chose to get an old acquaintance of mine, Alan Jones, to come and talk to the team the night before our opening match against Australia in Sydney."

Alan Jones had been the personal advisor to former Australian premier, Malcolm Fraser, and he was instrumental in establishing the successful sports academy system, which has made Australia the best sporting nation in the Commonwealth and one of the best in the world. From 1984 to 1988, Jones had also coached the Australian Rugby Union side, the Wallabies, to 89 victories in 102 matches.

The young and nervous South Africans did not have much of an idea of what to expect the following day in their opening match against the mighty Australians. And they were clearly intimidated.

Jones told them, "I will tell you the same thing that I told my rugby team once, before we played against Ireland in Dublin. We had to win one more game to beat the world record of 18 consecutive Test wins. It was the last match of a very successful tour to the United Kingdom and the lads were burnt out and tired. They were also getting very tense by now, as the pressure was mounting to beat this record. I told them what my mother used to tell me – that there are four things in life that never return: a spoken word, a shot arrow, time elapsed and a lost opportunity.

"Tomorrow you have the opportunity to make history or become just another footprint in history. My Wallaby team went on to beat Ireland the next day and they broke the world record. You have the same opportunity tomorrow to beat Australia, against all odds." Hansie quoted Jones's words in most of his speeches after that.

Jones looked at Allan Donald and said, "Tomorrow there will be 40 000 people packed into the Sydney Cricket Ground. The noise will be unlike any other noise you have ever heard. You may run in to bowl to Geoff Marsh and get him caught behind, but because of the noise the chances are good that the umpire will not hear the nick as the ball brushes the bat on the way to the keeper. If he says 'not out' then you will just have to turn around, get back to your crease and bowl as if nothing happened."

He added: "Make tomorrow your day. Just fix your mind on getting your job 100% right, 100% of the time."

Kepler Wessels recalled walking onto the field, after having won the toss and deciding to bowl first. "I looked closely at my team. They were white as sheets. No one said anything. They were so tense that I thought to myself 'We're gonna get slaughtered. I just hope that it's not too embarrassing.'"

Allan Donald had to bowl the first over. From their early days, Hansie knew that Allan's first over was always vital to his performance in any contest. "If things go well in his first over, then he is unstoppable. But if that does not happen, then the wheels can come off," Hansie used to say.

Allan turned at the end of his 18-metre run-up and charged in to bowl the first ball. The noise from the stands was deafening. As he let go of the ball, Allan knew that his rhythm was good. It was a perfect first delivery and it seamed away just enough from the batsman to get the outside edge, going straight through to Dave Richardson, who took the catch and started celebrating. A wicket off the first ball – a dream start! Allan and the team leapt in the air and started hugging each other. To their amazement, the New Zealand umpire, Brian Aldridge, indicated 'not out'. Marsh stood his ground as the replay on the screen clearly exposed the umpire's error.

Jones' pep talk echoed in Allan's mind. Incredibly, the prophecy had come true. "You will just have to go back to your mark and bowl the next delivery as though nothing ever happened." He turned, and followed Jones' advice. The rest of the team were up to it as well. Australia scored a meek 170 for 9.

Kepler went out to open and played a magnificent captain's innings, jogging steadily to his 81 runs, making his total of 2 000 runs in One-Day International cricket, enjoying every moment of the victory against his former team-mates. There is no finer revenge than playing well. Along with the experienced Peter Kirsten, he steered South Africa to a shock nine-wicket victory.

"Through sheer passion and desperation, we hit Australia so hard that I don't think they really knew what happened," recalled Kepler.

When asked recently how he, a loyal Australian could give a motivational talk to his country's arch rivals, Alan Jones replied, "Well, South Africa were not supposed to win, were they?"

However, the rest of the World Cup campaign almost ended in disaster, as SA lost to New Zealand and to Sri Lanka. But then they managed to beat Pakistan, admittedly in a game that was cruelly shortened in Pakistan's disfavour, because of rain.

Even though the batting and bowling were at times inconsistent, the South African team was beginning to make a big impression as a fielding side. It was a side full of youthful energy and agility, but the real spark came from young Jonty Rhodes. Jonty and Hansie would field on opposite sides of the wicket and keep everyone on their toes, greatly assisting Kepler, who knew he could rely on them to "captain" the close fielding, allowing him to focus on the bigger picture.

South Africa batted first and Hansie scored 47 not out. Pakistan was going along well with Inzamam-ul-Haq at the crease. It looked likely that they would beat South Africa. Inzamam, a big man, was not the quickest when it came to running between the wickets, but he was a hefty hitter. When the ball was dropped short, Inzamam hit it towards extra point and set off for a quick single. Inzamam started running, knowing little about the young man fielding at cover point. Jonty rocketed forward and fielded the ball. Then, instead of throwing it at the stumps, he ran and dived horizontally, with the ball extended in his right hand, crashing flamboyantly into the wickets.

The umpire at square leg stretched out his arm and pointed his right index finger in the air – Inzamam was run out. The slow motion cameras later showed that he was out by about two centimetres. A black and white photograph of a flying Jonty became a classic, eloquently exemplifying the new South African athleticism on the field. This run-out swung the match, which South Africa won.

Then it was South Africa versus India. Hansie hit the winning runs with a four and South Africa secured a spot in the semi-finals against England.

●

Hansie and Kepler soon became close friends, grounded as they both were in language, culture and the Grey College ethos. Hansie found in Kepler the ideal mentor, simply and utterly the right man, in the right place, at the right time. Kepler was also a Calvinist Christian, was committed to a high level of physical fitness, was a great tactician, and had a mind of steel. His tough-guy reputation was heightened by the fact that he was a boxer and a karate exponent, and worked hard on his mental toughness as well. Hansie's ideal hero, the first Afrikaner to play decent international cricket.

Kepler never seemed to get distracted by outside factors and opponents when he was batting. His leadership style was gruff, taciturn, inscrutable, stern and pedantic. His sphinx-like demeanour on the field was legendary. He led from the front and worked harder than anyone else. He expected the team to follow his example. He said little, and gave curt, to-the-point instructions. Team debate was not a characteristic of his captaincy.

Despite Kepler's dour and brittle exterior, he was a bit of a prankster, which further endeared him to Hansie. The South African team's long-standing physiotherapist, Craig Smith, commented, "In the context of the 'Englishness' of cricket in South Africa, Hansie and Kepler often made very Afrikaans comments to each other, and often they were the only two laughing at their own jokes with the other cricketers not understanding. On tour, the two of them would secretly get together and put sardines in air conditioner units, trash players' rooms and the like. Poker-faced lying about his guilt in the fun was a Hansie hallmark. They never seemed to get caught out as the culprits. Probably because people did not really expect something like that from either of them. Kepler was always very serious in public and even in front of the team. Most players were a bit scared of him. Later, the same was true of Hansie."

"Hansie," said Jonty, "worshipped Kepler. Kepler influenced Hansie the most. Kepler was disciplined to the max. He got where he was through sheer hard work. He trained like a man possessed. They would spend two hours together in the nets. Kepler always used to say that we must use the net practice like we were batting in a match. And if you wanted to practice your cover drives, or your cuts, you must take balls after net practice. For hours and hours. Hansie did this and had amazing stamina for it. He also had a desire to learn and Kepler was the only guy – because of his international experience – who Hansie could learn from. There was, simply, no-one else to teach him."

This was reminiscent of how Johan Volsteedt used to nurture them at Grey. He would identify two or three talented boys and then resolutely build relationships with them in the context of long hours of training.

It is clear that young Hansie modelled himself on Kepler. At times this imitation was taken to absurd lengths. The team laughed at Hansie at one stage, when he started throwing the ball just like Kepler did, "as if it were a javelin, or a shot-put", said Jonty.

In the evenings on tour, the two of them would often go out together and have a meal, or stay at the hotel and order room service. Hansie would often spend most of the evening talking about cricket, asking Kepler about various aspects of the game. Kepler never seemed to tire in this role. "Hansie," said Frans, "believed that a large part of cricket was learnt by talking about the game, especially when words of wisdom came from the likes of Kepler."

"Even at this early stage in his career, I could sense that Hansie's ultimate ambition was to captain the side. He did not just want to play in the team; he wanted to lead the side. I saw the potential in him and was very willing to guide him as much as I could," said Kepler.

Hansie set high but realistic goals for himself, and these included financial ones. He worked methodically with his money, investing judiciously. He did well. There was no peer in the team in this respect, throughout his career.

"After school he had set himself the goal of playing for South Africa. Then it was to be as fit as he could be. He was never one of the old-school players, partying after matches. After net practice he used to do push-ups and run. The guys laughed at him, but he changed world cricket with that attitude.

"He used to study leadership models and associate himself with leaders of all kinds, and he really tapped into Kepler," said Frans.

Perhaps because of his tight friendship with Hansie, Kepler was quick to point out that others in the team were always welcome to join them for dinner. This offer, however, was not often taken up. Perhaps because they didn't enjoy the desperate seriousness of it all, or didn't want to interfere in the Kepler-Hansie huddle. Perhaps it was both. Talking about cricket all night was not exactly the way of most of the other players, who simply wanted to unwind, to get away from the relentless cricket lore. Also, because Hansie and Kepler both wanted to be ultra fit, neither of them enjoyed drinking too much or frequenting nightclubs, so their apartness was inevitable.

But this separation also related to the differing sets of values and mores between the then traditional South African English way of cricket and the Afrikaans-Grey imperatives.

A cynical and unkind view of the old style of high-level cricket in South Africa, at least until the late 1980s, was that it was three months a year of boozing, smoking, womanising, good times and cricket. Many cricket players leaned towards degrees of agnosticism, or simply were quiet about their Christian feelings, deeming it unnecessary to "impose" personal convictions of this nature. Hansie, Kepler, Andrew Hudson, Jonty, team manager Allan Jordaan and others were to change that in some radical ways in the 1990s.

One of the players who did not quite share in Kepler's astringent personal convictions was Meyrick Pringle. Meyrick recalls with a smile an incident during the 1992 World Cup in Sydney. He had been out clubbing until 7am and had attempted to sneak back to his hotel room. As he furtively entered the hotel lobby, he saw, to his dismay, Kepler coming out of the lift with his jogging gear on, ready for his regular early morning run. Meyrick dived behind a nearby couch until Kepler was safely outside the hotel. As Meyrick stood up, coach Mike Procter walked passed him and commented dryly, "Why hide, Pring?"

Hansie and Kepler, believed fervently in God. They lived, or seriously attempted to live, by strict moral values, and were very self-disciplined and aggressively focused on and off the field. But Hansie also had an innate cunning and a strong and intelligent political will that he used to good effect.

Those who have observed Hansie's ways closely have said that he had "an exceptional ability to understand group dynamics, pinpoint power relationships and discern key social networks. Hansie was quick to read the political and social structures which underscored the national side. He recognised Wessels as the key to power within the national squad and began to align himself with the captain," wrote clinical psychologist Anne Warmenhoven in the course of her PhD thesis on Hansie's "emotional intelligence".

As Hansie modelled himself on Kepler, he was quickly drawn into the "leadership team" as vice captain. As he approached his own captaincy he seemed to start to cultivate a mystique, working at creating an aura of aloofness and a certain invincibility, despite the jokes and pranks and the easy-going, utterly friendly style he had with the public.

He never let the players get to know him too much, and seemed to do this on purpose. Even San-Marie felt this hard, curiously selfish edge, and disapproved at times. Once, when she was working as an estate agent, Hansie had bought a Bloemfontein townhouse that was on her books, from another agent. "I felt a little put out, I must admit. I found it strange that he hadn't consulted me about buying property. It hurt me. I felt I didn't know who he was anymore," she said.

"There were times when Mom felt far from him," agreed Frans. Hansie began to struggle with his persona, a struggle that lasted for a few years after he became Free State captain. He had to work out how to keep the balance between a stern captain and a friendly brother, son or friend. How to relate to family and to the media were sometimes vexing issues for him. But he soon managed to find the right balance and his relationship with his family and friends remained strong until the end.

Perhaps Hansie was influenced in his changing demeanour by his mentors, Johan Volsteedt and Kepler who had reputations for being grumpy at times. On one occasion, when Kepler was in the middle of a bout of poor batting form, Adrian Kuiper and others had attempted to "cheer up" the morose skipper by attempting to handcuff him in a mad jest. Kepler was ambushed by Hansie, Brian McMillan and Adrian and in the *melee* Kepler had fought them off wildly, headbutting Kuiper and even fighting off the bulky "Big Mac". The defeated threesome had quietly backed off, nursing their wounds. "Kepler was a lot of fun in many respects," Hansie is quoted as saying in *Hansie and the Boys*, "but we realised that there were times when he was best left alone. That was one of them."

Once, on the occasion of Hansie's birthday, one of his Free State team-mates had wrapped up a gift for Hansie – a box of tampons, in cheeky reference to his perceived moodiness. Hansie laughed thinly when he opened the box.

By the time the South African team ran onto the field to play England in the semi-final of the 1992 World Cup, they had matured exponentially, from young boys to a team of men who had the potential to be world beaters. "Unfortunately we made too many basic errors in the field against England," said Kepler. "But we had managed to get ourselves into a really strong position, when it suddenly started raining."

Before the rain began to fall in earnest and the players had to leave the field to sit it out, South Africa needed 22 runs to win off 14 balls. When they eventually walked back onto the field after a mathematical calculation called Duckworth-Lewis, the scoreboard read: "South Africa need 21 runs to win off 1 ball."

"We were devastated. Some of the guys had tears in their eyes. We sat in the change room after the match and everyone was just quiet," recalls Kepler.

After the dismal end to the game, they eventually left the change room and walked onto the field, where, to their surprise, most of the large crowd was still on the stands. When the team was lead around the ground by Kepler, they received a standing ovation.

A hero's welcome also awaited them when they landed in Johannesburg. The airport was packed with fans who screamed and shouted support for their heroes, who had emphatically made their mark on world cricket.

During the World Cup campaign in Australia an encounter took place back in Bloemfontein that involved a shy, blonde Afrikaans girl, called Bertha Pretorius. From the time they were little, Hansie Cronjé and Bertha Pretorius lived close to each other. Both families regularly attended the Universitas Dutch Reformed Church and sat in the same places, every Sunday, on one side of one of the two galleries. The two clans were on friendly terms, but were not close.

Back in 1991, Bertha was a first-year physiotherapy student. One day she was walking alone on campus. "I heard a whistle and turned round and saw a tall young man with dark hair driving a white Nissan Exa. He said 'Hello'. I kind of ignored him and gave him a half smile. It was the first time I had really noticed Hansie."

In those days, young Hansie sported a stiff black, curly 'mullet' hairstyle, then a fashion statement in Bloemfontein and totally in keeping with his flashy little Exa.

Early the next year, Bertha, 20, was struggling with a blighted three-year relationship with a young man. She and her best friend at university, Penny Middlecote, drove past 246 Paul Kruger Avenue and there was the dashing young gladiator, shirtless, manfully washing his car, smiling that boyish heartbreaker smile. Hansie looked up and waved at the young women and they waved back.

There inevitably followed a discussion about what a nice person Hansie was. Penny had heard her sister, Hester's best friend, mention that Hansie and Debbie Coleman "weren't getting along so well anymore". No one is exactly sure what happened next but word got back to Hester via Penny's sister, Nicky. Hester did her part and apparently asked Hansie, "Why don't you go out with Bertha?" Hansie retorted that she had a boyfriend to which Hester had countered, "Bertha is mad about you."

Bertha recalled, "Obviously that wasn't 100% true because I didn't know Hansie at all, never even spoke to him and I still had a boyfriend!" By then it was three days before Valentine's Day and Hansie was playing for South Africa in Australia in the 1992 World Cup. Interflora gave the team the opportunity to send their loved ones flowers, seeing that they wouldn't be home on 14 February. Hansie saw this as an opportunity to send Bertha some flowers without anybody knowing about it. But he didn't take into consideration that Interflora might want some recognition for their sponsorship.

On Valentine's Day, Bertha was at home in Bloemfontein when the phone rang. The person on the line explained that he was from the local newspaper, *Die Volksblad*, and wanted permission to take a picture of her. "Is this a joke?" Bertha asked.

"No, your boyfriend, Hansie Cronjé, has sent you flowers from Australia," the *Volksblad* photographer replied.

But Bertha was resolute: "I'm sorry you are making a big mistake, Hansie Cronjé is not my boyfriend and you can't take a picture of me."

Shortly after that, the flowers arrived, with a little note from Hansie, not signed by him, which Bertha can still recite from memory: *Somewhere in Aussie there's a little boy blue. Sending these flowers with love to you. No real message, no big fuss, just enjoy them, from all of us.* Bertha was delighted, but she tried not to show it, affecting a kind of nonchalance.

A few weeks later, Bertha and her brother Sybrand were driving to church on a Sunday morning when they spotted Hansie, alone, walking along, heading for the church too. Sybrand said, "We must stop and ask him if he wants a lift."

Mortified by the recent events, Bertha protested, "No! Just go. Don't stop!"

But Sybrand was determined: "I have to be polite. I must ask him."

Up to that point, Bertha had never spoken to Hansie. Hansie chatted brightly and then asked, "Can I come and have tea with you after church? I want to explain and apologise about the flowers." At that tea, they conversed politely and Hansie spoke about his first World Cup experience and how he was on his way to the West Indies and then England to play for a club side called Norden in the Central Lancashire League for six months.

Back in England, Debbie Coleman was waiting for Hansie to return to her. She was there on holiday and would meet up with Hansie after his tour to the West Indies.

"In our younger days, Hansie and I used to listen for hours and hours as some of our West Indian friends in Bloemfontein told us about their legendary players. Sir Garfield Sobers, Wes Hall, Viv Richards and the like," recalled Frans. "And they told us what the islands were like – Jamaica where Colis King was from, Barbados where Franklyn Stephenson and Sylvester Clarke grew up, Guyana where Alvin

Kallicharran used to play. For Hansie, going to the Caribbean was a boyhood dream come true."

At a party on the *Bajun Queen* river boat, Hansie, for once, had a few beers too many and had tipsily tried to insist on dancing with Kepler. It had been a particularly raucous party. The captain was apparently not amused by his protégé's embarrassing camaraderie. In the end most of the team ended up in the sea and some of them even had their passports and other personal belongings drenched with water.

During the tour, Kepler cut his hair short and Hansie promptly did so too. "It was Tweedledee and Tweedledum to such an extent that other players began to resent Cronjé as a nodding puppy on the captain's lap," wrote Edward Griffiths in *Kepler: The Biography*.

The series turned out to be a hard lesson in cricket for the young South African side, which lost the Test match, as well as the One-Day series.

From the Caribbean, Hansie flew to England for the English summer where he and Debbie stayed in a typical little semi-detached house in Lancashire, a fact that appalled Hansie's parents.

Frans and René were, happily, nearby – Frans was playing his first season of professional cricket in England in the Bolton League for the Westhoughton Cricket Club. Frans, René, Hansie and Debbie also frequently drove down to Leicestershire, where Gordon and Hester Parsons now lived – Gordon was a senior pro in the Leicestershire cricket side.

Jack Birkenshaw, the Leicester coach at the time, allowed Hansie and Frans to practise with the Leicester side from time to time. Practice facilities at English club grounds were often poor, or even non-existent. For Frans and Hansie, playing for English club sides was like a holiday – getting paid fairly well for basically working weekends only.

It was around this time, said Frans, that Hansie's first spiritual awakening began. "He started realizing that he was far from God, that his lifestyle was ungodly. There was, for example, his relationship with Debbie. Although he knew full well that she was not going to be his wife, he was living with her and that really bothered him – actually, it seemed to bother him from the start, given his religious upbringing."

One Monday afternoon, Hansie and Debbie were visiting Frans and René, for a lunch-time braai. René and Debbie were in the kitchen preparing the salad and Hansie and Frans were at the fire, braaing the meat. Frans had said to Hansie, "The English are such an ungodly nation. Their history is full of great men and women of the faith, yet only about five percent of English people attend a church regularly. Few Englishmen seem to even believe in God."

Frans noted that "almost no one" in his club side was Christian and that "some guys in the team even mocked me for going to church on Sundays before a match".

Frans continued in this vein, saying, "England is filled with the most beautiful cathedrals and chapels, but most of them have small congregations or none at all. Some cathedrals have even been turned into shopping malls."

Hansie looked at his brother and said, "Yes, I hear what you are saying, but aren't we also the same? The Bible says that a Christian's body and mind is like God's Temple. Aren't we also just as empty as these churches? Is our own faith in God at the moment not empty of substance too?"

Frans recalled, "I was stunned by his remark and immediately realised my own hypocrisy. Here I was being critical of other people, when the sad reality was that my own spiritual life (and Hansie's) was far from healthy. The only difference between me and the rest of the guys in the team was the fact that I attended church on Sundays and told people that I was a Christian. Like Hansie at the time, I wasn't walking the talking."

There followed a period of confusion for Bertha, as she wrestled with the possibility of a relationship with Hansie. He wrote polite letters to her from England, sending her postcards of Princess Di. "He did not profess love in those letters and I never replied to any of them," Bertha said. Around that time, Bertha and her boyfriend of three years broke up.

Back in Bloemfontein in the 1992/93 season, Hansie, energised by his international experiences, continued to drive his Free State team hard and they were well prepared for the new season. To Hansie's dismay, Eddie Barlow had accepted an offer to coach the Transvaal side and had left the Free State. He was replaced by Jack Birkenshaw. In those years, there was a One-Day knock out contest called the Nissan Shield and in November of that year Free State had to play Northern Natal in Richards Bay. Before leaving for Richards Bay, Hansie called Bertha and asked if he could come over on the Sunday afternoon to have tea with her. She was delighted and said yes.

There were no commercial flights to the town, and it meant that the team had to fly to Durban and then drive north from there for about three hours in two mini-buses. Hansie decided to hire his own vehicle in order to drive back to Bloemfontein straight after the match. He wanted to be back in time for a special event at church. Hester and Gordon's first child, Alexandrea, born in England during the English summer, was to be christened in the Universitas Dutch Reformed Church that Sunday morning. The Free State wicket keeper, Roger Brown, decided to join Hansie, rather than travel in one of the mini-buses. The team left some time before Hansie and Roger finally got on their way.

Roger recalled, "We left Durban at about 4.30pm and were travelling on the N2 towards Empangeni. The road was busy and about an hour and a half into our journey the light was beginning to fade as we passed a taxi. It happen so quickly. A little girl ran into the road and we hit her.

Hansie slammed on the brakes and he jerked on the steering wheel, trying to swerve, but it was already too late. I grabbed the steering wheel and held it firm to keep us from rolling the car.

"We slowed the car down and parked it next to the road. We both got out in disbelief, and I ran to the body. She was already dead.

"I covered the girl's body with a towel. We were both in shock. Hansie sat in the middle of the highway on the island, crying with his hands on his head. He blamed himself for the accident, but I reassured him over and over that there was nothing that he could have done.

"I tried to wave down the traffic for someone to stop, but it was only 45 minutes later that someone stopped. (There were no cell phones at that stage in South Africa.) Eventually the police arrived and informed Hansie that he would be charged with manslaughter – standard procedure in the South African criminal law system when the death of a pedestrian is involved. [A prosecutor later decided that Hansie wasn't guilty of any negligence.] Later, when the mother got there we explained to her what had happened and then we left for Empangeni."

It was a cruel irony that Hansie should find himself in church to witness a christening, a celebration of new life, the very next day. Hester recalled that he cried through the whole church service, absolutely shattered by the fact that he had inadvertently killed the little girl.

After a short tea with the family at 246 Paul Kruger Avenue, Hansie walked to Bertha's house. She recalls their conversation. "Hansie was distraught about the accident. He was cut up. He told me the accident had made him realise that he was not sure whether he would go to heaven or hell if he had died in that accident. He was also worried about the manslaughter charge. There were different emotions.

"I had just returned from a tour that entailed a group of young Christian athletes, called Sport for Christ Action South Africa, jogging in stages from Bloemfontein to Richards Bay (a distance of nearly 700km), and preaching the Gospel of Christ in towns along the way." During this time Bertha had an epiphany, which radically changed the direction of her life.

"I realised then for the first time what it meant to have a personal relationship with Christ, and I recommitted my life to Him. There was a big change in me. I was calm, peaceful and on fire for the Lord. My Christian faith deepened, I was reborn as a child of God. Christianity was a reality for me, not a social, cultural and merely religious habit anymore. I was more honest with myself and others."

Bertha's "born-again" experience, which curiously, miraculously, came at virtually the same time that Hansie was involved in the tragic road accident, equipped her well to help him through this difficult time in his life.

"From then on our relationship went to a different level," said Bertha. "I prayed for him that night. We prayed together and Hansie made a commitment to God. Basically he was also 'born-again' that night."

"Hansie joined my Bible study group, which was comprised of a few medical students from different churches who got together once a week at my parents' house." At his first meeting, he introduced himself as Jonty Rhodes. ("And one girl thought he was," laughed Bertha.) From then on, Hansie attended the study group whenever he was in Bloemfontein.

To understand Hansie at all it is important to understand what being "born again" would have meant to him, and what this belief required of him. Being born-again is a term that was used by Jesus in conversation with a Jewish teacher of the day, called Nicodemus. The account of this conversation is written in the third chapter of the Book of John in the New Testament. Nicodemus asked Jesus what he should do in order to have eternal life. Jesus answered that he should be spiritually born again.

The Bible says that no human is without sin and therefore deserves eternal death and separation from God. God, who created heaven and earth, created humans with the ability to hear God and speak to God. But through Adam and Eve's disobedience to God in the Garden of Eden there came a separation between man and God. God is a holy God and no creature can stand in God's sight if he or she has sin in their lives.

No amount of good works or religious rituals is good enough to fix this gap between man and God. The only way to restore this relationship would be through the sacrifice of a person without blemish or sin in his or her life. Through His wisdom, God knew all along that no mere human being would ever be able to perform this task, so He promised that one day He would send a Saviour (or Christ) to save the human race from eternal damnation. So 2 000 years ago God sent His only Son, Jesus Christ, to be born miraculously through a virgin, called Mary, to come to earth and fulfil the role of Saviour.

Jesus taught many things and then willingly handed Himself over to the Jewish and Roman authorities of the day to be tortured and crucified. He had concluded His conversation with Nicodemus by saying that "God so loved the world that He sent His only Son, so that all who believe in Him would not perish, but have everlasting life."

So to be born again you first need to realise that you have sinned and then be willing to turn away from that sin. Secondly, you need to believe that Jesus died in your place so that your sins could be forgiven. And then thirdly, you need to make a decision to commit to living a life of obedience to God. This doesn't mean that being born-again makes you perfect. You will continue to stumble and sin at times, but it's how you deal with that sin that matters.

So Hansie and Bertha (and later most of the Cronjé family) were 'born-again' with a firm belief that Jesus is their Saviour and by believing in Him they would spend eternity in heaven and also have a living relationship with God, even while living on earth.

The accident was not the only blow Hansie was to receive then, although this second blow was hardly comparable to the first. Hansie was left out of the South African team to play against India at Kingsmead in Durban. The selectors felt that he was a really good One-Day player, but doubted his abilities as a five-day Test batsman.

"For two months solidly, Cronjé worked on his fitness. He had never trained harder in his life. He went on a diet, drank only mineral water, and brought his weight down from 93 kilograms to an ideal 83 kilograms. He knew he was under pressure from players like Roy Pienaar and Mike Rindel ... Hansie went to a team training camp in Cape Town where he proved to be the fittest player," said Rodney Hartman in *Hansie and the Boys.*

The Kingsmead Test was drawn and the second Test was at the Wanderers in Johannesburg. The selectors then changed their minds and Hansie was selected to play. The Test was drawn and Hansie managed only 8 runs in the first innings and 15 in the second, but while in Johannesburg, he met another mentor who would leave a huge imprint on his life.

Kepler invited Ray McCauley, the pastor and founder of the influential Rhema Church in Johannesburg, to speak to the team. Ray had left school two years before matriculating to pursue his body-building career, but later studied to become a pastor in the USA and started Rhema in his garage in 1972 with 12 people. Today the Rhema church in Randburg seats 35 000 and is filled every Sunday. Ray also heads up a group of hundreds of other churches that relate to Rhema. He was involved in the political transition from the old apartheid government to the new ANC government. Even former President Mandela asked Ray for advice on several occasions.

Because Hansie always tried to make time for his sponsors and for the media,
it became increasingly harder to find time to relax.

Top: At the Durban
Dolphinarium.
Middle: Relaxing at home.
Bottom: Hunting in the Karoo.

Right: A life-long dream came true when South Africa beat the West Indies 5-0 in the Test series in 1998/99. Here, Hansie shakes Brian Lara's hand.

Left: Bertha and Hansie with Poppy and Goolam Rajah. Hansie and his team-mates felt Goolam was the best manager the SA side ever had.
Below: Coach and captain – an innovative combination

Hansie had a true affinity for his nephews and nieces. Above: Walking off the field in England after a match with Alexandrea. Right: With Frans's children Marié and Ewie Jnr. Below: Getting a huge kiss from James.

Above: Ewie's 60th birthday. On the sofa, from left to right: Gordon, Bertha, Hansie, San-Marie, Alex and Ewie.
On the floor: James, Hester, Frans, baby Marié and René.

Above: Bertha's family join the Cronjés for lunch at 246 Paul Kruger. Clockwise, from left: Surene and Sybrand
Pretorius, Oom Kosie, Liesie, Bertha, Ewie and Gordon.

Above: Pieter Strydom, Herschelle Gibbs and Hansie.

Paddy Upton and Hansie after Hansie's bungee jump from the Storms River Bridge.

Shaun Pollock, Paul Adams, Hansie and Craig Matthews.

*Receiving the trophy from President Nelson Mandela after
beating England 6-1 in the 1995/96 One Day International series.*

Meeting Queen Elizabeth at the start of the 1994 Test match at Lord's, London.

*The public often saw only the stern
face of the captain ...*

... but Hansie's team-mates all talk about his infectious smile and the many pranks that he liked to play.

A relaxed moment on tour with Gary and Deborah Kirsten.

Kate and Jonty Rhodes, Hansie and Shaun Pollock.

The King Commission.

Above: Graffiti in Bloemfontein.
Left: A braai during the King Commission at advocate John Dickerson's house.
Below: Raymond van Staden and Hansie.

Fancourt in George
Above: 18 Eagle Drive.
Right: Hansie and Bertha's
house is on the far right.
Below: Hansie's favourite – the
17th hole of the Montagu Course.

Studying for his MBL at Herold's Bay.

Garth le Roux and Norman Minaar at the Members' Bar at Fancourt.

Gordon and Marge McNeill at their lovely coffee and gift shop, Meade House.

From a young age Hansie had compassion for people who were less privileged than he was. After the King Commission he became president of SWD Sports Association for the Disabled. After his death, his family formed a trust in his name and through this trust they support various organisations. The bus below was donated to the SWD Sports Association for the Disabled.

A percentage of the profits from this book will also go to this trust.

HANSIE CRONJÉ
CHARITABLE MEMORIAL FUND

"Ray is a great guy and a tremendous motivational speaker. He was a champion body builder and understood the sporting environment well. I got him to speak to the whole team to get them motivated, and then he stayed on to lead a Bible study with those players who chose to attend," Kepler explained.

Ray's association with top Christian sportsmen was already well established by then and would be assiduously cultivated. "I have always enjoyed cricket and was happy to help where I could," he said. "The cricket players travelled a lot and many matches were played on Sundays. This meant that they often did not have the chance to attend their own church, or any church for that matter. I was burdened to help them out, to strengthen their faith."

In a sense, Ray soon became the chaplain of the South African side, a de facto office he held until the King Commission a decade later. His role in Hansie's development as a young follower of Christ was pivotal, his personal example and strong, well-articulated advice to Hansie was deeply influential. For many years, he was Hansie's principal spiritual mentor and Hansie would always respectfully refer to him as "Pastor", despite the fact that most men associated with the cricket team simply referred to the churchman as Ray.

When Ray was first introduced to Hansie, the two of them spent a lot of time talking about the little girl who had been killed. "His sensitive counselling helped Hansie tremendously. It was the start of a long and happy relationship between Hansie and Ray," said Frans. "Although Hansie always had a generous side to him, I think his relationship with Ray strengthened his empathy with those in need. I think that Ray is one of the most generous people I have ever met. You never visit Ray without him giving you some gift."

Hansie's "born-again" experience was soon broadcast widely. He sometimes spoke about it bluntly to friends and acquaintances. A South African Christian magazine called *Joy* featured Hansie on the cover in 1993, and inside was a short interview. Part of that interview read: "After the accident where the little girl got killed I asked myself the question. 'If it was me that died in the accident, where would I have gone after dying? Would I go to heaven or to hell?' I knew that my relationship with God was not right and that was one of the major reasons for committing my life to God. Since committing my life to Jesus I have total peace about dying. We are constantly travelling on the road and in the air, I now have perfect peace that should I die in a plane crash, I would go to heaven."

Hansie's "new-fangled" Christianity was greeted with frowns by the Cronjé clan. They didn't understand this "born-again" business. "The attitude of most traditional Afrikaner Christians in the Free State, especially back then, was that if you were born into the Dutch Reformed Church, then you were automatically a Christian of a high order," explained Frans. "They didn't see the need for this strange new 'born-again' way. The way that things get done at charismatic churches like Rhema is vastly different from the traditional ways of the Dutch Reformed Church. Four years after Hansie, I too had a born-again experience and it also happened to be in a Rhema Church. It was only then that I truly understood that the institution that we grew up in was not necessarily the only place to learn the truth. My grandfather, Oupa Hansie, always told me that in the old apartheid days you did not have much of a chance in life if you did not vote National Party and attend a Dutch Reformed Church, even though he supported the United Party. Fortunately this is one of the things that have changed for the better under the new government." The views of many Dutch Reformed Churches have changed considerably in the last ten years. And, as Bertha said, "What's important is not which church you attend but that you have a personal relationship with God."

By now, Hansie was connecting spiritually not only with Kepler, who was also a born-again Christian, but his relationship with Jonty was developing too, fuelled by a variety of factors, including Jonty's similarly strict Christian upbringing in a sports-mad traditional college, extreme self-discpline and infectious and utterly good nature.

A small group of "born-again" South African players would get together almost weekly for Bible study and prayer, initiated by team manager Alan Jordaan and two players, Andrew Hudson and Kepler Wessels. Jonty and Hansie were regulars. Fast bowler Fanie de Villiers was an occasional visitor. "Once, Brett Schultz walked in on us by accident and was too embarrassed to leave – that was quite funny. The guys used to come and go, but we had these weekly devotions right throughout my reign as captain," said Kepler.

The third Test match against India was at St George's Park in Port Elizabeth. This was Hansie's third Test, and there were still critics who said he did not deserve a place in the side. Hansie had scored a prolific amount of runs in One-Day cricket at provincial level, but not that many in the three-day matches.

Hansie proved his critics wrong, scoring a magnificent 135 of the team's 275 runs; the only other batsman who managed to score more than 50 was Andrew Hudson with 52. Kepler scored 95 not out in the second innings, and South Africa won the match. With this hundred Hansie established himself as a number three batsman in the side, and he was never left out again.

●

In August 1993 the South African side toured Sri Lanka. For the first time, Hansie was appointed vice captain, one month before turning 24.

He played badly in the first test match but managed to retain his place for the second. At this stage the South African side had great difficulty batting on the slow wickets of the sub-continent, and were greatly troubled by the spin-bowlers. Hansie was under pressure to score runs.

The evening before the start of the second test, Hansie got a surprise phone call from his older cousin, Frans Cronjé, known as Groot Frans.

Groot Frans was then a professional tennis coach based in East London, on the south-east coast of South Africa. In 2005 he was considered to be South Africa's top tennis coach. His speciality was mental toughness.

One of Groot Frans's tools was a short video entitled *Mental Toughness*, psychologist Jim Löhr's analysis of the United States tennis star Jimmy Connors. It was a video that Hansie had watched several times. Basically, the video emphasised eye control (focus on nearby objects, don't let your eyes wander around as you prepare for each delivery); positive body language (emphasise your power to your opponents); physical rituals (such as doing set and precise little routines before facing the ball); mental rituals (for example, thinking about the same thing before facing each ball); controlling the pace of the game (for example, getting the spin bowlers to take their time before delivery); "bat up" (carrying the bat like a sword, instead of dragging it behind you); controlled breathing when hitting the ball; and relaxed intensity (getting the balance between relaxation and intensity right).

Groot Frans recalled his conversation with Hansie before that second Test in 1993: "I told him to remember what the video said and encouraged him to try and implement its principles when he went out to bat. Sports like cricket, golf and tennis are similar in one way. In all these games there is time to think between deliveries, points or shots. This can cause players to think too much and to be their own biggest enemy. Having mental toughness helps you to overcome this problem and the great players all have this attribute. Hansie was born with natural mental toughness but, like all humans, had to work on it as well."

Hansie took Groot Frans's advice to heart. He went out the following day and hit a brilliant 100, grappling well with the spin, and South Africa managed to win the Test match and the series. Hansie was quick to give Groot Frans the credit for his 100 in the post match interviews.

One more thing Groot Frans told Hansie to do in order to help him with better body language, was to flip up his shirt collar before going in to bat and to keep it up during his innings. He did it and subsequently kept up this habit.

Hansie's growing global prowess needs to be measured alongside his incredible ability as Free State captain. The province became South Africa's top outfit, winning the Currie Cup and the Total Power Series (formerly the Nissan Shield). His Currie Cup average was 98.75. The 1993 Protea Cricket Annual called him "a national treasure". In his maiden first-class victory over Western Province, he scored 161 not out.

"Hansie," said Frans, "knew how to intimidate people and opponents. When I played for Border, playing against Free State was not a problem. But with Hansie in the side it was a different story. Opponents were clearly intimidated by a powerful presence."

The upright batsman, superbly fit, tall and physically powerful, would be unfriendly without discourtesy. He would often avoid eye contact, and the body language would be grim, taut with controlled energy. His hazel-brown eagle eyes would glint menacingly under ferocious eyebrows. Winning the game for Hansie, was a desperately serious business.

●

South Africa then played in a One-Day International series, called the Hero Cup, in India, without much success.

This was quickly followed by a 1993/94 back-to-back series against Australia. The first half of the series was to be in Australia and the second half in South Africa. The Australians were beginning to establish themselves as one of the best teams in the world, and there was a lot of eager anticipation for the tour.

In Australia, the South African team received a lesson about the media's relentless, seemingly orchestrated, onslaught against the opposition. Andrew Hudson once commented, "They [the media in Australia] seem to decide on a specific strategy to unsettle the opposition. They do this very well, without being too slanderous. For this tour, they built up Allan Donald as 'the fastest bowler in the world' and called him 'White Lightning'. All this hype, predictably, had a negative influence on Allan's performance, as it made him very tense."

The first Test was drawn. The second Test was in Sydney, and on the fourth day Kepler broke his finger, trying to scoop the ball up near the ground. Even the tough Kepler could not play with the fracture, and Hansie had to take over as captain. South Africa, though, did not score enough runs and when they took the field on the morning of the last day, Australia needed 60 runs to win, with 6 wickets in hand. A mere formality. South Africa had virtually no chance, especially with their captain sidelined. But Hansie had other plans.

Leading from the front, he displayed some remarkable leadership skills. His field placing and change of bowlers was innovative and successful. With Allan Donald hobbled by the reverse psychology media hype, fast bowler Fanie de Villiers was the main wicket-taker.

When Glen McGrath was caught and bowled by Fanie de Villiers, Hansie and the boys had pulled off a remarkable win, by nine runs. Hansie promptly picked Fanie up and carried him from the field on his shoulders. Kepler was the first to run onto the field, followed by Mike Procter and the rest of the South African contingent. Hansie and Kepler embraced as they met, and the team swarmed around them, jubilant. It was an historic climax in the companionable journey of Kepler and his protégé.

Kepler was ruled out for the rest of the tour, and had to fly home. Hansie was made captain in his stead, even though most players were older than he was. The experienced Peter Kirsten, who was not playing for South Africa at this time, was flown to Australia to open the batting with his younger brother, Gary.

In what many South Africans saw as one of the worst displays of umpiring in Test cricket, by Australian umpire Darryl Hare, South Africa lost the third Test and the series was drawn. It was, of course, a big disappointment, but nevertheless a good result for the young side. Typically, Hansie was gracious about the umpiring and never made a big deal about it. Such tact and diplomacy would become a hallmark of his unusually mature and level-headed leadership style.

Then there was the One-Day International series between South Africa, Australia and New Zealand. South Africa lost the first two matches against Australia and New Zealand respectively, and then won the following two matches, to win a place in the best-of-three finals against Australia.

In one of the matches, Peter Kirsten walked onto the field at Perth during the pre-match warm-ups and proclaimed, "What a lovely day! It's great to be alive!" An hour later he was carried off the field on a stretcher, after a delivery from Glen McGrath hit a crack in the pitch and crashed into Kirsten's face, fracturing his cheekbone.

South Africa won the first final, but then lost the second and the third, in Sydney. Hansie lost the toss in two of the matches and it probably played a big role in the results. "Hansie," said Frans, "was very irritated when a South African journalist called the South African side 'chokers' for losing the last match. He felt that this was hugely unfair."

Australia then came to South Africa. "This," said Frans, "was most probably Hansie's best-ever series. At the end of it, Hansie had scored a total of 700 runs against Australia in 12 appearances.

In the first ODI at the Wanderers, Hansie scored 112 runs off 120 balls and hit the great Shane Warne to all corners of the "Bull Ring". It was the first ODI in which Warne did not manage to take a wicket and he eventually conceded 56 runs in his 10 overs. Hansie and Jonty batted together for the majority of the South African innings to a partnership total of over a hundred runs.

This innings became so famous in South Africa that it prompted Standard Bank to use Hansie in a television commercial which showed him, at night, hitting the ball into a bank of lights on one of the pylons, which caused a power failure in the city. When the camera focused back on Hansie, he grinned mischievously, as only Hansie could, and said, sheepishly, "Sorry." This cute little piece of marketing is an enduring and classic image in the mind of the cricket fans of South Africa, and neatly symbolises the glory and boyish charm of the young star in his prime.

Hansie went on to score 97 in the ODI at Centurion Park, in Pretoria, the following day and a huge banner in the stadium, displayed by a supporter, read "HANSIE FOR PRESIDENT". Although he was barely 24 he had become an icon to many, a role model to millions and an inspiration to an entire nation – all ethnic groups, cultures and religious groups included.

By now he was earning a handsome amount of money from a range of different sponsors – Adidas made a line of Hansie equipment and clothing, Modern Clothing brought out a Hansie range of casual clothing, Gray Nicholls and then, County were his bat sponsors; later on BMW sponsored his cars – and so the list grew. He was incredibly loyal to his sponsors and always walked the extra mile to insure that they got the maximum amount of mileage out of him.

South Africa won the first three ODIs and then they had to play three Test matches before concluding the ODI series. Hansie's form continued as he scored 122 in the first Test at the Wanderers. Up to now, he had scored three centuries in his first nine Test matches, and South Africa had won every time he scored a hundred.

Australia won the second Test match, the third Test was drawn and the series was again tied, one all.

In between, Australia played a match against the Free State in Bloemfontein, and the words of Allan Donald best describe Hansie's innings of 251: "He hit those Aussies so far and so hard that one wondered if they would ever be able to recover from the pasting."

Sadly, South Africa lost the last three ODIs and also drew the ODI series. Once again the South African press started throwing the "chokers" insult at the team. Hansie was beginning to get seriously miffed at this, and anger at what he perceived as unpatriotic and insulting mischief began to boil up to the surface.

When Hansie was still at Grey College, he had enthusiastically said to headmaster Johan Volsteedt, "Mr Volsteedt, if I ever play for South Africa against England at Lord's, I'm going to buy you an air ticket and pay for your accommodation in London to watch."

On 21 July 1994, Kepler Wessels ran onto cricket's holy of holies at Lord's. It had been 23 years since South Africa had faced England at that august venue. In the stadium were Ewie, Hester, Gordon and a proud and glowing Johan Volsteedt. Hansie had remembered his promise.

Kepler was man of the match after scoring 105 runs in South Africa's first innings and South Africa won the match. It was a fantastic experience for Ewie and Johan Volsteedt – the culmination of decades of work by at least three different generations. During the match Hansie, "Vollies" and Kepler posed for a photograph together and this picture still hung proudly on the wall inside Volsteedt's office at Grey College in 2005.

Unfortunately, Hansie struggled with his form throughout the series. Kepler recalled that for the first time there was conflict in his relationship with Hansie. Kepler was angry with Hansie for "getting negative about his form and letting it affect the rest of the team too much". Hansie's mind, according to Kepler, seemed much too preoccupied with the succession issue.

In England, Ali Bacher had approached Hansie, saying, "I just want you to know that you're definitely going to get the job [of captain]. If anyone should ask you about this, don't say you're not ready or anything like that. Just tell them you'll be happy to take it when the time comes."

At the same time, Kepler felt that he had reached the end of his long and fulfilling international career and he communicated this to the UCB. He was 38 years old and his troublesome right knee had started "playing up". Hansie was waiting eagerly in the wings, ready to step out of Kepler's shadow. The UCB seemed to be on the verge of appointing him captain.

England went on to beat South Africa in the ODI series. The second Test was drawn and the England fast bowler, Devon Malcolm, blasted through the Protea batsmen during both innings in the third Test match at The Oval in Surrey. The series ended in a draw.

Due to Hansie's poor batting form, the UCB asked Kepler to continue captaining the national side in Test matches; Hansie would be captain of the ODI side. It was a time of great uncertainty for the old warrior and his protégé, and the UCB seemed to bungle the leadership transition from the start, insensitively changing their minds and unilaterally revoking agreements with Kepler.

"I was sitting at home in Port Elizabeth and I got a phone call from Peter Pollock and he said to me, 'We want you to fly up to Johannesburg'. So I asked why. 'We want you to take the team to Pakistan.' I said, 'No, we had an agreement.'

"Peter told me, 'Hansie's playing so badly that we don't want him to captain and in fact, we don't even want him in the team'. So I said 'That's got nothing to do with me. If you think that he's the guy to lead the side, there will be a time in his captaincy when he's going to not play well. If you believe in him you've got to go with him.'"

In Johannesburg, Kepler sat down with the selectors. Half of the players were injured, including Allan Donald. There was also conflict between the team and coach Mike Procter relating to the coach's perceived lack of technical skills.

"Hansie said at the meeting that he wouldn't be part of the equation if Procter was the coach. The whole thing was a mess. I should have just stuck to my guns and said that I would not be the captain.

"The selection meeting went this way and that, and I went back home and no decision was made. But the UCB kept on saying I had to be the captain, and I kept saying 'I don't want to'." Eventually a reluctant Kepler was persuaded.

On 9 September 1994, the UCB confirmed Kepler as captain for the triangular Pakistan tour, which included Australia. Peter Pollock told the press, "It's a matter of timing. We don't think that now is the right time to make Hansie captain." Former England Test cricketer, Bob Woolmer was appointed as the new coach in place of Mike Procter.

Just before leaving for Pakistan, Kepler said he received another call from the UCB, asking him to consider continuing in both forms of cricket. This further rumpled Kepler, and he thought long and hard about it, and said that he would decide in Pakistan.

South Africa had a poor tournament and although they came close to winning on a few occasions, they lost all nine matches. Hansie, still batting at number three, scored 354 runs in six innings, with a highest score of 100 not out against Australia, at an average of 88.8. He did so well against Australia that one of the Waugh brothers eventually walked passed Hansie as he walked in to bat and asked, half sarcastically, "So how many runs are you going to score today?"

"Hansie always had great admiration for the Waugh brothers," said Frans. "He felt that their upbringing was similar to ours and apparently their dad was also very involved with sport all his life."

Hansie was back in form and this pleased Peter Pollock and the selectors, prompting them to change their plans, deeply upsetting Kepler's refined sense of fair play and due process. In Rodney Hartman's *Hansie and the Boys*, Hansie is quoted as follows: "I think Kepler saw us [Pollock and Hansie] talking and thought we were trying to push him out or something. It wasn't the case at all. Peter simply asked me whether I would still like to have Kepler in my team once he stepped down. I said there was no question about it. He was still a very good player, and in Test cricket he would continue to make a big contribution because of all his experience. I wasn't too sure that he would make himself available for the One-Day games but for the Tests there was no doubt that I wanted him."

At a team meeting, Hansie also voiced strong opinions about the best approach to One-Day cricket. "I said that we needed to score runs more quickly, and particularly at the start of an innings. I wasn't being critical of Kepler, but I think he believed I was."

Kepler had always had a reputation for being too cautious, of making sure his side wouldn't lose, rather than adventurously making sure they would win, a perception endorsed by the likes of Volsteedt. In fairness to Kepler, though, Hansie's captaincy was one that included a side with extensive international experience, and Kepler's teams were mostly raw and untested on the international fields. Kepler's cautious style was exactly right for his times, as Hansie's would be for his.

The UCB made a mistake that South African sports administrators often still make to this day – lack of, or poor, consultation and bungled communication with the players involved in such sensitive issues. Without any proper discussion with Kepler, they announced that Hansie would become captain of the Proteas (as the South African team was now nicknamed) in both forms of cricket, after the completion of the Pakistan tournament.

Just before that, Kepler, after much thought, had made up his mind that he *would* accept the offer to continue his role as a captain in the Test side. But towards the end of the Pakistan tour, Peter Pollock had come up to Kepler at the breakfast table and announced, "As soon as the tour is over you must hand over your captaincy."

"The UCB's decision made me lose my temper completely, as it was in direct contradiction to the discussions we had before we left for Pakistan. I felt betrayed and hurt, and felt that I wanted nothing to do with South African cricket again," said Kepler.

In the midst of this unfortunate and probably unnecessary emotional back-drop, when the last ball of the last ODI in Pakistan was bowled, Hansie, 24, knew that he was finally going to be the South African captain.

Hansie and Kepler, who had travelled together so far and so fruitfully, were now estranged – a sad and inappropriate conclusion to their companionable and wonderful journey in international cricket.

"Hansie was very, very determined to captain the team," Kepler said. "I always wanted to be a good player first and the captain second; he was the other way around. He was always focused on the captaincy.

"I then stepped away from Hansie. Things were never the same. I decided that my influence on the team was finished. It was now time for him to take over – to stamp his authority on the side. I pulled back from it. If I look at it objectively, it wasn't so much him and me. It was the environment created around us by the UCB – it made things unnecessarily complicated.

"We never had a fall-out. We never snubbed each other or anything like that. But what should have been a very simple handing-over process, with no stress or tension surrounding it, was bungled."

The UCB later asked Kepler to continue playing Test cricket, batting in the number three position, but he angrily refused, although he continued captaining Eastern Province for four years.

Hansie and Kepler would later be reconciled through Ray McCauley.

On the eve of his appointment as national captain on 7 November 1994, at the age of 25, Hansie led the Free State team in a Currie Cup match. Facing defeat against Natal, he was given out on 21 to a disputed catch. Hansie harshly disputed the umpire's call. He was hauled over the coals for the first time in his career, fined R500 and given a suspended sentence. Free State lost by nine wickets. It was an uncharacteristic lapse, possibly brought on by the troubled succession issue and the urgent enthusiasm of a young lion finally let loose on the world.

Before New Zealand began their first tour of South Africa in 33 years, Hansie spoke out about Kepler. "Kepler and I have a lot in common. I have learned a lot under his captaincy, but I have a few ideas of my own that I want to try out. The last thing I want is for the responsibilities of captaincy to change my identity. I have always played the game aggressively and that's how I want to continue."

CHAPTER EIGHT

POWER AND GLORY

The Captaincy Years

Wherever Hansie went, happiness surrounded him.

— an assertion made by Les Sackstein (Hansie's lawyer).

In India, Hansie Cronje is not a cricketer; he's not a hero. He is a god.

— A South African sports television cameraman, cited by Johan Volsteedt.

Hansie's way of conducting his public life, his philosophy of manhood, was deeply influenced by the Rudyard Kipling poem "If", which he would quote regularly during his many speeches. The verses were his mantra, his orientation in the public eye, especially the last verse:

> *If you can walk with crowds and keep your virtue*
> *Or walk with kings – nor lose the common touch;*
> *If neither foes nor loving friends can hurt you;*
> *If all men count with you, but none too much;*
> *If you can fill the unforgiving minute*
> *With sixty seconds' worth of distance run –*
> *Yours is the Earth and everything that's in it,*
> *And – which is more – you'll be a man my son!*

It came as no surprise when, a month after his 25th birthday, Hansie was formally offered the ongoing captaincy of the national team. He became the second-youngest person ever to be appointed to that position since Murray Bisset in 1899.

Hansie was born to lead, had learned throughout his life to lead, and he had always confidently stepped into leadership roles. Allan Donald had known for a long time that Hansie was destined for greatness, but he saw it even more clearly in the match against Australia, when Hansie had to step in after Kepler was injured. "When he captained on that last day against Australia, that's when I realised it fully, and I said it to many. After Kepler broke his thumb, Hansie captained in a pressurised situation. Not one of us wanted to make bowling changes at that stage. But Hansie did. Who would want to make a change when it was going well? I knew then that he was destined for great things. Hansie's goal, when he became captain, was to break records that no one would match."

Through the years Hansie and Jonty did not only become heroes in South Africa, they also became very well known in the cricket playing countries, especially in India. It was almost impossible for either of them to walk the streets of India without being recognised and quickly finding themselves surrounded by tens of people asking for autographs or just wanting to shake their hands.

It was the start of the Golden Era of Hansie: 1995-1999.

Coinciding with his elevation was the September 1994 appointment of Warwickshire coach Bob Woolmer, a former English Test batsman, in the year that his team won the County Championship for the first time since 1972.

Bob's innovative character complemented Hansie's neatly. "I think one of the reasons why we work well together is that we are both willing to try things. We both like to be innovative and try different things," said Hansie in 1995. Initially, Bob had worked with Kepler, but his destiny was to be Hansie's right-hand friend in the promising years ahead.

Kepler had laid a solid foundation and Hansie now had the opportunity to take the team to "the next level". From the start, Hansie was somewhat different, yet strikingly similar, in certain aspects, to Kepler in his leadership style.

Jonty Rhodes said that "Kepler was perfect for his time, given the international inexperience of his team – but Hansie was required to head a new and adventurous age, after Kepler had laid down the foundations. In Kepler's day, it was pretty much Kepler's way, or no way. In truth, no one knew as much as Kepler did and it was laid down, and accepted, that Kepler was the law. There was no room for debate under Kepler."

In fairness to Kepler, Hansie now had the luxury of internationally experienced players like Daryll Cullinan, Jonty Rhodes and Jacques Kallis, who could be relied upon to deliver the goods. Such depth was something that Kepler could never really call on.

But the Kepler personality was still firmly stamped into Hansie, especially when it came down to his emotional life. The rigid John Wayne-style of leadership, quiet and strong, but internally suppressed, did affect Hansie deeply. Hansie often had great difficulty in articulating any inner turmoil and frustration appropriately, or at all, especially when his drive to win was being thwarted. "Hansie needed to express himself more, but that was Kepler's influence as well," said Jonty.

"We never really knew what Kepler was thinking. And he would not want to tell anyone what he was thinking either. Kepler was intimidating. If he told me to do something, I'd do it quickly, without comment or chirping. But with Hansie, he communicated with us, listened to us and got us to believe in what we were doing. It wasn't about dragging the guys with him. He empowered us to believe in ourselves. The biggest inhibitor in a cricketer's life is fear of failure. It's the most destructive force. You're tense enough as it is. He made you believe that you're the right guy for the job, whether it's ball in hand or bat in hand."

Hansie's innate optimism was another factor in the curve of successes. There was "never, never anything pessimistic about him", said Boeta Dippenaar.

"He always thought that things would work out," echoed Craig Matthews.

Johan Volsteedt described him as "one of the most optimistic people I ever knew. He did not think there was a challenge he could not meet".

"If we set a ridiculous target, he believed he could get it ... I'll never forget the one game – Free State was playing Natal, and they had to chase down about 430. I was watching some of the game on TV. I just saw Hansie come in to bat, and I knew straight away he was going to get this total. He was brilliant that way," said Gary Kirsten.

Clinical psychologist Anne Warmenhoven, whose 2005 PhD thesis was entitled *The Emotional Intelligence of Wessel Johannes "Hansie" Cronjé: A Psychobiographical Study*, talked glowingly of Hansie's "self-efficacy", a magical quality that he transmitted to team-mates, arguably his best quality as captain.

"He really believed in his own ability and he backed that," said Jonty. "This was key throughout his leadership. It gave the rest of us confidence too. He gave the players ownership of their own domains. He radiated confidence when you were batting with him. He backed your ability, saying 'We are gonna come through here' and he would be the one to take the risks. Hansie would say, for example, 'OK, this is the over, this is the bowler, we're gonna take it and get the rate down to under five an over'. And he'd do it. He'd identify and analyse. He would take the risk."

Jonty believed that Hansie's calmness on the field of play emanated from his rugby days. "In rugby, the team that panics loses. In cricket you want to be aggressive, to dominate, to stamp your authority, but you must never go overboard in this regard otherwise you lose equilibrium. Hansie was skilful, competitive and aggressive on the field. His presence was intimidating, much like Shane Warne's was."

But it was inspirational leadership that, according to Warmenhoven, stood out above every other competency in which he excelled. "His ability to inspire, motivate and encourage his colleagues was considered invaluable and translated into the unique gift of being able to get the best out of his players, especially in pressure situations. Hansie was able to excite the hearts and minds of his team to strive passionately towards a shared vision by graphically, memorably and compellingly painting a picture of the desired future. And clearly his own enthusiasm was contagious."

"He just got so excited about his dreams and ideas that you kind of got swept up into them with him," said Bertha.

●

Before South Africa's first matches under Hansie, the new young captain had phoned Kepler. "He wanted to thank the old skipper for what he had done for him on a personal level and for his overall input in helping to shape the team," wrote Rodney Hartman in *Hansie and the Boys*. "I asked him if he still wanted to play in the Test team, and he said he would think about it and come back to me. He never did, so I presumed he was no longer available," Hansie is quoted as saying.

Shortly after taking over the captaincy, Hansie and Bob Woolmer called for a team meeting. Those at the meeting included players like Hansie, Fanie de Villiers, Richard Snell, Craig Matthews, Brian McMillan, Daryll Cullinan, Clive Eksteen, Andrew Hudson, Gary Kirsten, Dave Richardson and Jonty Rhodes. Bob presented the question: "Where are we now, and where would we like to be in five years' time?"

During a long and intense discussion, the team decided that, by the end of 1999, they wanted to:

1. Be the No.1 Test side in the world. (At that stage the SA side was not rated highly in Test or One-Day International – ODI – cricket.)
2. Be the No.1 ODI side in the world.
3. Win the 1999 Cricket World Cup.
4. Have a team that is culturally representative of all South Africans, on merit.

In order to get there, they realised that they would need to set certain goals. Bob told them that to improve they didn't need "to do one thing 100% better, but rather do 100 things 1% better". The team then identified something like 67 items they could improve on in ODI cricket, and worked out a specific plan to improve on them, by a small margin, every single day.

Some of the things that Woolmer highlighted for their ODI campaign were:

1. Pick our best One-Day team at all times.
2. Identify each individual player's role in the team.
3. Become the fittest team in world cricket.
4. Encourage innovation and back players to play their shots.

"In order to achieve the above we prepared an 11-page document on the discipline of One-Day cricket. We paid attention to the finest detail and our catch cry was 'one run can make a difference'," said Woolmer.

Significantly, the team realised that most ODIs were either won or lost by less than a 10-run difference between the opposing teams' totals (that is between 2-7 percent in total). In the last 13 ODIs that the team had lost, they came close to winning many of these. So, it was postulated, that if every player could work hard to save "one run" in each game, then that would mean saving 11 runs in total. That, it was said, could mean the difference between winning and losing.

With this "one run can make the difference" attitude, the team started training and worked harder than ever – the captain, as usual, always leading from the front and pushing the rest of the team to the limits. The aim was to become the fittest and the best fielding side in the world. Athleticism of the highest order was to become part of the brand of the team, and no one worked harder at personal fitness than Hansie himself.

"For 1 825 days, that's all we thought about, ate about, drank about, slept about, practised. We studied the opposition, watched videos, tried to improve one percent on things every day, tried to cut one run … and we slowly started working our way up," Hansie said during a speech in Stellenbosch in 2001.

Hansie set himself training goals constantly, for example always trying to improve on his time for the four-kilometre run, or push more on the bench. For each gym session, he would set himself a specific goal.

Once, Hansie was running alone on the road in Bloemfontein when he had spotted a person running in front of him, at a good pace. He thought he would catch up with the person and ask if they could run together. He really struggled hard to get close enough, before he realised that it was the ex-world champion long-distance runner Zola Budd. After that they sometimes trained together.

The Sports Science Institute in Cape Town tested the squad twice a year for physical fitness. "The testing not only allows players to compare themselves to each other, but provides baseline values that further tests can be measured against and also points out areas that need to be prioritised," wrote Hansie. Justin du Randt, who had been the manager of the Discovery High Performance Centre at the Sports Science Institute, and was still employed by them in 2005, said, "I tested the national cricket team in April 1997. Hansie had a good general fitness profile but he had exceptional cardiovascular fitness. He ran a level 15.9 (151 shuttles) on the bleep test (multistage shuttle run) this is equivalent to having a vo2max of 66.6 ml/kg/min. The team average that year for the bleep test was level 13.4. No provincial or national player has bettered this score for that specific test in the last ten years."

This truly is a remarkable illustration of Hansie's drive and will to succeed, when one considers that he was not a natural runner.

Gary Kirsten learnt the hard way just how fit Hansie was. Brought in as a replacement during an Australian tour, Kirsten was eager to impress his then vice captain. Hansie had invited Gary to join him for a run around Sydney Harbour. "Completely in the dark about Hansie's running skills, I confidently set off from the hotel, looking forward to getting to know Hansie better. By the second kilometre I began to realise that any form of conversation would be useless for two reasons: firstly we were running so fast that talking would've ... probably resulted in my premature death! Secondly, he was so far ahead I would've needed a loudspeaker. As he took a detour up the Opera House stairs, I had a much-needed breather at the bottom and it gave me a chance to realise what a fool I'd been. The team later laughed at my stupidity. Hansie believes he can run a top 10 finish in the Comrades Marathon ... I'm just one of the few that has taken a bet with him that he won't succeed with his bizarre proposal. But, knowing Hansie, he's capable of anything."

"Capable of anything." That was always part of the aura of the star.

Diet was important too, although this is one area that Hansie and the boys mostly battled with – Hansie's penchant for Big Macs was legendary. "I tried to keep up with the diet given to us by Paula Volschenk (the team's dietician), but the choices weren't always available. Paddy Upton (the team trainer) tries to keep us off the chocolates, shakes, cakes, pizzas and other fatty foods and to get us to choose vegetables, fruit and muffins instead. A beer or two isn't bad as long as it doesn't mean peanuts and chips with it! I'm generally quite good and try to maintain a constant body weight of 85kg and a fat percentage of nine," Hansie stated in his benefit-year publication (1997/8), *Hansie: This is your captain speaking.*

During Hansie's reign a number of innovations were introduced. In September 1997, Hansie's brother Frans was appointed head coach of the Natal Dolphins and during his time in Durban he commissioned and directed the design of a sophisticated video analysis system. The system was probably one of the first fully digital video analysis computer systems used in world cricket, and had the ability to capture the video clips and relevant statistics of every single ball that was bowled during a match. The data were recorded onto the hard drive and then stored on DVD.

Back in 1997, few had ever used digital video-capture cards, let alone recorded video to DVD. Frans and computer specialist Mauricio Radovan showed a prototype of their system to Bob Woolmer, who was about to buy a similar English system – at a very expensive price – which was then still in analogue form. Bob was excited about the potential superiority of the South African system and prompted Tony Kirkbride at the South African Council for Scientific and Industrial Research (CSIR) to tweak it into shape within weeks.

This system was used comprehensively by the squad. (In 2005 it was still being used by the Proteas, as well as in Pakistan and the West Indies.)

Bob and Hansie, for instance, could ask the laptop at any time in the season to show all the cover drives that Jonty hit for 4. Or to show Jonty's dismissals. "This was an intelligent way for players to analyse themselves and learn from their mistakes, but it was also a great way for players to look at all their best shots while they were at the peak of their performance. Bob and Hansie found this to be useful in helping players regain confidence while they were going through a bad patch," said Frans. Of course, it also helped to clinically analyse the opposition's strengths and weaknesses and work out specific ways of countering adversaries.

In 2005, Bob Woolmer (at that time, national coach of the Pakistan cricket team) sent some interesting comments about Hansie from his hotel room in Kanpur, the very city where the Indian bookies first made contact with Hansie. "Hansie led from the front in everything he did. He was as thorough in preparing about the opposition as he was about making sure that his team was prepared. On the field he was innovative, proactive and he never let the game drift. He handled people extremely well and every player gave his all for Hansie. In short he was an excellent captain for the modern era."

One of Hansie's more controversial innovations was the introduction of an earpiece worn by cricketers on the field. This allowed players to listen to one-way advice from the coach. There was strong criticism of its introduction during the 1999 World Cup and the ICC banned its use after the first match. No one even knew about it until Allan Donald asked the umpire to hold his earpiece, along with his cap and jersey, while he was bowling. The umpire asked the match referee, and even though there was no mention in the rulebook about the use of such a device, the match referee decided that it was not in the spirit of the game.

●

The early support framework around Hansie was formidable and it contributed greatly to his ongoing successes. For example, Peter Pollock, chairman of the selectors, was a man who was willing to defend the rights of players, especially when they came up against political and inappropriate interference along the road to victory. When Pollock retired at the end of 1999, things changed markedly for the worse, as political motivation took preference over physical ability and form.

Pollock's selection panel chose their core players – and stuck with them, allowing players to settle down and establish their credentials. This created confidence and meant that they could grow together as a team. Peter Pollock consulted closely with Hansie and often gave Hansie and Woolmer their way.

According to Warmenhoven, commenting on how Hansie almost clinically managed the process of leadership in her 2005 PhD thesis, it is clear that he used his business-school background to "develop a strong service orientation. He treated his team as though they were his customers, and made every effort to ensure that their needs were met at all times. Hansie also viewed the media, his fans, his sponsors and the UCB as further 'clients'."

Warmenhoven said he consistently and conscientiously worked at keeping and increasing his clients' satisfaction and loyalty by making use of particular "conscious strategies", such as the following:

"1. He made his 'clients' look good, by acknowledging them in his speeches and in any other way possible.
2. He made his 'clients' feel like a significant part of the team and its successes, encouraging a team mentality.
3. He often allowed others to take credit for a job well done.
4. He was loyal and never ran team members down publicly, even if they had performed badly.
5. He constantly monitored 'client satisfaction'."

Hansie had been offered the national captaincy ahead of many other competent cricket players who exceeded him significantly in years and experience. Because of this, "he initially adopted a more democratic and inclusive type of captaincy style, and made every effort to learn as much from these men as possible, and to include them in the leadership process until he won their acceptance and respect. He selected a group of the most mature and experienced players to act as his 'middle management'," wrote Warmenhoven.

"You had guys like Brian McMillan, myself, Jonty … you had leaders in their own right in the middle of the thing. And he made sure the 'middle management team' were giving him information," said Craig Matthews.

"Hansie wisely recognised that in order to rise quickly to a position of confidence and proficiency from which to lead the national squad he would need to draw on their expertise and experience," said Warmenhoven.

Jonty was not just a remarkable fielder; he was also an inspiration to his team on and off the field. Hansie made this clear in his speech in Stellenbosch, in September 2001: "The best team player that I ever played with and against is Jonty Rhodes. If he wasn't contributing with the bat, then he would win the game in the field. Even when he had a bad day with the bat and in the field, he still stayed positive in the change room and urged the rest of the team to go out there and do better than their best.

"Jonty always put his team-mates first and was willing to be humble and serve the rest of the guys. Even at the age of 33 and a senior player, he would be the first to help unload the bus, or pack the heavy cricket cases into the bus after a match. He is a truly great example to follow," Hansie said.

The team looked to Jonty to set the pace at his familiar backward point fielding position and they were also willing to work just as hard as he did at practice to lift their fielding skills. In his quest to empower the senior players, Hansie appointed some of them as captains of specific areas. The obvious captain of the "fielding side" was Jonty.

Gary Kirsten became the "captain" of the top order batsmen and Hansie's old friend Allan Donald became the "captain" of the bowling side.

●

The South African public aligned themselves staunchly with Hansie's captaincy, and the world's media generally sang his praises whenever he played.

It is true to say that in the cricketing nations of the world from 1995, Hansie was a particularly bright star. A personal encounter with Hansie, however small, was gilded with the light of his smile, his warm and focused words. He radiated a quick sense of friendship and intimacy with groups of people from every socio-economic stratum, culture, religion and age group. His diplomacy and tact in public, his well-constructed and stirring speeches, his natural and easy way with everyone, his cheeky bonhomie, were just some of the traits that contributed to his recognition as a national and international icon. Many fans, especially those on the Asian sub-continent, had clearly adopted him into their pantheon of glittering heroes.

But Hansie's elevation worried his family at times. "I used to get calls from moms and dads – one woman said, 'Please ask your son not to spit on the cricket field. My youngest son idolises Hansie, and now he's also spitting on the pitch,'" said San-Marie.

For San-Marie, there came a time when the public idolised him too much. "They put him up on a pedestal and he shouldn't have been up there. When Hansie was selected as captain, my mom nearly had a heart attack. She said, 'They're going to kill this child. He's too young to handle it.'

"People made a god out of Hansie, forgetting that he was a normal person with weaknesses like you and me. Later, when they saw him stumble, it enraged them, because their idol had fallen. What I so often wanted to shout to the public was 'Get your children's eyes off sports heroes. Get them to realise that they are only people, only men. Rather encourage your children to worship Jesus.' It's sickening the way we South Africans, indeed the world – idolise sports people. In England and India it's even worse."

Did this "idolisation" of Hansie make him reckless and arrogant at times? "No, never arrogant. But I felt that that was where the UCB could've helped the up-and-coming players by educating them on how to handle themselves," said San-Marie.

But fame can be an odd thing, and sometimes Hansie was brought back to earth. On a holiday in Mauritius with Bertha in 1997, two youngsters had spotted him in a clothing shop as they walked past. They had stopped on the pavement, gazing at him intently and then had walked expectantly up to him in the shop. A smiling Hansie, meeting their gaze of recognition, had his pen out, ready for an autograph. "Excuse me, Sir," they had said, "are you Pete Sampras?"

The following morning, Mark Thatcher, the son of Lady Thatcher, was lounging at the hotel pool where Hansie and Bertha were lodged. One of Hansie's friends, as a joke, approached him and declared, pointing at Hansie, "Have you noticed that Pete Sampras is here?"

Thatcher calmly lowered his newspaper and said, "No it's not. That's Hansie Cronjé."

Hansie's rapport with children was especially remarkable and a great and consistent feature of his personality, a fact that even his sternest critics would not debate. "We'd finish a game of cricket – a Test match, and we'd have been out on the field for five hours. And then he'd go and stand on the field and play cricket with the kids," said Nicky Bojé.

Hansie would often walk up to a child and strike up a conversation, especially during the quiet moments on tour.

His cheeky sense of fun was childlike. He enjoyed sticking his finger in a plate of jelly on a dining-room table, and he would incite his little niece, Alexandrea, to do the same, given the opportunity. Such simple nonsense endeared him to kids everywhere.

Frans's wife, René, confirms that Hansie had a special relationship with his nieces and nephews. "All four of the kids were always very excited at the prospect of spending time with Hansie and Bertha. As they were still very young they knew nothing about their uncle's fame. It was just his (and Bertha's) way with kids and people that made him so popular."

"I spent a lot of time with Hansie, doing work with charities, hobnobbing with larnies… I saw this guy's heart. He didn't have a bad bone in his body. I never saw him swear at a kid, misuse his authority as a captain. Never lorded it over anybody," said Jonty.

"The things he did for people, the way he talked to people, he shook hands with them … the guy had time for them, he had time for the kids, he signed autographs. He never rushed away from people … If he was busy, he'd always say, 'I'm terribly sorry. I can't do it now. If you come back at two o'clock I can help you'. He would always have time for people," said Bob Woolmer.

Many still talk about his "compassion" and "common touch". Pastor Ray McCauley's son, Josh, just before his 10th birthday, asked his father if he could invite Hansie to his birthday party.

"Josh's idea was to invite his friends and that Hansie would play cricket with them," recalled Ray. "I tried to explain to him that the national cricketers were really busy, and besides, Hansie was supposed to play a match for Free State at the Wanderers that weekend."

Ray left it at that, but had jokingly relayed the story to Hansie when Hansie visited the Rhema Church. On the birthday, it poured with rain and Hansie's cricket was cancelled. "Later that day, as the party started, the door bell rang and it was Hansie. He had a wrapped cricket bat in his hands for Josh. Hansie then played cricket with the kids for a long time in the back yard before he left again to join his team. The following day he took Josh along to 'assist' in the Free State change room, and Hansie gave his cricket shirt to Josh. Compassion was a part of his character."

Ray also says that Hansie was always willing to "make appearances and give talks at some of the charitable projects that Rhema managed, such as orphanages and soup kitchens".

Wendy Sherrin, who works in the South African film industry, told the story of the reaction from Hansie, Allan Donald and Fanie de Villiers when she told them about a former South African cricketer, Xenophon "Bally" Balaskas, who was old and bed-ridden at the time. The following day they asked her to arrange a visit to Bally. He "was totally overwhelmed with emotion" when the three walked into his room. "He really enjoyed the visit and the three cricketers patiently listened as he gave them 'advice' on how to play. Bally told them that he was unable to watch cricket any more, due to his ill health and not being able to get to the lounge where the TV set was. The next day a brand new TV and wall-mounting bracket arrived and was installed in his room," said Wendy. Hansie had organised the gift. Bally died in front of the television, watching South Africa play Australia.

Hansie had a particularly soft spot for The Reach for a Dream Foundation – an organisation that arranges for children with terminal diseases to live out a particular dream of theirs. Often these "dreams" were to meet Hansie, and he would always oblige.

René Cronjé related how Hansie, visiting them at their new home in Durban, wanted to buy them a dishwasher straight away when he saw that they did not have one, and it took some time to talk him out of it. "He always recognised the needs and started making plans to meet them. Mostly at his own expense." She continued, "One evening in 1999, Hansie spent the night at our home in Stellenbosch. He arrived late in the evening and only wanted a cup of coffee, to download his e-mails and then go to bed. Knowing his hectic schedule and the politics raging around his head at the time, I couldn't help noticing how exhausted he looked. I told him that I felt sorry for him and asked if he was OK."

Hansie's response was very firm: "I never want anyone to feel sorry for me. Do you realise that it was my childhood dream to play cricket for South Africa? And now I am living my dream! I was given the greatest honour to captain the South African side and I am riding a huge wave. It comes with excitement and with strain, but I have to make the most of it while I have the opportunity … It won't last forever. One of these days I will be standing on the shore and I don't want any regrets. Never feel sorry for me!"

With South Africa still being relatively new to international sport after the isolation years, sponsors were willing to pay huge sums of money to sponsor the team and also to sponsor the likes of Hansie and Jonty individually.

Sponsors were delighted by Hansie's commitment to them. The head of sponsorship for South African Breweries Limited while Hansie was captain was Norman Minnaar. He said at Fancourt in 2005, "I think, from the sponsorship point of view, you couldn't have a better captain. He conscientiously looked after the sponsors' interests. We never had to ask him to go and put a cap on for an interview or to say something about the sponsor – which contrasted with a lot of other guys in the team. If we asked him to do something, he just did it, and would make sure that the rest of the team did it as well."

But sponsors are demanding and, perhaps unwisely, Hansie had signed up with about ten. This income flow came at a high cost, and Bertha had to pay for it too, seeing less and less of Hansie, even during off-season, as he shuttled around, pleasing the sponsors. Hansie felt an obligation to look after all of his sponsors and his obligations to them kept him spinning around endlessly during what should have been his free time.

What made the pressure worse was the fact that Hansie was also required to make appearances for the UCB sponsors.

Generally the South African media supported the new captain, and the early reports spoke highly of his character and abilities. He was willing to give out his cell number to anyone, and the media would sometimes phone him in the middle of the night while he was on tour. For years he was known by the media to be one of the most accessible and approachable captains internationally.

Television commentator and freelance journalist Andy Capostagno, for example, dedicated his book, *Memorable Moments in One Day Cricket*, published in 2004, to "my good friend Hansie Cronjé".

But "the Australian press were ruthless. They always targeted the captain, teaming up against the visiting side. They would ask tricky questions. Hansie was so good at press conferences, so calm and cool, saying for example, after a tricky question, 'We're not here for this'. Hansie was always the perfect diplomat, who knew how to deflect contrary questions. He wouldn't react to the nonsense," said Allan Donald.

While Hansie generally handled the media fairly well, he tried in vain to remain oblivious to the negative opinions that on occasion came his way, or his team's way. "The media are cruel ... Hansie didn't bother to read the papers. If we would tell him something that this guy or that guy had said, he would say, 'I'd prefer not to know, not to be aware of it'," said San-Marie. Yet there were many times when he could hardly ignore negativity, given the fact that it impacted on the sensitivities of his squad, and sometimes affected the mental equilibrium of some players singled out for criticism.

There were two types of media personalities that irritated Hansie severely. The first was "the small group of ex-players from the national cricket side who became so 'clever' after they played, and so critical," said Ewie.

The other group were those "who knew very little about the game of cricket, yet felt they had carte blanche to express their opinions freely in the press, to the detriment of the players", said Frans.

The desire to protect his players from unnecessarily harsh or warped reviews led to a few incidents that resulted in negative publicity for Hansie. The most famous of these was when the Proteas were on tour in Australia. Neil Manthorp, the official South African reporter during the Test series, had harshly criticised Daryll Cullinan's seeming inability to cope with Warne's "flipper". When Manthorp ventured into the change rooms after the report, Hansie swore at him viciously, and forbade him access to the players. Daryll Cullinan said in 2005 that he felt the entire team lost their trust in Manthorp and some other reporters. "We were always willing to give journalists inside stories, but it seemed that Manthorp was after sensation. He also misquoted me in the Shane Warne story. Later some of his family members apologised for the way he wrote certain articles."

Frans said, "It took a lot to make Hansie lose his temper, but on the rare occasions that he did, he really lost it." This is illustrated by another incident with Manthorp on the same tour.

In 2005, Manthorp gave his version of the story: "An article had appeared in the *Cape Times* after South Africa had lost the 'best of three' One-Day final against Australia in 1998 (having won the first game) in which they were labelled 'chokers'.

"It infuriated the coach and the whole team, particularly as it had the cowardly 'Own Correspondent' byline. Because it was in the *Cape Times*, and I was the only journalist on tour from Cape Town, Bob Woolmer assumed it was me and told the players that.

"Straight after the One-Day finals, we moved to Adelaide for the third Test where Bob and I had a very, very firm exchange of views and he accepted that the article had nothing to do with me. Then, on the final day, Mark Waugh was given 'not out' despite treading on his stumps, avoiding a Shaun Pollock bouncer. An hour later Hansie put a stump through the umpires' door.

"On his way out of the media conference I followed him to make sure he knew I hadn't written the article. As he started climbing a metal staircase to return to the change room, he turned around to face me, spat at me, saying he was going 'to *&%#$ kill me'.

"Later, when we returned to South Africa, Peter Robinson recognised the article as one he'd written for *The Star* but which had been horribly 'adapted' for the *Cape Times*.

"I was shaken by Hansie's behaviour and upset. I returned to the press box and started writing my report for the *Mail & Guardian*. I asked a close friend and colleague from Australia, Jim Tucker, whether I should mention the incident and he advised me against it. I never wrote about it and never thought much of it, after a couple of days."

●

Corrie van Zyl was appointed deputy coach of the Proteas, three seasons into Hansie's captaincy. "When I started my new job, the buzz in the team reminded me strongly of the early years of Hansie's captaincy of the Free State team. I could see he wanted to instil the same ethos: keep it simple, work hard, the coach and the captain are large and in charge, and you must do what they tell you, and do so enthusiastically.

"Like that old Free State team, the Proteas were struggling to get 'in' and realised there was a mountain to climb. We all worked hard together and a sense of mission, of camaraderie, of family, began to gel. With Hansie in place, I wasn't surprised by the way things were going. Hansie called the shots, but he allowed debate. There was always debate (then). He didn't mind constructive criticism. He led by example, and where others would not see a positive result in a game, he would see one. Many times a result would come because of his confidence, because of his belief in still winning from a bad situation. Hansie would show the way to victory.

"His communication was good, and each team member knew exactly – in fine detail – what Hansie required of them. He would say to each player: 'If we are going to win this match, then this (whatever it was) is the contribution you will have to make.'"

Allan Donald is particularly well placed, because of his long and personal history with Hansie, to comment on his captaincy: "In a huge way Hansie's captaincy changed the nature of cricket in South Africa. For starters, there was less drinking and more practising. In 1995, Meyrick Pringle was dropped by Hansie because he came back late after a night out during the second Test match against England at the Wanderers. It was not his first offence and Meyrick was never picked again. With Hansie's tremendous emphasis on fitness, he even influenced the way cricket was played around the world."

"Where Hansie's captaincy had initially been more democratic as he got down to the task of winning the respect of especially the senior players and learning the finer points of international captaincy from the more experienced cricketers in the side, his style of captaincy began to change as he became more comfortable and confident in his leadership role," wrote Warmenhoven. "Having obtained buy-in and commitment from every team member, he began to 'raise the bar' for his cricketing colleagues, becoming more demanding of individual and the team performances. This new 'pacesetting' style was the perfect approach to the high demands for success placed on teams competing at international levels – and Hansie demonstrated that he had mastered it to perfection as he managed to obtain a fine balance between empathy for his team members, and remaining focussed on the goals to be achieved."

Clearly, this more exacting pace was something that the team needed to adjust to, as illustrated in the following story, told by Allan Donald. "We were playing in Auckland on a very flat, glued pitch. I had bowled my heart out all day and at teatime we came off the field for the break. I was lying on the floor, with my feet up, and I said, 'Gee, this is hard work'.

"Hansie didn't appreciate that. He didn't speak to me for a week and a half. He blind-eyed me completely. The next morning we played touch-rugby and he aggressively shoulder-barged me, sending me spinning. I was angry, and nearly threw the ball at him. I thought, 'What's your *bladdy* problem man, what have I done wrong?'

"At Christchurch, in the lead-up to the One-Day game, he came up to me and said, 'Listen, we gotta talk.'"

Allan was still hurt, still furious, and told Hansie to get lost. Hansie explained that he didn't appreciate that "my senior player lay on the ground and moaned, sending out the message that he couldn't be bothered about all the hard work to be done".

Later, Hansie eventually forced himself into Allan's hotel room, and said, "Listen, I'm not here to make war. I'm here to chat." The old friends then made up.

"Although Hansie had become more demanding, his more commanding style also brought with it a sense of security for the team members. Hansie was very clear on what his expectations were of each player, and he was also very good at communicating this to each one, leaving no-one confused about what they needed to be working towards," said Warmenhoven.

Allan agrees. "With Hansie, I always knew exactly what my role was. If Hansie threw the ball to me on the field, I was 'there'. I wanted to be the man who made the difference for him.

"We all knew we had a captain who was in total control of what went on around him. It was that quality of his that made us so relaxed; we had so much confidence in him, we placed our trust in him, in the sure knowledge that he would make the right decisions, every time.

"He was brilliant at switching on and off. He'd ride the sledging and the tension. He could play. He was so dangerous when he had settled. Hansie wasn't the best starter as a batsman, he was actually one of the worst starters, but once he was in he was in.

"Hansie also knew how to wind up the opposition. I remember when I was playing club cricket against him, and he was batting, he shouted at me, 'Put a bowler on!' He loved to stir up the blood a bit."

Hansie's high expectations of others were complemented by one of his strongest assets as a captain – his belief in leading by example. "This strong conviction was evident in numerous cricket settings: he would be the fittest man on the field, he would be the first at the nets for a practice, he would be the last to person to leave, he would celebrate the success of others, he would sacrifice personal goals for team goals, he would remain calm and focussed under pressure, he was prepared to put his body on the line for the team (for example, fielding at short leg), he would never back down against opposition, and he would remain optimistic even in the face of defeat," wrote Warmenhoven. "Clearly, he embodied the principles, standards and visions of the teams or organizations he led and was never prepared to ask anyone to do anything which he could not, or was not prepared to do himself. Instead he pushed himself hard to show his team a better way and to inspire them through what he was able to achieve. Leading from the front was thus also one of his greatest motivational tools as a captain, as it won the respect of every team member and spurred them on to try to attain the same heights which they saw their captain reaching."

"At times Hansie was harshly criticised by the press for occasional loss of self-control, but those who knew and understood him explained such incidents as the direct result of the immense pressure that national cricketers – and especially captains – are placed under," wrote Warmenhoven.

"It is simply not possible for anyone to exaggerate or over-estimate the pressure of international captaincy, both on and off the field ... It is unreasonable and unrealistic for people to expect the captain's performance not to be affected ... it is difficult for people to imagine just how many extra duties Hansie had to fit into each 24 hours. The emotional strain is enormous," said Craig Matthews.

Added to this pressure was Hansie's insatiable will to win. "Achievement drive – the will to win – is the cornerstone competency of the world's most successful individuals. And Hansie was no exception," said Warmenhoven. In everything he did, he tried to build in an element of competition. He had always, always, hated losing. Even losing a card game with his wife Bertha and brother Frans would irritate him, so much so that friends would sometimes refuse to play games with him. "I'm a bad loser; I'm really grumpy when it comes to losing. It takes me a couple of days to get over that. But it makes me more determined to do well next time," Hansie said in 1995.

According to Warmenhoven, "Hansie was also an individual who set extremely high goals for himself, and he placed tremendous pressure on himself to achieve these. Hindrances to meeting these objectives were met with severe disappointment. It was a combination of these factors which sometimes led to certain indiscretions by the captain," as the following example, alluded to earlier by Manthorp, illustrates.

In Adelaide, Australia, 1997/8, after some spectacularly bad umpiring in South Africa's disfavour, Hansie carrying a stump at the end of the match, passed the umpire's change-room. He hit the door in frustration, and the sharp end of the stump made a hole in the door. He was reported and fined for it. From then on, South African TV commentator and good friend, Darren Scott, affectionately called Hansie "Spike".

Hansie understood that international captaincy was about winning, and this complemented his personal deeply aggressive will to win. However, this sometimes brought him into conflict with the UCB bosses and others as the years of his captaincy rolled by. He had commanded, at times even demanded, the necessary power to achieve victory, and for years it had mostly unconditionally been provided by the likes of the chairman of selectors Peter Pollock, the CEO of the UCB Dr Ali Bacher and coach Bob Woolmer, men who had learned to trust the captain's judgment and the sensitivity and wisdom with which he wielded the authority they had given him.

However, as the political climate in the country began to change, so did the demands on the sporting arena, and such freedom was no longer in the hands of the cricketing authorities to give. It was at such times that sharp conflicts arose between a victory-hungry Hansie and those in cricketing administration. Disputes were also apparent when Hansie believed that he held the better solution, but felt unheard by those above him.

"In 1998 he and Bob had a go at each other. Why, I don't know," recalled Corrie van Zyl. "On two occasions there were screaming matches between the two men and I found Hansie's behaviour unacceptable at that time." Corrie went to Hansie as a result and said, "Hansie, you can't do those things. You must behave respectfully towards Bob."

Hansie had meekly replied, "Corrie, you're right. I'm stupid, and I shouldn't have behaved like that."

"Hansie then made amends and apologised. They went out, had a meal together and sorted things out. Hansie was human."

It was the year before the 1999 World Cup, the prize to which four years of total, dedicated focus (if not his entire life) had been devoted, and the pressure was beginning to tell.

Hansie felt the weighty responsibility of bringing home a victorious team for South Africa. This pressure, together with the escalation of his own will to win, knowing that a personal life's ambition was within his reach, led to him taking an even tougher approach with himself and his team. "He was hard on himself and hard on the team as well," said Craig Matthews.

"As a superbly disciplined and diligent individual, Hansie admitted that he had always struggled to find a balance between enjoyment and seriousness. His capacity for hard work had always been exceptional, but as this major life goal drew closer he seems to have driven himself and the team almost obsessively," said Warmenhoven.

In the opinion of Craig Smith (the team physio), Hansie would actually "draw on the discomfort from injury and turn it into a motivating factor". But where Hansie may have had the capacity and endurance required for this, there were some who did not function optimally in such an environment.

"One of the big things the players would say is, 'Do we have to go to practice again?'" recalled Bob Woolmer. "And I would say, 'Listen, the practice is optional – you don't have to come.' And then I sat down with some of the players and the players said, 'If we don't come, you won't pick us.' So I said, 'Well that's a deception, not a fact. It's got nothing to do with that.' They said, 'Well what about Hansie?' And I said, 'No – Hansie wants to go and practise every day, but you don't have to. If you want to rest, take a rest.' And eventually … we got players to take rests … But Hansie would always be at the practice. He would never take a rest …

even when he injured his knee and Gary Kirsten took over as captain for one Test match, Hansie was there every single day... "

According to Warmenhoven, Hansie adapted his leadership style frequently throughout his career, according to the situation in which he found himself. Sometimes he asked for advice from his players (and, in the early years, from ex-coaches) and sometimes he made the call on his own.

Jonty said, "Hansie told me once that it sometimes became very difficult to decide on a specific strategy. For example, when Shaun Pollock was vice captain he often provided Hansie with so many useful options that Hansie had to choose the best of four or five possible solutions. The fact is that the captain still needs to make the final call and there may have been times when players interpreted this as autocratic. I never saw it like that."

Hansie's willingness to adapt his way of thinking was strongly tempered by his achievement drive. He knew that in order to meet the goals that they had set as a team, they would need to remain on cricket's cutting edge continually. Thus, he was not prepared to experiment with ideas which he was not absolutely convinced would work. At all times, Hansie was also very focused on 'service orientation'. That means that he clearly understood that his first priority to the country was to deliver victory. Anything that might jeopardise this outcome was rejected.

"If you didn't come to him with practical proof that it [a new idea] would work, he wouldn't go for it. I remember there were a number of guys giving him advice – sports psychologists and kineticists and he would tell them bluntly: 'They're theories, go and test it at a lower level until you can prove that it works, then we can implement it on the national side,'" observed Frans.

Naturally, this did not always endear him to the experts who were there to assist the team. Hansie's powerful dominance appeared to amaze and frustrate them at times.

At some stage Hansie started having disagreements with Professor Tim Noakes in connection with the scientific team's involvement and status. Hansie felt that they were demanding too much say in the way that the team trained; he felt they were also trying to influence team selection. "My perception was that Hansie was not always good about receiving criticism from people like Noakes, and started becoming much more dictator-like in his approach," said team physiotherapist Craig Smith.

Professor Noakes, a widely respected sports medicine expert from the Sports Science Institute in Newlands, Cape Town, had worked closely with the Proteas until October 1997. In 2005, Noakes said he believed that he had been sidelined in 1997 by Hansie's actions "at the very time we were beginning to make a measurable difference".

Even as the pressure was turned up, Hansie's fun-loving nature would shine through at times.

He always loved a party, for example. "He would stay with the best of them until 2am (if there wasn't a match the next day) but he normally wouldn't drink much at all, just one or two beers. The team used to have a forfeits ritual where squad members would have to down beers. Hansie would down milkshakes instead and would sometimes make teetotaller Shaun Pollock down two or three milkshakes in a row," said Norman Minnaar of the team sponsor, South African Breweries.

During the World Cup of 1996 in Pakistan and India, Hansie went down to breakfast before any of the team did. The previous day the fitness trainer, Paddy Upton, had played a prank on Hansie and Hansie was determined to strike back. He told Professor Noakes that he would hand out the medication for the day. He also asked Noakes for two sleeping pills. (Earlier, Hansie had noticed that the malaria and sleeping tablets looked very similar.) Hansie then proceeded to distribute the medicines to each team member as they came to breakfast, and when Paddy arrived he swapped the malaria pills for the sleeping tablets.

During the bus trip to the stadium Hansie told Bob Woolmer that he wanted to take the team through their stretching session at the start of practice, and wanted to incorporate some "mental exercises". So after a lap or two around the ground, Hansie ordered them to do stretching exercises before saying they must lie on their backs, with eyes closed, and imagine some tranquil place. This was not a part of the normal drill and the team all started wondering what Hansie was up to. When Hansie eventually told them to get up, Paddy was supine, fast asleep.

The team then had a good practice and Hansie was all for leaving Paddy in the sun for a few hours, until he eventually woke up. A sleep-addled Paddy, on rubber legs, then tried to help the guys with fielding and running practice, which provided for some hearty laughter.

"One of the competencies which Cronjé's colleagues hailed as exceptional was his ability to maintain a balance between closeness to, and distance from, those who followed him in order to maintain a level of respect as a leader. He worked hard at achieving this balance because he recognised that if an individual needed to be reprimanded, he needed to have slight aloofness in order to speak with authority," said Warmenhoven.

"Although he was one of the boys, he was never so part of the team that his team-mates saw him as an equal … He was very good with that … He'd just get close enough that you felt you could trust him … but never close enough that you could take advantage of his position," said Boeta Dippenaar.

"He was social, but … there was always a distance. That's important in a leader … You've got to have respect … He had the respect of the team in every way … guys would not overstep the mark when he was around," agreed Gary Kirsten.

The largely self-imposed loneliness of Hansie's captaincy was heightened by the fact that on tour he hardly ever shared a hotel room. "Hansie," said Bertha, "used to say to me it was difficult to be seen to have favourites. He distanced himself on a personal level, never wanting to get too close to anyone because, being the captain, he often had to tell the players who wouldn't be playing the next day and it was one of the most difficult things for him to do." In addition, he was a very private person, yet the anomaly was that "everybody that met him felt that they were one of his best mates. But in truth he never got close to anybody, even the guys on the team, and wouldn't open his heart to them," said Bertha.

"During his years as captain, not too many people took the liberty to speak to Hansie when he stepped out of line. I think because of his growing stature, people were too afraid to do it, or they may have just felt that he was doing fine anyway. This is a common occurrence with celebrities. One person that could speak to him, though, was Ray McCauley. Hansie had a huge amount of respect for Ray and he always listened to him. Unfortunately, due to some of his own pressures, Ray started spending less time with the team later on during Hansie's captaincy," said Frans.

In 2005 McCauley said, "It is so difficult to spend enough time with cricket players. They are always travelling and very seldom have time to attend their own church. When you consider everything that has taken place over the last few years in sport, I think that it is really necessary to appoint a full time pastor to travel with the team."

"In a sense, this meant that Hansie was unknowingly entering a 'danger zone'. Because of the lack of mentorship, Hansie remained largely unaccountable to anyone. There was also no one close enough to Hansie to be able give him feedback and to guide his actions – and thus no one to warn him of the dangers of his misguided exploration into the world of the bookmakers later on," said Warmenhoven

Hansie's drive to win, his extreme conscientiousness, his massively busy schedule meant that he also had little time to reflect on his life and on his values, Warmenhoven observed. "It caused a lapse in his usually healthy self-awareness. Early on in his career, he frequently took time out, he made time to assess the last few days and then learn from his own mistakes… Hansie was a person with very strong principles and a well-developed value system. He also had incredible discipline and integrity. But when a person loses self-awareness their values often become skewed."

One of the flaws in Hansie's personality, an inability to say "no" to the public's demands, exacerbated the situation. "As he accepted more and more speaking and public engagements (over and above his already unbelievably demanding schedule as national captain), he became so busy that there was absolutely no time for any kind of reflection, which hampered his personal growth – and spiritual growth. "It seems that as Hansie's values began to shift, his ability to distinguish between, for example, 'healthy balance/moderation' and 'excess' began to blur – making him especially vulnerable to crossing the line between 'living on the edge' and doing something that was totally wrong," said Warmenhoven.

This left Hansie wide open and exposed to temptation.

⬤

Most of the following section is taken from the statement that Hansie read during the King Commission in 2000.

While the Proteas were in India in 1996 a person by the name of "Sunil" contacted Hansie and asked if he would be interested in fixing some matches. Hansie told him that he was not interested.

On the evening of the third Test match in Kanpur, Hansie received a surprise phone call from the Indian captain Mohammed Azharuddin, who was friends with a few of the South African players. He asked if he could meet with Hansie in Hansie's room. (Sometimes in Test cricket the captains meet during the match to discuss a possible declaration when it looks like the match is evenly balanced, but at this stage the South Africans were already in such deep trouble that they were almost certain to be bowled out the next day and lose the match.)

"When he arrived, the Indian captain introduced Hansie to Mukesh Gupta (MK). Azharuddin left the room almost immediately and MK remained to speak to Hansie. MK then asked Hansie if he would speak to the remaining Protea batsmen about throwing away their wickets to ensure Indian victory. Hansie told MK that India were almost certain to win in any case, but MK said all he wanted was that there be no heroics from the players and that Hansie could make some money out of it

"Hansie then made what was probably the worst decision of his life. He thought to himself, 'Well, we will lose the match in any case, and I would not even have to speak to the players about under-performing'. He told MK that he would speak to the players and then received US$30 000 in cash from MK. He never spoke to any of the players and never had any need to tamper with the natural result of the match, which South Africa lost, as predicted.

"Although this really bothered Hansie, he rationalised his actions, saying to himself that he didn't really do anything wrong and that it was somehow acceptable to take the money. This was a serious compromise of his ethics, let alone his Christian beliefs. I think in 2000, as Hansie looked back on this incident, he realised just how wrong it had been to accept the money," said Frans.

The rest of the tour was tough for the team. What made matters worse was that the UCB had suddenly and unilaterally agreed to let the South African team play in a benefit match at the end of the ODI series. The squad members were furious as this came at the end of a long and hard slog. Mentally, they were all geared up to go home.

The Indian authorities had asked if the match could be upgraded to full ODI status. Again, the UCB obliged without consulting the players. To add insult to injury, it would be Hansie's 100th ODI for his country – and it was going to be played with half a team – several key players and Bob Woolmer were injured or sick – at the end of a really tough tour in a foreign country.

"Hansie," said Frans "was very upset", all the more so because his 100th ODI was scheduled to be at his beloved Springbok Park in Bloemfontein. "For some time he had been focused on this historic occasion on his home ground – and Hansie was always highly tuned in to such milestones, very mindful of traditions like that."

At this critical moment, MK called Hansie with an offer of US$200 000 to the team, if the Proteas would ensure that they lost to India the following day. Again, instead of just dismissing the offer, Hansie, now thoroughly angry with the UCB, and their absurd match, decided to speak to the team about it. The entire team was present during the discussion, and the offer was turned down. Three members who were particularly outspoken against the idea were Andrew Hudson, Daryll Cullinan and Derek Crookes. (Jonty Rhodes and Allan Donald had already returned home due to injury.)

After the meeting, a few of the players, mostly the more senior players, remained behind and talked about the offer.

It has been said that the Proteas viewed the bookies' approach as a bizarre "coming of age", proof that they'd made it into the big league.

The players who remained behind after the team meeting were curious to see whether MK would raise his offer. They "kind of joked" about the idea and said to each other that their team was so weak at that time that they were almost certain to lose in any case. Hansie called MK and told him that the team wanted to know if he would raise it to US$300 000, but MK said the maximum amount would be US$250 000. "No deal was made, and that was the end of the discussions," said Frans.

The bedevilled match turned out to be even viler than expected. While the Proteas were fielding, the crowd began pelting the team members on the boundary. This was something that the South Africans had grown accustomed to in India, but during this match it got out of hand. Spin-bowler Paul Adams was targeted the most – at one point a battery hit his head. Paul ran to Hansie with a handful of the objects that were thrown at him. There were stones, rocks, batteries, oranges and soft-drink cans.

Hansie immediately walked over to the umpires and told them that if the outrage didn't stop he would take his team off the field and refuse to play. A public announcement to this effect was made to warn the crowd, but they continued as before and when Adams again ran up to Hansie, he angrily called his team together and they left the field.

When they got to the dressing room, Hansie started packing his bags and told the team to do the same. "He had no intention, then, of continuing the match," said Frans.

The Proteas' manager, Robbie Muzzell, came storming into the dressing room, furious with Hansie. Hansie was amazed that Muzzell was not supporting the team decision. During the fracas, an Indian official came into the dressing room and kept on standing in Hansie's way, demanding that Muzzell tell the team to get back on the field. "Hansie," said Frans, "then completely lost his temper, picked up the Indian official and promptly threw him out of the dressing room. He was shaking with anger, and another sequence of shouting with Muzzell ensued." Incredibly, the team eventually went back onto the field but, not surprisingly, lost the bizarre and blighted contest. The players were very fond of Muzzell, but they felt that he always took the side of the UCB in disputes. This match, forced on them with short notice at the end of a long tour was an example.

"No money was ever received by any South African during or after this match. And Hansie did not keep the team meeting about the money a secret," said Frans, who recalled how Hansie told him in detail about the meeting and some of the players' reactions to the offer. Bob Woolmer also noted the incident in his tour report that was sent to the UCB.

MK again contacted Hansie at the end of 1996 when India toured South Africa. Hansie's statement at the King Commission read as follows:

19.1. I was asked by MK to provide information in respect of the first and second Tests, on which I understood he wished to place bets.
I understood that MK would pay me an (unspecified) amount if he won anything. The amount would depend on his winnings.

19.2. In respect of the first Test, I supplied him with the team selections and a daily forecast.

19.3 In respect of the second Test, I was only asked to tell him when, and at what score we would declare. I did this. After the second Test MK transferred a sum of about US 50 000 dollars into my NBS Savings Account...

19.4. South Africa won both the first and second Tests in this series and the third Test was drawn. None of these results was fixed or manipulated.

19.5. MK had asked me to speak to the players about losing the third Test and promised to pay me US 300 000 dollars if I did so, but I refused.

It is of importance to note here that Hansie then had no further contact with MK or any other bookie until January 2000, when Marlon Aronstam approached him during the final Test match against England.

●

Later, much would be made of Hansie's robust brand of materialism. This is a complex issue, and part of the complexity is that Hansie was a young man whose lifestyle and personality was still a work in progress. When the bookies started their global frenzy in the mid-1990s, Hansie was, it needs to be remembered, a young and naïve international captain aged 25. His life experience had only ever really related to the narrow and peculiar confines of the world of professional cricket.

"One must also understand that Hansie was a bright and inquisitive individual, and as a result he often complained of boredom during the long tours abroad. To stimulate his mind he was constantly exploring, foraging for new information, and looking for new challenges to meet... which brought him to the doorstep of the bookmakers," said Warmenhoven.

"People who are unable to spend time understanding their emotions and determining their values often develop a skewed sense of what motivates them," Warmenhoven wrote. "When their values become clouded they are prone to make the wrong 'gut' decisions. For Hansie, who had always been a strongly principled individual, the decision to become involved with bookmakers was clearly value-incongruent." It also meant that, for Hansie, making money became more important than it should have been.

Hansie himself later confirmed this: "I've always enjoyed making money. That's why I studied financial management and I studied commerce. I want to go into business ... You have to try to balance it all... sometimes the balance was tilting over to greed and the lure of money."

"The lack of mentorship in Hansie's life also meant that when he began to dabble in illicit behaviour – indicating a shift in his values – there was no one close enough to him to warn him of the dangers of his, in a sense, 'naïve' and misguided exploration, and to help him extricate himself from the 'web'," said Warmenhoven.

Since 1995, every move Hansie and his team had made had been in preparation for the 1999 World Cup. There were many highlights and many disappointments but, as the years went by, the South African team grew into a formidable unit. As the Proteas boarded the flight from Johannesburg en route to the 1999 World Cup, the pilot called Hansie to the cockpit and showed him the latest copy of an international cricket magazine. South Africa was now officially rated as the best team in Test and in ODI cricket. Two of the objectives from that long-ago team meeting had been achieved.

When Hansie got back to his seat, he looked around at his team and there were Makhaya Ntini, Herschelle Gibbs and Paul Adams. Three players of colour were now in the team on merit – the third of their objectives met.

All that remained was to fulfil the fourth by winning the World Cup, and they were favourites to do so. But this put an enormous amount of pressure on them. Would they be able to bear it and win?

"Tension boiled over," said Corrie van Zyl. Ewie recalled that Hansie was so tense during this World Cup and wanted to win so badly that he burst into tears during a telephone conversation, after beating Pakistan in one of their second round matches.

South Africa looked unbeatable in the first round, beating India, Sri Lanka and England, but slipped badly when they suffered a shock defeat to Zimbabwe. South African-born Zimbabwean Neil Johnson was Man of the Match.

In their second-round match against Australia, South Africa batted first and scored 271 runs. This was a good total and Herschelle Gibbs scored a magnificent 101 runs from 134 balls. Australia was in trouble at 48 for 3, before Steve Waugh came to the crease. When he was on 56, with Australia still 120 short and by now 4 wickets down, Waugh clipped a ball off his toes and the ball lobbed straight to Herschelle at midwicket. Herschelle had an unfortunate habit of catching the ball, and then nonchalantly tossing it away within a fraction of a second. He had been warned about this showboating on numerous occasions but, incredibly, when this ball was hit to him he tried to do the same thing, and in the process dropped what was an easy catch. Ricky Ponting, who was batting with Steve Waugh at the time, remarked, "You've just tossed the World Cup away, my son!"

Australia went on to win the match by five wickets in the final over, and this meant that they sneaked into the semi-finals. South Africa would have to play them again in the semis and Australia now had an advantage over South Africa, because they had beaten them in the previous match.

The semi-final, at Edgebaston, England, is one that South Africans would like to forget. Australia batted first and scored 213 runs. Hansie was given out, caught for a duck (even though the ball came off his big toe and not his bat), but eventually both sides were tied, and South Africa needed one run to win.

"Before I went out there that afternoon," remembered Allan Donald, "before I got my gloves on, Hansie came to me and put his arm round my shoulder, and said, 'Listen, whatever happens you were not meant to be there, this wasn't your job. But also know, if you go out now, people will never remember that you got four wickets today.'"

Allan was batting with Lance Klusener and in an awful mix-up, which included inexplicable hesitancy and confusion on the part of poor Allan, he was run-out, which effectively meant that South Africa was out of the final. (Because Australia won in the previous round it meant that they would go through to the final, even if they only tied the match.)

"Straight after the run-out, I saw Australia jumping all over each other, and I wanted to find the deepest hole ever, and dive into it and never come out. I got into the change room and didn't even unpad. I went straight into the physio's room, locked the door, and cried there, alone, for half an hour. Later, Hansie knocked on the door and I let him in. He repeated what he had said earlier and said, 'Look, try and forget about it. I know it's tough, but it wasn't your fault'."

Soon after the Australian captain walked in and said, "I don't want to be you."

"I was bitter. It was the biggest disappointment ever, the worst mishap in cricket that I have ever been involved in," said Allan.

San-Marie said, "The UCB did not provide the right support that Hansie as a captain needed. For example, when we lost that 1999 World Cup at Edgebaston, there was no support system whatsoever. The team was down and out. Hansie, alone, had to pick them up. This, I feel, was too much to ask. He was totally devastated, because they didn't win the World Cup."

Bob Woolmer said, "I guess I have never seen Hansie and the team so disappointed in my life, but to this day I will remember Hansie getting the team together and saying to the team that they should all stand proud."

Bob continued, "Our motto was 'one run can make a difference' …and unfortunately in the end, one run made the difference."

Many months later Hansie was at a function where people were asked to name their dearest wish. Hansie replied, "All I want is one run."

The reader, of course, will note that this chapter has not closely tracked the historic course of Hansie's cricketing captaincy. It is not the intention of the book to do so. Such an effort would've bloated the middle of the book with seemingly endless technical and ball-by-ball, match-by-match detail.

The highlights of his mostly illustrious career, with in-depth commentaries, have been well described in many other books by cricket writers well qualified to do so. Such books include those by South African Rodney Hartman, especially his two *Hansie and the Boys* volumes, which deal with Hansie's career from the start, right up to 1999.

During his international Test career, Hansie scored 3 714 runs at an average of 36.41 per innings. With his right-arm medium-pace bowling, he took 43 Test wickets at an average of 29.95 runs per wicket. He was more successful as a One-Day player, scoring over 5 560 runs in 188 matches at an average of 38.64. (Source: www.cricinfosouthafrica)

Hansie's obituary printed in the *Wisden Cricketers' Almanack 2003* includes the following quotes:

"With his aggressive batting, intelligent medium-pace bowling and brilliant fielding, Cronjé was a formidable competitor… His armoury against [swing] included a ferocious slog-sweep over mid-wicket, played on one knee. When he made what was then Test cricket's third-fastest fifty, off 31 balls at Centurion in 1997-98, he reached it by hitting Muttiah Muralitharan, the world's best off-spinner, for 4-6-6-6 off successive balls… His captaincy record brooks few arguments: South Africa won 27 and lost only 11 of his 53 Tests in charge, with series victories over every opponent except Australia; in 138 One-Day Internationals there were 99 wins, as well as a tie."

In 25 ODIs versus Australia, with Hansie as captain of the South Africans, the Proteas won 13, lost 11 and tied one.

South Africa won five of the six Tests in which Hansie scored centuries. He once scored 642 runs in 17 days, in South Africa, against Australia in 1993-4: 112, 97, 45 and 50 in successive ODIs; 44 and a career first-class best 251 in the Free State, and 21 and 122 in the first Test. He led South Africa in 53 (a South African record) of his 68 Tests. His Test average stood at 38.98 (3 587) runs, six centuries and 23 fifties.

During the British summer of 1997 Hansie played for Ireland for three months, and in the process helped to record Ireland's first-ever win against an English county side.

He gave up the captaincy of the Free State at the end of the 1995-96 season after leading them to seven major domestic titles in six seasons.

Hansie was Leicestershire's overseas player in 1995, scoring more than 1 300 runs following an approach by Jack Birkenshaw, who had previously worked in South Africa for the Free State. "For me, he is one of the best players I have ever been associated with. He did well for us and was a gent really," said Birkenshaw. "I have never known anyone to work harder at his game. He was dedicated and he was a top bloke."

He was 21 when he first led Free State and 24 when he first led South Africa.

He shares with Allan Lamb, Daryll Cullinan, Gary Kirsten, Adrian Kuiper and Garth le Roux the honour of being SA Cricketer of the Year three times (1992, 1995 and 1998).

(Source: *SA Sports Illustrated*)

Gary Kirsten said in 2003, "You're talking about a guy who, as far as I'm concerned, was the perfect leader… He was unbelievable. He was to me a classic example of a leader in any walk of life."

●

IF

If you can keep your head when all about you
Are losing theirs and blaming it on you;
If you can trust yourself when all men doubt you,
But make allowance for their doubting too;
If you can wait and not be tired of waiting,
If, being lied about, don't deal in lies,
Or, being hated, don't give way to hating,
And yet don't look too good, nor talk too wise;

If you can dream – and not make dreams your master;
If you can think – and not make thoughts your aim;
If you can meet with triumph and disaster
And treat those two impostors just the same;
If you can bear to hear the truth you've spoken
Twisted by knaves to make a trap for fools,
Or watch the things you gave your life to broken
And stoop and build 'em up with wornout tools;

If you can make one heap with all your winnings
And risk it on one turn of pitch-and-toss,
And lose, and start again at your beginnings
And never breathe a word about your loss;
If you can force your heart and nerve and sinew
To serve your turn long after they are gone,
And so hold on when there is nothing in you
Except the Will which says to them: "Hold on";

If you can walk with crowds and keep your virtue
Or walk with kings – nor lose the common touch;
If neither foes nor loving friends can hurt you;
If all men count with you, but none too much;
If you can fill the unforgiving minute
With sixty seconds' worth of distance run –
Yours is the Earth and everything that's in it,
And – which is more – you'll be a man my son!

— Rudyard Kipling

CHAPTER NINE

THE POLITICS OF RACIAL CRICKET

A Captain's Colours

It's because of all the political nonsense. It has now become impossible for me to enjoy cricket, or to do well.

— Hansie, on resigning his captaincy in January 1999.

From the start, Hansie's commitment to post-apartheid development cricket was clear and has been praised by many. Hansie had supported the need for "affirmative action" of a reasonable and intelligent kind, but not at Test or One-Day International levels.

Jonty said, "Hansie believed in transformation, but he did not think that the national team should be used as an 'academy' to teach players about international cricket. They needed to be ready when they were selected to play, not learn as they go, as it was not fair on the team, or the individual player concerned."

"Free State cricket was always very supportive of cricket development in underprivileged areas," said Ali Bacher in 2005. "In 1987 I took cricket to the 'township' of Rocklands, near Bloemfontein. It was mid-winter – I'd never known cold wind like this – it was a Saturday morning and they were all there to start this development programme in the township. Joubert Strydom, Hansie, Frans, Corrie van Zyl, Ewie, Johan Volsteedt, they were all there – and you could just see that the spirit was fantastic.

"On one occasion there was to be an opening of a sports field in Sharpeville, near Johannesburg, and Steve Tshwete [the former Minister of Sport] was going to be there. I phoned Hansie, who was in Bloemfontein, and asked him if he could attend. He said, 'No problem'. He must've left early in the morning to make the four-hour drive to Johannesburg. He was there, said a few words to motivate the kids and drove back home. There was no payment involved.

"Often," said Ali, "when Hansie had some free time, he'd phone the UCB and say, 'Tomorrow morning I'm available. Get some kids and I'll go and play with them.' He was proactive in this area, there's no question about it."

Yet another example was that Hansie spent three weeks early on in Makhaya Ntini's career, sharing a room with him, in order to mentor Makhaya's entry into the side, and to guide him personally. While this may not seem a big deal, it is to be noted that a firm global tradition is that the captain gets a hotel room to him-self on tour.

Bacher said that Hansie was the most willing to give of himself when it came to cricket development, without asking for anything in return. "Hansie, more than anyone else in the team, had the ability to see the bigger picture," he said.

In 1999, national selection based on merit was no longer politically correct, although the UCB tried to hide the fact of the ANC-imposed directives by the public denial of that reality. For the politicians, whether within or outside the UCB, the "transformation" issue was much more important than mere selection on merit.

At the start of the 1998/9 season, after losing the earlier 1998 Test Series to England, Hansie had set his mind on dealing with the West Indies at home and then continuing to prepare for that all-important 1999 World Cup, via games against New Zealand in that country.

At the start of the Test Series against the West Indies, a Durban-based writer, Ashwin Desai, who was involved in KwaZulu-Natal Cricket at the time, wrote a derogatory article in a Durban newspaper. Desai blatantly called Hansie a racist and said that it was his wish that Curtley Ambrose would demolish Hansie and the rest of the team as a punishment for their role in apartheid. It infuriated Frans who was then coaching the KwaZulu-Natal Dolphins and had been instrumental in the transformation process in the province. "His article made me mad. To call Hansie a racist was ludicrous. It was made even worse when no one at Natal Cricket or the UCB took any stance against his remarks. I felt that his comments were against the spirit of unity that we were all striving for in the country. If a white person had made such comments, he would have been banned and fined severely."

Hansie chose not to react publicly to Desai's article, in the same diplomatic manner that he also treated post-match presentations after shocking umpiring displays. One such poor display had taken place during the final Test Match at Headingley, against England in the 1998 Test Series. Bacher referred to this match during the King Commission.

(Christopher Martin-Jenkins, in the *Electronic Telegraph*, reported as follows on the umpiring: "The Pakistani umpire Javed Akhtar – whose decisions have been the subject of much debate – gave South Africa's last batsman Makhaya Ntini out leg before wicket to provide Gough with his best-ever Test bowling fig-ures of 6-42. Akhtar gave nine of the ten LBW verdicts in the match, seven of them against the tourists. Afterwards, the South African captain Hansie Cronjé revealed that he has been asked to submit a report on 'how umpiring can be improved' to his home cricket board 'when we have cooled down'. But he refused to blame the umpiring for this defeat." Hansie himself had been one of Akhtar's unfortunate victims.)

South Africa won the Test series against the West Indies 5-0 in magnificent style. At the start of the ODI series, Hansie and Bob Woolmer, of course, had their minds set on making sure that the squad for the West Indies and New Zealand matches was essentially to be the squad they'd be taking to the World Cup. This was seen to be a natural and vital process in the run-up to the World Cup.

During the last day of the Centurion Park Test match, Peter Pollock told Hansie that they had picked the squad to play the West Indies in the ODI series. The squad consisted of 17 players – and three of them were affirmative action players. This was due to pressure from the government. Hansie disagreed strongly, but after a lengthy discussion he decided to go along with this decree.

"Hansie didn't like the quota system at all. He really hated it, because he was so goal-driven. He wanted to win; he wanted to do well at all costs. He never had a racial problem, but he didn't like being told who to pick and who not to pick, because at that level, the difference between winning and losing is so desperately small that if you go and put yourself at such a disadvantage, you've got no chance," said Ray McCauley.

"Hansie was also tremendously frustrated with the double-speak of the UCB's top dogs. He believed that Ali had to tell the media in all honesty that they had been forced to include players of colour by government diktat."

Ali would not, and he resolutely maintained to the media that the team was "selected on merit". "The South African players knew this was untrue," said Ray.

Hansie felt hamstrung. How could one possibly beat the world's best when racial background rather than form and ability were used to choose players?

"Hansie was never against developing previously disadvantaged people, but he felt that the way the UCB went about it was not fair towards the team and not fair to the players who were forced into the side – many times to their own detriment.

"Hansie himself had worked hard to get to the top. He believed that young black players (like the white players) had to prove themselves by a hard-earned work record, with a proper mentoring process over time, and given opportunities when they were ready and able, no matter what their race or culture," said Ray.

Another glaring problem was that in almost every national squad, worldwide, one always has 14 players, but of course only 11 can play on the day. This meant that in any contest there were always three disgruntled players sitting on the bench. This routine and arguably necessary irritant was bad enough, but now Hansie was facing having to tell six players every time the squad played that they had been excluded.

After receiving the news, Hansie's relationship with Bacher began to unravel. At one point, Dr Bacher met with the team at their hotel and outlined his vision for "transformation". The players argued against it, with Herschelle Gibbs and Paul Adams also expressing misgivings. "The core of their argument," wrote Trevor Chesterfield and Jack McGlew in *South Africa's Cricket Captains*, "was how lesser players, filling the place of the proud men who had worked hard to play for their country, could weaken the side."

"Hansie was also upset that Bacher seemed to care more about the politics than he did about the fact that South Africa had just beaten the West Indies 5-0," said Frans. After Bacher left the room, the players discussed the issues amongst themselves. Hansie was resolute in his opposition to selection without merit. He then told Woolmer that he would never play for South Africa again.

Hansie was appalled and disillusioned. A few of the senior players then decided they did not want to continue playing in the national team either, but after some meetings they decided to bite the bullet and stay.

Hansie, however, handed his new kit in to team manager Goolam Rajah, hired a car, handed in his resignation as player and captain, and left for Bloemfontein.

"As soon as Ali heard about Hansie's resignation, he phoned me and told me, 'Your captain has just resigned'. I then phoned Ray McCauley and asked him to speak to Hansie," said Peter Pollock. Bob Woolmer phoned Frans and asked him to do the same. "Bob told me that he couldn't go to the World Cup without Hansie." Frans was in Bloemfontein at the time and Ray flew there, at his own cost, and the two of them met up with Hansie at Springbok Park.

Ray asked Hansie why he had resigned and Hansie had replied, "It's because of all the political nonsense. It has now become impossible for me to enjoy cricket, or to do well."

"I asked him if he would play if it wasn't for the 'political nonsense' and he said, 'Yes, of course.' I then told him that I thought he should continue to play, because he shouldn't stop playing because of outside factors. 'Other people should never determine your destiny; rather be in charge of your own destiny, bearing in mind submission to God.'"

In the end, he decided to play again. Amazingly, Hansie was gracious enough not to go to the media with his frustrations and no one knew about the resignation then except the team – who decided it was best to keep the matter confidential.

"The issue was finally resolved in my office at Rhema Church. With Ali and a few more UCB members present, Hansie officially withdrew his letter of resignation and the UCB promised him that they would give him much more say in the future," said Ray.

South Africa won the ODI series 6-1. One of Hansie's childhood dreams had become a reality. He had played against and beaten the West Indies. He remarked afterwards that this tremendous achievement was marred in such a way by the politics that it almost took all the enjoyment out of the victory.

●

In New Zealand in February 1999, South Africa lost the first One-Day International and promptly dropped Herschelle Gibbs, which meant an all-white team for the next game. (On tour, it should be remembered at this point, that the selection panel consisted of the coach, the captain and the vice captain.)

Ray White, then president of the UCB, phoned Peter Pollock and suggested that they have a word with Hansie about the matter. The UCB had agreed at their last board meeting that there should be at least one player of colour in the side. "Peter told me that if I felt strongly about it, I should speak to him," said White in *Ali: The Life of Ali Bacher* by Rodney Hartman.

By the time White phoned Hansie, South Africa had played a second game without Herschelle. "When I eventually got through to him at 7am, he was still fast asleep. I tried very gently to explain the selection policy because I was aware of how volatile he could be. He just went off pop."

"Cronjé was angry on two counts: (a) that no one had bothered to give the team a copy of the new selection policy after the 5 December board meeting; and (b) that the team selections reflected the experimentation that was underway to find the best combinations for the 1999 World Cup in England in three months' time," wrote Hartman. "White recalls 'a ghastly board meeting' at the time. 'The mob was baying for blood – Pollock's, Cronjé's and mine. John Blair made the nonsensical suggestion that we should bring Cronjé home. All sense had gone out of the window.'"

What the UCB didn't bother to do was to ask why Herschelle was left out for the second ODI. Allan Donald explained the incident in 2004. "While the team was partying during a tour, Hansie would often be planning the next match. He made us all realise that cricket was a serious business. 'I need you guys to take care of yourselves tonight,' he would say. Lack of due 'care' was ruthlessly dealt with. Herschelle Gibbs snuck back to the hotel late the night before the first ODI, and he didn't have a great game. Bob and Hansie promptly left him out of the side for three matches, to discipline him. The decision was made with no fuss, and no sharing of this backdrop with the media."

Hansie was very good friends with Herschelle, but it didn't stop him from applying discipline when it was needed. Back in 1995 when Meyrick Pringle was left out of the team for a similar offence, the UCB executive never asked any questions. This time however, the politics inside the UCB prevented a simple disciplinary procedure from taking place.

Frans said, "Hansie told me after the tour that he was saddened by the fact that the UCB were quick to jump down his throat for dropping Herschelle, but that none of those guys called him to congratulate him after South Africa won the series."

⬤

"Hansie had planned to retire after the 1999 World Cup," said Jonty. "We would have both retired had we won the World Cup and we even discussed this with our wives. He had already signed a contract with Glamorgan County Cricket Club as coach for the following season."

Ali Bacher recalled it this way. "Just before the 1999/2000 season, I got a phone call from a journalist in the UK, a guy from the *Telegraph*, asking me for comment about Hansie being the Glamorgan coach. My response was, 'Hansie signing for Glamorgan? What? You're talking rubbish.'"

Bacher said he then contacted the chief executive of the Glamorgan Cricket Club and said to him, "How dare you go behind my back, my board's back, signing up our nation's captain?"

"I then got Hansie to tear up the contract," said Bacher.

"With Bob Woolmer retiring as coach after the World Cup, it was understood that Hansie was going to be given almost carte blanche as captain and would determine, in a large way, who would be in the team for the following World Cup in South Africa in 2003. Bacher told Hansie that the UCB wanted him to remain captain until the 2003 World Cup. Based on this Hansie agreed to Bacher's request," Frans recalled.

A few days after this conversation with Bacher, the new convenor of selectors, Rushdi Magiet, announced in the newspapers, before breaking the news to Hansie, that the selectors had decided to keep Hansie in the side, but he would be under probation for three matches. If his performances weren't good enough, then he would be dropped as player and captain. This was in direct contrast to Bacher's words.

"From the ... latter half of 1999, uncertainty and cluttered thinking cloaked some of the selection policy. Where there had been tight parameters and a philosophy understood by most, the psyche had changed to a less tangible focus. Cronjé had been put on probation, a decision that did not sit at all well with the players, as there was no clear reasoning behind it – unless Magiet, or the selectors, were trying to make a policy statement. Was it an oblique attempt to break the captain's power base?" wrote Trevor Chesterfield and Jack McGlew in *South Africa's Cricket Captains*.

In the months after this incident, Hansie was again contacted by two bookies. This was the first contact that he had had with any bookies since January 1997. This time the approach came from people whom Hansie had not had contact with before.

In April 2000, Australia was due to play three ODIs in South Africa. "Hansie told me he was going to play in them, and then announce his retirement after that," said Frans. But the accusations of match-fixing and Hansie's atom-bomb confession would explode just days before the first ODI was due to be played.

●

In early 2005, the former Anglican Archbishop, Desmond Tutu, called for the abandonment of the quota system in sport, saying that a serious attempt to improve facilities for deprived sections of the community would be a better way forward for South African sport. He said, "I don't want tokenism, it's an insult to everybody. And there are so many occasions when it seems black players are there to satisfy demands for transformation. That is not good for the morale of the individual, or the team. People talk of two or three black players in a team but what is the difference between two, three, five or six? If they are good enough, they should be there, of course. I don't like our guys carrying this additional baggage, it is too much of a burden."

The Chairman of the South African Parliament's sports committee lashed out at Tutu, implying that anyone who wanted to scrap the quota system was a traitor, although he later said that his comments had been blown out of proportion.

Writing in the *Sunday Argus*, respected cricket commentator Rodney Hartman said, "South African cricket is awash with paradox. Its policy makers are black, but the national team has fielded only one black player on a consistent basis for the past four years. Black clubs and players outnumber whites, its showcase games are played to predominantly white audiences… Coloured players (those of mixed-race descent) seem to be flourishing, but around the fringes of the game there are whites who believe they are driven away through politics and those of Indian descent who claim they have been marginalised by both white and black."

In South Africa in 2005, a quota system required a minimum of four players of colour in every professional franchise eleven, and at least five in the amateur provincial teams. Officially, there is no quota system for the national side.

CHAPTER TEN

BERTHA'S OUTENIQUA

Then Moses said to him, "If your Presence does not go with us,
do not send us up from here."

Exodus 33:15

I spoke to Bertha, over four days at number 18 Eagle Drive, Fancourt, George, in the large four-bedroomed, thatched home that she and Hansie built in 1999. Conversation with the athletic, petite blonde widow with her sweet, girl's voice, bright mind and soft smile was punctuated by her regular self-deprecation, her balanced and thoughtful reverence for her husband, her concern for the feelings of others.

When the good times were remembered, Bertha's large green eyes would flash and her pure blonde locks would shake, waves of yellow cream, as she suddenly laughed loudly at the happy times spent with a man who she only really came to know in the last two years of his life. Cricket had robbed them of each other for most of their married life.

Sometimes her small voice would almost disappear as she spoke through the heartache and answered the hard questions. But there was a curious toughness, a rigid resilience about her, in striking contrast to her apparent fragility.

The Fancourt Hotel and Country Club Estate, arguably Africa's premier housing and golfing synthesis, is impressive, or oppressive, depending on your opinion of such mushrooming opulences on the western, eastern and southern coasts of South Africa, estates that continue to swallow, for good or ill, vast tracts of South Africa's coastal land and scarce fresh water.

Fancourt: four golf courses of top international standard, including a links course; the magnificent Outeniqua mountain range soaring heavenwards close by; endless green lawns and fairways; beautiful and large thatched and other strictly-styled mansion-unit clusters arranged tastefully over a canton-sized area, bordered by high electrical fencing, and security-boom entrances. Ponds, dams, sculptured and obsessively maintained fairways range everywhere. There is no sign of the beautiful town of George in which it is located – the views around the golf courses are pure natural landscape, a self-contained world, an indulgent, manicured planet for the seriously rich. *Soort soek soort.* This was Hansie's last earthly home, a cosy nest with Bertha, away from the strife and trouble. Away from cricket, the media, away from inquisitive acquaintances, away from the curiosity of strangers.

In the winter of 2004, I reclined in the inevitable giant brown leather arm-chair, Bertha similarly seated next to me in the lounge, a little tape recorder balanced on a wide armrest between us. Cups of coffee steamed nearby. The strong and pleasant smell of open thatch permeated the air. Adding to the expensive and groomed rusticity were the poplar beams of the roof structure, the beautiful teak furniture, dark grey slate tiles, the Persian carpets underfoot and several fresh flower arrangements. Large oil paintings of flowers, and various expensive interior-decorating flourishes were thoughtfully arranged throughout. Nearby stood a long, baronial dining-room table. There was a wide and well-furnished, long L-shaped covered veranda outside. Upstairs were more bedrooms and a mezzanine floor, which once was Hansie's study.

No cricketing memorabilia were evident, anywhere, at first. It was as if cricket had been blotted out. As if it were some kind of anathema, unsuitable for the embellishment of a decent haven.

But the memorabilia were there. Hansie had always been a hoarder, to an obsessive and magnificent extent. In a large bedroom tucked away in one wing of the house, were countless boxes, trunks and loose piles of paraphernalia. Bats, balls, jerseys, caps, shirts, photographs, giant piles of magazines, albums of all kinds, press clippings, trunk loads of a lifetime of school, provincial and international cricket. Bertha simply had no idea of what to do with this mountain of earthly chattels; those dried and desiccated flowers, those now-brittle mementos. It obviously pained her to even think about these collections, much less rummage through the piles, or even be in the room, so eerily packed with the sad remains of a past life, however glorious.

Later, I spent an hour or two mulling over the hallowed debris. Free State cricket bats, scoured with the imprints of Allan Donald-delivered balls. "Coffins" full of ageing and well-used pads, gloves and green helmets. Numerous cricket shirts signed by famous cricketers. Cricket stumps, claimed triumphantly by Hansie after winning countless matches, signed by the vanquished, signed by the victorious, were abundant.

In one corner lay a dilapidated black duffel bag. Inside was one black brogue, first worn on Hansie's wedding day. The shoe was scuffed and curiously torn. It had been retrieved from the saddle of a mountain a few kilometres away, one sad day.

●

The house was on the edge of a pleasant fairway. Nearby, a lone winter weeping willow mourned over a small water trap, picturesquely complete with mallards and other waterfowl. Hadeda flocks tramped resolutely along the fairway, probing with their big curved beaks for earthworms. The soft whine of passing golf carts and the raucous cries of the ibises mixed with intermittent silence. Fairways seemed to stretch from horizon to horizon, to the foot of the soaring grey and blue Outeniqua Mountains close by. "Outeniqua" in the Khoikhoi tongue, referred to a Khoikhoi (also known impolitely as "Hottentot") tribe that once lived there. The word means "man (or men) laden with honey", as the mountain Khoikhoi used to remove rich stores of honey from the swarms of bees flourishing on the nectar of the yellow, pink, orange and red wild proteas, gladioli, ericas, watsonias and other fynbos, a fire-adapted heathland, flourishing on the slopes.

Visible from the side of the house was that mountain saddle, over 1 000m high, falling down between the great George and Cradock peaks – in the path of a fatal approach to the nearby George Airport.

●

After three months of dating, Hansie asked Bertha in November of 1992 if she would be his girlfriend – but by that stage they were already kissing and holding hands regularly, smooching enthusiastically in the parked Exa near the cricket grounds at Grey College when Hansie was in town. But to Hansie's question Bertha had teasingly replied, "No, but you can ask me that question in a month's time."

"Hansie never asked me again and I got a bit worried! I was genuinely unsure about our relationship because he was away so often. And it had always taken me a long time to make up my mind about important issues," said Bertha.

At this point Hansie's natural naughtiness comes out clearly, despite his revitalised Christianity, which, according to some, should have made him more circumspect. Bertha took some time off from varsity to attend a match in Cape Town, where South Africa was playing India in a One-Dayer. "I went on the understanding that I was going to stay with Craig Matthews' wife at their home. At that time, I understood that Hansie was sharing a hotel room with Fanie de Villiers."

While Bertha was waiting in the Cape Sun hotel lobby, the shy *Afrikaanse meisie* was suddenly confronted by blustering, joking Fanie, who said, alarmingly: "*Ja, nou skop jy my uit my kamer uit!*" (Yes, now you're kicking me out of my room!)

"I was very embarrassed and did not understand what was happening," recalled Bertha. "I was very nervous about this development. I thought, 'I can't stay in the same room as Hansie. What will the people say?'" Hansie, at that point, was at practice, so he couldn't be confronted about this twist of events.

"I wanted to phone my mom because I didn't know what to do next. I realised that I couldn't stay at the hotel in the same room. My mom told me to stay calm when I phoned her. She told me to ask for another room and to tell Hansie that I was uncomfortable with sharing, but she did say, 'If you have to stay in his room for one night that's fine.'"

Bertha replied, "Don't tell Dad."

At the Hard Rock Café in Sea Point, that evening, she discussed her misgivings with Hansie. "He said he understood, but that it would be 'difficult' to change the arrangement for that first night and that Kate, Jonty Rhodes's girlfriend, was arriving the next day and that I could share a room with her."

It is hard to imagine, of course, that Hansie had not manipulated this situation somehow. He was, after all, a young man. However, Bertha reported that while she brushed her teeth in the bathroom of the suite, Hansie had moved the two single beds apart and when she entered the bedroom, he seemed to be asleep. It was only later that he told her he'd been pretending. Bertha was happy to report that Hansie "behaved himself that night".

Bertha's influence was positive, on several levels, from the start. And a new zest and lust for life took hold. At that match in Newlands, Hansie took five wickets, his best-ever bowling performance in international cricket. To cap it all, he hit a six to win the game.

The couple spent the New Year of 1993 in Cape Town and Bertha had told him, "It's now 1993, you can ask me again to be your girlfriend."

"No," said Hansie teasingly, "it's your turn to ask me now."

Bertha had shyly asked him and Hansie, of course, had responded positively, that white toothy smile lighting up the world.

The romance began in earnest from that point, although because of Hansie's incessant travels and commitments they barely saw each other. This was to be the pattern of their life together, bar a brief stint in England and the last two years. During their courtship Bertha continued her studies at the University of the Free State and qualified as a physiotherapist.

In the middle of 1994, Bertha spoke to Hansie about her desire to work in either the UK or the United States for a while. Hansie responded to this by saying, "If we got married, would you consider not going overseas?"

This question was not really answered by Bertha, although acquiescence was thick in the air.

After Bertha finished her studies she went on the traditional end-of-studies bash with ten girlfriends. During this time, Hansie was playing for Free State in Bloemfontein and would phone Bertha four to five times a day. "It was a standing joke between the girls, who would be woken up by that first call so early in the morning," laughed Bertha.

While she was away, Hansie also phoned Kosie, Bertha's father, saying, "*Oom*, I want to come and talk some *lobola* [a South African term for 'bride price', usually paid in cattle]."

Kosie replied, "Come when you are ready."

"Hansie did go, but he was so nervous that he never asked my dad anything!" Bertha told me.

Bertha finally arrived back in Bloemfontein, and Hansie suggested a "quick bite at the Spur [a popular family restaurant franchise in South Africa]".

While Bertha went to the ladies cloakroom, Hansie ordered champagne from their tiny two-seater table and put the ring in a filled glass. The matter was settled. Hansie's words to Bertha, when she saw the ring, were, "Promise you won't die before me."

The happy couple then went to Bertha's parents' house, where Hansie still had to ask formally for her hand. "We sat at the kitchen table and Hansie told my dad that he would like to marry me." The announcement was greeted with joy and no great surprise. Hansie's parents were telephoned and joined the happy celebration. Both families approved totally. Two beautiful young people in love. And neighbours too. What could be better?

Bertha, although happy, wanted some confirmation from God that this was what He wanted for them; that they should get married. "One Sunday night, Hansie and I had arranged to go to a little 'on fire for the Lord' Methodist Church that we went to regularly then. Hansie was playing cricket and was held up and I waited for him before I left, but he didn't arrive. The little church would get full quite quickly, so I left without him to make sure that I got a seat. It was packed when I got there and I had to sit right in front. The sermon had already started when Hansie arrived. Everybody turned round to see who had entered. Embarrassed, Hansie nevertheless pushed his way through the distracted crowd to the front and sat next to me. This was quite a thing for him, but he knew how important it was to me, and I knew how important it was to him to be in the Lord's house with me," she said.

After the interrupted sermon the minister had prayed a blessing over Hansie and Bertha. The confirmation Bertha had been waiting for.

Wessel Johannes Cronjé and Bertha Pretorius were married on 8 April 1995, at the Universitas Dutch Reformed Church in Bloemfontein, by *Dominee* Johan Lombard. The text for the sermon was Exodus 33:15: *Then Moses said to him, "If your Presence does not go with us, do not send us up from here."*

When the date for the wedding had been set, Hansie had told Bertha, "There's no way Free State is going to make the Benson & Hedges Day-Night final." But Hansie was wrong. The cricketer bedevilled his own honeymoon plans by unexpectedly knocking up a century in the semi-final against Western Province, thus qualifying for a place in the final against the mighty Eastern Province, slap bang at the start of their planned honeymoon. The day of the final arrived and it was raining. But the weather cleared the next day and lowly Free State, totally out of the blue, won the match.

Eventually, after these happy and unexpected interruptions, the couple left on their honeymoon, which included a visit to a private game reserve.

Throughout his life, the boyish pranks continued. On one occasion in their early relationship Hansie went to lunch at Bertha's folks' house after the Sunday morning church service. As usual, he frolicked with the family dog, Domino, and the family stood around the swimming pool in their formal church clothes, chatting. Domino jumped into the pool and Hansie took off his shoes and socks, rolled up his smart trousers, and stood on the pool step, playing with the dog. Liesie, Bertha's younger sister, noted this and decided to give Hansie a sly push into the pool. She quickly and quietly moved forward to do so, but Hansie noted this out of the corner of his eye. As she lunged towards him to give him an almighty shove, Hansie suddenly ducked, and Liesie went tumbling into the water, in her church frock. There was great hilarity. But true to form, Hansie immediately felt sorry for her, jumped into the water in his Sunday finery and fished her out, laughing heartily.

Yet, despite the good humour, the jokes, being Hansie's wife was to prove a great challenge for the shy and religious physiotherapist, cocooned as she had been in white Afrikaans Bloemfontein. Leicester, England, was going to be the first stop in that long journey of self-discovery. And discovery about her man.

Hansie played for Leicester County for a season in 1995. "It was very difficult for me. My English was poor; I didn't even want to speak in English in front of Hansie, I was so embarrassed about it."

The pair ensconced themselves in a little semi-detached double-storey house near Leicester Forest East. Fortunately for Bertha, her sister-in-law, Hester, and her family were just 20 minutes away. The *boeremeisie*, typical of middle class privileged whites in Bloemfontein, had never had to cook, iron or clean house before. Now all of this was required of her, besides a host of other cultural adjustments. "When we went to our first grocery shop, I was confused. I couldn't understand some of the English on the packaging, I didn't know what exactly to buy for the house... After moving down five aisles, I still had nothing in the trolley. I think Hansie saw my face because he put his arm around my shoulders and whispered in my ear, 'You must put something in there you know!'" The following day Hansie bought Bertha a book called *How to Boil an Egg* as a present.

The young Christian couple found England hard going. "We tried going to church, but there was the Sunday League. We had little contact with Christians at that time. Really, we hardly came across any in the cricketing world."

Chronic cynicism about her faith challenged Bertha in the circles in which she now found herself moving. She had never really come across this before and the fact that she couldn't converse adequately in English made matters worse in this contested area of ideas. "One night, at a cricketing dinner, I told a guy that I prayed about everything, even asking God to help me find a parking space."

The critical Englishman replied, "I have to doubt your commonsense and sanity then." This had shocked Bertha deeply.

Bertha found being in England tough, hard and cold at times. But it was good for her. She practised her English and her faith in God, forced as she was to consider and reconsider her own beliefs, compelled to argue the toss for God, to interpret the sometimes complex meanings, hard truths and often not-so-clear consequences of "a personal relationship with Christ".

It was also good to get away from Bloemfontein. Here they could be alone, unrecognised, free to amble their way through life at times without being constantly greeted and recognised by friends and acquaintances. It was to be a rare period of extended intimacy in their lives, and was arguably one of the happiest periods ever for the couple.

When they returned to South Africa, Bertha got a job at Universitas Hospital and the couple settled down in Bloemfontein. Or, one should say, Bertha did. Hansie's cricket playing and the demands of his rapacious sponsors swallowed up what should have been time with his young wife. Their relationship was hardly allowed to grow.

Things continued in that vein for several years, but in Hansie's benefit year in 1997, things got even worse. "In that year, Hansie only spent 37 nights at home," said Bertha. He made a large amount of money during his benefit year, and this amount remains one of the largest for a benefit year of any South African cricketer. Three years later this amount, which had grown exponentially because of careful investment, was held against him and offered as "evidence" of ill-gotten gains.

With his sharply intelligent focus and single-mindedness, dedication, enthusiasm and networking capabilities, it was inevitable that Hansie would make a success of whatever he did. His careful investments had the potential to grow into considerable wealth. By the time he graduated from the University of the Free State, at the age of 22, he already had an impressive investment portfolio, which included two Bloemfontein houses, stock market shares and substantial cash investments.

At Fancourt I asked Bertha, "Did you feel at any time that Hansie had an unhealthy obsession with money?"

"No," said Bertha emphatically. "He was always interested in shares, in property investments, in business ideas and businesses, and loved to talk about these things. It was more than a hobby. It was who Hansie was. Business and especially investment was his passion, and he always intended to pursue this full-time after his cricketing days ended. He read books about it regularly, especially when he started planning his retirement from cricket. He knew that the cricket would come to an end. He used his cricketing prowess, not cynically, but wisely, to advance his business interests. There was never anything wrong with that."

However, there was, almost from the start, cause for concern in this arena. Bertha worried that Hansie would be misunderstood. He frequently talked about business deals, about wealth accumulation, about the stock market. It was often on his mind.

Hansie was certainly no spendthrift. He would do his own laundry at hotels to cut back on the hotel bill, for example, so that he had more money for phone calls to Bertha. Rather than go to fancy restaurants, he would delight in going to McDonald's. "He was particularly fond of McDonald's – he admired the company's innovative business ideals and he liked the food," said Bertha. "I did worry that some people might think that he had an unhealthy interest in money. This was partly because he made a lot of jokes about 'being stingy'. What he was saying, in jest, was that he was prudent and careful with money. Collecting it, assembling it, investing it, became a lifestyle. I never experienced any stinginess, either towards myself, or to others, ever. Hansie would even leave his credit card with me when he went overseas."

It is true to say that wherever Hansie went discounts were invariably offered; expensive gifts would be placed before him. This is not unusual – most top sporting celebrities experience such generosity – but Hansie was probably the most powerful of all South African sportsmen then. Owners were thrilled if he visited their establishment and, of course, there were certain marketing opportunities if he did so, too.

He got used to being treated well. He went where he knew he would be well received, although Bertha told me that Hansie "would never actively pursue a discount".

"At the start of our relationship, I would try and explain Hansie to people. When we were with people we knew well, he would sometimes drift off – his mind would be a million miles away. I didn't want people to misunderstand him."

Eventually, Bertha gave up explaining Hansie to her friends. "I later realised that I didn't need to explain Hansie to others. I just needed to love him."

All this is not to say that Hansie was not a "people person". He was that and then some. "Hansie," said Bertha, "used to greet everybody. Wherever we drove. At road works, for example, he would hoot and say hello to the workers. He loved people, he was very aware of them – really seeing them. He always had kind words and jokes for the high and the low. He amazed me by always finding something to talk to people about, whoever they were."

I asked Bertha whether he was ever intoxicated by all the adoration and the fuss over him. "No," she said emphatically. "He was one of the most humble people I've met. On rare occasions people who were clamouring for autographs and the like would irritate him. But he was never rude. I did wonder sometimes, especially when he was under pressure, whether he appreciated the adulation enough. His brother, Frans, used to, quite rightly, point out to Hansie that he must enjoy the adulation while it lasted and be grateful for it.

"Hansie," Bertha continued, "was one of the first people I met who was always the same. He was always even-tempered, with a love for life. He was always positive and saw the best in other people. He would see the Lord in everyday things. I only saw him lose his temper once: the result of a personality clash with Corrie van Zyl." Corrie was then a tough-minded Free State fast bowler and player-coach. This "temper" was simply evidenced by Hansie throwing his sunglasses into the cubbyhole of a car. That was it.

By 1996, Bertha had her own Bloemfontein practice, with two other young women. This freed her up somewhat to travel with Hansie on occasion, but to build up the practice it was necessary to put in the required hours there, and Hansie supported her in this. "Hansie encouraged me to fulfil my dreams and plans; he was just as enthusiastic about my practice and job as he was about his own. When we were setting up the practice, he helped with the sewing of the cubicle curtains, and spent long evenings at the practice while I tried out the new physio machines on him.

"He was keen that I should have my own life, that I build a career for myself. He knew that the cricket wouldn't last. I felt strongly about my independence, about not just being Hansie Cronjé's wife."

The first night she spent alone in their new Bloemfontein home, she heard strange noises near her bedroom window and phoned San-Marie in a panic at 11pm. The noises proved to be wind-blown reeds scraping against a wall, and from then on in the early years of her marriage, she would often stay with San-Marie or her own mother when Hansie was away.

The long absences had consequences. "When we had time together it was quality time, but it wasn't a real life. The periods together were like honeymoons. In a normal relationship, you get to know each other, you bump heads, you sort things out, you debate issues between yourselves.

"Hansie used to come home for a few days and it would be great. The first few days after his departures were so lonely and dreadful, but after a while I'd get back into my comfortable routine and numbness would set in. Then Hansie would return again, doing things differently. For example, I was used to putting the garbage out, feeding the dogs, backwashing the swimming pool etc. And then, when he was back, I would be on my way to follow my little routine and find some of the things were already done. It was confusing at times but wonderful to have him there, to have someone to help with the everyday chores."

Did she ever worry about Hansie's fidelity when he was on tour? "I never used to worry about Hansie at all. I trusted him 100 percent. Hansie was one of the most loyal people ever in his own way. He was morally upright and responsible. But I did worry about his quiet times. I knew how busy he was and how full his programme was, but I also knew how important it was to maintain a relationship with Christ. I never used to worry about whether he was drinking or womanising. But the truth, I suppose, is that Hansie would've been tempted to join in the 'boys will be boys' stuff. And maybe he did that on occasion. I'm not sure. I worried about the temptations he would have to endure and prayed that these would be overcome.

"Hansie never used to talk out of the change room. We never talked about cricket. The office stayed at the office. I never used to hear about any shenanigans. If I asked him about things like that, if I'd heard unpleasant rumours, he would try to talk it away, to change the subject. Maybe I was ignorant and naïve. I never used to think anyone in the team would do terrible things. I still don't."

It needs to be pointed out here, as an aside, that a golden rule of cricket, amateur or professional, is that "one never talks out of the change room". Wine, women, song and the like were not for the ears of wives and girlfriends back home, not for the ears of family, and certainly not for the likes of the dreaded media hacks. Did Hansie break that rule? Was that one of his chief offences? In breaking the code of silence, was he breaking his own back?

Frans Cronjé later told me at Fancourt, as we emptied pails of golf balls on one of the driving ranges, "For all those who were disappointed by what Hansie did, there were equal numbers who could not forgive him, not because of what he confessed to, although that shouldn't be minimised, but because he broke the code of silence."

CHAPTER ELEVEN

VENTURE TO THE INTERIOR*

Al die paaie wat jy loop

Al die draaie wat jy stap

Al die strikke wat jy aftrap

Al die grond wat jy koop

Gaan sit in jou knieë en die klere aan jou lyf

En klou aan jou treë en trek jou rieme styf

Al is jou spore vergete

Al is jou sole verslete

Al is die pad lank en swaar

Die skoene moet jy dra

Al die spoke wat jou jaag

Al die spore wat jy trap

Elke keer wat jy aanstap

Elke hek wat jou vertraag

Skiet wortel in jou bloed en rank tot in jou vuis

En kleef aan elke voet wat jou dra tot by die huis

Jou verlede klou verbete

Aan die veters van jou gewete

Die skoene moet jy dra

— Valiant Swart

This song, by the celebrated South African songwriter and musician,
was included in a Laurika Rauch album called *Die Mense op die Bus*,
which Hansie played frequently at home in Fancourt.
He identified strongly with the lyrics, according to Bertha, which concern consequences.
Literally, wherever you go, you'll have to wear these shoes.

---

*also the title of a book by Laurens van der Post

While Hansie was in India, Bertha moved to Fancourt towards the end of March 2000. It was supposed to be the start of a refreshing new chapter for the couple.

But perhaps Hansie was already anticipating the approaching onslaught and was prudently seeking shelter at the Fancourt hideaway, before the approaching black clouds unleashed their deluge. One way or another, some hatches were being battened down.

After the Indian tour, the team went straight to Dubai for the Sharjah Cup. The wives were allowed to meet the players there, because by then it was ten weeks since any of them had seen their husbands. They all flew back to South Africa on 1 April 2000.

Hansie and Bertha went to Bloemfontein to collect their last few belongings, before driving to Fancourt. "We went to see our lovely home in Bloem one last time and, as it stood empty, emotions welled up in Hansie. It was the first time I'd seen him so affected. The day we left with the two cars to drive down to George, saying goodbye to his mom and dad, and even my mom and dad, Hansie was overwrought. It was like he was saying goodbye to Bloemfontein where he'd lived all his life," said Bertha.

When he saw their newly completed Cape Dutch-style house at Fancourt for the first time, Hansie was quite tearful, standing in front of the almost clinically serene abode, speechless.

After their first day together in their new idyll, the couple walked across the golf course to the Fancourt Country Club restaurant. "We are so blessed and privileged to be here," Hansie said, as they walked arm in arm across the fairway. After five years of marriage, they still openly showed their affection for one another. After the matches in South Africa against Australia were over, they anticipated some freedom. They would have at least two to three months with no cricket and, for the first time, Bertha was not working during Hansie's off-season. She had sold her shares in her physio practice before they moved to George and was planning to do locum work when Hansie was away playing cricket. Hansie was considering the possibility of ending his career and making a new start, suggesting an appropriate time might even be as soon as after the three matches against the Aussies, the first of which would be played on Wednesday, 12 April 2000.

On Friday, 7 April, at about 11am, Bertha was downstairs getting ready to go to the beach with Hansie. The 8th of April would mark their fifth wedding anniversary and they had planned to spend a romantic two days together before the start of the Aussie series. Above her, in the balcony study, Hansie was on the phone. She heard him saying, "No, Doc, that's rubbish!"

Ali Bacher had phoned to say that he had been told by international press agencies that Hansie and three of his team-mates were under investigation by the New Delhi police for match-fixing. K K Paul, New Delhi's Joint Commissioner of Police, had chaired a press conference in the Indian capital at which damning "transcripts" of an alleged conversation between Hansie and a London-based Indian businessman, Sanjay Chawla, were presented.

Bertha called out to Hansie, her little voice softly wafting upwards and disappearing into the open thatch of the roof, "What was that about?"

Hansie came down to her and said, "They say I was involved in match-fixing. It's nonsense. Nothing to worry about." Bertha was shocked, but reassured by Hansie's dismissive, curt manner.

"I was a bit puzzled but didn't even think twice about it after Hansie had told me that it was nonsense. I thought to myself that it was probably a media mistake or some misunderstood comment someone made somewhere that had been pulled out of proportion by the media. But after we got to the beach at Victoria Bay, I saw that Hansie was looking worried and not happy at all. There was very weak cell phone reception in that area, but some of the players managed to get through," Bertha remembered.

When the calls came, Hansie wandered off when he spoke, making sure Bertha did not hear everything he said. She could see he was upset. Eventually, she asked, "Are you all right?"

"No," came his terse answer. Hansie had never found it easy to express his emotions. His reputation for openness was more aligned to a friendly bonhomie, rather than any proper articulation of inner feelings.

"I started to get worried about Hansie and these allegations," said Bertha. When they returned to Fancourt they watched the evening news, which was full of the match-fixing allegations. The New Delhi police claimed that Hansie had struck a deal on behalf of himself and three team-mates: Herschelle Gibbs, Nicky Bojé and Pieter Strydom. (Henry Williams' name was mentioned in the transcript of the tapes but not in the original statement made by the Delhi police.) The Deputy Commissioner of Crime Prevention in New Delhi, Shripradeep Strivasta, according to the South African *Sunday Times*, said that "police would prove Cronjé's voice was on the tapes", which were in his possession. He said that "the tapes had been sealed and locked away in a safe in New Delhi and would be produced only when the matter came to court".

When Frans Cronjé, who was then based in Stellenbosch, heard about the accusations, he was with former South African all-rounder Trevor Goddard. Both of them dismissed the media reports outright. The two men prayed for Hansie's protection against the "lies of the press". Meanwhile Allan Donald, who was in England, had heard about the allegations. "I thought it was the biggest prank. I repeatedly tried to phone Hansie, but eventually got through to Frans. "Don't worry about it," Frans said. "It'll be sorted out in a day. There is no way that Hansie was involved in it." Soon after that, English cricketers started ribbing Allan mercilessly about the "scumbok" allegations. Allan told them, with some short Anglo-Saxon words, to take a hike.

●

The next morning, the anniversary of their wedding day, Hansie wanted to stay at home. It was hectic, with the phone ringing repeatedly. Then the front doorbell rang. Hansie and Bertha froze. Who was that now? They were not expecting any visitors. Fanie Heyns, a reporter from *Die Burger* and Coenie de Villiers (a friend of Frans's), had got through Fancourt's security. Usually people who had not been specifically invited by residents were kept away. Fanie didn't seem to want an interview; he appeared to be there simply to comfort. "Are you disappointed about how you're being treated now, after all you've done for South African cricket?" he asked.

Hansie replied, "I don't want to say anything now." Fanie then prayed for Hansie, asking that the Holy Spirit would guide and protect him.

That afternoon another friend visited, and while Hansie was standing next to him in the driveway, he opened the boot of his car to get something out and there, lying in full view, was a front-page newspaper report about a New Delhi businessman, Rajesh Kalra, being arrested for match-fixing. The report said that Kalra was claiming that the recent one-day series between India and South Africa had been fixed, involving a large sum of US dollars. Hansie, stood, transfixed, staring into the abyss.

Later that day, a reporter from South Africa's largest-circulation weekend paper, the *Sunday Times*, arrived and a barefoot Hansie, dressed in shorts and a white T-shirt, told the reporter, "I deny accepting any money from anyone for match-fixing." He then reportedly told the journalist that he had been instructed by the United Cricket Board of South Africa (UCB) not to speak to the press.

Around that time, the UCB released this statement, "No Indian official has yet contacted the UCB... The UCB is dismayed that the integrity of South African cricket and its players is called into question." The South African government also called on India to release the tapes so that it could judge their authenticity.

That night Hansie didn't sleep well. His agitation increased. Bertha did what she could – she prayed for her husband, hovered around him, trying to comfort him, but not knowing how to do so. Hansie wouldn't open up. On Sunday, Bertha took Hansie to the airport. He had to go to Durban to play in the One Day International against Australia. "We prayed together before he left; he asked me to pray because he couldn't. I prayed for strength and wisdom and for the Holy Spirit to guide him," said Bertha. Increasingly distraught, she asked her parents to come and stay with her while Hansie was away.

Hansie joined the team in Durban. At a team meeting the media vortex was discussed. Hansie boldly asserted that he had never lost a game on purpose, had never thrown a game. The team publicly responded as one, "We believe you, Hansie. We're right behind you."

In the course of the day, Hansie told the media: "I am stunned. The allegations are completely without substance."

At 6.30pm on Sunday, Hansie was called into a meeting with Clifford Green (the UCB's lawyer and then still Hansie's commercial agent), team manager Goolam Rajah, the UCB's communications manager Bronwyn Wilkinson, and Nicky Bojé and Herschelle Gibbs who were allegedly mentioned in the "transcripts". Hansie repeated his denial: he had never thrown a match, his bank accounts were open and available for scrutiny, and he had never ever approached any of the players, an assertion which Bojé and Gibbs supported fully then.

"I never spoke to any member of the team about throwing a game. I've never received money for any match I've been involved in. I've never approached any player and asked them if they wanted to fix a game. The only way to clear my name is to speak to the players and check my bank accounts," he told the media assembled at the press conference held in the Kingsmead Presidential Lounge. He admitted that his team was offered 250 000 US dollars to throw the last match of the 1996/7 tour of India. "A team meeting was held to the offer but the players laughed it off."

"The issues at stake are the lack of protocol used on this most serious issue, and the bugging of phones used by South Africans while in India," Dr Bacher was quoted as saying.

On Monday, 10 April, there were "urgent talks" between the Deputy Minister of Foreign Affairs, Aziz Pahad, and the Indian High Commission in Pretoria.

Hansie phoned Bertha from Durban at 8pm – on someone else's mobile phone. "Don't be alarmed," he said. "I know it sounds strange, but I'm talking about legal money here. Go upstairs and look for a blue bag in the storeroom. There's some cash in there." Bertha quickly did so and dread rose in her throat when she found the plastic bag of US dollars.

Bertha put the phone back to her ear. "Sherbert! Hans!" was about all she could say.

"Bertha, they are coming to look through the house. Give the money to your mom and dad," Hansie said. He told Bertha it was meal-allowance money. Bertha reluctantly and fearfully agreed, but it never got to that point. After the cryptic and brief call, Hansie put the phone down. He was in a hurry, he was on his way to a team meeting, he said. He hadn't said who "they" were. In his mind, Hansie saw the police ransacking his house, looking for evidence. A thick wad of foreign currency would not look good.

Stunned by this and not really knowing which way to turn, Bertha took the money and counted it. With shaking hands she counted, then miscounted. Eventually she reckoned there was 15 000 US dollars. Or was it 10 000? Too much for a simple meal allowance, she thought. In a daze, she put the notes under a bed. Where was she to put this strange and offensive package? Eventually, at Hansie's urging, she would take it to Les Sackstein.

At about 2.30am on Tuesday, 11 April, the phone rang at Fancourt once again. Bertha knew it was Hansie. "Bertha," he said calmly, "I wasn't honest with you. I did receive some money. I want you to please phone my mom and dad and tell them that. Phone Kate and Jonty. They'll take care of you. I think it may take a week or two to sort out. I am so sorry, Bertha," he said.

"It doesn't matter," Bertha responded, as fear gripped her heart. "Just tell the truth. That's the main thing."

Hansie's emotions spilled out, his voice starting to break. "I'm writing you a letter that I will fax." The same fax was sent to Les Sackstein, Dr Ali Bacher and Ray McCauley. It was hand-written by Hansie and was five pages long. The letter simply referred to "you".

"It wasn't a public letter. It was very personal, it was private, intended only for those it was sent to," said Bertha later. "It was never meant to be a public letter."

Its curious public-private nature remains a source of confusion for the family. Hansie had made no reference in his letter to it being "private". Frans, who later read the fax, says, "It was a letter of repentance. Instead of just praying and saying 'Lord forgive me', he decided to act decisively. The letter wasn't addressed to a specific person but it was never meant as a public statement."

The day before Hansie was due to testify at the King Commission, the fax was leaked to the media. It is not certain who the guilty party was.

"Hansie," said Frans, "told me that he had faxed the letter to others and not just to Ali Bacher because he thought Ali and the other UCB administrators 'would try and squash it and nothing further would happen'. He wanted people to know that that was going on. Hansie wanted it in the open. He didn't want it to be swept under the carpet. I was present later on when a high-ranking government official actually told Hansie that it was a pity that he had made it public, as they could have easily 'handled' the affair privately and swept it under the carpet. I believe Hansie wanted to atone, he wanted a few trusted people to witness the letter of confession he had sent to the UCB, but that letter was not for public consumption. It was a very private document."

Les Sackstein said, "Prior to the news breaking, Hansie had spoken to me. I warned him that I felt he had done more than he admitted to me. I urged him that if he was lying to me he should speak to me first before communicating with anyone at all. He ignored this advice and wrote that fatal confession that destroyed his career."

As soon as Bertha had read the fax, she phoned Ewie and San-Marie, who were stricken, although at that point Ewie was not unduly surprised; he had known that his son was in trouble from the moment the allegations hit the media.

At 3am that morning Dr Bacher had received a call from Hansie, who told him: "Doc, I haven't been honest with you." A stunned Bacher, who had been resolutely, even aggressively defending his captain up till then, asked Hansie if he had ever taken money from bookmakers. "Yes," said Hansie. Bacher asked him what the amount was: "Between 10 000 and 15 000 US dollars," Hansie replied, adding firmly that no other players had been involved. Mortified, Bacher quickly contacted Percy Sonn and in the small space of 30 minutes the pair had decided on a radical course of action: to remove Hansie from the team to play Australia; to request that the government institute a judicial commission of inquiry into the matter and to apologise to the public and the Indian police for the UCB's angry defence of Hansie. (*Ali: The Life of Ali Bacher*, by Rodney Hartman, refers.)

If Bacher had had any intention of sweeping anything under the carpet, as has been insinuated, Hansie's semi-public letter of confession and his unpredictable and growing propensity to openly confess to at least some of his transgressions had effectively tied his hands. Who knew what Hansie would do next? What he would say next? And to whom? There was now no real chance of a quiet little Australian-like closed "disciplinary hearing", and the ICC and the UCB probably felt compelled to pursue the matter resolutely, and make a global example of Hansie.

Bacher then told Hansie to wait in Durban for him. But there was to be no waiting around for Bacher, with whom Hansie had a dysfunctional relationship due to political interference with team selection. By now Sackstein was fully activated and engaged, a raging legal bulldog, ready for a protracted battle in defence of Hansie. He put fear into Hansie by referring to the possibility of criminal charges. "My first responsibility," Sackstein said, repeatedly, "is to make sure that there are no criminal charges against you." He begged Hansie to keep his mouth shut, which seemed to have little effect.

Bertha meanwhile had phoned Kate Rhodes. Jonty remembers Kate saying, "Huh? He's done what!?" Jonty was fearful, his first concern being that Hansie would do something to himself, like jump out of a window. "I knew that the hardest thing he was going to face was his family's disappointment. And by family I also mean the South African cricket team, especially the members of the close-knit team that had been together from 1995 to 1999."

At 10.45am, the UCB announced that Hansie had withdrawn from the One-Day series and that he had not been "entirely honest" in his media statements. At 3pm, Bacher called a press conference and announced that Hansie's contract had been suspended and that the captain had admitted to receiving 10 000 to 15 000 US dollars during the triangular One-Day International series against England and Zimbabwe earlier that year. He had taken the money, which he had not banked, in return for "information and forecast" for a London-based bookmaker. Bacher said Hansie had told him he had been "harassed by bookmakers" on the Indian tour, but "denied involvement in fixing matches".

"We are shattered. The UCB and the government have been deceived," said Bacher, who added that the UCB had asked the Minister of Sport, Ngconde Balfour, to institute an inquiry.

During the course of that day, almost all Hansie's sponsors, without speaking to him, announced the immediate termination of his sponsorhips and endorsements.

At that point an important new figure in the drama now appeared in Hansie's life.

Raymond van Staden is a qualified forensic investigator and electronic counter-surveillance expert. He was trained as a South African Defence Force intelligence officer, and later recruited by the South African Police intelligence unit. Based in Europe for five years, he resigned in 1993 and started a business as a consultant, specialising in corporate investigations and counter-intelligence, with operational bases in Durban and Johannesburg.

Well built but with a mild manner, he laughed at the public perception that he was Hansie's bodyguard. This big man with a soft and friendly voice admitted, however, that he "hung around Hansie and was very protective". Somehow, he often managed to appear stern and threatening, his chubby round face acquiring a strangely eagle-like, ferocious, tense expression.

In the early hours of 11 April 2000, Van Staden had received a call from the UCB's security chief Rory Steyn. "Please come to the Holiday Inn; someone needs to go to Pretoria." Van Staden picked up one of his colleagues, Mike Domoney, and they made their way there, not knowing who they were supposed to help.

Hansie had by now asked to see the Minister of Sport, Ncgonde Balfour, and then later also requested to see Aziz Pahad, the Deputy Minister of Foreign Affairs. Hansie seemed determined to run with his confession, putting distance between himself and the UCB in doing so, seeking the counsel of others. He also wanted to apologise to both of these men. Possibly he was thinking about the quality of life in an Indian jail, and that Pahad could prevent a possible extradition. Although there was no formal extradition treaty between the two countries, the South African President could override that, and extradition treaties between India and some other countries, such as England, could make any overseas travel dangerous.

In a hotel suite, Van Staden and Domoney met Hansie, the national team's manager Goolam Rajah and Rory Steyn. They were told that Hansie needed to go to Pretoria to see Minister Pahad. With that, Hansie left with the bodyguard Domoney, for Pretoria. Van Staden made his way to the hotel foyer after being told to wait there by Rory Steyn.

"Rory came down and said, 'Listen, the story is bigger than you know. It's not just a case of taking him. We believe now that the minister is not going to be in Pretoria, but in Cape Town today, so take him there instead." Perceived threats to Hansie's safety included nervous and angry Indian bookies and their musclemen, and renegade members of the public.

Van Staden phoned Domoney and said, "Turn around and go to my house." Domoney did so and travelled with Hansie to the house in Amanzimtoti.

Van Staden went home and waited for them. While he was there, Goolam Rajah phoned and told him that the UCB had booked tickets for two – Hansie and a minder – to go to Cape Town.

Carol and Raymond van Staden's house is a medium-sized double storey, a modest home, but perched on a hill overlooking the crash and whisper of Indian Ocean waves about 100m away. The front door gives onto a flattish concrete verandah offering a panoramic view of the sea. Directly in front of the house is a typical sub-tropical explosion of thick, impenetrable coastal thicket hiding the beach.

Hansie arrived and Van Staden suggested that he go and rest in a cottage at the back of the property. He declined the offer and sat in a chair on the veranda. He crouched low in the chair, with his back to the sea, staring at the ground. He never looked at the ocean, restlessly shimmering below him. He asked for water. Van Staden recalled thinking, "Here is a man with big problems."

Soon afterwards, Van Staden and Hansie were on their way to the airport. Hansie started making calls on his cell phone. He kept on saying to various cricketers, "Keep your mouth shut. I'll take the rap." He said that to everyone he phoned, said Van Staden. Hansie gave all of them his word. He would be the whipping boy. Who else?

Van Staden phoned Sergeant André de Villiers of the South African police at the Durban Airport, saying, "I've got Hansie Cronjé with me. I need to get him on a plane without the public seeing him. Can you help?"

At the airport, Sergeant De Villiers quickly and quietly spirited Hansie to the VIP lounge, while Van Staden acquired the tickets. The police sorted out Hansie's baggage and got it onto the plane. Van Staden waited until all the passengers were seated before he took Hansie up the steps into the aircraft. The plane was nearly full, barring a few empty seats in business class. To his horror, Van Staden noted that he and Hansie were in economy class, in separated seats. He looked at Hansie. Pale, gazing at the floor, a man drowning in shame and fear. Hansie desperately needed someone to hang on to.

Van Staden approached the cabin controller and said to her, "Please Ma'am, can you upgrade us? I'll pay cash now."

"No, came the reply.

"I've got Hansie Cronjé here," Van Staden pleaded.

The stewardess said curtly: "I don't care who it is."

"Ma'am. Look at the man." His distress was plain. "We don't even want to eat food. We just want to be away from people." Eventually, she capitulated. Hansie and Van Staden sat down in the last row of business class. Van Staden put his hand on his charge's shoulder. Tears were running down Hansie's face. Van Staden took a blanket and gently put it over the captain's head as Hansie began to sob bitterly, uncontrollably.

After that, Hansie, who had been speaking to Van Staden in English, switched to Afrikaans and calmed down somewhat, even slept a little. By now it had been three days and two nights since Hansie had rested properly.

When the plane landed in Cape Town, Raymond noted the police vehicle sidling up to the plane, as arranged. After business class had cleared, stout Van Staden blocked the aisle while Hansie made his way to the tarmac and into the police car, which transported them to the VIP lounge.

After seeing the letter of confession, Ray McCauley had phoned Frans and told him that Hansie was on his way to Cape Town. "Meet him and keep him there. Make sure he doesn't leave until I get there."

When Frans got to the airport, he tried to find Hansie, without success. He was not listed on any flights. Frans couldn't get through on Hansie's phone. Eventually someone told him that the VIP lounge had been cleared and Frans guessed that that was where Hansie was. When he walked in, only Hansie and Van Staden were there. When he saw his brother, Hansie simply said, "I'm sorry," and started to cry. The brothers held each other and sobbed for about five minutes. After that, Hansie showed him the letter.

Ray McCauley and his right-hand man, Ron Steele, then arrived. Ray's first words were to Frans were said with a smile. "We should never have talked him into playing again in 1999, when he resigned." He then said to Hansie, "Don't worry, people make mistakes. What you have done is wrong and it is not God's will, but God promises in Romans 8:28 in the New Testament that He can let all things work together for good to those who love Him. Tell the world what you've done. Let's address this issue and get it over with."

They all began to discuss the meeting with Minister Pahad. They were told that he was flying into Cape Town shortly and would meet Hansie. It was agreed with the police that the VIP lounge would be used for the meeting. The police told them that a horde of media representatives was also at the airport, hunting Hansie down.

Aziz Pahad arrived with his entourage and was very friendly and tried to put Hansie at ease.

Hansie said, "Minister, I'm sorry. I'm sorry for the embarrassment I've caused you and my country. I'm sorry." Hansie went on and on in this vein. Pahad kept on repeating the phrase "My boy, my boy," hugging him on occasion and remained steadfastly friendly and empathic, not condemning him.

Van Staden remembered, "McCauley and Steele held a mini-conference on the phone with Ali Bacher, worrying about what they were going to say to the media." Frans also talked to Sackstein about the statement.

Eventually, Steele advised Hansie, "Just tell the media what you've already said to the minister. Don't tell them anything more at this stage."

Earlier, in a phone conversation with Les Sackstein, Hansie had been strictly cautioned once again: "Don't speak to anybody," an injunction that Hansie mostly ignored as the media circus continued. Around this time, Hansie announced that he wanted to speak to Minister Balfour as soon as possible. Balfour happened to be at the City Park Hospital in Cape Town, blighted with kidney stones. On hearing of Hansie's wish, Pahad informed the group that he was up for a visit to Balfour too.

Meanwhile, the media horde seethed just beyond the doors of the VIP lounge. A woman member of the press corps eventually broke through, but she was sternly escorted away by Van Staden. They had barricaded the door to the lounge with their bodies, making it physically impossible for the group to get out.

Instead, Hansie and those with him were whisked away through the door that leads onto the runway, and headed to City Park Hospital in several cars. Frans was in the second vehicle behind Hansie and, as they left, Hansie pointed to his ring finger as they were separated in the melee, vainly trying to indicate to Frans that he should phone Bertha.

The group arrived at the hospital and went up to a waiting room near Balfour's private ward. Outside the room, standing next to Van Staden, McCauley was on his mobile to Ali Bacher. Raymond heard, "Yes, I know you want to strangle him. I also would like to strangle him." McCauley tried to pacify Bacher, whose anger seemed to be growing by the minute.

A rumpled Balfour eventually met them, dressed in his gown and pyjamas. Like Pahad, he was empathic, comforting Hansie, who of course couldn't tell Balfour the whole truth – he was trying, as he would for months, to keep his word to his team-mates.

Meanwhile, the media had arrived again and were all over the hospital. Balfour exclaimed, "What am I going to tell the media?" He was swearing and cursing the press, recalled Raymond.

Eventually, Balfour gave his press conference in an 11th floor lecture theatre at the hospital, flanked by Hansie, Minister Pahad and Ray McCauley. It was declared that all questions would be directed to Balfour only. Strangely, according to some media reports, Balfour said that Hansie's bank accounts had already been submitted to support his claim that he was never paid, this in seeming contradiction to Bacher's and Hansie's earlier statements. It had been agreed that Balfour would make a statement after speaking to Hansie, but Bacher had gone ahead and made his own statement, before Balfour's media conference.

Journalists at the scene commented that Hansie was sombre, and seemed to indulge in "trance-like staring". Balfour said that Hansie denied all match-fixing by himself or his team-mates, and was adamant that he had received no financial reward during the recent tour to India.

Balfour said Hansie was "still my captain", that he had admitted "an error of judgment" in "playing along" with individuals who had tried to coerce him into accepting bribes. "In the meantime, as South Africans, we need to give our undivided support and attention to Hansie, the team and the players as they prepare to face Australia in the One-Day series. Until Hansie is proven guilty I will still call him my captain."

At the conference, Hansie released a brief statement. He was quoted in the *Cape Times* of 12 April as saying, "I wish to emphasise that the allegations of match-fixing by myself are devoid of all truth. The wrong that I committed was having had these discussions in the first place, and wrongfully mentioning players' names. I have never thrown any game and never will. However, I do admit to having some discussions with individuals, which could have led to the wrong impressions being created.

"Earlier this year, I was contacted by a South African during the series with England and Zimbabwe, which was about three weeks before the tour to India. While I was in India I was again contacted.

"I wish to apologise to all South Africans, the team, especially the players singled out, the UCB, the government as well as my wife and family for my involvement in the matter."

That was it. It only whetted the media's appetite for detail. It begged a thousand questions.

According to Rodney Hartman's *Ali: The Life of Ali Bacher*, Balfour later summoned Bacher and Sonn to his house in Cape Town. He raged at them for holding a press conference in Durban, on the same day, without due consultation with him, in which it was announced that Hansie had lied and had been removed as captain. To dispassionate observers, it was a farcical laugh a minute.

In England, Allan Donald was contacted by Sky News, who told him that Hansie had admitted to taking money from a bookmaker. "After thinking it was nonsense at first, I later saw a press conference on TV in which Hansie admitted to taking money. I was shattered. I felt incredibly let down. I didn't think Hansie would ever do a thing like that. Ever." In the wake of that Allan issued some scathing comments about Hansie. "I felt let down. I was bitter, and very, very angry."

Shaun Pollock was duly installed as the new captain. Days later, at the Wanderers in Johannesburg, where the South African team clinched the series against Australia, many banners of support for Hansie waved among the 30 000 strong crowd. One of them simply read "Long live Hansie".

The new captain, Shaun Pollock, told the crowd, "We've got a lot of respect for Hansie." The crowd cheered loudly and Shaun got into trouble with the UCB for his words.

●

After the hospital conference, Van Staden walked up to Hansie to say his goodbyes. Hansie said, "Where are you going?" Van Staden replied that he was only hired to take Hansie to Cape Town.

"Please stay with me today," Hansie had pleaded.

"It's not my call. I was hired by the UCB," said Raymond.

Hansie, apparently, genuinely feared for his own life and the lives of his family and wanted some professional security. Paranoia danced with a growing realisation of the magnitude of his offences and the effect it was having on the media. And would the corrupting bookies and their dark servants seek to silence him somehow, or exact revenge?

Hansie then got Rory Steyn to phone Ali Bacher and request that Van Staden remain with him for the time being, as he now wanted to go to Bloemfontein to be with his family and meet with Sackstein. Reportedly, an irritated Bacher said, "Give him whatever the hell he wants!"

Before starting on the trip to Bloemfontein, it was decided that Hansie would spend the night at Frans and René's house in Stellenbosch and Van Staden was installed in a nearby B&B. Van Staden recalled having supper at a nearby restaurant, while the TV news was on, and how the restaurant patrons had reacted. "They couldn't believe what was happening. They said Hansie had been framed. They said he was taking the rap for others." This seems to sum up public response at the time.

The next morning Van Staden picked Hansie up at Frans's house at about 5am and hit the N1 to Bloemfontein. After some formal niceties, Van Staden said, "You'll have to forgive me, I know nothing about cricket." This seemed to please Hansie.

Hansie then asked, "How do you think it went yesterday?"

"I will give you my honest answer: it went crap," Van Staden replied. Hansie was quiet for about five minutes. When Hansie asked why, Raymond responded, "You have opened yourself completely here."

"What," asked Hansie, "would you have done in my place?"

"I would never have given anyone any ammunition against me. I would've kept dead quiet. I would've taken legal advice."

Hansie retorted, "No. All those people are trying to help me."

Van Staden was by now fired up. "Hansie, what I saw yesterday… I think it was people trying to feather their own nests. I refer to everybody: Bacher, Balfour, McCauley, Pahad. They're playing political and personal games, a game for their own groupings. They weren't thinking about you. Those guys have their own agendas. Each of them wanted the limelight. They are only thinking of No.1." He added: "You should never have faxed that letter to anyone. That stuff is personal."

Later, he added, "There are two people you must tell absolutely everything – your Big Boss upstairs and your lawyer."

Hansie flopped back into his seat and sighed, "I've got problems."

As the sun began to rise, the media had somehow got hold of Van Staden's cell-phone number. He told them he was still in Cape Town. Hansie took a few calls, one from the respected Afrikaner politician Roelf Meyer and another from tender-hearted Goolam, who phoned repeatedly. They both expressed their utmost concern for his wellbeing.

As the pair travelled, Hansie kept on with his overflowing remorse, repeating that he didn't want to get anyone into trouble. He admitted to Van Staden that he had taken money, but gave Van Staden his word that he never, ever threw a game, an assertion he repeated until the end.

From their discourse, Van Staden understood that Hansie had seen his flirtation with the bookies as "another game he was playing, nice easy money on the side, a sort of insider trading".

Hansie also focused on the issue of his impending punishment. "Raymond, what's it like in prison?"

"Hansie," Van Staden had said, "why are you asking me this?"

"I'm going to jail. Find out for me what it's like in prison," Hansie had pleaded.

"Nonsense," countered Van Staden, "stop being so negative."

Whenever the car they were travelling in went through a town, Hansie slid down in his seat and pulled his jacket over his head.

As they approached Colesberg, just before the Free State border, they were travelling at 140km/h, over the speed limit. They went through a speed trap and a traffic officer stepped out into the middle of the road and pulled them over. It was a classic moment, the cop walking slowly and menacingly up to them, glaring malignantly through his aviator-style sunglasses.

He sternly asked for Van Staden's driver's licence, looking at Hansie with a growing recognition. The cop then walked around to Hansie's side of the car and stared at him through the open window. Hansie then said, "Officer, we've got to get to Bloemfontein urgently, man."

The traffic officer, silent for a few seconds, replied, "Sorry, Mr Cronjé. Yes, of course. My apologies."

He then proceeded to give them advice: "From here to the Free State border it's clear. Be careful at the first bridge you cross after that – they normally trap there. After that it should be clear all the way to Bloem." Hansie offered his thanks, waving goodbye as the car drove off. In the rear-view mirror the cop stood, his hand up in the air, in salute to his captain.

"Hansie," said Van Staden, "loved to tell his 'Jammer, Meneer Cronjé' story. That cop was the only person who spotted us on that long journey and he never split on us."

Hansie started working his mobile, calling his family in Bloemfontein, telling them that he'd explain the situation when he got there. Van Staden cautioned him, "Don't speak through any land-line connection. Mobile to mobile is the safest."

As they were closing in on Bloemfontein, Ewie called, "The E-TV news team is parked outside our house and keep on moving around the area." Raymond wondered if he should put Hansie in the boot, or just get him to lie down at the back of the car. Eventually it was decided that Hansie would simply slouch down in his seat and they would go to Bertha's parents' house through a side gate. Ewie and San-Marie would meet them there.

Van Staden delivered him without incident, gave Hansie his card and said his goodbyes. He never thought he'd hear from Hansie again.

Media crews were patrolling the Universitas suburb; landlines and mobiles rang incessantly at the Cronjé and Pretorius homes. Neighbours and friends of the Cronjés volunteered to stand outside the houses and repulse unwelcome visitors. The E-TV news crew, parked outside the Cronjé home, was told to move on by family friends, which they did – only to return later.

Bertha, smuggled into her parent's home on the floor of a minibus, was there to greet her husband, as were Ewie and San-Marie, who were also smuggled in on the floor of a car that zipped into a side entrance to the Pretorius home.

Hansie was very quiet, sometimes avoiding eye contact. No anger was directed at him. Compassion and, yes, disappointment were there, certainly. Bertha felt sad that her husband had chosen to carry his burden without sharing it with her.

After a miserable lunch, with Hansie saying little other than meekly and vaguely apologising for what he had done, it was decided that Bertha and Hansie were to be secreted at the home of their close friends Wouter and Louise Klopper in Waverley, one of Bloemfontein's upmarket suburbs. The Kloppers' home was a tranquil haven, with a large and pleasantly manicured, secluded garden, with several outdoor living spaces at the back, hidden from public view.

Impeccably groomed and poised, Louise had for some time acted as Hansie's personal public-relations officer, handling his fan mail, among other duties. She is Waksie's older sister. Wouter, part of the large and prosperous Bloemfontein Klopper dynasty, was a Grey man too.

Hansie and Bertha hid there for ten days.

"When Hansie arrived, he was tense, quiet. He paced in the garden, walking up and down, doing an endless circuit. We worried about him, worried about his sanity," said Louise. "The remorse was endless. I wanted him to stop. Enough already." Hansie seemed compelled to apologise to any member of the public at hand. Louise's friendly domestic worker, Jane, received some of his remorse too. "Jane," he said, "I'm sorry about what I did. I did a terrible thing."

Exactly what that "terrible thing" was, was not articulated much. He spoke in general terms, saying he was "sorry about the whole situation" in which he had put Bertha and his family. Louise was getting frustrated. The media were calling her at her office, wanting a response from Hansie, but Hansie said nothing much, and Louise was still in the dark.

At one point she said to him when Bertha was out, "You must tell me the truth. I want to know."

Hansie had simply paraphrased what he'd written in his fax: "I took money from bookies. I never threw a game. I never lost on purpose."

"I believed him," said Louise. "I could see he was telling the truth." While this vague confession seemed to satisfy Louise, the appetite for detail raged on outside the Kloppers' sanctuary.

"Hansie," said Louise, "was always naïve. And he loved to push boundaries. He flirted with the bookies and was naughty." For her, it was always as simple as that, as if Hansie were a bright little boy who simply needed a caning and then it would be over. Most of Bloemfontein would have agreed with her. Many of his South African fans were of that opinion too.

The caning was just beginning though. It was far more vicious than Hansie had anticipated, and it never seemed to end.

There were a few tranquil moments while Hansie and Bertha were holed up. With Hansie hunkering down inside a minibus, the Kloppers took them to nearby Rustfontein Dam on Sunday, 16 April. The dam was almost deserted and the group played around on water skis and had a braai. Back at the Kloppers' home, Hansie would kick a ball around the garden with little Thabo Klopper, finding his familiar happy space, even if just for a few simple moments. The Klopper children had been sworn to secrecy about Hansie's presence, and they revelled in the cloak-and-dagger proceedings. Besides, they had their beloved Hansie to themselves and Hansie's rapport with children seemed heightened by his troubles.

Hansie and Bertha would drink a glass of wine or two in the evenings, and he would relax just a little. On one occasion, while the foursome were watching a video, Louise and Hansie laughed heartily at Wouter and Bertha, who had fallen asleep on a sumptuous brown leather couch, snoring loudly, in unison.

●

Meanwhile, Les Sackstein travelled to Durban and Cape Town, consulting with advocates Malcolm Wallis SC (Senior Council) and John Dickerson SC. Sackstein had been a larger-than-life Bloemfontein fixture for half a century, and a figure that loomed large in Hansie's life. When he was interviewed for this book in 2004 his pale blue eyes seemed cold, hard and ironic. Of girth and gritty aggression, he could inspire awe (and fear) in ordinary folk and judicial officers in courts of law.

He was an attorney who had an excellent reputation as a lawyer's lawyer, who had friends in high legal places; you didn't want to get on the wrong side of "Oom Les". He was the sort of guy Hansie had a deep respect for. Tough, successful and intimidating. Sackstein at times functioned as a second father, who steered Hansie through those two awful years with a strong and forceful hand. A "father" who loved cricket and who loved Hansie with a passion. He had been handling Hansie's legal affairs since 1994.

His simple and unpretentious office spoke volumes about a man at ease with himself, confident in his own intellect and personality. His rooms were in a modern 1980s office block near the historic Raadzaals.

Sackstein's imperial presence was heightened, yet amusingly distorted by many photographs of his "children", pedigreed bulldogs, who was leered pugnaciously from various parts of his office. Seated behind his large and long, teak desk, "Oom Les" reigned comfortably in an exquisite old leather swivel chair of magnificent proportions.

Les Sackstein arrived as a little boy in Bloemfontein in 1940, shortly after his father received some agencies as a commercial traveller. Little Les was soon enrolled at St Andrews School in Bloemfontein and went on to study law at the University of the Orange Free State. Bloemfontein, being South Africa's judicial capital and the site of the Supreme Court of Appeal, is an excellent place to practise law.

One would have thought that the fervent anti-Semitism of some sections of Afrikanerdom during the Second World War years and beyond would have been hard going for a Jew in Bloemfontein. But it was not so. "Bloemfontein is the only major centre that has never needed a Jewish Sports Club. Anti-Semitism has never been an issue in Bloemfontein for me," Sackstein said.

He did, however, punch a guy once for an anti-Semitic remark. Such pugnacity has stood Stackstein in good stead during a long and distinguished career, a career that was pivotal in Hansie's painful duel with the South African legal system and the cricketing authorities.

●

Ali Bacher phoned Ewie on Monday, 17 April. He told him, "Ewie, I feel for Hansie, I feel for you and the family." He sounded very down, Ewie recalled.

Louise's landlines hummed with calls and faxes. Her mobile rang incessantly. Where was Hansie? What was he doing? How is he feeling? How about an interview or a press release? At that stage, the media may as well have dropped their questions and requests into a black hole. Eventually, Louise felt compelled to engineer a press conference for Hansie at Sackstein's office, in which Hansie simply paraphrased what he had said already after the bombshell confession, and repeated the core of his assertions: "I have always played to win." It became his mantra, right to the end. I always played to win. I always played to win. To a man, those who knew him believed him.

Hansie had intense meetings with Sackstein, who played hardball. "I must say again," he reiterated, "that my first duty, is to keep you out of jail. What you have done is deeply serious. You could be charged with criminal offences". Such offences could have included fraud and the breach of the country's foreign-currency control regulations.

After ten days, the Kloppers realised that Hansie could not hide in their home indefinitely. It was resolved that the four of them would travel to Fancourt together and they proceeded to do just that, Hansie lying low in the minibus, behind dark glasses and a baseball cap.

The family and the cricketing world waited for the commission of inquiry to be appointed. It was duly constituted in early May 2000. On 11 May Bacher phoned Ewie again, to find out how the family was doing.

Interviewing Ewie Cronjé at his home in 2004 about the time span surrounding the breaking of the scandal was difficult. His spirit groaned inwardly as he revisited the shattering sequences of shock, some disbelief and disappointment – and raw compassion for his beloved son.

When he did share emotion, it was sparse, given out slowly and fearfully, reminding one of a jittery opening batsman judiciously defending his wicket at the start of a match.

On Friday, 7 April, when the allegations first broke, Ewie had heard on the radio news that the Indian police had named Hansie, Nicky Bojé and other players. He had phoned Hansie and asked him if he was involved in any way. "No, Dad," Hansie had said.

Later that day, Ewie phoned Hansie again. Again Hansie denied any involvement with the bookies. After Ewie had received several phone calls from the media, he phoned Hansie a third time. Ewie ventured, "Isn't it just the Aussies up to their tricks?"

Hansie's response had been oddly flat in tone, and brief. "No, Dad, it's not the Aussies."

"When Hansie said that, I knew that something was not right. If the allegations were untrue, he would've said something like 'yes, it's the Aussies playing their psychological games again'.

"His reply shook me. I thought: hell, there's something going on." Forgetting that he had not switched the phone off after he said goodbye to his son, Ewie had said to San-Marie, listening nearby, "There's something wrong here."

Hansie heard this remark and said to Frans later, "*Pa het geweet daar's iets fout*" (Dad knew that there was something wrong).

When Ewie phoned Hansie on the next morning to wish him a happy wedding anniversary, he could hear that Hansie was down. On Sunday, Ewie had wanted to go with Frans to support Hansie in Durban. After discussing it with San-Marie he had decided not to. Hansie had thrice begged him to stay away. "To this day I regret not going," he said when interviewed. "My brother said to me that our father would've gone if it had been one of us, whether we had wanted him to come or not." Frans also blames himself for not flying to Durban.

With growing angst, Ewie watched the news reports on TV, watching his son at first baldly deny the allegations. He thought his son had come across "quite well", but he felt increasingly uneasy. Ewie spoke to Hansie at midnight on Sunday and Hansie had said that he had wanted to speak to the then acting president of the UCB and deputy national director of the Scorpions, South Africa's version of the US's FBI, Advocate Percy Sonn, but for some reason had been unable to do so.

"He never got the chance to speak to Percy," said Ewie. "It was of little use speaking to Bacher. Hansie and Ali had parted ways 18 months before that."

On Monday morning, Ewie tried unsuccessfully to get hold of his troubled son and had phoned his agent, Clifford Green, also the UCB's attorney. He asked Clifford where Hansie was and Clifford had replied that Hansie was sitting next to him. "How is he?" Ewie asked.

The answer came, "He's not well."

Clifford passed the phone to Hansie. "He cried like hell. I knew then, finally," said Ewie.

Ewie later phoned the team's assistant coach, Corrie van Zyl, and said to him, "Corrie, give Hansie some sleeping tablets. I know he hasn't slept for at least three nights. Hansie can't play on Wednesday if he is in such a state."

Corrie said, "Oom Ewie, we had the practice and the team talk. He's fine, there's no problem."

Somewhat reassured, Ewie went to bed on the Monday night and slept quite well. But at around 5am, he sat bolt upright in bed. "I hadn't been awake for five minutes when the phone rang. It was Bertha. She said that Hansie had phoned her at about 3am and had admitted that he had received money from the bookies."

At this point in the interview in the winter of 2004, Ewie broke down and tearfully looked at San-Marie, sitting nearby. "This is difficult. I can't. I can't." Ewie wept quietly.

"It's good to talk about it," said San-Marie soothingly. "You haven't spoken about it for such a long time."

"I can't, my wife, I can't..."

CHAPTER TWELVE

WHIPPING BOY

To understand why the King Commission came to be in the first place, it is important to know something of the history of the match-fixing scourge.

Modern allegations of match fixing in international cricket surfaced in the mid-1970s. Former Pakistani captain Imran Khan told Australian TV Channel 4's Liz Robertson, after the King Commission, that in the latter half of 1990s "bookies went wild and the players went along with it".

The epicentre of this underworld is in Mumbai, India, and the criminal bosses were and are also involved in the drug trade, among other nefarious activities. From these gangsters, called the Mafia, spread thousands of betting shops across the sub-continent, where bets can be placed on literally anything concerning cricket, such as who will win the toss, how many players will walk onto the field wearing dark glasses, and the amount of runs any one cricketer will achieve.

During the research for this book we interviewed an expert in cricket betting who wished to remain anonymous. According to him, in India alone, this illegal business is probably worth two billion US dollars a year. Betting on horse racing is legal in India and the government receives a handsome percentage from this industry in the form of taxation. One of the main reasons that gambling on cricket remains illegal is to avoid the same kind of taxation that the horse-racing industry is subject to.

This same expert explained that most of the betting takes place on the telephone, so it doesn't really matter in what country you live. You have bookies and you have punters. The bookies are the people who determine the odds and the punters place their bets with the bookies. Our expert, who lived in South Africa, was a punter and he told us that, due to his frequent betting he had built up a credit rating of 100 000 US dollars. This meant that he could place bets to the value of 100 000 US dollars by simply calling one or more of the bookies in India.

So what happens when you do not pay up after losing your bet? It is said that some individuals who haven't honoured their bets have ended up seriously injured or even dead. Most of the time you just lose the right to place future bets.

The source said that knowing conditions like the kind of pitch, the weather, etc. was of limited use to a bookie or punter, but he was of the opinion that bookies (and punters) use the payment for this information to get cricket players hooked for more information later. However, if you knew for sure that a player would score less than a certain amount of runs or which team would win, you would stand to make a fortune. The most popular bribe would be to get the favourite team to lose the match against an obvious underdog. With a scenario like this, one could place a really large sum of money on the underdog and still get good odds.

Our expert's theory was that when Hansie, Williams and Gibbs did not go through with their agreement during the One Day International in India, the punters (or bookies) must have lost big money. That may have caused them to decide to leak some information to the Indian police in order to get their revenge on Hansie or make an example of him. He did not believe that there were in fact tape recordings of their conversations with Hansie.

He had one further comment, "As far as I am concerned, Hansie's biggest sin was admitting that he was involved at all. If he had just kept quiet, nothing would have ever happened to him, or anyone else."

Vishwa Gupta, a senior income-tax commissioner in India, said in Liz Robertson's television programme, entitled *Fixing Cricket*, that he believed that "no match-fixing can take place without the connivance of the Indian cricketing authorities". Gupta also claimed that Indian captain Mohammed Azharuddin over the years might have taken up to 50 million US dollars in deals related to match-fixing.

An ICC fax sent by ICC CEO Dave Richards to the Pakistani cricketing authorities in 1995 urged them to be discreet in their handling of match-fixing investigations. Rashid Latif had blown the whistle on Pakistani captain Salim Malik in 1994, claiming he had been offered 25 000 US dollars by Malik to under-perform, among other things. Soon after his accusations were made, Latif was dropped from the team.

Also in 1994, Australians Shane Warne, Tim May and Mark Waugh were offered 200 000 US dollars when they toured Pakistan, an offer which they declined. In 1998, it emerged that the Australian Cricket Board had covered up the fact that Warne and Mark Waugh admitted taking thousands of dollars in 1994 for giving information to an Indian bookie on the "weather, pitch conditions and team morale" during the Australian tour of Sri Lanka. After their internal disciplinary hearing, behind closed doors, they were slapped on the wrist and continued their careers. (Waugh was fined 10 000 Australian dollars and Warne 8 000 dollars.)

In the late 1990s there were strings of such allegations, involving Pakistani and Indian cricketers especially. The ICC kept silent and seemed to be in perpetual denial, bleating "where's the evidence?" When allegations were investigated it was done behind closed doors, offences were frequently denied and inquiries were white-washed, accused cricketers sometimes giving award-winning performances as they pleaded innocence.

In 1997 the Indian cricketing authorities set up a commission to investigate match-fixing allegations and at the end of that they gave Indian cricket a clean bill of health. The ICC received the report and seemed to concur with the bizarre conclusion. Among the panel of ICC experts who examined the report was (South African Constitutional Court judge and African National Congress hero) Albie Sachs, claimed Liz Robertson.

So why was Hansie singled out with such mercilessness?

Dr Ali Bacher said that in 1999, prompted strongly by the Warne and Waugh wrist-slap, the ICC instituted a regulation that made a life ban mandatory for any cricketer found guilty of match-fixing, or any involvement in paying players to under perform. None of the players interviewed in 2005 had any recollection of being made aware of this ICC resolution.

Interviewed in a Wanderers boardroom in 2005, Bacher replied to questions about this issue:

Was it necessary for the ICC to request a government commission of inquiry into the allegations brought against Hansie?

Bacher: We made that decision.

The UCB made that decision? Why?

Bacher: Because – I'd been to the sub-continent on quite a few occasions and every now and then there was a little chatter about malpractice, but the bottom line was always: "Where's the evidence?" I brought it up twice at ICC meetings ... the first time I brought it up was in 1997 [at a meeting of Full Members chaired by Sir Clyde Walcott]. And then in 1999 I was told two World Cup matches were thrown. Majid Kahn, the CEO of Pakistani cricket, kept on telling me, "Ali, it's happening." So our strategy was to internationalise this problem ... and to give it credibility, it had to be away from the UCB. We were too near.

You had to park it somewhere else and the government was the only agency?

Bacher: I was too much involved. It was such a big, serious issue. Once we did that, I had to keep my distance from Hansie, unfortunately.

Looking back now, do you think the UCB could have handled Hansie differently? Do you think the process was reasonable and fair?

Bacher: I think once it came out in the open, I think we did the right thing in the interests of world cricket... the whole fabric of the game was under threat here. Sponsors were withdrawing ...

So, historically, I suppose, Hansie did international cricket a big favour by his confession?

Bacher: What happened in South Africa started a process, which may well have saved the game of cricket ... Saved the game of cricket.

The irony is that Hansie's greatest contribution to cricket was probably telling the truth about his involvement with the bookies.

Is it true to say that Hansie, albeit unwittingly, forced the cricketing world to acknowledge the universal problem in an open external hearing televised live? Hansie's own confession seemed to compel the UCB to deal with him harshly, and make an example of him. Hansie was a whipping boy. Part of the reason for this was that he simply told the truth, albeit in instalments, mostly because of his great reluctance to drag team-mates into the mess.

In the end, the only real evidence against Hansie was his own confessions. The "tapes" in 2005 remained curiously elusive. The "transcripts" remained an exhibit of little consequence, as it was not ever proven that they were based on a real conversation. If the tapes had existed, why didn't the Indian police produce them? And why couldn't prosecutor Shamila Batohi bring them back, despite her desperate visit to India?

From George, Hansie and Bertha shuttled between Bloemfontein, Durban and Gauteng, visiting Les Sackstein and advocates Malcolm Wallis and John Dickerson, as the legal processes ground away. The couple spent many long months of "negative energy" acquiring and collating bank statements going back to 1991, in attempts to prove the veracity of Hansie's assertions about the sources of his income.

It can be argued that the King Commission was an expensive ICC/UCB road show – paid for by the South African taxpayer, Hansie's estate and all cricket fans who pay to watch matches live or on TV. In the end, the damage it did to South African cricket probably outweighed any global usefulness it may have had in "making an example" of the beloved South African captain.

Maybe Bob Woolmer's comments summarise it best: "I cannot subscribe to Hansie's involvement with the bookies as captain of the national side. However, I thought the King Commission was South African cricket's worst nightmare; it was a tragedy to see so many players having to speak publicly about what was a very messy business. It stood out as a massive publicity stunt. The fact that it finished unresolved and in a mess showed how thoughtless it was."

Hansie's relationship with Les Sackstein was based largely on a stern father-pliant son dynamic and Hansie mostly listened carefully to him, with a deep respect.

During the King Commission, Advocate John Dickerson regularly invited Hansie and Bertha to his home in Tokai. For a time a Saturday *braai* was a standing arrangement, often in the company of their friends and minders, Raymond and Carol van Staden. "Hansie trusted and liked Dickerson deeply," said Bertha.

Hansie also developed a special relationship with Dickerson's son Ally, who has cerebral palsy. Hansie would always take him aside, talk earnestly with him and play around the garden with the boy, who was delighted with Hansie's attentions.

His relationship with Sackstein was complicated. This tough lawyer treated Hansie's spiritual convictions with a worldly dose of cynicism. Hansie and the Cronjé family were contacted on several occasions by lawyers and advocates who suggested that because they professed to be Christians they should represent Hansie, but Hansie remained loyal to Sackstein and was very grateful to him for all his help.

●

The media played their part in the relentless two-year whipping of one of South Africa's most loved and admired heroes of all time. The fact that Hansie was a Christian seemed to make his crimes even more colourful and juicy. One can hardly blame them though for simply reporting on the events that unfolded, but it was often the tone, the sensationalist rantings and clever-dick, cynical distortions of some hacks that hurt so much. And Hansie didn't help matters by glumly releasing the truth in instalments, as he battled to protect fellow team-mates. Not to mention his obvious frustrations with Batohi.

"Hansie felt he had been hurt by many of some of his erstwhile friends in the media. He had always been accommodating to many of them, taking calls in the middle of the night without complaint, for example," said Bertha. "He had considered many of them to be his friends. He knew that they had a job to do in reporting on the King Commission, but it was the way in which they wrote their reports that wounded him."

Hansie had said in his faxed confession, leaked to the media during the King Commission, that he had "taken his eyes off Jesus and had been tempted by Satan". The gleeful distortion in the media played out as "Hansie says: 'the devil made me do it.'" One of the reporters even wore a mask of a devil with two horns when he reported on this. This, in particular, saddened and upset Hansie, but there were many times when he felt he deserved such approbation.

Much was made of his "love of money". During the King Commission, Hansie had said that he liked money, an admission that most people in the world would make. "The media went on and on about this. Hansie meant that he was passionate about business, which of course is all about the accumulation of wealth," said Bertha.

The crazy media distortions included a Radio Oranje news report which stated, "Hansie Cronjé has committed suicide", a broadcast that Hansie himself heard as he had travelled around Bloemfontein. At least that raised a bitter laugh for him.

It wasn't only journalists who had hurt Hansie, a few retired national team players commentating and writing in the press, also at times joined in the media chorus of damnation. Even Allan Donald lashed out. Allan recalled Hansie's attempt to mend the breach: "I sat and cried and talked to him for two hours in Bloemfontein. He acknowledged he was greedy, but assured me he had never fixed a game. I believed him and always will. Our friendship was renewed."

Frans has a very strong view on the media: "As Allan Jones told the South African team back in 1992, one of the things in life that never returns is the spoken word. Once something is said it remains said. The same is true of the written word. I wish that commentators and journalists would just think a bit before they wrote. They never seem to consider what impact their words may have on people's lives.

"Over a period of five months after the King Commission six or seven reporters from different newspapers and magazines phoned my dad and asked him to apologise to Hansie for their harsh words – words that were often written to get their articles placed and to help sell their publications. All people make mistakes and it's great that those guys expressed remorse. We are still good friends with them today, but I do not agree with the process of writing a critical article that is read by millions around the world and then feeling bad about it and apologising in a private letter. If you need to apologise privately then do it. But then you need to also be man enough to admit your mistakes openly to the same audience that read your first article."

"Because of Hansie's position of influence he had a large responsibility. By getting involved with the bookies he compromised that. But I believe that when you're in the media you also have great influence and therefore a responsibility to report acurately and with integrity. When journalists twist facts for the purposes of sensation, they are shirking this responsibility to the public."

While Neil Manthorp didn't think it was necessary to apologise for any of his articles about Hansie, he did try to explain to Hansie how he felt in a letter.

Recalled Manthorp, "I wrote it when I returned to my office on the day of the King Commission when Hansie appeared and broke down. It was a page and half long and I said that after six or seven years touring together I took no pleasure in witnessing his pain. I said that I hoped we could put everything behind us and that, although I knew he hadn't liked some of the things I had written, I hoped he understood why I had written them. I gave the letter, in an envelope, to Leslie Sackstein at the lunch break of the following day's proceedings and asked him to pass it on to Hansie. He put it inside a brown leather folder and nodded his head saying 'okay'. My relationship with Sackstein had been tense, to say the least."

⬤

The King Commission became a regular public whipping in the town square, watched by a sullen crowd who mostly disagreed with the punishment.

Sympathy and support among the public seemed to grow with every blow. Good grief, enough already! Let the poor guy get on with his life, man. Whenever Hansie ventured out in public he was met with goodwill, sympathy and kindness. Ordinary people loved him, forgave him, wanted to embrace him, shake his hand, express their concern. Bertha cannot recall one incident in which this was not the case. The media however continued to torment him, right to the end.

There were seemingly endless global news reports, features, exposés, in-depth investigations, special reports and time-lines. The media stories and musings dragged on, re-stimulated by each new turn in the legal processes, in which judges, advocates, lawyers, prosecutors and politicians played their part, some of them vying for peer approval, others for the approval of their bosses. The black robes don't mind lengthy and convoluted proceedings.

Hansie's labyrinth of pain included the hostile UCB, especially the UCB's then president, Advocate Percy Sonn, who strangely was also the deputy national director of the Scorpions, the special police department that handles high-profile corruption cases. But after a while, some of the UCB officials, such as Ali Bacher, seemed to become somewhat detached spectators, too, rather than willing participants in the King Commission with its toxic and ponderous meanderings, all watched live by a global television audience.

For many, the match-fixing inquiry became too much "Hansie's trial"; there was a sense of overkill, that it was a lopsided luxury for the world's cricketing lords.

Les Sackstein issued the following statement about the truthfulness of Hansie's testimony at the King Commission:

A factor that troubled Hansie and his legal team enormously was the apparent misconception in the minds of the press and others as to what the indemnity in fact was. Malcolm Wallis and I had no doubt that the evidence which Hansie gave before the Commission [was] given in terms of an indemnity which was in place as soon as he gave the evidence but was conditional in the sense that it could be withdrawn if Hansie did not make a full disclosure to the Commission, or that he was honest and truthful.

The point is that the indemnity was in place and it was solely the decision of the National Director of Public Prosecutions (NDPP) as to whether the indemnity, in terms of which his evidence was given, could be withdrawn for non-fulfilment of either of the aforesaid commissions.

Malcolm Wallis said to Bulelane Ngcuka, the then NDPP, that it was unnecessary to canvas the contrary views asserted by King during the course of the Commission, because in his view King's interpretation of the correct legal procedure was flawed.

It is most significant that throughout Hansie's cross-examination by Batohi, it was at no stage suggested by her or anyone else who cross-examined him, that he was not being truthful, or his evidence was contradictory or that he had concealed anything from the Commission. Batohi never even pointed to any conflict between his testimony and the testimony of other witnesses, nor did she ever accuse him of lying or withholding information from the Commission.

It is crucial to know the importance of challenging the evidence of a witness in cross-examination if any finding is to be sought that he is being untruthful or less than forthcoming... this was stressed by the Constitutional Court in the matter in which the former president Nelson Mandela took the South African Rugby Union to that court. It was also emphasised by the Supreme Court of Appeal in the Boesak case.

The conclusion that one had to draw was that the absence of such challenge in regard to Hansie's evidence is a strong pointer to the fact that it should be accepted as truthful.

The overall position accordingly was that Hansie gave evidence under oath before the Commission and that evidence was never attacked either in regard to his credibility or in regard to its completeness and no suggestion to the contrary was ever made.

●

On 15 June, Hansie read out the following statement.

I, the undersigned, Wessel Johannes Cronjé, do hereby state that:

1.   I have been a full-time professional cricketer since 1988. I was a member of the South African cricket side from 1992 until the 11th of April 2000. I captained the South African team from the third test of the Australian series in 1994 until the 11th of April 2000. I played in a total of 68 Test matches, 53 of which as captain. I also represented South Africa in 188

One-Day Internationals, 138 of them as captain. Ninety-nine of the One-Day Internationals under my captaincy were victories.

2. It is time for me to try to repay a part of the enormous debt that I owe to cricket and to try to repair some of the damage which I have caused the game, South Africa, my family and team-mates, and the cricketing public.

3. My initial denials of involvement made publicly and to the UCB were untruthful in a number of respects; and so too was the subsequent press statement issued on my instructions. I misled the United Cricket Board of South Africa and members of the South African government and those who tried to defend me. I also withheld facts from my legal representatives, I was not honest and apologise unreservedly.

4. I have also decided to sever my connections with the game and I will not play cricket again at a representative level.

5. Words cannot begin to describe the shame, humiliation and pain I feel, in the knowledge that I have afflicted this on others. To my wife, family and team-mates in particular, I apologise.

6. The greatest honour that can be bestowed on any cricketer is to lead his country's national side. I have failed in my moral and professional duties. Hopefully, I can contribute some small measure of redress by placing before the Commission the information that follows in this statement. Until now I have not named or implicated any other person, and I fear that the revelations in this statement may create serious implications for my personal safety. I have already received death threats.

7. I wish to disclose all the information I have and, in the emotional state in which I find myself, have dredged my memory as best I can in order to place the facts before the Commission.

8. Since the first revelations made in the Indian press and, in particular, the morning of 11 April of this year, I have known that my days as a cricketer are over. There were however others – namely Herschelle Gibbs, Pieter Strydom and Henry Williams – who have their playing careers before them and whose futures have been imperilled by my inexcusable actions. Foolishly, I tried to suppress disclosure of their involvement and, in doing so, encouraged Herschelle Gibbs and Henry Williams to conceal their role. I hoped to save them from the predicament in which I had placed them: instead I compromised them and worsened their position. It would be a tragedy if any of these players were to be lost to South African cricket because of my wrongdoing. I beg the Commission and the cricketing authorities not to deprive the game of their talents and beg the UCB to reinstate both Herschelle and Henry to the national squad.

Herschelle lied to the UCB, his employer, at my request. Herschelle, forgive me.

9. I will attempt to deal with the matters which form the subject of this Commission's terms of reference in chronological order ... Before doing so, however, I would like to deal with an approach I received to influence the result of the first one-day international against Pakistan in the Mandela Trophy in January 1995. Pat Symcox mistakenly said, in his evidence before the Commission, that this occurred in 1997.

1995: THE MANDELA CUP

10. Shortly before the first One-Day International final against Pakistan in the Mandela Cup in Cape Town in January 1995 I was approached by an Indian or Pakistani man, who described himself only as "John". (I believe he may be the individual of the same name who was referred to by Shane Warne and Mark Waugh during their hearings before the Australian Cricket Board.) He offered an amount, I think about 10 000 US dollars, for the team to throw the game. I subsequently discussed this with Pat Symcox. We agreed we should not even put it before the team, and that was the end of the matter. I did not approach any other players. In the event, we won the match.

11. I recall that when I walked onto the field for the match, I was asked by Salim Malik (the Pakistan captain) whether I had spoken to John. It was evident to me that he knew about the approach I had received. I felt ashamed and embarrassed and, wishing to avoid even talking about the matter, merely nodded.

12. Before the second One-Day final in Johannesburg I was again contacted by John who asked if anything could be done in respect of the second game. I told him I was not interested. We also won that game. I never spoke to him again.

13. I subsequently heard rumours that Pakistani players had been involved in match-fixing during the Mandela Cup, and in Zimbabwe in 1995. South Africa had not been [involved].

THE SOUTH AFRICAN TOUR TO INDIA IN 1996

14. During our tour in Pakistan in 1994, Kepler Wessels told me that he knew of offers which had been made to Australian cricketers, I do not know to whom, to lose a test match in Karachi.

15. During the 1996 Indian tour I was approached by "Sunil". He had befriended some members of the team earlier that year during the Sharjah

Cup. Sunil asked me if I was interested in fixing matches. I said I was not. No offers or financial proposals were received from him.

16.   On the evening of the third day against India in Kanpur, I received a call from Mohammed Azharuddin, who was friendly with a number of South African players. He called me to a room in the hotel and introduced me to Mukesh Gupta (MK). Azharuddin then departed. MK asked if we would give wickets away on the last day of that test to ensure that we lost. He asked me to speak to the other players and gave me approximately US 30 000 dollars in cash to do so. I led him to believe that I would. This seemed an easy way to make money but I had no intention of doing anything. I did not speak to any of the other players and did nothing to influence the match. In the event, however, we lost the test. I had effectively received money for doing nothing and I rationalised to myself that this was somehow acceptable...

17.   Before the final one-day international MK asked me to speak to the players about throwing the game, which I agreed to do. By that stage we were exhausted, it was the end of a long and arduous tour, and a number of key players were suffering from injuries. MK asked me to convey an offer of US 200 000 dollars to the team to throw the match. It was a long time ago and I cannot recall the exact sequence of events, but as far as I can recall it was as follows:

17.1.   I spoke to some of the players beforehand, advising that a team meeting would be called to consider the offer.

17.2.   A team meeting was held the evening before the match, attended by all the players in the squad. I conveyed the offer to the team, which rejected it. I recall, in particular, that Andrew Hudson, Daryll Cullinan and Derek Crookes spoke out strongly against it. It was agreed that the decision had to be unanimous or not at all.

17.3.   After the meeting a few players remained and we chatted about the matter. We were curious to see whether the offer could be increased. I telephoned MK and told him the team was not interested but asked whether he was prepared to increase his offer to US 300 000 dollars. He replied that this was too much but that he would increase it to US 250 000.

17.4.   The next morning before the match, there was a very brief meeting at which it was confirmed that the offer was rejected. Bob Woolmer, the coach, heard about the offer and he was very angry about it...

18.   I then telephoned MK and told him the offer was rejected. No money passed hands. I did however tell him that the team was sub-standard because of the number of injured players. I received no benefit or offer of payment for this information.

19. I had no further dealing with MK, John or any other bookmakers or punters on that tour. However, when India toured South Africa at the end of 1996, early 1997, MK came to South Africa. He was in Durban for the first Test and in Cape Town for the second. I am not sure whether MK is a bookmaker or punter. I believe, however, that he was one of the bookmakers, referred to in Dr Bacher's statement, who were in the presidential suite.

19.1. I was asked by MK to provide information in respect of the first and second Tests, on which I understood he wished to place bets. I understood that MK would pay me an [unspecified] amount if he won anything. The amount would depend on his winnings.

19.2. In respect of the first Test, I supplied him with the team selections and a daily forecast.

19.3. In respect of the second Test, I was only asked to tell him when, and at what score we would declare. I did this. After the second test MK transferred a sum of about US 50 000 dollars into my NBS Savings Account...

19.4. South Africa won both the first and second Tests in this series and the third Test was drawn. None of these results were fixed or manipulated.

19.5. MK had asked me to speak to the players about losing the third Test and promised to pay me US 300 000 dollars if I did so, but I refused.

20. After the 1996/7 Indian tour to South Africa, MK contacted me on a few occasions. He requested information (I think this was during the quadrangular One-Day International series in Pakistan involving South Africa, Sri Lanka, Pakistan and the West Indies). I refused. I cannot recall speaking to MK again.

21. I do not recall any further contact with or from bookmakers or punters until the fifth Test against England at Centurion Park earlier this year (2000).

RECEIPT OR PROMISES OF PAYMENT

22. The facts ... are set out below.

23. The fifth Test between England and South Africa was held at Centurion Park from the 14th January to the 18th January 2000. Play commenced but was disrupted by protracted rain and it became clear that it would play out to a draw. The match itself was not significant, as the series had already been won.

24. On the fourth day during the rain interruption, a meeting was held between me, Nasser Hussein (the English captain), Dr Ali Bacher, the match umpires and the match referee in the library of the Northern Titans. Dr Bacher was anxious to save the game as a spectacle. There was pressure

to turn it into a One-Day International, but this was apparently not possible because of a clash of sponsors. [Test matches and One-Dayers have different sponsors.]

25.   ... on the evening of the fourth day, I received a call on my mobile. The caller identified himself as Marlon Aronstam. I do not know where he got my number and I had not previously heard of or spoken to him.

26.   ... Marlon said he was a cricket lover and wanted to see action on the field. He said that my image as captain was poor and that I was perceived as a conservative and negative captain. We also spoke about my recent form, which had not been good: I had had two ducks in a row. Marlon urged me to speak to Nasser Hussein about an early declaration to make a contest of it, saying that this would be good for both me and cricket. This is something that is often done, for example, in county cricket in which each side forfeits one innings. It had never before been done in a Test match.

27.   Marlon revealed that he was involved with NSI, a listed company, which I now know to be involved in sports betting. I did not know this at the time and only became aware of it in April this year.

28.   Marlon said that if we declared and made a game of it he would give R500 000 to a charity of my choice and would also give me a gift. We did not discuss either which charity or what the gift would be. He asked whether we could meet at my hotel, which we did that night. He wanted to call Nassar Hussein, who was in the same hotel... I refused because I did not want him involved. We spoke about cricket and the Centurion Test. I was impressed by his knowledge of cricket. He said a forfeit by each side would be a positive move for cricket. He genuinely sounded as though he wanted to see a cricket contest and I was not asked to influence other players to perform badly, or to influence the result. Marlon's suggestion seemed to make perfect sense from an entertainment point of view. It was nevertheless wrong for me to have entertained the offer of a gift for doing something in respect of which I was required to make an independent decision as a captain.

29.   Marlon had asked me to call and let him know if and when we decided to declare. The morning of the fifth day the question was raised and discussed by the respective team coaches and captains. The England team and management seemed reluctant, and I called Marlon and left a message that there would be no declaration. There were discussions between the two teams about a realistic target to be set, and once this was settled it was agreed that we would declare. There were mixed views within the team about the declaration. Some members were opposed and others were in favour. I think it was the correct decision.

30.   I then sent an SMS to Marlon advising that "the game is on", or words to that effect. He subsequently told me that it had been impossible for him to get any bets on the game, as he had been advised too late to do so.

31.   The match was a closely fought encounter with a lot of action, which made for good entertainment. Had Paul Adams not been injured during play ... we would have almost certainly have won. Dr Bacher called me the following morning to thank me for saving what would have been a disastrous Test. So did Mike Procter and Richard Harrison (president of the Northern Titans).

32.   After the game Marlon visited me at the Sandton Sun, where we were staying, and gave me a leather jacket and R50 000 in cash amounts (R30 000 and R20 000) on consecutive days. I believed this to be the gift he had spoken of. He said it was in consideration of me giving him information in the future, but did not specify what this information would be. The R500 000 which had been promised to a charity of my choice did not materialise and was never mentioned again.

33.   I should never have entertained the discussion with Marlon and it was wrong to have accepted anything from him. It has only served to discredit what I believed was recognised as a good move for cricket. I was not asked by Marlon or anybody else to "throw", lose or otherwise fix any results or performances in the Centurion Test. The declaration was a genuine attempt to save the game as a spectacle, which was agreed to by both teams. I was also anxious, because of my bad form, to have an opportunity to gain public support. I truly believed that we could win, given the declaration, and requested Pieter Strydom to try and place R50 on South Africa to win. He was unable to do so. The match delivered a genuine result and was in no way manipulated but that, of course, does not justify my conduct.

THE TRIANGULAR SERIES

34.   The day before the first One-Day International at the Wanderers, ie on 20 January 2000, I was approached on my way to the nets by an individual known only as "Hamid". He had been a regular hanger-on around the team for a few years and was always handing out biltong for team members and asking for tickets. I have subsequently discovered that his full name is Hamid Cassim. He is known – not by the players but apparently in his own circles as "Banjo" and runs a sweet shop in Johannesburg. I'm also aware that Hamid is a friend of Mohammed Azharuddin.

35.   Hamid said that if he had known that I was going to declare in the Centurion Park Test he could have made himself some good money. My response was "why didn't you ask?"

36.   At the beginning of February I travelled with the team to the Beverly Hills Continental at Umhlanga Rocks [near Durban]. We were due to play the fourth One-Day International in the series against Zimbabwe in Durban on the 2nd of February. Hamid was at the hotel... He introduced me to a man known as Sanjay, whom he said was from London. I was not told he was a bookmaker and was not told he was a punter.

37.   They indicated that Sanjay wanted me to supply them with information, but did not specify what information. They also said I could make a lot of money if we would lose a match. I said I was not prepared to do it unless we were assured of a place in the final of the series. I was spinning them along as I do not think I had any real intention of throwing a match. Sanjay handed me a cell phone box containing US dollars in case I changed my mind.

38.   I did not count the money, which was kept in a filing cabinet at home, together with my prize money from the World Cup, the Kenya tour, and leftover subsistence allowances. It was subsequently counted, not by me, on 11th April, when I confessed to receiving it, and I was told that it was about US 10 000 dollars, but may have been US 15 000 dollars.

39.   It is difficult to say with certainty which of the monies kept in the cabinet had come from Sanjay because it was kept together with dollars derived from my winnings, allowances and advance payments I had received from player's signing on fees, deposits and travel allowances for what proved to be an [aborted] benefit tour to the sub-continent in April this year.

40.   All of these monies were handed over to the South African Reserve Bank through my attorney. I am told that they amounted in all to US 10 000 dollars, plus a further sum of about US 37 000 dollars. This sum of US 37 000 dollars was made up in the following manner:

40.1.   On or about 15 February 2000 I had received, in advance, US 25 000 dollars in Bloemfontein as an advance on the payments due to the South African players participating in the benefit matches. The payment was for the signing on fees, the deposit, and the travel costs of the players. I annex a certificate from the promoter who arranged the series. The payment was made in Bloemfontein in cash.

40.2.   The balance of the dollars was the residue of my World Cup and Kenya winnings and subsistence allowances which I would have converted to dollars. It may also have included dollars left over from previous tours and overseas trips.

41.   It was not initially my intention to throw any games or to fix results. [I] was driven by greed and stupidity and the lure of easy money. I thought

that I could feed Sanjay information and keep the money without having to do anything to influence matches. In fact there was no manipulation of games or results in South Africa, and I supplied no information in respect of the matches in South Africa.

42. I realise now that the purpose of the payment was to "hook" me for the Indian tour... as set out below, on the Indian tour in February and March 2000. I was increasingly pushed to manipulate results, and found that I had got into something from which it was very difficult to get out.

THE INDIAN TOUR 2000

43. In India I was contacted by Sanjay who gave me a local SIM card so that he could call me for information and which would also be helpful for Internet connectivity and emails. This was not compatible with my mobile and could not be used. I later received a mobile sent up to my room, with which it was compatible.

44. I had initially no intention of involving other players and thought I could satisfy Sanjay by accurately forecasting outcomes. Sanjay was not satisfied with this, and pressured me to speak to some of the other players to manipulate results. In the build-up to the tests, the pressure on me increased. I received calls on a regular basis from Hamid and Sanjay. Even when the mobile was switched off, calls would come through to my room as late as 2am and 3am. I felt increasingly trapped. I had already taken money from Sanjay and it became increasingly difficult to resist his requests to speak to other team members and manipulate results.

45. During the Indian tour Marlon also phoned on a few occasions to encourage the team to win and to congratulate us on wins but, apart from general discussion, did not request information or offer me anything.

46. I spoke to Pieter Strydom before the first Test in India. His account of this discussion, contained in his written statement to the Commission, is correct. At the time of speaking to him I was already wracked with guilt, and his remarks about doing his best for South Africa shamed me and he in no way indicated that he was interested in receiving money. I did not speak to any other members of the team. Therafter I tried to pass off the whole incident with Strydom as a joke.

47. Under further pressure from Sanjay I subsequently made faint attempts to approach other players in respect of the second Test. I spoke to Kallis, Boucher and Klusener. The rebuffs were immediate, but I think they thought I was joking. I did not approach any other players in respect of the

Test matches and the results in the second and subsequent Tests were not manipulated.

48. I then told Sanjay that perhaps I could do something in the first One-Day International in India, thinking that if we could get the match out of the way that might satisfy them. My intention was not to involve other players, but merely to forecast which way the match was going to go, looking at the pitch and conditions. Sanjay was adamant, however, that this could not be done, so I suggested that I would speak to some of the other players, lying to him to get rid of him after the first match.

49. I ignored Sanjay and Hamid the night before the first One Day at Cochin but [then] I was phoned the next morning and urged to go ahead. I told them we would lose and that I had spoken to other players (which was untrue). We were supposed to lose the match but I couldn't go through with it: I decided that I couldn't not try and would give it my best shot. As it happened we got 301/3 and I got 19 off 20 balls, but India won quite comfortably after Hayward was injured. I honestly tried to win the match, even at that stage, and believe we would have done so if Hayward were not injured.

50. When I got back to the hotel Sanjay was upset because we got too many runs, and I blamed the Indian wicketkeeper for three chances that he missed, obviously not revealing that the South African players concerned had not been involved and in fact none of them knew anything about it. I did not receive any money for that match. I believe Sanjay lost money.

51. Hamid kept phoning me and saying that I should speak to Sanjay, who was now worse off than before, that he needed to win some money, and that I would have to deliver something. So intense had the incessant nagging become that I was pressured to fabricate a story that the players were angry with me for not getting their money. He said not to worry, he would make up for it during the rest of the One-Day series. However, no other players and none of the One-Day matches were involved, except for discussions with Gibbs and Williams in respect of the fifth One-Day International, which I will deal with in due course.

52. During the second, third and fourth One-Day games I was really only fore-casting what I thought would happen, as I wanted to win the series. I received no money and did my best throughout.

53. The pressure on me to produce information and results was increasing. I was not only being repeatedly phoned by Hamid but also by Sanjay. I tried to deal with this by lying about having spoken to players and [saying I'd] done things which I had not in fact done. I cannot recall all the names that I mentioned and I cannot remember all the figures and amounts.

54.   I cannot recall all the conversations, the times and the dates, and what was said on each occasion. Also, a great deal of what I told Sanjay was untruthful, particularly about the involvement of other players.

54.1.   Prior to the third One-Day International, I had untruthfully told Sanjay that Bojé, Strydom and Gibbs were involved. He therefore wanted to know if they would be playing in the third One-Day International and if further players could be involved. The first portion of Annexure BAW2 to Wilkinson-Luck's statement, if it is an accurate transcript, probably concerns this conversation.

54.2.   A discussion with Sanjay took place the night before the fifth One-Day International, during which we discussed Gibbs's score, a total of 270 runs, and Williams's bowling figures. If the results were as agreed, Sanjay was to pay US 140 000 dollars into my NatWest Bank account.

54.3.   Since playing for Leicestershire in 1995, I have had a bank account at NatWest Bank, Granby Street, Leicester. This was used for my foreign earnings.

55.   None of the results, including the fifth One-Day International at Nagpur on 19 March 2000, dealt with below, were fixed. No money changed hands in respect of any of the matches in India, all of which were a true result. That applies also to the fifth One-Day game, despite the earlier agreement to manipulate the result.

56.   By the end of the tour I was under severe pressure to provide some results, and my attempts to string Sanjay along were no longer effective. He and Hamid had become increasingly upset by the fact that I had not delivered the required results, in consequence of which they had been losing more and more and more money.

57.   The morning of the fifth One-Day match at Nagpur Sanjay phoned me and urged me to go ahead with fixing the match, and I gave in. I told him that I would go ahead. I was required to ensure that Gibbs would score less than 20 runs, that Williams would bowl poorly and go for more than 50 runs during his ten overs, and that the total score should be no more than 270 runs. I was to be paid for doing this. I spoke to Herschelle Gibbs and Henry Williams, as described by them in their testimony.

58.   The fifth One-Day International was not fixed or thrown. Although it appears strange in the light of what I have already said, once we went onto the field we were not able to carry out the plan. I know that Herschelle batted as well as he could: the offer quite clearly went out of his mind once he walked onto the field and, in fact, it was one of the best knocks I have seen. He scored 74 off 53 balls, and Henry Williams, until his injury, bowled well. At lunch I told Williams that we must win the game, and that we should

give our best. I tried my best, and scored 38 runs off 31 balls, before falling to a very good catch by Dravid. We not only scored more than 270 runs, but the total of 320 was South Africa's highest One-Day score against India.

59. While this does not detract from what I have done [to] the game, I do believe that once we set foot on the field, we [could] not go through with it and did our best – as indicated by Herschelle's unbelievable run-out to win us the game.

60. I have not spoken to Sanjay since the Indian tour and – apart from the money I received from him in Durban – received no payments from him or Hamid after the Indian tour.

61. After the 2000 Indian tour, whilst I was in Dubai for the Sharjah Cup in March of this year, I was again contacted by Hamid. He indicated that Sanjay wished to resume contact with me, along the same lines as in India. I had by now developed sufficient resolve to put it all behind me, and told him that I was not interested. I thereafter had no contact with Hamid after the incident described above until April 7, when I telephoned him and told him that news of what had happened in relation to the One-Day games in India had broken.

62. Sunil was around and about during the Sharjah Cup, asking for the odd bit of information and news on the team. He never paid me, or offered me any payment or benefit, nor did I receive anything from him. I gave him nothing out of the ordinary.

63. The night before the final of the Sharjah Cup I received a phone call from a man, who did not name himself, who wanted to speak to me in the team's room about "a promotion". He enquired whether Lance Klusener and I would promote some of his products and tried to set up a meeting for the next day. He also said he was willing to give us US 100 000 dollars now and US 100 000 dollars after the match, if we would play badly. I told him we were not interested. This was never conveyed to Klusener.

64. I apologise to the officials and members of the Department of Sport, including the Minister of Sport, for the embarrassment that my conduct has occasioned.

65. On the morning of 11 April I knew, and decided, that I could no longer live with myself or with the situation I had created. I wished to unburden myself. However, I had created problems for other people and players and it was not only a question of myself. I truly wished to protect those players whom I had compromised and found myself torn between conflicting emotions and responsibilities. I must however acknowledge that I was also activated by a measure of self-interest.

Hansie and Bertha loved having the family at Fancourt. Pictured here shortly after the King Commission in 2000.

Louise and Wouter Klopper at their home in Bloemfontein.

One last time. After the visit when these pictures were taken, Ewie and San-Marie never saw their son alive again.

Above and below: Pictures of the wreck taken the day after Hansie died.
Left: "We miss you, Hansie" – a bouquet left at the Cricket World Cup, Newlands Cricket Ground, January 2003.

The funeral at Grey College,
5 June 2002.
Below: Peter Pollock

Herschelle Gibbs, Gary Kirsten and Jonty Rhodes.
Frans and Ali Bacher.
Ewie and a friend of Hansie's, John Kolver.
Johan Volsteedt and Bertha.

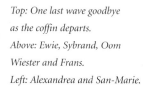

*Top: One last wave goodbye
as the coffin departs.
Above: Ewie, Sybrand, Oom
Wiester and Frans.
Left: Alexandrea and San-Marie.*

Below: People from all over put bouquets in the fence at 246 Paul Kruger Ave until the Bloemfontein florists ran out of flowers.
Right: West Indies captain, Carl Hooper, placing flowers at the wall of remembrance at Grey College in 2003.

Wessel Johannes Cronjé
Hansie

25 September 1969
1 Junie 2002

The Lord bless you and keep you,
the Lord make His face shine upon you
and be gracious to you;
the Lord turn His face towards you
and give you peace.
(NUMBERS 6:24-26)

TERMS OF REFERENCE A4.1

66.   As set out above and in the written statement by Pieter Strydom, I attempt-
       ed to place a R50 bet on South Africa winning the truncated fifth Test
       against England at Centurion Park. The only other bet that I have made in
       cricket was during the World Cup, when I placed one pound on South
       Africa to win at 4:1 odds.

GENERAL

67.   I hope that my experience will serve as a lesson to all other cricket players
       and administrators. My only consolation is the knowledge that despite
       my inexcusable behaviour, South Africa has in fact never thrown or fixed
       a match.

68.   I cannot exaggerate the level of temptation that is placed in front of a
       cricketer who is offered money for doing, or not doing, what can easily be
       accepted as furnishing information. Once money has been accepted, even
       for what appears to have been something innocuous, one is compromised
       and it becomes difficult to turn back.

69.   I think a serious effort should be made to educate and warn players –
       particularly before tours to the sub-continent – of the dangers posed by
       sports betting and gamblers. Most young professional cricket players have
       little experience of the hard realities of commerce and the gambling world.
       They are easy prey.

70.   As long as there is gambling on sports events – legal or otherwise – players
       will continue to be approached, pressured and tempted. I was wrong in suc-
       cumbing and worse, I encouraged others to be drawn in and to try to cover
       up. I do think it is important, however, that every effort should be made to
       prevent it from happening again. Team hotels, change rooms and practice
       areas should be monitored to ensure that gamblers and hangers-on are not
       afforded direct access to players. The players should be properly briefed and
       prepared about the risks and problems, so that they can deal with the
       inevitable approaches which they will receive and the cricketing authorities
       need to impose management procedures to try and address the problem.

15th June 2000. Signed by WJ Cronjé.

CHAPTER THIRTEEN

GOD'S ANVIL

The King Commission was a butchery. Hansie was
cut to the bone and the wounds were never closed up.
It was a bloody dissection of my son.

— San-Marie Cronje

Hey, Hansie! Life is Great!

— Herschelle Gibbs, shouting to Hansie during the

King Commission, as he drove past.

The Centre for the Book, the venue for the King Commission hearings, is a stately old building next to the first European garden in southern Africa. The Company Gardens, first planted and laid out near the Cape Town Castle by the Dutch East India Company in 1653, is a wide ribbon of trees, shrubs, lawns and flowers, many of them exotic plantings. A generous pedestrian pavement, a kilometre-long straight, is flanked by oak trees, and is alive with squirrels and, unfortunately, not a few rats, who seem to scuttle in and out of the nearby Houses of Parliament.

The immediate setting is one of Dutch and British colonial architectural and landscaping splendour, containing as it does Cape Town's High Courts, the South African Museum, the South African National Gallery, the South African Library, Government House, built in 1699, the South African Cultural Museum, which originally was a slave lodge, and St George's Anglican Cathedral, among many other notable buildings. The picture is one of gracious European achievement and glory – solid, orderly, pompous and pristine.

Other powerful colonial monuments abound, including two massive statues of arch-imperialist Cecil John Rhodes, one of which stands and points solemnly to the hinterland, dramatically declaring Rhodes's intention to pave a British highway from Cape to Cairo. A bulky, rock-like statue of Jan Christiaan Smuts, the Boer warrior, World War II Field Marshall and international statesman, who was a founding father of the League of Nations, enthroned magnificently on its pedestal.

194

Behind him, just a few hundred metres away, looms Hoerikwaggo (the Khoi name meaning "Mountain of the Sea"), commonly known as Table Mountain, South Africa's premier landmark. Seen for the first time on a clear day, the one-kilometre high, three-kilometres-long mountain is a soaring massif of grey sandstone that completely dominates the city, its presence felt, even when it is not actually in sight.

New Agers talk of its special magnetic powers, its spiritual dynamism, which they say make it one of the most exciting and magically charged places on earth. It has been likened to a fortress, a throne, God's Anvil. For some it suggests a sleeping goddess, or a towering Buddha. It is and was the Portal to Africa, Watcher of the South and Guardian of the City, and is described as the 'old Grey Father of Colonialism and the Silent Witness of Apartheid' in *Hoerikwaggo: Images of Table Mountain*, published by the South African National Gallery (author and curator Nicolaas Vergunst).

Hoerikwaggo stands, immovable, God's created sentinel, a compelling symbol of His infinite, irresistible and certain sovereignty over all human affairs. Over the Dutch, the British and the "new" South Africa, over Hansie, the King Commission, the bookies and their minions. Over the diverse peoples of Cape Town, who walk up and down the Gardens every day – the stream of Eastern Cape Xhosa migrants; refugees from the Democratic Republic of Congo, Nigeria, Angola, Zimbabwe, the Sudan and Ethiopia; the Dutch, French and British descendants; the "Cape Malays" descended from the slaves and political prisoners brought from places like Singapore, Malaysia, Sri Lanka, India and Madagascar; the "Cape Coloureds" of thoroughly mixed race; and the few ravaged and scattered descendants of the once-proud original inhabitants, the Hottentots, or Khoikhoi, whose numbers are now tragically few but whose aboriginal fire still glows in the hearts and bones of the large mulatto populations of the Cape of Storms.

The Centre for the Book auditorium, the best example of Edwardian architecture in Cape Town, with its Spartan domed interior, was a fitting venue for the "trial" of the golden son, placed as it was in a nexus of southern African history. The inquiry was, in the end, the ritual shaming of a flawed Afrikaner prince. It was supposed to be a general inquiry into cricketing irregularities. From the start, though, it was really all about Hansie. A complex sub-text and interplay added to the fascinating drama, and those who loved him were transfixed by a ceremonial evisceration.

Hansie's appearances at the King Commission at the Centre for the Book in Cape Town were misery itself for the Cronjé clan, a kind of sadistic, legalistic farce, watched live by millions. One can hardly imagine a more shameful and tragic end to a top international cricketing captain's career.

The day before the hearings started, Bob Woolmer's perspectives on Hansie and match-fixing were quoted in the media. In the *Cape Times* of 6 June 2000, Woolmer said:

"The danger always is that if you become successful and you are given a lot of leeway and rope, you start to feel as if you are untouchable, that you can do anything... My view is that he fooled around with the bookies. When I say that, I mean that he would tease them... Knowing Hansie as I do, I just reckon he dabbled too much and got caught. I would perceive that he got too much power and felt invulnerable... If you look at his career during the five years we had together, he gradually took more and more control and he was given terrific powers by the UCB, and particularly by Bacher... He had this devil-may-care attitude, but he was always going to have a troubled conscience because of his religious beliefs."

That neat summation of Hansie and the bookies probably rang true for many fans and critics who were privileged to observe him closely.

Kepler Wessels, writing in his column in the Johannesburg *Saturday Star* around this time, said, "It has been more and more evident to me over the past few years that there had crept into the national side an arrogance and defiance towards others which I found disturbing. Whenever I said so I was shouted down. Ray White (former President of the UCB) accused me of 'trying to split SA cricket down the middle' because I dared criticise a player's attitude. I saw these worry-ing trends developing some time ago. Ignoring them, glossing over them and playing 'happy families' as many in the media seemed glad to do, has helped con-tribute to this shambles."

Without Hansie's proper consent, Ray McCauley made some comments to the press when he was interviewed, thinking that he was helping Hansie, when in fact the comments made it harder for Hansie's legal team who suggested that until the Commission was over Hansie desist from having discussions that could lead to adverse publicity. This meant that he had no contact with Ray until the end of the King Commission. "This was really difficult for Hansie," said Frans.

Before the King Commission started Hansie was in the midst of writing essays and studying for his Unisa MBL qualification. Exams started on 15 May and ended on the 28th, adding enormously to his stress load.

The King Commission proceedings got underway on 7 June.

San-Marie watched fearfully as her stricken son grappled with his studies at the family home in Bloemfontein. He would rise at 2am in the morning to get some hard work and studying in before breakfast. A week or so before the Commission started, she went to talk to him in the study where he'd been working. "Hansie was completely drained. He had collapsed and had slumped down in a chair and seemed unconscious. His face was grey. I said to him, 'Son, are you all right?' He couldn't answer. He couldn't get any words out of his mouth. I had never seen anyone in a depression like that before."

She said to him, "Hans, I don't think you must write that exam tomorrow."

Bertha and San-Marie later conferred and Bertha had said, "Mom, let him go and write. If he passes one subject that will boost him, lift his spirit."

In the end, Hansie passed all his subjects, to the complete amazement of his family. Arguably, that was one of the hardest fought battles of his life, easily rivalling any of his great Test cricket victories.

●

Still in a haze of depression, which lifted just a little now and again, Hansie was taken by Les Sackstein to meet Senior Counsel Malcolm Wallis in Durban.

By some accounts, he was grilled to the point of breakdown. This was absolutely traumatic for him. These sessions were repeated several times in Cape Town. Raymond and Ewie were sitting outside Dickerson's office during one such session when Dickerson emerged and said to the two men, "Please, come and comfort Hansie." They found Hansie lying on his back, crying like a baby.

Raymond van Staden had been asked to continue in his role as security consultant and was, as usual, there to comfort as well.

Hansie requested that everyone leave the office the day before he testified and asked to speak to Raymond alone. He was very distressed and told Raymond he was very scared and he wanted to know what he should do. Raymond said to him, "Partner, remember what I told you in the beginning: there are two people you trust and you tell everything to – the Big Boss Upstairs and your lawyer. If you have not yet told them everything, now is the time to do so. It is your choice; whatever your decision is I will stand by you no matter what."

Raymond recalled, "Hansie then opened up to the legal team. I never realised what my words meant to him until the 29th of August 2000, when he wrote on a photograph of him and me entering the Commission for the first time: *Dear Partner "I will stand by you no matter what!" Those words will always be close to me – just like you! Thank You.*

●

As always, Hansie had good and powerful friends looking after his interests. Raymond and his wife Carol stayed with Hansie and Bertha throughout the entire King Commission and their help was immense. Secret and secure accommodation was essential to counter any possible attempts on Hansie's life. Tich Smith, a friend of Hansie's, had a mate, businessman Terry Rosenberg, who owned a luxury beachfront holiday apartment in Clifton, which was secure and private. The media and other unwelcome guests could not gain entry, or indeed any view of the apartment from the land, or, it was hoped, even notice a vehicle containing Hansie deftly ducking into the almost invisible garaged area beyond the secured entrance. Hansie and Bertha, with their now entrenched "bodyguards" and friends, Raymond and Carol, would stay there during the King Commission and its associated travails.

The media never found out where Hansie's hideaway was.

Clifton is arguably South Africa's most expensive real estate, sheltered from the south-easter, perched on cliffs overlooking the Atlantic Ocean, its beautiful white beaches, and curious, large rounded boulders are often littered on warm days with sun-baking bodies. The sea is brutally cold, and hardly anyone ventures into the water.

From the hideaway, the tranquil sea view and the bustle on the beach helped to soothe Hansie's dark emotions and deep depressions.

During the King Commission, a local security expert, Vaughn Brazier, assisted Raymond van Staden with Hansie's physical security and movements around Cape Town.

Part of Raymond van Staden's task was to assist Hansie's legal team, which included attorneys Les Sackstein, Clem Drucker and advocates Malcolm Wallis and John Dickerson, and flesh out profiles on the likes of South African bookies "Banjo the Biltong Man" Hamid Cassim and the wily Marlon Aronstam. "Hansie, in some cases didn't have phone numbers, and just had first names. That's all I had to go on. He obviously didn't know them well at all," Raymond said.

Bertha stuck by her man and watched in dismay as Hansie battled with his relentless trauma, before and after his court appearances. "At the apartment, I often had to change our sheets in the middle of the night, because he was sweating so much. His sweat soaked right through to the mattress. I've never seen anything like it. Hansie also hardly ever spoke. I put Bible verses and Christian sayings on the mirror in the bathroom, like: 'God is in control'. He ate very little; usually he just had a coffee and a chocolate, if anything."

Bertha asked Hansie if he wanted her to attend the hearings. Hansie said, "No." She was greatly relieved. The family decided that just Frans and Ewie would attend the King Commission hearings. Ewie sat there on his own through all the hearings. Frans stayed with Hansie during the day, which meant that he only attended the King Commission when Hansie had to be there.

Raymond's services to Hansie during the King Commission, bar the first day of his duties, were given freely. "Hansie was like a brother to me. I couldn't charge him. He was my friend," he said. The security expert, adept as he was at surveillance and intelligence gathering, soon had a batch of information on Aronstam and Cassim, even on Bacher, the investigator Jeff Edwards and chief investigator Shamila Batohi.

Hansie also had Raymond checking telephone lines and premises for bugging devices, one of Raymond's fortes. None was detected.

"He was like a yo-yo. Down one minute, then jokes. We sat in lawyers' offices hour after hour, day after day. All of a sudden Hansie would get up and start tidying the table, energetically throwing stuff in dustbins. He wouldn't eat. It worried us," said Raymond.

In the evenings, Bertha, Carol, Hansie and Raymond would sit together and Raymond spent a lot of time coaching Hansie, preparing him mentally for the King Commission hearings, trying to keep him calm.

●

Much was made of "death threats" against Hansie during this time, but in the course of research for the book I was told of only one, the circumstances of which make a somewhat humorous story.

Calls on Hansie's mobile were not taken, but voice mails were monitored. On 11 June a death threat came through during the King Commission.

From the accent, Raymond concluded that the caller was a young Durban Indian male. With the co-operation of the mobile network provider (via "Advanced Caller Line Identification" on the phone, which picks up the number of the caller, even if they have blocked it), Raymond traced the mobile phone number of the caller, and with a little investigation, the name of the caller and his address. He then phoned a reporter on the Durban *Sunday Tribune* and gave him some details of the "death threat", which were duly published. In the article Raymond had hinted at dire consequences for the caller, who was known to him.

Raymond decided to have "some fun" with the caller and dialled the number. When the call was picked up, Raymond said: "It's nice to make threats. Hey? When you think people don't know where it's coming from?"

"Who's this? Who's this talking?" came the shocked response.

"It's nice. Nice to play games with people when you think you're anonymous?"

"Who's this? Who's this? You're scaring me."

Raymond: "My friend, I'm your worst nightmare. I'm coming for you."

"What are you talking about?"

Raymond: "You stay in Parlock."

"How do you know this?"

Raymond then read out his name and his ID number to him.

Raymond: "I know everything about you my friend."

"Oh, but you're scaring me."

Raymond: "Do yourself a favour. Look at the *Sunday Tribune*. Go and get yourself a paper and you'll see what I'm talking about. And I'm phoning you back." Raymond then hung up, and phoned the little weasel an hour later.

Raymond: "It's me again."

"Who are you? Who are you?" (The young fool then started crying.)

Raymond: "My friend, I'm coming for you. You've got problems, hey. Ja."

Raymond concluded his story by saying, "Hansie was considered fair game, and I wasn't prepared to let Hansie be just fair game. It was just a prank by some stupid youngsters, yes, but they needed to be taught a lesson. It was also a lesson to others and the lesson was: 'Don't think you can hide your number and get away with it.'"

The "death threat" they sent was: "Hansie you fucker. You are a fucking dead man, you bastard. South African fucking traitor."

Raymond's investigations had revealed that Hansie's mobile, which had been damaged after being dropped weeks before, was handed to a Nokia Customer Care Centre in Durban. While a technician was repairing the phone, he copied Hansie's contacts list and made a note of Hansie's number.

Raymond later visited the men involved in the seedy affair, and this time confronted the caller in person, who grovelled in shame, apologising profusely to Hansie, saying he had "learnt a lesson" and would never do such a shameful thing again. His apology was taped and given to Hansie.

At least that raised a little smile on Hansie's face.

●

San-Marie and Hester stayed with Frans and René during the King Commission. San-Marie couldn't bear to watch Hansie being interrogated on television. She sat in the car outside the house, and listened to it on the radio. Bertha did watch the parts of the King Commission that were televised, but often she'd switch off the set. It was just too painful for her to see Hansie suffer. "I had lots of quiet times with the Lord and I kept myself busy, cooking lunch for the four of us. I used to eat digestive biscuits with cream cheese and fresh chillies (a combination I discovered through Carol) – and the more it burnt me the better I felt.

"I spent a lot of time talking to the Lord, writing about my feelings and emotions in a diary. God answered my prayers in many ways for Hansie and our marriage."

"Did you," I asked, "feel that now he had told you everything?"

"I never asked him if he had at that time. He had too much to deal with. I waited for him to tell me."

Carol had warned Bertha about the fact that Hansie had approached players to influence games. Hansie had not shared this with her up to that point. "He tried to protect you," said Frans.

●

Judge Edwin King, retired Judge President of the Western Cape, was appointed by President Thabo Mbeki to handle a general inquiry into match-fixing and other irregularities in South African cricket, and the Commission's initial terms of reference were confined to the period between 1 November 1999 and 17 April 2000, the period covered by Hansie's initial hand-written confession. But the terms of reference broadened because of new revelations outside the time frame as the "inquiry" proceeded.

On Wednesday, 7 June 2000, the King Commission began. About 40 people had been subpoenaed to give evidence. Every official involved in the 1996 tour to India and in international matches between 1 November 1999 and 17 April 2000 had been summonsed. The only ones spared were Bob Woolmer and Allan Donald, who were living in England.

From the beginning, the state tried to get hold of the alleged tapes from the Indian police and seemed confident in doing so. They were doomed to fail, however, and grew increasingly frustrated as this vital evidence seemed to be withheld by the Indian police. Or were the tapes in fact non-existent?

On the Wednesday, Judge King was on the bench and leading the investigation was Advocate Shamila Batohi, who had previously prosecuted some high-profile investigations into hit-squad activities in KwaZulu-Natal. Young and beautiful, she became a media darling of sorts at first, although not to many in the Cronjé camp.

The King Commission opened proceedings with a legal argument to overthrow Judge King's decision to bar television cameras and recording equipment. There were separate legal teams for Hansie, Derek Crookes and Daryll Cullinan, the rest of the players, the UCB (represented by widely respected and feared Advocate Jeremy Gauntlett) and the state.

Initially, only live radio broadcasts were allowed.

Neil Andrews, a gambling expert, gave evidence on the nature of sports betting and Advocate John Dickerson, representing Hansie, asked, "And would you agree that there is a significant difference between forecasting and betting?"

"Indeed, significant," replied Andrews.

"And would you agree that that although betting always involves forecasting, forecasting does not necessarily lead to betting?" Again, Andrews agreed.

Judge King then asked his own question, "I'm trying to work out why a book-maker would pay for information that he could get for nothing."

Andrews then gave a long reply on the values of early, inside information and how inexact the craft of forecasting was. Earlier, one of the UCB's legal represen-tatives had established via Andrews that spread betting was largely limited in South Africa to three aspects: how many runs a player would make; how many runs a team would make in the first 15 overs; and how many runs in the entire innings. On the Indian sub-continent "everything" from who would open the bowling to who would bowl at first change would be up for a bet. In effect, almost any aspect of the game could be bet on in Pakistan, India and Sri Lanka.

On Friday, 9 June, the second day of the Commission, Pat Symcox, Herschelle Gibbs, Derek Crookes and Daryll Cullinan gave evidence. Gibbs came clean on Hansie's bribery attempts, and admitted he had lied eight times "to protect Hansie Cronjé and because I was scared of the consequences".

Gibbs told the hearing that Hansie had repeatedly told him to lie about the fact that he had accepted an offer of 15 000 US dollars to score less than 20 in the One-Day International at Nagpur in India. In the event, Gibbs had scored 74. Consequently, Gibbs was never paid.

"LIES, LIES, LIES AND MORE LIES" was one of the headlines in a South African newspaper. The *Cape Times* reported on its front page: "... Gauntlett, as head of the UCB's legal team, is clearly under instructions to cut to the bone to get to the truth. The way he examined Symcox and Cullinan must have struck the fear of God into all the players ..."

Daryll Cullinan had given evidence that Hansie's actions had been "a stroke of genius". "It was his way of testing the team... We left the meeting a better side, clear in our minds there was no way we would entertain those ideas."

However, Cullinan was tied into some knots by Gauntlett: "Mr Symcox testi-fied that he was approached by Mr Cronjé about an offer to throw a game in 1995... Do you think this was a private moral test being laid for Mr Symcox?" There was no answer from Cullinan.

On Friday, 9 June, Hansie's faxed confession dated, 1am, 11 April, was handed to the King Commission by the investigators. It was a photocopy of the handwritten statement, missing one page, for some unknown reason. This evidence had been leaked to the media and was published the same morning.

On Monday, 12 June, Dr Ali Bacher took the stand and spoke of "death threats" that both he and Hansie had received. He said, "There is an urgent need for the ICC to deal promptly and effectively with [corruption] if the game is to survive." Dr Bacher alleged that the cricket Mafia had been linked to the death of a Pakistani bookie who was shot 67 times in Johannesburg in May 1999. The bookie had been an associate of former Pakistan captain Salim Malik.

Other allegations were that Malik, who had been banned from the game for life for match-fixing, received two-million US dollars through match-fixing; that at least two 1999 World Cup matches had been fixed; that Pakistani umpire Javed Akhtar was paid to influence the result of the Test between England and South Africa at Leeds in 1998; that the Australian authorities were aware of match-fixing in their midst; that match-fixing is "simple" and costs about one-million US dollars, and that arrangements were made through team captains.

Dr Bacher focused on providing the context to match-fixing and associated irregularities globally. He refrained from lashing out at his former captain, not interested in joining in the flogging.

Bacher was backed into a corner when he denied that he knew about the 1996 incident, where the team was offered $200 000 to lose the match. Bob Woolmer had made it very clear that he had included the incident in his report, but that nothing was ever done about it. In an interview in 2005 Woolmer also added, "The fact that Colin Bryden from the *Sunday Times* wrote about the approach in the paper in 1997 and that Ali sent me a copy of that newspaper is proof enough that he knew of the approach. (He read every newspaper every day – he was a great publicist.)"

On 12 June, the UCB's Jeremy Gauntlett asked Dr Bacher one final question: "... is there, for you, any final lesson which emerges from all this?"

Dr Bacher replied: "I would sum up my feelings as follows: that if the bookmakers can get to Hansie Cronjé, they can get to anyone in world cricket."

Rodney Hartman, in his book *Ali: The Life of Ali Bacher*, noted, "According to Gauntlett, there were various aspects of Bacher's testimony that might have exposed him to attack by Cronjé's legal team, but nothing of the sort was forthcoming. In fact, he was asked only five questions in the cross examination by Senior Counsel John Dickerson. Included in his answers was his confirmation that he had received threats of physical violence... he believed the match-fixing menace went to the heart of the criminal underworld. Bacher also acknowledged under cross-examination that he had never felt that the South African team under Cronjé's leadership was not trying its best to win.

Sackstein explained, "A problem that Hansie's legal team had at this stage was that Malcolm Wallis, as lead counsel, was in the UK and everybody wanted him to lead the cross-examination of Bacher. Certain other aspects had come to light that made Wallis's cross-examination of Bacher all the more attractive.

"Firstly, it was thought that it would be best for Bacher to be examined after Hansie had given his evidence. Secondly, several people had phoned the lawyers at different times – some of them anonymous – giving information in relation to Bacher and the UCB, which had to be carefully checked before these facts could be put to a witness in cross-examination. It was therefore decided not to examine Bacher at this stage, but to reserve the right to recall him at a later stage. Everybody involved knew that this was the tactic which the lawyers had decided upon."

Many of Ali's allegations were subsequently furiously denied and some of those named threatened legal action. Akhtar said in the media that Bacher's claims about him were "a load of rubbish" and he said he intended taking legal action.

Former Pakistani captain Imran Khan, on 20 June, lashed out at Bacher. He said that Bacher should be expelled from the ICC and sued for "millions of dollars" for making allegations based on "hearsay". "Bacher is a two-faced man and I have no faith in his credibility. Bacher is vindictive towards India and Pakistan," Khan said, rejecting Bacher's allegations of match-fixing during India's win over Pakistan in the 1999 World Cup.

Charles van Staden, a South African Reserve Bank official, told the hearing that the bank had been given two separate amounts in foreign currency by Hansie's legal team: 10 000 US dollars and another amount of 37 000 US dollars. "I requested information for the money but have not yet received [it]," Van Staden told the Commission.

On the same day, a nervous Lance Klusener told the Commission he had been approached by Hansie, as had Mark Boucher and Jacques Kallis (both of whom corroborated his statement), before the second Test in India in 2000. He said he had turned the offer down.

On Tuesday, 13 June, Dave Richardson gave evidence about his role in the 1996 incident in India when a financial offer was made to the team to throw a match. "At the time it did not seem a big issue for the team. It was a novelty; it was a big deal in the sense that we too had now been made an offer. With hindsight I agree that it should have been brought to the management's attention." (There followed a dispute about whether Woolmer had included mention of the players' meeting about the match-fixing offer in his report to Bacher at the time.)

Richardson called for the appointment of a father figure in the mould of a Morné du Plessis (a former Springbok rugby captain who was involved as the rugby team's manager for many years), to protect the integrity of the UCB and its players.

On Wednesday, 14 June, Hansie agreed to his testimony being broadcast live on radio and television. "There is no precedent for the kind of pressure he is under and it is potentially dangerous for his health for this to continue. [But] he wants to get on with it," said Hansie's lawyer Clem Drucker. (Live Africa Network News had launched an urgent application to allow radio broadcasts of the hearings after Judge King had ruled that live broadcasts would be "an inhibiting factor" for witnesses.)

On Thursday, 15 June, Hansie appeared before the Commission for the first time. After he read out his statement, the hearing was postponed to Tuesday, 20 June. It was noted in the media that Hansie could be prosecuted under the Corruption Act if Judge King refused him indemnity on the grounds that he withheld information, or lied.

Before Hansie read his statement, Judge King said to him, "Mr Cronjé, I know you are under strain. I want you to know you have my understanding of your situation. I want you to be frank and honest with me. Before I swear you in I would like to refer you to Chapter 8, St John's Gospel: 'The truth will set you free.'"

Hansie's reading of his statement was later broadcast to a global audience.

Some time after Hansie had testified, Sackstein entered a lift on his way to Dickerson's office. While he waited for the lift doors to close, Herschelle Gibbs suddenly breezed into the lift – he was visiting someone else in the building. They greeted each other and Gibbs asked, "How's Hansie?"

Sackstein replied, "He's in chambers right now. Would you like to talk to him?"

Gibbs said he most certainly would.

Hansie and Gibbs shook hands and embraced enthusiastically. Hansie said, "I'm sorry man."

Herschelle replied, brightly, "I got myself into it anyway. Who gives a f—k? Shit happens."

After the short reconnection between the two comrades, Herschelle left Hansie to his legal tangles in chambers. Later, Hansie and Frans came out of the building together. They heard a shattering bass coming from a monster sound system and gazed in the direction of the hip-hop blasts. They were coming from Herschelle's fancy cabriolet, which was moving towards them. As he came around the corner, Herschelle slowed down and screamed above the noise, punching the air: "Hansie! Life is Great!"

"Hansie," said Frans, "was greatly refreshed by this. Hansie was really fond of Herschelle and they remained good friends way beyond the King Commission."

One of the few moments of respite during the mad roller-coaster of the hearings was organised by Johan Fourie, an Old Grey who happened to be the head ranger of the West Coast National Park.

Hansie had a grand day, although he said little. At one point, as he, Bertha and

Johan had sat on a white beach enjoying the pristine coastal renosterveld, Hansie had suddenly stripped down to his underpants and had run into the sea, screaming and laughing as he enjoyed (and endured) the frigid winter Atlantic.

●

John Dickerson and Malcolm Wallis submitted to Judge King that Hansie was taking strain and needed to rest for a day or two. They tried to convince King that Hansie was not in a fit state of mental health for such prolonged trauma, and produced a psychiatrist's report to this effect. The psychiatrist, Ian Lewis, said that Hansie was suffering from "severe depression" and would be unable to focus his mind and answer questions adequately.

Judge King was unimpressed and refused this request.

Raymond told of a humorous incident: "On the day of Hansie's assessment, Hansie was spirited into Dr Lewis's consulting rooms at a Cape Town Shopping Centre by me and Vaughn Brazier. Our arrival went smoothly; the exit was another story. While sneaking Hansie out of a rear entrance at the centre, we inadvertently triggered an alarm on the back door. With the siren blaring, we all just burst out laughing and ran to our vehicle. A group of vagrants were sitting close by and one said, "*Wie is dit daai* – Cronjé?" (Who's that, Cronjé?) To which his mate replied, "*Ny man*, but it must be someone important."

On Monday, 19 June, the issue of live television and radio coverage of Hansie's cross-examination had still not been sorted out. The Live Africa Network News (Lann) court application was heard by a full bench.

The finding of Judge President Hlope of the Cape High Court was that the ban on radio coverage was unconstitutional. The issue of television broadcasting was left to the discretion of Judge King.

So Hansie's cross-examination, which began on 21 June and continued for three days in total, was broadcast to the world. His cross-examination days were staggered, and the stop-starts played havoc with the lives of the Cronjés. Investigators delayed proceedings at times for days, grappling with the fact that they still didn't have the tapes.

A report in the *Cape Times* was fairly typical of the print media's coverage of the proceedings. Under Thursday, 22 June's page 1 headline, "Hansie tells of love for money", reporter Judith Soal introduced the lead story after the first day of Hansie's cross-examination as follows:

"Former South African captain Hansie Cronjé is by his own admission a money-grabbing miser whose love for money overcame his passion for cricket and his country. The once-proud young sportsman, who earned about R1,5 million a year until recently, told the King Commission how he regularly skimped on expenses, free-loaded on the generosity of his fans and was prepared to do almost anything – even illegal [sic] – for cash."

"I never knew you were this big. I thought you were just 'Hansie,'" was one comment from a fan on a radio broadcast at the time.

"In the eyes of the media," said Frans, "Hansie's sins were doubled simply because he said he was a Christian. His declared Christianity seemed to send them into a frenzy."

●

During cross-examination by Marlon Aronstam's counsel, Itzie Blumberg, who had pushed Hansie hard about his alleged match-fixing, Hansie said, "I'll tell you straight about ... the unfortunate love I have for money. I do like money, but I promise you that every time I walked onto the field I gave my all for my country." When he said this, Hansie was suddenly very emotional.

During this period of the Commission Hansie admitted that he would "probably" have not told the truth about offering money to team-mates Herschelle Gibbs and Henry Williams if Gibbs himself had not come clean.

By now, Hansie sometimes spoke in a dull monotone, appearing drugged to some, an assertion that has always been denied by the Cronjé clan, although after the King Commission hearings, Hansie did take anti-depressants. Reported the *Cape Times*: "the crowd squirmed" as Hansie "repeatedly misunderstood simple questions".

On Thursday, 22 June, the second day of Hansie's cross-examination, Batohi launched into the fray. Her interminable duels with Hansie formed much of the drama of the King Commission. At stake on this day in the proceedings was the veracity of the "transcripts" of the conversation Hansie allegedly had with Sanjay Chawla.

Judge King intervened regularly during the proceedings in an apparent attempt to make sense of exactly what Hansie was saying. Hansie appeared to be unable to explain why he had been in constant contact with "Sunil", "Sanjay" and "Sundeep". He didn't seem to know why he had accepted an offer one day and refused a similar one three days later, and why bookmakers should suddenly agree to leave him alone. "I know it seems strange when you look back, but I have no explanation," Hansie said.

Referring to Marlon Aronstam, Batohi said to Hansie, "You told him that you were prepared to throw a match between South Africa and England?"

Hansie replied, "If the conversation went in that direction, I suggested I would be prepared to, if South Africa had already qualified for the final."

"No," countered Batohi. "He [Aronstam] will say you referred to the first match."

"That's incorrect," answered Hansie.

As his self-confidence grew and his occasional humorous and sarcastic asides increased, Batohi especially grew increasingly vexed.

During the proceedings it was apparent, too, that Batohi was deeply troubled by the non-appearance of the tapes, which in their "transcripted" form were disjointed, and seemed patched together. The disjointedness was obvious to anyone paying close attention to the proceedings. They, whatever "they" were, weren't much use to her at all.

During his son's appearances, Ewie often sat slumped in his seat, head down, eyes on the floor, shattered by the spectacle, by what he was hearing from, and about, his beloved son. However painful it was, Ewie felt obliged to stand by his boy. For some, the essence of the tragedy unfolding was the sight of Hansie's noble and widely respected father, crumpling slowly, as the ritual "butchery" dragged on, and on.

●

According to the Cronjé family, Hansie said after the three days of his cross-examination, "If I wasn't so emotionally drained I could've answered the questions a lot better."

The repetitive nature of Batohi's questioning of Hansie frustrated him severely. He countered it by the odd absurd joke, or angry and bitter remark.

Shamila: Do you recall the conversation recorded on this transcript?

Hansie: I had many conversations with Sanjay, this could well be one of those.

Shamila: What does Sanjay mean when he asks whether Strydom and Gibbs are "playing"?

Hansie: "Playing" means whether they are participating in the match.

Shamila: So why do you say you can't get anyone else to "play"? Doesn't "playing" refer to participating in match-fixing?

Hansie: No. I agree it sounds strange. It sounds kinky to me to have Gibbs and myself playing with each other. (Hansie laughs.)

Shamila: But you said this conversation could've taken place?

Hansie: Yes. I had many conversations with Sanjay.

Shamila: So what does it mean?

At this point, Malcolm Wallis said, "I really must object to this line of questioning."

"Hansie made it a lot worse for himself with his jokes and snide remarks. If he had explained himself in Afrikaans it would've come out better," said Ewie.

On one occasion, Judge King told Hansie, "I'm not threatening you. But please answer the questions as they are asked."

When King asked Hansie about a conversation he had with Bacher, he replied, "I don't ask you personal questions as to what you talk about at lunch-time."

Hansie's legal team were unhappy with him at times and Sackstein told him, "Stop trying to get clever."

During one of Batohi's questions, which related to whether Hansie had said anything to Bertha about the money he received, Hansie had replied, "No. She would've cut my testicles off."

After Batohi had questioned "Banjo the Biltong Man", who made a pathetic witness, but perversely managed not to incriminate himself much, The *Cape Times* of 27 June, reported, "Batohi, who has received widespread criticism for her muddled approach in cross-examining Cronjé, took her gloves off when it came to Cassim. Once she'd finished, there was little doubt that the sweet shop owner had been less than forthcoming…Cassim spent the day trying, with little success, to convince the Commission that his role in the relationship between Cronjé and the paymaster Sanjay Chawla was one of matchmaker, not conspiring match-fixer. He claimed that he had introduced the two, at Chawla's request, but was 'to this day' not sure what transpired between them."

"I was amazed at the lack of resources made available to Batohi," said journalist Neil Manthorp. "She was clearly ambitious but knew little about cricket and had just two assistants. Compared to the resources available to, and hired by the UCB and Hansie, she was clearly going to come third. Then, a senior legal figure at the Cape Bar told me that that was exactly what was supposed to happen. Commissions of Inquiry, he said, were supposed to 'put awkward issues to bed, not dig them up'."

Referring to the contention that he had aided and abetted Batohi in her work at the Commission, Manthorp said, "She interviewed me before the Inquiry began but, once it had started, she asked me no more than two or three questions – technical issues relating to the dates of matches, bowling changes and batting orders – that sort of thing. Otherwise our contact was limited to one-liners, such as when she repeated my assertion on E-TV that her questioning of Hansie had been like 'being savaged by a sheep'. She neither 'leaked' any information to me, nor provided me with 'a story'."

●

Towards the end of Hansie's cross-examination, his exhaustion and sense of relief at the sight of the finish line unleashed tears. "We Cronjés are very emotional beings," said Frans. "Hansie got up and walked out, followed by his legal team, Raymond, my dad and me. As we got to an empty room out of sight of the public, Hansie just fell on the floor and lay on his back crying."

THE HANSIE CRONJÉ STORY

"We all cried then. I think even the legal team had tears in their eyes," said Raymond.

All in all, Hansie endured three days of questioning. After his final grilling, Ewie approached the media and said, "Please give my child the time and space to construct a new life for himself. The past 12 weeks have been a very tough time for the Cronjé family and hopefully we will emerge from it stronger people... The fact that Bertha, my wife and my daughter have not been at the Commission during Hansie's evidence should not be seen as significant. They have all supported Hansie away from the public, but being at the hearings might have been too much for them. Both myself and Frans have been present throughout Hansie's evidence. We have seen Hansie admit that he has done wrong and that he must be punished for it. He has also made an apology without reservation to everyone and I hope that the country and the game will accept it."

At the same time, Hansie made the following statement: "... I am bitterly sorry about what I have done and the pain that I have caused. It is not my intention to seek to excuse myself for what I have done. There is no excuse and I have let the UCB, the team, the fans, and the game down and this will be the bitter truth that I will have to live with for the rest of my life. I draw some consolation from the fact that I know that I have never fixed a match. Every single game that I played in was a genuine contest and what the records show correctly reflects a 100% effort by the South African side."

Hansie's own admissions – principally via his handwritten confession faxed to various people on Tuesday, 11 April, and the statement he read during the King Commission – formed the basis of all the hard evidence that the King Commission had. Hansie's evasiveness prior to the Commission seemed to relate principally to his desire to protect team-mates and to his consistent contention that he never threw a game.

Sackstein said in 2005, "One must pause to say that Hansie and his legal team were at all times very doubtful about the evidence which Batohi said would be forthcoming, particularly the tapes from India. Batohi went to India in September and when she came back stated that her trip, which was a further burden on the taxpayers, had been successful. Tapes or transcripts would be available.

"By now acrimonious correspondence had passed between Judge King and me and I had made it clear that I was utterly dissatisfied with the manner in which Batohi, in particular, had spoken to the press and that King had described her as a prosecutor."

The legal team began to believe that the Commission of Inquiry into match-fixing and other irregularities in SA cricket was degenerating into a witch-hunt against Hansie and this was carefully documented in long and detailed correspondence.

Once Batohi had returned from India, Hansie's legal team demanded delivery of the tapes. When these were not forthcoming, the lawyers concluded that there simply were no tapes. Wallis and Sackstein decided to adopt an aggressive approach and to take whatever steps they deemed necessary to bring the Commission to a conclusion.

A recent judgment in the matter of the South African Association of Personal Injury Lawyers vs Heath and others, assisted Hansie's team. The Constitutional Court held that somebody in the position of a judge, such as King was, is "constitutionally incompatible with leading an investigatory unit and that it is inappropriate for a judge to become involved as part of the criminal investigative process or even to become closely engaged in work which is an adjunct to the investigatory and prosecutorial functions. A letter to this effect was delivered to King dated 14 December 2000," said Sackstein. "King disputed the correctness of Wallis's interpretation of that judgment but in the end, closed the Commission by issuing a very interesting press statement on the 22 February 2001. He said that he had taken the decision because it had been precipitated by the threat to challenge the constitutional validity of his appointment. Hansie was thus spared the further stress of waiting to see what would happen in so far as further hearings of the Commission were concerned – so too, of course, were a lot of other witnesses who would otherwise have had to be called."

●

Raymond van Staden had some noteworthy comments to make about the King Commission, which deserve reflection.

"President Thabo Mbeki set up the King Commission to investigate irregularities in the UCB and cricket in South Africa as a whole, and not only to investigate Hansie Cronjé. Before the start of the hearings, Judge King referred to Hansie Cronjé as 'the defendant' to all the legal representatives of concerned parties at the Commission. This was supposed to be a commission, and not a criminal trial. It created the wrong impression from the beginning.

"On Friday, 30 June 2000, at 6.55am on SAfm (the state broadcaster's premier English-language radio station), in an interview with John Perlman, Judge King made the following comment: 'The investigating team has worked very hard, as have the prosecutors, but it's a continuous operation.' The Commission made no concerted effort to rectify the perception that it was a commission to investigate Hansie. It was supposed to be an inquiry into cricketing irregularities. The perception was created that Batohi and her assistant Vincent Botto were 'prosecutors' and Hansie was 'the defendant' or 'the accused'."

Les Sackstein observed at the time: "We find it strange that [King] uses words like 'prosecutor' whilst he is referring to a Commission of Inquiry. I decided to take King on and an exchange of acrimonious correspondence followed. All sorts of irritating incidents occurred: Batohi gave an interview to one Paul Martin, which was published in the London *Sunday Times* on 3 June 2001. She said that she had been misquoted and had no problem in publicly repudiating the incorrect and untruthful portions of that report. This was symptomatic of the problems that Hansie and his legal team faced in dealing with the Commission. During December, contrary to specific arrangements made, the commissioner decided to re-commence hearings of the Commission that month, which was the only month of the year when Sackstein and Wallis were unavailable. Efforts to persuade Judge King to postpone the matter until February when they were all available were fruitless and this led to Hansie having to bring an urgent but costly application to the High Court in the Cape, to have the postponement ordered by the court.

"Judge King entered the lists as a litigant and was resoundingly defeated in the judgment delivered by the Honourable Mr Justice Jali, who ordered costs to be paid by the State. Again, a huge amount of tax payers' money literally went down the drain as a result of a completely unnecessary court application precipitated by the determination of the commissioner and the investigators to bring the matter on in December when everybody was available in February, and in view of the previous delays, nobody could have been prejudiced by the delay."

During the King Commission, Scotland Yard officers, Detective Superintendent Steven Gwilliam and Detective Sergeant Martin Hawkins, were present.

An approach was made to Raymond for the detectives to meet with Hansie. A discreet meeting was arranged and took place with Sackstein and Raymond present. The detectives were grateful for the meeting. Contact was maintained with Raymond as the go-between; Detective Constable Bruce Horbury was nominated to liaise with Raymond.

On one occasion at New Scotland Yard in London, Detective Superintendent Gwilliam told Raymond that the British approach to the investigation was different from that of the South Africans. They viewed the cricketers as witnesses, not suspects.

For months afterwards, there was always a chance that the King Commission would reconvene. Batohi eventually told King that there was no new evidence. In the end, he said he was still not sure whether Hansie had told the truth or not, and therefore he could not reach a finding. After everything, after all that trauma, there was a non-finding.

"King never said Hansie lied. But he never said Hansie spoke the whole truth either. King was meant to give a final declaration of some kind, and Hansie was kept waiting for that. It never came," said Sackstein.

Despite the lack of resolution, the UCB decided to ban Hansie for life. King's preliminary report came out in August 2000.

Sackstein commented, "The preliminary findings that the Commission made were regarded by many as fatuous. The commissioner decided that telephonic access for players should be strictly controlled and their phone calls and e-mails should be monitored. He recommended that there be an obligation on players to – as the commissioner described it – split or whistle-blow on their friends and colleagues and it should be made clear to them that this was not disreputable conduct.

"He also thought that under-cover agents should approach players in the guise of bookmakers with bogus suggestions of match-fixing. He suggested that players should contractually authorise the undergoing of the lie-detector tests, which should be undertaken at random.

"This, and suggestions that bank accounts, not only of the players, but also of their wives, companions or families, should also be open for inspections led people to believe that the practicability of such a report was, to say the least, doubtful."

●

After the King Commission adjourned for the first time, in August 2000, Hansie appeared in a three-part mini-series featuring himself, Bertha and his parents on the South African pay-TV channel M-Net.

The interviews were conducted by former Australian and Transvaal cricketer Mike Haysman and Olympic swimmer Marianne Kriel. The questions were carefully vetted by Hansie and his advisors beforehand. It was, consequently, a rather bland public-relations attempt and was perhaps justifiably criticised by some in the media, who said the programmes were "tame and unrewarding".

The media's blood was up against Hansie and he further infuriated them by appearing in an Australian Channel 9 interview, which by some accounts was also somewhat "sycophantic" and "boring".

Hansie was paid for the Channel 9 and M-Net interviews. He used the proceeds to pay his enormous legal fees. "Hansie was not keen to do the interviews. But he could've been broken financially by the legal costs," claimed Raymond van Staden.

A Basic Timeline

7 June 2000: The first day of the King Commission. Pat Symcox alleges that the team were offered 250 000 US dollars to lose a one-day game.

8 June 2000: Herschelle Gibbs says Hansie offered him a bribe to under-perform. He tells the Commission he agreed to Hansie's offer of 15 000 US dollars to score fewer than 20 runs in a one-day match in India.

10 June 2000: Hansie is offered immunity from prosecution by the state if he makes "a full disclosure".

15-23 June 2000: Hansie admits to taking large sums of money from bookmakers and to asking some team-mates to under-perform. But he insists he never threw or fixed a match. He breaks down and cries after three days of cross-examination. Hansie confesses to receiving 110 000 US dollars and R53 000 in total from bookmakers.

27 June 2000: Former Commissioner of the London Metropolitan Police Sir Paul Condon is appointed as the ICC's new anti-corruption investigator.

August 2000: Gibbs and Henry Williams are banned from international cricket for the rest of the year for their involvement in the scandal.

11 October 2000: The UCB decrees that Hansie is banned from any and all cricketing activities, for life.

14 October 2000: Les Sackstein points out that the life ban prevents Hansie from earning a living in the media or even coaching under-privileged children.

2 November 2000: The UCB softens its stance, saying that Hansie might be allowed back into the sport in the future. "We acknowledge that, with effort, people are able to rehabilitate themselves over time," says UCB president Percy Sonn.

10 December 2000: Hansie's legal team lodges a court application to overturn the life ban, saying it is "unconstitutional".

22 February 2001: After a three-month campaign by Hansie's team to declare the King Commission unlawful, the Commission comes to an abrupt halt. Judge Edwin King says he is unable to reach a conclusion about whether or not Hansie told the truth.

1 April 2001: The UCB says Hansie can coach privately, but not at any UCB affiliate. (All schools, clubs and provincial teams are UCB affiliates.)

July 2001: Hansie says in the media, "I think that one day when it comes along I would certainly like to have that [the position of national coach] because I certainly tried my entire career to make South Africa the number-one cricket playing country in the world."

26 September 2001: Hansie opens his campaign to get the life ban overturned in the Pretoria High Court. He is not present at the hearing, but in an affidavit he accuses the UCB of interfering with his personal life and with his attempts to earn a living.

27 September 2001: On the second day of the hearing, the UCB's senior counsel, Wim Trengove, says Hansie is free to practise as a journalist by attending a match as a spectator and reporting for the print medium.

17 October 2001: The court rejects Hansie's review, but says he can take part in "certain coaching and media activities. He was also granted certain interdicts that he asked for".

*Adapted from a BBC Sport web page dated 1 June 2002

CHAPTER FOURTEEN

FANCOURT DAYS

A Golfer on Fire

After the King Commission hearings wound down, Fancourt's security boom entrances and its high, electrified fences made it difficult for the press to corner Hansie. The complex's guards paid special attention to his need for privacy, his need for security, and kept an eye out for the paparazzi especially. They made sure that Bertha was safe when Hansie was not around.

From fortress Fancourt, Hansie could carefully choose his initially very few public appearances in the town of George, his early furtive forays to the golf courses.

His isolation effectively kept strange visitors and uninvited media away, bar two instances: a photographer was asked to leave when he was found hiding in a bunker while Hansie was playing on the course, and on another occasion an Australian lensman took some cheeky pictures of Hansie and Bertha while they were sitting at the dining-room table, inside their home. Hansie and Bertha's bedroom had tilting blinds; they had been unaware that passers-by outside could sometimes see them clearly. Hansie joked about this and said that now he realised why the security guards were willing to patrol their home 24 hours a day.

For the first year at Fancourt, Hansie was at sea, emotionally and spiritually. Bertha recalled, "He was dumbstruck. Initially Hansie was too scared to make any decision by himself; he was scared he would make the wrong one and it would make matters worse. Before he was a strong husband who made all the important decisions in our lives. Now he relied on me. He constantly asked for my advice. 'What should we do?' he asked regularly. I used to say, 'We must pray about it', and he used to reply, 'You pray about it'. He couldn't speak to God. He felt too terrible to even approach God. It was difficult for me because I was so used to Hansie making most of the descisions and hardly ever the wrong ones. It is difficult for me to make up my mind at the best of times; I am always scared to make the wrong choice . And so it takes me a long time to make a descision. I would have to pray about each one and find out what the Lord's will was for that area of our lives. And even then I found it difficult to take the step. I was desperate for Hansie to pray with me, to hear from the Lord and to once again take his place as the head of our family (and as its spiritual head as well)."

After Hansie's confession, Bertha was initially disappointed in Hansie for not having confided in her, as a husband should. She would have liked to have shared his burden. "I felt great compassion for him and wanted him to be freed from the weight of living with what he'd done. But I also realised that he was ashamed and embarrassed and in a way he wanted to protect me from anything harmful or wrong."

Hansie tried at times to get his spiritual life sorted. He meditated on Psalm 23. As he did so, he fasted for three days and on the third day a neighbour came to visit and was so frightened by Hansie's gaunt appearance that he immediately called a doctor to examine his friend.

Bertha feared at times that Hansie might be suicidal.

She said, in 2004, "From the time that the news broke, one of the most difficult things for Hansie was to go out in public. I remember when we wanted to change our dining-room table for a bigger one. I asked him to go with me to one of the antique shops in George. He couldn't. Eventually I had to take a picture of the table I'd chosen, so that he could at least see it before we decided to buy it.

"When we approached people I would feel his hand holding mine tighter. He would look carefully; very sensitive to any kind of gesture, a look of resentment or disappointment in their eyes, and then he would relax. We spoke about it often, I used to tell him that the people were amazing in their support of him, and that he should accept it and take comfort from it. After all, the public support said a lot about his personality.

"I told him often to look at the thousands of letters, the cards and books of encouragement. They love you and support you, I'd tell him. Hansie's reply would be, 'It makes me feel worse about what I have done. I have let so many people down, disappointed so many people.' He couldn't read the letters, couldn't even open them. Initially I tried, because I thought it would encourage him, make him feel better, but later I realised that it made him feel worse, and I knew that he would in his own time, read them and realise that there were millions who understood, who forgave and who loved him…

"Going out in public was hard and difficult for him, but it did get better with time, like most things…"

His early fears of public attacks of any kind were largely unfounded. George citizens generally loved him, forgave him. But somehow, Hansie never quite felt "forgiven" by his fans. The constant push of shame and fear and the pull of fame and friendly social engagement never quite went away. This ambivalence never ended, and it is important to understand this complexity.

John Robbie, the South African talk-show host and former Irish rugby player, made an intriguing comment about Hansie's popularity and his fall from grace. "Why so many people were so cross with Hansie, and seemed to hate him so much, was that they never liked Hansie. They loved him. If it had been just an 'ordinary' member of the national team, people would have just shrugged a bit and moved on." Robbie's point was that when someone you love lets you down, it's always much harder to take. Yet that public anger seemed to dissipate quickly. There were very few who had loved him and who did not forgive him, and certainly this was so in George. The people of George adopted him as one of their own. *Onse Hansie. Almal se pêl.* (Our Hansie. Everyone's pal.)

After an initial period of morbid hibernation, Hansie began to make time for people, and make time for a semblance of a renaissance. His famous and genuine interest in people, whatever their station in life, started to emerge again. With Hansie, the legend went, you would always realise within 20 seconds of meeting him that he was genuinely interested in you, and even the Fancourt caddies could attest to this.

Whenever he drove around George in his little silver BMW (with personalised number plate – Dot Com WP), people would wave. And Hansie would wave back. The whole town knew his car and his bright and toothy smile.

●

"Hansie made a mistake. He sinned. He learnt from it. But he had to live with it," remains one of Bertha's favourite sayings.

Hardly a day passed by without Hansie apologising again and again to Bertha. "I know I've done wrong. I've lied to you. I've tried to regain your trust, but I can't do any more than I've done already," Hansie said.

I asked Bertha, "Did you express your concern that if he lied to you about this, he lied to you about other things?"

Bertha replied: "Not in so many words. I did ask him many times if he was sure that he had told me everything because I wanted to know. He said 'Yes'. He got tired of saying 'yes'," laughed Bertha.

Hansie, paralysed by his unresolved guilt, relinquished his old-fashioned husbandly role and leaned heavily on Bertha. She wanted him to fix his broken relationship with God, and to take his place as head of their home. Part of the problem seemed to be that Hansie couldn't forgive himself and he was not at all sure if God had forgiven him. In comparison, his problems with the media were miniscule.

The dynamic between Bertha and Hansie, especially during their early months in Fancourt, is well illustrated by the following:

Hester and Gordon and their two children were visiting them and the two couples had travelled to nearby Mossel Bay to look at a new housing development there. The site had a security boom entrance and casual visitors were prohibited from roaming around the area.

The guard at the entrance had stopped their car and Hansie was asked what his business was. Hansie had lied, "We know someone who lives here, we are on our way to visit them." With that, they were let through.

Bertha was furious. As they drove along she said, "Hansie, when we go back through that gate you must apologise to the guard and tell him that you told a lie."

Deeply embarrassed, Hansie had meekly said: "Bertha, it was just a white lie."

"Hansie! *Jy jok nie meer nie!* (You don't lie anymore!) You WILL apologise. You must never lie again. Not even little white lies," she said. Bertha's frustrations with Hansie's poor spiritual state, along with his own feelings of guilt began to have a powerful effect and Hansie eventually began to realise that he needed a spiritual guide, a mentor who could somehow help him get back on track.

Tich Smith is well known in South African Christian circles, especially in Durban. Tich played cricket and rugby for Natal. He is not unfamiliar with shame and disgrace, having caused pain and suffering to himself and those closest to him, through his addiction to alcohol and gambling. There was a time in his life when he felt that the world was judging him. And it did. He knew what it was like to be a social leper.

In 1986 Tich had his life changed by the acceptance of Jesus' claims in the Word of God. The Lord helped him to stop gambling and drinking and he has devoted much of his life to spreading the Good News of the Gospels. He has also become a successful businessman. Tich learnt his Christian belief from that luminary Peter Pollock, with whom he had a good friendship. Tich is a strong, no-nonsense character who shoots from the hip, like Peter. The two men were the kind of battle-hardened, gutsy Christian men who could do Hansie some good, men who could cut boldly through the layers of wordly compromise.

"When Hansie's troubles hit the news, I felt that I had to get alongside him," Tich told me in 2004 at his large, burgundy house on prime sea-front real estate in Umhlanga Rocks, near Durban. Tich then proceeded to do what he believed God wanted him to do. He made contact, and offered his friendship.

"I was upset by the actions of the media and a lot of the cricketing fraternity. They were so harshly critical, like they had never done anything wrong in their lives. They did not want to forgive Hansie. The criticism seemed especially harsh simply because it involved money, as if that particular sin was worse than adultery, for example." Tich was quick to add, "I didn't condone one thing Hansie did. I still don't."

Tich, who was building a house at Fancourt, had been friends with Hansie for a number of years, but their relationship deepened during this time. They spent hours on the Fancourt golf courses together, playing golf, but they would also talk about life. "Hansie would often break down and cry," said Tich.

He cried about "letting people down. Cricket fans. South Africa. Bertha. His family."

Tich recounted how Hansie would say, "I cannot believe I got that low in life." "I don't believe people will ever understand how broken he was. He was still in the process of learning to forgive himself. His public face was a front. He was wearing a mask. He couldn't be the Hansie he wanted to be."

On the phone, at home in Fancourt and on the fairways, Tich listened carefully to Hansie's outpourings. "What amazed me about Hansie was that he never said a bad word about anyone. He didn't battle to forgive his persecutors; he felt that they had a right to be harsh. But he battled to forgive himself. I told him that the Lord forgives our sins if we forgive those who sin against us. And that includes forgiving yourself."

Hansie told Tich about his crooked dealings with the bookies and Tich came to the conclusion that Hansie's understanding of gambling was very limited. "I gambled at casinos and racetracks for 17 years. In my eyes Hansie was naïve when it came to gambling."

According to Tich, Hansie's relationship with the bookies began to unravel when he started incorrectly forecasting a result and the bookies started insisting that he get other players involved. The second line that Hansie crossed was when he approached other players to share in the unholy conspiracy. "Hansie was way out of his league. I don't think he ever realised the magnitude of money that he was involved in. I don't think he ever knew the magnitude of money that is involved in cricket betting."

⬤

Inch by inch, Hansie began to crawl back to God. "This was mainly because of Bertha and his family's relentless encouragement," said Tich. Many people phoned from all over the world telling the Cronjés that they were praying for Hansie.

In August 2000 Hansie contacted Peter Pollock and Tich Smith and had asked them to come to George, as he now wanted formal instruction about reconciliation with God. He felt he wanted to confess. He required spiritual guidance. "Please come to Fancourt and stay for a while," Hansie had pleaded.

Peter and Tich dutifully booked flights to George. The day before the flight, Peter had phoned Tich. "I'm not going. I've prayed about this. I think the time of pandering to Hansie Cronjé must stop. Too many people have been at his beck and call for too long. If he is genuine about wanting to change, he must come to Durban and come to see us," said Peter.

Tich agreed with this and phoned Hansie. "If you want to change and get your life right with the Lord we're available – in Durban." Hansie vacillated. He was still hiding from the public and going to Durban would mean getting on a commercial flight. He wasn't sure if he could do that.

San-Marie later phoned Peter and said, "I'm so worried about Hansie. Can't you help him?"

Peter had replied, "He has an open invitation to come to me when he's ready. We must leave him to walk through the desert by himself."

Soon after that Hansie phoned Tich. "Bertha and I fly to Durban tomorrow."

On 29 August 2000 Peter Pollock met with Hansie and Bertha at his home. Hansie and Bertha stayed with Tich and his wife Joan.

Tich and Peter played hardball with Hansie. "You've been playing games with God. How can you say that you love the Lord Jesus and behave like you have? You have lied. And the lies have multiplied. Now you're in this situation. If you're serious about being a Christian, you need to confess your sins before Him and repent."

The two men spoke long and hard with Hansie, especially about his attitude to money. Tich said, "If you can cheat about money, you can cheat about anything." Hansie confessed his sins that afternoon.

Peter, ever the stern evangelist, told Hansie, "When you were 10 you knew it was wrong to take money from a bookmaker. It's no good comparing it with what Shane Warne and Mark Waugh did. It's time to stop rationalising and looking for extenuating circumstances or excuses. It was wrong. It's time to repent, to turn, and make it right with Jesus. It's time to acknowledge that it's not just a decision of the intellect, but also a decision of the heart and will. It's the biggest decision of your life. You need to love Jesus with all your heart, mind and strength."

A tearful Hansie didn't say much except "I know, I know."

The two men told him that the Lord would forgive him anything, if he repented and came clean. They talked about money. A lot. About what the Scriptures said about money. Hansie broke down, wept profusely. They cautioned: "Think carefully about what you're doing. Don't rush into this. It's not a glib, instant fix. This really is about life and death."

Both Tich and Peter suggested that if Hansie wanted "total commitment, a unilateral declaration of dependence on Jesus", that he be baptised. Hansie wanted to do it there and then, but they told him to go away and think about it carefully before he took that step.

Hansie said little after the gruelling confession, which lasted about two hours.

Baptism, as explained in the Bible, symbolises cleansing and the death of the old life, and the raising up of a new life in Christ. This act also publicly states a thinking person's declaration of faith in God.

The next day Hansie and Bertha went to Inez and Peter Pollock's house in Mountain Ridge. Once again, Hansie was crying, his whole body was shaking. Clutched tightly in his hand were a blue Speedo and a towel.

Peter asked Hansie, "And now?" to which Hansie replied, "The old Hansie needs to die and the new Hansie needs to rise." (Hansie hadn't been baptised after he was born-again in 1992, and felt he had to be baptised now.)

Peter put on his swimming trunks and led Hansie into a small swimming pool in the garden. He moved up to Hansie and stood close to him. Hansie bent his elbows and put his fists against his chest as Peter put one hand on the penitent sinner's back and another on Hansie's wrists. "Hansie Cronjé, on the confession of your faith and at your own request, I baptise you in the name of the Father, the Son and the Holy Spirit." With that Peter pushed Hansie backwards into the water, as Hansie flexed his back and felt the cool blue water envelope him.

Hansie rose up again, gazed at the sky, and then at Bertha. "The new Hansie emerged from the water and that familiar, bright smile returned to his face," said Pollock.

San-Marie always remained grateful for Peter Pollock's gruff pastoral concern for Hansie. "To my mind that is somebody who really contributed to Hansie's rehabilitation. With an open mind and strong vision. He didn't spoon-feed him like some Christian ministers do. In some churches repentance is too glib, too smooth, too easy."

Despite the tonic of general public acceptance, the media storm around Hansie got worse as insinuations and further accusations became an almost daily diet for Hansie and Bertha. Especially after his baptism, Hansie was praying regularly and reading his Bible as he grimly tried to make his way through the seemingly endless media babble and harsh official sanction. But the more the press harangued him, the more the ordinary public's empathy seemed to grow.

Bertha said, "It was terrible for both of us. I remember how a feeling of anxiety or uneasiness would take hold of us especially on a Saturday night, all because we didn't know what would be on the front page of the Sunday paper the next day. Initially we would go on the Internet in the middle of the night, just so that we would at least know when we faced people the next day, either in the street or at church, what was said or written about us. It got better later, much better. Never easy though.

"It would mostly be news to us as well, and that would make us feel helpless and devastated at times, but we learnt through it all. I saw Hansie realise that it actually didn't matter any more what [the media] came up with. In the beginning, he wanted to put the lies and the false accusations right, even the half or twisted truths frustrated Hansie. Although it stayed difficult and took a long time, he eventually, we eventually, let it go… The truth will set you free, and as long as you know who you are in Christ, nothing else really matters."

Hansie was also keenly aware of his awkward status as a high-profile Christian, and at one stage felt that he shouldn't even show his face in a church, fearing that the charge against him of "hypocrisy" would somehow transfer itself to a church congregation as well. He also worried about confrontation with other Christians, a fear that only on rare occasions was actually realised. Admittedly, he tended to avoid putting himself in a position where such attacks were possible. But Hansie knew that he required regular fellowship with other Christians.

●

Bertha and Hansie scouted around George for a church family and soon found Pastor Dave Hooper and the Patria Church, a respectable, charismatic Christian church in George, which they attended every Sunday, whenever they could. Hansie would often sit upstairs in a corner, not wanting to be noticed, and such furtiveness in closed spaces in public remained with him to the end. He often needed to approach the public on his own terms, one eye on a quick getaway.

Over Easter of 2001, Ewie, San-Marie, Hester, Gordon, Tich Smith and his wife Joan visited the Patria Church with Hansie and Bertha. A young visiting preacher had spoken about forgiveness. In the front of the church were two large wooden crosses. He invited the congregation to write on a piece of paper: "'Jesus died on the cross to forgive ... for …" Members of the congregation were to insert their own names and then list their sins, all the sins they'd ever committed. The young preacher then invited the congregation to come forward and use a hammer to nail their confessions on the cross.

The entire Cronjé clan did this.

Hansie had sinned of course, and had fully deserved damnation, eternal separation from God, like all of us who have sinned. But, the Bible says "if we confess our sins, He (God) is faithful and just to forgive us our sins and to cleanse us from all unrighteousness". To Hansie's self-righteous enemies in the cricketing fraternity, the media, and elsewhere, one could have issued the same challenge Jesus made to the religious leaders of his day: "let he who is without sin cast the first stone".

If truth were told, there were many long months of hurled abuse, and Hansie stood, meekly contrite, taking the 'stoning' without bitterness.

"The King Commission, the pressure and the dire consequences of his sin would not disappear. But now, more importantly, a repentant Prodigal Son had returned to his Father's house and was welcomed with open arms. Plenty of those 'elder brothers' – the intellectual moralists – would be around to express disapproval, but God's Word and His promises stand, despite the thoughts, philosophies and judgments of men," said Peter Pollock.

In early 2001, Hansie was asked by a group of pastors in George to be the chairman of the George Transformation Committee. The committee was to organise an event in the town, which was to be a part of the first South African-wide Christian Day of Prayer for Africa. Faithful Christians around the country would gather at many stadiums on the day to pray for a troubled and divided continent. (By 2005, the Transformation Day of Prayer for Africa had spread across the world to become a Global Day of Prayer.)

Hansie had declined the invitation, feeling that he was unworthy of such a task and he feared that the media would criticise the committee for appointing him to such a role. At first (during a meeting with Hansie present) the committee accepted his refusal to be chairman, but 20 minutes later during the meeting, one of the Xhosa pastors suddenly stood up out of the blue and said, "This man has turned away from his sin and we have all forgiven him. With all of his experience and ability as a leader he is the right man to chair the organising committee. I say we make him chairman."

On the day of the rally, 21 April 2002, Hansie left Fancourt at 6am to offer whatever practical help he could at the local stadium. When Tich arrived at the stadium at 10am with Peter Pollock, Hansie was one of the ushers in the car park, directing traffic to parking areas. He later directed people to seating in the Outeniqua Stadium, helping wherever he could, in small ways. He had designated this task to himself without making any kind of fuss about it or drawing any attention to this fact.

He was dressed in a tracksuit, had not wanted a jacket and tie and the public platform, which was offered to him. He sat on the ground of the stadium, participating in the rally like any other Joe Christian in the assembly. "That took guts. When I saw that I realised that he had humbled himself," said Tich.

●

Bertha got a job as a physiotherapist at the beginning of 2001, at the Carpe Diem School for the Disabled. Carpe Diem started in June of 2000, founded after the need arose for such a school in the George area. Physically and mentally disabled children from pre-school through to about 16 years old attend the school.

"I was doing some locum work at a practice in George at the end of 2000, when the occupational therapist at the school, San-Marie Vosloo, contacted me and asked if I would be interested in applying for the job of physiotherapist at the school. The post was advertised and Hansie and I were not sure what to do, seeing that our lives were so unsettled at that stage. The morning of the last day that the applications had to be in Cape Town, Hansie and I sat in the car in front of the Postnet in George. He prayed that the Lord would take control of this and that the application would be there in time, if that is where He wanted me to be.

"It got there in time, and when I had to go for the interview, Hansie waited in the car outside for me. We prayed together. I was very nervous, especially with everything that had happened in the past year. We both knew that the Lord was in control, no matter what we tried to do ourselves. I got the job. Hansie was very excited for me.

"I always found it very difficult to get up early in the morning, I'm not a morning person. So, Hansie would wake me up and make us some coffee. We would sit outside on the veranda (especially in summer) and read a piece out of the Bible. Some mornings we would pray out loud and other mornings we each had our own quiet prayer time. We used to discuss what we read for a short while and talk about our day and what we needed to pray about for each other. Hansie sometimes made me a sandwich for lunch, and got my car out of the garage so that I only had to jump in and go, seeing that I was usually running a bit late! He would stand in his gown on the driveway, waving goodbye, before turning his attention to the morning's golf, and later, fitness programmes.

"Hansie came to the school often. Some of the children used to recognise him, but most didn't have an idea who he was. He would sometimes leave a chocolate on my desk with a message in my diary if I wasn't in my office. Some days he would bring us two Kentucky Rounders when it was break time – it was one of our favourite things to do on a Sunday night, buy Rounders and watch the 8 o'clock movie on M-Net in bed. We both loved take-aways…" Bertha still treasures her desk diary that contains Hansie's last message to her: "Ek is lief vir jou." [I love you.]

"I think it was hard for him," continued Bertha, "knowing his personality and the way he used to think about looking after and providing for his family. But he was brave; he tried to be positive and made sure that he was always at home when I got back from work at 3pm. It was a wonderful and precious time together. Some after-noons, especially during September, October and November 2001, I used to get home and he had everything ready to put in the car to go to the beach. Herold's Bay was one of our favourite spots. To have three hours together there, 'braai' some chops and 'wors', and have a glass of wine, watch the sun go down… We did that often.

"Other afternoons we would have a cup of coffee together and go to the gym, sauna and Jacuzzi at Fancourt. Hansie also tried very hard to teach me golf. Sometimes, after I got back from work, he took me to play a few holes, or went to the driving range where he desperately tried to coach me!

"It was precious time and on a Sunday afternoon, after a nice sleep in the afternoon we would walk across the fairways, reminding each other how blessed we were that through everything that had happened we still had each other."

For the first time in their married lives, Hansie and Bertha could spend quality time together; live a kind of "normal" life. At first they didn't go out of their way to make new friends, they just wanted each other.

There was no Sports Club for the Disabled in George, or for that matter, in the whole of the South Western Districts region (SWD). The disabled athletes who wanted to participate more seriously in their sport had to go to Cape Town to participate and compete for Western Province colours. The people at Carpe Diem School soon resolved, with Hansie and Bertha, to form a sports club for the disabled in George.

The Carpe Diem Sports Club was duly constituted, with Hansie as chairman, and was initially affiliated to the Boland District, which meant that Hansie and vice chairman, Pieter Koekemoer (a very talented disabled athlete) had to travel to Worcester, near Cape Town, once a term to attend meetings.

Below is the bottom section of the last page taken from the application that Hansie and the committee drafted to form the new provincial body for disabled sport in the SWD. It was foreseen that clubs in that region would join this body rather than the Boland one.

The main aim of this body is:

To organize sport for the disabled person in this region.
To provide equipment and facilities to these athletes.
To assist with the classification of athletes.
To assist financially wherever possible.
To help athletes compete Regionally, Nationally and Internationally.
To allow social interaction and leisure activities for disabled people.
To represent disabled athletes in the SWD area at National Meeting

…We ask you to consider the above material carefully and to bear in mind that all we are trying to do is to leave something behind which was far better than what it was when we first got here. Charles Swindoll once said, "We are all faced with wonderful opportunities, brilliantly disguised as impossible situations." A few months ago it looked an impossible task to establish such a body in the SWD, but now we are ready for these exciting challenges.

We thank you for taking the time out to read this document.

Kind regards

Hansie Cronjé
Chairman

Hansie had a new goal and threw his time and effort into this endeavour. Bertha said, "He really got involved in the practical things as well. For the athletes to qualify for the SA Championships they had to have qualifying times. George does not have a tartan track and if the wheelchairs were timed on a grass track the athletes would struggle to qualify. We took a whole lot of them over to Oudtshoorn to participate in a meeting.

"Hansie went with all of us, and helped to lift some of the athletes out of the minibuses and onto their wheelchairs. He even ran a 200m race with two of the disabled athletes, seeing that they were the only participants.

"These experiences helped him get a perspective on his own troubles. After that day, on our way back home, he said to me that he realised how blessed and fortunate he had been. Here these guys were, struggling so much to practise their sport, while Hansie and his team-mates sometimes used to take everything that was done for them and that they received for granted."

For SWD to become a province there had to be three sports clubs. Hansie was also involved in establishing two more clubs in the area: one in Oudtshoorn and one in Mossel Bay. Now SWD could function on its own as a province and the athletes had no more need to affiliate or travel to Boland or Western Province in order to practise their sport.

"Hansie was voted in as chairman for SWD Sport for the Disabled on 23 November 2001. It was a wonderful day for all of us," said Bertha.

From 24 to 27 March 2002, the South African Championships for the Physically Disabled were held in Kimberley. It was the first time that SWD would be represented at this championship. Bertha drove a minibus to Kimberley with the athletes and Hansie later joined them there, for a day and a night, staying in a hostel with the athletes. They were over the moon that their hero was with them and at such close quarters.

Hansie helped to get various sponsorships and donations for the sporting body and later on Bertha also donated the Hansie Cronjé Floating Trophy. It is presented annually to the person who has tried the hardest and inspired the most people on and off the track.

It is true to say that for the first 18 months after the King Commission, Hansie played golf. Lots of golf. After cricket, golf was his game. At one stage he had a handicap of 3.

One of his regular golfing buddies was the former South African fast bowler and national cricket selector Garth le Roux, whose own brilliant cricket career ended in 1990.

Garth remembered playing against a young Hansie in the Free State team in 1988/89. He later met up with him occasionally when commentating, and still later as the Fancourt property salesman who had pitched his wares to the South African cricket team. Hansie had been impressed by the presentation and had tried to encourage team-mates to buy property there, with little success. But he had seen the investment potential and had bought a plot, which soon soared in value by more than 300%. Garth had met the team at a Cape Town hotel in 1999. "They could've bought a Fancourt lodge for R1.6 million then – four bedrooms en-suite. We've just recently sold one like it for R4.5 million," said Garth.

When Hansie came to live at Fancourt, around the time of the start of the King Commission, Garth tried to "give him a little bit of assurance that he wasn't alone. That we were hoping that he would come through."

"The Fancourt guys made a point of asking him to come and play golf, knowing that he didn't want to be anywhere near Joe Public, but at least it was a change of atmosphere, hitting a golf ball. Even if you are going through a tough time, at least you're out there and it's life. He needed something like that. Otherwise you end up sitting in a hole or jumping off a cliff."

Garth's rough and spicy humour and his love of sport provided a great antidote to Hansie's troubles, to his often astringent Christian impulses and friends. The following anecdotes, recalled by Norman Minaar, perfectly illustrate this. "Garth le Roux, Hansie and myself went crayfishing off Misty Cliffs near Cape Town one weekend, and we put the boat in the water. Hansie was not too keen to go out to sea because he got seasick. The Atlantic was flat, it was a perfect day but Hansie started getting sick after about five minutes. He vomited over the side and Garth and I were laughing at him – he was laughing as well, in between the purging. Eventually I said to him, 'Hansie, if you tell us the truth, we'll take you back.'

"He just laughed. Later, when we went back to shore – we had caught some crayfish – Hansie was still sitting in the boat. Garth was pulling the boat up the slipway when two Marine Coastal Management inspectors suddenly appeared. One of them said to Garth, 'I'd like to check the boat – have you got a permit?' So Garth turned round to the guys and said, 'I know why you want to check. It's because you think we're *skelms* because Hansie's here. You think we're stealing crayfish as well now!' It was classic, because Hansie had the balls to laugh at that.

"On another occasion Hansie and Bertha invited us over to their place at Fancourt in the heat of the Commission. A crowd of us went for dinner and Garth took along some US dollars and put them under the cushions of the couch. Halfway through the dinner – everyone was having a chat and everything was quite serious – and Garth suddenly said, 'Hansie, are you sure you haven't got any cash lying around here?' And of course, Hansie was thinking 'don't be ridiculous' but the next thing Garth pulled a wad of US dollars from under the couch! Hansie just collapsed – he just laughed. It was great."

Interviewed at a lovely Fancourt country club restaurant in late 2004, Garth had some harsh words for some of Hansie's critics. "I would've liked to see Hansie get some more support from the cricketing people themselves. We have this thing in South Africa where we have to show the world how 'righteous' we are. They get you, they strip you naked, they put you on the cross and they beat your arse for the entire world to see. That's what happened to Hansie.

"If you look at any other irregularities that've happened to sportsmen, these rugby players that come over here and tear telegraph poles and parking meters down and beat up prostitutes… They go back home and nothing gets done. We have one poor South African player in a nightclub in New Zealand, calls some ex-South African a name – and he's banned! It goes in the press and a big issue is made of it – it wouldn't happen anywhere else! But by damn, it happens here."

After some time had passed for Hansie at Fancourt, Garth had one day closely observed Hansie as he bought a round of drinks in the members' bar after golf. "Hey Hansie," he shouted, "*jou boude lyk nes 'n polisieperd s'n*." (Your backside looks just like that of a police horse.)

"You know," Garth explained, "in his cricketing time, Hansie set the example as far as being fit was concerned. Now with all this stuff happening, he got big. He wasn't training and he had a wide backside on him." Hansie was well stung by the comment.

"The next day, he was training, baby. He was running and was in and out of the gym. Now he had another 'project' and he was working hard. He used to go and get his friend Gordon McNeill and make him go on long bicycle rides, because it's easier with a mate."

At that stage Hansie had put on an astounding 11 kilograms from the time of the King Commission. On Kate Rhodes's recommendation, he joined Weight Watchers. "The lady at Weight Watchers was very kind to him and allowed him to go and weigh in when the other ladies weren't there. He eventually lost all 11 kilograms again," said Bertha.

Like many others, Garth was particularly struck by Hansie's raging competitiveness. "Hansie simply hated losing on the golf course. If he played badly, or opponents played well, he'd really get upset."

Tich had also remarked, "If he was losing, he'd get cross. A lot of guys wouldn't play with him, especially when he played with Garth. Of course, many simply wanted to play with him because he was Hansie Cronjé. But it was often unpleasant when he didn't play well. He would get grumpy. He would be in a silent rage, often throwing his sticks viciously into the bag.

"Frankly, Hansie wasn't the easiest bloke. He was also a strong person in the sense that if he had made up his mind about something, it was not easy to change it."

Hansie played golf regularly, nearly every day, but he never played when Bertha was not at work, which excluded him from playing in the league. This irritated some Fancourters.

"He was highly competitive on the golf course, in any sport or competition, always. He was impossible on the golf course if he didn't play well. There was no such thing as a 'social round' for him. Gordon Parsons, Dad and I played with Hansie at Fancourt once. After three or four holes, Gordon and I were leading. Hansie was getting grumpier and grumpier, so much so that we stopped chirping him, fearing he would become truly enraged," said Frans.

On one or two occasions Hansie took Bertha onto the course. "He would get irritated if she didn't play well. She would get nervous and worried. The family used to have a good laugh about this."

The caddies at Fancourt adored him. Hansie's common touch was probably his greatest asset, his strongest weapon against the harsh criticisms of the cynical high-ups and the sarcastic intellectual moralists.

He engaged the caddies, spoke to them about their lives, got involved with them and offered his friendship. Some of the caddies knew that they could pop in anytime at Hansie and Bertha's house to watch sport on satellite TV, or use the computer for their personal needs.

Jean Safers, who was regularly Hansie's caddy at Fancourt, liked the way Hansie used to talk about "us", quickly and in a jocular fashion establishing a sense of teamwork.

Jean recalled finding Hansie in Golden Valley, a poor, coloured section of George, the kind of place whites avoided because it was "dangerous". "I found him in the street with kids. He was sharing food with them from the open doors of his silver BMW. For me this was a great thing to see, because nowadays white people feel very scared to come into my suburb, you know, and here's the man sitting in the middle of the street, feeding the kids. That really impressed me.

"Hansie's door was always open for me," Jean said. "He was always full of smiles."

When Jean discussed his chronic lack of cash in the off-season, Hansie had suggested to him that he get a coin-operated pool table and put it in the caddies' lounge. Within a week Hansie had bought the table. "We had an agreement that I should pay him back in instalments, when I could. There was no hurry. That pool table comes from a legend. It's not an item that just comes out of the hand of any-one. It has great sentimental value for me."

Jean told me: "If you look at the history of cricket, there was no replacement for him. In the sport, he made a great impact on and off the field. And as a person, I think he was one of the greatest cricketers that ever existed. I will never forget him for his leadership and inspiration."

Jean got married on 1 June 2002 and asked Hansie to drive him and his wife to church in his BMW. Hansie agreed, but had to call Jean to tell him that he had missed his flight to George but would try to get to the wedding on time. Hansie was determined to get to the wedding though, even if it was a bit late…

Hansie and Bertha made a few other excellent friends at Fancourt – Tina and Garth le Roux, Gordon and Marge McNeill, Franklin and Pam Stern, and Norman Minnaar. The McNeills had lived in Fancourt since 2000, having moved from Johannesburg where Gordon ran a successful off-shore investment business for a large Irish financial services group.

Still young, healthy and fit, the couple spun out their days in the wonderful ambience of the Fancourt lifestyle. Their large and light-filled home has extensive views of the Outeniqua Mountains and is truly luxurious. For many, the McNeills were the epitome of success, living the good life. Hansie certainly concurred with that and valued their friendship highly.

Gordon was bright, cheerful and had always been an intense golfer, a golfer who also fell in love with cricket shortly after his arrival in South Africa in 1995. Hansie's star was on the up, and excitement about the future of the national team was increasing. Gordon was captivated by South African cricket in general and Hansie in particular.

In 1995, Hansie was a guest speaker at Gordon's golf club in Johannesburg, and Gordon and Marge went to fetch him at the airport. The couple were charmed. "He was so normal, so easy to talk to. So accessible."

His speech at the club was warmly received, as his simple and well-constructed deliveries always were. Hansie had stayed on after the dinner, had more than a few beers, posed for innumerable photographs, and told jokes at his table. Gordon and Marge were smitten. They felt they had really hit it off with Hansie.

The couple periodically bumped into Hansie in the 1990s as the McNeills often watched the national team play, and often stayed in hotels where the South African team was lodged. Just after the King Commission, they met up with him again, renewing their acquaintance at the opening of yet another nearby Western Cape golfing estate, Sparrebosch.

They felt for Hansie that night, they noticed his "displacement". At Gordon's table a man had said, "I don't know how Cronjé can show his face in public."

While Hansie had not heard the remark, there were more than a few who were murmuring and muttering about his presence, throwing sour looks. Hansie, said Gordon, had felt this, was very aware of it. A formal England cricket player was also there and later in the evening was in private conversation with Hansie. "I will play golf and have a drink with you anytime that I am available, but I want you to understand that I will never forgive you for what you have done to cricket," said the person.

How did Hansie take it? "He took it. He bit the bullet and brazened it out. His attitude was: 'dish it out if you want to'." Hansie's presence there, his courage, had simply increased the McNeills' admiration for him. "We really admired him for stepping out and saying: "Hey! I'm here!"

Soon after that the McNeills met Bertha and a strong friendship between the couples began to grow. They noted the love between the Cronjés, how their closeness was evidenced by the constant kissing and cuddling, how resolutely supportive Bertha was of her man.

In the winter of 2000, shortly after Garth's unkind remark about Hansie's bottom, Gordon and Hansie started a fitness-training programme together.

Hansie had insisted that the training start daily at 7am. "That was Hansie. It couldn't be 9am or 8am. It had to be 7am."

The first morning they went off on a long bicycle ride – Gordon, about 20 years older than Hansie, was fit though, and a regular cyclist. Hansie had suggested cycling to Herold's Bay – a distance of some 50km there and back – and Gordon had said, "That's a big climb back up, Hansie. Are you sure you want to go to Herold's Bay?" Hansie was adamant.

"Of course, Hansie flew down the hill at 100 miles per hour, and I'm sort of white knuckles, holding on, behind him. So we get down there and then he said, 'Right, I'll race you back to the top' and I said, 'I'm not racing. I tell you what; I'll see you at the top. You just go'."

Off Hansie went pumping for all he was worth, with Gordon in an easy gear, making his way slowly and sweetly. A couple of kilometres up the hill Gordon turned a corner and noticed that Hansie was off his bike. The hill was very steep at that point and Hansie was knackered. Because of the gradient he couldn't get back on and pedal, so he started running with his bike. Together they raced to the top of the seemingly endless hill, Hansie running and Gordon pedalling. Of course, Hansie still won. "That," said Gordon, "is one of my favourite memories of him."

Hansie's competitiveness and pranks were also in evidence at the gym. The two men started to go there together every day. "God help anybody who was there, because he just took over," recalled Gordon. "Hansie would say, 'Right, this is what we're gonna do', and as he's talking he's sorting all the weights out and the pieces of equipment. 'We're going to do this, this and this. We're gonna do repetitions', or whatever it was. 'We're gonna do 50 seconds on the treadmill, 50 seconds on this and then back onto the treadmill and then back onto this, and back onto this', and the like, and he'd quickly and assertively set up the circuit for everybody."

On one occasion Gordon and Hansie were busy with such a circuit, and Gordon was exhausting himself trying to keep up with the Hansie-calibrated pace, incessantly moving as they were between the treadmill and the weights. The pair went through the paces for about 40 minutes, and Gordon was on the verge of vomiting and giving up. "I'm on my knees, Hansie. I can't take it," Gordon had panted. Hansie was laughing loudly. "Gordon, didn't you see me notching up the treadmill speed for you every time I got off it?" Gordon started the circuit on 8km/hour, but by the time they had finished the speed was up to over 12km/hour without Gordon noticing.

Interestingly, during his two-year friendship with the McNeills, Hansie said little about his Christianity. "It was always Bertha who introduced the subject," said Gordon. That said, it was clear to the McNeills that "Hansie was a strong, Christian family man. A man's man, but very polite and respectful when women were around."

When women weren't around, he'd enjoy a beer or two with the guys around a braai and crack the odd rude joke like one of the boys. A favourite was delivered in a bizarre accent: "I'm not really a gynaecologist, but I don't mind taking a look..."

Gordon believed that Hansie had seen himself "in the top 1% of his profession, one of the most famous cricketers in the world and I think he felt that he deserved more financial reward, especially when he compared his income with that of golf and rugby stars, for example. He never really articulated this, but I had this clear impression that he felt it keenly.

"I never got the impression that he wanted big cars or big houses. I just think he wanted to be successful. And I think he measured success strictly in financial terms."

The McNeills often witnessed his natural and eager rapport with the public. In Franschhoek once, said Gordon, an old Xhosa woman had rushed up to him and hugged him tightly in the street. "Don't you listen to anything anybody ever says to you! You're the best," she had said. Hansie, of course, hugged her back. By now, the adoration of fans had almost ceased to fan his guilt. Now it often fortified him, increased his resolve to get a life, to stand up for himself.

Shame was slowly morphing into a kind of righteous anger against some of his harshest accusers. There comes a time when a bloke simply has to get up and fight for himself. One can endure a deserved whipping for a while, but what kind of man can put up with a whipping every other day, with no end in sight?

Franklin Stern in 2005 was a recently retired successful corporate retail business-man who owned a lodge at Fancourt. "I never met Hansie while he was playing for South Africa, but dearly wanted to speak to him after the King Commission to encourage and support him. So I wrote a letter to him and Bertha that Garth le Roux kindly handed to him." His feelings expressed below typify those of many South Africans at the time.

23 June 2000

Dear Hansie,

I know you will have no idea who I am, and no doubt (and I certainly hope) you have received much mail of positive support for you and Bertha and the rest of your close family, therefore I'll be just one of much correspondence that you receive.

Let me introduce myself by saying I'm a great cricket fan (in fact a sports fanatic generally), an admirer of your leadership and dedication/commitment and your natural ability. I'm also a part-time 'neighbour' of yours in that I'm a lodge owner, and spend a bit of time at Fancourt (fairly irregularly). But most importantly I want to introduce myself as someone whose admiration for you has grown immeasurably over the last few days. I've recently had surgery and have been confined to bed this week and have therefore followed the King Commission quite extensively.

Let me at the outset say that no doubt many people have made mistakes in life, and you know and have conceded what a mistake you made. I further believe that not many have come forward to "come clean". You need to be commended for this. You have my (and I know many, many others') sympathy in the way the commission has tried to 'try you' through the media. You have been so patient in repeatedly answering the same questions, put sometimes by the same person, other times by different people from "different angles" in order to try and trip you up. You have in the main remained incredibly calm and polite (as we've always known you to be). You are now telling the truth ... consistently. How can they trip you up? You too have shown incredible support for your teammates... you could easily have named senior players who never refuted your offer outright. In fact, at times, and maybe I'm wrong, I do feel you may be holding back, simply not to incriminate anyone else.

I say this to you. For me, and no doubt many others, you have fast restored your credibility, even although you made a mistake. Through the Commission your true colours have once again come out. I have no doubt that you have learnt from your mistake and we all know nothing untoward would happen for you in the future ... in fact I firmly believe the way you've rectified the mistake will once again make you a role model for others to follow in the future. Your true colours that I referred to, that have once again come out at the Commission, are your honesty, consistency, high intelligence, compassion, care and concern for others, calmness under provocation, sense of humour, genuine emotions and leadership. You also weren't scared to [say] your piece.

All I wanted to say to you and Bertha in this note, which I asked Garth le Roux to kindly deliver to you on my behalf, is that you still have someone (amongst many, many – I'm sure) who still has a huge amount of respect and admiration for you. You have taken enough 'punishment' for your mistake, and now people need to support you so that you can re-build a happy, healthy and successful future (I am sure there are thousands and thousands, if not millions who are supporting you). I HAVE NO DOUBT YOU WILL RE-BUILD. Your true colours/values will once again come to the fore, and you will go from strength to strength. In fact as I write this, I can think of so many ways you can make such a positive contribution to the future of so many (including yourselves). I'll even be so bold as to say DON'T RULE OUT SPORT ... sport needs Hansie Cronjé. In any event, as I said, besides sport, I just have a picture of you in one of many leadership roles in many different spheres of life here in South Africa.

We say to you that you have 'friends' in Lodge 729 at Fancourt, who without us imposing on you or your privacy, want you to know, that when we are at Fancourt (or anywhere else for that matter) and you perhaps want to have a drink, have a "gesels" [talk], take a jog around the estate, play some golf or tennis, have a braai or whatever, we could think of little else better than to spend some of our time with you.

You have been, you still are, and definitely will continue to be a very special human being.

My wife, Pam, and three daughters join me in these sentiments.

I just felt I needed to write this to you. Good luck. G-d bless.

Franklin Stern

Hansie and Bertha were receiving thousands of letters that were similar to this letter from Franklin. At the same time huge amounts of letters were received by Hansie's parents, Frans and Hester. All of these were sent to Hansie, but sadly he never got to read all of them. The picture that Hansie had in his mind of the general public's view was the one that he saw on television and in the newspapers. It was one of harsh criticism and unforgiveness and it took him a long time to come to realise that the majority of the public had the same feelings that Franklin Stern had.

Hansie and Bertha did, however, phone Franklin and became very good friends with the Stern family. Franklin spoke fondly of his friendship with Hansie. They regularly used to jog together and fairly often played golf as well. One of his most enduring memories is of an evening when Hansie and Bertha went over to the Sterns for a braai. There were a number of guests there, but Hansie befriended a young nephew of Franklin's, Paul Rawraway, who was partially mentally challenged. Hansie realised this early in the evening, and, Franklin said, "that was Hansie for the night – he spent nearly all his time in discussion with Paul, and early the next morning he arrived back at the house with a signed shirt of his... 'To Paul, best wishes, Hansie'. He never did this to draw attention to the fact – he did it because he cared."

Another incident of note took place in the summer of 2000. Ernie Els was often at Fancourt (which was his home course at the time). Franklin said, "When Ernie was at Fancourt it was always a treat to occasionally drive a few holes and watch him in his 'practice' rounds. As the entire world knows, he's a great guy and doesn't mind this at all. On this particular day Hansie was due to play with Ernie, making it even more special. Also playing were Ernie's dad, Neels, and Mike Hargreaves. They played on the Montagu course. Hansie was magnificent. He was so competitive and the tougher the competition, the better he performed. You could see and almost feel Hansie lifting his game – as he always did for the big occasion. I remember him having nine consecutive pars on the first nine, then a couple of birdies, with the odd dropped shot. At the time he was playing off a 6 handicap, he ended with a brilliant 2-over par-74." A few weeks later, Hansie played his best round of golf ever when he shot a 3-under par 69 during the Ernie Els invitational at Fancourt.

The golf games that Franklin and his twin brother Hilton Stern played with Hansie would always start with lots of jokes and chitter-chatter, particularly when Hansie and partner were leading comfortably, but on the odd occasion when the game was close and there was a chance that Hansie might lose, the friendly banter stopped. A determination came over Hansie. "Trust me," said Franklin, "Hansie never ever played to lose! But on the very odd occasions that he did, the R40 bet was settled with humility and very sportingly."

●

Eventually, Hansie knew that the King Commission and its toxic aftermath would not go away. The legal process was open-ended; there was never any real closure for him. At times he had to spend days on end trying to get back seven or eight years of bank statements to prove to the revenue service that his earnings were legal. Hansie used to comment how terrible it was to spend so much time on negative things. He waited patiently for over 18 months for Judge King to conclude the Commission, so that he could move on with his life, but it never happened. Towards the end of 2001 Hansie realised that he had to move on, find a new course, even a job, unrelated to cricket. But who would have the grit to employ him?

His BCom (Hons) and an almost finished Masters in Business Leadership (MBL) obviously qualified him for a job in the financial services sector, at least.

"He looked at options in George but came to the conclusion that options were limited. He spoke about opening his own business too," said Bertha. The couple also talked about the possibility of moving to Pretoria and building a new life there. Nothing seemed to gel in his mind though, as the months rolled by.

On New Year's Eve of 2001, Jonty and Kate were having dinner with Hansie and Bertha at Fancourt. Hansie told them that he thought that it was time to get a job and that he would like to get it before the schools re-started later in January. "Hansie and I prayed together and asked for the Lord's help in this," said Bertha. "The Lord answered our prayer and by 22 January, Hansie had a new job.

"I remember that we both discussed this job offer at Bell, the day before Derek Crandon came to see us in George. We were wondering about a salary, etc. We decided to look at our budget and see what we needed in a month, we prayed about it. After Derek left, a proposal was e-mailed to us. Hansie read the e-mail and I was in the bedroom. He printed it out, and as he came into the bedroom, I could see he was amazed. He asked me to guess what they had offered him as a salary. It was exactly what we needed a month. It strengthened and encouraged us both."

Interviewed at Bell Equipment's strikingly plain Durban offices, situated in a very ordinary looking little light-industrial park, Company Chairman Howard Buttery comes across as a no-nonsense character, unafraid of the opinions of others, confident in himself and his successful global business of selling yellow heavy-duty machinery.

Hansie had, in the early months of 2000, and even during the King Commission, completed a study on Bell as part of his MBL. Tich – who looked after Bell's insurance, pension and provident fund monies – had phoned Howard and said, "This Hansie Cronjé chap needs a bit of a break." Buttery had responded, "Well, he doesn't need a break from me. He's just a student. If he wants to use Bell as a study, I don't care if he's Hansie Cronjé or Donald Duck or whoever. Providing we can accommodate him, I'm happy to agree to it."

During Hansie's studies, he visited Bell five or six times and met Buttery. During discussions with Hansie at Fancourt about his future, Tich had thought of trying to get him "in" permanently at Bell. He had a word with Howard, "I told him Hansie was looking for a job. Howard was amazing, he quickly said: 'Listen, we can look after Hansie.'"

During a game of golf with Hansie that Tich had organised, Howard had asked, "Hansie what are you going to do this year?"

Hansie replied, "I'd like to get a job."

"Doing what?" Howard asked.

"Well, anything, but you know with my current status – I'm not easily employed."

"You can start with us, if you like," said Howard, quickly.

"What do you mean?" asked Hansie.

"Let's not waste any more time. Start next week if you like. I'll check with my board, since you are a 'personality'. I have to make sure they have no objection, and then you can fire up as soon as you're ready."

Hansie was amazed. "What will I be doing?" he asked.

"Go and find something. I don't know, you're an intelligent fellow, go and find something," said Howard.

Hansie began working at Bell in January 2002. When he signed the contract he noted that he only had 17 working days leave a year. Hansie chirped to Tich later, "When I was playing cricket I used to have 17 days leave a month!"

On the first day of the job, Howard told Hansie, "There are a couple of things that you don't do if you work for me: you don't drink at work; you don't put your fingers in the till and you don't screw the boss's secretary." He added with a smile, "Cause I'm too old to do it myself. And because of your reputation, I don't need you spending your life running to the newspapers getting publicity about trying to get reinstated as a cricketer. Forget about that part of your life."

When Hansie visited the Bell factory after his appointment, he spent an hour signing autographs for the workers there.

Soon after he started, Bertha noticed a marked improvement in Hansie's mood. "That's when we started really talking, and at that point I saw that he was happy. For the first time since the whole thing started, he had purpose again."

"He also enjoyed studying for his MBL and he continued to devour books on business and successful business owners."

But he was also frustrated by his perception that he had a lot of "catching up" to do. Hansie said to Bertha, as he was packing the dishwasher, "I'm so way behind my peers. Guys my age have up-and-running careers and here I am starting a new job and sharing an office with four people."

Bertha had responded, "Don't be silly. You've got so much going for you and have so much experience in leadership." Ever the competitive player, in whatever game it was, Hansie felt that he was losing the match, that he was starting "at the bottom".

The previous morning, Hansie had a meeting with Howard, and they had talked of his future in the firm. He was told he would get his own office, and would be one of the managers of Bell's Sub-Sahara region. There was talk of Hansie going overseas on business too. "Hansie was greatly cheered by this," said Bertha.

Predictably, Buttery was heavily criticised by some in the media. "The business press had a go at us. The *Financial Mail* said that by Bell employing Hansie Cronjé, we had created an 'irrevocable breakdown between the business sector and government'."

Buttery reacted to this comment thus: "I had the same thought that you would have about it, I'm sure: 'it's raining in Bulgaria on Thursday afternoons, but the bullets are west over the duckbins in Peru' – you understand me? What has the government got to do with me, and what difference does it make to me?"

Howard admits he was "naïve" about the fuss around the man. "Having had a Springbok rugby captain [Gary Teichmann] work with Bell, I didn't see a cricket captain as having so much more impact. There was this huge charisma about him, from his past, but I never really understood it properly then.

"When the media used to phone me and hammer me, I used to tell them all to go and get stuffed. There was a whole pile of articles in some Australian publications – I've got them here somewhere but who wants to read them? There was a whole supplement about Hansie in *The Australian* and they tried to drag me in as a 'mysterious benefactor'. It was so far from the truth. He was a university student who had come to work at Bell who showed a lot of bloody interest in our company and who had some bloody good ideas. Man, let's rather have that bugger working for us than for the opposition. And that's it – there's no magic to it beyond that. People would like to think that I had some dream at 3 o'clock in the morning to employ him, but I'm afraid I don't have that story for you ... Maybe Ali Bacher can tell you that story.

"I mean, this was a young guy who came and had a bit of a troubled past, but we've had guys work for us who used to smoke dagga and had been around bad women in their lives and we've employed them and they stabilised and became reasonable, responsible employees."

At the time, I saw a young fellow who was clearly bright, competent, and in a company such as ours with 2 500 employees, we're constantly looking for young brains to come and help our business. We employ 10 to 12 new graduates every year and he happened to be one that came to my office, and I liked the look of the fellow. I simply employed him in Bell's interest."

Buttery seemed to reject the idea that he employed Hansie because of any perceived "positive marketing spin-off" for the Bell company. "I didn't box him because he came along as Hansie Cronjé. He came along as an employee to Bell and he had an employee number and he worked with the team.

"I thought he had some bright ideas – he'd come up with a very interesting strategy for our finance team and I thought, 'Hell, this bugger's given some thought to this and he's got a bit of brainpower'."

Hansie's job at Bell entailed selling finance packages and insurance policies to companies that bought Bell equipment, and part of the job was to organise Bell golfing days around the country, as a marketing tool for this enterprise.

After his first month at Bell, Hansie phoned Tich, saying, "Some guys contacted me and said they'll pay me R10 000 a month if I let them put my name on a cricketing score update delivered to mobile phone subscribers. What do you think?"

Tich said, "Hansie, you've just started a job at Bell. They've broken everybody's rules; they've bent over backwards to give you a job. You definitely can't do this thing." Hansie agreed.

An opportunity for another income stream soon presented itself. Chris Potgieter, a diamond mine owner, had bought a Fancourt plot and wanted to build a big house on it. He was an unreconstructed Hansie fan and had wanted to give Hansie a hand, but didn't want to just give it to him as a gift. He contrived to get Hansie to oversee the building of his house, in return for a handsome fee.

Hansie was approached about the deal and he discussed the offer with Bertha. Bertha simply said "no". Hansie discussed the matter with Tich, who said, "It's fine, Hansie. Go for it, as long as it doesn't involve your working week, you can do it on weekends.

"I knew Hansie would do a proper job, as always. He would count every brick. Bertha was shocked at my advice, but I said to her, 'You can't just keep on saying no to Hansie. He can be a real help to this guy. It is a partnership which will have no impact on his work at Bell.'"

Later, Hansie sold two Bell machines to Potgieter, also handling the finance packages and the insurance policies related to the transaction.

When Hansie first started at Bell, said Howard, "He was like a young boy on his first day at school. Ja, he looked a little bit vague.

"He was a very respectful man, coming as he did from a strong Christian background. You didn't have to tell him anything twice. He made an effort to understand every aspect of our business. He was a hard-working bastard. When he started working for us, he was very clear to tell me that he had zero business experience. He used to earn more money from an appearance than he earned in a month from us. So he'd come into this whole new world. He'd never played on this wicket before. He'd never held this kind of bat." In his last few years as captain Hansie's minimum fee as a guest speaker was R10 000. Often companies were willing to pay far more than this. The only exception to this was when he spoke at events in aid of charity, in which case he wouldn't ask any appearance fee.

As Hansie's confidence grew, Howard decided that he would take him on a trip to Europe to show him aspects of the Bell business there and even naïvely contemplated taking him to India. "At that time I didn't realise there were these political consequences ... some people in India got terribly nervous when they thought I was going to bring him to India with me," said Howard. Hansie himself was afraid of going to India too, and even a trip to Britain was fraught with danger, like the prospect, however remote, of arrest and extradition.

Buttery said that Bell never regretted the decision to employ Hansie. "He only worked for us for five months and quite honestly his impact on our business was neither here nor there, really. But he made a solid contribution, especially in his work with client liaison and the golf days. That had a huge impact. He certainly created good relationships with every client he met. I never had one client telling me that they were unhappy about us employing him. He had barely started his work, but he was on his way to the top and had been earmarked for that."

Because of Bertha's employment at Carpe Diem School, she was not able to join Hansie in Pretoria straight away. She did however eventually hand in her resignation and was to join Hansie in Pretoria after the July holidays.

Gordon McNeill had a few interesting perspectives on Hansie's new deal at Bell, which entailed being based near Johannesburg Airport, living in Pretoria during the week, and flying back to George every weekend, in between travelling around the country on duty for Bell.

"I think there was an acceptance there that this was his life now, but the loss of cricket was something he never got over. I don't think his new life came very naturally to him. He made a tremendous effort with the Bell job, to make it work and he was very positive about it. But he had a great ability to play the game and pretend everything was fine.

"Marge and I worried about this whole Bell thing because it was such a departure. But he knew he had to do it, he had to prove it to himself and to Bertha; he had to make a clean start and try something new. He wasn't going to get back into cricket. It just seemed, I think – it just seemed so alien to him."

●

"All Hansie ever wanted to do was to plead for forgiveness, especially to the cricketing fraternity," said Tich. "To be forgiven. That's what he longed for. I think he eventually accepted that his deeds were so wrong that he just couldn't get involved in cricket in any formal sense, although he had so much to offer the game.

"Hansie just wanted them to say, 'We understand. You've been sentenced, and you're serving your sentence, but we still love you.' He desired that so badly.

"He led people to believe that there was still more that he needed to confess.

He never lied to protect himself. He lied to protect others. He never challenged any sentence. He never said he was being ill treated. And the treatment meted out to him went far beyond the crime, in my eyes."

Pastor Dave Hooper of the Patria Church in George came to know Hansie and Bertha quite well in their two years at George.

He, like so many others, was surprised by Hansie's lack of bitterness, his lack of self-pity. "He wasn't even angry about how he was punished. And Hansie spoke a lot about his deep regret about decisions he'd made. He never tried to put the blame on anyone else except himself."

Dave made the observation that Hansie did not, at first, realise that the impact of what he did would be so huge and long lasting. "I think he had the belief that after speaking to Ali the whole thing would blow over in a couple of weeks. To the end, he was truly stunned and overwhelmed by the consequences of what he had done."

For Dave, Hansie's enduring characteristic was his bright, child-like humour and his love of people. "He'd do things like reach down suddenly and untie your shoelaces with one hand, snapping his fingers with the other as he did so."

In a shop in George once, a group had spotted him and started shouting, "Hansie! Hansie!" Hansie had been with Dave and Bertha, and had abruptly left them and engaged the group, leaving his wife and friend standing for many long minutes while he attended enthusiastically to his newfound friends.

"That was Hansie," said Dave. "He did that sort of thing as a matter of routine. He never did it for cameras. He was there for people. He encouraged me in that, tremendously. In the end, he wasn't the captain of the Proteas. He was just Hansie," said Dave.

CHAPTER FIFTEEN

THE OUTENIQUA CROSSING

It was a beautiful, early autumn afternoon in Pretoria, South Africa's capital city, on Wednesday, 15 May 2002. The Highveld sun shone brightly in the windless air, warm enough to take off any edge of coolness. The frosts had not yet arrived and the city's lawns were still green, the veld grass on the koppies around the city had yet to turn to straw. The hosts of summer's purple-blossoms, the jacaranda trees, still had their leaves.

Pretoria's imposing British colonial Union Buildings, the administrative seat of the South African government, the massive and curious squat bulk of the stone Voortrekker Monument, and the monstrous modern building housing the University of South Africa (Unisa), Africa's largest university, each commanded skylines on hills at various points around the historic, sprawling old Boer metropolis, full of the stolid, monolithic architecture erected when apartheid was in its prime.

It was Frans Cronjé's birthday and he had travelled from Stellenbosch in the Western Cape to Johannesburg for a meeting. He was on the steering committee of the Volunteer Management System for the Cricket World Cup that was hosted by South Africa in 2003. A few months before that Frans had called Ali Bacher, who was now the CEO of the World Cup Organising Committee, to ask him if they had any need of volunteers. Ali replied that indeed they did, but as yet they had not had a chance to start organising any, Frans suggested that his organisation, Sport for Christ Action South Africa, would volunteer to get the process started. He further told Ali that they would appoint a full time manager in Herman Beetge, to manage the volunteer system at no cost to the World Cup Organising Committee. And so Frans and Ali's relationship was restored through this new project, which proved to be one of the biggest success stories of the 2003 World Cup.

Frans did not want to spend his birthday alone in Johannesburg, so he drove to Pretoria and spent the evening with Hansie. "It was a really special evening. After a brief visit to my dad's cousin, Oom Wors Cronjé, we went to a restaurant called *Cynthia's* for dinner and I noticed that Hansie walked into this public place with his old confident manner for the first time in two years. He chirped the owner on the way and actually stopped to say hello to a few people who recognised him.

"He told me how tough the first few months at Bell were, but that he had finally signed his first deal on the previous day. This was for the two machines that he had sold to Chris Potgieter. Along with this, the golf days that he had organised for Bell were a great success. He had managed to get a group of professional golfers to participate in most of the seven golf days; many of them were good friends of his, and this exposure had helped him to realise that there was a general feeling of acceptance amongst the public.

"He was also excited about the fact that Bertha would soon join him in Pretoria. They had grown so close over the two years since the King Commission and he found it really difficult to be away from her during the week.

"We also spoke about how privileged we were to have such a close family and such loving parents. I think Hansie was still thinking that he had let my parents and our family down. By the way, we never felt that Hansie had let us down or brought any shame on the family. People make mistakes and the most important thing is how you recover from them. We were always proud of how he tried to rectify his mistakes and I could see that Hansie was just about back to normal.

"He was living in a small bachelor flat in the backyard of Dr Charles Niehaus during the week and he only had one double bed in the flat. We both slept in the smallish bed, but fortunately we were too exhausted not to sleep well."

Ten days later on 25 May, Grey College was to play the Afrikaans Hoër Seunskool, also known as "Affies", in Pretoria. It was an important match. If Grey won, they would officially be the top school rugby team in South Africa.

Bertha was in Pretoria for the weekend and many of Hansie's close friends with Grey connections were also there for the match, including Wouter and Louise Klopper. Earlier in the week, Wouter had contacted Hansie, and urged him to come along and watch the game. Hansie had agreed, but on the Friday morning before the match he phoned Louise and said, "I'm not going to the rugby. I don't know if I'm up to seeing all those Grey people."

Louise had not accepted this. "Of course you're going," she said.

In the end, when the match started, Hansie was there, sitting in the stand with Bertha, the Kloppers and Johan Volsteedt. He smiled his nervous, cautious smile. At first he was quiet and said little, preferring others to do the talking. But the general acceptance and support that he got from the Grey boys and parents soon got him out of his shell. He had just come from an early Saturday morning meeting with one of the Bell directors and told Bertha how excited he was about his future at Bell.

"It was a helluva game," said Louise. "In the first ten minutes Grey was 14-0 down. At one stage we were 17-6 down, and then the score was 21-12 to Grey at half time. We eventually beat them 46-17. Hansie was ecstatic, standing up and cheering the team on with the rest of us. He was in his element." Throughout the game he would send text messages from his cell phone to Ewie to give him the latest score.

"It was one of his best days. It was fantastic; everybody was so good to him. It was like old times for Hansie," said Louise. "The Grey fraternity were openly friendly, greeting him enthusiastically. Everyone was happy to see him there." Hansie started to relax, looking people in the eye and chatting a little.

After the match, a South African Broadcasting Television crew, who had filmed the match, had asked for an interview. Hansie accepted, but simply spoke glowingly about the match and how well the Grey boys had done. In answer to one question he explained what made Grey such a special school. Then came the Grey supporters' function on a nearby field. "I was sceptical about taking Hansie with us. There would be intense social interaction and I worried for his sake. All it would take for him to crumple would be one unkind word, one hard question. He was still very nervous about mixing with the sports fraternity," said Louise.

When the Grey First XV began to say their goodbyes at the function, Hansie ambled over and shook all of their hands, congratulating them on playing so well, on a fine win. The captain, Andries Strauss, said of that occasion, "It was the best day of my life. I couldn't believe that Hansie actually came up and talked to us."

Hansie relaxed even more. He had realised, once again, that the people he loved most were accepting him, had never rejected him, still loved him, and wished him well, despite everything. A hero forgiven.

After the function, as they walked back to their vehicles, Hansie spontaneously joined some young kids who were kicking a rugby ball around the field. "Hardly anyone saw him do this. It was dusk. He wasn't doing it to show off. He did it because that was always what Hansie did. The kids he was playing with were very excited, enjoying his play with them enormously. They couldn't get enough of their hero," said Louise.

That evening the Kloppers, Hansie and Bertha went back to Hansie's flat for a braai and Hansie was very chirpy. He refused to let the Kloppers go home, and he made Dom Pedros for everyone after the meal. The previous evening they had all been to Cynthia's where Hansie had won a bottle of Blue Label Johnnie Walker Scotch in a lucky draw. He laughed while making the drinks, because he could just picture Les Sackstein swearing at him for using this expensive bottle of Scotch for something like Dom Pedros.

Charles, the owner of the cottage was away for the weekend, but he had told Hansie that if he needed anything, he was welcome to borrow it. Hansie didn't have any wine glasses so he went and got four from the cottage. He urged everyone to be very careful, as he wasn't sure whether these glasses were part of Charles' collection of rare wine glasses. Unfortunately, Wouter managed to knock one of them over, breaking it. When Charles got back, Hansie got all his courage together and went to apologise about the glass, hoping that it wasn't one of Charles's most valuable collector's items. Charles politely told him not to worry at all (though he did show Hansie which glasses he could use in future). Hansie immediately phoned Wouter and told him that he'd broken one of the last glasses taken off the top deck of the *Titanic* before it sank!

Hansie and Bertha spent that Sunday together. "We stayed in bed a little longer. We spoke about our plans, dreams and the week ahead. Hansie told me all about the meeting he had had with Bell earlier that morning and he looked, for the first time since April 2000, happy and excited. It wasn't the same as with cricket, it was different, but he was positive and upbeat again. We decided that I was going to resign and come to Pretoria to be with him at the end of June. Hansie helped me to write my resignation and we also talked about his goals for the South Western Districts Sport for the Disabled, of which he was still the chairman.

"He wrote down the goals, and asked me to take them to the vice chairlady, who worked with me at Carpe Diem. I still have the piece of paper where Hansie wrote this. They were having a meeting at the end of the week and he wanted her to look at his suggestions before then. We also read from our Bibles and prayed together. There were so many new things going on in our lives, and I remember Hansie's prayer so well. He specifically prayed for the Lord's blessing upon the golf day in Cape Town the following day, and he prayed for good weather as well (it had been particularly bad in the Cape). The other thing he prayed for was our safety. He asked the Lord to keep us both safe and bring us together, safely back in George, the following weekend.

"The Kloppers came by to say goodbye to us. Then we took a long drive to look at possible future homes in Pretoria. After that we went for lunch at a restaurant in Brooklyn. We went back home after lunch and had a Sunday afternoon snooze. We went to Loftus (Pretoria's main rugby stadium) to meet up with Tommy and Riana Smook. Tommy was the doctor of the Blue Bulls rugby side and there was an opportunity for me as the under-19 team's physiotherapist.

"We both got quite excited and things were looking up for us. I was coming to Pretoria, it seemed like I was going to have a job not too far from where we would be staying initially, and Hansie felt excited about his future. As we were driving back home, he asked me what I wanted for our life. I remember telling him that I wanted to be with him, even work with him. As we got back to the cottage, he wrote down a ten-year plan. I still have that piece of paper, too.

"He wanted to work hard and then maybe move back to George. We never realised that there wouldn't be another ten years. Not even another ten days. We spent the Sunday evening quietly at the cottage, talking, and we both felt a bit down. Hansie's mom phoned and I remember him saying that we had the Sunday blues because I was going back to George the next day. He also thanked her for the rusks and biltong that she had sent him. We had the rusks and biltong with coffee for supper and went to bed early."

Hansie took Bertha to the Johannesburg International Airport where they said goodbye and hugged each other. Kissed each other. Bertha flew back to George and Hansie took a flight to Cape Town to attend the Bell Golf Day, which he had organised. It was at the Mowbray Golf Club and Frans met up with him there after Hansie had played a brilliant first nine holes, leading some of the professional golfers. Frans joined the party for lunch at the club and sat with Hansie and pro golfers, James Kingston and Hendrik Buhrmann, a Grey College Old Boy and family friend.

After lunch, Hansie asked Frans to walk with him for a while, but he had to leave. Hansie teed off on the tenth and hooked the ball into the bushes. Frans laughed at this, ribbed him a little and then said what was to be a final goodbye.

On Monday, 27 May Hansie faxed the following letter to Johan Volsteedt and he read it to the boys, during assembly on the Friday.

Dear Mr. Volsteedt
I have often heard the cliché: "In my day" or "remember in the good old days…"
This obviously refers to almost all of us who often look back at our earlier lives when we believed that things could never get better than what they were back then.

I can honestly say that these two sayings were well and truly destroyed on Saturday, whilst sitting at the rugby ground in Pretoria. I am not referring to the 46-17 winning margin, but I am referring to what I "experienced" sitting in amongst the fellow Grey gentlemen and afterwards with some of the Old Boys and staff.

Jack Welch talks about the essential four E's of people working for General Electric, being Energy, the ability to Energize others, having the Edge, and being able to Execute it. The P that coincides with these E's is Passion.

When I left Grey in 1987, I really battled to believe that it could get any better. How wrong I was!! I thought Lappies was irreplaceable. Roelie van Heerden would be missed. Chain could never be replaced. Like other schools in SA, I thought Grey might go the inevitable route of sliding backwards … how wrong I was!! Others have slipped back, but Grey has leaped forward every single day for 15 years.

The grounds and facilities are superb, the staff now has a greater passion than ever before (the tears in most eyes gave it away on Saturday), the singing and the cheerleading (Dixie and Pieter) was better than ever, the stand was left spotless afterwards, the hockey side have beaten teams again and again, and dare I say it, the rugby was awesome. To the coaches I take my hat off, because to find attractive rugby on 72 channels on TV is impossible, but 60 minutes of watching you on Saturday was enough to last me another winter. I am not saying this to blow smoke up your asses, but merely to celebrate small victories with you, and to inspire all of you to greater heights. Savour the moment, but only for a moment, as tomorrow will be tougher than yesterday.

*How wrong I was … how I wish that 15 years would not go so fast.
Proud of you, and particularly of you, Vollies. You are a Champ.*

Kind regards, Hansie Cronjé

●

Hansie had intended flying back to George on Friday, 31 May, at 8am. But he had to attend a function on behalf of Bell at the showgrounds in Schweizer-Reneke, so he changed his flight to one at 4pm.

That day, Hester, who lived in nearby Potchefstroom, received a call from her brother at about 6.45am – he was travelling with a Bell colleague through Potch, he said. Hester urged him to pop in for a visit, but he declined, saying he had no time. Hester persuaded him to stop by on his return trip. "We're having pancakes at our nursery school. Stop by and have a pancake with the children," she said. She knew that Hansie had always loved pancakes and was always glad to be with children.

While Hansie was moving around the Schweizer-Reneke area that day, a Cape Town radio station, Cape Talk, contacted him by telephone and requested an interview to be broadcast that evening. Hansie agreed.

Here are excerpts from the interview:

Jon Maytham (of Cape Talk): Personally, how are you? You sound fine to me. Are you well and happy and strong?
Hansie: Yes, I am well and happy and strong. I'm enjoying the new challenges of the job. I'm very excited about the prospects of working with Gary, Pete and Paul Bell and the family.
Maytham: I know you don't want to focus on the past, but is it something that you have, other than in your dark moments, put behind you?
Hansie: I don't think that you ever put it 100% behind you. The minute that it happened, I knew that I would have to live with it for the rest of my life, and it's just a case of how you manage that. It would be foolish to say that I'd put it all behind me and moved on, it doesn't happen like that. There is a song, "Die Skoene Moet Jy Dra", which means whatever you do in your past you will have to carry with you for the rest of your life. I'm not saying that it's pulling me back; you've just got to manage it and carry on looking forward.
[Maytham recounted an anecdote of Hansie stopping to help push a motorist's car after it had broken down and asked if he was still that person.]
Hansie: Absolutely. I don't think I've changed. I still think I made a horrific mistake, or three or six, in my life. I'm not proud of it, but it doesn't change who I was, or who I am and who I will be in the future.

Later that day, Hansie phoned Hester again and said, "Sus, we're running late. We haven't even left the showgrounds yet. I'll miss my flight if I stop over and visit you." Hester was disappointed, but not surprised. That's how it used to go with Hansie – always on the move, running late. She used to look forward to seeing her brother and then she'd either see him for a few precious minutes or the arrangement would melt away. "I was disappointed and I told him so."

Hester then suggested to her daughter Alexandrea, 9 years old: "'Let's go and stand by the side of the Johannesburg road and wave as he drives past'." Hester remains angry with herself for not going there with her little daughter, who loved Hansie so much, and waving to her beloved brother, the beloved uncle, one last time.

In the late afternoon, Hansie's radio interview was broadcast in Cape Town. (It was broadcast again the following morning.)

At every opportunity, Hansie would fly back to George from Johannesburg to be with Bertha. He had already had to postpone his 31st of May flight once. Now, as he drove to the airport a severe thunderstorm broke out that left him stranded in the traffic on a Johannesburg freeway, so close and yet so far from the airport. He eventually got out of his car and, standing next to the BMW, phoned his mom. They had an unusually long and loving chat, about the little, important things of a family's doings. He told her how sad he was at having to take leave of the study group with whom he had been associated for three years. He had just attended a farewell gathering of the group the previous day. San-Marie told him how proud they were of the guts he showed by pressing on with his studies through that difficult period of his life.

●

It was a serene day in George. Clear and mild. Bertha and a friend who worked with her were having coffee on the veranda. She was looking at the Dutch irises she and Hansie had planted. The previous year they didn't come up and now they had just started flowering. Hansie phoned. He told her he was stuck in traffic in the hailstorm, and couldn't get to the airport on time. "You won't believe it! I can see the airport, it's so close."

Bertha had replied, "Hansie, get out and run!" and Hansie had laughed. He eventually got to the airport, only to be told that all the day's flights had been cancelled.

When Hansie told her of the delay, Bertha said, "Fly back tomorrow morning." But Hansie couldn't wait. He never could wait.

"I was a bit upset – irrationally irritated by the situation and disappointed that we were going to miss one precious night together. The weekends were so short and I missed Hansie terribly during the week. Over the previous two years we had got so used to being together. Also, we had a dinner date with Marge and Gordon McNeill at Fancourt," Bertha said.

Her friend, Alba, had listened to the conversation and said to Bertha, "You know, it's not his fault. Phone him back and say you're not upset with him and that it is just the situation." Bertha didn't. Later that evening, Alba phoned Bertha, "Have you phoned Hansie yet?" Bertha had not. Her friend was right. She needed to phone her husband. When she explained her reaction to him, Hansie said, "I know you're disappointed, Bers. I'll hitch a ride with the cargo aeroplane [Air-Quarius Aviation] and see you at 7 tomorrow morning."

"I told Hansie to rather have a good night's rest and fly first thing on Saturday morning because flying on the cargo plane meant that he had to get up at midnight. He didn't want to hear any of that; he was desperate to get home. He loved George and Fancourt and said that he would rather have a whole day at home."

Hansie phoned Marge to tell her of the delay and apologised in advance for his absence at the dinner. Bertha proceeded to the Irish banker's mansion at Fancourt and the three of them enjoyed a meal together, toasting Hansie with his favourite wine, a dry red from the Rust-en-Vrede Estate. Rust-en-Vrede (the name means Rest and Peace) belongs to the Engelbrechts and Hansie was good friends with their son, Jean.

Gordon phoned Hansie at 8.30pm and told him, "We're drinking your favourite wine, Hansie, and we're drinking a toast to you." He then put Bertha on the line and they had a brief conversation. Bertha could hear that Hansie had been asleep, because he had gone to bed early.

"*Ek is baie lief vir jou, Engel,*" (I love you a lot, Angel) Hansie said. Those were the last words he ever said to his wife.

He was never keen to stay over anywhere if he could get home. When a cricket team would overnight somewhere in South Africa, Hansie would often be the only one to hire a car and drive through the night to get home, before and after his marriage. He had so little time with Bertha – an hour or two made such a difference.

Bertha and Hansie had a private arrangement with AirQuarius Aviation pilots, which entailed providing bed and breakfast accommodation at their Fancourt home for the pilots after their night freight-transport flights from Johannesburg to George. Hansie knew the pilots well. After returning to Pretoria and discussing his frustrations with Niehaus, he called the AirQuarius pilots on his mobile. "Any chance of a seat?"

"Join us," they said. "We leave at 2.15am from Lanseria Airport."

Before 2am Hansie boarded the 1982 Hawker-Siddeley, with pilots Ian Noakes, 50, and Willie Meyer, 69. After one hour and 37 minutes of flying, they landed at Bloemfontein Airport to offload some freight before continuing onwards. The flight to George from Bloemfontein was expected to take about two more hours.

At 6.56am the Hawker-Siddeley flew over George at an altitude of 8 000 feet above sea level. Willie Meyer radioed George Airport and informed them that the aircraft was joining the holding pattern and would be descending to 3 500 feet. The George Tower was unmanned and the unmanned field communication procedures were in force.

Bertha had been up since 5am, and now she was brewing the coffee and cooking the eggs and bacon for the pilots and Hansie. She was a little nervous. The arrangement with the pilots was still new and she wanted to please and impress. The men would be hungry. She looked out of the kitchen window, "I remember opening the bedroom curtains. It was still dark outside. I remember the rain against the window. I thought to myself that yesterday had been such a perfect and beautiful day, with no sign of rain. That morning it was totally different."

The weather was terrible.

She thought she heard, faintly, the drone of the Hawker-Siddeley. They'll be here soon, she thought.

The night before, Bertha had asked Hansie if he needed her to fetch him from the George Airport, or if he was coming with the pilots. "Come and fetch me. The pilots have got paper work to do. I'll send you an SMS as soon as the wheels touch the ground," he had said. George Airport was five minutes from Fancourt.

Hansie's father Ewie was hunting at a huge game farm in Cradock in the Karoo, nearly 500km away from George, not contactable because there was no cellphone coverage in the area. Curiously, for a man who grew up on a farm, Ewie never enjoyed hunting. He only went on this trip because his old friend and colleague from the university sports office, Tat Botha, had persuaded him to go along for the relaxation. At breakfast, Ewie had strangely and unexpectedly said, "Today is the 1st of June, and I've a feeling that something is going to happen today, but I don't know what, because there is no rugby or cricket being played." When he said that, it was 7.15am.

Bertha continued to wait. "At 7.30am I started to feel a bit uncomfortable. The plane was never this late." She phoned Hansie's cellphone but it was on voice mail. At 8am she took Julie, one of her domestic workers, back to her home. As she was driving back to Fancourt, she was getting more and more concerned. She thought, "Maybe his mobile's battery is flat. Maybe the plane has been delayed somewhere."

Back at home, she climbed back into bed, not sure what to do next. She took out her Bible. She opened it at random and read the first thing she saw on a page: "… and Samuel died." Fear gripped her heart. And then the phone rang.

"I picked it up quickly, silently hoping that it was Hansie. The man on the other line said that his name was Gavin Branson from AirQuarius. I felt sick to my stomach. I knew that something was seriously wrong… "

He asked, "Have you heard from Hansie?"

"No," said Bertha.

"Listen," he said, "don't panic, but the plane's missing. Maybe they've diverted to Oudtshoorn."

Bertha said, "No. Hansie would've phoned me instantly if they had done that; he knows that I am waiting for him."

"I got up, went to the dining room and stood in front of the big windows overlooking the fairway in front of our home. The realisation of what might have happened took my breath away, and an unbearable pain went through my body. I called out to God and I sobbed. It was so painful that I put all those thoughts out of my mind immediately. I phoned Gavin back and asked him to explain to me exactly what he knew had happened up to that point. He simply said the plane had tried to land, but couldn't. It followed the procedure for a missed landing and that was the last they had heard."

The hollow, interminable minutes moved by. And Bertha waited…

She didn't want to phone Hansie's mom and dad before she had more news. "I was hoping that Hansie would phone in the meantime and say that he was in Oudtshoorn, and that his cellphone was not working or something like that. At 8.45, I knew I had to let them know before it somehow got out in the media. I phoned Gavin and asked him if he thought it was necessary for me to phone Hansie's mom and dad. He said yes. So I phoned my mother-in-law immediately."

The Tuesday before, San-Marie had had a bladder operation. To add to her discomfort she had had oral surgery too and was recovering from the procedures at home in Bloemfontein. She had spent days in bed, but that Saturday morning she had decided to get up. Shortly after this Bertha called her with the bad news. San-Marie was perplexed, because she thought Hansie had already arrived in George the previous night. Bertha then explained his decision to fly with AirQuarius.

At about 9am, Frans's mobile rang at his home in Stellenbosch. It was his cousin, Hettiën, who had stayed over at 246 Paul Kruger Avenue the night before. She was with San-Marie, who by now was in a state of horror. "Pray for Hansie," she said. "They don't know where his plane is. It's already two hours late."

Frans replied, "Ag, you know Hansie. They'll be fine. He always gets out of everything."

Frans phoned Bertha and she said tearfully, "I don't know what to do. There's no trace of him. Something is seriously wrong."

Frans was initially annoyed. "I thought to myself 'Now you've missed the plane. Why are you not answering your phone? You're up to mischief and causing all this fear and alarm'."

But half an hour later, the plane was still missing and with cold dread Frans realised that there must have been a crash. The plane would have run out of fuel by then.

Tearfully, Frans had told me on one of our road trips to Bloemfontein from Cape Town: "René and I were praying and praying, crying out to God for protection. But it was like praying against a wall. We felt emptiness as we were praying. It was as if we knew that we were asking for something that was not going to happen. I said to René, 'I can't handle this waiting.'" He quickly packed a bag and went off in his Isuzu double-cab diesel bakkie, heading at speed for George, his cell phone at hand.

"I phoned Gavin. He was in the Lanseria control tower and said he didn't know where the plane was."

Hester and Gordon Parsons at that time were on their way to a wedding in Klerksdorp. En route, they received an SMS from Frans: "Please pray. Hansie's plane missing."

Hester then phoned San-Marie, who told her, "We didn't want to tell you until they had found Hansie's plane." Hester was known to be emotionally the most volatile family member.

Hester and Gordon arrived at the church, but couldn't go in. Hester was sobbing uncontrollably.

As he drove, Frans kept phoning Bertha, San-Marie and Hester, keeping in almost constant communication. Ewie was still not contactable.

San-Marie recalled, "At about 10.15am I realised that they couldn't have landed anywhere else. We would've heard about that. They didn't have the fuel. I immediately started praying: 'Just not the sea, Lord. Not this, Lord. Not this. I want to know where they physically are'." While she prayed, San-Marie received an SMS from Ewie: "*Daar is 'n koue, droewige suid-weste wind wat waai.*" (There is a cold, depressing south-westerly blowing.)

San-Marie knew then that Ewie was in cellphone range. He happened to be sitting on the only koppie on the farm that had a signal. When Ewie answered the phone, his wife asked, "Are you alone?"

"No, Tat is with me," Ewie replied, perplexed.

"I want to speak to him," she said. San-Marie told Tat that Hansie's plane was missing, explained the whole situation and asked him to tell Ewie.

Tat broke the dreadful news, and the two men prayed together, kneeling in the veld.

By now different search and rescue teams, ground and air, had been activated, involving about 30 people. The weather was just beginning to clear, but visibility was still poor. At 10.16am a helicopter pilot spotted the wreckage, the broken fuselage pivoting on a mountain peak. Two hours into Frans's dash to George, Gavin Branson phoned him and told him that a helicopter had sighted Hansie's plane. There was no sign of Hansie or the pilots, and the helicopter pilot couldn't land anywhere near the wreck in the precipitous kloof.

"He told me that there was still hope and that they might be alive, but I now realise that he didn't quite know how to tell me how bad it was. He said that they were sending a rescue team to the crash site," Frans said.

By that time, Bertha had phoned a clinical psychologist friend, Christie Els, and told her about the situation and Christie dashed over to be with her.

"The rest of the day is a blur. One big nightmare," Bertha said.

She stayed by the phone; it offered some kind of comfort. Many people came to the house. Some just parked outside. "They didn't want to come in, they just wanted to be close," said Bertha.

Bertha's mind raced. "At one point I thought, 'Maybe he's disabled. That's why I had to work at the school for the disabled. Maybe he's a paraplegic and is going to win a disabled sports championship.' I never let the thought that he might be dead cross my mind."

Before Frans could phone her with the news, San-Marie received a phone call: "It has been confirmed. The plane has just landed safely in George," a voice said.

San-Marie was ecstatic with happiness, and had barely started to celebrate the good news when Frans phoned, "Mom, they've found the plane, wrecked, in the mountains. There's no sign of the pilots or Hansie."

San-Marie just cried out, "My son, my son!"

Frans phoned Hester and René with the news of the sighting of the wreck. "I kept on hoping that he was still alive, but deep down I started doubting," said Frans. Meanwhile, Hester and Gordon had left the wedding to go back to Potchefstroom. They then left immediately for Bloemfontein.

Frans was still travelling along the N2 to George, constantly answering his cell phone as people across the world started calling. It was all over the news that the plane was missing and people wanted to know what was happening. "A Cape Town journalist called and asked if I had any comments about Hansie's death. By now we only knew that the plane had crashed, but it was not yet confirmed whether the pilots or Hansie had survived. It made me furious that the journalist had the nerve to call at such a time and I snapped at him. I shouted at him that they [the newspapers] had been trying to kill Hansie while he was alive, why would they like any news now? I felt really bad after he had hung up, and I treated subsequent calls from the media with much more patience."

"My cell phone battery was getting low and there was still no word from Gavin or the rescue team – and then just before reaching Buffeljags [about half way to George], Gavin phoned. He said that he was really sorry, but it had been confirmed that Hansie and the two pilots were dead. He also asked if I would call Bertha and my parents, as he didn't know how to tell them.

"I first phoned Bertha and somehow managed to get the words out that 'Hansie didn't make it'. Then I phoned my mom, and then also managed to get through to my dad. I had just enough battery power left to call my wife, René, before my cell phone shut off.

"It was the hardest thing that I had ever had to do and I just burst out sobbing as I drove."

René then called Hester to tell her the news.

Ewie arrived back at 246 Paul Kruger Avenue, heart-broken. Then the tidal wave of press and people started flowing into the house, a wave that continued throughout the weekend. "It was a strange thing," recalled San-Marie. "I didn't mind the press and all the people around me. They were looking at me with different eyes. Rugby players started arriving. Cricket players. There were people everywhere. The house was a mess. Friends started arriving and they just took over, making tea, answering the phone – the super-support system from Bloemfontein was out of this world. Bunches of flowers started flowing in – we couldn't take any more into the house."

People stopped and put flowers on the front-yard fence. Soon, it was packed full of blooms. Florists in the city ran out of stock. That night, Bloemfontein kept vigil outside the house. Candles were lit, hymns were sung, prayers were said. Grey College boys and University of the Free State men and women came to visit and offer their prayers, wanting to help.

By the time Frans got to George, seven hours after the crash, the sun was shining. There wasn't a breath of wind. The Outeniqua Mountains shimmered purple and blue in the bright light.

At 3.13pm, doctors at the scene examined the three bodies and proclaimed them all dead. They put the bodies, all intact, in bags and on stretchers. Monster Wilkins, who was part of the rescue team, was one of the first at the scene. "It was an unpleasant sight, very final," he said. The team had to abandon the scene because of poor light and bad weather conditions. They had to return to Vandalanskloof on Sunday morning to rope up the stretchers and take the bodies to a morgue in George. "It was really hard for my mom to know that the bodies were still on the mountain that evening, but I told Gavin to tell the rescue team not to risk their lives trying to get the bodies off the mountain before dark," said Frans.

When Frans had phoned Bertha, her pastor, Dave Hooper, answered the call. "As I was coming down the passage, I saw Dave holding out the phone to me. He smiled at me, and there was a peacefulness about him that made me calm, and I realised that Hansie was dead," said Bertha. "All Frans said to me was, 'Bers, *Hans het dit nie gemaak nie.*' [Hans didn't make it.] I gave the phone back to Dave and walked out into the garden and started to sob. I phoned Kate. All she managed to say to me was, 'I am so sorry. I am so sorry'. I just cried and couldn't speak."

The last time Jonty had seen his mate was about a month before. "Hansie had been in Durban with Bell and spent a Sunday with us. For once, Kate and I had him selfishly to ourselves. We sat together at the pool, our feet dangling in the water and spoke about his life. He was perfectly happy. It was clear to us that Hansie had made his peace with God."

Kate and Jonty had only received news of the missing plane at around noon as they had been staying on a farm that had no cellphone reception. Kate's mother had phoned the farm on a landline to tell them that the plane was missing. They then travelled back to Durban and when they got back into cellphone range, Kate had picked up a string of SMSes from Bertha, such as "Chickie 1 to Chickie 2 [the code the two friends used for each other]. Pls fone me" and then "Hansie's plane is missing".

When a doctor arrived to attend to Bertha, all she wanted to do was to go to the Outeniqua Beach, where she and Hansie had a special spot against a dune, close to the crashing Indian Ocean. There they would spread a blanket on the yellow, crunchy sand and have a glass of wine. Alone, still in love. Happy to be away from others for a while.

Frans was with her now. Friends from Mossel Bay arrived as well. Brian McMillan and his wife Denise. Jacques Kallis. Herschelle Gibbs. They sat together, watching the news on TV. For the first time, Bertha saw the wreck on the side of the Outeniquas. It felt so unreal.

That night, her friend Christie and Frans stayed with Bertha. Early on Sunday morning, hours before sunrise, Bertha awoke. Silently she walked downstairs and opened an outside door. It was cold. "I walked to the 17th hole of the Montagu course, Hansie's favourite hole." It was still dark and Bertha sat there on a little bench at the tee, in her tracksuit and slippers, until sunrise. "I looked up to the Outeniqua Mountains and cried for Hansie. My heart ached and I called on the Lord for comfort."

●

The South African Civil Aviation Authority Accident Report, 110 A4 pages long, signed by the investigators only on 5 May 2004, stated that the twin-engined Hawker-Siddeley 74B (AZS-OJU) "was on a scheduled freight flight ... Poor weather conditions prevailed over the George area and the pilots had to execute an instrument-guided approach for the landing. The ground-based Instrument Landing System (ILS) on Runway 29 at George Aerodrome was intermittently unreliable during the approach. The pilots decided to execute a missed approach.

"They flew the aircraft into a valley and crashed into the side of the mountains north-east of George."

It was as simple as that. Not the slightest shred of evidence in the tedious and meticulous report of any malicious tampering with the aircraft or assassination of Hansie by mad bookies or some such rogues, a rumour that did the rounds world wide for a long time, even in some usually reliable newspapers.

The "probable cause", the report said, was that "the crew deviated from the missed approach during an attempted ILS landing on Runway 29 at George in Instrument Meteorological Conditions and lost situational awareness, aggravated by the presence of strong upper south-westerly winds. They allowed the aircraft to drift off course, resulting in a controlled impact with terrain 6.7 nautical miles north-east of the George Aerodrome."

The exact location of the crash was Vandalanskloof in the Outeniqua Mountains at S33 degrees 54' 42" E022 degrees 28' 33.6".

There was no air-traffic controller on duty at the George Tower during the radio calls – his hours of duty only began at 8.30am, more than an hour after the crash.

The South African pilot, Mr Willie Meyer, was 69 years old and had no record of previous accidents and his health status was moderately good. The British co-pilot, Ian Noakes, aged 50, also had no record of previous accidents. The plane itself, said the report, was generally in good nick and all papers relating to its operation were in order.

However, the autopilot, gyro and other instrumentation had been known to be defective in 2002, and probably had not been fixed, according to the aircraft's flight folio. In addition, the localiser of the ILS on Runway 29 had malfunctioned. This means that it was at least likely that no Localiser signals had been properly received by the aircraft's instruments. Such marred functionality on the ground and in the air is not all that unusual.

"There were several defects relevant to the serviceability status of the navigation equipment of the aircraft entered into the flight folio which were not cleared. This rendered the aircraft technically unairworthy" and "the pilots did not follow the approved procedure for a missed approach. This resulted in them losing their situational awareness, furthermore, they disregarded the warning flags that indicated that the (ILS) facility was not reliable," said the report.

All in all a complex web of events, with some defects on both the aircraft's and the control tower's instruments, coupled with foul weather.

Several eyewitnesses, who included pilots, observed the weather at the time as being overcast with low-level clouds and rain. Visibility was poor towards the aerodrome, and they observed a strong westerly surface wind. They saw the aircraft from time to time between the clouds and saw it disappearing into the clouds when it flew over the town in a north-easterly direction. The mountains were covered with clouds and it was raining in the area north of George.

A meteorological report indicated that the accident site probably had cloudy conditions with rain, and icing would have occurred on the aircraft. Visibility would have been zero. The calculated wind strength at point of impact was 45 knots.

The co-pilot flew the aircraft, up until the last minute and a half of the flight, when the pilot-in-command took over. It was clear, the report said, that the Ground Proximity Warning System (GPWS) on board was operational and had issued warnings.

"The nose of the aircraft rolled in underneath the forward part of the wreck and burst open during the impact. The lower areas of the cockpit, including the main instrument panels, were scattered underneath and to the left of the forward wreckage. The nose landing gear, cockpit centre pedestal and the pilot-in-command's body were found in the area to the left of the nose wreckage. The co-pilot's body was stuck in the left-hand side area of the cockpit wreckage."

Hansie's broken, 32-year-old body was found in its seat. The rear fuselage had come to a standstill, pivoting on a rock. The wings had folded around the curved side of the mountain.

Medico-legal post mortems were carried out on the pilots' bodies. The accident was deemed not survivable. The cause of death was multiple injuries. No alcohol was found in their blood. No medical factors could be found as the cause of the accident. At the moment of impact the aircraft was flying at 115 knots, carrying motor spares, and postal packages.

Cockpit Voice Recording Transcript from the report – the last few minutes:

5:16:33 CP (Co-Pilot): "Speed a bit high for the flap."
5:16:56 Ground Proximity Warning System (GPWS) signals PULL UP
GPWS PULL UP
GPWS PULL UP
CP: "Pull up my chum."
GPWS PULL UP
GPWS PULL UP
CP: "What's that there?"
5:17:18 CP: "Ten miles still."
PIC (Pilot in Command): "OK that's bearable."
CP: "OK."
5:17:25 CP: "That's what they say max nine miles. Get that pull up."
PIC: "*Ja, O my Lewe* (indistinct) *man*." (Yes, O my life… man)
CP: Indistinct.
5:17:40 GPWS PULL UP
GPWS PULL UP
GPWS PULL UP

5:17:55 PIC: "OK, how is your flags now?" (flags on the instrumentation panel, warning of a faulty ILS)

CP: "They're OK at the moment."

CP: "OK, two and a half thousand."

PIC: "OK."

5:18:06 CP: "That, the glide slope [possibly the directional beacon link-up with the George Aerodrome] is out now, it's all out again."

PIC: "And we must go down."

5:18:35 PIC: "Let's just take a bit more power there." (sound of engines spooling up)

5:18:35 ALERT SIGNAL

PIC: "Let me take it."

CP: "You got it."

PIC: Indistinct (possibly "O shit"), then "man".

5:19:05 ALERT SIGNAL

5:19:29 GPWS PULL UP

GPWS PULL UP

GPWS PULL UP

ALERT SIGNAL

5:19:50 GPWS PULL UP

ALERT SIGNAL

GPWS PULL UP

THE PLANE CRASHES

(CPVRT ENDS)

Note: The CPVRT time line is Co-ordinated Universal Time (UTC). South African Standard Time (SAST) is UTC plus two hours. So the moment of impact was ten seconds before 7.20am (SAST) on 1 June 2002.

＊

Bertha never saw Hansie's body afterwards. "Frans went to identify Hansie. A family member had to do it and I couldn't. I asked Frans to bring me Hansie's wedding band."

Frans nervously drove to the morgue at about lunchtime on the Sunday afternoon. "I walked into the room where they had laid his body. The undertakers had put the open coffin behind glass, but I wanted to be close. As I saw his body, I had perfect peace. I somehow knew that the Lord had always known that the 1st of June 2002 would be the time to take him home. By His grace he had exposed Hansie's sins, and had given him two years to set things right. Our family has never felt the pilots, AirQuarius or the airport were to blame in any way for the accident."

"It was a strange feeling to be there. It was not hugely emotional, but very peaceful. It really helped me to get finality about Hansie's death and to deal with it." With the help of a policeman, Frans took Hansie's wedding ring off, and searched Hansie's pockets for other belongings. His brother's body was stiff, flesh still chilled by the icy mountain air and rain. Hansie's face was not disturbed. His right leg had been smashed though and his whole body was crushed from head to toe. On his right wrist, where his watch used to be, there were purple marks.

"It was about 1pm when I left the morgue and went back to Fancourt. When I got there Jonty and Kate had just arrived. I walked in and just embraced Bertha and then Jonty. We just stood there crying.

"Still today I sometimes dream about Hansie and cry at night," said Frans. "But flesh is flesh, and spirit is spirit. Our earthly bodies are just temporary, but the breath of life, our spirits, will live forever."

San-Marie wanted her little boy to come home. "Don't leave him there. Bring him home to Bloemfontein," she pleaded. After the undertakers had prepared the body and it was moved to Bloemfontein, San-Marie and Ewie went to see him. The coffin was now closed, except for the hinged lid exposing only his face, which had a serene expression.

●

Lost in the remote kloof are one of Hansie's size 10 black brogues, first worn on his wedding day, his watch, the hard-drive of his laptop, and his wallet and its contents. They were never found and probably still lie among the bushes and rocks of Vandalanskloof. The other brogue, scuffed and torn, was found some distance away from the body, with shredded little fynbos flowers and stalks inside.

An entrepreneur bought the plane wreck and airlifted it off the mountain, planning to use it as some sort of grisly museum piece. The Cronjé family has consistently refused to have anything to do with this venture and tried to stop it, but he still continued with his plans.

CHAPTER SIXTEEN

'ONSE HANSIE'

My hart is seer; ek sal jou nooit vergeet nie.
Jy was my vriend en mentor by Grey Kollege.

— Varkie Greyling

Hansie is in heaven. He is playing cricket there.
God is in his team – and Hansie is the captain.

— an apocryphal quote from a little boy, after learning of Hansie's death

Here was a young man courageously and with dignity
rebuilding his life after the setback he suffered a while ago.
The manner in which he was doing that ...
promised to make him once more a role model of
how one deals with adversity.

— former President Nelson Mandela's tribute to Hansie

On the Sunday night before the funeral, Dr Ali Bacher phoned San-Marie and expressed his condolences. He said, "Your son was the only one who spoke the truth." Angrily, San-Marie replied, "Why tell me now? All Hansie wanted to hear, all he asked from you, all he wanted from you was for you to say publicly: 'Hansie spoke the truth'."

Bacher also spoke to Ewie. "You must tell me if you and the family don't want me to attend," he said.

"Anybody can come," Ewie had replied. Despite everything, he bore no malice towards Ali, and recalled times when he and Ali had been good friends.

The decision some of Hansie's sternest critics had to face was: dare I attend the funeral? Even those who had slated him, worked and conspired against him, found that his death put things into perspective. Whatever one thought about Hansie's latter reign, one had to acknowledge his monumental, historical captaincy and the shining times, when he had led his team-mates to victory time and time again.

Emotions were running high among Hansie's fans and there was a possibility of, at the very least, unpleasant incidents against perceived persecutors and hypocrites. Some family members – indeed Bloemfontein itself, blamed Ali Bacher for many of Hansie's troubles. And then there were the likes of Percy Sonn, John Blair, the bookie fraternity, the media, and some fellow players who had raged against Hansie. Personal opinions, public perceptions and the Cronjé clan's feelings had to be weighed carefully.

Although some of the Cronjés were still struggling to forgive Bacher and company for the harsh way they had dealt with Hansie, Frans said, "I feel sorry for Dr Bacher because I believe that he wanted to patch things up with Hansie. Unfortunately, I think he wanted to wait until after the World Cup to do so and then he missed the opportunity."

In 2004, the author put the following to Bacher: "It seemed that you softened your attitude towards Hansie halfway through the King Commission, but Percy Sonn, John Blair and other UCB officials were very harshly outspoken against him. Did you at any time think that you didn't agree with their public statements, such as Sonn's assertion that if he had his way, Hansie wouldn't even be allowed to play beach cricket?"

Bacher replied, "Hansie phoned me and said, 'Is that your viewpoint too?' and I said 'No'. There's no question that I differed with Blair and Sonn on the intensity of the aggression. My ultimate hope for Hansie was that he would continue to contribute to South African cricket, but time would have had to pass before that could've been realised. Hansie played in three World Cups. He wanted to do commentary work but the whole focus would've been on him. It wouldn't have been fair to the country.

"After the World Cup of 2003, I would've said, 'Hansie, townships. I've got no obligations; I can do what I want now. You come with me; let's go to the townships.' And I'm sure by doing that, he would've matured and got his confidence back and his credibility. That's the advice I would've given him."

The family wanted a private funeral at Grey College. They were adamant and wanted the funeral over quickly, with a minimum of pomp and ceremony. There was to be no hijacking of, or even participation in, the process by the authorities they had come to distrust, indeed, to dislike deeply, in some cases. If some of the government officials had had their way, the funeral would have probably been a quasi-state funeral, complete with overseas dignitaries, state officials, a mass choir singing the national anthem, and many other bells and whistles befitting an international hero, a noble African son. The traditional funeral for a hero would have been very different from the relatively understated and "private" notions held by the likes of Bertha, Frans, Hester, San-Marie and Ewie. Hansie would be remembered in a service of humility, eloquence and simplicity, in the bosom of his cultural home: Grey College, in Bloemfontein.

"It wasn't a time for politics or even a time to acknowledge dignitaries. It was a time to glorify the Lord Jesus Christ. That's the way Bertha and the family wanted it. The moment had arrived. It was time for the God story," Peter Pollock said in his book *The Winning Factor*.

"At the time there was night around Hansie, night around us. Death had become something holy. We questioned God. 'Why take him away now, just when he was beginning to stand up?' But we realised that he was never going to be the old Hansie again," said San-Marie. "I would never have declared it, but I always knew that Hansie's time would be short. He was too much of an angel-child."

Ewie concluded that Hansie's death had been unreal, "unworkable", in his heart and mind. "I couldn't process it properly. Without God, I could not have dealt with it at all; I would've gone mad. I have friends who have lost children. The pain never goes away. The memories stay."

However, Ewie, a man of few words when it comes to his emotions, affirmed, quietly and carefully, "When I think about Hansie, I am not overcome with pride because of his achievements; I'm simply thankful for his life. Mostly, Hansie had a good life and I'm grateful for that."

At first, Frans and Ewie consulted with Les Sackstein, the family lawyer. At that stage they certainly did not want any member of the United Cricket Board (Dr Ali Bacher at that time was technically not a member of the UCB) to attend. The wounds of Hansie's perceived unending and gruesome persecution were still raw. Unresolved anger was in the air. Together with Sackstein they compiled a fax to be sent to the UCB, telling them explicitly that they were not welcome at the funeral. "I think it was more a case of fearing violent public reaction at the funeral, than not wanting the UCB officials to be there," Frans explained.

The fax was sent and received. In a subsequent family debate, Bertha disagreed with this prohibition. Hansie, she said, would have liked them to attend. Hansie was not malicious, and bore no grudges. No one was to be barred from coming. "Bertha is really one amazing woman and a shining example to us all, and the whole family knew she was right," Frans said.

He quickly asked Louise Klopper to contact the UCB and inform them about the change.

"Please ignore the previous fax. Everyone is welcome to attend," she said. They then sent off a second fax in confirmation, saying explicitly that anyone was welcome to attend, and the UCB was certainly not barred. Louise understood clearly from her communication with the UCB that the first fax had not been passed on, and had been torn up and thrown away. In fact, this first fax had somehow been circulated to all members of the UCB and was released within minutes to the media, which reported on this snub widely. When news of the second fax eventually broke, it was simply placed among the hubbub of reportage on the funeral arrangements, and a degree of confusion reigned among the media representatives, who seemed unable or unwilling to adequately process the "all welcome" signal.

Les Sackstein phoned Ewie the next morning, very upset about an article insinuating that the family said that all were welcome at the funeral, but blaming Sackstein for sending out a fax to say that the UCB were not welcome. Eventually, Ewie held a press conference to clear up the matter.

Bertha stayed at Fancourt until the Tuesday morning. "When we had to decide on everything for his funeral on the Monday after his death, it was so unreal. I woke up at 5am on the Monday morning. Kate was staying with me in the bedroom. I got up and went to Hansie's study. She immediately went to wake Jonty, and the three of us sat in front of the computer. My head was working over time. There were so many things going through my mind. Silly things. For example, that it was the beginning of a month, the 3rd of June, and Hansie used to pay all the bills – what was I going to do? My salary at the school would never cover all our expenses."

"All of a sudden, I just couldn't take it anymore and I collapsed into a heap. Kate and Jonty were right there beside me. She gave me a calming tablet. Jonty jumped in and started to organise some of the bills and after a while I started to feel a bit better.

"That day was one of the worst days of my life. There were so many things to do. I was in constant contact with Frans and the rest of the family, deciding about what to sing at Hansie's funeral, who was going to lead the service, finding a picture to put on the funeral bulletin and then, one of the worst things of all, deciding what Hansie would wear in his coffin. I remember standing in front of his cupboard and I felt sick to my stomach. As I took out his favourite Fancourt shirt, I couldn't come to grips with the fact that I was organising my husband's funeral. It was one of the most exhausting days for all of us. It was almost too much to bear."

As most of the florists in Bloemfontein had run out of stock, the family asked Sackstein to open up a special bank account, called the Hansie Cronjé Charitable Memorial Fund. They asked the media to tell the public that instead of sending flowers, they could donate the money that they would have spent on flowers to the fund. All the money that has since been paid into this account has been donated to the SWD Sport for the Disabled (75%) and to the Reach for a Dream Foundation (25%). Later, five different musicians wrote songs in tribute to Hansie and they also donated money to the fund. Since Hansie's death, Gordon McNeill has organised an annual Hansie Cronjé Golf Day at Fancourt around the 1st of June. This golf day and many similar events have enabled Bertha and the Cronjé family to keep donating money to these charities. One special gift was the purchase in full of a new Mercedes Sprinter Bus, with all the right fittings for the disabled sporting people of South-Western Districts.

Bacher recalled his road trip to the funeral in Bloemfontein in the lengthy paean *Ali: The Life of Ali Bacher*, by Rodney Hartman. "During the journey he [Ali] received word that somewhere ahead of him was another car transporting his friend and former colleague Hoosain Ayob, to the funeral. There was however, another occupant in the car, and his name was Hamid 'Banjo' Cassim."

Cassim was "the Biltong Man", the man who, in January 2000, had introduced the bookmaker Sanjay Chawla to Hansie in a hotel room in Umhlanga Rocks, near Durban. Sanjay had notoriously featured in the obstinately missing tapes of an alleged conversation with Hansie, which Shamila Batohi had so tenaciously relied on at the King Commission.

Ali said in the book that he called Ayob on his mobile and said, "... I want you and your passenger to turn around immediately and go back to Johannesburg."

Raymond van Staden, Hansie's erstwhile security consultant, had a different recollection of the matter, which does not necessarily negate Bacher's story. Raymond, en route too, had spotted the car and its occupant, and had stopped it. He told Cassim, after consulting telephonically with some of the family, "We can't guarantee your safety." Cassim, who had loved Hansie, had eventually turned back, with tears and a heavy heart.

Bacher was shocked to see, when he drove into Bloemfontein, newspaper posters that screamed at him: "*BACHER JY IS NIE WELKOM NIE!*" (Bacher you are not welcome.) But as she arrived at the funeral, San-Marie embraced him and received him warmly, as did Frans and Ewie.

However, it is probably true that the worst thing Bacher ever said publicly about Hansie was that he had "erred grievously". In his statement to the media after Hansie's death, Bacher said, "... Hansie's honesty at the King Commission of Inquiry facilitated a process for world cricket to address the problem [presumably of alleged match-fixing and related bookie interference in the game of cricket] and start stamping it out."

On Wednesday, 5 June 2002, more than 25 million people around the world watched Hansie's funeral, televised live from Grey College's Reunion Hall. About 1 000 people packed into the school's hall, another 1 000 were seated in and around a nearby marquee with a TV monitor. Hundreds of others sat on chairs outside the hall, in the mild winter afternoon sunshine.

Seated at the front and near the front were the Minister of Defence Mosiuoa Lekota, the Minister of Sport Ngconde Balfour, Premier of the Free State Winkie Direko, Mayor of Bloemfontein Pappie Mokoena and Webster Mfebe, the MEC for Sport in the Free State. They weren't mentioned, or officially welcomed in any of the several speeches made. Some of them afterwards expressed their disappointment and thinly concealed pique at this.

But Frans said, "It was a private funeral. We didn't send out invitations. We said that anyone was welcome to come. The family meant no offence in not following certain protocols, like acknowledging the dignitaries present – we just didn't give it a thought."

Bertha was dressed in a yellow-khaki coloured jacket, white blouse with a flamboyant flounced neck, black trousers and gold earrings, her long blonde hair in a simple, natural style. A red rose was on her lap. At one point during the ceremony, the sun shone brightly through one of the many large windows, dramatically lighting up her golden hair. She sat in the middle of the front row, with her and Hansie's family members and special friends, tightly gripping Kate Rhodes's hand. "As I walked into the hall at Grey College, I felt an amazing peace, 'the peace of the Lord that passes all understanding', and as I was thinking this Kate whispered in my ear, 'Can you feel the peace?'"

Heart-broken, Alexandrea Parsons, Hansie's beloved niece, sat on Hester's lap throughout the proceedings. It was her 10th birthday.

Behind them sat the South African cricket team in their green striped blazers, a phalanx of tearful and grim fortitude.

The service began with the singing of a mournful *Onse Vader* – the same hymn that was sung at Hansie and Bertha's wedding. Just off centre stage was Hansie's metallic blue coffin, decked with Leonardo roses in shades of red. In front of this was a Tinus Horne portrait of Hansie, smiling, in his South African cricket colours. White daisies were arranged near another painted portrait on cloth, which hung from the lectern, placed there by an anonymous admirer.

On the walls in the front, at the sides and the back, were the school's honours boards, on which the Cronjé family name featured so often.

Pastor Dave Hooper of the Patria Bible Church in George was the unassuming, gentle MC. During his discourses he quoted from various Bible passages and eventually concluded with the last verses of Ecclesiastes, "Let us hear the conclusion of the matter: Fear God and keep His commandments: for this is the whole duty of man. For God shall bring every work into judgment, with every secret thing, whether it be good, or whether it be evil."

The Welsh folk hymn *Guide Me, O Thou Great Jehovah* was then sung, the song a little boy had been so familiar with, as he watched the great heroes of Welsh rugby on endlessly re-run video tapes, all those years ago.

The main sermon was, of course, delivered by the popular evangelist and cricketing man, Peter Pollock.

He proclaimed that it was "an honour and privilege to have been intricately involved in Hansie's 'Decade of Destiny'. Hansie saw his job and his goal simply to give the fans what they wanted – victory. He was single-minded about his task and he took his country to the top. The statistics speak for themselves. They are indelibly written for all time. He won over 70% of his One-Day Internationals, which ranks him amongst the truly great international captains. He won 51% of the Tests. Surely a testimony of greatness.

"Then came the fall. There was an unprecedented and relentless media onslaught. At times I cringed. At times I cried. Would it ever quit? Christians never claim to have it all together. In fact, they know they are lost without Jesus Christ. That's the gospel.

"The truth – that's all we advised Hansie. The truth shall set you free, says the Bible. It's the only way. There are just no options. Typically he tried to protect others. Biblical principles govern the world. Don't ever make decisions that are contrary to Biblical principles because they will collapse sooner or later. Sin reaps its consequences, but God forgives the repentant sinner. What Hansie did was wrong. But he didn't make excuses. He took his medicine.

"Times were tough, life was hard, but Hansie reaffirmed Jesus as His Lord. It was uphill, into the wind. The wicket was dead, the ball was soft, the bowlers tired and support was scarce. But Hansie put his hand on the plough. Looking back was not an option. It never was with the captain. Jesus never promises that it will be easy, but He does promise: 'I will be with you'. There was a mountain to climb and, typically, Hansie was determined to climb it.

"Last Saturday Hansie made alternative arrangements to 'get home'. Ironically enough, he did in fact 'arrive home' on top of that mountain. He is finally home. He is with Jesus at last. He is now experiencing that peace and joy that is beyond the understanding of this world.

"Like mighty King Solomon, Hansie discovered the hard way that life isn't about fame and success. God is in the people business and the family business. Life moves the goalposts. It strews the path with temptations. There is no pot of gold at the end of the rainbow.

"A famous American actor once said, when asked about fame, 'It's a puff of dust, a mirage in the desert. You aim, you achieve, there is a moment or two of exhilaration. Then the dust settles, the mirage clears and all you have is emptiness.'

"The absolute truth is that life is meaningless, a chasing after the wind, if you have not found God."

Peter concluded by saying, "I thank God for Hansie, his life and achievements and his testimony. They will all live on. I thank God, too, for all those multitudes of fans who forgave Hansie long, long ago."

He quoted from Philippians 1: "I know that this will turn out for my deliverance through your prayer and the supply of the Spirit of Jesus Christ, according to my earnest expectation and hope that in nothing I shall be ashamed, but with all boldness, as always, so now also, Christ will be magnified in my body whether by life or by death."

After Peter's sermon, the ten-man multiracial Grey College musical group, Indomitus, sang *Time to Say Goodbye*, backed by two mournful cellos, two violins and a flute. Bertha said, "We heard Andrea Bocelli for the first time with Wouter and Louise. Hansie instantly got us the CD and the DVD – he loved his music and soon knew most of the words, especially those of *Time to say Goodbye*."

The national team made their way up to the stage, Makhaya Ntini, Jacques Kallis, Lance Klusener, Allan Donald, Boeta Dippenaar, Corrie van Zyl, Jonty Rhodes, Shaun Pollock, Mark Boucher, Steve Elworthy, Neil McKenzie, Herschelle Gibbs and Bob Woolmer. Jonty was first to speak and managed a smile when he said that Hansie always told him that Grey was a great school, but after hearing those boys sing, he now also believed it. Then-captain Shaun Pollock battled for a while to find composure before he could start. He recounted the good times, providing little anecdotes about Hansie's good nature, his common touch, and his pranks: the Vaseline on door handles, aftershave on toothbrushes, the tranquillisers he gave to Paddy Upton, who thought they were malaria tablets... He paid his respects to "an outstanding leader, cricketer and friend... We are proud to have served under your leadership. Hansie, we'll miss you."

The headmaster of Grey College, Johan Volsteedt, provided a sombre and articulate tribute, and spoke of Hansie as a "true South African sporting gentleman... Little boys who play cricket today all want to be either 'Hansie' or 'Jonty'." He noted Hansie's common touch – evidenced by the fact that the biggest bouquet the family had received was from the Fancourt caddies. "Hansie," he said, "made us proud to be South African, a pride that was much-needed". Volsteedt was talking from the same stage and same platform where Hansie had stood at the end of his school career in 1987 to deliver his farewell speech as school captain of Grey.

After Volsteedt's speech, Bertha struggled gamely up the steep stairs to the high podium. Jonty Rhodes recalled afterwards, "I thought, how on earth is she going to get up that staircase? For months on end I was wracked with guilt because I hadn't helped her."

After eventually reaching the platform, her small frame rested awhile, as she steadied herself on Hansie's coffin. Behind her, Volsteedt protectively stood, a picture of decorum and grief. In a quavering voice, Bertha said, "For the past two years I wanted to tell the world. I wanted to shout it out. I wanted to explain to people, that even though Hansie made a mistake, he was still the same Hansie. A kind and loving husband, a genuine friend and an honourable man. Over the last couple of days, I've come to the wonderful realisation that actually nobody forgot the special qualities that I knew he had. Therefore I would like to thank Hansie's parents for the special person they raised. It was a privilege being married to him."

As she made her way down the stage, the whole hall rose to their feet and applauded.

The militant war cry of the Church, *Onward Christian Soldiers*, was then sung, for a special reason, San-Marie had explained to me. "Before the King Commission I had a dream one night. Hansie was standing in front of a huge cross, with his back towards me. Later, during the King Commission, I had a dream about Jonty and Hansie, who were standing and singing *Onward Christian Soldiers.*

●

At the conclusion of the service in the hall, the pallbearers came forward: Ewie, Frans, Bertha's brother Sybrand Pretorius, Hansie's uncle Wiester Strydom, Bertha's father Kosie Pretorius and Hansie's brother-in-law Gordon Parsons.

The casket was taken through the doors behind the stage, down a wooden staircase and carried through the columns standing at the entrance to the school, through a guard of honour made up of Grey's first cricket and rugby teams. As the hearse moved away, the boys burst into song: "Hansie is our hero, he shall not be moved…" And the television commentator Christo Olivier read the poem "If" by Rudyard Kipling to end the television coverage.

●

For Bertha, Ewie, San-Marie, Frans and Hester there were endless media interviews and scores of house-callers. Phone calls, faxes, e-mails, poems, mementos of various description, letters, cards and specially-made albums of tribute poured in from all over the world. The family, in the midst of their grief, tried to read at least a good portion of these. For weeks the flow continued, piling up into little mountains of mourning.

At the end of 2004, many trunks and boxes of these heart-felt outpourings were stored at Fancourt and at 246 Paul Kruger Avenue, warehouses of not only South Africa's grief, but also valedictory volumes from Hansie fans around the world.

A few days after Hansie's funeral, on Saturday, 8 June, Frans, Ewie and Tich were given tickets to watch the South African rugby side play in a Test match against Wales at the Free State Stadium in Bloemfontein. "It was a very emotional experience for Dad and me," said Frans. "Prior to the start of the match a Welsh male choir sang *Guide Me, O Thou Great Jehovah* and then the Welsh National Anthem. They had always been two favourite songs for Hansie, Dad and me. Then, just before the kick-off, the announcer asked for a minute of silence in honour of Hansie. Within ten seconds of this minute of silence, the entire crowd broke out chanting, 'Hansie, Hansie…' We just stood there with tears running down our cheeks."

Hansie's body was cremated on Friday, 7 June 2002. It was decided to lay the wooden box containing Hansie's ashes in the wall of remembrance at Grey College. This wall was built soon after Hansie's death, for Old Greys and their families should they wish to be laid to rest there. Hansie's ashes were the first to be placed and the ceremony was held on Saturday, 2 November 2002.

Ewie, San-Marie, Bertha and her parents Kosie and Elize were there. "I remember my mother-in-law saying that we should go there on the Saturday morning at about 7am, because that was the time the plane went down. It was a beautiful morning," recalled Bertha. "As we walked to the wall, I held the wooden box in my hands, and to this day I remember Hansie's mom's comment, 'Did you ever think that you would carry Hansie like this in your hands? He was always the one that carried you in his arms.' Nobody spoke. We stood in front of the wall. That same peace that I felt at the funeral was there again. It was quiet, with just the noise of the birds."

San-Marie said a prayer and Bertha placed the little wooden box in the wall.

"I remember thinking that I hope there is enough room in that little hole in the wall for me one day as well. I said thank you to the Lord for Hansie's life, for the precious time we had together, especially over that last two years, and I thanked Jesus for not leaving us, nor forsaking us, especially through this terribly difficult time."

The inscription on his plaque simply reads *Hansie Cronjé Psalm 23 The Lord is my shepherd.* "The Lord was Hansie's shepherd through everything, right to the end," said Bertha.

⬤

On the Vandalanskloof in the Outeniqua Mountains, malachite sunbirds hovered about, attracted by the nectar of bright orange ericas, king proteas with their massive dark pink bracts and scarlet gladioli that bloomed in the winter sunshine, among the jagged stone precipices, among the small pieces of wreckage left behind. The Indian Ocean was a serene dark blue ribbon on the eastern horizon.

From the time of the King Commission until Hansie's death, the willow tree he had claimed as his own as a six-year-old at 246 Paul Kruger Avenue slowly withered and died. It still stands there, a memorial stump to a bold little boy who was once so full of enthusiasm and passion for an ancient game.

As the willow died, a small olyvenhout tree sprouted spontaneously from its trunk, lush and strong, bright green leaves thrusting boldly towards the sun.

CHAPTER SEVENTEEN

CRUCIFIXES OF LIGHT

F rans Cronjé and I travelled to Bloemfontein from Cape Town on Friday, 30 July 2004, in the late afternoon. The towns of the Karoo – Matjiesfontein, Beaufort-West – spread far apart on a long, straight, flat and wide road, sped by. We repeatedly passed pantechnicons, as they moved ponderously along on the N1, the national highway. They politely fell back and hugged the road shoulder, allowing us to pass. Every time they did this Frans would activate his hazard lights to say "thank you". Without fail, the truck drivers would flash their headlights as we passed, as if to say "my pleasure". Such mutual politeness on the road was unusual in my South African experience. Road idiocy and arrogance, I had come to believe, was a national sport. I was impressed.

After Colesberg, as we crossed the great Orange River into the Free State Province, Frans rejoiced. He was back home.

Hansie's big brother remarked regularly about the landscape, the fauna, and pointed out farm dams in particular, as many a Free State *boereseun* would. "Look at that dam. Isn't it beautiful? I'd love to have a dam like that on my own farm," he would say. I would then gaze at some little earth dam next to the road, with a few small trees and bushes around it in a flat and monotonous dry winter land-scape, amused by his romanticism.

The Free State can be a thirsty land. Many "rivers" are simply winding beds of parched yellow sand – until the little floods come in summer. Rivers are some-times called Sand River, or Dry River, or Salt River, or Bitterfontein. Rivers that mostly aren't rivers. The dams can be lifesavers for livestock here.

Among other African antelope grazing like tame sheep near the road, Frans pointed out some very rare almost black springbok as we passed the many game farms and nature reserves of the province. The sub-desert plains of ochre, orange-brown and tan earth, dotted about with hardy, low and small bushes, were relieved occasionally by khaki koppies and small mountains and crags crowned with large crenellated ridges.

Earlier, we stopped at the Three Sisters roadside farm stall to check out the bil-tong. There was kudu, springbok, blesbok and beef, of the finest quality and at a good price. Frans bought a monster packet of beef biltong, which had a generous crust of fat on it. He attacked this with deep enjoyment. I bought some of the dried kudu meat and chewed with equal content. Top quality, not too-dry, lean venison, veld fragrant with the herbal tang of the indigenous bush. It had a good, deep-red colour inside and was seasoned lightly with coriander, salt, pepper and vinegar. We stood outside the stall on the dry and dusty plain, in the growing dusk of the arid scrubland. The heat of the day had subsided and the cold air began to fall down from the sky. Bright evening stars glittered in the dimming dome.

As we continued our journey, Frans, as usual, was juggling conversations and SMSes on two mobiles, fiddling around frequently with a large packet of rusks, crunching away happily, and drinking coffee in between. "Keep your eye on the road, *jou donner!*" I admonished, half-jokingly, as he on occasion crossed the mid-line of the road. Frans laughed politely at my "old woman" attitude and we ribbed each other in a way that only men can do without causing offence.

Past Donkerpoort, in the far distance, we could see a lonely crucifix in the blackness, near Trompsburg. Lit by hundreds of white globes, the 10-metre-high cross was perched on a small koppie next to the road. The shining symbol of absolute shame and disgrace – and yet the sign of redemption, of God's only bridge to Himself for all men and women.

Sins have to be paid for by sacrifice, by the shedding of blood, God's Law asserts unequivocally and repeatedly in the Bible. Jesus was the Lamb of God, who took the sins of the world upon Himself and faced His Father's wrath in our stead. God had never, would never, tolerate sin. Christ was sacrificed, once, for all. But God's redemption plan comes with a proviso: it must simply be accepted, as a free gift and repentance, a turning away from sin, must take place. The cycle of accelerating renewal of a relationship with God is a process in a human life that can only be triggered by a dogged and simple faith in the message of the Messiah's life, death and resurrection, as recorded in Holy Scripture. Jesus declared, "I am the Way, the Truth and the Life, no-one comes to the Father, but through Me." There was and is and always will be only one way to God. If the opportunity of salvation is rejected, eternal separation from God will result after death. Heaven and hell are not fairy tales. This is what the Christian Bible teaches, and Hansie believed all of this, with all of his heart and mind.

I commented on the cross to Frans. "Church communities along this road erect and pay for these crosses," he said.

It was not the only cross we sped past that night, as we travelled on to Edenberg. The closer we got to Bloemfontein, the more crosses there were. It was eerie, yet strangely comforting, the crosses first appearing many kilometres away on the straight and flat highway, slowly growing and brightening as we approached. Lonely, stark givers of light in the darkness.

It was my first visit to Bloemfontein in the course of research for this book, and the crosses spoke to me about Hansie and his Jesus.

Shortly after my arrival and warm welcome into the Cronjés home, I heard that, coincidentally, Peter Pollock, was to be the guest speaker at the Universitas Dutch Reformed Church the following Sunday. He was, I was told, going to speak about Hansie in his sermon. Frans, Ewie and San-Marie, of course, would be there too.

On the Sunday morning, Frans, Ewie and I drove to a nearby bed and breakfast establishment to fetch Peter, who had travelled the day before from Durban. Ewie was, as is his wont, grey-suited, Frans in a large and long, black-leather jacket, making his tall bulky body appear even more imposing, his neatly cropped coarse bush of sandy-grey hair crowning his head. Like Hansie, he had a powerful physical presence, a gravitas, balanced with a disarming smile. Peter Pollock came out of his rooms, black-suited, balding, his lively pink face crackling with energy, despite his age. He greeted Ewie particularly warmly and he and the Cronjés bantered about cricket, about friends.

We arrived at the church and met up with San-Marie, the picture of an attractive and refined Bloemfontein grandmother, with her understated tartan skirt and jacket. We lingered for a while outside the church, typical in many ways of other Dutch Reformed Church buildings – some vertical stained-glass panels of many pale colours, in abstract design, formed part of the large windows in the front entrance of the church. A tower rose up from the squat building, which had an architectural air of solid, self-conscious simplicity.

Friends were greeted at the entrance for several minutes and then Ewie went in with Peter to sit on the right-hand side of the high and canopied wooden pulpit where the other elders sat. The pulpit seemed to soar upwards, backed by a fan of panelled hardwood. In the foyer, there was a framed stained-glass cross, which bore the legend underneath: *Leef voluit tot eer van God* (Live completely to the honour of God).

Inside were long oak pews and green-carpeted aisles. No banners or embellishments, the interior was harsh and plain. The church was nearly full as I sat at the back, next to San-Marie, with Frans on her other side. The balconies slowly filled up, too, with young married couples, children, teenagers, but mostly elderly folk.

We sang *Kom dank nou almal God* ("Now thank we all our God"), the verses of which were on an overhead screen. The congregation sang lustily, loud and clear. Invisible in the gallery above us, an ethereal choir sang *Kom en loof Hom, Kom en prys Hom, Kom en loof die Heer se naam*. I gazed upwards, to the right, where Hansie always used to sit, as the organ music and the beautiful voices swelled.

The congregation recited the Apostles' Creed. Some babies and older children were then christened by the *dominee*: Dane Pieterse, Gabrielle Venter, Christine Esterhuizen, and Nathan Charles Young, in a ritual that involved Bibles, lit candles, sprinkled water, and much oohing and aahing, while parents and grandparents looked on proudly. About 34 years ago, Hansie was christened in another Bloemfontein church very similar to this one.

The guest speaker was introduced. Peter Pollock rose and mounted the high pulpit. He spoke in English.

His text for that morning was Luke 15, verses 11 to 32, Jesus' Parable of the Lost Son. In a loud and piercing voice, Peter read, "A certain man had two sons ..."

The reader may know the story as that of the Prodigal Son, but it probably bears repetition at this point for those who do not, or recall it imperfectly. It is the story of a younger son who goes to his father and asks for his inheritance so he can go out into the world. He squanders all his money on "wild living" and is eventually penniless and starving, working on a farm. When he finds himself so hungry that he's longing to eat the food he feeds the pigs, he decides to return to his father, beg his forgiveness and offer himself as a labourer. His father sees him coming, runs to meet him and embraces him. The son says, "Father, I have sinned against heaven and against you. I am no longer worthy to be called your son." But the father calls his servants to bring fresh clothes and prepare a feast to celebrate his younger son's return.

When the older son returns from the fields, he is furious. He asks his father to explain why, after all his years of hard work and obedience to his father's orders, he has never been given so much as a goat to enjoy with his friends; yet when his younger brother, who has wasted his inheritance, slinks home, the fattened calf is killed for him. The father replies, "My son, you are always with me, and everything I have is yours. But we have to celebrate and be glad, because this brother of yours was dead and is alive again; he was lost and is found." (Quotes taken from the *New International Version* of the Bible.)

Peter referred to verse 12, when the younger son said, "Father, give me my share of the estate."

"Me. Me. Me," Peter said. "ME. ME. ME. Gimme. Gimme. The biggest problem we have with God is the trinity of sin: I, me, myself. We live in a world today of 'building up self-image seminars'. The world repetitively asks the question: 'What's in it for ME?' Personal fame and success have replaced God. Ego has become ogre."

Peter, in his inimitable and authoritative manner, went on. "The world cries out for 'freedom'. But what the world means by this is freedom from discipline, freedom not to show respect, freedom from obedience. God is in the discipline, respect and obedience business.

"The 'freedom' the world talks about is another word for rebellion and anarchy. The freest cell in the body is a cancer cell. It doesn't obey the rules."

Peter went on to talk about those who appear to be Christians, but who don't change their patterns of behaviour. "If there's no change, there's no Jesus.

There is no excuse for man. He sees God in creation. The human race knows there is a God."

Peter noted that the Prodigal Son was "handed over to the consequences of his own decision. Destiny is where the heart is. My fate is my choice. Obsession with fame, obsession with money means that God will hand you over to the consequences of that. You and I are in a place that we've chosen to be. You can't blame anyone for where you are – or aren't – in your relationship with God."

Peter went on to talk about a fickle world, fair-weather friends, the "pseudo-values of superficiality and deception", and how the world's commandment was "Thou shalt not get caught".

"The joy and peace that is to be found in God is beyond the understanding of words," said Peter. "What the world understands about 'joy and peace' is that it is the state that exists when 'I am making money, when I am successful materially, when I'm on top'. But true joy and peace is a supreme confidence in a sovereign God even when things are dark, when famine is at your doorstep. Emptiness and desperation is the lot of the world without God. When are we going to believe that emptiness is in us? We don't want to admit this. Most of us know about God, but we don't want to know Him. We can get so positive about the things of the world that we go into denial about God."

Peter reminded the congregation that the Prodigal Son was handed over to the desires of his own heart. And that caused him to end up in the pigsty. He had joined the world. "The ultimate degradation in the eyes of God is to be in the world, and of the world. Separation from God is the ultimate degradation. We are all in the pigsty if we are separated from God. The Prodigal Son in the pigsty is the picture of spiritual death and disconnection from God. The lost son understood clearly where he was and how he had got there. The thing is, we don't like to acknowledge that some of us are there too, but we need to come to the point where we say, 'I have sinned. I am unworthy.' We can't blame our parents, we can't blame the government, we can't blame the Church, we can't blame apartheid. I have sinned. Only when you understand that you are the problem, not others, not your circumstances, and that God needs to be on the throne of your life do you achieve the key revelation. Only the dead to self truly submit to the will of God. We need not just to know *about* Him, we need to know Him. We need to come to Jesus."

With those words, he launched into a section on Hansie.

"He was a favourite son. The world was his oyster. He had everything. Then came the fall. There was an unprecedented onslaught, vicious in my opinion. When I saw him on TV at the King Commission, breaking down, I thought: 'Hansie is well and truly in the pigsty.'"

Peter recounted the story of Hansie's confession of faith, his repentance and his subsequent baptism on 29 August 2000. "What happened to Hansie there, only God could do." He spoke of Hansie's death and said, "Hansie is home. Many of us here are still in the pigsty."

Next to me, San-Marie was quietly weeping. Frans's eyes glittered with tears. They were not alone. I noticed many wet eyes in the moved congregation. Ever the evangelist, Peter concluded his sermon by calling on the crowd to acknowledge their sinfulness, the fact that many of them were in the pigsty, too, and needed to run back to the Father and beg for forgiveness, to restore their relationship with God. "Stand up where you are if you hear God talking to you now. Acknowledge your sin and turn to Jesus. If you need to commit your life to Him I will pray for you now."

More than half the congregation stood up. Stiff old, grey-haired academics, teenagers, prim matrons, young married couples. Standing meekly.

Peter prayed the sinner's prayer before the service was brought to a close. Somberly, the congregation filed out into the winter sunshine, heading for the Sunday roast, the steakhouse lunch, the mutton-chop braai. For some, the repentances would fade, dimmed by the relentless and overwhelming habits of the world, by expedience, by comfort and ease, by fear of ridicule and exclusion.

Some weeks after the sermon, I browsed through Hansie's little blue paperback New Testament, given to him by the Australian cricket team's chaplain and the Bible Society of Australia "on the occasion of the January 1994 2nd Cricket Test: South Africa – Australia".

There were many under-linings in blue pen throughout the book and some notes in Hansie's hand. A few verses in the Prodigal Son parable were underlined, including "...younger son" and "...wasted his money".

In the following chapter, Luke 16, the Parable of the Shrewd Manager, Hansie had underlined Jesus' words: "No servant can serve two masters; he will hate one and love the other, he will be devoted to one and despise the other. You cannot serve both God and money." Hansie had written at the top of the page, in bold capitals: "*KAN NIE GELD EN DIE HERE DIEN NIE.*" (Can't serve money and God.)

San-Marie walked up to me and held my arm affectionately as we strolled to the nearby parking lot. She loved people – much as Hansie did – and she embraced those around her with grace and simplicity. I had a sense of Hansie's arm on mine, too, my spiritual brother, whose life's journey I had come to know well.

We said little as we drove back to 246 Paul Kruger Avenue. She had heard the message of the Gospel of Christ many times, but it always stirred her deeply. Like Ewie, she looked forward to the day when she, too, would be home, living in her Father's house, with Hansie.

BIBLIOGRAPHY

Alfred, L. *Lifting the Covers: The Inside Story of South African Cricket.* Spearhead, 2001

Bulpin, TV. *Discovering Southern Africa. Struik,* (Fourth Edition), 1986

Chesterfield, T and McGlew J. *South Africa's Cricket Captains.* Zebra Press, 2003

Cronje, WJ. *Hansie: This is your Captain Speaking* (Benefit Year Publication 1997/98)

Gledhill, E. *Veldblomme van Oos-Kaapland.* Department of Nature Conservation, 1969

Green, LG. *Karoo.* Timmins, 1984

Griffiths, E. *Kepler: the Biography.* Pelham Books, 1994

Hammond-Tooke, D. *The Roots of Black South Africa.* Jonathan Ball, 1993

Hartman, R. *Hansie & the Boys.* Zebra Press, 1997

Hartman, R. *A Year On ... Hansie & the Boys.* Zebra Press, 1998

Hartman, R. *Ali: The life of Ali Bacher.* Penguin, 2004

Joyce, P. *The South African Family Encyclopaedia.* Struik, 1989

Lewis, CS. *The Great Divorce.* Harper Collins Publishers, 1946

Pearce, J. *Wisdom and Innocence: A life of G K Chesterton.* Hodder and Stoughton, 1996

Picton-Seymour, D. *Historical Buildings in South Africa.* Struikhof, 1989

Poland, M. *Iron Love.* Viking, 1999

Pollock, P. *The Winning Factor.* Christian Art Publishers, 2004

Reader's Digest. *Illustrated Atlas of Southern Africa* (1994)

Reader's Digest. *Illustrated Encylopaedia of Gardening in South Africa.* 1994

Reader's Digest. *Illustrated Guide to Southern Africa.* Fourth Edition. 1986

Reader's Digest. *Illustrated History of South Africa.* Second Edition. 1992

Schirmer, P. *The Concise Illustrated South African Encylopaedia.* CNA, 1980

Struik. *Birds of Southern Africa (Struik* 1997)

Vergunst, N. *Hoerikwaggo: Images of Table Mountain.* South African National Gallery, 2001

Warmenhoven, A. "The Emotional Intelligence of Wessel Johannes "Hansie" Cronjé: A Psychobiographical Study". 2005

N1: National highway stretching from Cape Town to Pretoria

alles sal regkom: everything will be all right

baas: boss

bakkie: pick-up truck

Biltong: Dried meat that is highly salted and spiced (not unlike beef jerky). Early farmers made biltong from beef and game, because they had no cooling system for storing fresh meat. Biltong is now an expensive delicacy in South Africa.

blesbok: an antelope of southern Africa

bloomen: probably from the English intensifier "blooming" – a euphemism for bloody

boerekos: traditional Afrikaans ("farmers") food

boeremeisie: farm girl, or even a city girl that is very Afrikaans

boerenooi: farm girl, a term often used to describe naïve Afrikaans girls

boet: "brother", also a term of affection

braai: barbecue

Cricket terminology for those who are not familiar with the game:

Simplified explanation of the complicated game of cricket

Cricket is always played between two teams with 11 players in each team. A cricket field is usually shaped like an oval and is roughly 150 meters in diameter. The pitch (as described on page 31-33) is in the middle of the oval and there is a set of 3 stumps (called a wicket), at both ends of the pitch.

There are always two batsmen batting at the same time. The batsman that is facing the ball stands in front of the one wicket. A bowler is allowed to run in and bowl the ball to the batsman and he may bowl as fast or as slow as he wants to. The bowling action must always be with a straight arm and the ball is only allowed to bounce once on the pitch, before hitting the wickets or the batsman. The bowler tries to hit the wickets with the ball, but is also allowed to hit the batsman's body to intimidate him (the fastest bowlers bowl at about 150km/hour or 95 miles/hour). The ball is made of hard leather, with cork on the inside and a brand new ball is rock hard and can seriously damage, or even kill a batsman. A bowler bowls 6 balls at a time, called an over. Then another bowler bowls an over from the opposite side, before the previous bowler can bowl again.

The batsman tries to protect his wicket and at the same tries to score as many runs as possible. Runs can be scored by hitting the ball to any part of the oval and then running to the other side of the pitch, with the batting partner running in the opposite direction. When the ball is hit out of the oval, it is 4 runs if it bounces inside the oval and 6 runs when it is clears the oval without bouncing first. A batsman is out if the ball hits his wicket, if he gets caught out, if he is run out or if he is leg before wicket (LBW – the ball hits his body and is judged by the umpire that it would have hit the wickets, if it didn't hit the batsman's body).

When a batsman scores 50 runs in an innings, it is considered a milestone, but reaching 100 runs is the preferred measure of a great innings by an individual. When a bowler takes 5 wickets in an innings, it is usually considered a similar achievement as scoring 100 runs.

There are two main formats of cricket

The traditional format is played over several days: 5 days when two countries compete (Test Cricket); 4 days when the competition is between two provinces, counties or states (First Class Cricket). Both teams have two innings in which they can bat for as long as they want to. There is no limit to how long a batsman may bat or how many overs a bowler may bowl. An innings comes to an end when the batting team has lost 10 wickets (it is called a wicket when a batsman gets out), or when the batting team's captain decides to declare. The team that scores most runs in the two innings wins the match, however if neither team gets bowled out twice during the scheduled duration of the match, then the match is declared a draw. Both teams wear white clothes and the ball that is used is red.

The other format is called one-day cricket (One-Day Internationals, or ODIs when two countries compete) and the entire match is completed on the same day. Both teams bat for 50 overs (300 balls) and try to score as many runs as possible. A batsman may bat for the entire innings if he doesn't get out, but each bowler is restricted to 10 overs. Unless rained out there should always be a winner. Each team wears coloured clothing that is unique to their own team.

Terminology used in book:

deep square leg: fielding position at about 9 o'clock from the facing batsman
midwicket: fielding position at about 10 o'clock from facing batsman
long-on: fielding position at about 11 o'clock from facing batsman
point: fielding position at about 3 o'clock from facing batsman
cricket coffin: the preferred way to carry all cricket kit – in large, rectangular, coffin-like cases
batting average: the total amount of runs scored by a batsman in a period of time (i.e. a season or career), that is divided by the number of times that the batsman lost his wicket (a batting average of more than 40 is usually classified exceptional)
bowling average: the total amount of runs that a bowler conceded over a period of time, divided by the number of wickets that he took (a bowling average that is lower than 25 is usually considered exceptional)
Not Out: when a batsman completed his innings without getting out

dominee: reverend

groot: big/large/senior (as in Groot Frans = Frans snr)

hardekop: hard-headed

ja: yes

kleilat: children's game where tiny balls of clay or mud are flicked from a stick at someone else
kom ouens: come guys
kraal: an enclosure for livestock

Ma: Mom
meisie: girl

olywenhout: wild olive
Oom: Literally, 'uncle', but also respectful form of address for an older man. Most Afrikaans-speaking people still call older people (the rule is usually more than 10 years older) *Tannie* (aunt) for any woman, or *Oom* for any man that they speak to. This is done even if these older people are not relatives.

Pa: Dad
pap en wors: *mieliepap* is a porridge made from maize (corn) meal and is a traditional staple food in South Africa. *Mieliepap* is a favourite accompaniment to 'braai-ed' meat. *Wors* (short for *boerewors*) is a thick, spicy sausage made from mince meat.
plaasjapie: boy or man who lives or grew up on a farm
platteland: countryside, rural districts (literally, the "flat land")

rooinek: "red neck", a facetious name for an Englishman (the British usually had very fair skins on their arrival in Africa and soon got "red necks" and arms in the harsh African sun.)

School captain: At Grey College the term 'school captain' is preferred over 'head boy', but has the same meaning.
sjambok: a heavy whip of rhinoceros or hip-

popotamus hide
skaapplaas: sheep farm
soetveld: sweet grasslands
soort soek soort: Afrikaans, equivalent to: birds of a feather flock together
stoksiel alleen: totally alone

Tannie: Literally, "aunt", but also respectful form of address for an older woman. Most Afrikaans-speaking people still call older people (the rule is usually more than 10 years older) *Tannie* for any woman, or *Oom* (uncle) for any man that they speak to. This is done even if these older people are not relatives.
township: a part of the city where black or coloured people were forced to live apart from white people during the apartheid years

trekbokke: term used for migrating springbok

verligte: enlightened (or liberal in a political sense)
Volksblad: The only major, daily Afrikaans newspaper that is issued in the Free State (literally, people's page)
volk and vaderland: countrymen (particularly fellow Afrikaners) and homeland
Vierkleur: the flag of the old Transvaal Republic, literally "four colours"

wag-'n-bietjie: a type of tree that grows abundantly in the Free State (literally, wait a bit)
windgat: cocky

INDEX